£7.60

D1457484

THE
GOVERNING
PASSION

Cabinet Government
and Party Politics in Britain
1885–86

Frontispiece

Gladstone in his study at Hawarden, late 1880's: 'It is easy to view his policies as overtures leading naturally towards home rule, but they can equally well be read as leading in a different direction: towards diminishing the independence and strength of Irish Nationalism, so as to benefit the Liberal party and his position in it.'

THE
GOVERNING
PASSION

Cabinet Government
and Party Politics in Britain
1885–86

by A. B. Cooke
Research Fellow, The Queen's University of Belfast
and John Vincent
Professor of Modern History, The University of Bristol

THE HARVESTER PRESS 1974

The Harvester Press Limited, *Publishers*
50 Grand Parade Brighton Sussex BN2 2QA England

First published 1974
© A. B. Cooke and J. Vincent 1974

ISBN 0 85527 492 1

Designed by Sheila Sherwen

Printed in Great Britain by
Western Printing Services Limited Bristol

To Marigold

Contents

vii

List of Illustrations

Acknowledgments

We are indebted to Her Majesty the Queen for her gracious permission to consult the Royal Archives at Windsor Castle, and for allowing certain passages to be cited. We are most grateful to Miss Jane Langton, the Archivist, and her colleagues for their guidance.

The evidence on which this book is based consists largely of the private, unpublished papers of the politicians who governed Britain in 1885–86. Some of these papers have now found their way into libraries or record offices up and down the country. Accordingly we have had occasion to draw upon the time and experience of a large number of archivists and librarians. We would like to take this opportunity of thanking them all collectively. In particular we wish to mention Mr Alan Bell, a Keeper of the Manuscripts at the National Library of Scotland in Edinburgh, and Mr A. G. Vesey and Mr C. J. Williams of the Flintshire County Record Office, who have given us sustained help going far beyond the call of duty.

Many collections of papers we have studied still remain in family hands. We are indebted to these families for their kind co-operation in making the relevant documents available to us, and for providing us with facilities for research in their homes.

Dr Andrew Jones of the University of Reading kindly let us have sight of his authoritative *The Politics of Reform, 1884* before it went to press. We also had the stimulus of seeing 'The Formation of Liberal Party Policy, 1885–92' by Dr M. Barker of the University of Leicester (unpublished Swansea Ph.D., 1972) at an early stage. We are glad to acknowledge their good offices and also those of Professor M. R. D. Foot, Mr A. F. Thompson and Mr G. ó Tuathaigh concerning various points of scholarship. Finally, we would like to thank Mr M. Stenton for his assistance in research.

Preface

In order that the reader may grasp what this book sets out to do, it is necessary to say something about the stages by which it reached its present form. Originally the authors had intended to discuss cabinet government and party politics in 1885–86 only as an insubstantial by-product of their previous work together as editors of two unpublished memoirs,* one Liberal, one Conservative, both of which cast light on ministerial politics at that time.

Thus at first it seemed that no more need be done than to collate readily accessible information relating to the day-by-day functioning of the cabinet. It was hoped merely to settle such technical but unexplored questions as the date, place, and duration of every cabinet meeting, together with the names of those ministers attending, throughout two years of unusual political tension. This task was soon completed, though the status of a few ministerial meetings continues to defy classification.

At this point, two further considerations emerged. It became apparent that there was no sharp line dividing what happened at cabinet meetings from a continuous but less formal process of discussion and intrigue from which policy also emerged. It also became apparent that the construction of a precise timetable for meetings in Downing St was a strong incentive to build up a list of topics discussed on each occasion.

Even when these arguments had been accepted, it was not initially obvious that anything more was required than a highly compressed article, more or less in tabular form. This, at least, would certainly

* 'Ireland and Party Politics, 1885–87: An Unpublished Conservative Memoir' published in three parts in *Irish Historical Studies*, vol. xvi, nos 62–4, 1969: *Lord Carlingford's Journal: Reflections of a Cabinet Minister, 1885* (1971).

have been the case had attention been confined to the most obvious records relating to the cabinet, i.e. those documents in the Royal Archives at Windsor, in the Gladstone Papers, and at the Public Record Office, together with information in the press, which bear directly on the subject. Even when studied closely and related to a precise chronology, this body of evidence could yield only an inadequate and even partial view of central government decision-making, and it certainly could not answer any of the really interesting questions.

In seeking to remedy this, one was able to take advantage of the very large number of collections of private political papers which, for this period, are only now becoming fully accessible for the first time. For instance the leading previous writer* on this subject had to contend with the difficulty of being largely confined, as regards original sources, to the Gladstone Papers, and not even all of those were at his disposal. Since then, the situation has been transformed. In the case of the Liberal cabinet of 1885, the authors were able to inspect the papers of all but two ministers, out of a cabinet of sixteen. As regards Salisbury's ministry of 1885–86, papers have been traced for every minister in a cabinet of sixteen, with the single exception of Lord George Hamilton. In 1886, of the fifteen men who sat in the home rule ministry, only three have failed to yield at least some documentary records. Six political diaries showing inside knowledge of cabinet business, all previously unused for this period, have also been located and studied, as have several diaries of backbenchers.

At this point, a possible divergence of aims emerged. The material available, though sometimes disconcertingly fragmentary, was not merely rich but too rich. On the one hand, one was led towards an attempt to explain and interpret motives and meanings throughout an enormously involved episode. On the other hand, one could produce a piece of work which would fall in the genre known to French scholarship as *documents pour servir*. It was clear, in fact, that no document would be serviceable unless there was a proper balance, even within a text arranged in the form of a chronicle or diary, between simple presentation of evidence, its arrangement in meaningful ways, and some measure of elucidation, comment, and interpretation. In short, there was no possibility of restricting our work to the barest form of chronicle.

The crisis of 1885–86 was peculiarly complex, both as regards the number of issues involved, and the number of ways in which an unusually large collection of politicians of the highest talent tried to turn them to account. Any speculation on the great matters

* J. L. Hammond, *Gladstone and the Irish Nation* (1938).

at stake which are not preceded by minute analysis on a day-by-day basis cannot hope to get at essentials except by pure good fortune. In saying this, it is not to be thought that such complexity is the normal characteristic of political situations at this period, or that our approach here would be appropriate for studying a parliamentary system in ordinary times.

In Book One, we give our opinion about some of the meanings behind the events set out in detail in Book Two. There is no absolute sense in which our opinions are necessarily entailed by our chronicles, and it is to be expected that other interpretations consistent with these will inevitably emerge. No attempt has been made to give a complete interpretation of everything in the chronicles.

The chronicles themselves are incomplete. In some cases we do not regret the omissions, because they relate to episodes which require microscopic scrutiny by a mind unoccupied with other tasks. The most obvious examples of this are the role of Manning and the Catholic hierarchy in the central board scheme: the negotiations between Liberal leaders between June 1885 and the elections (labyrinthine, sterile, and bitter to a degree): the Hawarden Kite: the confused and ultimately abortive tangle of negotiations with Chamberlain in spring 1886: the role, if any, of such shadowy and self-important intermediaries as the O'Sheas and Labouchere: and the technicalities of the way the home rule and land bills were put together. To these problems of English politics, which are at least in principle soluble, must be added a problem which may not be soluble, namely the elucidation of political motive among Irish politicians. The difficulty here is partly archival, in that Irish politicians simply did not use and keep letters as English politicians did: and partly a matter of the deliberate reticence and ambiguity of the Irish leaders on their own ultimate intentions, so that, for instance, there is no way of assessing Healy's claim that Parnell did not want home rule.[1] The only questions that can be answered satisfactorily about Irish politics at this time are those relating to party organisation, and these have already been well dealt with elsewhere.[2]

What we do regret is our inability to trace the way in which cabinet discussion was embodied in the work of government departments. There are three good reasons for this omission: one archival, one to do with historical reality, and one arising from our human frailty. The archives relating to politics are generally as separate as can be from the archives relating to public administration. Further, all our evidence tends to show the rarity of contact between politicians and administrators, and the degree to which politicians lost interest in questions once they had turned from matters of cabinet antagonisms into administrative grind. Finally, to extend this study into the machinery of the departments, would have required another year and another volume. But the problem, a real one, remains.

Book One: Commentary

'In a democracy,' said Mr Pinfold with more weight than originality, 'men do not seek authority so that they may impose a policy. They seek a policy so that they may achieve authority.' – Evelyn Waugh, *The Ordeal of Gilbert Pinfold*.

I

The Structure
of Political Action
in 1885–86

'The (Reform) Bill is a frightfully democratic measure which I confess appals me. Its effect will not be felt at once but in a few years it will come with a rush. I don't see any hope for the Tories anywhere or anyhow.' – Harcourt to his wife, 2 December 1884, Harcourt MSS.

'The time is coming when our party (of three or four) must have a programme and know exactly what it is aiming at. Anyone who has anything definite to propose has a good chance to be hailed as a Saviour. But have we a Gospel?' – Chamberlain to Morley, 19 May 1883, copy, Chamberlain MSS 5/54/505.

At the beginning of 1885, the politicians had just called a new electorate into existence. It would be natural to think, therefore, that the relation between this new electorate and those engaged in politics would provide the essential dimension for analysing political action. However, this is not the case. It is true indeed, that politicians were concerned about the electorate. It is true, also, that they worked within certain stereotypes about what the future held in store for them under the new conditions. Their view of the electorate was, most commonly, that it was an aggressive democracy. Their view of the future envisaged a long succession of liberal governments.* (The elections of 1885 did in the event produce a

* Two senior ministers even forecast the election virtually correctly. On 16 July 1885, Harcourt predicted Lib. 355, Con. 235, Parnellites 80 (Herbert Gladstone MSS, B.M. Add MSS 45992 f. 9). On 22 August, Childers wrote to Knowles forecasting Lib. 330, Con. 250, Parnellites 90 (*The Times*, 14 Dec. 1885). No senior politician forecast a Tory victory in 1885.

majority of Liberals over Conservatives which was, where Great Britain was concerned, much the same as the previous Liberal majorities of 1865, 1868, or 1880). Conservative politicians were just as prone to these beliefs as Liberal ones. From early 1885 until close to the election, Conservative leaders expected a Liberal victory, and disagreed primarily on the lesser question as to whether the Liberal ascendancy* should be met by offensive or by defensive tactics. Lord Bath's description of Salisbury as a pessimist by nature who thought his mission was to fight a hopeless battle well, could be equally well applied, not only regarding electoral calculations but also to their sense of history, to most other Tories. Politicians of all kinds however felt little need to react in a clear-cut way to what they saw as their general historical situation.

They had their reasons. They believed politics was ultimately about the organisation and presentation of the parliamentary community in such a way that the working class could be contained. They knew of four or five ways of doing this, and did not propose to add to them. They did not, however, believe in discussing specific responses to events in working class politics. For example, there is no traceable discussion of why a former artisan, the stone-mason and trade union organiser Henry Broadhurst, was given junior office in 1886, even though no working class leader had ever taken office before. Similarly, the Trafalgar Square riots † (occurring almost at the same time) were not considered a political talking-point except in so far as they permitted acid reflections on an unpopular colleague's departmental reputation. ‡ Though politicians academically and conceptually accepted the idea of an 'aggressive democracy' confronting them, they did so in a purely general way. All their picture of the situation meant in practice was that they expected the parliamentary community to go on arranging parliamentary affairs *as if* 'aggressive democracy' defined the situation in the world outside. The politicians did not mean that they had seriously to think about overt agitation among the less well off. Apart from Chamberlain's campaign, the two relatively successful extra-parliamentary agitations of 1885–86 were the Fair Trade and Church-in-Danger movements which arose ephemerally, and with

* The electoral régime set up by the reform bill of 1884 and the redistribution bill of 1885 did not in fact produce straight Tory party majorities more than twice (1895 and 1900) during the eight general elections when it was in operation.

† '... the first time a mob has actually pillaged shops and attacked property on principle' wrote Wilfrid Scawen Blunt delightedly (*The Land War in Ireland*, 1912, p. 27).

‡ The death of a Tory candidate in June 1886 following a rough election meeting in London, was also taken with calm, as befitted an event which *The Times* in a leader calculated would swing votes to the Unionists.

acknowledged electoral impact,* at the 1885 election. These movements (perhaps precisely because they had little association with particular classes) were treated by parliamentarians as a momentary eccentricity, and were soon forgotten in the turmoils of 1886, despite their wide interest to the electorate. This was pardonable enough, for the cross-currents were so perplexing, especially in Lancashire, that even the most pliant politician would have had great difficulty in defining what he was being called upon by the electorate to do. Liberal leaders, moreover, were liable from long experience to regard unexpected behaviour by voters as some new kind of unscrupulous Tory ruse. Thus, if the boroughs registered no enthusiasm for the Liberals at the 1885 election, it was an easy matter to regard this in terms of the vagaries of the Irish vote. And so, from these causes and from the press of events at Westminster, the 1885 election, in which electors had struck out on their own account in quite interesting ways, was pronounced by the parliamentary community to be an event that led nowhere.

The deep concern of the politicians as to how the parties should bring parliamentary politics into the life of the people, was partly a concern about laying down terms of reference within which popular political activity could safely be encouraged, and partly a concern about keeping the people out of politics, in the sense of ensuring that the electorate would not want to exercise any initiative in deciding what politicians ought to be doing. These preoccupations could best be sorted out, not by talking directly to electors, but through the medium of clubs, the lobby, the dinner table, the race meeting, the visit to dine and sleep, the morning call, and the stroll in the park. This was where political work was really done. Leading men rarely discussed matters of party machinery: still less commonly did they relate the management of the extraparliamentary organisation to the decisions of parliamentary life or public administration. Speeches, of course, were increasingly common, and politics in 1885–86 was beginning to be, as it has remained, something of a permanent campaign. The Corrupt Practices Act of 1883 had made its mark, and one of its consequences was the constituency weekend speech in lieu of electoral beer. Extra-parliamentary developments of this sort did not, however,

---

* Gladstone ascribed the urban defeats in 1885 to 'Fair Trade + Parnell + Church + Chamberlain' in that order (Gladstone to Grosvenor, 27 Nov. 1885, cited Hammond, op. cit., 398). Cf. Gladstone's published letter to Lord William Compton (*The Times*, 12 Dec. 1885): 'The present has been a wonderful election. It will prove, I think, that we have decidedly gained on the Tories since 1880 if allowance be made 1) for a balance of 5 seats given them through double candidatures and 2) for 15 seats – a very moderate estimate – given them by Mr Parnell.'

determine the content of such political discourse, only its increasing frequency. The machinery and texture of aristocratic politics were therefore never more relevant or more hard-worked than when, not just the internal divisions of the parliamentary world, but the possible transformation of the old arrangements, stood on the agenda.

There is a curious point to be made here. This is that the English working class was in an unusually turbulent state in early 1886. It had been a hard winter, trade was depressed and unemployment, especially in London, was high, employers were forcing through reductions of wages and resorting to lockouts, and there were prolonged industrial disputes in the cotton, shipbuilding, and metalworking industries. The Welsh quarries were in a very disturbed state indeed, and troops had to be sent there from Manchester. Even the normally secure railwaymen of Crewe, 6,000 of them, were put on short time. There was, indeed, a typical capitalist crisis, but this time with the difference that working class resentment expressed itself in riotous or political forms, often under quite capable revolutionary Socialist auspices. A spectre should have been haunting the parliamentary community, faced with its first experience of militant socialism, the more so as socialist disturbances were virtually world wide that winter. In fact there was no spectre and no haunting.

The most obvious response to 'dangerous' pressure from below was a display of good nature. Donations flowed in for the unemployed after the West End riots, while the Liberal landslide in the counties in the 1885 elections led to a stream of announcements by great landowners about allotments given to or planned for their labourers, and this at a time when landed incomes had just dramatically diminished. Laudable motives apart, the determination of the political élite to maintain class collaboration intact was probably strengthened by the challenge of explicit class antagonism.

The mental blocks preventing a recognition of elemental class hostility were too powerful. It is often remarked how the working class was controlled by its fixation on parliament as the only relevant locale for political action. The same applied to their social superiors. Working class pressure, focussed in the traditional way through a parliamentary leader like Chamberlain, did indeed frighten sensible men of property and education: but working class pressure on the streets, even if substantial by the standards of, say, the Reform League in 1867, by itself did not have much effect. The day-by-day chronicle of events in the *Annual Register* appears to be dedicated to showing that all history is the history of class conflict. On 20 September 1885, 2,000 attended a Socialist meeting at

Whitechapel, and on 27 September, 30,000 heard the Socialists at Limehouse. On 3 November election riots took place in Maidenhead, Guildford, Penzance, Glamorgan, Suffolk and Dorset. On 4 January 1886 troops were sent against the Welsh quarrymen. On 8–10 February there were serious riots in the West End. On 11 February, there were serious riots at Leicester, followed on 15 February by Socialist riots at Birmingham and unemployed riots at Yarmouth. On 21 February a Socialist meeting in Hyde Park was said to have drawn 50,000. On 26 February there was rioting again by strikers in Birmingham. Finally, in Manchester there were large and potentially dangerous unemployed and Socialist demonstrations on 28 February and 18 March. If anyone wished to draw alarmist conclusions about the imminent breakdown of the existing social order, they had ample material to support their case, without looking across the Irish Channel. Yet what apprehensive reactionaries were concerned about at the time this was going on, was writing letters to *The Times* to prove that life on the western seaboard of Ireland was a little irregular,* and doing so as if the fabric of English society depended on that issue alone. Even the ordinary voter failed to take much notice of the working class demonstrators, for a fair number of by-elections in the first three months of the year showed only that party loyalties remained little altered. (It was only in April 1886, when working class pressure abruptly died away, that the Liberal vote started to look insecure). People saw what they expected to see, and having made a firm choice that their contemporary reality was going to be the spectacle of the Irish question, they were not to be put off by the worst outbreak of working class disaffection for at least twenty, and perhaps for forty, years. Their thought had so definite a structure to it, that it could not be simply modified or adjusted to take into account some new predicament like class tension. They needed to believe, in order to maintain their central myth of the supremacy of parliamentary activity, that class tension, the destructive element in social experience, arose from right or wrong conduct within the parliamentary situation itself. News which did not fit this scheme, had to be eliminated, or re-defined as non-political (i.e. as matters of police

* By far the worst Irish disorders in 1886 were in Belfast, but here again the reality singularly failed to attract proportionate public notice, probably because the Belfast situation did not permit romantic identification with an oppressed landlord minority, as did the news from the west of Ireland. The Belfast situation was so confused it was by-passed by the main stream of controversy. Writers in *The Times* in 1886 were much troubled by undoubted cases of destitution among Irish gentlewomen accustomed to living on small agricultural rents, and this at a time when the bottom had apparently fallen out of the English domestic economy: clinically, a curious case of transferred insecurity.

or charity), or projected on to supposed threats among the parliamentary community like Chamberlain or Gladstone. When the
unemployed sent a deputation to Salisbury at his private house
on 5 February 1886, it was entirely proper that he should tell
them of his wish for ministerial action to start major relief
works around London (something that his own ministry, only
a week out of office, could have provided if it had wanted to). In
short, Salisbury felt that a relaxed treatment in a disingenuous
public relations manner was the right response to working class
crisis.

In this treatment, it must be admitted, the working class were
at least put on the same low footing as the capitalists. What
Salisbury meant by giving the latter the Royal Commission on the
Depression of Trade, apart from its being a move designed to
embarrass the Liberals and detach some of their support in the
chambers of commerce, was that the aching slump of the mid-
eighties was going to be of little importance in politics. The
chambers of commerce may have submitted numerous and emotional memorials urging the opening up of new markets, especially
in Burma, but Burma was annexed for traditional reasons of state
which most Tories would have accepted, slump or no slump, at
any time since Theebaw's accession. The cabinet did not take
cognisance of the slump, or discuss remedies. It was outside their
mental picture of what was to be dealt with, except when they were
dealing with Ireland. They knew that politics in Ireland was a
matter of harvests and prices, and they thought closely about the
political implications of these. They did not transfer the habit of
mind to English industry. 'Fair trade' and a Royal Commission
were for playing to the gallery. Only Chamberlain believed and
feared that the slump could involve politically dramatic consequences: 'Two bad winters and we shall see the people taking the
bit between the teeth.' Such comment stands out because it is
almost unique. The anxieties of politicians were focussed, not on
demotic unrest, not on organised labour, not on economic decline,
not on petty collectivism, but on the danger that the Liberal left
might become the dominating force at Westminster. This, and this
only, was the 'threat to society'.

Another notable development was that the trades unions had
ceased to be a political topic. This was an unexpected change, for
in the period 1860–67 the darker shadows of the debate on democracy were as often as not filled in with forebodings about organised
labour. It was a bogey: it was also a very real fear. Since then, the
depression of the later 1870s had weakened the unions: the legislation of both parties had given them, first respectability, then a

more privileged recognition of their needs: and their name was no longer linked with industrial terrorism. Union leaderships took on a more bipartisan tone as the old Reform League militants fell away, and their members had been politically invisible for a decade or so. In a world which contained the perfidious Mr Gladstone and the dangerous Mr Chamberlain, no professional speculator upon evils lying in store would want, in 1885, to waste ink on decrying trades unionism. As in print, so in private letters: politicians neither had practical occasion in the present to think about unions, nor did they envisage that politics in the years to come would involve some important problems about relating unions to the party and parliamentary system. Trade unionism, as an institution, could not have counted less if it had been a minor nonconformist church: indeed, in 1886, some politicians thought it a fine prize to win over the great preacher Spurgeon, but no one ever mentioned the TUC. Indeed, when the TUC held its conference, almost unnoticed, at Hull in September 1886, the opening address was given by an outgoing president who was a Tory: while his successor, urging a more activist line on the Congress, put forward a programme of free schools, more numerous sanitary inspectors, and opposition to Sunday opening of museums. The politicians' letters of the period would have to be searched hard and long for any suggestion that trades unionism even existed, let alone that it might one day be a force in the land, and those who believed that the future contained a radical democracy, had just as little to say about it as everyone else.

Politicians did not expect, in general, to find the future agreeable. Argyll's apprehension that 'we have a greater crisis before us than any since the Revolution'* over-dramatised a widespread sense of misgiving. However they did expect that they would have no difficulty in guiding that future and that political leadership would be supplied by those who had customarily supplied it. In so far as they seriously considered dealing with the electorate, they thought this could best be done by retaining the identities they had been used to presenting under the previous system. Salisbury, Hartington, Gladstone, and Chamberlain, the makers of party character, decided that they could best ensure their position vis-à-vis the new electorate by taking no particular steps to modify

---

* Argyll to Gladstone, 9 Dec. 1885, printed, George Douglas, eighth Duke of Argyll, *Autobiography and Memoirs* (1906), ii 399: Argyll did not mean the Irish problem. The Duke some time later illustrated the amorality of the common man by telling a recollection of Wordsworth. Walking in the Lakes, the Duke had pointed out a mountain and asked 'Whose land is that?' The poet replied 'I had never heard that it was anybody's land.'

their previous image. What they owned was a public impression of themselves as a personified virtue, and that was too valuable to put aside or experiment with, and perhaps was beyond their power to modify. Hartington embodied (to the great public) practical sanity: Salisbury, intelligent traditionalism: Gladstone, moral authority: and Chamberlain, energetic subversion. These were their trades, as they were to some extent their genuine private selves. The general election of November 1885 up to a point justified all four of these men in their views that no new response to the electorate was needed. (They had in the Tory–Irish alliance a ready-made excuse to explain away Liberal failure in many urban constituencies). Hartington in particular found that it paid handsomely to be orthodox in the old Free Trade, non-radical manner in his own industrial Lancashire seat, despite the trade depression and despite the fact that he was challenged by the leading Fair Trader, W.F. Ecroyd.* Similarly Chamberlain's 'unauthorised programme' merely served, as it was intended to do, to confirm and strengthen the ideas always held about him. In so far as there was a positive response to changed conditions it came from small groups centred around Goschen and around Churchill who attempted to formulate new conceptions of what the Liberal party should be and what the Conservative party should be. Their actions were distinctive, not only because they failed but because they provided unusual examples of politicians basing their actions on a view of what the electorate wanted.

In 1885 the essential conflicts therefore were within the parliamentary world. The most serious issue before the London dinner-tables was the reconstruction of the Liberal party. Even this was a disagreement within narrow limits. Both Whig, Radical and centre factions accepted Gladstone's deep conviction that the working class electorate could best be guided and controlled by constructing a middle class consensus agreed on a policy of limited concessions to, and emotional solidarity with, the manual working class. Whigs and Radicals differed only in degree as to how this should be done. Whigs were in general much closer to the Radicals, than they were to those like Goschen who advocated dealing with the working class by forming, in overt opposition to it, a middle class party of resistance.

Throughout 1885 Whigs and Radicals were looking for an issue to fight over, not primarily because they were Whigs and Radicals, but because they were united in a belief that cabinet politics was about the cut-and-thrust of personal competition. They tried in

---

* Rossendale, 1885: Hartington L. 6060
Ecroyd   C. 4228

turn to quarrel over Egypt, the budget, the Sudan, and Ireland. In no case did it prove difficult to find compromises which everyone could have accepted, had the disagreements arisen only on the merits. The real question is to determine the function that this disagreement had for the Radicals. They did not envisage an early Radical take-over of the Liberal party. They were entirely willing to accept Hartington as leader of the party, on terms which recognised their importance. It was because they anticipated and indeed wished to bring about a Hartington leadership that the Radicals fought so hard in order to establish their bargaining power. The 'burning social issues' which served as Radical ammunition in cabinet and on the platform were of secondary importance, not least to their exponents.

Chamberlain's personality was not torn between an interest in social reform and an interest in parliamentary intrigue. By 1885, whatever may have been the case in his earlier days, the social reform existed to serve the intrigues, but the intrigues did not exist to serve the social reforms. There is no evidence in his papers of continuous interest in or repeated study of social matters during 1885. His papers include a file on the temperance question, 1876–1891 (ten documents!) but there is no file on the burning topic of the housing of the urban poor, then being considered by a Royal Commission which issued its first report on 9 May 1885, offering ample material for any genuinely concerned campaign. In fact Chamberlain's interest in the question as a public topic remained strictly limited, and his campaign in autumn 1885 said much less about better urban conditions than did his abortive effort of January 1885. For a president of the board of trade, he was remarkably underemployed throughout that year, and his speeches did not draw much from his administrative experience. What lay behind his speeches was not Fabianism or municipal prowess or trends towards collectivism, but the political tactics of the moment. His speeches on social policy were not foreshadowed in his correspondence, as were his schemes for a central board. There was no obliging lackey of the Capt. O'Shea sort at work for him here: Morley, his tame littérateur, actually opposed his paymaster on collectivist topics, while Collings was a one-issue man. What has to be explained is not a timeless, situation-free assertion that Chamberlain supported social reform, but the fact that in 1885 Chamberlain gave brief campaigns to the subject at two specific times, while the rest of the time neglecting the subject. In January 1885, taking advantage of Churchill's absence in India, he made a bid for the favours of a supposedly collectivist new electorate. At least, that was on the surface what he was doing: but the bold

11

moves on his part were probably a response to his discovery a few days before of imminent reconstruction under Hartington (which he favoured), in which an adequate place had not yet been found for him. Similarly, Chamberlain's autumn campaign on chiefly social issues was probably a hasty replacement for the dramatic Irish campaign which he and Dilke had been planning in June and July as the centrepiece of the election. Throughout 1885 Chamberlain wished to limit his attempts to construct detailed policies to the sphere of Irish devolution, his activities in other directions being confined to the creation of a mood of aggressive depredation which left him free from specific commitments and which, at least metaphorically, could be worked out on the train going down to the meeting. Chamberlain's studiously vague principles were not meant to stand in the way of Chamberlain, but only of other people, and were intended to be operative only at specific times for specific purposes of Chamberlain's own choosing. He inveighed against the lack of milk for the urban poor: he did not suggest actually giving them any milk. The topics of the Unauthorised Programme were defined with midday clarity: the when and how of their achievement, and the degree of Chamberlain's commitment to them, were carefully evaded.[3] Though Chamberlain (not Dilke) temporarily had to take a line aimed at controlling the Liberal Left, he was not interested in creating a Left Liberal party (as Labouchere mistakenly thought he ought to be). He wanted a broad-based, multi-faction party with a wide range of contemporary meanings, just like Hartington did, and his tactics in 1886, again like those of Hartington, only become intelligible when it is realised that he sought throughout 1886 (and much later) to lead a non-Tory majority party, rather than (like Harcourt or Gladstone or Morley) to lead a faction.

Chamberlain's power within the system rested on various elements, all of them flimsy. There were subordinate considerations, such as the shrewd Tory belief that he was their best vote-winner. Salisbury, for instance, wrote of the new electoral régime 'I think we shall suffer a good deal in the first instance: but Chamberlain is doing his best to save us',[4] and later thought that 'Chamberlain does good wherever he speaks'.[5] This meant he never lacked publicity from opponents. The main point, however, was that he was supposed to be prepared to act upon a realistic knowledge of the desires of an 'aggressive democracy'. This, and his general trenchancy of manner, inflated his status enormously – for the time being. It certainly concealed how little lay behind his assumption of authority. While it may not be surprising that his desk at the Board of Trade was not piled high with work in hand, it is more to the point that he did not establish a radical junta till summer 1885, and still more that he neglected the task of welding backbench opinion into an effective bloc. He was probably further from the ordinary backbencher than most ministers: and he spent too much of his evenings talking to fellow intriguers and to Society figures, to make himself easily available to the ordinary decent Liberal M.P. He saw the road to power in traditional terms, as something to be trodden by a few kindred spirits, craftsmen in manipulation, rather than through general solidarity. He may or may not have believed that the National Liberal Federation was a reliable weapon which meant he need not cultivate ordinary parliamentary popularity. He liked to be felt as a threat, and could not quite see himself in other roles. He was curiously unclear that, for a person like him, the Liberal party in the House of Commons was a very important body. He preferred to concentrate on the intricacies of personal realignments in cabinet. In short, the Whigs had educated him to their way of thinking, in which he excelled. But he could only play their game so long as his insight into popular politics was still accepted as given.

The 1885 election left this reputation in rags. The party did peculiarly badly in areas like London where Chamberlain had hoped to do well. As Michael Barker has pointed out, Chamberlain neither anticipated nor desired that the balance within the Liberal party would be shifted from the towns into the shires. His anti-landlord propaganda on rural themes was chiefly aimed at swaying urban audiences, not at winning rural constituencies. Chamberlain had indeed advised a prospective candidate to seek out borough constituencies and avoid county seats. Chamberlain's impieties about the Church of England turned out to be singularly maladroit: Dilke found in London 'the Church could beat the non-cons out of the field'.[6] By the end of the election, Chamberlain was utterly nonplussed: 'The boroughs do not care for our present programme, and I confess I do not know what substitute to offer them.'[7] He had shown that he did not know about the things he was supposed to know about – the inducements that would win the popular mind. Dilke, campaigning in London, simply had to disavow the Chamberlain programme:

'Even my Nonconformist friends come to me to implore me to pledge myself against disestablishment ... and free education is unpopular. I'm now fighting the election entirely on City guilds, and against protective duties – these are the only two questions on which I find our views popular... I fancy this applies all over London.'[8]

13

The root cause of Chamberlain's failure was that he had overrated the ideological prejudices of the electorate and under-estimated its financial self-interest. As Mundella told him, 'Our Philistines are dead against increased rates',[9] and he had to lecture Chamberlain on the elements of city politics:

> 'It is a fact that some of my best supporters who are radical on other questions are not yet convinced about Free Schools... I have seen some of the candidates in the London School Board who are advocates of Free Education ... *not one of them* ... had had the courage to mention it in their addresses... The significant thing is that the Liberal Organisations stand aloof from the Liberal members of the School Board, because they are so unpopular.'[10]

One therefore has to face the fact that, whatever Birmingham may prove, Chamberlain as an urban politician could be disas-trously mistaken, and that the 1885 election only brought this to light. The election produced a fairly advanced (but good-humoured) majority among the new Liberal M.Ps, combined with a clear absence of radicalism among electors in Chamberlain's own urban Liberal area of support.* The new parliament wanted Chamber-lain's policies from Gladstone's leadership. Chamberlain's old formula of progress through confrontation was a non-starter in early 1886, partly because the election results had shown that he was far from being, as he claimed, a man who had his finger on the pulse of the Nonconformist vote and of the urban elector. The Liberal backbenchers might want progress, but they preferred the soothing and painless brand of 'progress tomorrow' being offered by the official leadership in early 1886. It could therefore be fore-cast that, whatever happened about Ireland, Chamberlain would during 1886 look for new sources of support outside traditional radicalism. The coming of democracy left Gladstone, Salisbury, and Hartington with their roles unaltered, but forced Chamberlain to set off in search of a new one. His search could only be successful if one of the established leaders vacated the central ground that

---

* Cf. Goschen to A. Grey, 1 Dec. 1885, Grey MSS: 'What a crushing defeat Radicalism has sustained. I agree with you in thinking that the elections are a complete justification of moderate Liberals': and ibid., 12 Dec. 'There will after all be a large brigade of good Liberals outside of Chamberlain's circle...' According to *The Times* of 15 Dec. 1885, the new parliament contained 111 Oxford graduates (37 from Christ Church) and 82 Cambridge men (52 from Trinity). As regards schools, Eton supplied 72, Harrow 46, Rugby 27, Westminster 8, Winchester 8, and Charterhouse 4. Such figures, though interesting education-ally, indicate little politically.

they all occupied after the 1885 elections. Chamberlain, therefore, had little to gain by giving further thought to radicalism, or by doing anything to prevent polarisation over home rule.

When this is seen, other things fall into place. Gladstone's studiously vague election campaign in 1885 takes on a masterly instead of a senile air. The politicians to the right of Gladstone who sensed a need for the popularisation of reaction become interesting figures, not just prisoners of their reactionary class background. The apparent stupidity of some very inscrutable politicians like Hartington should be interpreted as a wise attempt to cope with a situation where the entire absence of reliable information about electorates made any assumption of insight most imprudent.

In those circumstances Gladstone was everyone's enemy. From one way of looking at it he stood in the way of a deal between Whigs and Radicals which would settle policy differences. He also stood in the way of a deal in which the more powerful ministers would all promote themselves at the expense of the less powerful ministers. The Whigs found Gladstone too quietist (or simply weak) in foreign policy and too radical in home policy, whereas the Radicals found Gladstone too inclined to be drawn into international arrangements overseas while in home policy he was quite unable to give the new lead which they saw as necessary. A further point which told against Gladstone was that the ministers specially associated with him (Derby, Selborne, Childers, and Granville) were thought to have become a political liability, so that both wings of the party were keen to see Gladstone's dependants disappear in his wake. In January 1885 Gladstone was as clearly marked for the axe as any prime minister can be. There were signs that he accepted this. There were many times during 1885 when he, without prompting, very nearly threw up politics in an irreversible way. In view of this, the problem of how in 1886 Gladstone was able to conduct the most successful party purge in British history becomes a most striking one. The problem of how his lieutenants were to displace Gladstone was solved in 1886 by Gladstone displacing his lieutenants. In the process, Gladstone won not only a personal victory but determined the character of the party for a long time ahead, if only by ruling out the most interesting positive possibilities along with those who embodied them.

The politicians of 1885–86 were dealing seriously and adequately with the main problem confronting them, namely that of presenting themselves and the world of parliamentary activity generally in a sufficiently attractive, necessary and interesting way to maintain a general consent to their hegemony, and so maintain the political system they had been used to since 1868.* The secondary and really rather different problem facing them, that of mediating the specific demands of the electorate, received less attention and insight, but at least it was not neglected, and in the area where it was most possible to do simple things simply, i.e. social reform, the politicians found no difficulty in intimating that the construction of an era of good feeling was not beyond them, indeed that the courteous service of farm labourers, crofters, and miners was something to which they had long sought to devote themselves.

This was a matter of achievement as well as of intention. It comes as a surprise to find that any legislation at all was passed during the turmoils of 1886, but it was so. The problem, perhaps, was why so much good was done with so much stealth, no one pluming themselves on what had been, by ordinary parliamentary standards, an unusually fruitful session. The main reforms, on outward show at least, did correspond to the sentiments and sections of a slightly radicalised Liberalism. Humanity reigned. The crofters were attended to, and the agricultural labourers, in lieu of allotments, got an act dealing with payment of their wages in cases of bankruptcy. The miners got an amended Coal Mines Regulation Act. Children were protected from the sale of liquor by one act, and from guardians by another. The medical profession was reformed. A measure gave facilities for helping the mentally impaired. The Irish labourers received legislative attention, as did the Irish destitute poor. The hours of labour of children and young persons in shops were limited. Finally, on a rather different but still ostensibly progressive point, the nonconformist conscience won the formal repeal of the contagious diseases acts, thanks to a direct intervention by Gladstone which reversed the procrastination of his whip.[11] In all, no less than 59 public general acts received the royal assent in 1886. All that was required was the virtual absence of high politics from the Commons for much of the session, the benign indifference of the leaders, and the total absorption of the great men in problems of party structure. It must have been purely in a general sense that the Gladstonian régime had any collective knowledge that it was a socially progressive ministry, yet that general sense was quite decisive. Virtually without discussion, the old political managers had adapted to the kinds of things the new backbencher and the new Liberal voter were supposed to consider

* Cf. Kimberley to Derby, 14 Dec. 1885, Derby MSS, unsorted: 'This House of Commons is not Radical, and if the Irish difficulty could be tidied over would support a Liberal Cabinet in settling many urgent questions in a reasonable manner. If their settlement is postponed, the new voters will get angry and may become revolutionary.'

important. Whatever backslidings occurred afterwards, the time in 1886 was 1906, when read by the Liberal clock. One newly elected Liberal long remembered 'the eager and multiform hopes and projects of that wonderful Parliament of new men, in deadly earnest'.[12] The Liberal party at large felt younger in spring 1886 than it had done for a long time.

When one turns to Ireland, all is different. While the British policy of politicians can and must be explained in terms of general ideas about a British political and social system, the Irish policies of British governments at Westminster cannot be explained in terms of Irish circumstance. They must be explained in terms of parliamentary combinations. Obviously, British politicians were not trying to influence Irish audiences (even Orange or Liberal Protestant ones); less obviously, they were not (in 1885–86) sensitive to the rising power and developing branch structure of the National League, the imminence of dark winter nights or of turbulent quarterly rent demands. Before the Plan of Campaign, the rhythm of seasonal disorder in a peasant society had not imprinted itself on Westminster, where statistics of outrages were little more than the playthings of debate. The monthly returns of crime in Ireland were not awaited with the concern and interest given to, say, modern balance of payments figures. Within broad limits, the situation in Ireland could fluctuate up or down and no one would notice very much.

Politicians did not know about Ireland. The public mood had, since the early 1880s, included a horrified awareness of the drama of the Land War in its most sensational aspects, and as members of the public politicians shared this awareness, and perhaps privately added to it, as when Trevelyan brooded on Irish threats to abduct and mutilate his young children. However, this awareness included little of Irish reality, and in particular it excluded preoccupation with the problems of the British machinery of government in Ireland. Dublin Castle, like Simla, was expected to consume as well as create its own difficulties, leaving only the causes célèbres and the questions of parliamentary combination to be dealt with at Westminster. The stream of anxious propaganda about Ireland came from amateur sources (the Irish Loyal and Patriotic Union, and Buckle's *Times*), and had its chief effect on amateur, female, and academic opinion: naturally so, since the chief premise of their argument, that a Parnellite takeover was an imminent possibility, was never accepted as plausible by the professionals. *The Times* news coverage of Ireland was as scanty as its editorial and polemical treatment of it was excessive: and the historian can get virtually no idea of what was actually going on in Ireland, what speeches the Nationalists were making, and so on, from the politicians' chief breakfast-time reading. 'English opinion about Ireland' was manufactured in England for home consumption, had nothing to do with Ireland, and everything to do with England.

The cabinet did not regard Ireland as its collective business in the sense that it did so regard such questions as the enfranchisement of the police, the promotion of the Duke of Connaught, or the situation in Bechuanaland. Even in the talkative Liberal cabinet of 1885, talk did not get round to Ireland till the end of April, and then it was diverted, somewhat against usual practice, into a cabinet committee. In Salisbury's cabinet, we can only weigh the written words, and not the spoken ones, but even so there are telling signs of, at best, detachment. Salisbury seems to have filed his ministers' letters with care, and the only ministers, outside the Irish government, who mentioned Ireland even in passing in their correspondence with him, were Northcote, Beach, Churchill, Smith, and Cross. Of these, the efforts of Northcote, Smith and Cross were scanty and belated, and the only systematic discussion of Ireland going on was that carried on by Salisbury, Beach, Churchill, and the Irish government, who were all (except Carnarvon) greatly more concerned with party alignments than with Irish unrest. Unless a politician was actually required to administer Ireland, he would see no reason to think about it as a country presenting problems of government, unless he saw himself as an entrepreneur of party tactics who could turn substantive questions of government into the gold of party gain. Very few Tory ministers did see this as their job. The 'Irish question' was the temporary and particular name given in the 1880s to a continuous and permanent existential problem which party managers inflict upon themselves. This is the task of finding party lines, divisions, and alignments, and then rationalising these for the benefit of that great majority of even their senior colleagues who hold themselves bound by habit, honour, loyalty, and decency to an essentialist view of party, definitions of which they then loyally expect the moral entrepreneurs of the party to evolve for them from their own inner nihilism.

Public opinion about home rule was a phenomenon in itself. On the Gladstonian side, it is fairly understandable how what was morally reprehensible in November 1885 became a matter of facing cruel necessities in January, a struggle of classes in Gladstone's manifesto of 1 May 1886, and emerged in the campaign rhetoric of the summer as a sacred trust, ripening over succeeding years of coercion and eviction from a question of justice and autonomy, to one of sentimental humanitarianism. This process presents no problem. On the other side, however, it is much harder to account for the excitement of those Unionists to whom home rule presented an apocalyptic threat. Those who became really emotional about the danger, were chiefly underemployed journalists, academics, and members of the upper classes whom for one reason or another life had excluded from a political role. The more a man cared about the fate of Ireland, the more certainly he would be excluded from the counsels of those who guided Unionist intentions. If one is to look for a total absence of alarm, one must look to the Unionist headquarters (even if it is as far away as the Riviera, where Salisbury spent the spring of 1886). Sincere and decent Unionist peers like Westminster and Cowper, who were horrified by what might happen in Ireland, and cared little for party considerations, were only allowed a walking-on role in the political drama. 'Unionist opinion' as a phenomenon as distinct as possible from Unionist politics, involved the whole apparatus of 'grand formal receptions and garden parties, long business gatherings, stirring propaganda meetings, demonstrations, publications, protests, election campaigns and all the rest' as Mrs Fawcett of the Women's Liberal Unionist Association put it. In addition there were such consummate exercises in amateur agitation as importing 800 Irishwomen for an Albert Hall demonstration.

These manifestations of spirit in search of consciousness indicated, not only the usual blind reliance on a moribund tactical tradition, but vague tendencies to disoriented activism among the unoccupied. For some years the Primrose League, the Women's Liberal Federation, the various moralistic pressure groups, the Bulgarian atrocities campaign, and even perhaps the mock parliaments such as that in which Bonar Law perfected his reticence, had in their different ways indicated certain needs for an assertive amateur political arena. The Corrupt Practices Act of 1883, by suppressing various strictly male and mercenary kinds of political professionalism, had turned politics into a game, like bicycling and lawn tennis, which had the enormous advantage that it could be played by both sexes. The certainty that they were doing important work was a valuable rationalisation of their own existence for the unimportant members of the leisured class. For these, and other reasons, it is fair to say that the vast army of militant amateur Unionists, often with a non-party background, had never been so happy as in 1886. They needed the crisis more than the crisis needed them. They needed the crisis in a way which made it impossible for them to see there might not be a crisis. The phenomenon belongs to the pathology of political virginity. The curious may extend their view to that public which was roused to agitation by *The Times*, in the hope that it represents 'public opinion on home rule'. It does not: it represents a closed system of self-coopting articulateness which found itself able to exist without relation to the power structure of high politics, or to the opinion of the various non-political publics. *

The same kind of limitation applied even to hardened journalists. They were part of the system of high politics, in that they might be summoned from on high to leak information or fly a kite. For instance, Churchill liked to speak of the *Morning Post* as 'my paper'. What they did not have, however, was an independent power of finding out what was going on, or a view of themselves as concerned in the continuous formation of policy. A later generation of journalists did indeed have this quasi-ministerial status, especially in the Liberal party between 1900 and 1920. They towered above any backbencher. The editors of 1886 were lesser beings. Only Cooper of the *Scotsman* and Wemyss Reid of the *Leeds Mercury* stood out as men thinking and acting like politicians. Editors were still editing, rather than running a moral constituency or engaging in dialogue with ministers.

It is rather harder to evaluate extra-parliamentary party organisation. For one thing, such bodies hardly gain a mention in the papers of major politicians. For instance, if it ever mattered who won control of a party machine, it mattered in May 1886 when Chamberlain lost control of the National Liberal Federation. Yet there is scanty evidence that his rivals were sitting on the edges of their chairs waiting for the decision (as they did indeed wait for the outcome of Chamberlain's meeting of backbenchers of 31 May). Again, there was very little political and social contact between Schnadhorst and party leaders. The draper was not asked to dinner, or to help cut down trees at Hawarden.

There was no direct equivalent to Schnadhorst in the Conservative party. Middleton, the agent, had not really had time to establish himself following the abrupt resignation of his predecessor in March 1885, and Middleton's interpretation of his task was always a narrow one. There was a similar change in the whips' office, so that in 1885 the Tories went into the election with a new

---

* E.g. those who voted at by-elections in spring 1886, who were wonderfully unconcerned about the prospective dismemberment of the empire. Mr G. ó Tuathaigh's work on constituency politics (Cambridge Ph.D. in progress) demonstrates seat by seat the predominance of economic, confessional, personal, regional, and local issues over the Irish question in the by-elections of 1886. Drops in the Liberal vote (e.g. at Ipswich) were not necessarily due to the impact of national issues. The voting public was fairly obviously not convulsed by home rule: *The Times* and its public were. We are indebted to Mr ó Tuathaigh for guidance on this point.

chief whip (Akers–Douglas) as well as a new national agent. Following years of neglect at constituency level under Winn's régime as chief whip (1880–85), the Tory machine could hardly be said to be in prime order in 1885, though there were almost certainly sweeping improvements by the time of the 1886 general election.

The National Union of Conservative Associations was less a help than a hindrance. Organised originally to do the work of a supporters' club, it had developed in the mid-1880s into an arena where pro-Churchill and pro-leadership factions fought inconclusively but with singular malice. Its function was in fact to divide the great body of Conservatives in the country on the lines that divided Tories in the House of Commons.

Faced with such tangles, Salisbury simply left much of the general oversight of party work to junior colleagues. In England, he relied on Edward Stanhope, a hardened anti-Churchill campaigner who was also a clear-minded organiser, and in Scotland on Reginald Macleod (who got the job because he was Northcote's son-in-law and kept it because he was at university with Arthur Balfour). The interesting assumption behind these arrangements is not that a purely informal designation of responsibilities was preferred, but that party management was thought to require the close attention of only one fairly junior minister (and one who was very isolated from his colleagues other than Salisbury). As to the tone of the campaigns in 1885–86, Salisbury simply made his own decisions.

What has to be stressed here is not the familiar proposition that the lower levels of political parties are unimportant compared with the higher ones, but that the two levels are simply not in close connection. For instance, the National Liberal Federation was remarkably like the National Liberal Club: a kind of House of Lords for provincial notables who did not seek a parliamentary career, but who wished for some institutional recognition. The sense in which various spheres of life (e.g. party organisation, the press, the organised working class, the Ireland of peasants and priests, and so on), all things important in themselves and to those in them, were politically unimportant in 1885–86, was that the politicians' world of the time was a closed one. It was closed to those outside, in terms of direct access and influence: it was closed also in that politicians were bound to see more significance in the definite structure of relationships at Westminster, than in their contacts with the world outside. In short, a politics of dialogue was not to be expected so long as the public understood very little of Westminster, and Westminster felt itself remote from the public.

21

Explanations of Westminster should centre not on its being at the top of a coherently organised pyramid of power whose bottom layer was the people, but on its character as a highly specialised community, like the City or Whitehall, whose primary interest was inevitably its own very private institutional life.

2

A Synopsis of Events
1885–86

The reform bill crisis of 1884 involved a period of intense concentration which not only obliterated the political themes of previous years but left politicians without any sense of direction when it was over. They also needed a rest, some of them taking this during the Christmas holidays, some extending their political convalescence well into spring 1885. When politics began again in January, party leaders had not had the usual autumn discussions on the coming year's work, as a direct result of the reform crisis. They were therefore flung unprepared into the business of a new session, in its three main branches: the handling of public affairs, the construction of well-defined relationships among themselves, and the playing to the gallery necessary in what was certain to be an election year. The only settled point in a universe of flux, was the knowledge that the seats bill could be relied upon to consume a great deal of parliamentary time, even though the only leaders from whom it required continuous attention were Dilke and Northcote. Since the terms of the bill were a foregone conclusion, frontbenchers and backbenchers alike had to look for significant activity outside the normal parliamentary routine.

At the start of 1885, both the extraordinary parliamentary lull, and the extreme difficulty of the negotiations over Egyptian finance, which passed all understanding, were driving Liberals to think harder than ever before about the ever-present problem of replacing Gladstone. There could have been no more sensible occasion for retirement. The premier had just marked up a great public success in carrying through the reform bill*: his health, and particularly

---

* 'He never quitted London in greater personal triumph. No one could have

23

his nerves, had subsequently given way quite badly: and for the first time he himself had to admit that he found a financial problem, that of Egypt, almost beyond his powers. Moreover, his will to continue was visibly wearing thin.

The answer to the Liberals' problem ought to have been simple. They had in Hartington a generally acceptable successor. No other names were seriously canvassed. The one question which absorbed his abler colleagues was the terms on which they would be able to join his ministry. Hartington wanted the job and rightly saw himself as entitled to it. He was certainly the best prime minister the country has never had. He was trusted, respected, and did not make mistakes. He was the only British politician able to impress himself upon the public as strong and resolute. He had over twenty years of political life in him. He could work extremely hard. He was, in fact, the ablest Whig since Palmerston. (His interesting private life did nothing to detract from his popularity). What really needs to be stressed is how, much of the time, Chamberlain and Dilke were looking forward to taking their place in his government.

Three methods of easing out Gladstone were available. There was, first, an extensive and secret plot among senior ministers in spring 1885 to oust him and share out his inheritance. There was also personal harassment of Gladstone as an old, tired, and ill man, over the finer points of Egyptian finance. Finally, inspired by just the same motives, the lieutenants also tried a policy of blandishments on the premier, the chief example being the brotherly love which developed between him and Hartington during their Holker Hall visit in early February. Those who wished to retain Gladstone were few and far between, and also lacked the standing to do anything on his behalf, even had he wished it. Immediately prior to the fall of Khartoum, it was becoming extremely hard to think of any basis on which Gladstone could continue much longer as leader. The movement of both wings of the Liberal party against its centre was irresistible.

All this was before a Sudan crisis was really expected. Profound complacency prevailed at the War Office and elsewhere until the last moment. The difficulty about Egyptian finance had melted away, chiefly owing to changes in French and German politics, but also owing to fine and hard work by Childers, Granville, and Lyons. Other anxieties were also absent. There was virtually no visible tension over Ireland, and no discussion of it in cabinet before late April (due to Gladstone's use of pressure of events to postpone consideration of a large scheme of Irish reforms sub-

achieved what he has done and at the same time kept his party completely in hand' (E. Hamilton's journal, 6 Dec. 1884).

mitted by Spencer for cabinet use late in January). If there was an Irish question, the country had lost interest in it. One further soporific was the absence of opposition attack. The liberals consequently experienced the centripetal strains of what felt like a one-party system.

Subsequent developments in 1885–86 cannot be fully appreciated without exploring in detail how closely Gladstone's career came to being totally wrecked in the early months of 1885. At two points, separated by the crisis over Khartoum in early February, the leading members of his cabinet, Whig and Radical, were on the verge of reaching a clear understanding as to what the successor ministry should look like in terms of policy and personnel. This was worked out in some detail, as such plots go.

Security was excellent. Gladstone and his main associates remained in the dark throughout, and therefore put up no apparent resistance. Hamilton's diary, which rarely missed anything of importance, had no inkling of what was going on, and does not refer to the plot at all. Indeed, Hamilton remarked with some surprise that Chamberlain and Hartington were seeing eye to eye over Egypt, whereas the crux of the reconstruction was that both men regarded themselves as able to forego their well-advertised opposition at the drop of a hat. It was presumably also felt, wisely, that it would be no use trying to incorporate Granville in the cabal. In any case, his early departure from the scene was one of its prime objectives.[13]

The press, however, had some idea of what was afoot, if only because Gladstone's poor health in early January was public knowledge. Press speculation centred on the idea that Gladstone's retirement was imminent, that Hartington would take his place (no other successor being canvassed, privately or publicly, during the whole episode) and that Granville, Selborne and Derby would depart along with Gladstone. What the press did not scent was the part being played in the reconstruction by Harcourt, and still more by the Radical ministers. Chamberlain's speech at Birmingham on 6 January appeared a well-timed obstructive effort designed to show that a Hartington ministry could not get off the ground.[14] In fact, Chamberlain's concern here was to convince the public that he had nothing to do with a plot which in fact he was quite willing to see succeed:

'Above all things we have to avoid the possible suspicion that we have joined in any intrigue against Mr. G. His retirement is possible and may be necessary. Hartington and Harcourt can bring it about – but let us be very careful not to enable them to say that we have been engaged with them in dividing the lion's skin.'[15]

Chamberlain's 'socialistic' speeches in January 1885 were, to nearly all observers, so obviously what was really going on, that they provided the perfect cover for a great deal of activity which entirely negated the 'socialism'. Chamberlain's wish to pre-empt certain positions at the next election still left at least half his mind available to pursue an entirely unrelated set of calculations at the level of cabinet politics. Derby and Selborne were particularly outraged by Chamberlain's doctrines, Selborne protesting that the lot of the town artisan was a thousand times harder to bear than that of the agricultural worker, and Derby spluttering 'In the eyes of some of our colleagues the great crime seems to be to *own* anything'. But these, be it remembered, were the reactions not of a compact Whiggery at bay, but of individual political innocents whom Whigs and Radicals generally united in wishing to drop. The reconstruction that Chamberlain and Dilke wished to see was not radical in character. Its most specific feature, probably, was an agreement to move towards a more Palmerstonian policy overseas. In explaining Liberal cabinet politics in 1885, the rift between Peelite and Palmerstonian ideas in foreign policy was deeper and more lasting than that between Whig and Radical ideas on domestic policy: while neither source of tension mattered as much as that simply caused by competition among able men acting in a necessarily unstable situation of collective leadership.

When Dilke returned from France on 3 January, he found intrigue already in full swing. Already that day Harcourt had told Carlingford that he and some others were 'determined to break up the government'.[16] Any thoughts that this might be accompanied by a simple Radical withdrawal from the cabinet, followed by a Tory caretaker ministry, were ended when on 4 January Chamberlain wrote to Dilke refusing to resign over Egypt, as Dilke had urged. From then on, for the Radicals, any change centred on the departure of Gladstone, to be followed by a strong new Liberal ministry. Chamberlain probably turned down any idea of resigning himself, because he had wind of what was afoot. On the morning of 4 January, Harcourt had spent two hours with Hartington at Devonshire House deciding who was to be in the new Hartington ministry.[17] The prospects were thought enticing by all who viewed them. Their imminence was believed to be hastened by Gladstone's ill-health, and by the offence it was thought he would feel at the way the cabinet had mauled his proposals after his early departure from the cabinet of 3 January. The altered despatches had been sent overnight to Hawarden, not without a hope that they would precipitate Gladstone's withdrawal from politics.

On 5 January Dilke called to see Harcourt, 'much delighted at the idea of being foreign minister under Hartington'.[18] Harcourt told Dilke that Gladstone and Granville were going to resign, and that he (Harcourt) would be lord chancellor in the new Hartington ministry. About 6 January Chamberlain described Harcourt as 'a most loyal friend, though he cannot be expected to agree with us in everything'; given his past rows with Harcourt, this shows Chamberlain's willingness to wipe the slate clean as opportunism dictated. On 7 January Chamberlain, Trevelyan and Dilke met to discuss the terms on which they could join a Hartington government. The only really difficult points, it was thought, were Egypt and an inquiry into the civil list, though Chamberlain added the proviso that Parnell or some other Irishman should be chief secretary. The revised terms formulated by the Radicals at this meeting were less stringent than those previously put forward by Chamberlain, speaking for himself only, when he had called for support for Collings' proposed inquiry into the illegal appropriation of land and commons, an inquiry into the position of labourers, and into charitable endowments.[19] On 10–12 January Dilke was the guest of Hartington at Hardwick, where he was supposed to be going to coach Hartington on the impending seats bill, although in the end Hartington did not raise the matter.[20] Dilke's ideas on reconstruction were clear:

> 'Mr G seems likely to go. Lord Granville [will] go with him and I think the Lord Chancellor. In this case Hartington [will] move Lord Derby, take in Rosebery etc. I suppose I should have to move. I think Kimberley ought to go to the F.O. as I think it should be held in the Lords, but some people want me there. *I don't.*'*

At this point we can consult Harcourt's account, as given to his son,[21] of the Liberal plot to rid the party of Gladstone and Gladstonianism. (Dilke, to whom the plot had from the start allotted a plum job, did not feel impelled, as Chamberlain did on hearing of negotiations which gave him no definite promotion, to

---

* Dilke MSS 43894 f. 163, dated 9 Jan., and closely paralleled by an entry in the Diary of Dilke's secretary Bodley, probably of talk on the same day: 'As Dilke was going to Hardwick, I asked him if it was likely that Hartington would have any talk about the office he should take supposing Mr G. retired at once, and Hartington became premier. He told me he thought Lord Granville would decline to serve under H. and that he (Dilke) would be offered the Foreign Office' (Bodley's diary, 11 Jan., in Shane Leslie, *Memoir of John Edward Courtenay Bodley* (1930), 98).

raise his bridal value by 'socialistic' displays of Jacobin irreconcilability.)

'The object of the meeting between Hartington and W.V.H. this morning was to consider the formation of a new government in that event. They decided that Granville, Derby, Selborne and Carlingford should be left out, W.V.H. to be Lord Chancellor, Dilke Foreign Secretary, Forster Colonies, Goschen Chancellor of the Exchequer. Chamberlain's place is not settled, Rosebery would come in as Lord President and Privy Seal, Northbrook would remain at the Admiralty, Childers might take Hartington's place at the War Office, Lefevre would probably have the Local Government Board and John Morley the Post Office or vice versa, probably both with a seat in the cabinet.

'W.V.H. said Dufferin is the proper man for the F.O. but we could not ask him to give up India to join a government which would only last for about two months. I dare say the Tories are not particularly anxious to turn us out before the next General Election, particularly after Gladstone has gone, because with him the greater part of the animosity will disappear. Kimberley and Trevelyan will keep their places at the Indian Office and the Duchy of Lancaster. It would be difficult to find an Egyptian policy on which Hartington, Dilke, W.V.H. and Chamberlain can unite. Hartington would like a protectorate, but none of the other three are likely to consent to this. W.V.H. told him plainly this morning that if that was to be his policy, he would not join him but suggested they might combine on the following: England to remain in Egypt as at present, not guaranteeing the debt, but undertaking to make up the deficit as long as we are there; a guarantee for the loan for the Alexandrian indemnities, and an understanding that we are to remain in Egypt so long as Wolseley and Gordon were there, but when they could be got away, then the whole future of Egypt would be settled by Europe by a conference in London or at Berlin. This Hartington seems inclined to adopt and W.V.H. thinks Chamberlain and Dilke might be inclined to agree to it, though no doubt it would be difficult. There is no office sufficiently tempting for Chamberlain. I suggested the Home Office, but W.V.H. said "Oh no, that could never be. The Queen would never consent to have him in a place of constant communication with her. Fancy Chamberlain at the accouchement of Princess Beatrice!" There is some difficulty in finding a new Home Secretary, unless Henry James would take it, which W.V.H. does not believe. If he does, Herschell will be Attorney General and Horace Davey Solicitor

General. If the government is formed without Gladstone, Granville and Derby, Bismarck is quite likely to turn round again and support our proposals as his cantankerous behaviour is entirely due to his hatred of those three men, and to a certain amount of pique about the way they treated him about Angra Pequena.'

The first half of the anti-Gladstone plot took place between the New Year and the fall of Khartoum. On balance, it went well. A remarkable degree of agreement and eagerness was achieved. The only flaws concerned the failure to find a good berth for Chamberlain in the initial plans, which led Chamberlain to make demagogic speeches designed to show that a general reconstuction (of which he otherwise approved) could not take place except on his terms. His point was made, but not without a certain amount of annoyance to Hartington, who in the period 22–28 January turned back with greater sympathy to the old arguments that he must lead one section on the right of the party, with Gladstone holding the scales in the middle. At any rate, Hartington began to be agreeable to Gladstone, except behind his back: but this has to be seen in the light of Gladstone's improved health. The first phase of the plot had depended on his insomnia to a high extent: now, with that taken away, Gladstone had to be cajoled into leaving office (an impossibility after about 5 February), or a new 'patriotic' consensus about the handling of foreign affairs had to be found which would exclude Gladstone.

The first phase of the intrigue was intended to appear as the normal process of replacing a sick prime minister: the second phase was based on the idea of replacing a discredited foreign policy with a more 'Palmerstonian' one, by playing on the mood of national emergency. The actual incidents of the plot over the next few months are, naturally, a little hard to piece together, but cajolery of Gladstone, quickly followed by the idea of a 'patriotic' Liberal party, were the keys to the matter.

In middle and late January, Chamberlain and Dilke at least were relatively inactive, Chamberlain because of illness, and Dilke because he had good reason to believe that the fruits of power would fall into his lap all the easier if he was not seen to be exerting himself to get them. With little to be found in their normally copious papers, therefore, developments become increasingly hard to follow at this stage. The plot may be regarded either as having lost momentum, or as being almost entirely tied up at this stage: and it was possible for Gladstone to spend six days (Friday 30 January–Thursday 5 February) under the same roof as Hartington at Holker Hall without embarrassment and without arousing surprised comment among the other conspirators.

The problem is to decide to what extent Gladstone's long visit to Holker (which would have been longer but for the fall of Khartoum) should be seen as more than simply a relaxed period of convalescence. Gladstone gave out that he was seeking a rest, and did indeed shut himself away from visitors while at Holker. It was not difficult to find quiet in a household dominated by the recluse Duke of Devonshire, whose days revolved round prayer meetings and carriage rides. Gladstone certainly had not arranged beforehand to meet Hartington at Holker, and was quite surprised to fall in with him on the train from Liverpool, where the premier had been staying for the marriage of his son Stephen to the daughter of a Liverpool doctor on 29 January.[22] But that an invalid premier should shut himself away in a north Lancashire stately home for a week in February with the most philistine of his colleagues, his colleague's recluse father and unhappy widowed sister-in-law, can hardly be explained by a need for fresh air and rest that would obviously have been best met by remaining where he was, at Hawarden. Though chance may have brought them together, Hartington and Gladstone inevitably turned it to political account, discovering quickly how much they had in common when away from the rush of business. Each morning Hartington came to Gladstone's dressing-room, and the two men remained closeted together for hours with the latest telegrams. It all seemed infinitely more pleasant than cabinet routine.* Capping it all, Gladstone broke with habit and, gun in hand, accompanied Hartington on a shooting expedition.

However, this interlude of good feeling did not necessarily mean that Hartington no longer had the premiership in mind. It might equally well show that he was aiming to capture both the succession, and Gladstone as an honoured Nestor. The only safe way to depose Gladstone was by cultivating him: and indeed after a few days of intimacy, Hartington could write that Gladstone was 'really looking forward to his retirement soon'.[23] Events on the Nile shattered this hope. On 5 February news arrived of the fall of Khartoum, and the same day the first meeting of ministers to consider the central Asian question took place. These two contingencies marked the end of suitable opportunities for intrigue for some time.

The fall of Khartoum did wonders for Gladstone's health. As

---

* 'Lord Hartington in full swing with Father without any [idea] of calling in Downing St or writing' (Mrs Gladstone to Mary Gladstone, n.d. but c. 2 Feb., 46223 f. 179).

the burden of his labours increased dramatically, so all suggestions of his unfitness disappeared. It was, in fact, Hartington who came near to breaking physically under the strain of the succeeding months. It is difficult to judge how far, and how quickly, Gladstone had recovered during the latter part of January from disorders which were as much nervous as physical.* When the projected reconstruction of the ministry was aired again in February, therefore, after a decent interval for the flurry after Khartoum, it could not be done on the grounds of Gladstone's own best interests. The desperate character of the international situation was used instead, as a suitable pretext for a series of promotions which those concerned had wanted well before the international horizon became seriously troubled. Hartington was to be pushed by the Radicals into forming a war ministry, nominally non-party, a scheme being hawked round the cabinet by Chamberlain: 'Childers was much taken with my idea of a "Patriotic Minister" (Hartington) carrying on the War with of course loyal support of the outgoing Ministers.'[24]

Hartington, so Childers was told, would be given 'the loyal support of those of us who went out with Mr Gladstone', or more vulgarly, Childers would not find himself without a job. Chamberlain, according to Dilke, next proposed to defeat the government on anti-imperialist grounds, in order to force forward a reconstruction on relatively imperialist lines:

'On 25 Feb., Goschen having asked for assurances as to the Berber railway, Chamberlain wrote to me[25] saying that if Hartington gave them, it might be a sufficient cause for our resignation, as we were not prepared to commit the country to establishing settled government in any part of the Sudan. Chamberlain proposed that he should resign before the division, and that the government being beaten there should be brought about the establishment of what he called the combination or patriotic government, which meant a Hartington administration. I, on the whole, preferred to go on as we were, so I stopped a box of Hartington's which was going round the cabinet and

---

* Gladstone's doctor was 'mightily pleased' with his condition on his return from Hawarden, 20 Jan.; and on 29 Jan. the doctor again gave 'a most satisfactory account' of Gladstone's condition (Gladstone to his wife, 20 Jan.: E. Hamilton to H. Seymour, 29 Jan.: both Glynne-Gladstone MSS). On 17 Feb. the premier was 'most wonderfully calm and well' (Herbert to Henry Gladstone, loc. cit.). On 18 Feb. the diplomat Morier 'almost wept' at the 'complete indifference' shown about the Sudan crisis by Gladstone, whom he found on meeting to be 'as jolly as a sand-boy' (Milner to Goschen, 18 Feb., Milner MSS box 182).

proposed an alteration of form which prevented Chamberlain going out.'[26]

Following the decision, which was supported, however reluctantly, by Dilke and Chamberlain, on 28 February that the cabinet should retain office, the itch to resign remained strong with the Radicals, but its context was different. It was not now a question of reconstructing the ministry, but of finding an opportunity to break away from it, preferably in association with Gladstone, so that they could approach the coming election free of all ties and making a claim to be the only true Liberals. Chamberlain had to take Dilke with him; and Dilke had invested too much of his reputation in the seats bill to wish to push ahead with resignation pure and simple, except in very advantageous circumstances. A further consideration was that a Tory minority government would be doubly undesirable, in that it would give its leaders a better chance to woo the new electors, and because a precondition of its existence would be an undertaking to treat the Tories with consideration.

The fall of Khartoum in February, followed by the Russian crisis in March and April, not only revived Gladstone's will to rule but restored the Liberal party as an effective force and a formidable government which could handle major problems with deliberation and skill. The opposition was shown up by the same events as weak and divided, incapable of providing an alternative government and, within six weeks of Khartoum, it was Northcote, not Gladstone, who had lost control of his party.

Gladstone, in even greater degree than other senior ministers, handled the appalling overseas situation in spring 1885 with astonishing force and judgment unclouded by emotion. He showed himself, once again, able in the most serious crisis to work harder than anyone else and to produce correct and agreed solutions at exactly the right moment. Faced with continual threats of resignation from most of his cabinet, he did not in fact lose a single minister, yet his policy in public appeared strong (perhaps too bellicose, in the Russian case), patriotic, and was difficult for the opposition to oppose. For the last time, it was shown that the best political minds in England were concentrated in a largely Whig cabinet. Government by dispute (even by competitive resignation) proved an extremely effective method of handling great imperial issues, and the personal jealousies of a cabinet of prima donnas one of the best motives for sound work.

The exception was Chamberlain. His lack of departmental or national contribution to government was outstanding. He had not Dilke's excuse of absorption in the seats bill. He could not deal with sustained competence with overseas issues in the way the Whigs did. With marginal exceptions, he kept to the modest role of a domestic politician. His speeches on social questions in January were quite unrelated to any programme of reform he might have wished to put before the cabinet. They were magnificent (or at least very unusual, even for him), highly courageous, successful in polarising politics at press level, and helped to stop the Liberals winning the election. Their full purpose is uncertain, but they must be seen in the context of Chamberlain's simultaneous attempt to win a good berth in the Hartington ministry. (The reason that such a good berth was not offered him was not because of any wish to exclude him, but for the contrary reason that he was so well regarded that there was some difficulty in finding a post good enough for him.)

The question of what Chamberlain was trying to do in 1885 is nevertheless an interesting and not an obvious one. His attempt to make urban social reform a central issue in party warfare in his January speeches was a palpable failure, not least because Dilke cautiously stood aside from his campaign. As a minor minister who had to find his sphere of self-assertion within domestic politics, Chamberlain thereafter had little choice but to involve himself with Irish matters. His dabblings in Irish affairs in January and February 1885 were pursued at a low level of intensity, as was appropriate considering that only by a leap of the imagination could they be seen as germane to a Hartington reconstruction. By mid-April, Gladstone was again so firmly in the saddle (and Hartington was showing understandable signs of exhaustion) that any question of a change in leadership had to be temporarily forgotten. Only Gladstone continued to remind people of the possibility, as a means of underlining his indispensability. All this had its consequences for Chamberlain. He had to turn to Irish questions, because there were no other issues to be seized upon that had not already been seized upon by others: and indeed he was so far from having a substantial and secure personal following on the Liberal backbenches,* that he (like Churchill) had to look to the Irish as the only possible way of giving himself command of a numerically substantial vote. In turning to the Irish, he turned away from Hartington, not because Hartington personally was reactionary (of his private views we know little), but because Hartington as a politician wished to represent broad English

* The Liberal chief whip, indeed, was able to claim that only five opponents of the second reading of the home rule bill were Chamberlainites, though this was probably wishful thinking (Arnold Morley to Gladstone, 19 June 1886, 44253 f. 13).

opinion. Thus for several months, from late April until sometime about July 1885, Chamberlain's activities centre on an attempt to capture Gladstone and to detach him from his other senior colleagues, by identifying him with plans widely believed to have emerged from Chamberlain's pocket. Chamberlain sought to achieve this by the most varied means: by bludgeoning Gladstone, by bludgeoning Spencer, by refusing proposed Irish reforms, by going to extremes of flattery in public speeches about Gladstone, by seducing Rosebery from the Whig camp, and by resolutely stamping out all prospects of a conciliatory settlement of Irish questions within the cabinet. In the end, he had to use the budget as a means of bringing down the ministry and preventing peace (on the Irish issue) breaking out in the party, even though such a peace would have been largely on his own terms.

What Chamberlain was doing, unwittingly, was to give Gladstone an easy way of solving his problems. From May onwards Gladstone was in the curious and perhaps rather strong position of having no obvious reason for retiring and no obvious reason for remaining. Indeed, he was able to put it about that he was staying on – *if* he was staying on – at the request of his colleagues, in order to save them from intense divisions. Those divisions had been neatly put into the centre of political discussion by Chamberlain, when had it not been for his machinations, the Irish problem need not have become a major source of tension. Gladstone maintained tension, by keeping the issue alight as something that had to be fought over by Liberal leaders, while presenting himself as the embodiment of possible agreement. The central board scheme enabled Gladstone for months afterwards to impose his own interpretation of the Liberals as a deeply divided party only held together by a reluctant leader, expert in conciliation.

Chamberlain had provided Gladstone with a formula for survivvival: what he had not done, in his various inexpert forays between January and July 1885, was to find a basis for fighting the election, either for his own use or for the party generally. Dilke, after a year in which, diligently sticking to his parliamentary chores, he had appeared as Chamberlain's shadow, initiating little except private and explosive rows with Gladstone, finally foundered late in July 1885 on the rock of the Crawford scandal. Despite the slowness and uncertainty with which the case developed, it was recognised by the informed from very early on that the scandal would be fatal to Dilke's career for the foreseeable future. Whatever future role Chamberlain may have envisaged for Dilke, the calamity which fell upon the latter in July must have seriously limited the things Chamberlain could hope to do. By autumn 1885, therefore, it was clear that Chamberlain could neither provide effective guidance for his party nor escape from political isolation.

While the Liberals marked time during the summer and autumn of 1885, the Conservatives had gained suddenly in purpose and self-respect. They indeed needed such a transformation, for in the early months of 1885 they were in a very sorry shape. The reform settlement of the previous autumn had not only removed all landmarks, leaving them nonplussed and potentially resentful, but it had left them with nothing to do. They did not know whether to be democratic or anti-democratic (even if the Goschen and Chamberlain wings of the Liberals did not seem to public view to have pre-empted both roles) and they did not know what else to be. The only possibility of achieving a dramatically new line in home policy lay in coming out for Fair Trade, and that had come to be seen as the penchant of Northcote and some minor figures who lacked the nerve and the promotional audacity to bring off such a major change. In such a situation, a party without a role usually repairs matters by presenting itself as an effective alternative government, and no more. Since very few Conservatives saw themselves in such a light, this, too, was difficult. Their position had to get worse before it could get better, and get worse it duly did, with the fall of Khartoum as the occasion of the biggest Tory reconstruction for a generation. The Mahdi transformed the Conservatives, after much travail, into an effectively-led party.

The debate on the vote of confidence (24–28 February) over Khartoum revealed unexpected resilience in the Liberal party, and complete confusion among the opposition. Contrary to all probability, the disaster on the Nile had a far more unsettling effect on the Tories than on the government, because it exposed them as a party without an effective and acceptable power structure. The debate on Khartoum, and its repercussions in following weeks, marked Northcote's political death, and ended the period in which the lieutenants of Disraeli ('the gouty brigade') formed a fairly established ruling group who quietly controlled the Tory party despite intermittent sniping from Churchill.

Disraeli's heirs were old, ill, incompetent, and on holiday. Northcote, because he happened to be competent and not on holiday, was the only major leader available as a target for Tory unrest in the Commons, and he had therefore to bear the brunt of criticism. With Salisbury taking things quietly in the south of France and Florence; with Cranbrook at death's door during spring 1885; with the party Nestor, Cairns, suddenly dying;[27] with Cross becoming a ludicrous, even bibulous figure; with Carnarvon idling at Portofino; with Manners and Richmond wanting nothing more than valetudinarian quiet, the lieutenants of Disraeli had ceased to be a credible ruling group. Only Northcote stuck to his duties, stumping his constituency in Devon, and forcing through the redistribution (or seats) bill in the Commons. It fell to Northcote to enforce loyalty to the inter-party compact on redistribution of autumn 1884, and thus to many of his party, already seriously disturbed by the constituency changes themselves, he came in spring 1885 to sound little better than a Liberal whip.

The Tory rank and file longed for office with a deep instinctive thirst. They longed for the unremitting 'rapier and rosette' partisanship of Churchill (then enjoying himself tiger-shooting in India, showing no desire to hasten home, or to have the ministry brought down while he was away from London). They could hardly fail to compare the supposedly vague and nerveless tone of Northcote's leadership, with the biting acidity of that of Salisbury (even if Salisbury's initial role in the Khartoum crisis was to demand decisive action from the government in private letters written from Florence, while his subsequent role consisted chiefly in very firmly preventing his party from taking an expansionist line over the Sudan).

In these circumstances almost any incident could have provoked trouble. It just happened to be, first, Khartoum, and then redistribution. On 24 February a meeting at the Carlton condemned Northcote's resolution on Khartoum as vague and weak, meaning that it might not secure office for the party. Salisbury was present to soothe them by stating that if they won, then a conservative government would be formed. Northcote's line in the debate (24–28 February), which was to demand a statement of war aims from the ministry without committing the opposition to anything, was openly challenged by Beach (acting, it should be noted, without any prompting from Churchill) who said Britain should not leave the Sudan without settled government. (Beach's convictions on this subject faded immediately on his taking office, if not before). Tory speakers in general diligently avoided proposing 'a new India in the centre of Africa.'

The division perhaps showed that Northcote was right in choosing a resolution which kept the emotional temperature down. With the government majority down to only 14 (302–288), the writing was certainly on the wall, and yet, happily for the Tories, there was no cast-iron pretext for resignation. An analysis of the division prepared for Gladstone[28] showed that slackness and indifference contributed a certain amount to the advantage of the Tories. Twelve Liberals voted against Gladstone, including Goschen, W.E.Forster, and Ebrington, all future Unionists. Ten

Irish Liberals and 44 home rulers voted against Gladstone, but, curiously, 17 Nationalists, including their whip, voted for him. Of those present, eight Liberals and one Tory abstained. Those absent altogether included six British and three Irish Liberals,[29] three home rulers, and five Tories. The immediate reaction in the House was confused, the result being seen as neither one thing nor the other.

The main effect of the Khartoum debate was to enhance Conservative difficulties. A series of minor divisions on the redistribution bill showed complete lack of loyalty to Northcote. It did not help matters that Salisbury had scored a personal success in the upper house with his vote of censure on the ministry, thus gaining the first opportunity since the redistribution compact of the previous autumn to show that party opinion accepted his part in that arrangement. On 16 March, Northcote called a meeting at the Carlton, essentially to secure better discipline over divisions on the seats bill. Many of the 150 members present, led by Beach and Chaplin, took a dissident line, (again of course unprompted by the absent Churchill), and it was clear that not much remained of Northcote's leadership after this supposed 'flagellation at the Carlton Club'. The following day, on a trivial motion, Beach led 47 Tories against Northcote and Dilke (about the same number as the 35 whose revolt on 15 June forced a crisis in the formation of Salisbury's government). The willingness of Beach to break up the Tory party, acting on his own initiative and in an election year, was testimony enough of its inner decay.

Tory ex-ministers were on the whole relieved that they could continue the not over-exacting life of an opposition. Carnarvon wrote 'It is a terrible prospect to succeed to such a heritage of blundering misfortune, and I shudder at the idea of a return to office.'[30] Beach, earlier on, could only say that the Tories 'may be obliged to beat them if they ride cleverly for a fall' but rather hoped to avoid this,[31] and it is not easy to say that Beach or any other Tory ex-minister unequivocally wanted a return to office. Richmond was quite typical in writing 'I think it very fortunate that the Govt had a majority in the House of Commons. We should have been placed in a very awkward spot if the Govt had resigned.'[32]

The attitude of Salisbury himself was quite consistent at all stages after his return from the Mediterranean on 12 February. Whether or not Northcote wanted passivity, Salisbury on balance preferred that course. On 19 February, before the debate, he wrote that Northcote's anodine motion 'will do very well' and, while paying lip service to the idea that the opposition should oppose, added by way of qualification 'however disagreeable and injurious to us as a party, such a result might be. But I do not expect that we shall succeed'.[33] On 5 March his attitude was far clearer 'I cannot say with what a sense of individual relief I heard of the division on Saturday morning. Whether the result has been good or not in a party sense may be open to question. On the one hand, as you say, there is the loss of such advantage as we might perhaps have gained by a dissolution on the old franchise: on the other, we should have been made responsible for the heavy budget and for the ever-deepening trouble into which the Empire is gliding.'[34]

Northcote himself was even more cautious. His initial reaction to Khartoum was 'I am afraid we must have a vote of censure...',[35] the fear being that 'we may be forced to turn the government out'.[36] After the division, Northcote was clear that he had gained what he wanted, that it to say a weakening of the ministry; 'I think last night ended on the whole unsatisfactorily and at all events very uncomfortably for the government. They will hardly have any strength to carry all their plans, if indeed they have any.'[37] Northcote and Salisbury, and nearly all their colleagues, were agreed with only minor variations of emphasis that whoever acted responsibly, it must not be the Tories. It was for this view of matters that, ironically, Northcote was hounded by his rank and file, who saw in him only an excessively responsible attitude. It was significant that both whips, Winn and Akers–Douglas, were among those siding with rank and file demands for activity. It is interesting that Churchill could so totally misread the situation as to write, from India 'It is quite clear to me that Salisbury and the Goat played to come in.'[38] The real interest of the increasing resistance to Northcote in spring 1885, however, was not personal, but was a symptom of well-grounded disbelief in the leadership's ability to maintain a competitive party system.[39]

After the Carlton Club meeting of 16 March 1885, the days of Northcote and the 'Old Guard' were gone for ever. A firm, new control over policy was established by Salisbury and Beach, with Churchill being allowed to appear (certainly in private correspondence, probably not in reality) as if he were the éminence grise who gave the (in fact formidable) Beach his orders. The relationship between Beach and Churchill is simply inscrutable, more so than that between Dilke and Chamberlain. By mid-1885, the dual leadership, in each House, of Beach and Salisbury had replaced the dual leadership of Salisbury and Northcote. (It is hard to know whether Salisbury wanted this). The 'Old Guard' were retained as party ornaments, to provide continuity and easily managed subordinates. Only Northcote, too competent to be a mere ornament, was harshly treated. No consideration was shown to him even after his displacement, and he simply became a forgotten man who ceased to have any effect upon politics, until the shortage of capable Tories resurrected him as foreign secretary in August 1886.

On 7 April 1885, Churchill returned to England from India, after having been absent since the previous November, to begin what was virtually a new career in politics. There is little trace of him in April, but in May he began to strike out on quite new lines. Indeed, his ideas came so thick and fast at this time that the most wildly unorthodox schemes were linked with his name.[40] The change in the Tory leadership caused a change in Churchill's political strategy. Under Northcote he had tried to appear as the right-wing alternative to a crypto-liberal leadership. In 1884, he was still uncertain whether his fortune lay in appealing to his party, which he thought wanted reaction, or to the public which he thought wanted liberalism but from non-liberal sources. With Salisbury firmly established from May 1885 onwards as an authentically Tory leader, Churchill had to veer round to a more progressive line, given plausibility by his real sympathies with Ireland. Throughout 1885–86 Churchill was looking for ways of seeking agreement with some part of Liberal or Irish opinion as a means of strengthening his hand in the Conservative party.

Churchill knew Ireland at first hand and understood politics there perhaps better than he understood politics in Britain, and probably better than any other British politician. Although his desire for a strengthened Tory party, a Tory–Irish alliance, or perhaps even a 'National' reconstruction of parties arose from his situation vis-à-vis Salisbury, he nevertheless reflected seriously on Irish questions, showing some willingness to pursue ideal solutions for their own sake and at some personal cost. If any British politician can be said to have acted from a genuine feeling for the Irish, it was Churchill. Had Churchill ever been allowed his head on Irish matters, he would have had a better chance than any other British politician of reconciling Ireland to the Union.

The origins, precise terms, and negotiations involved in the Tory–Irish understanding from May 1885 onwards do not particularly matter, especially as regards explaining the events of 1886. If there is continuity between the two years in Tory history, it lay in Churchill's wish to expand his sources of support outside normal Tory circles, and in Parnell's well-judged desire not to lose touch with the Tories. Salisbury, whose substantive views on Ireland are simply non-existent or unascertainable, had to consider the Irish problem as a Trojan horse led into the cabinet by Churchill with a view to his overthrow. Churchill, for his part, disguised his substantive views beneath a tactical indifference as to whether his Trojan horse should contain Parnellites, Whig dissidents, or Radical dissidents.

Throughout the Conservative ministry of 1885–86, the only real point at issue was the relative position of Salisbury and Churchill. This does not mean they personally disliked each other, and found it hard to establish a good working relationship. On the contrary, they formed a close partnership and enjoyed savouring each other's political intelligence, as was to be expected of men who stood head and shoulders above their colleagues. Between them they left little for the rest of the cabinet to do, and the latter were duly thankful to be absolved from non-departmental responsibilities. Most of them, had after all, been picked and trained by Disraeli to be accommodating nonentities.

The general election of November 1885 is of interest to the story only because it created a stalemate. The ideas of both parties showed the poverty of their thought as to how to approach the electorate. The latter body put forward some novel and interesting ideas of their own, like Fair Trade, which were, however, muffled almost at once after the election by the din of Westminster politics. The economic depression, though deeply felt, remained submerged beneath verbal manoeuvre. In December 1885, therefore, electoral considerations behind them, politicians turned inwards upon themselves to discuss the internal order of their own world. Ireland, which had been a peripheral issue at the general election, became the ideal instrument by which politicians could evolve new relationships.

Though the first election results were in by 25 November, the outcome remained in doubt till the very last. As late as 3 December, Salisbury still hoped 'we may be above low water mark'[41] (i.e. for a Tory–Parnellite majority), indicating perhaps that this was still the direction of his mind. Despite this prolonged uncertainty as to the arithmetical balance of parties, however, Churchill began as early as 30 November to engage in a constructive political manoeuvre to make something out of the election results. At this stage, Churchill's attention was turned chiefly on directly stated ends (i.e. acceptance in principle of cooperation with the Liberals) to be achieved by rather unspecified means: after this approach was slapped down by Salisbury on 9 December, Churchill turned to arguing for highly specific means (i.e. procedural reform) to rather undefined ends. Both before and after Salisbury's douche of cold water on 9 December, the point at issue was the same – whether it was time to explore the possibilities of an understanding with some Liberal leaders. This was what the cabinet was really turning down on 14–15 December, though Churchill paid little heed to their decision and continued till late in January, along with Beach, to look for a strategy of active mastery of the situation with which to meet the new parliament. Churchill's efforts (15 December– 2 January) to retain the tactical initiative by giving priority to reform of parliamentary procedure, in a way which had strong though discreetly unstated implications for party collusion, (and even in the end for a Churchill-inspired centre party) are outlined separately below. What concerns us here is his much more direct attempt to negotiate an arrangement with the Liberals, in the period between the elections and the first post-election cabinet (14 December).

Churchill's efforts were on a strikingly wide front and were as strikingly successful, at least until his colleagues, instigated by Salisbury, determined that they should be thwarted. At the time of the decisive cabinets of 14–15 December, Churchill had gone far towards being able to assure his colleagues that Chamberlain and Hartington would do nothing to harm them. He could not, however, make his colleagues do anything but shrink from such assurances, remarkable as they were. It was Churchill's need to find terms, any terms, with which to create a Liberal cave and perhaps thereby a Tory reconstruction, which led him to take an anti-home rule line after the elections. He rationalised this as a return to true Toryism, when in fact it was just the reverse: it was being led by what he believed was wanted by potentially dissident Liberals. Churchill rejected well-meant plans from Irish friends for a bipartisan approach to an Irish settlement, on the lines of the bipartisan settlement of reform in 1884. He placed his rejection on grounds of party interest and the wish to dissolve against Gladstone on the Irish issue. At the same time he admitted that 'no great change in the state of parties might result and the Tories would be definitely and decisively beaten on a distinct issue.'* This concealed an inner intention of a quite simple kind. Very few Liberals, in early December, wanted a pro-Irish bipartisan solution: but some of them might look at an anti-Irish one. Hence Churchill at times in December stressed the need for a 'true Tory', hard-line approach to Ireland: but he did so quite largely on Liberal grounds. 'Playing the Orange card' was not simply a reaction to the election results,

* For Churchill's elaborate but bogus formal grounds for spurning apparently centrist solutions of the Irish problem, see Maud Wynne, *An Irishman and his Family* (1937), 113, and Churchill to Morris, copy, Churchill MSS x 1145. Lord Chief Justice Morris had urged the announcement in the Queen's Speech of a committee of peers and M.Ps on home rule, and 'a sort of understanding between leaders' as in 1884 (Morris to Churchill, 5 Dec., Churchill MSS x 1137: Morris to Carnarvon, 6 Dec., Carnarvon MSS, PRO 30/6/55/38).

it was a fusionist tactic aimed as much against Salisbury as against Gladstone. Similarly, the wish entertained by Carnarvon immediately after the elections for an immediate resignation, urged on purely tactical party grounds as a way to confound the Liberals, was probably prompted by a non-partisan desire to stop the Tories coming out against conciliation whilst still in office.[42] With both Carnarvon and Churchill, displays of pure party feeling have to be interpreted as having almost opposite meanings.

Chamberlain emerged as more than ready to go in the direction Churchill wanted. Churchill's major task with Chamberlain was simply to find ways of conveying to an inattentive cabinet that Chamberlain wished to see them take the parliamentary initiative. The exact means by which Churchill sounded out Chamberlain hardly matter. No letters between Chamberlain and any Conservative leaders have survived from this juncture, but on the other hand it had been commonly understood for some time that Churchill and Chamberlain were on terms of unadvertised if unconcealed intimacy. Labouchere, moreover, although his own views, as early as 1 December, were for an Irish–Liberal majority government, was always standing by to facilitate this union of minds: and Churchill's unheralded visit to Labouchere on 3 December at once assumed the purpose of direct negotiation with Highbury, carrying to a higher level the line of thought first sketched in his overtures to James on 30 November. No campaign, perhaps, was necessary, the citadel having fallen and Chamberlain maintaining throughout December his own very clear idea of how the situation should be handled – on lines wonderfully close to what Randolph wished to engineer.

Strong convictions were not allowed to replace fundamental requirements of manoeuvre and window-dressing. Shortly after the first talk about a Centre Party reached Highbury, Chamberlain had his radical junta of five (himself, Dilke, Trevelyan, Lefevre, Morley) to stay (5–7 December) – the last time this group met. The primary purpose of summoning them was to instil into them the line that true radicalism required the Tories to stay in office, a line with which even Morley only half disagreed, and with which Trevelyan agreed strongly. With the Radicals in his pocket, there remained the question of instilling confidence into the Tory cabinet. Chamberlain's speech at Leicester (3 December) had only gone a little way in this direction, and that chiefly aimed at preparing the minds of the faithful: Dilke's speech at Chelsea (12 December) was much more obviously beamed at the meeting of the cabinet on 14 December. Dilke spoke strongly in favour of leaving the Tories in, using the language of extreme radicalism to put this case. Harcourt was also brought in on the scheme, Chamberlain visiting him on 8 December, and Harcourt speaking at Lowestoft about leaving the Tories 'to stew'.

Chamberlain held to this analysis consistently throughout December, not varying his views to fit in with correspondents like Morley and Labouchere whose minds were slipping away in other directions. There were other factors in his attitude. He let it be understood that he was incensed by a conviction that he had caught wind of negotiations between Gladstone, and the Tories and the Irish, negotiations which were wrongly withheld from him. What is odd is that Chamberlain was taking this line *before* either the Hawarden kite (17 December) or the Gladstone–Balfour interview (15 December). At the very moment when Churchill's proposals for a creative exploitation of the new situation were being turned down in cabinet, Chamberlain's loyalty to Salisbury was at its high water mark. Chamberlain, it was said, was determined not to take office, and to have nothing to do with Gladstone's home rule scheme. 'He has made up his mind to support the Tories, so long as they behave themselves, and to help them pass Liberal measures...'[43] The deeper question, whether Chamberlain's complaisance towards the Tories was designed to engineer the radicalisation of the Liberals, or whether he saw in it the chance of a creative 'centrist' coalition – rather like the 'National Government' he had tried to contrive in February 1885 – is one for which there is no relevant evidence save Chamberlain's own actions, which leave both those doors wide open.

Chamberlain's wish to be captured, then, exactly coincided with the cabinet's decision not to make anything much of Churchill's proposals for creating a situation which would capture him. Chamberlain, too, wished to be captured by specifically Churchillian means: 'I should warmly support any proposals for amendment of procedure which gave more power to the majority...', he wrote to Labouchere (meaning, of course, to Churchill) on 4 December, undertaking *en passant* to keep the Liberals too disunited to take office. Chamberlain had no thoughts of formal coalition, but every thought of a tacit one in which the real power travelled along the Churchill–Chamberlain axis. The ministry would continue to be a purely party Tory one, for a period which Chamberlain estimated at various times in December as one session, two years, and ten years.[44]

Churchill and Chamberlain were acting in reasonable and intelligent concert in the first half of December, with Churchill probably priming the pump a little to start with, particularly with such ideas as taking up the time of the new house with reform of

43

parliamentary procedure. Their relations, however, were probably essentially based on exchanging information. It is in another relationship that one sees Churchill at his best as an effective Liberal leader.

His influence upon Henry James is easy to trace. James, though important as a messenger while there was still bad blood between Churchill and Hartington, mattered enough in his own right, and he fitted easily into Churchill's schemes. Churchill had close links with James. He had come to believe that the two of them had master-minded the Reform crisis of 1884. James had reconciled him to the Prince of Wales in February 1885. James and Churchill, travelling decidedly *en garçon*, had taken a jaunt to France together in May 1885. Correspondence of September and October continued, on a note of boyish banter, to arrange *tête-à-tête* dinners. Not until 30 November, when James' re-election was known, did Churchill make his plan for James clear: 'I see that you and I will have to make another great arrangement as we did over the Reform Bill', modest words, indeed, and signifying a tacit centre coalition in which Churchill would be the moving genuis, whatever formal arrangements might be retained. There is little reason to doubt that James played along willingly with this: still less that it was Churchill who, rudely and abruptly, broke off all that the two had projected, and that he did so because to him the tenor of discussion in cabinet on 14–15 December, however apparently pedestrian the tactical issues under review, appeared clearly prohibitive of further intelligent direct negotiation with Liberals. Henceforward Churchill and Beach concentrated on attempts to construct a short-term tactical situation in which the Liberals need not be opponents, but to do this without bringing the Liberals directly into the scheme. Churchill, however, never gave full credence, as Beach did, to this latterday development of the collusive theme, so far as one can judge by his remarks that there was no way of avoiding conventional party warfare. The most serious point is whether Churchill was able to make his view of policy attractive to Hartington. At first sight this looks improbable: Churchill had made a dead set at Hartington in election speeches and Hartington had taken it badly. There may have been more private causes of rivalry at work also. However, manoeuvre has precedence over hatred, and Churchill received encouraging replies from his approaches[45] to Hartington through Henry James and Chaplin, but after failing to convert Salisbury (9 December) allowed the momentum to run down. The most difficult contrary piece of evidence is a remark by Churchill on 7 December 'Lord Hartington's animosity towards us grows more intense': this is, however, a straw untouched by the wind, and it may have preceded receipt by Churchill of more favourable tidings. At any rate, at no time after the election did Hartington indicate any wish for the Tories to be turned out.

To sum up, Churchill spent his time between the election and the cabinets of 14 and 15 December in trying to think of situations which would enable Liberals to support the government, and to find out whether Liberals in fact wished something like this to happen. No other minister went into the matter or even gave signs of thinking in this way: Beach's interest in inter-party collusion becomes important only after 15 December. By the 14th, Churchill was able to report wide Liberal interest (if not more) in maintaining a Tory regime – and Churchill had detailed tactical proposals for embodying this strategy, despite Salisbury's prior dismissal of collaboration. Churchill's tactical proposals were then discussed in cabinet on 14–15 December, probably without most ministers grasping their bearing on general strategy. His scheme for an elaborate reform of parliamentary procedure was there defeated at the level at which he understood it, though it was later allowed to live a shadowy life unrelated to general considerations of inter-party collusion. Churchill came away from the cabinet clear that more had been shelved than his pet ideas on procedure (later revived, but in an isolated context). His attempted resignation over this belongs to the same pattern of goals: it was seen, by colleagues, as an attempt to break up the ministry, and must be considered as such, as much as a sign of temperament. Both the very sudden fall of the ministry – sternly opposed in a casuistical homily by Salisbury – and its prolongation on Liberal sufferance meant the same thing: enormous possibilities of negotiated 'centrism' with Churchill as the master-mind, and Salisbury isolated from general politics by an inevitable posting to the Foreign Office. It was the latter condition from which the cabinet, especially Salisbury, drew back: Salisbury and Manners both mooted the case for a Hartington–Tory coalition on 26–27 January – but under conditions in which it would not have been a Churchill-inspired affair.

Little emphasis has been placed in this explanation on the actual content of Churchill's procedural proposals. Even this little, however, may be too much. It would be possible to place the proposed reforms in the perspective of developments in procedure during the 1880s, or to relate them to certain bees buzzing in their author's head, as in the case of Churchill's dislike of late (parliamentary) nights and his palpable anxiety about his health. All this, however, is beside the point politically. The issue before the Tories, from the elections onwards, was not how they should act in relation to the Irish: that was by then a matter so secondary that its formal termination eluded definition. The only material decision for the Tories was whether they should find an issue on which they could act in conjunction with some Liberals. All specific actions of theirs must be seen as having this extra dimension.

Thus, in the first stage after the elections, there was Churchill's hope of establishing in a more or less direct manner, a Liberal cave. His colleagues having put paid to this in mid-December, the same project arose again in different guise. By putting procedure (it could have been any other item of major business) in the centre of political attention, one could, provided there was Liberal collusion, exclude the Irish issue till further inspiration arose. It was not even necessary that Liberals should agree with Tories over procedure itself, provided they agreed on its priority over other business.

By mid-January, it was clear that the question of coercion in Ireland was inevitably coming to the fore, and that procedure must take second place. It was, however, possible to juggle with coercion as formerly with procedure. Three policies were possible, all of which might have involved putting some Liberals under the embarrassing necessity of supporting the ministry. One could continue with a policy of douceurs, denouncing all attempts at coercion, and doing some window-dressing with Irish local government and university bills. (It was the active presence of this possibility that kept alive in January 1886 some appearance that the Tory–Irish alliance might yet live,* and even forced the Parnellites to act with regard to that possibility, even though its chief function now lay in Tory–Liberal relations alone). A policy of not having coercion, while laying some stress upon the fact that this was not at all a pusillanimous omission but rather part of a carefully considered riposte designed to kill home rule by kindness and specific conciliatory measures, would chiefly have been aimed to strike at the hearts and minds of the Liberal right, though it would have affected the Liberal left as well. The Liberal right wanted to be Liberal, anti-Gladstonian, and anti-Irish, in that order: and a Tory policy of conciliation to Ireland would have offered them as good an excuse for keeping the Tories in, as a reactionary one. The second possibility was to carry through a coup of some kind in Ireland before parliament met, facing the Liberal party with the bitter choice of having to decide whether to *restore* disaffection in Ireland. This

---

* Because there were virtually no ministerial speeches between the end of the 1885 elections and the debate on the Address (21 Jan.), it was exceedingly difficult to judge whether there was or was not a Tory-Irish alliance still in shadowy existence. When Lord George Hamilton spoke at the Croydon by-election (16 Jan.) he was as Delphic as Salisbury had been at Newport in October. There was no public sign given, by Hamilton or anyone else, of changed views.

second possibility was embodied in the proposal for the simultaneous arrest of all the nationalist members on a charge of high treason, allegedly originating with Halsbury and taken up by Churchill and Smith about 16 January, when spice was added by Churchill's suggestion to Salisbury that he, Churchill, would be a good man to fill the vacant Irish secretaryship.[46] The third possibility was a carefully worked out, apparently moderate coercion bill, backed by a united cabinet and put forward as soon as parliament met as its main policy, with the Liberal right sounded as to its provisions.

It may seem hard to reconcile Churchill's resolute opposition to coercion at one moment, with his demands for it to be carried through *à outrance* only a day or two later or earlier. (It should be noted, by the way, that his talk of playing the Orange card, and his visit to Belfast in February, both of which originated in his presence at an ascendancy house-party near Dublin on 28–31 December, had little bearing on his conduct in January, when there were at least two distinct and substantial phases when his policy was 'green' without a fleck of 'orange' about it). In fact Churchill was as consistent, in everything save externals, as was Salisbury. Churchill pushed in turn all possible policies, whether substantively pro-Irish or anti-Irish, whether sensational or responsible, so long as they pointed towards some hope of joint action with the Liberals or towards an eventual possible reconstruction of the Tory party. Salisbury, for his part, was unwavering in his support for whatever was necessary to maintain the distinct identity of the Tory party, its leadership, and his position in it. In practice, this meant that Salisbury's position on coercion was never a position about policy in Ireland, but about parliamentary alignments at Westminster. The only function which Salisbury required of coercion was that it should be brought forward in such a way as to frighten off potential allies among reactionary Liberals, these at this time being nearly all convinced that traditional coercive legislation would not work, and thus help Salisbury to achieve his short-term end of a Gladstone home rule ministry. Salisbury was, conversely, equally opposed to sudden and decisive action against the nationalists, obviously partly on prudential grounds, but more because when parliament met, it would afford an intolerable inducement to 'patriotic' Liberals to keep him in power. Within this general framework of basically simple calculations, it becomes possible to understand the otherwise intolerably complicated and fluid situation within the Tory cabinet in January 1886.

Compared with Churchill and Salisbury, Carnarvon's position was simple indeed. His position on party structure and leadership was that he had no position, or rather that he was so much an orthodox Tory that he did not give thought to such things. Carnarvon's problems were about inessentials: personal grumbles, and the immodest initiatives that he continued to take in matters of Irish administration, such as university bills, which always fell through because they were essentially unrelated to the parliamentary world. As for his home rule leanings, Carnarvon did not feel them as separating him from the party in which his life was rooted, or as matter for intrigue. He wanted his views fairly discussed in party circles, but could not see how discussion could get anywhere in the short term. For, as he remarked to Mrs Jeune, 'how can it be carried? Such men as the Duke of Richmond and Lord Cranbrook in the cabinet and Knightley and Manners in the House would never agree to it – Knightley would resign his seat.' (Knightley, considering a Tory home rule bill possible in December 1885, had indeed decided to do just that).

In the first half of December, Carnarvon was out of spirits, and probably wanted to leave office before his party declared firmly against conciliation in Ireland. Carnarvon came over to England on the 10th and went round speaking very openly in favour of some home rule initiative, leaving rumours rippling in his wake. In the mid-December cabinets, Carnarvon's policies were finally put to the axe, and Carnarvon returned to his lesser schemes of amelioration with renewed interest. He was more interested in Ireland as a social situation than in the cabinet as a political situation, and probably thought, indeed, that cabinets ought not to be political situations.

On the 12th, he called on Cranbrook, who was extremely perturbed to find that Carnarvon, whose policies he detested, might 'upset the coach' by leaving office on grounds of expense and health, and because of his private agreement with Salisbury on taking office (not known to other ministers) that he would only hold office until after the elections. Cranbrook agreed that the expenses of Carnarvon's office were serious, especially since his Hampshire rents had fallen to a quarter of their former level. Cranbrook took Carnarvon's complaints at their face value, and both men acted without guile despite entirely contrary views. Cranbrook felt 'the greatest surprise and irritation will ensue' if Carnarvon went. None of the hard-line anti-Parnellites in the cabinet at any time showed any wish to hasten the departure of their home rule viceroy.[47]

What the impasse in Conservative policy-making in December 1885–January 1886 led to was the creation of an opportunity for Gladstone such as he himself could never have imagined, anticipated, or contrived. It is true that Gladstone, for his part, did avoid mistakes or commitments which might have hampered his return to office, and his handling of his own party cannot be faulted. His task, nevertheless, was a hard one, and the extra sense of urgency and inevitability which in the end, and only by the narrowest of margins, bounced him back into office, could only have come from Conservative failure, for complex internal reasons, to select any one of several reputable lines of policy. The Conservatives had failed to produce a partisan policy that made sense: they had given only derisory attention to the possibilities of a bipartisan Irish policy, whether on the (presumably, though not self-evidently) progressive lines proposed by Gladstone to Balfour in their talk at Eaton on 15 December, or on more anti-Parnellite lines such as most of the Liberal leaders would have liked. The failure of the Tories to interest themselves in either partisan or bipartisan policies left it open to Gladstone to come forward as an accommodating bipartisan figure who could also with ease impose his own reading of the situation on his party.

It is customary at this point to refer to the loftiness of Gladstone's motives. Certainly there can be no suggestion that in this episode he acted only from gross or opportunist motives, or with the degree of egoism he had shown in 1859 or 1880. On the other hand, it completely misstates the position to suggest that he was making a noble and altruistic sacrifice of position and authority for the sake of a cause. It is both unflattering and untrue to suppose that his handling of his party and colleagues, including Hartington and Chamberlain, was anything but highly felicitous from the point of view of the ends he had in mind. On the other hand, the extreme view that he used home rule to cleanse his party of radicalism can be largely rebutted by reference, firstly, to his successful policy of killing radicalism by kindness in early 1886, and secondly by his own precipitate adoption ('unauthorised', so far as his colleagues went) of an intransigent Radical tone in his manifesto of 1 May 1886. It was, of course, Gladstone's job as leader to cut Chamberlain down to size in 1886, but that was not because he was Chamberlain or because he represented a strong radicalism, but because he represented an apparently weak radicalism from which it was in the best interests of the Liberals to move away.

Gladstone's position on Ireland may be seen in many ways, some of them more fruitful than others. For instance, one can look at his views over a very long period of time, and on that basis assess him as a man who had early foreseen and privately sympathised with the emergence of home rule. This view is supported by the absence of hostile references (with one exception at Aberdeen in

1871) in his public utterances. It is also supported by selective recourse to private documents and to his correspondence with leading intellectual contemporaries, including Acton and Manning, where the Irish issue could be examined *sub specie aeternitatis*. This kind of evidence primarily establishes what is not in any case in doubt, that he was a tactful, sensitive, and wise man. It does not establish what Gladstone would personally have liked to do, or thought it might become possible to do, about Ireland.

There still remains, however, the question whether home rule in 1886 was not the cunningly designed culmination of previous phases of Gladstone's Irish policy. There is, indeed, a sincere Liberal tradition to the effect that Gladstone's Irish reforms formed a single coherent programme. In fact, only one measure looked suspiciously like a stepping-stone to national autonomy, and that was the reform settlement of 1884–85. It is now clear that Gladstone was primarily responsible for the inclusion of Ireland in that bill *pari passu* with Great Britain. This certainly strengthened the Parnellites both in Ireland and at Westminster. Whether Gladstone at the time valued such a prospect, or whether he simply took the line on which it would be easiest to secure cabinet and parliamentary support, is highly doubtful.

In other areas of policy, there is more discontinuity than continuity. It is often implied, for instance, that because Gladstone had passed one land bill in 1870, that he was inevitably dedicated to passing another at some future opportunity. In fact, this was far from being the case, for a revision of 1870 (as later of 1881) could only be an admission that his handiwork had been at fault, especially in those qualities of permanence which he had claimed for it.

Far from being eager to disturb his own Irish settlement, Gladstone in the late 1870s and at the start of his 1880 ministry was apparently willing to ignore the subject until it was forced on his attention. In the Midlothian campaign, Ireland was not put forward as one of those topics about which every Liberal elector should be thinking. Unlike Afghanistan, it was a far-away country for which the incoming Liberals had no programme or sense of mission. So far as there was any new thinking on devolution, it came from W. E. Forster, not from Gladstone, whose Land Act of 1881 was in political terms an act to break the Land League, and to detach Ulster from Irish nationalism. In 1881–82, the cabinet contained no stronger supporter of coercion than Gladstone, and the eventual release of Parnell was accompanied by the preparation of a new coercion bill, which was enlarged but not initially created by the Phoenix Park murders of May 1882. From 1882 there was

some tendency for Gladstone to see, rightly, in Parnell a conservative nationalist who could usefully be turned to account at some
future date. This preference, which was purely a comparative one,
for Parnell over the dynamite gangs and pure separatists, does not
imply so much a wish for home rule as a wish, strong and consistent, to bring Ireland under some reasonable degree of control.
By the time he left office in June 1885, Gladstone was no longer
willing to exert himself to secure coercion, but his ideas on autonomy were still quite restricted, not going beyond those of
Chamberlain and many others, including some Whigs. In a private
talk with his son Herbert on 4 August 1885, Gladstone stated:

'... He will not lead *quâ* Liberal v. Conservative. He will not lead
a section or division of the party. But he is ready to fight the
general election if matters shape favourably in two directions.
1) The Irish party must formulate a practical scheme of local
govt. for Ireland including a Central Board or Nat. Council calculated to work efficiently and which the Liberal party might
agree to accept. They must undertake to cooperate in this scheme
in its passage through parliament and in its actual working in
Ireland. 2) The Liberal party must be practically united in their
Irish policy. Apart from Ireland the difficulties are not so great...
Father still believes in Parnell and holds that his ... [past record]
entitles him to some confidence in his intentions and courage.'[48]

This document shows more than the fact that Ireland was viewed
in a context of deep party calculation. It shows that Gladstone, at
one of the last points where he had considerable freedom of choice,
really wanted the Irish, in crude terms, to come to heel. Indeed, he
actively lobbied Parnell through Mrs O'Shea with that aim in
mind.[49] It is easy to view his policies as overtures leading naturally
towards home rule, but they can equally well be read as leading in
quite a different direction: towards diminishing the independence
and strength of Irish nationalism, so as to benefit the Liberal party
and his position in it.

What has tended to escape notice about Gladstone, because he
was an obviously charismatic figure, is how similar his views were
to those of other people. He used the same assumptions about Irish
society, judged its turbulence by the same narrowly English standards, took the same instinctive dislike to the Parnellites whether
as individuals or as a potential government. He had little room for
optimism in his assessment of the Irish situation. He was not a
holder of extreme and unusual opinions, but above all a partici-
pant in an unusually wide consensus that there was no alternative
between home rule and coercion. His deepening sense of Ireland

as a maltreated nation in December 1885 is very interesting, but it was not the operative reason for his having to prefer home rule to coercion. There was nothing peculiar in Gladstone's behaviour except the long uncertainty about whether he would adopt home rule as a *sine qua non*, an uncertainty which suggests that, rather than be guided by any very strong personal views, he left his policies to be formed by the political situation as it developed. As Gladstone said 'it is a case of between the devil and the deep sea'.[50]

Not unnaturally, from December 1885 Gladstone was jotting down, purely for his own benefit, outlines of home rule bills[51] (which differed in crucial respects from what he proposed in April 1886). What we do not know, and still more important, what he could not know, would be the political context in which these useful contingency exercises might become the basis of legislation. They might (as was first intended) be tacked to a land bill. They might, separately, run as junior partners of a land bill. They might even be linked with coercion and a land bill. Context would be everything, and it would be impossible to see home rule emerging as front-runner in an Irish programme until the last moment. It is impossible to say when Gladstone decided to make home rule the centre of his Irish policy for 1886, but it could have been very late in the spring. The land bill, it must be remembered, looked during February as though it would smother home rule, and yet within weeks it had been quietly pigeon-holed. The case of the land bill is not the only example to show the difficulty of fixity of intention for one in Gladstone's position. The other glaring instance was Gladstone's sudden discovery of class warfare at the end of the Easter recess in 1886, having spent the previous winter carefully establishing himself as a preacher of one nation (and having done his best to establish a ministry of the Liberal Right to boot).

His interest in Ireland was an abstract one. He loved the principle, not the flesh. As with Bulgaria in 1876, the country was remote but eternal justice near. It was enough for him in 1886 to know Ireland through Dublin Castle officials, through correspondence of tactical intent with Irish landlords, and to 'get up' the subject in the way parliamentarians and draftsmen do get up subjects. It was second nature for him to deal with the subject as a parliamentary topic, once it had again become such: but it did not mean that he was in some special way uniquely close to the problem. What was more central to him in his fight against age, his fight to be, was his sense of Ireland as an appropriate area for moral energy. The following extract gives some sense of the situation. While staying at Eaton in early December 1885, Lady Cowper called at Hawarden and talked alone with him on Ireland:

'He was very civil: asked me about Ireland and whether we ever talked of it. Then asked me if I knew whether rents were being paid; and when I said they were not, then asked *judicially settled* rents; I said no; and he answered "if that can be proved, it would be a very strong point". He evidently knew nothing about it which struck me as so odd; and he got so excited when he talked to me about Ireland, it was quite frightening. He ended the conversation by saying "Well, it has come to this, we must give them a *great deal* or *nothing*". And I answered with some warmth "then *nothing*". Upon which he pushed back his chair and with his eyes glaring at me like a cat's, he called to his wife that it was time to go out ... I saw his table covered with MS of an answer to Huxley upon some religious subject.'[52]

There is plenty of testimony similar to the above as to Gladstone's beliefs. The problem is however to know whether they refer to the political world which Gladstone inhabited as a practising party leader, or to the religious and moral world which he dwelt in as a great Christian man. There is no understanding of Gladstone which makes sense which does not stress his ability to move rapidly from one world and atmosphere to another and perhaps incompatible one, forgetting for the time all the other contexts in which he operated. This was greatness, and we only fail to recognise it if we try to assimilate what the virtuoso practitioner of the politics of parliamentary manoeuvre thought about the Parnellites, to what Gladstone as a religious man, conscious of wrong in a high historical meaning, thought the righteous individual must believe about the grievances of Ireland.

Gladstone did not in fact enter upon home rule in a state of incandescence. He did not have Parnellites to dinner: indeed, with one or two possible secret exceptions, he refused point blank to meet them socially or politically. His recorded conversation at the time shows no trace of good feeling towards them, and suspicion of their motives which readily turned to disparagement. He barely preferred them, politically or personally, to Chamberlain. His entry towards home rule had no happy or generous note about it. He was not buoyed up and in high spirits, as Peel had been in December 1845, by the knowledge there was great work to be shaped. There was, in 1886, no union of hearts. From Gladstone's own point of view, the home rule fiasco is to be seen not as a tragic failure to achieve a potentially excellent settlement in Ireland, but as a not at all ineffective means of preventing that dire worsening of the situation over there which he had half convinced himself was imminent in January 1886.

Nor can one look to John Morley for a display of pristine idealism and enthusiasm. He was comically worried when T.P. O'Connor got hold of an invitation to one of his Newcastle meetings, urging his constituency chairman 'he ought not, I think, to have been asked, and I begged him not to come ... we must have no Irishmen prominent...'[53] He initially tried to harness home rule to popular dislike of the Irish, by presenting it as a scheme, first and foremost, of disfranchisement and political repatriation. He said some very unidealistic things about not wishing to take office under Gladstone (perhaps for the very obvious reason that he had to pay £805 for re-election, with 'another election this year a certainty',[54] and his pocket did not easily stretch to such things). What Morley showed in intimate political conversation at this time was fear, defeatism, and at least outward acceptance of the primacy of personal calculations. His later attempts to keep Chamberlain out in the cold, by threats of resignation if necessary, showed even more clearly how loyalty to John Morley came before loyalty to passing the home rule bill.

In a pleasanter way, it is important that Gladstone was less obsessed than on some previous occasions by his 'cause' of the moment, at least until the election campaign of June 1886. Seldom can a premier have had a more enjoyable short ministry. Absorbed only in problems which stimulated him, he dined out almost continuously, far more than in previous years. At the dinner table, he was almost always in capital form, and he chose his company more with a view to pleasure than to political effect. His conversation frequently centred on the trivial and anecdotal. Conventional accounts written in the shadow of party warfare entirely fail to convey how much Gladstone in 1886 was a sane, balanced, good-humoured but old-fashioned old gentleman whose life contained much more private pleasure than public anguish.

Simple and absolute commitment to the Irish cause by Gladstone can be read into the evidence by those (the great majority) who look for it. A remarkable lack of commitment until late in the day is however almost equally compatible with the evidence. For instance, some visitors to Gladstone in mid-January 1886 formed the impression that he might act sternly against the Irish: other visitors in mid-February surmised that he might lead a cabinet which rejected home rule. It is certain that he could not have known when the home rule ministry was formed, whether it would accept home rule. Because Chamberlain on 13 March forced the issue before the cabinet, none of whose other members showed any wish to discuss it, Gladstone was presented with an opportunity of securing his ministers' assent to the principle of the exclusion of Chamberlain (*alias* home rule). Whether Gladstone's drafting work in February 1886, and his initial production of a land bill, prove that he was committed to doing more than go with the majority of his cabinet on home rule (either for or against) is a question about assumptions as much as about documents.

It must be remembered, moreover, that had his cabinet 'of examination and inquiry' consisted of those he wished it to consist of, instead of those who were admitted by default, then there would hardly have been any chance of their agreeing to present a home rule bill. It may be that the build-up of expectations about his Irish policy in December and January, encouraged by Gladstone, in no way pre-empted his future course except in so far as it enabled him to form a government quickly, with Irish support, and with a completely free hand. It may be that, having formed his government, he did not see the situation as permitting him to go further with home rule than to work over the materials with the officials. (In doing this, he was doing less, not more than the previous government). Seen in this way, it was only Chamberlain's (surely unexpected and unpredictable) challenge on 13 March that enabled him to bring home rule forward as a question that could serve to unite his cabinet and increase his command of the party. The home rule bill, as hastily put together as a Disraeli reform bill, was hardly meant to establish home rule. All the classic objections – the Lords, the lateness of the session, the drafting problems – were obvious. The bill was however meant to unite the Liberal party by committing it to the principle of home rule and to prepare it for further protracted struggle in which there would only be one possible leader.

The best view of Gladstone's motives that may be obtained at present, would be one based on a distinction between his long-term hopes for the Irish cause, hopes which bore the full impress of a sternly just man, and his short-term political appreciation of what it was possible to achieve with the Liberal party and the Parnellites in the course of one or two parliamentary sessions. His short-term appreciation of the possible must be expected to have varied greatly from month to month, and even by the purest home rule criteria he would not necessarily have been wrong if he had seemed to prefer winning unchallenged supremacy over his party, to specifically Irish considerations.

All that in the end can be said about Gladstone's short-term political motives, is that he wished to recapture control of his party, control which he had had to share with powerful colleagues in 1880–85. It could be said that he wished to dismiss Hartington or Chamberlain because he disliked them. But he did not dislike Hartington (rather the contrary, he just found him rather young) and though he did dislike Chamberlain, he could cope perfectly well with uncongenial, indeed maddening, subordinates like Harcourt, chiefly by keeping away from them socially. A careful advocate might not find it difficult to imply that all the steps along the road to home rule were taken just after ascertaining that they would be unacceptable to Chamberlain: but this would probably be the fallacy of coincidence. Home rule need not have been meant to make Chamberlain a pariah, but it could not have failed to make him either that or a subordinate. Chamberlain would not necessarily have resented a subordinate role in a home rule government, had Harcourt not occupied the relevant ground, almost entirely by chance. Harcourt hated home rule as volubly as Chamberlain, he resigned more often from the home rule ministry, and yet he became Gladstone's loyal henchman while raging against the very idea of the bill inside the cabinet far more fiercely than Chamberlain dared to criticise it outside. Chamberlain went because Harcourt stayed, and Harcourt stayed because Chamberlain went.

The Liberal dissidents of 1886 are discussed in another chapter. They were a collection of small and not very friendly groups which would have looked distinguished had they been backed by average party opinion, but which when separated from the context of Liberal orthodoxy looked very makeshift and lightweight affairs. There were the ostensibly non-partisans, like Goschen, Argyll, and the Queen, selling each other goods none could deliver. There were priggish young Whigs who believed they had discovered a kind of modernising nationalism which would transform class politics. There were traditionalist Whigs who were not reactionary, and there were reactionaries who were not in the least like traditional Whigs. There were the inveterate 'clever' backers of reversionary interests, preferring the rising sun of Hartington to the setting sun of Gladstone. There were men with constituency problems. Somewhere in the background, the Rothschild interest was closely involved, whether at a spiritual level only none can say.

The dissidents had a hard task. Their task was not to defeat the bill, but (far more important to them) to create a winning parliamentary combination. To the right, they were faced with the towering figure of Salisbury, with whom competition was fruitless. To the left, Gladstone had moved over, helped by his opponents' alarmist rhetoric, to occupy the radical territories from which Chamberlain had been ousted. Both Gladstone and Salisbury thought they could best control their parties by polarising politics, and hence left no opening for Hartington or Chamberlain to lead an alternative party of moderate progress or of moderate resistance. The dissidents were left in limbo, and Gladstone showed no undue desire to extricate them. Had he taken certain steps in May 1886, Gladstone might have put Hartington in power, at the head of a Liberal majority sympathetic to Irish demands,* for the next generation. It is not clear that Gladstone did make this *gran rifiuto* knowingly, and he took care to avoid discussion of the point. His analysis of the situation must have included awareness of the possibility.

The other reason why there could not be a Liberal 'cave' in true alliance with the Conservatives, was that such projects were all expected, by both sides, to be linked to Churchill, and hence were almost automatically opposed by Salisbury and Tory orthodoxy. Saving the party and its power structure came before saving the nation from the common danger. It was actually necessary to Tory orthodoxy, not on far-sighted electoral calculation, but on leadership grounds, to risk the Union by creating a home rule ministry and preventing projects of coalition which never got off the ground.

Tory leaders did not show anxiety about the bill. If anything, they were simply contemptuous of what they saw as a phantom ministry. 'There never was a government', Beach told Salisbury on 27 March 1886, 'with less control over its nominal supporters: on general questions they depend solely on the Irish: and Labouchere could carry any revolutionary proposal against them any night, if we did not take some trouble on such occasions to help them.'[55] The Tories had to wait for a change in by-elections before throwing down the gauntlet: but in parliamentary terms they never felt pessimistic.

What did perturb them was the possible accession to power of Hartington. This they did act fiercely to destroy, by deliberately identifying opposition to Gladstone's bill with reactionary Toryism of the old school. They stripped Hartington of his Liberal garb and made it appear that he had passed quite outside the pale of orthodox Liberalism. Disraeli's greatest triumph had been to make Gladstone look left-wing. Salisbury's generation in office was founded on his verbal dexterity in making Hartington look right-wing in May 1886.

---

* Cf. Hartington to Chamberlain, 27 Mar. 1886, Chamberlain MSS JC 5 /22 /3, '... It seems to me that if it were possible to make some settlement of the Irish Local Government question, the land purchase question might be allowed to go on, on the very liberal basis established in the Act of last year.' Had Hartington been looking forward to a reactionary role, he would probably have put land rather than devolution first.

The Easter recess (19 April–3 May) had sharply divided the period of the debate on the first reading of the home rule bill from that on the second. The problems of the two periods were quite different. Until May, there was no question of the government being brought down, unless it were by cabinet dissensions, because the Tories were not ready for an election. By May the Tories were ready for an election, and therefore the situation was basically a pre-election situation. What went on in the House, therefore, had only a limited significance. Whether the bill scraped through (it could hardly do more) or was defeated, it would equally lead to an election in no long time. Similarly, a resignation by Gladstone would probably have led to a dissolution by the incoming ministry, if only to take advantage of Gladstonian disarray. To the 'House of Commons man' from whom our evidence mainly comes, the month between 4 May and 8 June was an enormously exciting drama of coups, plots, and fluctuating calculations of majorities. While Liberal Unionist managers consistently hoped for a majority fairly similar to what they actually got, on the Gladstonian side the barometer rose and fell with bewildering rapidity. The chief prospect, of course, was the belief that a reconciliation with Chamberlain was perfectly possible. Senior backbenchers like Whitbread and Vivian found it difficult to believe that their party could be split, and the parties to the quarrel had to pay lip service to their belief. Moreover, Chamberlain's group never deviated from a professed belief in Irish autonomy. But a return to the fold never had much to commend it from Chamberlain's point of view. Had he returned before 15 May, when the most active negotiations were taking place, he would have thrown away his chances of the central place in a Hartington-led government which then seemed imminent. Had he made his way back later, he would simply have come back (presumably outside the cabinet?) apparently committed to a Gladstonian regime which, even were it to survive, he could have influenced little. A further point, perhaps, is that had he changed sides, so few might have come over with him that the bareness of his cupboard might have been revealed for all to see. The belief that the numbers in his group were sufficient to have given Gladstone an adequate majority in the event of a reconciliation is based far too much on simply accepting Chamberlain's propaganda at its face value, and on unwillingness to suspect that his meetings were very carefully staged.

An election, then, there had to be. Gladstone and his cabinet, with few exceptions wanted it: the Tories wanted it. The Queen had her instructions too. What Hartington wanted we do not know, except that by late May there seemed no chance of his getting anything but honour.* The Liberal Unionist militants could hardly not want an event for which they had spent their whole political career (of several months) preparing. They were, too, in funds, and their seats, it was generally assumed, would be safer in an immediate snap election than in a few months' time. The only question was whether the election would settle anything.

In the first place, the election was not a national verdict against home rule. From a politician's point of view, it did not mean that home rule joined, say, temperance, in the doghouse of inherently lost causes. The Unionist majorities of 1886 had by 1887 become a flowing tide of home rule by-election successes. Moreover, it was a very curious election. While Gladstone's Irish programme differed from speech to speech, it was possible to find Liberal Unionist opponents who held ideas of devolution more radical than his, just as there were Gladstonians whose addresses bore little resemblance to those of their leader. Regions and countries pulled different ways. Psephologically, the election was like 1874: emotionally it had all the passion of 1880, if not more. Above all, the election threw no light on whether the English urban working-class was a disturbing or a conservative element in the land. Each side, in fact, drew different conclusions from their experience.

What was highly unlikely from the start was that the election would return any one party with an overall majority, which is after all what elections are supposedly about. Despite the euphoria, the Tories had only 316 seats. The Irish and the Liberal Unionists had between them 162 members, and their alignments could not be predicted. Some, but not all, Liberal Unionists had been elected by fairly Liberal constituencies to behave like Liberals. The election therefore decided nothing. It simply underlined the fact that power lay in very delicate inter-party understandings made in parliament itself. The opportunities for Chamberlain and Churchill to make mischief therefore were infinite. Barring human error, these two should have been the main beneficiaries of the election, and six months afterwards, for a brief moment, the world seemed at their feet.

In July 1886, however, the Tories had an advantage. They knew exactly what they wanted, and that was to keep Liberal Unionism in limbo. In this somewhat risky venture, they were positively aggressive, and their offers of a paper crown to Hartington need not be taken seriously. Churchill's leadership in the Commons was the best way to keep Churchill securely inside the party and Hartington

---

* Up to the last moment, however, Hartington was hinting that he was ready to take over if Gladstone resigned after defeat on the second reading (Ponsonby to the Queen, 7 June 1886, Royal Archives RAC 38/113).

securely outside. Their ministry reflected no positive purpose except *esprit de corps* and a rather diffuse good-will towards Ireland. As in the previous August, three or so able and sensible members of a Tory cabinet ran, partly for personal enjoyment, their own Irish policy, which ran counter to the probable wishes of the cabinet as a whole, which was drifting again, as in August 1885, towards coercion. The novel party situation did nothing to shake the confidence of Tory ministers in their traditional lack of method.

3

The Character of Conservative Government

Previous studies of Victorian Conservatism have largely centred on the theme of the deliberate traditionalism of the parliamentary party created by Derby and Disraeli, despite the growth, especially in the 1880s, of new sources of urban support. This accepted view requires little change, and it is another dimension of analysis that is examined here.

The first issue, to be considered in the light of the 1885–86 ministry, is the relationship between behaviour and state of mind. Salisbury's ministry, like other right wing ministries at other times, was predominantly reactionary both in sentiment and in action: but there was little relation between the two phenomena, and certainly no necessary relation. The reactionary sentiments of the ministry did not lead to reactionary policies: while the reactionary policies of the caretaker government arose from almost everything else but its prepossessions and sentiments. In short, the 'political culture' of the party was no guide to anything but its political culture.

The prime example of this highly indefinite relation between Tory feelings and Tory actions lay in the case of the alleged Tory–Irish alliance, though any such phrase assumes a clarity of knowledge on our part which does not and cannot exist. Nevertheless, an investigation of relations between Parnellites and Tories in 1885–86 affords the best chance to measure the opportunism, self-deception, and inner nihilism of the Tory leadership at that time.

The third point to be noticed is that the Tory cabinet at this time practised an idiosyncratic style of government, (whose motto might be 'the less said the better') which sharply distinguished them from the Liberals. There were, indeed, two separate systems and meanings of cabinet government at this time – the 'collective leadership' style of the Liberals, and the deliberate lack of personal interaction of the Tories. The Tory style of government no more derived from their being the party that accommodated the Right, than the Liberal style related to their ambition to accommodate all men who were not of necessity Tory. More simply, it was a case of two groups of men, having the opportunity to arrange their mutual relations in quite different ways that did not depend on party creed, going ahead and taking up that opportunity in a quite stylised way.

The fourth point is epistemological. Epistemology asks, not what was the government like, but what is a government? Epistemology is more than technically useful in such social matters because the certainty of the historical practitioner that the answers are as clear as day, tends to prevent central questions ever coming forward. Now if a government is simply popular ascription of (or popular willingness to ascribe) a general fullness of powers to certain leading men to the exclusion of other men, then the term is a phantom more to be sought by psychical than historical research, for its meaning is independent of its actual existence. For the sake of academic productivity, then, it is more fruitful to consider government as the act of governing. Now governing is communicating: to remain still in one's chamber is not government. Governing is the use of words, chiefly in speech, and chiefly to colleagues, in private surroundings, in groups of two or three. If government is, literally not metaphorically, conversation within certain kinds of popularly ascribed contexts, what is to be said of a government like that of 1885–86, where the mutual solicitation of opinions and actions by leading Tories fell away to a very low level (Churchill's largely Indian correspondence with Salisbury excepted)? The point here is that if the state or government is a term inductively arrived at from empirical data, instead of a doctrinal (and recommendatory) borrowing from inherently centralising and systematising subjects like law and sociology, then it is and should properly be a very variable term indeed. The language available for political description is itself a structure built round the dogmatism that the differing actions of different men and different groups of men are, can be, and probably should be closely related. The disproof of this can only be taken *ambulando*, by long reading of long historical books: but the deliquescence of the conceptual core of government in the light of what politicians really do, can be pointed up quite well by the case of the 1885–86 ministry.

There, 'central' activity does not emerge as a distinct kind of activity, or as defined with any deliberateness as something that could have separate conceptual meaning. The Emperor's clothes may have existed, but there was no body to the Emperor beneath them.

In the case of the first problem set before us, that is of whether there was a definable Conservatism and whether, if there was, it tended to produce Conservative policies that would not in any case have been produced by free play of circumstances, must be seen against the national political mood which the opposition had successfully created in 1880–85. (They controlled this mood very much less once in office: if power is the power to determine the context in which the handlers of power operated, then opposition was trumps). The fall of Khartoum symbolised what the Tories as an opposition wanted to say. They wanted to create an obsession about Gladstone, about his vanity, lack of earthiness, dilatoriness, spiritual arrogance, and weak-kneed internationalism. The Tories succeeded in this at least, that they created a 'patriotic' mood in which Northcote's chances of leading a Tory ministry could at last be given the *coup de grâce*. For some Tories this may have been an underlying intention, for others an unexpected incident: and Churchill was provokingly absent in India, writing home to say how little interest he felt in current politics. It was one thing, however, for the 'Old Guard' who had inherited the Tory leadership in the 1870s to sweep away their representative official man, Northcote, on the grounds that he did not meet the (rhetorically defined) 'needs of the hour'. It was another matter altogether to supply those needs. Indeed, Tory leaders never thought it within the bounds of practical politics to satisfy the popular emotion which in large degree they represented, conjured up, and accommodated.

On the central issue of the Sudan, in fact, they drew the obvious conclusion from the fall of Khartoum, that British personnel must not be put at risk in remote portions of the globe. Their public condemnations of Liberal policy were carefully ambiguous,[56] not simply *révanchiste*. They dwelled on past sins of omission without clarifying the future. Salisbury wrote an academic treatise in a private letter to Manners proving that the British could never be sufficiently strong to govern a nation of Mahometan belief. Again when Lord Wemyss, acting independently, moved in the Lords for annexation of the Sudan, Salisbury was again careful to refuse any involvement. The Union Jack had become, in 1880–85, more essential to Conservative culture than ever before, but not above the level of electoral declamation.

In office the Conservatives were exemplary followers in the footsteps of the Little England school. Within days they had without demur spurned any idea of an autumn campaign, and decided to pull out not only of the Sudan but of the border province of Dongola as well, in both cases contrary to Wolseley's deepest hopes. The Liberals had very real excuse in the form of Russian pressure for backing down: the Tories much less so. Yet the Liberal cabinet took weeks of agonising, memoranda, and incipient resignation before it could decide to do over Dongola what the Tories did in days without apparent argument. As later when a victory over Mahdist forces in January 1886 was only turned to account to further a policy of inactivity, no member of the cabinet can be located as having been willing to speak up for teaching the Mahdi a lesson. It was British ministers who had been taught a lesson and they had learned it thoroughly. In the end, the only distinctively Tory contribution to policy on the Nile was that, while otherwise carrying out the policy of the Liberal Left with easier minds than the Liberals would have done, they decided in their first cabinet to bring the Guards regiments back from Egypt, initially to Cyprus, because Egyptian conditions were affecting their health and everybody's London season. The non-Guards regiments continued, despite vehement agitation by their Generals, to die like flies in upper Egypt throughout the ensuing months.

The caretaker ministry gained prestige chiefly from its record in diplomacy. It was never accused of softness where British interests were concerned. Yet its successful negotiations with Russia over the Afghan border were a footnote to Granville just as much as its recognition of a Greater Bulgaria was a footnote to Gladstone. In the Afghan case, indeed, much was achieved by paring down or casting aside what its Liberal predecessors had stood out for, and withering indeed were the Tory glances cast at the paper ramparts the Liberals had sought to erect in central Asia.

In Africa almost the only point the ministry had to decide was the future of Bechuanaland. Liberal ministers of all hues had by May 1885 reached a consensus in favour of annexation by Britain, (not by the Cape). The problem ought to have been relatively simple, but the Tory cabinet made heavy weather of it. Their attitude to it chiefly reflected two things, their own sense of how confused they were, and a desire not to be drawn into anything which might cost money. Beach, here as elsewhere, wanted nothing more than to be a severe Gladstonian chancellor. There was not a sign of any jingo brand of annexationism, any more than there was over Burma. Twice there were passing references, and as it would seem nothing more than that, to Burmese problems in the course of cabinets: but it would be stretching matters to say that Burmese policy ever properly came to the notice of, or received the approval of, the cabinet. Certainly the actual act of annexation was done quite without cabinet authority. It was the war of one Asian power against another. This, the most imperialist action during the ministry, did not arise from even minimal imperialist leanings on the part of ministers or party.

Tory ministers thought government policy should remain within a consensus established by a Liberal tradition of practice and expectation. They did so because they thought the Liberal consensus was right as regards content of government, if nauseously wrong as regards style and sustaining motives: and not because they were the prisoners of a Liberal majority, if indeed they were, for it is an imponderable point. This was so throughout the departments. At the Admiralty they scourged the outgoing Liberal, Northbrook, not for parsimony, but for recklessness in expenditure. In Scotland they accepted the current 'progressive' programme of the creation of a Scottish Office, giving it education to run, and undertaking to make laws for crofters. They produced a local government bill which was essentially Liberal in shape.

Behind all this there was an older, more private realm of atavistic Conservative sentiment. There were people like Jem Lowther and Manners waiting, as they had waited for forty years, for the imminent turning of the tide in favour of protectionism: there was Northcote, by no means any longer the intellectual liberal-conservative of the 1860s, declaring that elective county councils would be fatal: there was Lady Salisbury's breezy conviction that 'the only cure for the evils of Ireland is the total extermination of the inhabitants', a lady's joke, no doubt, but not a joke that a lady would make at Hawarden. Tories were different, very different, in the realm of private sentiment, but what they were asserting was a freedom of spirit and feeling only and not of conduct or action. There were indeed little pockets of upper class antinomianism up and down the country, Hatfield included, but what they offered, like the 'Souls' of the 1890s, was a political Bohemia, an area of dissent into which the realities of government, which were taken to be unalterably Gladstonian, need not enter, disturbing in their grossness the happy and entirely harmless sectarian enjoyment of contempt for the real world. Some members of the Tory leadership were of this breed of closet reactionaries, others were pure opportunists, others were representative men of position of their day who did not trouble to affect partisan humours, and yet others were at heart principled crypto-liberals. Such private details, however, concern the historian of political behaviour no more than the other (and equally inaccessible) private fantasies which come between a man and his pillow. The solitary individual cannot commit politics, and the member of a political group like a cabinet submits to enacting the roles the situation gives him and not the roles his fantasies give him. Hence we dismiss, not without regret, the fact that many of Salisbury's cabinet had private access to a distinctive Conservative subculture, as being as devoid of consequences as was their having the entrée to a good many other esoteric milieux. Ministers sought light relief in many directions: Salisbury in chemistry, family life, and thinking about Indian affairs, Carnarvon in Latin orations, Northcote in quarter sessions, Beach in work, Lord G. Hamilton in visiting his ancestral Ulster, and Churchill in light relief. It is a vain task to chase after the political implications of these modes of relaxation.

The one place, perhaps, where Tory sentiment was allowed to throw sand in the eyes of political judgment, was in their view of Gladstone. Instead of recognising him as a conservative tactician with no discernible strategy (and therefore a highly dangerous opponent, unlikely to make mistakes), they indulgently dramatised him as mad. They agreed, in fact, with modern Gladstonian writers, in thinking of him as quite unlike other politicians. Even senior ministers like Cranbrook thought madness a good explanation of Gladstone's conduct.* Lower down, Conservative folklore about Gladstone became a major part of their raison d'être:

> 'Sir Howard Elphinstone vouched for the following as a fact. Not long ago a man got out at Didcot and asked to be put in another carriage. The stationmaster went and looked into the carriage and said "Why, that's Mr Gladstone." The traveller replied "I don't care who it is. I have had the care of lunatics for 12 years and that man has all the symptoms of advanced lunacy." The other day Gladstone sent for Lady Wolseley, she naturally thinking it was about her husband: but after keeping her waiting for some time all he said was to recommend them to read G. Eliot's *Life*.'[57]

The question of what, if anything, was quintessentially 'Conservative' about the Tories, must however chiefly be judged by what they did about Ireland. Here again there were certain distinctly reactionary sentiments to be found, which tell one nothing. Some ministers, and especially Cranbrook, were in a simple way anti-Catholic, especially in such things as educational policy.

* At a Tory shadow cabinet, someone said 'Gladstone is so impulsive and excitable, that in some way he must be regarded as a kind of lunatic' (Ashbourne diary, 15 Aug. 1881, Ashbourne MSS).

However, this can be used to make a quite opposite point, namely that in any gathering of elderly English gentlemen at that time (or since) such sentiments will be found, but usually much more markedly than among Salisbury's ministers. Again, it is difficult to find open evidence of sympathy with Ireland among ministers, yet on the other hand there was a striking lack of the explosive abuse that the Parnellites provoked from the lips of the Liberal leaders. Immoderate emotion was absent, like much else, from Tory thought on Ireland, even with the inflexible hard core (Northcote, Smith, Cranbrook, perhaps Cross, Halsbury) who saw themselves as incapable of opportunism and yet deceived themselves sufficiently to sit at ease (and in ignorance) among a cabinet run by opportunists on opportunist lines. The specifically 'Tory' states of mind about Ireland to be found among ministers, did not actively create or determine Irish policy till January 1886, when the general party situation made it attractive for the cabinet opportunists to manipulate the latent Toryism of the 'honest men' of the Tory right. Generally, however, the Irish behaviour of the ministry did not arise from any underlying collective state of mind, whether reactionary or not.

Most views of the Tory–Irish alliance have been bedevilled by the wish to prove a point or draw a moral. No such definite objective is possible. One cannot arrange the events credibly with a view to presenting the Tories as liberal-minded opportunists who took up with Unionism on party grounds: or with a view to depicting the ministry as a set of hard-line Unionists playing at negotiations that had no more than an electoral purpose. The reason one cannot make such broad judgments is that there were too many separate negotiations going on at different times, for different purposes, on differing topics, between different people, for there to be anything more than, at most, a string of miscellaneous and limited 'Tory–Irish alliances' for limited and immediate purposes.* These limited ad hoc understandings did not result from a general and concerted policy of alliance, but on the other hand they did edge the cabinet towards that position. Secret and even conspiratorial negotiations there undoubtedly were, but broadly Salisbury's ministry did what it would have done anyway had there been no such negotiations. From the latter days of Forster's régime in Dublin, there had

---

* For instance, it was not decided until at least the middle of November 1885 that the Tory-Irish alliance would definitely operate during the election. On 16 Nov. Parnell was writing to his election manager in England that it was 'almost certain' but not finally settled 'that we shall have to vote for the Tories at the general election' (Parnell to T. P. O'Connor, 16. Nov 1885, National Library of Ireland, MS 15735).

never been any difficulty in seeing that impeccably orthodox Tory
front-benchers might prefer a 'green' to an Orange policy when
their turn came: and in this respect the Tories' policy in 1885 was
new only in that it was sustained. In the case of Churchill, his predilection for a Tory–Irish combination went back, nostalgically,
to his happy years in Dublin in 1878–80, his good friends in
Ireland, his recollections of successful Disraelian intrigue among
Butt's party, and his genuine affection for the Irish and for dazzling
political effects. By the time he returned from India on 7 April
1885, however, Churchill only had to accelerate a bandwaggon
already under way.

On the Sudan vote of censure in February 1885, the majority of
the Irish voted with the Tories. At the time, as later in June,
honourable Liberals started allegations that they had stumbled
across Parnell plotting with leading Tories in dark and deserted
corridors of the Palace of Westminster. There was indeed some
kind of dialogue afoot, in which Churchill, who was abroad, took
no part for once. It was in fact Rowland Winn, the Tory chief whip,
who wrote to Salisbury on 2 March 1885 enclosing a memorandum[58] dated 27 February 1885 'of interview this day with Mr
Parnell'. The two main points about this episode are that its bearing on the resumption of Tory–Irish discussions in May and June
must at best be very indirect, and secondly that it happened, with
Churchill abroad, under the auspices of the party leadership and
whip.

For years afterwards members of the Liberal party returned again
and again to these allegations in order to score cheap points off
their opponents. At least three M.Ps claimed to be first-hand witnesses, namely Mundella, Bryce and George Armitstead. However, it was not clear whether all three had seen the same incident
or whether they had each individually witnessed separate incidents.
Only Bryce was consistent from first to last, maintaining that he
had observed Parnell and the Tory chief whip deep in conversation
outside a committee room immediately before the defeat of
Gladstone's government on 9 June.[59] Armitstead was studiously
vague as to time and date in sharp contrast to his precise recollections as to place.[60] In Mundella's original account of his experiences the date was 27 February, immediately prior to the key
division on the Sudan, but by the time of the 1885 election this
had been altered to April or May.[61]

Most Liberals who created propaganda out of these allegations
wisely refrained from going into details. However one clumsy
attempt to marshal all the 'evidence' was made during the 1885
election campaign by Herbert Gladstone, who had himself had

secret dealings with an Irish M.P. in 1882.[62] He was immediately slapped down by Winn and Parnell, who never at any time endorsed the Liberal allegations although some other Irish M.Ps did so after 1886.

Not until May 1885 was there further evidence of any kind of contact, perhaps because there was no vote of confidence in the offing. Some time in May, however, unknown Tories, probably including Churchill or acting under pressure from him, threw out at least strong hints to the Irish that they would not renew coercion, though a formal frontbench decision to that effect was not taken till 17 June. This May offer was at any rate sufficiently credible to make the Radical ministers fight *à outrance* to outbid it with their Irish proposals, and to ensure, with little known further bargaining, that the Irish voted to put the Tories in on 9 June.

The defeat of the ministry on that occasion again led to reports by Liberals of their having stumbled on unholy intrigues in dark corridors between Tory and Parnellite representatives. These allegations can be given only slight weight in the general picture, not because they are not credible, but because no clue survives as to the content of the whispering. These Liberal rumours (or rather, smears) are also unsatisfactory in that they were written in some cases several years after the event, and tend to conflate or confuse the unrelated episodes of February and June 1885.

The first solid evidence of alliance is, again, under the most respectable auspices, had nothing to do with Churchill, and refers to conversations probably initiated only after the defeat of the Liberals on 9 June. R. Power, the Parnellite whip, had offered his counterpart Winn support in return for a labourers' bill and a measure eliminating sheriff's expenses in uncontested elections, the one being a worthy measure of social reform and the other designed to economise on Parnellite funds. Power also maintained that the Parnellite vote could and would give the Conservatives fifty additional seats in England, and five in Ulster. Winn reported this arrangement to Salisbury,[63] but not in a way which suggested that it fell outside the usual communication through the proper channels in which whips engage. It is not clear that the deal was ever made final, or carried through or reported to the cabinet, but this probably matters less than the habit of informal conversation which it showed. The labourers' bill was however approved by the cabinet, almost certainly on 4 July, and was then announced by Carnarvon as part of his Irish programme on 6 July. The episode might be taken as showing how small was the price that the Irish sought to exact in terms of Tory legislation. There is no evidence, for instance, that Ashbourne's land purchase bill was something that the

Parnellites had pressed for, or had discussed with the Tories at any stage. Holmes, who handled the land bill in committee in the Commons for Ashbourne, has left no record of any contacts with the Parnellites concerning it, though he gave full and candid reports of such contact in similar cases concerning other Irish legislation.

The other piece of evidence concerned the appointment of Sir W. Hart Dyke as Irish secretary in June 1885. It has been asserted that Dyke was appointed on Parnell's nomination, and this is not obviously implausible in that Dyke did at least do nothing subsequently to impair the smooth working of Tory–Parnellite relations. Unfortunately, Northcote left in his diary a circumstantial account of Dyke's appointment which does not tally. Northcote agreed that R. Power was one among many people consulted, but stated that Power, while not necessarily against Dyke, put forward another name as his first choice.[64] As the testimony does not agree, it is perhaps best simply to take note that senior ministers took it, in their varying accounts, as not in question that the Parnellites were and were rightly consulted, if not necessarily more than that, in the choice of Irish Secretary. This would have been a major ideological point in a Liberal ministry, but in a Tory one it started no hares.

The flavour that is missing in June 1885 is that of Churchill. This is not surprising, for Tory relations with the Irish grew out of the need of sensible men to establish sensible arrangements for a temporary government. This was not Churchill's game, for until the last moment he (and probably Beach) did not want the Salisbury ministry to take place, and therefore did not want its corollary, good relations with the Parnellites. Churchill wanted the process of attempting to form a ministry, to be one which damaged in turn Northcote, Salisbury, and then perhaps Northcote again, and if in the end he lent his name to a weak Northcote ministry after Salisbury had failed, this would be the quickest way forward to supremacy open to Churchill at that time. Churchill had the wit to perceive that he had no interest in creating a successful Salisbury ministry which would make Salisbury unsinkable, and accordingly started no helpful intrigues with the Irish, as he had done in May and was to do in July.

It was indeed Salisbury, not Churchill, who is reported as having flown the only home rule kite at this time. Salisbury, at lunch with Manners on 11 June, before he had received the royal summons, raised the possibility of giving Ireland provincial councils for private bill legislation only, hardly an exciting prospect, yet presumably his intention in talking like this (he is not known ever to have recurred to this suggestion) was to draw Manners, embodiment of the 'Old Guard', into stating his estimate of what Tory rectitude did and did not permit in the case of Irish autonomy.

The Tory programme for Ireland, as it emerged in July 1885, was a programme of unrelated fragments of widely differing origins, combining to create a general effect which one cannot say had been master-minded. The labourers' bill is the only item resulting specifically from known inter-party negotiations. Ashbourne's land purchase bill was there because the Tories believed in land purchase, and to show their disbelief in the Liberal idea of judicial rents. It also showed that their belief in Ashbourne was at that time still regarded as a policy in itself. The Irish educational endowments bill owed virtually nothing to the ministry, and was carried through nearly single-handed by an Irish Protestant judge acting under Churchill's patronage, assisted by secret talks with the Nationalist M.P, Sexton. In the case of the Irish bank crash, it was not surprising that Justin McCarthy should have had at least two interviews with the chancellor of the exchequer, one of them at 2 a.m.,[65] though it is not known whether they made any mark on policy. The non-renewal of coercion was partly, or nominally, based on technical features of crime control in Ireland, but primarily on the leadership's view of the necessities of the parliamentary situation, alliance or no alliance.

The Irish programme of the ministry showed nothing, one way or the other, about whether some central individual or group in the ministry had at some time decided for an Irish alliance, or even for systematic appeasement. However, the way the personnel of the ministry on its Irish side were put together did show more positively the disarray of intentions among those who later became the relatively pro-Irish group in the cabinet.

Salisbury wanted Carnarvon as viceroy from the start, knowing full well his autonomist leanings, and no one else was really considered. This did not mean Carnarvon was chosen on Irish grounds. He was able, weighty, impressive, a link with the past, and an upholder of the 'Old Identity' in Tory politics. He was basically a Salisbury man. He would not tamper with realignments of parties, which was why even when apparently acting with Churchill on Irish matters, he was not really his ally. Salisbury, for all we know, appointed Carnarvon as much for his basic orthodoxy, indeed pietism, in party terms, as for his unorthodox approach to Ireland. Churchill, Carnarvon's most weighty pro-Irish colleague, not only did not want or like Carnarvon, whom he found depressingly respectable, but according to Northcote, Carnarvon was among those whom Churchill specifically sought to exclude from the cabinet as

71

a condition of his joining: another pointer, incidentally, to Carnarvon's being seen as having an 'Old Guard' connotation.

At the time no one imagined that Carnarvon's appointment had helped substantially to smooth the way for the Tory–Irish alliance. On the contrary Carnarvon hardly functioned at the parliamentary level at which the alliance existed, placing his chief emphasis on the cultivation of good feeling in Ireland itself, particularly with the Catholic hierarchy. Inevitably as head of the Irish administration Carnarvon was given some of the credit (and more than he deserved) for the ministry's Irish legislation, but the policy with which he mainly identified himself was winning the assent of the Catholic church to a settlement of all outstanding questions relating to education, a settlement inspired and set in motion by Carnarvon himself with little encouragement from his colleagues. For a time he appeared to be on the way to a resounding personal triumph, even though Archbishop Walsh, the head of the church in Ireland, tended to mark time in the hope of obtaining a complete capitulation to his demands and a full recognition of the church's central role in Irish society. By the autumn, however, Carnarvon found himself working in competition with Churchill for the much coveted distinction of having finally allayed Catholic grievances, and Churchill immediately set about wrecking his plans by undermining his authority in Dublin.[66]

Despite the much publicised and not particularly important secret conference between Carnarvon and Parnell in August 1885, the former was not really interested in private understandings with the Irish party on details or on home rule unless backed by a united cabinet. Indeed, there were good grounds for doubting whether the Tories could simultaneously appease the Catholic church and the Irish party. As Churchill in one mood put it 'it is to the Bishops entirely to whom I look in the future to turn, to mitigate or to postpone the Home Rule onslaught'.[67] Nevertheless Carnarvon discussed home rule with such evident enthusiasm to all and sundry who cared to listen (including Parnell, Justin McCarthy and Dublin Castle officials)[68] that members of the shadow cabinet and clever young pundits, unaware of the peculiar idiosyncrasies of Conservative government, automatically drew damaging and incorrect conclusions about the intentions of Salisbury's cabinet. While Carnarvon talked home rule in Dublin, at Windsor, and over society dinner-tables, the majority of his colleagues were moving in a contrary direction in their minds (if they had minds) but not in conversation or on paper and therefore without affecting the situation at all. What was absent throughout the 1885–86 government was a strategy on Ireland to which individual acts of policy could be linked. Instead Carnarvon and Churchill were left to develop their own policies, unaware of the inconsistencies which cabinet discussion would have revealed, only to have all their work undone when their fully matured plans finally came before their dull and unimaginative colleagues. The fault did not lie with Carnarvon, who alone in the 1885–86 cabinet showed a warm regard for the principle of collective ministerial responsibility. Throughout the period from August 1885 to January 1886 when the future relations between Ireland and the Tory party ought to have been planned, Carnarvon repeatedly asked for a special cabinet to decide the broad framework of policy: the one that was summoned immediately had its attention diverted to other subjects and Ireland was never mentioned.[69] In the summer of 1886 the Tory leadership drew heavily upon its notable capacity for self-deception when, of its own accord and in a mood of blind self-righteousness, it successfully ruined Carnarvon's career and saved its own skin. The charge against him was that he had concealed his interview with Parnell. In fact all he had done was to exercise the free hand which he had been given against his own wishes.

The rest of the Irish team was put together rather inadvertently. Ashbourne, or Gibson as he then was, had earned himself a reputation in the early 1880s as the party authority on Ireland, and through this had an undoubted claim to a cabinet place. He was however initially offered the home office by Salisbury, turning it down with the characteristic plea that he had a large family to support. He thereby secured the Irish lord chancellorship, which carried an income which would outlast the ministry. Ashbourne, whose party reputation up till then had been that of a vigorous partisan, thus found himself a pillar of Carnarvon's regime in Ireland, slipping at once into a policy of sincere sympathy with Irish demands which he sustained until January 1886.[70] Ashbourne's appointments as law officers, Holmes and Monroe, did not suggest any awareness, in June 1885, of where Carnarvon was about to take him. Both were party promotions of the men next in line, both were stout loyalists with Ulster attachments, and it could not have been envisaged that they too would fit pliably into the context of appeasement. Holmes' political line, indeed, had been to attack the Spencer regime in Ireland as too soft on crime, but by December 1885 he was advising Carnarvon on possible ways of meeting the demand for home rule. Dyke, the chief secretary, was appointed through the interplay of diverse chances, and represented no hopes or intention except that Carnarvon, perhaps, should have a free hand. Dyke was believed to be a reliable official man who would do trivial work unquestioningly. In fact there were complaints of his exceptional idleness, and in the end he resigned without making his resignation intelligible. He did not get on well with Carnarvon, and the current of affairs passed him by. He was probably an 'appeaser' with regard to Irish demands, but it is hard to be sure. Very little is known about him or his views, and he survives as 'Billy' Dyke, the man who invented lawn tennis.

This leaves Churchill to be considered. Churchill, though very busy at the India Office and often in poor health, was involved in Irish affairs in a way no other minister was. He conducted an Irish policy of his own. He maintained an extensive private correspondence with leading officials and Tories in Ireland. He took under his wing men like Holmes, the Irish law officer, who was properly Carnarvon's subordinate and Ashbourne's protégé. He dealt directly with the catholic hierarchy. He was involved in three house parties devoted to Irish politics. In August 1885 he visited Ashbourne at his chateau at Boulogne, meeting there Holmes and his old friend Fitzgibbon: in October 1885 he went to stay near Dublin with Holmes, whom he told 'that he had many understandings with the Irish members which were faithfully adhered to on both sides but that he never either directly or indirectly countenanced home rule or hesitation in regard to it':* and thirdly he was present, as usual, at Fitzgibbon's traditional party near Dublin at Christmas. At a parliamentary level, Churchill was involved only once, but in a grand way, when he, Beach, and Gorst, acting in opposition to Carnarvon and the cabinet, threw over Spencer in the Maamtrasna debate, causing Parnell to remark 'This is the greatest thing we have ever accomplished'. Finally, there was a general impression, unsubstantiated at the time, that Churchill was somehow in close negotiations with Parnellite leaders, an impression he much later confirmed in this remark to James, who evidently believed it:

'I wondered constantly at [Parnell] remaining silent in 1886...
He was several times at my house (no. 2 Connaught Place) during the summer of 1885, and we arranged a great many things in connection with the General Election of that year, the most perfect confidence existing between us. When I went to Ulster

---

* Cf. statements by Justin McCarthy, M.P, in his *Reminiscences* (1899), i, that Churchill 'had always the kindest sympathy with Ireland ... we were often conspirators in some form of attack upon the government' in 1880–85 (p. 434): and that 'there were never any dealings between Lord Randolph Churchill and the Irish Parliamentary Party, the history of which might not have been published fully in all the daily papers ...' (p. 438). McCarthy notes an incident when he and Churchill deliberately engaged in intense conversation at a London reception in order to cause grounds for speculation.

and attacked the Parnellites all round, I fully expected that Parnell would disclose our conversations, but he never uttered a word, and has never done so since.'*

(In fact, at the time of Churchill's Belfast visit, Parnell talked of him as 'a young scoundrel but not as if he was cross with him', adding that 'we got more out of him last year than he ever got out of us').[71] Churchill's concern with Irish affairs existed in its own right at the highest level, and was not derived from parallel policies independently pursued by Carnarvon and Ashbourne.

Churchill's policies had a long-term basis, but not much of a medium-term background. They had always been in his mind, in a sense, but in a sense also he had given little attention to Irish matters until very late in the day. In Irish terms, Churchill was basically 'green' not 'Orange' in his whole orientation. His reference to 'those foul Ulster Tories who have always been the ruin of our party' was far more typical of him than this talk – very intermittent talk it was too – of playing the Orange card. The 'green' approach was after all the only one which gave much play to political intelligence and a sense of one's ability to construct situations.

Churchill had gone to Ireland in 1876 as private secretary to his father, the viceroy. After the vicissitudes of London society, he had found Dublin had its agreeable side. He formed what was the closest and most lasting of his semi-political friendships with Gerald Fitzgibbon, who knew the Irish situation inside out. He often entertained Isaac Butt. He relaxed at the congenial dinners of a Roman priest, with whom he became curiously intimate.[72] He published, in 1878, an improving pamphlet on Irish education. Because foxes did not live in Dublin, he necessarily saw much of rural Ireland, including the west where 'the peasantry ... live in their wretched mud-hovels more like animals than human beings'. He immersed himself in the work of his mother's Irish Relief Fund in 1879, and won respectful mention from the veteran Quaker philanthropist Tuke. He liked the Irish: in London he mingled with Radicals and stormed 'I hate the government'. It was a strange beginning for a Tory. He began his political life with a fuller grasp of current Irish moods than any frontbencher. Even after 1880, his

---

* At the time, however, Churchill produced two very convincing reasons for Parnell's silence: 'Labby told me that Parnell thought that I had behaved very badly to him and was awfully unscrupulous, but that he saw no good in making disclosures or accusations in the H. of C. 1. because they might fail for want of evidence and 2. because it might be necessary to try & negotiate again with the Tories' (Churchill to Salisbury, 9 Mar. 1886, Salisbury MSS). This letter also shows that Churchill was still at this date on close terms with Power, the Irish whip.

wife at least and perhaps her husband 'rarely missed paying a visit, either to the Castle during the season, or to the Viceregal Lodge for the Punchestown Races.' Churchill himself was invariably a guest at the Christmas house-parties of Fitzgibbon at Howth.

The general background was there to draw on when he wanted it. For much of the earlier part of 1885, he did not want it. He decided in November 1884 to go to India, leaving behind the debris of the reform bill crisis for others to clear up. He had no Irish enterprises afoot at the time. In India, except for making friends with the Dufferins, he avoided politically significant activity. The fall of Khartoum found him 'in camp in an immense forest at the foot of ,the Himalayas'. The political crisis, such as it was, of February 1885 did not accelerate his return. On Wolff telegraphing him to cut short his visit, Churchill wrote (17 February) 'he has crisis on the brain: and, in any case, no political contingency will hasten my return by an hour', and equally unenthusiastically, 'the Tories will try to come in: I wish them joy of it'. Churchill did not in fact return till the first week of April 1885, then to begin what was virtually a second career.

When he did bestir himself, in May 1885, to bring Tories and Irish into liaison, it is far from clear that it was his interventions that decided his leaders to let it be known that they would not renew coercion. In mid-May he even allowed himself to dream up a plan for uniting the Chamberlain Radicals with the Churchill Tories and with the Parnellites, in a coup against either or both of the official front benches: but nothing more was heard of this. Churchill's Irish policy, if he had one, was not very evident before July 1885. In a full sense it really began with Maamtrasna.

Churchill's Irish policy thereafter centred on two successive desiderata, embodied in two successive phases. Prior to the elections, he was chiefly concerned with an alliance focussed not on home rule, but on the coming elections. The bait offered to the Irish – to priests as well as Parnellites – lay in educational policy. Churchill probably wanted an election result in which the Tories depended on Irish support, rather than a straight majority where his peculiar qualities would no longer be at a premium, and there is no reason to suppose his vision extended beyond that. After the elections, Churchill's Irish policy continued to comprehend conciliatory and aggressive approaches to Irish problems, with the stress not decidedly in favour of either, but each being valued in so far as it made possible an interesting new relationship with the Liberals.

In the event, Churchill did not seriously play the Orange card. In December 1885 he talked momentarily like a precursor of Bonar

Law and arranged a Belfast visit for February 1886, but in January 1886 his interest centred on (a Liberal–Tory) coalition, rather than on mobilising Orange militancy. In February and early March 1886 he sounded the Orange note, no doubt for a variety of reasons: partly to make his peace with the Ulster members, partly to lure Salisbury to the far right and then leave him stranded there, partly from a debater's wish to draw out Gladstone, but probably chiefly because other leading Tories had decided to keep silent and Churchill had a chance to engross the role of party orthodoxy.

Churchill was not in the event a passionate or conspicuous opponent of home rule after the early spring of 1886. Though he remained in the public eye as a brilliant and active speaker, in the real private world of politics he was 'resting', no longer using the Irish issue to seek mastery in general politics. There may, moreover, be private reasons behind his relative withdrawal in March–July 1886: for one thing, he quarrelled seriously with his wife in March, and remained strangely distant from her throughout the summer, in a way perhaps connected with his health.[73] But political reasons alone could have fully explained his choice of course. He began quite early to disengage from the immediate situation in order to be free to act in its successors. In those future situations, he almost certainly saw himself as taking a 'green' approach. Other politicians, equally sophisticated, realised this possibility was perfectly open to him.* His basic inability to compete with Salisbury as a figure of orthodox reaction left little else open to him. By June 1886 he had arranged a Norwegian holiday to 'escape those beastly elections' intending 'to please myself by taking a very quiet part in the coming election.' When the Tories took office again, Churchill and Beach at once (before the new cabinet was even appointed) imposed an Irish policy of restraint, of 'soft words and hard cash', which was maintained, though wearing thin, till Churchill's departure. Out of office, Churchill's mobile political features became more mobile still. In February 1887 he made two approaches through Labouchere, as to how some way could be devised in which he could support Gladstone against Salisbury. Though nothing ever came of it, Churchill – just a year after Belfast – was attempting to devise a situation in which he would

---

* E.g. on 18 Aug. 1886 Justin McCarthy forecast to John Morley that the Tories would dish the Liberals by bringing in their own home rule scheme. Morley agreed this was possible, and in particular dwelled on the fact that Churchill had only declared against 'repeal' and, Morley said, 'we all declare against repeal, and we put whatever meaning we like on the declaration' (McCarthy and Praed, *Our Book of Memories* (1912), 47). In May 1886, the leading Parnellite T.D. Sullivan thought Churchill 'having no principles, might yet be a friend again' (W.S. Blunt, *The Land War in Ireland* (1912), 44).

tell the House that Gladstone and home rule were a lesser evil than Salisbury and unsound finance.

This sense of the way party structures could be remoulded overnight was basic to both Churchill and Chamberlain. One happy example can be cited to establish the kind of political thinking one has to look for beneath the surface throughout the 1880s. In June 1887, Chamberlain found himself confined on a Jubilee cruise in Channel waters with Hartington and the Churchills:

> 'Tired of inactivity, he was revolving at that time, in conjunction with Randolph, a scheme for a new party, which was to be called the National Party, and both were anxious that Lord Hartington should join it. The moment was thought propitious, and it was settled that Mr Chamberlain should speak to Lord Hartington. That afternoon I was sitting on the deck with the latter when Mr Chamberlain joined us. Drawing up a chair, he suddenly plunged into the matter without preliminaries and with his usual directness. Lord Hartington ... looked uncomfortable, and answered very shortly. Mr Chamberlain, full of his scheme, pressed the points home, taking no notice of the monosyllables he got in answer. But after a time the frozen attitude of Lord Hartington began to take effect, and the conversation languished and died. I believe the subject was never reopened.'[74]

The deliberate creation of new or National parties is a normal pastime only among first-rate politicians. In 1885–86 only Churchill (among Tories) gave serious and continuing attention to the possibilities of bringing about a fundamental change in the party system at a stroke. His eccentricity reflected his difficulties with the existing Conservative leadership. According to his colleagues Churchill's difficulties were largely of his own making, in that he believed conflict and competition were permissible and they did not. The interesting point is not that this was true, but that in a Liberal cabinet Churchill's way of behaving would have been the accepted norm. Ideology apart, Gladstone would have controlled Churchill while adapting his best ideas to the general purposes of government. Salisbury controlled Churchill, but by overruling him except as regards Indian matters where the two men formed a limited but successful relationship in line with Tory expectations as to how colleagues should behave. Because of the general estimate of Churchill's character formed in opposition, the well-informed proposals on Ireland which he made in government, were construed, and dismissed, as further attempts at egoistic intrigue. This uncomprehending attitude encouraged Churchill to persist in working to set up a party of his own. It made him in practice a more unreliable cabinet colleague than he wanted to be.

Disraeli's most enduring legacy to the Conservative party was a method of government by which questions of general strategy were decided by the party leader alone or at most with personal advisers outside the cabinet. The lesser lights inside the cabinet were expected to aim at providing a quiet life for each other by running their departments so well that no scrutiny was required. In view of the character of Disraeli's heirs, this was probably the best style for the Tory party to adopt in ordinary circumstances. But in 1885–86 everyone agreed that the times were out of joint in Ireland: in this situation Salisbury's best course was to reveal something of his mind to the cabinet so that guide lines could be laid down for Carnarvon and those who wished to think seriously about Ireland (effectively Churchill). In fact, however, Salisbury gave no lead on Ireland before January 1886, and the cabinet were not even asked to reach a collective view about the policy which would best serve the interests of the party. The only collective decisions taken by the cabinet in 1885–86 were essentially negative in character: to throw to the winds the plans to which Churchill and Carnarvon had devoted their best hours in office, and to rely on Gladstone to dig his own grave. By an over-rigid adherence to an established doctrine about avoiding cabinet discussion, the Tories delivered themselves into Gladstone's hands when the government met parliament in January 1886. The party was rescued just in time in May 1886 from the prospect of twenty years' opposition to a Hartington-led Liberal party, by a well-timed intervention by Salisbury acting entirely within Disraeli's rules for verbal manoeuvre above the level of political understanding of his colleagues and party.

May 1886, rather than December 1885, or the general election of July 1886, was the climacteric of the home rule crisis. The events of May determined the character of the successor régime, and this was a more important matter than whether a home rule bill was introduced or whether it was passed or received public endorsement at an election. Senior politicians cared less about what went on during the crisis of 1886, than about what was to follow it. By May 1886 – particularly with Gladstone's rediscovery of class war in his manifesto of 1 May – Gladstone firmly occupied the whole left of politics. The battle was for the right and centre. Traditional Conservatism found its existence threatened by the possibility of a reconstructed Liberalism, more dangerously than Gladstone could ever do. Salisbury, with Gladstone's assistance, put paid to this threat, not by using any of the machinery of politics, but by creating a verbal structure which left no room for moderates.

Addressing the party conference on 15 May, he showed how a speech could matter more in politics than anything else.

His speech was no formality, but a carefully constructed reply to Hartington's speech and meeting of the previous day. The essence of Hartington's speech had lain in his claim that Liberal statesmanship was capable of dealing with the Irish question. To prove his point, Hartington had Trevelyan and Chamberlain at hand speaking in his support. Goschen and James were not put on show, but no one doubted their readiness to serve under Hartington. 'A Hartington, Goschen and Chamberlain administration is talked of'. Those three, with James and Trevelyan in the background, (and all of them House of Commons men) could constitute the nucleus of a formidable Liberal ministry, beginning within days and lasting for years. A *Times* leader supported just such a solution. This new version of the Palmerstonian ascendancy of the centre was not what Salisbury wanted. Hartington had said nothing about Conservative statesmanship being capable of governing Ireland. He had said nothing about coercion, and he had not really ruled out some kind of limited settlement with Parnell, provided it was under his own auspices. He and Chamberlain had committed themselves to nothing inconveniently definite, except overthrowing Gladstone. Even that, perhaps, was to be blurred by the kind of feelers James was putting forward to make a bridge across which Gladstone could retreat. Hartington was not raising the emotional temperature. He was keeping open the possibility of acting within the same framework of understanding as Parnell and Gladstone. He was continuing to stress that his function was to lead a constructive, progressive Liberal party, and by implication that he saw the Conservatives as a reactionary party with an opposition mentality.

Salisbury could not, of course, enter into direct controversy with Hartington. It was part of the picture that the two leaders maintained an amicable understanding on patriotic grounds. That they did not much look like close political friends, could always be excused on the grounds of their utterly dissimilar characters. They had practical business to transact, at least through underlings. They could therefore for many reasons not afford an open show of difference, however much they were in fact in competition. Salisbury therefore had to do violence to Hartington's hopes in an indirect way. This he did in a speech which showed what a political speech can do. The speech, in general, was designed to strike audiences as a display of violent reactionary prejudice. Textually, it was technically fairly innocent, and it left scope for a subsequent quiet and careful speech (to the Primrose League, 19 May) saying that he had not said anything.

Salisbury's speech was characterised by opponents as 'manacles and Manitoba'. He said that the emigration of a million Irishmen ('Manitoba') would be better than land purchase: attacked the Catholic Church in Ireland: referred to the existence of races like the Hottentots which were incapable of self-government: and appeared to offer twenty years of coercion as the sole remedy for Irish ills. In conclusion, Salisbury emphasised that the Irish question could only be dealt with by the Conservatives, with the clear implication that Liberal support could be no more than incidental.

Salisbury did not say these things because he was carried away by partisan feelings. He said them simply and specifically because they would shock Liberal opinion. Each point was carefully chosen to prevent prominent Liberals acting in concert with the Conservatives. The refusal, or disparagement, of land purchase, even though a Salisbury cabinet would probably have favoured some further scheme of that kind, was peculiarly gratuitous, as all shades of moderate Liberal opinion wanted some kind of land settlement. Coercion was presented as unpalatably as possible, and no Liberal leader at this stage believed he could afford to defend coercion. No one was going to rush to undergo Spencer's ordeal of 1882–84. Yet here was Salisbury deliberately going out of the way to stress that the Irish issue was one which should be understood in terms of a Manichean battle between progress and reaction.

What Salisbury was doing was vetoing the formation of a Hartington ministry. Such a ministry would have been formed on the basis that in a complex question requiring sound judgment, a basically uncommitted ministry of the centre was the right answer. If, however, Salisbury could succeed in insisting that there was no middle ground, but only the eternal struggle of opposites within which the Liberal mind had customarily regarded history, he could make Hartington's hopes of reuniting the Liberal party (after a largely personal defeat of Gladstone) impossible.* The immediate danger to Salisbury was that the anti-Gladstone Liberals would reunite the party, probably on rather disagreeable non-Irish issues. Jesse Collings and his cows might after all march on Hatfield. That risk could not be taken, while the risk of a Liberal reunion under Gladstone was too faint to bother with. Salisbury had never in any case worried much about the actual fate of the bill itself.

Much depended on the Liberals rising to Salisbury's bait. They

---

* Cf. the relevant emphasis in Salisbury's comment when the news of the bill's defeat reached Hatfield at 2 a.m. 'It is too good, Gladstone will dissolve and not resign' he said, a grey Persian cat sitting calmly on his shoulder (Lady F. Balfour, *Ne Obliviscaris* (1930), ii, 56).

did as predicted. The Gladstonians became more self-righteous, and accommodation with the dissident Liberals became more difficult than ever for them. Chamberlain and Hartington had to stress their Liberalism and therefore their practical agreement with the man they were trying to overthrow. The chance of creating a new Liberal consensus about the Hartington–Chamberlain axis had gone, and what remained was simply a wrecking operation without prospect of opening up a road to power. Numbers of estimated supporters also fell.

On 11 May A. Grey expected a Unionist majority of up to 40 or 50: on 12 May he thought 'a division tomorrow would secure us a large majority': on 14 May he wrote 'we have now over 100 Liberal M.Ps whose vote can be relied on against the bill'.[75] On 12 May Chamberlain looked for a majority of 70.[76] Then, after Salisbury's speech, Grey wrote 'Salisbury's speech may I fear frighten away some Liberals and do more harm than good' (17 May) then later (19 May) elaborated: 'Salisbury's speech has done even more harm than I anticipated – the Radicals are delighted at it, declaring that it has revolutionised the situation... The Irish Conservatives are very angry.' Salisbury's speech was intended not only to maintain Gladstonian control of the Liberal party, but to inhibit a mood of coalition among Tories, and was so understood by some of them. Sir R. Knightley was 'much disturbed' interpreting the speech 'as meaning that Salisbury will not support a moderate Liberal government under Lord Hartington'. In support of this view, Lady Knightley noted how 'the Gladstonians are all gloating about it'. Indeed they were: John Morley thought the speech 'has been silver and gold to us', ensuring that the Chamberlainites 'will pretty certainly rally to Mr G and the bill when the time comes'.[77] As in January 1886, Salisbury's only strenuous exertions centred on the attempt to prevent the formation of a broad-based Unionist government, and when he sounded most reactionary, it was as a calculated feint designed to preserve the opportunist identity of the traditional Tory party.

The Tory impasse derived from first principles. The mass of the party consisted of honest men without guile, energy, or imagination, which was a sound reason for their being Tories. From a political point of view, their defect tended to be that they were whole human beings to whom the ordinary business of living meant more than the hothouse atmosphere of parliament. Such men (and Tory cabinets reflected their strength in the party) could only cease to be ineffective by submitting to the leadership of opportunists whose whole life was politics. This was not necessarily unfortunate for the party, had the honest men been able to show an intelligent appreciation of what the opportunists sought, and reacted accordingly. The Liberal party ran smoothly on the tension derived from the alleged irreconcilability of Whig and Radical. The Conservatives might have drawn a similar energy had the contradiction between opportunists and orthodox Tories been allowed to come to the surface, which it very rarely did. Because of the Conservative refusal to have rows, fruitful relationships were not formed in cabinet or elsewhere. Instead of openly arguing with the Tory 'Old Guard', the opportunists had to conceal their most important ideas from them (and from each other). The Tory party paid a heavy price for its belief in unity.

4

Goschen, Hartington and the Young Whigs

Historians have forgotten Goschen. They have also misunderstood him. They have seen him as a precisian and technocrat, an external supplier of reliable administration to the real manipulators of high politics. This aspect of him was quite secondary. In 1885–86, it was almost non-existent. It was only when he succeeded Churchill at the exchequer that he ceased to be primarily that most interesting kind of politician, the creative manipulator who is also a rigorous theorist. His decision to join the Conservatives at the end of 1886 was a conscious admission of the failure of his plans for reconstructing the party system. All he had to show for two years of unremitting labour was a group of 'leaders who want an army': they were now to be thrown over for 'the army that wants a leader'. *

* Alfred Milner to Goschen, 29 Dec. 1886, Milner MSS box 182. In 1884 Milner had become Goschen's private secretary, though without resigning his appointment on the *Pall Mall Gazette*, and an intimate political relationship began almost at once. In 1885–86 Milner was as close to Goschen as it was possible to get. As regards both overall strategy and immediate tactics they thought with one mind, and so the 30-odd letters relating to this period from Milner to Goschen which have survived in the Milner MSS may be taken as evidence of the ideas and ambitions motivating Goschen, whose papers have for the most part almost certainly been destroyed. (There are no Milner diaries for 1885–86). Milner went further than Goschen in that he regarded the creation of an obedient democracy mainly as a means to a stable and responsible foreign policy. He largely wrote the sections of Goschen's speeches which dealt with foreign and colonial questions, but otherwise he was content to feed Goschen's doctrines back to him, thereby helping the master to overcome his feelings of doubt and inferiority. At the 1885 election Milner unsuccessfully contested Harrow as a Liberal, studiously avoiding mention of Gladstone's name. In 1886

Goschen's theories were not, in the first place, about Ireland. His concern was the creation of authority in a democracy. So far as Ireland could be made to serve that end, it interested him. Otherwise, he was curiously uninterested in what actually went on in that country: and his indifference was only temporarily dispelled by the home rule crisis.* His approach to democracy was a fresh one, much more so than that of Chamberlain. Both men believed, entirely uncritically, that the third reform act had created a 'new democracy'. Because, psephologically, this misses a number of very important qualifications,[78] this does not mean they were wrong in their beliefs from the one point of view that mattered for them: namely that they, as politicians, had now to say new things. Goschen, out of office since 1874, did not wish to waste further time opposing democracy. He wished to govern it, and to govern it on the secure basis of a general idea. Moreover, he saw in the democratic situation itself the means of negating that very idea, and of creating a new basis of power for an anti-democratic ruling party. This party was intended to fill the vacuum left by Gladstone's political demise, an event which Goschen believed to be imminent when he made new plans early in 1885. As it happened some of his policies (as regards education and land for instance) were progressive in character and aim, but the important point is that they were policies given to the people by an authoritative figure, and not handed up from below.

England had never had a party of resistance. It had had two liberal parties, one of which was called Conservative, but both representing the striving of the territorial aristocracy and their associates for popularity and acceptance. Under democratic conditions, as they had arisen in 1885, Goschen saw this was no longer necessary. There was now no need to have two parties of flattery. Instead, the existing right-wing of the Liberal party should cease, domestically, to be a party of appeasement and accommodation: it should take, verbally, a strongly patriotic line abroad, calling on the people 'to take pains and make sacrifices for national greatness': †

he became a founder member of the Liberal Unionist Committee very much out of loyalty to Goschen for 'personally I don't care two straws about the Union' (Milner to Goschen, 25 Apr. 1886, loc. cit.).

* A number of long letters from Milner based on meticulous research during a tour of Ireland in autumn 1886 apparently evoked no response. The letters discussed the vital question of how the Liberal Unionists could dissociate themselves from the Tory policy of coercion and concentrate on some innocuous alternative such as 'fostering the material resources of Ireland' (Milner to Goschen, 12 Dec. 1886, Milner MSS box 186). Milner apparently had been sent to find out where financial help was most needed.

† Milner to Goschen, 31 Jan. 1885, Milner MSS, box 182. Patriotism,

it should be rigidly economical in name and programme: it should not offer anything much beyond the rule of social and intellectual authority, and it should exploit the fact that it was not offering anything much.* Goschen saw that such a party would have very wide popular appeal in the new conditions. From this point of view, he actually needed Chamberlain's radical onslaughts, because they established exactly the right simplification of what was happening. Goschen was convinced that there was a political fortune waiting to be picked up by becoming Chamberlain's leading antagonist. This conviction led Milner to proclaim at the beginning of 1885 that 'this is seedtime'. 'Chamberlain's decided fiasco the other day' he wrote, 'makes it all the more possible for Liberals of a different type to influence things their way.'† On the one hand, there were the politicians (the great majority in all parties) who did what people wanted, out of unlimited opportunism: on the other hand, there were the few (Goschen and his young Whig friends, ventriloquising through the mouthpiece of Hartington) who would not do what people wanted, but did what they thought right – again, out of unlimited opportunism and because they thought such a style offered greater rewards. To understand Goschen's position in 1886, one must first see him as launching a radical new departure in response, not to Ireland, but to the change in franchise: as an innovator, not as one who wished to put the clock back.

In his calculations the traditional Toryism had no place. Its special bundle of idiosyncrasies were, in his eyes, all impediments to the creation of the kind of social and intellectual authority that the new democracy would recognise. (That he and the Tory leaders had no love for each other, only hardened his convictions). Property, to put Goschen's cause at its simplest, now had nothing

strength, and decisiveness were seen as qualities with wide limits in terms of substantive policies: Goschen's reaction to the fall of Khartoum was to urge strongly that the government must do one thing or the other in the Sudan – either withdraw completely, or commit themselves to a full-scale war (*R.J.*, 21 Mar. 1885). This fully accorded with the first principles of a successful foreign policy as laid down by Milner: 'limit your spheres of duty and interest and then stick to them' (Milner to Goschen, loc. cit.).

* It was clearly understood by both Goschen and Milner that the fairly specific statements that were made over a wide range of issues in Goschen's spring campaign of 1885 (often as debating points to score off Chamberlain) were not intended as the programme of a future non-Tory government of resistance.

† Milner to Goschen, 8 Jan. 1885, Milner MSS box 182. Later in the month he was writing: 'a good many Liberals and advanced Liberals too will be very glad if you give Chamberlain some hard knocks' (20 Jan., loc. cit.). A study of local Liberal newspapers, carried out in late Jan. 1885 by Milner, appeared to show that the vast majority preferred Goschen to Chamberlain (at a time when Gladstone's days were thought to be numbered).

to gain, and perhaps something to lose, by putting forward the Tory furniture of church, crown and land to occupy the place in popular respect that ought to be held by economic reason. Goschen was not, like W. H. Smith, a nervous Liberal going over to the Tories, but a confident Liberal who meant to absorb what was narrowly particular in the old Toryism and recast it into new and stronger generalities.

Nor, for Goschen, did Hartington matter all that much.* He was to be the great political asset: Goschen was to be the banker who made the asset fructify. Though Hartington did turn into an active Unionist, Goschen and his friends only sought that he should be a captive one. It was Goschen, not Hartington, who cultivated a circle of young Whig members, and talked to them of the great part that history called upon them to play:† it was Goschen who settled seat by seat with the Tory whip[79] which Liberals could be assured of Tory support for their return at the next general election: it was Goschen who was constantly seeing the Queen in spring 1886, in the intervals of whistle-stop campaign tours round northern towns which put his health at risk.‡ Hartington did not see the Queen at all between June 1885 and August 1886: he did not seek to form a party or to define his views, any more than Bright did, for it was because of their imprecision and their lack of association with any organised squadron that both Hartington and Bright could always be recognised as symbols of leadership, either when they chose or at times when others chose for them. For much of 1886, Hartington was led by his followers, and his followers were led by Goschen. Because Hartington took up an apparently categorical position on Ireland in December 1885, and again took up an uncompromising attitude in April–July 1886, it is easy to overlook that in the intervening months his name had been writ in water: that he had sedulously avoided commitment, and had seemed to his followers almost incapable of it; and that he

---

* This was Gladstone's impression at the time. When Goschen lost his seat in the 1886 general election, Gladstone wrote 'Goschen's defeat is ... a great event. He supplies in the main soul, brains, and movement to the body. Can Hartington get him a seat? Can he form a Govt without him?' (Gladstone to Granville 6 July 1886, Ramm, ii, 456).

† Cf. Goschen to A. Grey, 1 Dec. 1885, Grey MSS: 'I should be inconsolable if you were defeated.'

‡ 'I have slept very badly .. I am not up to the mark in health' (Goschen to Milner, n.d., but written from Edinburgh in mid-Apr. 1886, Milner MSS box 182). This is one of the very few letters from Goschen to Milner that have survived in the Milner MSS. On 15 Mar. Goschen was ordered to Hastings for a short holiday by his doctors (*The Times*, 16 Mar.), probably having been unwell since at least 6 Mar., when A. Grey reported him as confined to bed with a severe cough.

had taken no one in the 'Whig' section into his confidence as to his intentions or opinions, until it had become clear that his followers on the one hand, and general public opinion about his standing as the embodiment of simple rough-hewn honesty on the other, would no longer permit him to stand aside with impunity.

Thus, one of the main ways in which Goschen was able to change the situation, was by holding this pistol at Hartington's head: 'either live up to the public estimate of you, created by your followers' behaviour, or find yourself superseded by a more angular and militant version of the moderate man of principle: either come forward to act out my wishes by creating a Hartingtonian secession which will be a new focus for the principle of authority, or be left behind in a broad popular Liberalism which could by now be resisted better from outside than from inside'. Because Goschen consistently played the part of the loyal subordinate, working selflessly for a party leader who was resolved to stand firm against the disorder in history, Hartington in the end had to give in to the expectations that were created about him. Goschen's behaviour was a fine example of coercive loyalty in public, accompanied by discreet hand-wringing in private:

'I saw Hartington yesterday. He was not combative at all. But I hope that a letter will appear in Monday's papers stating that he adheres to all his electoral declarations. I have not wished to act before him or without him if it could possibly be avoided. I want *him* to act as the leader of the Moderates so long as there is any hope that he will'.[80]

To some extent, such utterances were only disguised and self-advertising comparisons, in which Hartington's great qualities as a leader were only dragged into the conversation in order to make the qualifying point that those qualities were far from visible in Hartington's practice.* Records of Goschen's conversation between December 1885 and April 1886 are peppered with such disparagements. Such simple rancour, however, by no means measured the deprivation which Hartington's followers were wishing on their leader. They proposed nothing less than the destruction of his career.

Hartington wished to be prime minister. This is to be taken as

* Cf. Goschen to Grey, 12 Dec. 1885, Grey MSS: 'I have had a more satisfactory letter from Hartington lately than any of his previous ones ... I hope Granville has not once more demoralised him. Unless I hear soon, I shall write to ask what has happened.' The effect Goschen uniformly sought to create was of a Hartington who could only act firmly if Goschen made clear to him what he had to do (e.g. as when he got Hartington to issue a public repudiation of the Hawarden Kite).

self-evident. There is no evidence whatever of *nolo episcopari* as a general tendency of his mind, his three refusals of the premiership occurring because acceptance at those particular times would have, on balance, been to his political disadvantage.

Hartington had no particular wishes about what he wanted to do with the premiership. This fitted well with the fact, which he perfectly appreciated, that so long as the Liberals were a permanent majority party, and therefore representing an extraordinarily wide spectrum, their party leaders had to be chairmen, and as such had to act within very clear constraints. Hartington wished to be premier: he wished the means of his premiership to be a permanent majority party of all colours and no colour: he did not wish to make the adoption of a pronounced political style the basis of his power. He certainly did not see it as his job to be an exponent of popular demands, but then he did not think it wise or in his interest to come out in opposition to popular demands in a way which distinguished him from all the other politicians who were searching for styles of social control. He wanted to lead the united party built by Palmerston and Gladstone, and he wanted his succession to the throne to be definitive and to take place without recriminations. His relations with Gladstone were usually as amiable as could be expected between two such dissimilar men, and his view in spring 1886 that he had everything to gain by being pleasant to and about Gladstone is hard to contest. Hartington was, in fact, far more agreeable to Gladstone in spring 1886, than in the previous year: a clue lies here, perhaps. The problem however lies elsewhere than in Hartington's intentions. In intention, as we have seen, Hartington meant to maintain the party structure, the ideology of class collaboration and so on, that he had grown up with: he did not, like Goschen, seek to destroy the past. The question is what forced Hartington's plans to go amiss. The answer is firstly, that Goschen and the 'young Whigs' defined the character of his personal support in a way that drastically redefined his possible scope as leader: and secondly, that Salisbury and Gladstone acted together to destroy him in May 1886, just as he was on the verge of leading a strong and united cabinet, backed by a broadly based moderate majority party, into inheriting the earth. Hartington, working within the old system of politics, won game and set by sheer good sense and with little effort, and failed only at match point.

It was, of course, impossible that Goschen, and Hartington, and Gladstone, could all succeed in the medium term. It was possible, however, for all to be relatively successful in the short term: Hartington in standing aside as the disinterested, friendly alternative leader waiting happily for the Palmerstonian future to fall into his lap; Gladstone in tying the cabinet and party with consummate skill to an *idée fixe* which necessarily entailed his leadership and yet, for him though not for his followers, was infinitely plastic and negotiable; and Goschen in making public-spirited disquiet among good party Liberals wear the features of an inevitable right-wing secession. All three leaders had splendid luck, and made hardly a mistake, in the first three months of 1886. Hartington stood aside without seceding, and in so doing won admiring speeches from Gladstonian ministers: while in private correspondence Hartington was inflicting friendly advice on Gladstone. He wrote on how to proceed on the Address, how to reform procedure, and on getting advice from Irish landlords, on this last point going to great pains to collect letters from Irish land agents which on the whole came out for general land purchase as the only solution to the land problem. As late as 15 March, Hartington was writing in the most solicitous way of his anxiety to assist Gladstone in buying out the Irish landlords,[81] a class of whom his family were prominent members. If there was any failure to follow up this opening, it was on Gladstone's side: and it is interesting that the letters were mislaid by Morley and only came to light recently. Had Gladstone not in fact avoided it, one would certainly have taken an agreement between Hartington, Chamberlain, and Gladstone on an Irish land programme to be unavoidable in the early months of 1886. The one decisive lead given by Hartington in the months preceding the home rule bill was to impose his view that premature partisanship must be avoided.* Hartington was as neutral and responsible in debate as in correspondence: in early March he condemned Churchill's premature attempts to stir up partisan excitement over Ireland as wanton.

Until at least quite late in March, then, Hartington and Gladstone were not really having a row at all, but creating roles which mutually sustained each other, just as they had always done, without affecting their real agreement as to what types of policies were possible. Both men agreed that, until an election created a fresh situation, any government had to have an Irish policy, and that an Irish policy had to be based either on Irish national unity, which happened then to exist, or on English national unity, which at a practical level did not exist in this context. Both probably regarded coercion as virtually impossible to carry out, though only Hartington really

---

* Thus Goschen was clearly given to understand that 'it is necessary to have out Gladstone's plan [and] that the country will not be unanimous enough in dealing with Ireland unless convinced that Gladstone had been allowed to try his hand and had failed' (Goschen to Sir R. Morier, 10 Feb. 1886, cited in Elliot, *Goschen*, ii, 15–16.)

stated this: both regarded a home rule scheme as a potential solution, though only Hartington said this clearly in late January. Both, however, preferred not to look to either extreme of the spectrum, but to fix on a narrow central range of possible policies which would unite an English consensus with a dominant body of opinion in Ireland. This meant, obviously, creating a new situation, something Hartington was quite content to leave to Gladstone. Hartington, pushed by Goschen, said something in reply to the Hawarden Kite on 22 December which sounded like a disavowal of home rule, but whose real function was to establish his claim to be a more responsible (since more reluctant) leader of average Liberal opinion where Ireland was concerned. Hartington's standing aside from the Liberal ministry on 31 January was also meant to serve the same function, as was his rather frenetic buttonholing operation on 23 January when he tried to make representative junior ministers grasp that, should Gladstone for any reason fail to form a ministry in coming weeks, they could nevertheless expect from Hartington all that they had hoped for from Gladstone – that, indeed, it might not be necessary to have a Gladstone ministry at all, and that above all it was important to see Hartington not as a secessionist but as a constructive and sympathetic interpreter of party opinion, though in a more cautious way than Gladstone. A year earlier Gordon's death had greatly increased Hartington's standing, although he was the responsible minister: and a minister who had extracted from that debacle a demand for a Hartington 'patriotic government' need not have been wholly innocent in his dissociation from further Gladstonian errors of judgment.

There were perhaps three occasions when Hartington made fairly genuine attempts to rule out the programme implied in the Hawarden Kite, on 22 December, around 1 January, and around 20 January. They were feeble efforts, not conducted as if they were really meant to deflect Gladstone: almost as though they were done for the record. They did, of course, establish a genuinely reactionary element in Hartington's thinking on Ireland, which is faithfully reflected among his papers at Chatsworth, and which closely corresponded to the public idea of what Hartington was like. This element, however, cannot be taken on its own, but must be seen in the context of behaviour pointing quite the other way; above all, his presenting modified home rule ideas in conversation (but not on paper) in late January, and his refusal to do anything to ease Goschen back into the ruling group in the Liberal party.

The pressure from Goschen did affect Hartington, but in a chiefly contrary way, pushing him towards the centre and forcing him to take up a position of positive disavowal of Goschen's cave.

The danger Hartington had to face and guard against in January and February 1886 was of public identification with a knot of 'Whig' dissidents who were anything but under his control, who had little regard for him, who subjectively and objectively were wrecking his orderly succession to the leadership of a united Gladstonian party, and who probably by no means shared his sense of what the Irish problem was. Hartington reacted as one would expect him to react, avoiding any appearance of being a party malcontent or leader of a wing, sounding as though he could lead the Liberals at least a little way in all possible directions, and adopting a posture of benignly evasive centrality. He did not belong to Goschen's party, and he wanted everyone to understand that. He was the next Liberal prime minister, and, if necessary when the time came, he would be a great, though moderate and reluctant, home rule prime minister. Gladstone was unnecessary, except perhaps in the very short run, just as unnecessary as Goschen's opposition to Gladstone. All one needed was a Hartington government.

Some records of the conversation of Unionist Liberals in mid- and late January make it possible to draw an important distinction between the points of view of Hartington and of Goschen. Goschen's idiosyncrasy lay in his desire for a land bill: Hartington's, in his weak but novel interest in Irish local government, with perhaps a land bill thrown in for good measure. As usual in 1886, the Liberal intellectuals, among whom Goschen (here modelling himself, perhaps, both on Argyll and Lowe) certainly wished to be numbered,* were far more passionate about the rights of land- lords than the landlords themselves, whereas Hartington was at this time quite relaxed about the land question, seeing it as secon- dary to the more general question of maintaining public order. Since Hartington's family estates in Ireland were having their share of trouble at this time †, his detachment showed considerable ability to stick to the essentials of maintaining his personal auth- ority and not being sidetracked into maintaining the authority of doctrines, as Goschen wished to do. There were also sharp dif- ferences in the degree to which they were opposed to home rule, and willing to rule by coercion.

Goschen was unequivocally opposed to any form of home rule,

---

* On 27 Feb. 1886, Goschen addressed an educational society at the Mansion House on the subject on 'Hearing, Reading and Thinking', in which he deplored the hurry of modern life, and the small time it left for thought and study.

† The Duke of Devonshire's Irish tenants had just demanded a 40 per cent rent reduction, rejecting an offer of 20 per cent by the Duke (*Pall Mall Gazette*, 13 Jan.).

but thought 'some very big measure for buying out landlords compulsory on landlords to sell and *on tenants to buy*, might be useful. Alternative according to him is something of that kind, or rigidly enforcing existing rights at all costs and continuously'.[82] Hartington showed no interest in land legislation, but doubted 'whether people who are all pronouncing strongly against home rule have looked at all the evils entailed by refusing it... He seems to think we must do something in the direction of local govt: though in present state of Ireland, the real governing [of] the country cannot remain with local bodies. "We must carry British opinion with us" '.[83] In view of such meditations, one must regard statements made by unequivocal anti-home rulers about Hartington's position with caution, as for instance when Goschen said 'Hartington speaks quite satisfactorily and decidedly on the matter'.[84] So no doubt he had, but not only to Goschen, and it was only in later months that the full two-sidedness of Hartington's tactics began to dawn on those hard-line Unionists who thought they knew from the beginning exactly what Hartington wanted. Trevelyan, starting from the conjecture that if Hartington had joined the ministry, Gladstone's home rule scheme could have been prevented, went on to discuss whether Hartington's withdrawal had implied a desire of his not to block home rule.* At the relevant moment, which was the fall of the Salisbury ministry, this would be far from a wild conjecture as to part of Hartington's motives. As experienced a judge as Samuel Whitbread thought at that time that Hartington would actually join the new Gladstone government.[85]

If one were to make a rough chronology of the ebb and flow of Hartington's position, it would take approximately the following form. His rebuttal of the Hawarden Kite (22 December) established that he was a man of principle who had made his position publicly clear. It left him free to do anything or nothing, while at the same time showing him as more 'straight' than Gladstone. It also neatly cut out Goschen's bid to lead the Liberal right on the pretext of organising support for Hartington. Once Hartington had declared against home rule, he would be more credible than anyone else if he slowly came round to that position, since such a change would be taken as indicating the extremity of the situation. It was from this position of basic strength that Hartington became involved in attempts to construct a broad ministerial front, principally through the Devonshire House meeting on 1 January, to control Gladstone. What else the front was to do was quite unclear: it could no more

* Elliot diary, 25 Mar. 1886. Trevelyan told Elliot that he himself had only joined 'to prevent them proposing any outrageous scheme'.

set about coercing the Irish than it could offer home rule. Hartington's involvement in the Devonshire House meeting arose from the need to control Gladstone, not from a wish to kill home rule. The need to control Gladstone arose from a view of home rule in which the degree of caution with which the subject was to be approached, became the main issue. On these terms, by being the most cautious of home rulers, Hartington could displace Gladstone as a viable Liberal premier: by being an anti-home ruler pure and simple, he could not do that.

Hartington soon accepted that ministerial pressure on Gladstone would not work in a situation where Gladstone was showing exceptional caution and was generally expected to be premier within the month. He then took the line that the situation was exceptionally difficult: his remarks to Elliot on 14 January show him sitting on the fence. In the period 2–18 January, he hardly ranks as an active opponent of home rule, or as a proponent of any course whatever. * About 19 January, under strong pressure from a handful of right wing Liberals who were more interested in stopping home rule, Gladstone, and 'revolutionary tendencies', than in achieving a broadly-based Hartington ministry fairly quickly and comfortably, Hartington attempted to make a stand, if only to prove to his own satisfaction that making a stand would not work. Hartington threatened to speak strong words on Ireland as soon as parliamentary opportunity occurred: Gladstone made it clear that in that case he would abdicate, punishing any attempt by Hartington to succeed him with the serious risk of a Gladstonian 'cave' inhabited by all possible kinds of malcontents. From 20 January onwards Hartington made no further attempt to block Gladstone forming a ministry. On the day of the division on Collings' motion his supporters were given no indication as what they should do. † It was a situation in which the reversion to the Liberal leadership was distinctly more valuable than the leadership: and had Hartington made it his aim to force Gladstone out in January, as he could well have done, he would only have enhanced Gladstone's power by making him the reversionary interest and leader of last resort, and

---

* Replying to a letter from the governor-general of Canada who was anxious to dispose of his large Kerry estates at the best possible price, Hartington said that 'for the interests of landlords I think that the best solution might probably be a Home Rule scheme combined with a fair land purchase measure', but because English opinion would only agree to an overhaul of county government as part of a simultaneous reform throughout the country, thereby alienating the Irish party, 'We may therefore have to struggle on for some time longer on the present system' (Hartington to Lansdowne 4 Jan. Devonshire MSS 340/1884).

† 'He took absolutely no trouble to get his friends to support him' (A. Elliot's Diary, 26 Jan.).

done himself immense damage. This was a point that his Whig followers were quite unable to appreciate. With startling naivety they interpreted the situation in sharp, simple terms. Thus it was possible for them to believe that had Hartington taken a strong line 'Mr. G. would have given up the lead of the party ... and retired to Hawarden'.[86] In practice, of course, Gladstone would have done no such thing. Yet in spite of the fundamental disagreement between Goschen's group and Hartington on the right tactics to be employed there were never any serious difficulties between the two leaders, and this harmony is an indication of the skill shown by Hartington in controlling Goschen while appearing to be genuinely in need of his advice.

From 20–27 January Hartington, having eliminated the possibility of resistance to Irish demands as a battle cry, tentatively went round talking to people about the need to meet Irish demands. He did not yet know what was in Gladstone's mind, that revelation (not that there was much to impart) coming on 26 January. Before then, though, Hartington talked home rule. On 20 January he and Trevelyan privately received a deputation of Irish merchants who wanted anti-boycotting legislation and a firm pledge on the Union. Trevelyan did not speak, while Hartington, presented with a good opportunity to make a 'patriotic' statement, chose to be totally reticent, leaving his intentions entirely ambiguous. Hartington 'was not prepared with a definite expression of opinion', but reminded them that the vast majority in Ireland wanted home rule. On 23 January Hartington talked persuasively on behalf of home rule successively to Sir U. Kay-Shuttleworth and to A. Grey. He converted the former to home rule, and deeply alarmed the latter by flying a home rule kite. At this stage he probably expected to join the next Liberal ministry and wished to enter with his principles showing, and perhaps even had some idea of pre-empting the policies Gladstone was still refusing to acknowledge that he had, and forming a qualified home rule ministry over Gladstone's head. What ended this phase is not clear, but probably Gladstone did enlarge on his Irish policies so diligently on 26 January that Hartington decided to drop out of that race also for the time being.

One can establish just how Hartington did indeed seem to be moving towards some accommodation with home rule throughout January, a process which would of course have been easier had Gladstone not acted as if to nip it in the bud. What Gladstone wanted was a conversion of those he wanted to see converted, as an act plainly stemming from Gladstonian initiatives: whereas what Hartington probably was reaching out to was an independent act of leadership aimed at drawing his own Whig following towards home rule, in order to emphasise his ability to do what Gladstone could not do. It was true that Hartington's Whig following, insofar as its articulate embodiment was a stage army of three or four restless young men of good lineage indoctrinated by and more than half belonging to Goschen, would really not accept any home rule at any price. But that Hartington was vulnerable to the sniping of his self-appointed supporters, and that he was lazy and so put off all decisions with remarkable consistency, are not the nuances one should choose to stress. More important was the absence of any process by which Hartington could be teased into modifying his own opinions, under the guise of being asked to decide others' opinions. Hartington's remarks on 23 January to Albert Grey show the direction in which drawing him out would lead, and it was only accident that the drawing out was done by a conspiratorial young reactionary. What Hartington may have said, we do not know, but Grey's rejoinder indicates the trend:

> '... having duly considered your remarks of yesterday, I still adhere as stoutly as I can to my original determination to fight as stoutly as I can [for the Union] .. such a Repeal of the Union as you contemplated when you spoke of getting rid of the Irish members ...' was of no value to anyone. '... I shall do everything in my power with Arthur Elliot and others to resist and fight against Repeal, and I only hope that in the battle we may be fighting behind you under your leadership, and not against you'.*

Curiously enough, another indirect indication of the impression Hartington was trying to make on people at this time is available, as it happens for the very same day as he spoke to A. Grey. It concerns the Lancashire neighbour and admirer of Hartington's, Sir U. Kay-Shuttleworth, whose memorandum on the history of his views is a riposte to an aggrieved G. O. Trevelyan, who had accused Shuttleworth of changing faith. Shuttleworth wrote (15 May 1886) agreeing that he had indeed been against home rule when the two men had first discussed the question in January 1886, but that his opinions had thereafter begun to change in a way consistent with his holding office. He dated the beginning of his conversion to a

* Albert Grey to Hartington, 24 Jan. 1886, Devonshire MSS 340/1915. Arthur Elliot was equally irritated by the failure of Hartington to act the part of the consistently reactionary leader whom they did not in fact actually suppose him to be: 'Hartington could rally round himself an immense amount of support if only he would speak out firmly and at once ... I am very much disappointed with Hartington in this great crisis. It is impossible for private members to put spirit into a leader without it' (Elliot to Selborne, 26 Jan. 1886. Selborne MSS 1869 f. 135).

chance conversation on 23 January 1886 with Hartington, which impressed Shuttleworth with the deep need for home rule.

Once Hartington's attempt to create a stop-Gladstone block in the ex-cabinet had failed, he adjusted quite rapidly to the realities of the situation. On Ireland he had much of Gladstone's realism, responsibility, and self-interestedness, all alike grounded in the classical view of man. There was, in fact, no strictly Irish question for him to decide. What he had to consider was whether there should be a short, purely Gladstone ministry whose inevitable failure would precipitate his coming to power a little later with the freest of free hands. The alternative was to have a ministry so little Gladstonian in character, that it would achieve the same results but more quickly. It was a nice judgment to make, requiring continual idleness to make it in. In not interrupting that idleness, the Gladstonians threw away their best card. Had they, with a pious gesture of languor or helplessness, indicated they felt it was a problem that only Hartington could resolve, they might have gained their man and won their cause. Instead, there is the least possible evidence of the future Gladstonians wishing to implicate Hartington in making decisions which, clearly given to him to make, would apparently have been made in their favour. A ministry formed by Hartington in late January 1886 would have been, in leaning and in direction, a home rule ministry.

What Goschen was doing, certainly from early 1885 onwards, and perhaps earlier in the 1880s, was forming a party round himself. (To some extent the party he formed to oppose home rule in 1886 and Chamberlain in 1885 was a resuscitation of the party, still glum and sore, which had unsuccessfully attempted to form a cave in favour of proportional representation from early in 1884)*. Whether he used that party for action under his own aegis, or whether he lent his nucleus of strength to Hartington in order to make him do what he wanted, depended very much on circumstances. In early 1885 when his ideas first took coherent shape he expected the 'mantle of Elijah' (i.e. the premiership) to fall on his own shoulders,[87] but when the 1885 election campaign began to bring Hartington within his orbit, he accepted that an element of self-effacement was required from him. Once Gladstone's home rule government had been formed Goschen was '*most* anxious that Hartington would take the lead and not I.'[88] Goschen depended for success on a general sense of Chamberlain as an economic

---

* Lubbock, Courtney, and A. Grey, but not Goschen, were among the small group which met on 16 Jan. 1884 and decided to launch a society in favour of proportional representation (Lubbock's diary, 16 Jan. 1884).

(rather than religious) threat, and also on resentment of Radical attempts to take over the constituencies. This gave Goschen a context in which to stand forth as strong, central, and wise. How convincing he was we can hardly guess. He certainly took immense trouble to proselytise. He had a circle of fairly close adherents of good standing: Sellar, Elliot, Albert Grey, Ebrington, Lymington, Lubbock, perhaps Brand, perhaps Courtney. These were good backbench names, no more, no less. They were mostly intelligent, often intellectual. Among colleagues of equal rank Goschen was quite isolated,* more by his choice than by any general sense that he was not a man to join with in political labours. Of the adherents, most is known about Albert Grey, M.P, the young nephew of the aged third Earl Grey, whom he succeeded in the title: and probably there was more to Grey's activities than to those of any other schismatic Whig backbencher.

Grey had charm, looks, athletic vigour, zest, joy in life, and money: and consequently had great ability to raise more money. He had already come into possession of the Grey estates in 1884. At Cambridge he had been seen as 'the beau ideal of manly English youth.' In society, his 'wandering eye' led observers to note his readiness to give himself to 'frank and catholic admiration of beauty – beauty of every kind.' The embodiment of patrician virture in its healthy outdoor aspect, he was an appropriate future Governor of Rhodesia and later of Canada: his engaging innocence led him into political intrigue which he treated with some finesse, with some thought for theory, but also with a glowing sense of sport. His First in law showed that he could work, if no more than that. To women, a future prime minister, to himself he was above all an exponent of Whig Democracy – that is, of the view that the democracy really wanted to vote Whig. He had some grounds for this, having come top of the poll for South Northumberland in 1880 with an appreciable personal vote, and having won Tyneside handsomely in 1885 without paying attention to radical shibboleths. †

In his part of the country, perhaps better than anywhere else,

---

* No particular significance should be attached to the incognito visit which Goschen made to Inverary in Sept. 1885. His object was probably to consult the Duke of Argyll on Scottish politics, before going to campaign in his Edinburgh constituency. There are no grounds for thinking that Argyll was ever invited to join Goschen's non-Tory national party. In part ill-health made any sustained exertion during 1885–86 impossible, but also he had little regard for Goschen whom he described as 'self-centred and doctrinaire' (Lady F.Balfour, *Ne Obliviscaris* ii, 49). Argyll's chief interest at this time was in sustaining an entirely unproductive correspondence with Gladstone. From Dec. 1885 to Apr. 1886 he was virtually *hors de combat* due to gout.

† 'You bearded the caucus and have conquered them' (Goschen to Grey, 12 Dec. 1885, Grey MSS).

Whigs could find and hold a popular audience, and discern that whatever ideas were put to a popular audience would be received quite well, so long as they were put and put confidently:

> 'I have attended five very important colliery meetings since the rising of the House and have found it perfectly easy to win for Hare's scheme (of proportional representation) an entry into the minds as well as the hearts of the people. . . I look forward with keen pleasure to the Chamberlains etc. of the party being dragged no long time hence at the heels of the Whigs.'[89]

The country, in Grey's view, was waiting for a cause and a man, and then the radical froth would be blown away with ease. Grey, like Goschen, held this view well before home rule became the issue of the day: and had home rule not presented itself, one can see Grey (and Goschen) moving through some other issue, like proportional representation or the empire, towards the same end, namely, a reconstruction of the Liberal party to become a party of authority and overt resistance to working class demands, supported, much more than were the Tories, by popular ardour, and sustained by vehement campaigning (Grey had formed his impressions of politics in 1878–80). In his impatience he could hardly bear to wait for the right situation before acting. In May 1885 he called on Goschen in 'fighting vein' and urged him to consider 'retiring from Edinburgh and endeavouring to bring a party together before the election.'* Goschen understood correctly that the time was not ripe for such a bold departure.

The key assumption in Grey's thinking was that the country would demand an active dialogue with its politicians. Had he been right in this assumption, he would have been well placed to turn it to advantage. His vocabulary of assuagement for those who lacked everything was rich in verbal treasure. 'Brotherhood', 'Christian love' and 'national greatness', were linked with the theme of a 'national party' to support 'a new crusade'. He valued highly certain kinds of social reform, not least because they could so happily be exhibited as dissociated from resentful radicalism, and opposed to the spirit of party competition which he painted as the evil demon of Westminster. Had a baring of the heart been what the situation required of the political class, Grey's would have been an eminently suitable heart to expose to the great British public. As it was, persuasion of the electorate was easy to neglect simply because all participants in the struggle for power were

---

* Goschen's journal, May 1885, cited A. Elliot, *Goschen* (1911), ii, 293. After the interview Goschen commented: 'I am extremely disgusted and do not see how I can go on'.

agreed that it was not a problem. Grey therefore had to switch his identity from being the Sir Galahad of the north-east coalfield, to being an aristocratic puppy in Westminster committee politics, a world where all young men were seen by all old men as a kind of useful private secretary with a purely contingent political meaning.

Grey, it was clear, would have acted anyway, with or without Goschen, just as Goschen would have acted anyway, with or without Hartington. Grey could not have achieved, and did not think to achieve, frontbench standing, and therefore in one sense he did not matter, being outside the possible combinations of governing men. On the other hand, he did make things happen. He could chance his arm in a way that Goschen was too senior to do. He did not mind, or did not know, whether he made a fool of himself. He did not care what happened to the Liberal party since it had to be rebuilt anyway on new principles: unlike Hartington, he did not just want Hartington to come in and do what Gladstone had been doing, even if under the slogan of twenty years of common sense rule. Grey's and Goschen's party was 'the moderates':* Hartington's, the Liberals. Goschen had expected a speedy demise to the 1886 parliament in any case, even before it was elected, and therefore all his plans were interim ones, awaiting the moment when the Liberals could be broken, preferably from the inside:

'I will tell you what I think the best plan ... I have told no one yet except my wife. It is to prepare myself, if the occasion arises, to join a cabinet † formed by Gladstone (of course if I am asked, which may be doubtful), then to keep Hartington up to the mark in resisting the radicals in the cabinet, to keep them strictly to the accepted programme put forward by Gladstone, and then when the latter retires, either to assist towards making Hartington the first power, or to split off: to keep up throughout the idea that the moderates will be as outspoken against radical schemes, as the radicals are in their favour, and to see to it that the cabinet does not drift. If all this could be done, the split, which must come, might find the Moderates in a stronger position than now:

* Cf. Goschen to Grey, 26 Sept. 1885, Grey MSS: 'I *may* speak too for Haldane ... He is one of the moderates'. They much preferred this term to that of Whig, which they rightly thought made them sound more traditionalist than they were. Moreover, a member of the select company had certain distinct characteristics which distinguished him sharply from a mere Whig. According to Milner's definition, 'a real moderate Liberal is a man whose moderation is based on principle, as strong, maybe stronger, and better digested than that of other more advanced men. But the moderation of the Whig is the result not of moderate principles but of having no principles at all' (Milner to Goschen, 21 Aug. 1884, Milner MSS box 182).

† He probably had the exchequer in mind here.

at any rate personally I should be able to act and come forward in defence of Moderate Liberalism, as one of the joint heirs of Gladstone and his "sound economic school" instead of as malcontent and outsider. Gross Conservative profligacy almost drives me to this course, and Gladstone's comparative moderation makes it possible. I shall take no one into confidence about this, but tell me how it strikes you...'*

This, then, was the master-plan: and it was made before the election, without reference to Ireland,† without reference to the Tories, and without regard to religion. Indeed, the implication was that it was for economics to supply the binding force once lent to social discipline by religion. As to Ireland, it is quite likely that Goschen had not really thought much about it at all until a very late stage, it not being till 2 January 1886 that he wrote to Grey on this subject, and then only in a most floundering manner.‡ There was no question of going over to the Tories, or coalescing with them: it was rather a matter of rejecting the ability of the Tories to act as an effective force of control in a secular industrial society. Looking many moves ahead, it was Salisbury's job that Goschen wanted: and to get it, he had to destroy the Liberal coalition, bring into isolated prominence the Radical wing, and ignore or disparage official Conservatism (this last coming easily to his cast of mind). The formal aim of all this was to rally average opinion under the Hartington umbrella, instead of dividing it between the two parties, but beneath that there was an indivisible mixture of ambition, resentment, and moral entrepreneurship of Goschen's part.

Goschen wanted Salisbury's job: that is he wished to make a right-wing Liberal party the dominant party of the right. He had no wish for political partnership with current Tory leaders. His

* Goschen to Grey, 20 Sept. 1885, Grey MSS: cf. Goschen to Grey, 18 Oct. 1885, ibid., on similar lines 'I intend *pinning* our Moderate leaders to their programme...'

† Goschen went for a walk round the woods at Dalmeny with Gladstone and Rosebery in Nov. 1885. Gladstone and Rosebery talked openly of their leanings to home rule, which they presumably would not have done if they had suspected Goschen's hostility. Goschen was silent throughout and gave no indication of his Irish views. In fact he may not have had any Irish views at that time. However, in retrospect, his conduct on that occasion was seen as a singularly unattractive flouting of the conventions under which political discussions took place. Cf. Harcourt calling Goschen 'a poisonous intriguer' (*R.J.*, 25 Jan. 1886), and Granville's wife doing a little dance when Goschen lost his seat in July 1886: it was a pleasure to dislike Goschen.

‡ Grey MSS: 'I think and read of nothing else but the Irish question from day to day. I am steeped in it now ...' implying previous lack of concern, and going on to state his sense of confusion: 'The forces are all so incalculable...'

soul, as well as his political instincts, shrank from Churchill. Yet
Goschen in practice confined his operations to surgery upon the
Liberal party. This was probably because they were the people he
knew. He did not try to draw on latent Tory support for his impending reactionary party of the centre. That support was however
there. Goschen made a deep impression on those Tories who
regarded themselves as honest and true men of principle perma-
nently fated to be led by opportunists. The archetypal squire Sir
R. Knightley looked on Goschen 'very much as his future leader'
while his wife was attracted by 'the moderate party under Mr
Goschen to which so many people look forward'. Balfour and
Dalrymple thought the Tories 'should hold out the hand' to
Goschen. W. H. Smith even offered to give up his cabinet place to
make room for him in any future Tory ministry, arguing that
Goschen had 'weight in the country if not in the House'. Lord
Bath could say of Goschen 'no man in England has been so straight
and honest' and consider the 'only chance' for the country was 'a
moderate Liberal government under Goschen'. Those Tories who
leant to Goschen were not defined by their being on the liberal
wing of their party, but by being 'true Tories' who were disturbed
by the radicalising effects of party competition. Like Lord Bath,
they wanted something like 'a moderate Liberal Government leaning on a modicum of Conservative support' as under Palmerston,
and they liked Goschen for offering the Tories a role as loyal
opposition working to create a system which, though under
Liberal hegemony, would be conservative in its general direction,
and would not attempt to accommodate supposed popular radicalism. There was, in sum, a substantial minority of Tory rank-and-
file opinion which was convinced, from clear-sighted reaction, that
what mattered was where the total political system was going, and
believed that a competitive Tory party was at this level a recipe
for disaster. A reconstruction of the right to produce a non-
competitive Tory party and a dominant right-wing Liberal party
was, as Goschen sensed, a widely desired possibility. Nothing was
done to make it come about at Tory rank-and-file level, in a manipulative way: but had a right-wing Liberal ministry got off the
ground, its effect upon the Tory army would have been exceedingly dangerous for those leaders whose only understood function
was to run a professionally competitive party.[90]

As regards the Liberal side of Goschen's operations, he and
Grey started from about the same theoretical position, though
Grey could give it an aura of ease, generosity, spontaneity and
birthright that Goschen could not. Goschen and Grey were moreover agreed that it was unlikely that they would find themselves in

disagreement, irrespective of the particular political situation: how this relationship had originated is not known. Grey did, however, make a distinctive contribution in the sphere of simple-minded crusading, enjoying the novelties of work and intrigue in a spirit of noblesse oblige.

Milner's contribution was much less obtrusive, at least in 1885, but in its own way it was just as vital to the smooth functioning of the machine. Between secretary and master the most perfect unanimity reigned. In every letter Milner wrote, Goschen found enthusiastic confirmation of his own beliefs and tactful encouragement to further exertion. Goschen badly needed both these things. *
On the other hand he was always careful to preserve the distance between them by allotting Milner a heavy load of routine chores. Mixing very little in society Milner had plenty of time to chase references, arrange publication of Goschen's speeches and sound out the reactions of his other employer, W. T. Stead, to the new movement. † When foreign and colonial questions were due for an airing Milner was called in to act as speechwriter. It was therefore entirely predictable that Goschen should find Milner a place on the Liberal Unionist Committee immediately after its formation in April 1886 not only to ensure that Grey did not make a mess of it, but to keep its operations within clearly defined limits. Whatever other talents he possessed Milner was valued for his qualities of loyalty and intellectual application. Grey had style and connections, but lacked discretion and judgement. In harness they made up a well-balanced team.

Grey's confidence was much increased by the 1885 elections, which were indeed regarded by Goschen as 'a complete justification of Moderate Liberals'. ‡ Whatever psephology may think of this view, what matters here is the subjective view of the electoral situation, and the subjective view taken by the non-radical Liberals of the 1885 elections was that, contrary to initial expectations just after the third reform bill was settled, everything was going to be all right. There was, it was true, an area of 'Lib-Lab' politics, much more clearly defined than before, but far from explosive, which

* In spring 1885 Goschen went through a period of deep depression during which he seriously considered throwing up his political work and emigrating to Australia (Goschen's journal, cited A. Elliot, *Goschen*, 1912, i, 294–5).

† One early result of these soundings was an article in the *Pall Mall Gazette* (Jan. 1885) in which Stead attacked Chamberlain 'very much on your lines' (Milner to Goschen, 29 Jan., Milner MSS box 182).

‡ Goschen to Grey, 1 Dec. 1885, Grey MSS. Cf. Goschen to Grey, 12 Dec. 1885, ibid., 'There will after all be a large brigade of good Liberals outside of Chamberlain's circle and every nerve must be strained to keep the advantage we have gained'.

the party leaders (including Rosebery and Gladstone) now believed they could win away from Chamberlain by a policy of dinner parties for working men,* minor but fastidiously prompt† legislation, and the general solicitation of deference by courtesy. In the case of the miners, for instance, a Coal Mines Regulation Act duly made its appearance in February 1886; and nothing could have been more natural than that Mrs Gladstone should have presented the great leader of the South Wales miners, Mabon, with a silver leek to mark the occasion of his first St David's Day as an M.P. later that spring. There was no problem about the working man, so long as he was not Chamberlain's working man‡: and it was becoming abundantly clear that the sensible thing for the Liberal establishment to do was to undermine Chamberlain's not very strong hold on the working men, on the party activists, and on the party organisation. This was to some extent going on steadily and gradually throughout 1885–86, and was only hastened somewhat by the parliamentary crisis. 'Moderate' [i.e. reactionary] Liberals reacted to the 1885 elections with relief and hope, feeling they could look forward to a better position in the party than they had supposed, and the relative failure of radicalism in the urban constituencies began a general revision of the cliches about 'aggressive democracy' on whose widespread acceptance Chamberlain's power was ultimately based. By December 1885 it was clearer than it had been for a long time that the Liberal party was worth staying in for moderates, and that Chamberlain was *in any case*, irrespective of Irish considerations, going to be cut down to size.

Grey was one of the few Unionists who felt it right to make continuous and eager exertions in the Unionist cause. In retrospect, speaking twelve years later at a presentation dinner in his honour, he went out of his way to stress that 'he was the first follower of Mr Gladstone who started the revolt against his home rule policy' by speaking out against Gladstone's plea, as 'an old parliamentary hand', for Liberal silence on Irish policy on the evening of 22 January 1886: and went on to recall that 'he could claim the chief credit which belonged to those who conceived the idea of and brought about the first great Opera House demonstration in

* The Speaker's special dinner (26 May 1886) for working class and miners' M.Ps to meet members of the social and intellectual élite, was paralleled by a number of other private dinners given by Liberal leaders.

† E.g. 'The business we are most anxious about is undoubtedly, the Crofters' Bill...' – Gladstone, *Hansard*, 9 Apr. 1886.

‡ Cf. Broadhurst's merits as the first working man ever to hold office: 'When I go to Birmingham' Broadhurst remarked 'I don't stay with Mr Chamberlain but I put up with a joiner' (Sir Shane Leslie, *Memoir of John Edward Courtenay Bodley*, 1930, 83).

London, where Liberals and Conservatives, for the first time in their history, stood side by side in defence of the empire'.[91] Whatever exaggeration had crept in over the years, it is true that Grey was a Liberal Unionist *contra mundum*, when no one else was. If anything, Grey wanted land purchase in Ireland, (where Goschen indeed wanted compulsory land purchase as a matter of urgency), because it would save the landlords and represented some kind of non-party consensus in English politics: but he decided, some time in early January, to invest a large amount of emotional energy in opposing home rule. He proposed, at first, to move a coercionist amendment to the Address, to show up the weakness of party leaders as compared with Grey Whigs:[92] and to assist in this project, he proposed to call together 'a small committee of independent men on both sides of the House' to obtain facts about Ireland on which to base his amendment calling for a hard line there.[93] His original proposal had to be laid aside as he learned more of supposed Tory plans for drastic action,* although talking to Irish Unionists like Saunderson strengthened his belief that '*abundant* bloodshed is thus the certain result of home rule'. (Saunderson had said confidently that he could bring 10,000 Protestants over from northern England in a week to fight for Ulster if necessary).

Had Grey somehow got a majority for an anti-Irish policy, he would have exerted himself to secure, not a Liberal, but a coalition government in place of the Tories. It was plain enough that, if one thought of Goschen as mattering, as one had to do if one took right-wing, public-spirited cerebral Whiggery to be a question of high principle, then one had little to hope for from a Liberal party where contact between Gladstone and Goschen was purely formal and virtually non-existent, and where even Hartington made not even a slight gesture to get Goschen taken back into the leadership:

'I asked him [Goschen] about Hartington. He could not tell. He had received no intimation that the Liberal leaders would be glad to admit him to the discussion of their affairs – and considering the agreement that exists between Hartington and him, he said that unless Hartington insisted on Goschen being admitted into the Councils of the Party, he, Goschen, would take it as a sign of Hartington giving way.

He is going to write to Hartington today to ask what line he proposes to take and to say at the same time that he Goschen is not going to drift, that he wishes to act with Hartington, but if

---

* Grey to Earl Grey, 15 Jan. 1886. On 31 May 1886, with an 'inspired' sense of timing, the *Pall Mall Gazette* published a detailed account of an Orange volunteer army, 73,000 strong.

Hartington is going to drift, he must know at once in order that he may have time to make effective arrangements...'[94]

There was, in 1886, no difficulty in seeing a place for Goschen as an admirable Liberal minister (rather like Lowe's return to the fold in 1868), and Goschen wanted that kind of party recognition perhaps quite strongly. But on the one hand, he was not much liked: he was competing for Hartington's role in a way that Hartington could hardly wish to assist: and he did not suit the immediate situation. Radicalism had turned out to be weaker than expected. In response, the party leaders had decided that instead of the anticipated fight against the left, they would simply be agreeable and create a cosy Lib-Lab atmosphere. They were, rightly, confident they could create this new atmosphere in which honest and pious men were touchingly deferential to the sentimental socialism of their natural superiors, provided that they steered clear of the acrid contempt which Goschen directed, on economic and practical grounds, to new tools of class collaboration like allotments. The objection to Goschen was that he did not understand what the correct ruling class riposte should be to very mild forms of endemic radicalism. The new politics consisted of giving a dinner to working-class M.Ps, and then getting back to the old politics: and Goschen did not operate that way.

Up to the second week in March, Hartington had broadly speaking evaded any partisan commitments. It is true that he had sometimes, privately, thrown sops to the militant anti-home rulers, as in his reassurances to the Ulster Liberals on 11 March, and his promise to Salisbury* that he would take a firm line in his speech to the Eighty Club on 5 March. Those who saw in Hartington at this time only an intrinsically dissident, but lazy and taciturn, Whig, because that was what they wished to see, did not take into account his friendly gestures of co-operation to Gladstone in February and March, his home rule kites of 20–26 January (which fortunately for him never attracted subsequent attention), and his steady refusal to set himself up as leader of the faction which wished ostensibly to follow him, in a direction to be determined by Goschen's ideas.

The first cabinet to deal with the Irish question was on 13 March. This altered matters, by bringing Chamberlain into play. From 13 March or a little earlier it was clear to initiates that Chamberlain

---

* Cf. Salisbury to Churchill, 16 Mar. 1886, Churchill MSS xii 1416: 'Hartington's speech differed rather widely from what he had told me, two days before, that he would say ... I suppose somebody has got at him ... I do not think it is necessary to make any more advances to them: the next steps must come from them...'

intended to smash the Irish bills, and with them Gladstone. Chamberlain may have been encouraged to stake his claim to be leader of disquiet on this issue, by the fact that Hartington had failed to do so. There was a niche to be filled, and Chamberlain was much more enthusiastic about fighting home rule in early March, when he had a chance of doing so at Hartington's expense, than in early April, when opposition meant playing second fiddle to Hartington. It is so unlikely that Chamberlain wished to play second fiddle to Hartington, in early March 1886, that one must look for some other picture of the situation: either a picture in which Hartington did not come forward effectively at all, or a picture in which Chamberlain drove both Gladstone and Hartington into extreme positions, leaving himself as the only leader acceptable to both wings of the party, using the existing Liberal majority as the basis for a great premiership. Certainly Chamberlain's Irish formulæ were designed to take central ground rather than to comfort the anti-home rule militants (who disliked his federal schemes almost as much as home rule). Chamberlain was angry and tense about home rule in March, but no more so than at any other period since December, and not enough so to make him wish to change from being the subordinate of an old man to being the subordinate of a young man. He was not in any case acting in practical concert with Hartington*: he was competing with him for the lead, not necessarily of the few young Whig patricians (though that was just possible) but of the much larger body of bewildered and unhappy opinion, of all political shades, which Gladstone's Irish proposals had created within the Liberal party. If all went well, Chamberlain could hope to be premier within months, offering Gladstone the lord presidency and a peerage, say, and Hartington the Foreign Office, offering the Radicals junior offices (there were no Radicals, if pure opportunists like Trevelyan be excepted, who could have taken senior posts), and carrying on as the party of government with some energetic progressive flourishes in the less politically sensitive areas.

It was the threat from Chamberlain that finally ensnared Hartington into commitment, where pressure from reactionary dissidents had largely failed to do more than impress upon Hartington the importance of making himself available to balance both

* Brand's attempt to invite Chamberlain on to the Liberal Unionist Committee in Apr. 1886 was a blunder which showed a tyro's misunderstanding of the different definitions of alternatives to Gladstone, which Goschen and Chamberlain were offering (Milner to Goschen, 28 Apr. 1886, Milner MSS box 182). Similarly, Chamberlain was absent from the great rally at Her Majesty's Theatre, and even his election address in June 1886 stressed his support for modified home rule.

wings of the party in the way Gladstone had formerly done, and was now omitting to do. There was a point about numbers, too, as Churchill said: 'No doubt Chamberlain's defection has increased Hartington's numerical following, and it has also rather fluttered him, for fear he should be cut out by Chamberlain taking the lead...'[95] Hartington had little choice but to give up trying to provide an alternative leadership of the centre on a basis of freedom from policy commitments, and to turn instead to the business of securing his hold of the traditional right of the party. With Goschen providing effective opposition to Ireland on Unionist lines, and Chamberlain threatening to lead an even more powerful anti-Gladstonian cave on modified home rule lines, Hartington was in danger of finding himself without support for his line of muted opposition on undefined grounds.

The accession of Hartington and Chamberlain to their ranks in mid-March left the activists free to turn away from politics, which puzzled them, towards political organisation, which was for most of them an entirely new game. The beginnings of a coherent Liberal Unionist organisation began to be visible about this time, though it is not now possible, and probably never will be, to say specifically what the Unionist activists were doing when they wrote of how hard they were working. Only the more incidental activities tended to leave a record. Albert Grey, for example, tried to get a stage army of Tennyson, Lecky, Bright, Tyndall, Huxley, and Argyll, to write anti-home rule pieces, chiefly aimed at the American press.[96] Churchill was rather taken with his own notion of getting the City Corporation, the City Guilds, 'and even the Universities' to petition the Queen against home rule.[97] Beyond this area of inconsequentiality, there was probably increasingly structured activity, left to Grey and his friends, relating to the management of the press, bargaining over seats and M.Ps' souls, and building up funds. As search for the early office papers of Liberal Unionsim suggests quite strongly that none have survived, except in Scotland, and the papers of the individuals involved do not throw light on matters of office organisation, only tentative points can be made. Firstly, the Liberal Unionists (especially before their merger with Chamberlain in August) were run by talented amateurs who were novices at party organisation. Secondly, absence of complaints by itself suggests they were fairly well supplied with funds,whose source, however, remains unknown. Thirdly, the leaders of the backbench secession felt mentally free to concentrate on the single objective of creating a well-run organisation, as something desirable for its own sake, because they felt confident by March that Chamberlain and Hartington had the situation in hand. 'If

Chamberlain leaves as well as Trevelyan, we shall beat Gladstone in the Commons.'[98] 'I think we shall defeat Gladstone in the Commons.'[99] Backbench rebellion could therefore happily accept that politics was a matter for frontbenchers, and get on with work in hand, such as printing notepaper headed 'Liberal Committee for the Maintenance of the Legislative Union between Great Britain and Ireland. Telegrams Consistent, London. 35 Spring Gardens, London S.W.' The young Whigs were running their own outfit at last: that it was a toy, that it was contingent upon decisions taken by leaders who did not enter into candid discussions with them, did not obscure the joys of energetic employment.* They tried to run by-elections, and got snubbed by the Tories for their pains. In the Bradford by-election (21 April), they had the Liberal Unionist, Evelyn Ashley, 'at full cock ready to go off as soon as a Bradford finger pulls the trigger',[100] but Hartington intervened, very significantly, to frustrate their plans. He wrote decreeing that 'nothing would be further from my mind than any attempt to dictate either to the constituency or to any portion of it or to suggest a candidate for their acceptance'.† In the end there was a straight fight between a Tory and a Gladstonian. They tried to oppose Kay-Shuttleworth's re-election in N. Lancashire (19 April) by putting up an Irish Whig, but had in the end to let the Gladstonian be returned unopposed (a sign, incidentally, of the general confidence in Liberal electoral prospects). Similarly, when the Tories won Ipswich by a hair (14 April), Grey's reaction was significant: 'Ipswich is a triumph – we did not expect to win.'[101] Unionist intrigue was confident, because it saw a flowing tide in the House of Commons, not because of electoral straws in the wind. They began to be electorally active, because they felt there was now little need to be so, high politics being about to settle such things in their favour anyway. The aristocratic dissidents had ceased to try to manage high politics, but they had revived a little Whig party which, in the late spring of 1886, was a pleasantly exclusive club.‡

* Cf. 'I am busy trying to catch Spurgeon and the *Wesleyan*' (Grey to Earl Grey, 6 May): 'I am busy as the day is long on the business of the Liberal Unionist Committee' (ibid., 10 May): 'I have been very busy all day about the Bradford election and about the meeting in the Opera House tomorrow' (ibid., 13 Apr.): cf. the remark of the indefatigable Milner, 'I have worked harder this week than I have done for years' (Milner to Goschen, 26 Apr., Milner MSS box 182).

† Hartington to Goschen 9 Apr. enclosed in Goschen to Milner, same date, Milner MSS box 182. Goschen himself wished 'a Liberal Unionist could be returned' (loc. cit.). Ashley had inherited Palmerston's estates in Sligo.

‡ Chamberlain, Grey wrote, was 'anxious that his followers should join Hartington's Committee in a body, but I am thankful to say his followers objected, the result being that our organisation will be distinctly Hartingtonian' (to Earl Grey, 21 May).

A more serious and professional approach to the problems of party organisation was provided by Milner whose vigour slowly rubbed off on the committee's secretary and only full-time employee, F. Maude. It was Milner who demanded that the office should be properly equipped with reference books and maps, though no one else seemed to care, and pestered Goschen until they arrived.* It was Milner who put the young aristocrats to work in a systematic way on drawing up lists of anti-home rule M.Ps and of prominent Liberal Unionists in the constituencies, creating order out of chaos. By 26 April he had established a simple code of procedure: 'We enter every name of an adherent as it comes in, in a little note-book, and then copy it into a big ledger'.[102] With a little further pressure it was possible to arrange for circulars and leaflets to be sent out in rich profusion, but that was about as far as Milner could go. There remained the problem of finding a continuing supply of money to cover the office running expenses. 'Where', Milner asked Goschen, 'are the Dukes with their long purses? It is monstrous that you should have had to subscribe more than half the whole sum given, £80 to save an Empire! !'[103] However, it was necessary to call on Albert Grey to deal with that particular difficulty.

In May 1886, however, the group of activists at Spring Gardens became more definitely concentrated on organising a general election. 'We are at work with the Conservative Whips in organising election contests in view of an early dissolution' wrote Grey as early as 11 May. On 21 May he reported that 'the task of getting together a Purse has been put upon me. I have begun with a contribution of £2,000 from one individual. I want to get £50,000 in the next ten days.' We do not hear whether he succeeded, but Grey certainly did have a happy touch as a fund-raiser throughout his life. At any rate, on 9 June 1886 the *Birmingham Daily Post*, with its special sources of information, was reporting that the Liberal Unionists had £30,000 ready. While he was raising his own funds, he was also crying stinking fish over his discovery that the whip of the party in office received from public funds £10,000 of secret service money, for electoral purposes. 'I think the indignation which has been called forth by the revelation of this fact, will force the government to discontinue the practice.' The practice was promptly discontinued.[104]

What was going on, as Grey and others played at being Schnad-

---

* 'Altogether we need apparatus, and as we have the money we ought to get it at once. Do please ask for these things' (Milner to Goschen, 28 Apr. 1886, Milner MSS box 182).

horst, with some lack of discernment,* was that Hartington was letting his less important followers congeal into an organised party, partly because they enjoyed doing so and he had no means of stopping them (his guiding hand in the operation of the infant organisation is nowhere apparent), but also partly because it kept them quiet. It left him free to resolve all the vital issues on his own. The fuller irony of the division of labour by which Hartington thought about strategies, while the secessionists managed a wide range of partisan activities, was that what Hartington was still mainly engaged in considering was whether there should be a secession (of a Whig or Unionist minority) at all. Hartington was still free to return, at the first opportunity, to running a broadly based Liberal coalition based on 'examination and inquiry' into Irish problems.

Indeed, Hartington's speeches on the second reading did not establish beyond doubt his opposition to some kind of home rule arrangement with the Parnellites. His speeches left a skilful impression of toughness, and many took it for granted that by May 1886 there was nothing equivocal about his position. In fact there was just enough in the small print of his speeches, had anyone looked, to leave him free to continue exploring the possibilities of circumstances. In his speech of 10 May, Hartington threw in a condemnation of the Dublin Castle system, and hinted at an interest in devolution step by step, while refusing Gladstone's challenge to declare his policy for Ireland by referring to the latter's practice of not declaring his hand in advance. His speech was not au fond reactionary. In his other major parliamentary speech, on 28 May, Hartington again avoided questions of substance and concentrated on the easy target of lack of clarity in government policy. Both Hartington and the Parnellites were studious, prior to the 1886 election, not to create the kind of animosity which would have made future negotiations impossible.

A few basic points about Goschen's Whig cave as it emerged as one of the facts of politics in January, 1886 should be noted. Firstly, Hartington gave it neither countenance nor encouragement. Secondly Hartington may have been deliberately, effectively, and intelligently working against it. Thirdly, Goschen's cave had very poor information as to the real intentions of leading men, and were prone to fall victims to every rumour and canard. Fourthly, Grey's instinctive euphoria apart, they felt themselves, quite rightly, to be in a hopelessly weak position. They did not on the

* 'We shall turn out Childers and Campbell-Bannerman in Scotland' (Grey to Earl Grey, 21 May). In fact Childers' majority was 1,500 and Campbell-Bannerman was returned unopposed.

whole expect to win over Hartington. * Finally, they did not receive help or encouragement from the Tories, but the reverse, Goschen's attempt to make a reactionary stand on the issue of 'expropriating' land to make allotments being deliberately repudiated by Balfour. The latter acted partly under strong pressure from Tory county members, longing to take a progressive line with their constituents, but probably also it was a calculated snub to any hopes of coalition entertained by the right-wing Liberals. The 'moderates' (i.e. reactionary Liberals) either walked out or voted for Collings' motion, not only because the Tories were too reactionary over coercion, but because they were not reactionary enough in their social policy. Nevertheless, they never doubted their obligation to oppose Gladstone: and whatever issue had been prominent in 1886, they would have done much the same.

Grey was certainly hard at work as parliament opened, immersed 'in interviews with Irish loyalists, and the duties of an amateur whip!'[105] He hoped for coalition, with Salisbury as Hartington's foreign secretary: he and Goschen hoped to tie parliament by resolutions in favour of the Union, coercion, and compulsory land purchase. This was pie in the sky unless Hartington was interested, and unless there was a good chance of a majority on dissolution. Neither condition applied. Hartington remained unsnared, the new parliament emerged increasingly as Gladstonian, and the evidence of by-elections gave the Tories (and the Irish, too, perhaps) every reason to avoid a dissolution. Grey noted 'a curious timidity' when he tried to get Liberals to make short speeches committing themselves against home rule, though Arthur Elliot made 'a good and plucky speech last night and if the debate had not collapsed I had got Ebrington and 2 or 3 other Liberals to back him up. Goschen undertook to move the adjournment last night ... but he was frightened by the success of Elliot's speech, and ran away!'[106] Goschen was reprimanded, more or less, by Grey for not risking a confrontation, one of the small indications that Goschen could only lead the young Whigs in the direction they wanted.

Grey's patrician sense of responsibility for his elders was shown in other small touches. On 25 January he was working on a detailed plan to get the best seats in the House, in order to cheer Goschen ('we suffer much from having no organisation') but

* Grey wrote to Earl Grey, 29 Jan., that he would 'not be very much surprised if he (Hartington) agrees to serve under Gladstone'. Hartington at no time before Mar. 1886 lent his countenance to Grey's backbench rebellion. Hartington's refusal to lead against Collings' notion was blamed by Grey for the small size of the Liberal vote against the motion (ibid., 30 Jan.).

found that the Parnellites reserved their places earlier in the morning than he did, a dirty trick which much shocked him. Brooding on the Parnellite success in manipulative politics, he drew the obvious conclusion: 'why should we not have an anti-Repeal League headed by Liberals, a good fund started, and lecturers sent all over the country?'[107] And thus, in opposition to Hartington and from dissatisfaction with Goschen, Liberal Unionism was born.

In the very short term Grey's attempts to set a Unionist tone in the Commons backfired. They forced Hartington to dissociate himself in a most overt way from their militancy: they annoyed Liberal frontbenchers, who found they could at least agree on the impertinence of backbench initiatives: and they encouraged a divided Tory cabinet to take a plunge towards coercion, which from the naive Unionist point of view disastrously divided the Tories from the moderate Unionists. (They had no suspicions that Salisbury and Hartington might intend just that.)

February saw Grey having to oppose the militancy to which he was congenitally prone. The reason was simply that 'the re-elected ministers have got abominably larger majorities',[108] this being most obvious in the case of John Morley's greatly increased majority at Newcastle (12 February). For the time being it was the duty of a tactically intelligent opposition not to oppose:

'The Ulster Party talk of moving an amendment on the Queen's Speech to the effect that the legislative Union ought to be maintained. I hope they may be prevented. To put Gladstone in a minority before he had disclosed his plans would be a fatal mistake. Everybody would say, if only the GOM had only had a chance given him he would have settled it all. He *must* show his Plan...'[109]

This throws light on why there was so little parliamentary pressure on Gladstone in February and March. Before he had taken office, he was able to unite the party, and to dodge the question of a vote on Irish autonomy, by his doctrine that the opposition should keep its own counsel. After he had taken office, his opponents had to assume that a defeat of Gladstone in parliament, might lead to their drastic defeat at an election. With a sufficient majority, the Liberals might be freed of the Irish, but whatever doubtful element of patriotic gain was contained in that, was not worth fighting for. Hartington and Salisbury wished to maintain the existing party structure, to remove Gladstone from it, and to prevent home rule, probably in that order, and to achieve these objects they had to stage a fairly viable home rule ministry, instead of threatening to remove it, as was at all times more or less possible, with an anti-home rule resolution.

Left to himself, Hartington might well have lain low till the Irish bills were put before parliament in early April. In fact, however, he moved from being a benign friend of Liberalism, to being the director of a Liberal faction, as early as the beginning of March. Partly, no doubt, he was a little perturbed by the sight of Gladstone doing so well: he needed to do something, however nebulous, to secure his own following. Much more clearly, he could not ignore speeches made by Churchill and Salisbury on 3 March. (Churchill's escapade at Belfast on 22 February could simply be ignored as juvenile delinquency).

On 3 March, however, Churchill spoke at Manchester, calling for a Unionist coalition. As with his Belfast escapade, this must be seen as a threat to Salisbury's authority within the party: Churchill was putting himself forward both as the gallant partisan of extreme Toryism, and as the man who would self-effacingly welcome new faces from moderate Liberalism into the Unionist leadership. It was Churchill also who got up Holmes' motion on 4 March, an essay in instant opposition designed ostensibly to draw Gladstone, but in fact designed to advertise Churchill as the real leader of Tory resistance to separatism. (Salisbury barely commented on the expediency of putting forward Holmes' motion).

Salisbury was well able to deal with these little forays. Speaking at the Crystal Palace on the evening of 3 March, he made an aggressive party speech designed to put paid to Churchill's machinations. There was no crude repudiation of the proposal for coalition. There was, instead, a vehement attack on land purchase as financially and socially disastrous. Salisbury may have believed this, but the political function of his reference to the topic was to eliminate the main area of potential common ground between Tories and moderate Liberals without appearing to do so. Goschen and Chamberlain, certainly, wanted to govern Ireland by land bills, as probably in his more inscrutable way did Hartington. Salisbury's message was that he would make it as difficult as possible for Liberal dissidents to act with the Conservatives, Churchill or no Churchill. Salisbury's speech emphasised, in the crudest way, the supreme importance to Ireland of 'country gentlemen'. As with Salisbury's famous 'Hottentots' speech in mid-May, this was a case of hitting exactly the note that Liberal Unionists would find it hardest to accept and, more important, to get their constituents to accept.

Salisbury knew what he was doing. He had an ex-cabinet which he could twist round his little finger, Churchill being the only exception. Only Churchill could challenge his position in the party. Churchill would never be his ally or augment his authority, however useful he had been against Northcote or at the elections. The isolation of Churchill within the party and the cabinet was therefore a matter of importance. If new, ex-Liberal faces were brought into a coalition of Unionists, Churchill could only gain. He could take up Liberal principles in a way that Salisbury could not, and manoeuvre against Salisbury from a central position. Alternatively, he could lead a revolt of true Tories against the coalition, in the manner of the 1922 revolt against Lloyd George. Which alternative Churchill had in mind, no one knew, least of all Churchill: but the danger could not be neglected. Calmly leaving time and the House of Lords to destroy home rule, if all else failed, and regarding it as somewhat of an unreal threat, Salisbury concentrated with great exactness on destroying the much more real threats of Churchill and Hartington.

It was in this context of Tory private ambitions that Hartington decided he must do something to keep his following together. At the end of February, he formed a shadow cabinet of Goschen, James, Brand, Wodehouse, A.Elliot, and A.Grey to meet at Devonshire House every Saturday, 'to talk over the business of the coming week, and decide what ought to be done'. This was not necessarily a step towards militant action, but might well have been conceived as a sop to followers whose lives were easily brightened by such empty gestures. There was, after all, not much business to settle, and Hartington would not have let others influence him on matters of weight. James, speaking to his constituents at Bury, made a limp speech on 1 March giving 'no clear intimation that he will take off his coat and go to work to avert the policy he dreads'. 'He [James] evidently contemplates surrender. He has made his protest and will now let the matter slide. If Hartington also throws up the sponge on Friday we are dished'.[110]

As late as 3 March 1886, then, it was possible for a well-informed organiser of revolt to think that Hartington might resign himself to the passage of home rule through the lower house, and that Gladstone's majority might be substantially unimpaired. Backbench opposition, in the eyes of its leading exponents, was ineffectual apart from Hartington: '... the chief difficulty in getting M.Ps to act strongly lies in their uncertainty as to Hartington's attitude... If Hartington declares himself openly as opposed to Repeal on Friday next, we ought to lead 100 Liberal M.Ps before the following Tuesday'.[111]

Hartington's action in gathering around him the Whig clique

which had been a main barrier to his claim to national leadership cannot be explained confidently. Putting aside hindsight, his motive may just as well have been gently to disabuse them of anti-home rule ideas, as to gird up his strength for the coming fight. James' speech at Bury on 1 March, given by a man who wished above all to be his master's voice, did not give any sense that Hartington was in a fighting mood. (It might have been a blind: but a blind of that sort would have been a self-inflicted wound).

Hartington was in fact in a fighting mood, but not about stopping home rule in the way the Whig clique hoped. Home rule would stop itself. In the meantime, he would fight his way to power by not fighting. He would leave fighting to Salisbury and Gladstone. The country did not want gladiators, and policies with sharp edges. It wanted normality, good will, and good sense. This was the leadership he would supply. It would bring him to power with a free hand, and then when in power it would be time enough to devise policies, or let James devise them for him. In this context, he might as well permit Goschen's faction to affiliate itself to him, since it wished to do so, and since its doing so would leave him unsnared. His immediate task was to establish that he was courteous, sincere, unemphatic, not given to blackguarding opponents, a little tired of Churchill's eccentricities (thus quietly putting off court Churchill's claims to be a bridge between middle opinion and the Tories), and entirely free from any commitment that could tie his hands in future or produce detailed criticism in the present. How could anyone differ from an open mind? how could Hartington not be seen as the coming prime minister?

At any rate, Hartington was not partisan enough for his clientele to have any idea beforehand what line he would take at this speech at the Eighty Club (a self-important group of slightly intellectual, ambitious, younger Liberal backbenchers) on 5 March. Nor were they much the wiser after his speech. The proposer of the vote of thanks uttered home rule sentiments which were coldly received, while the seconder taking the opposite line was well cheered. The speech was non-committal, reticent, nebulous, but conveyed a combination of firmness and vigilance tempered with fair-mindedness and freedom from petty considerations. It was, in short, very clever: it convinced his immediate clientele that he meant resistance,* but read on paper in a way that left him entirely free for the future. Above all, he did not reveal his real mind to his parliamentary following, and they were too much in awe of him to question him directly. This enabled him to meet his prime re-

* Arthur Elliot, for instance, thought it an 'important and admirable' speech (diary, 5 Mar.).

quirements, of sounding quite unlike a Tory leader, and of not needing to take any decisions.

In private, he may have been a little firmer. It came to light that the Ulster Liberals had been discouraged by Hartington's speech 'which they interpreted as a speech of surrender'. Hartington then gave an intermediary, Monteagle, an assurance to pass on, that the Ulster Liberals might depend on him to oppose as stoutly as he could if he could obtain support. Grey was involved in this manipulation of the Ulster Liberals.[112] In a case like this, however, private avowals matter less than public association, and Hartington fought shy of public association with Ulster, as he had done before when the opportunity arose in January. Precisely because he was who he was, he could not possibly let it appear that his Irish policy was shaped by an undue concern for the Liberal, protestant, or ascendancy elements in Irish life – that is, if he wished to carry weight with the Liberals in the Commons.

Other things indicated caution. His seat, Rossendale, was an industrial one. His constituency association asked him to explain his vote for the Tories on Collings' motion, as well as his attendance at Her Majesty's Theatre. His constituents did not censure him, but neither did they express approval of his explanation. Their comments did however suggest a wish for an effective party which had clear implications. In order to keep his seat, Hartington had to take pains to establish his Liberalism: Rossendale could not be won on a straight right-wing vote, and indeed in 1892 became a safe Gladstonian seat on Hartington's elevation to the peerage.

The attempts to replace Gladstone's hold over the electorate with a different kind of non-Tory majority party ended in failure. In some cases, failure was to be expected, as when politically inexpert backbenchers tried to make things happen by being furiously active. They acted in the tradition of the Anti-Corn Law League and of the Bulgarian atrocities campaign, and they did so because they were governed by having read that that was how things happened. In this belief, or error, they were for all their disavowals exactly in the tradition of those they opposed.

The position of the leaders was rather different. Goschen, Chamberlain, and Hartington cannot simply be said to have misread the situation. Goschen worked extremely hard, indoctrinated an entourage with success, and seized on the key position of a Queen with no one to talk to, because these were the cards a politician playing from weakness had to play. On the other hand, Hartington, playing from strength, was studiously careful not to do anything which might impede his role as leader of four-fifths of the Liberal party, or (always much less likely) as a dominant figure in a reactionary coalition. Hartington's successes in 1886 lay in what he did not do. On a different level of appreciation, his dignified absence of reaction in May 1886, when the high hopes held by him and his entourage of his forming a government were suddenly dashed by the extreme lengths to which Salisbury and Gladstone were willing to go to prevent this, showed truly ducal ability to play high and lose well.* The failure of Hartington's plans made him appear a truly honourable figure, willing to lay down his career for the sake of an Irish minority for which he had in fact never thought of fighting, when all he had wanted to do was be prime minister.

If we are to look for personal misjudgement, we must turn to Chamberlain, who also wanted not less than everything and ended up with Birmingham. It is difficult to place his error exactly in time. His Irish line (moderate concessions with a dash of resistance) was as attuned to party feeling and to Irish practicalities, as was Hartington's line of moderate resistance with a dash of concession (and Hartington was careful to do nothing which in the last resort might make the Irish prefer to put the Tories back in office). Chamberlain's wish to replace Gladstone's appeal to the electorate with a similar appeal, based on a little more class conflict and a seasoning of Palmerston, was sound in the sense that it wished to continue the traditional basis of the system of Liberal predominance.

In a more complicated way, one can argue that it was a case of too many cooks spoiling the broth, and that it was not a question of their individual strategies, but of the mutual effect they had on each other. If Goschen was right in thinking that he ought to break up the Liberal party, the only possible time was in January 1886: and in the event he never made the attempt because of the need to capture Hartington. Similarly, Hartington, who wished to remain free from identification with any particular section of the party, became much too identified with the Goschen group to remain a person into whose hands the destinies of the party as a whole could pass. Hartington was also affected by pressure from Chamberlain, whose resignation took away from Hartington the option of remaining benignly in the shadows and forced him to come out and challenge Gladstone directly, thus polarising politics between Gladstone and Salisbury both of whom were determined to leave no central position for him to occupy.

* Cf. E. Hamilton's journal, 9 May 1886, 'One never hears him (Hartington) say an unkind or embittered word'.

5

The Whig Ministers

The real work of governing was, and was expected to be, largely in the hands of highly experienced Whig ministers who were nevertheless often not much more than names to the public. This was, of course, partly because they took their jobs very seriously and were too busy to indulge in public engagements, which appeared trivial compared with their daily work. The outcome has been neglect on the grounds that their lives lacked colour and meaning, and that their day was over. Apart from the fact that their public function was indispensable (as Salisbury's twenty years of weak ministers was to show), they in fact concealed interesting personalities beneath devotion to duty. It must be realised, above all, that they cannot easily be understood.

There were those who were successful, interesting, and made almost an art of remaining in the shadows. Granville clung to an advisory role as most politicians clung to power. Spencer's interest lay in solving difficult administrative problems without interference from colleagues. Kimberley, who appeared to be a bluff and rustic understudy foreign minister, was a scholarly, self-reliant, self-controlled administrator, an 'Imperial handyman', who could be set to work on any overseas problem in the knowledge that he would not commit blunders, and that he could be relied on to leave party politics to the party leaders. Ripon was also unassertive in party matters in a way that signified strength of character. A specialist in defence policy, he was sensitive to general budgetary requirements in a way that service ministers often were not. Though fully informed about general questions, he was content to meditate these in a mind fully able to draw on the higher traditions of the religious and secular thought of his age. He also shot, incontinently, holding a record for birds killed in one day. What is striking about these men is the absence in them of any unruliness of the will, or of concern about political advancement.

The contrast with Dilke and Harcourt could hardly have been more great. They were not exactly ballast to steady the ship. They ordered their lives around personal ambition. Disraeli's view of Harcourt left little unsaid. Asked if Harcourt would rise, Disraeli replied 'Certainly. He is a man of old family, of fine presence, eloquent and learned and absolutely without principle.'[113] Harcourt had been many things in his time. He had fought a by-election as a Conservative, emerged in 1868–74 as a brilliant radical, and had then become mainly a Hartington man who looked on Gladstone's return to power in 1880 with anything but pleasure. As home secretary in 1880–85, he took a stern unbending line on all departmental questions, including law and order in Ireland and Scotland. He was the hard man of the party. In 1882, he black-mailed the cabinet into accepting an extreme coercion bill by threatening to resign, join the Tories, and make a speech revealing Parnell's love life as uncovered by Home Office detectives. In 1883 or thereabouts he abruptly became a man of principle and a devoted follower of Gladstone. He sought single-mindedly to be Gladstone's right-hand man, and, there being no competiton, succeeded. Not a man to miss an opportunity, he saw the need for a dishonest broker between the Whigs and the Radicals, acting in liaison with the premier. The position he coveted was the Wool-sack, some said because he needed to pay for his new house at Malwood. Harcourt's isolation made sense on other grounds, since his very obvious unreliability would have made him an object of suspicion in any role other than that of go-between. Moreover, his Little England outlook was not only odd and extreme, but oddly and fanatically expressed without any regard for its effects upon his colleagues. A born misfit, his behaviour would at times not have been tolerated anywhere except in a Liberal cabinet.

Dilke does not really concern us here. During 1885 he was absorbed in the grind of the seats bill, which was ending just as the Crawford scandal began. Except for a few cabinet rows, Dilke was therefore *hors de combat* in 1885 from start to finish, and his few speeches struck no distinctive note. It therefore is impossible to tell how far, in other circumstances, he might have been something more than Chamberlain's echo. Dilke resembled his Whig colleagues more than he resembled Chamberlain in that he believed in the necessity of almost obsessively hard administrative work (the attractions of which for Chamberlain have not been established) and felt the importance of 'abroad' as providing the main part of ministerial tasks. Chamberlain's *Radical Programme*, after some shuffling, had simply ignored overseas issues.

But every cabinet contains personal tragedy – men who, already seeing death at the end of the tunnel, can contemplate neither past nor future with satisfaction. In 1885, this class was represented by Carlingford, Childers, and Northbrook. Even their political future was dim, for Northbrook and Carlingford, close friends since college days, were aged 60 and 62 respectively and expected no more than to see the government out. Both had fallen foul of Gladstone in striking ways in 1884, and his unconcealed contempt weighed heavily on them. Childers' offence was partly his unexpected independence of mind in 1885 itself, partly a long record of departmental misfortunes and a congenital inability to play to the gallery. He had no allies in politics, where he was generally seen as Gladstone's Jack-of-all-trades, a fact which led to mutual ill feeling between him and the premier. All three ministers were scarred by family bereavements: Carlingford and Northbrook were widowers living in gloom. Carlingford was to be seen weeping on his wife's tombstone in the village churchyard. All three ministers wanted a spirited imperial policy to brighten their lives, and spent much of 1885 learning that such thoughts were idle dreams. To present them thus is to invite the disrespect which they indeed suffered at the time, but they were nevertheless very clever men. Carlingford was perhaps the most widely read politician of his day, so far as serious modern literature was concerned. Childers' mastery of financial minutiae was only matched by Northbrook's command of Indian and eastern affairs. All ought to have provided rich seams of wisdom for any cabinet which had the sense to make use of their strengths as adeptly as it seized upon their weaknesses. But the strong were not strong enough to do without them as failures.

Three more unusual ministers, only loosely to be classified as Whigs, need to be looked at particularly closely in order to see how little there was of the generic in their conduct. All, by the standards of the world, were remote, shy, bookish men who were not easy to know, and whose position was the only thing about them intelligible to the public. Selborne (aged 73 in 1885), Derby (aged 59), and Rosebery, then 38, showed how it was possible to be a major public figure without revealing anything of one's political nature even to the wider parliamentary world, which invariably misunderstood what really mattered to them. Their elusive qualities are therefore worth discussing at length.

The lord chancellor, Selborne, was a notable addition to the folk-lore about lord chancellors. Though in a prosaic light he could be seen as simply a very successful, diligent and clever career lawyer who had made his way up from humble beginnings to the top of his profession, that certainly was not how he appeared to contemporaries. No one would have thought of suggesting that his refusal of office on ecclesiastical grounds in 1868 could have been connected with a need to continue at the bar to finance difficulties incurred in developing his estate: or that his views on Ireland had ever been affected by his professional connection with the Londonderry Company. Rather, he was in every way impressive in the way a lord chancellor should be: aged, austere, learned, pious, landed, wealthy, a Sunday School teacher, somewhat obscurantist (for instance, he could date an ordinary letter 'King St. Charles's Day), and in short altogether a man of principle and distinction.

This convenient apparition did not lie wholly in the eye of the beholder. Selborne, as a narrow and devout high churchman, with a rare gift for disapproval, could easily have let himself become simply a man with a grudge against the modern spirit and the tendencies of the younger men around him.

This lack of sympathy for the modern world certainly existed but it did not stop Selborne acting effectively by the standards of that world. In 1884–85, for instance, he was engaged in a far reaching programme of legal reforms, involving the reconstruction of the lord chancellor's department, and the passage of a judicature bill: he arranged a new circuit system: he settled the scale of fees payable in the higher courts. When he left office he was engaged in consolidating the courts of Chancery. Thus departmentally speaking, Selborne was undoubtedly, even at the end of a five year ministry, playing the part of an energetic reformer, more so perhaps than any other minister. However, neither he nor anyone else dreamt of seeing him in that light. For one thing, his high churchmanship was far more simple and naive than Gladstone's in its relation to politics. Selborne, like Gladstone, put the church before the Liberal party but, unlike Gladstone, he did so honestly and overtly. The consequence of this was that, though he rarely had occasion to act while a minister in defence of Anglican supremacy, everyone was aware that he would so act if necessary, and this marked him out as a man apart from the other ministers. Gladstone, consequently, could not afford to be identified with Selborne.

This explains a number of things. It explains why there was no close working relationship with Gladstone before autumn 1885, despite the ties of age, churchmanship, and past victories. Also

Selborne only once, and then in a minor way, exerted himself on Gladstone's behalf, this being in an attempt to find a compromise with Spencer in June 1885. The reason for this was not really political. It was not due to Selborne's political inflexibility so much as to his human isolation. For instance, he was one of the few members of Gladstone's cabinet who made no attempt to resign during 1885, even when he might have been expected to do so. He confined himself to reasoned argument: he gave way to no emotional outbursts. He was never noticed as saying anything striking. As with Childers, no general political reason prevented him from striking up understandings with most of the less extreme members of the cabinet. That he did not do so, must be ascribed chiefly to a strong preference for solitariness.

Selborne did believe in a certain kind of paternalistic rural society. He believed that farm labourers were a hundred times happier than town artisans. Where Granville awarded Chamberlain the title of the Prince of Opportunists, Selborne was naively horrified at what he regarded as his very real Jacobinism. His reactionary attitudes, because they were indeed what Chamberlain would have liked Whig attitudes to be, separated him from his leading Whig colleagues. Because he had clear beliefs, he was morbidly apprehensive. Disraeli's ritual bill of 1874 made him wonder 'if blood were one day to be shed in a religious war in this country'.[114] Not having been born a landlord himself, he felt more strongly than any other minister, except perhaps Hartington, the need to defend landlords' rights. He showed an unusual degree of concern about the proposed increase in estate duties in the 1885 budget. In the case of Ireland, too, he was much more concerned about maintaining the Irish landlords than about maintaining the union. It is also likely that this trait in his thinking led him to take a strong interest in the proper, non-commercial colonization of backward areas, with a view to securing for the natives of New Guinea and Africa those benefits which English landlords provided for the labourers on their own estates.

His attitude to imperial policy therefore began from the same Christian premises as that of Gladstone but went on to reach far more expansionist conclusions. He was the only minister to give sustained attention to native welfare as a criterion of policy. His main reason for wanting to occupy the Sudan was to suppress the slave trade. In general he deeply regretted the necessity of British expansion even when he was urging it. Yet considerations of honour and prestige were as much on his lips as ones of moral duty: indeed he synthesised religion and *amour propre* into his own personal brand of imperialism.

It is difficult to grant him the status of a full reactionary where Ireland is concerned. In May 1885 he treated Dongola as far more important than the Irish schemes then before the cabinet. There is no sign that at any time he seriously thought about Ireland as a country in disarray. He was on the other hand more than zealous in using Ireland as an occasion for hunting down 'revolutionary tendencies' within his party of which he thoroughly disapproved. After the Hawarden Kite, Selborne did indeed take a very hard line (as who did not?), but better indications of the limits of his thought are given by his trimming during the few days when Gladstone held out hopes of office to him, and by the curious fact that his son Lord Wolmer, the future unionist minister, went remarkably far in accepting home rule at this time.[115]

Selborne momentarily nourished cautious hopes of returning to office. Once these were dashed, his inflexibility became unbounded, although he found only limited pleasure in consorting with Hartington and Salisbury, and no pleasure at all in being aligned with Lord Randolph. His disappointment found vent chiefly in two enormously long letters to *The Times* (23 April and 3 May), chiefly on the unfair treatment of Irish landlords, but also lashing out biliously in all directions. Selborne's distaste for his colleagues on both sides of politics, with the partial exception of Northbrook, makes it hard to tell whether inactivity and isolation on his part stem from political judgement or from old age and poor health. For instance, he made no speeches of any consequence in the Lords during the 1886 parliament, and his two outdoor speeches in the summer of 1886 were very minor efforts: presumably he could have done much more had he wished. After 1886, he became a regular campaigner.[116] However, despite a breakdown in health in December 1884, there is no sign that he was feeling his years in 1885–86, a holiday of about four months in Italy in summer 1885 no doubt contributing to this. More important, probably, was the death of his wife in April 1885, but even here the most noticed feature of his bereavement was the strong Christian faith which enabled him to return almost at once to active cabinet work.

The main reason Selborne did not join the home rule ministry, was not home rule, but because Gladstone did not want him to. 'Selborne nibbled at the offer, but I felt it would not work and did not use great efforts to bring him in' Gladstone later wrote.[117] Gladstone's first letter to Selborne on the subject (27 January 1886) was a clear bid to get Selborne to forswear office, on church, Irish, and other grounds.[118] At the same time, Gladstone was assuring James that Selborne was no longer in the running for the Woolsack.[119] Selborne did not give the desired reply. He did not admit the church problem to be insuperable 'or even difficult': his absence from the shadow cabinet dinner had no political intent, but was due to his bereavement: and, as to Ireland, 'I did not, I do not (to use your words) "intend to shut myself out from considering whether there are practicable conditions which would warrant and recommend the creation by statute of an Irish legislative body for Irish affairs." '[120] This was cautious, but on 28 January it went as far as anyone at that time did towards home rule. It meant that Selborne wished to exercise his enormous capacity for disapproval from within, not without, the new cabinet: indeed, to play a role in it not far different from that subsequently taken by Herschell. Selborne had, however, two great stumbling-blocks: he wanted exclusion of Irish members (believing Gladstone to be for retention 'from what I hear') and security for landlords (probably knowing little of Gladstone's embryonic land plans).

Gladstone's need to bid farewell to Selborne days before sitting down to forming his ministry generally, arose from the delicate position of James, a smooth and pleasant career lawyer who managed the House well, obeyed orders, and had no particular political commitments beyond friendship with the great. (He taught himself racing in order to communicate with Hartington). Gladstone wanted James as the major figure in his Commons team. But James' marginal seat was in danger, if he took a Commons post, and it might be necessary to dangle a vacant Woolsack before him from the very start of negotiations. Selborne, that barnacle-encrusted figure from the past, was redundant, not because Gladstone was looking in a Radical direction, but because Gladstone wished to move the Liberal party back towards respectability and centrality, and James advertised that wish, without provoking Radical counter-claims.

By 30 January 1886, prospects of getting James were looking poor, though Gladstone was still avoiding Harcourt so as to leave himself room for keeping the lieutenancy for James if at all possible. Gladstone briefly became anxious to secure Selborne, especially after James' refusal at 12.30. Having summoned Selborne by telegram early in the day, Gladstone later sent him a persuasive letter by Queen's Messenger, urging him to come up to town that afternoon. Gladstone said the new cabinet would have 'an entirely free hand' on exclusion of Irish members, on which his mind was 'entirely open': and that Selborne should talk over Irish land with Spencer.[121] In short, Selborne was receiving the treatment. Whether he received Gladstone's letter before setting off for London is not clear. His interview with Gladstone in the late afternoon resulted in a polite negative, and almost immediately afterwards the Woolsack was offered to Herschell. This was a puzzling outcome. There is no direct evidence to show whether it was Selborne or Gladstone who changed course at the last moment. Did Selborne, hoping to be pressed, and reassured as to his bargaining position by Gladstone's volte-face in his letter earlier that day, overbid in the face of a Gladstone who realised that 'it would not work'?

Selborne himself thought, just afterwards, that his refusal had nothing to do with home rule *per se*, nor with Irish land, but arose because he could not get a satisfactory undertaking to exclude the Irish members, and because of the 'distinctly revolutionary' objects of Chamberlain.[122] Had Gladstone wished, he could have thrown down bridges here – pointed out the weight of feeling for exclusion among likely ministers, and intimated that Chamberlain and the Liberal party were different things. Gladstone certainly did not give Selborne the kind of chance to join his government that was offered to almost everyone else. One must conclude that though no longer, as on 28 January, urgently interested in having Selborne's place available in order to carry out a specific window-dressing exercise in terms of personnel, Gladstone when forming his cabinet still wished on quite general grounds to manoeuvre Selborne into retirement. No one has ever accused Selborne of opportunism over home rule: Gladstone never really gave him the chance.

Lord Derby was an enigma in public and in private life. A somewhat sad and lonely man of six foot two, his reputation in 1885 was firmly behind him, and he knew it. He may not have cared, if as Mrs Humphry Ward believed, he 'was perpetually brooding on social reform ... interested as to what Labour was going to make of Christianity'.[123] Loathed at Hatfield as 'Titus Oates', he had married, at 44, the step-mother of Lord Salisbury, two years after the death of Salisbury's father. Derby was a man who had hopelessly lost his avenue of retreat to the right.

It would be an illusion to think that Derby broke off his connection with the Liberal party, some time after the fall of the second Gladstone ministry, as a reactionary gesture against the spirit of the times. True, in the summer of 1885 he spoke of giving up politics, but that, after all, was not a meaningful choice for an Earl of Derby. What is true is that his connections with the Liberals remained as tenuous after June 1885, as they had been before. He remained politically intimate with Granville, and Gladstone continued to make it clear that he wanted Derby in the leadership. It was clear that any reshuffle that removed Gladstone would also remove Derby, and this not only because his office was bound to bring him highly critical public attention. Few other leading Liberals had ever wanted Derby as a colleague in the way Gladstone had, as a man versed in sound traditions, a 'representative man' at least in appearance as Hartington was, but with far more Gladstonian inclinations, a man whose standing with the right could be used by Gladstone as a counterpoise to both Hartington and Salisbury. Derby had been brought into the Liberal leadership for special purposes, and he lacked the nature and the desire to impress himself on either his Whig or his Radical colleagues, generally speaking. He preferred the company of intellectuals to that of politicians. He was quiet, deliberate, intelligent, and slow to reach decisions. He was at his best as chairman of quarter sessions in Lancashire. His detachment from ordinary human problems was Olympian, if well-meaning. This is reflected in the dearth of correspondence to or from him at ministerial level on matters of general politics. Derby, a humane, decent, and unambitious man, himself took no part in cabinet intrigue throughout 1885–86, and his frequent parliamentary speeches in January–June 1885 were limited to departmental themes.[124]

As a colonial minister, Derby was much more firmly expansionist than Gladstone, much more firm in standing out for British interests than the press gave him credit for (and his conflict with Bismarck, supposed to show Derby acting out the 'weak' stereotype of him that had grown up in the 1870s, was in fair degree caused by Derby's stubbornness and Granville's unwillingness to override him). But all these differences were differences of degree within a context of fundamental agreement on an overseas policy of *quieta non movere*. Even when Derby was an activist, as in Southern Africa, it was on the traditional prudential grounds which had proved themselves in the 1860s and 1870s: 'If Bismarck breaks out in a new place and annexes any more territory in the neighbourhood of our colonies, I think we shall have serious trouble.'[125] Derby did not want African colonies, but he did want peace with Germany. His reaction to the press campaign against his handling of affairs early in 1885, was certainly not apologetic; taking it as a radical ploy to discredit Whigs, he made it clear that he had no intention of accepting retirement for carrying out 'the result of our deliberations in common'.[126] His relative failure at the Colonial Office led him to identify more, not less, closely with the Liberal party and with Gladstone as 1885 wore on, since that was the only way apparently open to him of carrying out his objective of remaining a major politician acting on Gladstonian lines.

In fact, Derby acted exactly as a rather solitary Liberal senior minister should, right up to the formation of the home rule ministry. He took over responsibility for questions in the Lords.[127] He made known his general support for the party at the time of the election.[128] His loans helped to keep Granville afloat financially, and the two men continued an intimate epistolary discussion of Liberal prospects and Gladstone's vagaries throughout July 1885–January 1886. He went to stay at Hawarden in the early autumn:[129] he had earlier received Gladstone's last thoughts on the Irish central board scheme.[130] In return, Derby considered the post-election situation entirely within the context of his remaining an influential Liberal leader.[131] His choice was indeed not a hard one, if he really believed his own assertion that 'the Liberals were likely to govern England for a good many years to come'.[132] Whatever he thought in private, he was quite prepared to wear the public face appropriate to the party of the left. He had no objections to any of Chamberlain's 'advanced' proposals: he derided weak-kneed capitalists who took fright at the first hint of socialistic legislation.[133] His loathing for Chamberlain was a motive that made him more, not less, ideologically flexible than before. Because of Chamberlain's highly publicised desire to drive them over to the Tories, many Whigs who otherwise would have drifted to the right, moved sharply to the left (in terms of slogans) late in 1885, in order to make it clear that Chamberlain was not God's gift to the new electorate to the extent he thought. With Derby, this pattern produced a tendency to support Gladstone rather than Hartington: 'Your address has produced exactly the effect... You have intervened just in time. The party is united again but it will not remain so 24 hours after you leave it. I am afraid there is no possible release for you from the cares of leadership.'[134] If anything, the impact of the new democracy on Derby was to make him commit himself far more firmly to Gladstone than before.

It should be remembered that a rapprochement with Salisbury, who, as Derby's successor at the Foreign Office, had shown him up most woundingly, was unlikely on almost every ground. Derby, for instance, was the only Liberal Unionist to come straight out against coalition in July 1886 because of overt objections to Salisbury's innate malignity.

Derby was far from being thought a deeply committed anti-home ruler at the time of the formation of the 1886 Gladstone government. Gladstone asked Granville for news of him, as soon as he began work on forming a ministry; and Granville had called at Derby House to collect him within the first hour or two of cabinet making.[135] That Granville and Gladstone should be so emphatic in sounding Derby on 30 January (whether the purpose of that emphasis was to elicit a refusal or otherwise), when Gladstone had received Derby on 27 January, and had almost certainly been in touch with Derby around 13 January [136] on the same subject, does rather suggest that no doors had been firmly closed. Moreover, Derby, if not now then later in life, was 'pretty firmly of opinion that Home Rule would come'.[137] Indeed, he once loftily told Froude that 'kings and aristocracies can govern empires, but one people cannot govern another people'.[138] It is true that Derby could not agree, *tout court*, to home rule, but then, as befitted the future leader of the Liberal Unionists in the Lords (1886–91), he regarded the whole affair when put into context very much as a non-problem:

> 'I suppose Gladstone considers himself pledged to Home Rule (that is, an Irish Parliament): and I do not see myself assenting to it. So in all probability Downing St will not be graced by my presence. If he tries to go on, he will fail in the Lords – and I don't see how an English agitation is to be got up in favour of Irish independence.'[139]

Delving a little further back, Derby's attitudes become more equivocal. Whether by accident or design, he missed the meeting of anti-Gladstonian malcontents at Devonshire House on 1 January 1886: a trifle perhaps, as is the strong suggestion that, in so far as he took a much stiffer tone about Ireland after the 1885 elections, it was because he objected to Gladstone acting behind his colleagues' backs.[140] (It is also worth noting that he was rather less inclined than Granville, Spencer, or Harcourt to agonise about the horrors of Irish nationalism). At the end of his life, he noted that he had only spoken 'five or six times in all' on Ireland, and on these occasions he 'felt most wretchedly the irksomeness of saying over again what other people had said'.[141]

What is fairly clear is that Derby was strongly hostile to home rule in December 1885 (that is, when most future home rulers were at their furthest point from any kind of acceptance of Irish nationalism), and again after the formation of the Liberal ministry in February. His hostility in the latter period to home rule was important enough to cause what he thought of as a rather unreal and temporary* severance from his party, but not important enough to make him ever think, do, or say much about Ireland. It would

---

* He wrote to Sir U. Kay-Shuttleworth, 9 Feb. 1887; 'I would do much, if much were in my power, to make up the quarrel... That the situation may soon alter, is as earnest a wish of mine as it can be of yours' (Shuttleworth MSS). Shuttleworth had just asked Derby to pay his subscription to the local (Gladstonian) Liberal organisation.

be misleading, however, to deduce his attitudes before December 1885, and in January 1886, from what is known of his Unionist career, and of his feelings in December 1885. He may, conjecturally, have floated strangely* in January 1886. What is clear is that his position in December 1885 (and in later life) as compared with some of Derby's earlier views, represented either a palpable change of heart, or a spasm of personal irritation over Gladstone's secretive tactics.

Of Derby's considered utterances on Ireland, the most remarkable is what was also probably the most genuine:

'I think the plan of having four separate centres of local government preferable to the establishment of a central board... There is much to be said in favour of treating Ireland like Canada. I do not like the notion, but I could accept it as a necessity. By that method we should get rid of the Irish members...'[142]

Derby, in putting forward Granville's nostrum of provincial councils, here had in mind the obvious tactical purpose of both quashing and outflanking the Radicals' central board scheme: but the important point is that he started exactly from where Granville started, that he had no discernible reason for parting company with him, and yet he ended up as leader on the other side of the House. Hence one would specifically like to know what passed at his interviews with Gladstone in January, 1886.

There was after all no reason why Derby should not have been offered a post in 1886, as indeed, despite lack of evidence, he may well have been: Goschen and Northbrook were both considered or approached, and *The Times* stated confidently that Northbrook, a future scourge of the Gladstonians, had accepted. However, nothing survives on paper as regards relations between Gladstone and Derby at this time. (It must be remembered that there were sound reasons unconnected with home rule for not including Derby in any ministry of whatever complexion, after the bad press he had received in 1882–85). Derby's eventual appearance on the public stage in April 1886 as a central Liberal Unionist leader appears to have been the result, not of any action on his part, but of initiatives taken behind the scenes by young men† whose

* E.g. Derby to Harcourt, 9 Jan. 1886, Harcourt MSS box 11: 'It is impossible to have a satisfactory government for home rule or one against'.

† A. Grey to Derby, 27 Apr. 1886, asking him to lend his name to the Liberal Unionist Committee: Hartington to Derby, 19 Apr. 1886, asking Derby to chair the forthcoming Unionist demonstration, which was also essentially a case of militant backbenchers organising lazy frontbenchers. Derby certainly was remarkably inactive, not speaking in parliament between June 1885 and Aug.

approach to politics differed from that of Derby far more than Derby differed from Gladstone. There is, in fact, not even scanty evidence that Derby wished the Liberal or Liberal Unionist parties to be parties of resistance to social change, parties of truculent nationalism and imperialism, parties tied to traditional privileges (such as those of the Church on which Selborne deplored his 'weak tone').

Why then did Derby leave the party? He had prepared himself astutely for a post-election situation in which Gladstone would need friends of a Gladstonian temper to protect him from the Radical tide. Derby had indeed backed the right horse, but with the wrong bet. After the elections, the Radical tide flowed out, not in: Gladstone found himself lumbered with rather shopsoiled Gladstonian friends, and therefore was chiefly concerned to get *soi-disant* Radicals or Whigs. There was a cry about for new men: it was all the easier to assume Derby's star had set, because he had never come out against Gladstone, and therefore his acquisition for a home rule ministry would represent no triumph. One could be sure that Derby would be an ineffectual opponent, as indeed he was. Whether Derby was dropped by Gladstone in 1886, or whether Derby set too high a price for inclusion (not realising that no real bid was to be made), one is left with the conclusion that, as with Selborne, home rule *per se* had little to do with Derby's failure to take office in 1886.

Rosebery was very close to Gladstone in Irish matters in the winter of 1885–86. His closeness in turn enabled him to realise, more clearly than others, that it was being close to Gladstone that would matter in future.* Only Herbert Gladstone knew more of what was passing in the old man's mind. The relationship was not the obvious consequence of Rosebery's own political position, for he was at this time the forgotten man of frontbench intrigue. There is no evidence in either Whig or Radical correspondence that it was thought important to know Rosebery's views or to try and influence him. Indeed, in the period of frantic consultation after the 1885 elections, Rosebery met no one except Gladstone, Spencer, and Labouchere, in any politically significant context. Rosebery performed for Gladstone the function, later taken over by Morley, of putting forward clear ideas on policy while at the same time giving Gladstone unqualified support and approval.

1886. Out of doors, he confined himself to making two election speeches for the Liberals in 1885, and one against them in 1886 (Derby MSS).

* 'Rosebery declares himself certain that Gladstone will lead! Hartington thinks the opposite' (Goschen to A. Grey, n.d. but Oct.–Nov. 1885, Grey MSS).

The picture is one of extraordinary harmony between the two men, in full agreement on a major issue for the first and probably the last time. Rosebery was in Scotland for much of December, and he steered clear of the various Whig conclaves that were being held in London, including the meeting at Devonshire House on 1 January to curb Gladstone, which he refused to attend. When Rosebery came south, it was to show his loyalty to Gladstone, not to fraternise in Brooks's. Rosebery did rather isolate himself at this, as at most other times, but his information was none the worse for it. On 12 December, for instance, at Gladstone's bidding, he met Labouchere to ensure that that great negotiator kept his skills under control, and in so doing heard all Labby's gossip about subterranean Irish manoeuvres. In subsequent lengthy and fascinating letters, Labouchere gave Rosebery all the benefits of intrigue without any of its inconvenience.[144]

The basic accord between Rosebery, Gladstone, and Spencer was established during a visit to Hawarden in the first week of December 1885, and was not affected by the vicissitudes of the next two months. Gladstone treated Rosebery not only as a confidant, for instance reaching agreement with him almost at the beginning over the undesirability of Granville going back to the Foreign Office, but as a wise adviser. 'I wish we could meet daily' he wrote on 24 December. Rosebery had a clear and simple line: that home rule was desirable, and nothing should be done about it. In fact so clear was Rosebery as to the rightness of this course, that during the Midlothian campaign of November 1885, when Gladstone was at Dalmeny, Rosebery made his mentor sit down and pledge himself in writing[145] to a policy of inactivity until the Conservatives had fully declared their intentions. In subsequent months, Rosebery seldom allowed Gladstone to forget this theme. Rosebery strongly backed the idea of putting the onus on the Conservatives, and saying nothing: 'I agree most strongly that I must remain obstinately silent as to my plans'[146] wrote Gladstone on 13 December, and this agreement on policy remained unaffected by the Hawarden kite, which Rosebery took in his stride much more than most of his colleagues. Thus on 20 December Rosebery wrote in the same vein as before 'I should like you to stand aside and let the whole matter simmer till parliament meets, then call your party together and take them to some extent into your confidence.'[147] Rosebery's optimism was grounded in his belief, held from the start, that 'I thought there were irresistible forces ... which would compel Parnell to side with us',[148] and that precisely because of this, the Liberals should confine themselves to urging the Tories to deal with the question. To this general scheme

Gladstone added the rider, that, when Ireland was raised, it must be by the Liberal leaders, and not by Parnell; a stipulation so fully observed that Gladstone's success in achieving it has largely gone unnoticed.

However, the fundamental point that needs to be stressed here is that Gladstone obtained consistent support from Rosebery for a policy of inactivity at a time when he was being badgered by his colleagues and his family to make definite pronouncements. Gladstone always needed to be told he was right: at the end of 1885 it was Rosebery alone who provided him with this essential reassurance. Further, the clear implication of this new relationship (no less tangible for being unspoken) was that Rosebery would now follow in any direction in which Gladstone cared to lead after the meeting of parliament. For Gladstone this was a quite unexpected boon, in view of Rosebery's past obstinacies and his consistent advocacy of Scottish, not Irish, claims, which he had reaffirmed in a major speech at Paisley as late as October 1885. With remarkable suddenness, Rosebery now turned his back on Scottish affairs, even refusing to help smooth the way for a defeated cabinet colleague when an Edinburgh seat became vacant shortly after the general election. On wholly unforeseen grounds, therefore, Rosebery was the first to enter the Gladstonian camp, remaining loyally inside at a critical period and asking nothing in return except intimate consultation.

After having been so close to Gladstone, so deeply involved in the inner workings of his mind, it must have been a shock to Rosebery to find himself treated as outside the central counsels of the party when it came to the crucial work of forming the 1886 ministry. Rosebery was simply left alone to play tennis. The flow of confidence and intimacy suddenly dried up, and Rosebery was not slow to feel such things. It is therefore hard to tell whether his extreme withdrawal during the 1886 ministry was due to some resentful desire to show that he too had no need of the intimacy, or whether it was due to the burden of the Foreign Office of which he made so much. His diary entries showed continuing latent affection for Gladstone, but perhaps more as an endearing old man than as a confidential colleague. At one point the premier went six weeks without talking to his foreign secretary, which is both odd and a measure of trust. What is hard to be sure about is whether Rosebery would not have, without undue fuss, joined a successor Liberal régime under Hartington had Gladstone resigned in May 1886. His need to give affectionate support to a senior figure clearly meant much to him, certainly more than Ireland, about which, as he very properly emphasised, 'my practical knowledge is almost nil'.[149]

6

Small Men and Lesser Archives: The Unimportance of the Unimportant

In the Liberal government of 1886, every minister was kept in the dark some of the time and some ministers were in the dark nearly all of the time. All ministers accepted that Gladstone's intentions were the firm and concrete centre of the situation, yet the more one examines that centre, the more it turns out to lack definable content, just as, to do him justice, Gladstone had always protested was the case. It was a government of examination and inquiry, in which the actual examination was done by Gladstone, Spencer, and perhaps senior civil servants in the Treasury and in Dublin Castle. This was just what ministers expected examination and inquiry to mean, and their occasional protests at Gladstone's methods of work turned really on *amour propre* rather than on a desire to work on different lines. Some ministers secluded themselves in their departmental business, as with Rosebery and Mundella. Rosebery's supposed *mot* 'Ireland is not yet a foreign country: when it is, I shall look after it',[150] slightly exaggerated his non-involvement in Irish affairs, but corresponded accurately enough with the impression of non-involvement that he successfully set out to foster. Others, like Granville or Mundella again, had long spells of illness, while Childers, Gladstone and Spencer had lesser spells of illness or exhaustion. Childers was probably the only minister to suffer a bereavement, but it was a heavy one. Many ministers were unfamiliar to their colleagues. Ripon and Stansfeld, though respected and competent figures, had been called out of political limbo. Morley's only real colleague was Gladstone: other ministers could hardly have come to know what kind of man he was. Spencer said that he knew nothing of John Morley. The only political relationship which Granville kept up, was with Gladstone, and after their cooperation in forming the ministry, even this became very desultory.

Some ministers, therefore, and in particular Ripon, Rosebery, Granville, Kimberley, Campbell-Bannerman and Mundella, were hardly in the cabinet so far as the Irish legislation was concerned. Even Morley and Spencer, who were supposed to carry this load on their shoulders, were not vouchsafed any total sense of Gladstone's strategy. Morley was, properly, given little say in the framing of the land bill, while Spencer was only one among many colleagues who created the government bill. Both men, too, were thrown over on major points in quite casual fashion, Morley on exclusion of Irish members, and Spencer on the arrangements for land purchase. Morley might say in May 1886, though not in April, that he did not mind modification, though his preference for exclusion was clear enough, and even strongly emotional. Spencer, however, suffered more cruelly. He came into the ministry above all to secure adequate arrangements for the landlords. He was defeated first over the amount of the purchase money, secondly over the precedence between the two bills, thirdly over the implicit shelving of the land bill, and then finally when Gladstone, in the autumn, put the blame for the failure of the home rule bill squarely on the unpopularity of the land bill, and in effect dropped it altogether from his Irish policy.

Gladstone had a permanent problem with his cabinet, which never became serious. His cabinet was never really a home rule cabinet. Many ministers had strong reservations about particular points, or schemes of their own to press (as with Childers and Stansfeld). In a sense there was at most only a bare majority for the home rule bill within the cabinet, even after the resignations of Chamberlain and Trevelyan. Yet there was never an anti-Gladstone lobby, though this was not simply out of respect, as Childers' wrecking game with press leaks in April showed. The general situation was one of contradiction and paradox: to an exceptional degree, ministers were making it clear that they accepted Gladstone's monopoly of interpreting the needs of circumstance, yet at the same time Gladstone was trying to base his policy, to an exceptional degree, on finding out what people wanted him to do.

In 1886 large political meanings were contained in small gestures, in hesitancies, in table talk, to such an unusual extent, that one wants far more than usual to note every leaf that stirred upon the tree. Yet, to do this effectively, one needs to direct one's inquiries in the light of some provisional guiding theory as to where significant action took place; and the archival report which follows here, is designed at least to show the stringent limits imposed on the value of the surviving evidence, by the character, as well as the archival habits, of the lesser politicians.

The way forward in defining how a government worked, is to sift the surviving correspondence in the light of the single crucial distinction between politicians who just did their particular jobs, and politicians who took it upon themselves to create the general situation. On the whole, the archives follow the roles, i.e. the big guns have left papers of wide-ranging interest, while the small fry have failed to record even gossip just as they failed to cut a dash politically. Discussion of the major participants is dealt with elsewhere in this book, in terms of more sophisticated political analysis: the other figures in the Liberal party, however, can best be placed in terms of a rather pedestrian survey of their archives and what they suggest as to their authors' significance. The theme, therefore, of what follows below, is largely to establish the unimportance of the unimportant in an English parliamentary party and ministry in its length and breadth, rather than leaving it to be stated by default as usually happens; and by doing this, to make the singular and determining importance of the few significant individuals all the clearer.

The materials relating to the cabinet proper in 1886 are elusive. There is no regularly kept diary of much use. The diarists in the cabinet were Gladstone, Rosebery, and probably Kimberley: and definitely no one else. Rosebery's journal for 1886 is of very limited interest for most purposes, and many of its better passages have already been printed by biographers. Whether Gladstone's diary for 1886 is or is not a valuable political source, only time will show: but access to it did not enable J. L. Hammond to produce a rich and many-sided version of politics from the inside. Kimberley's papers, located but not open to examination by scholars at the time of going to press, have been in limbo for a generation, and, though broadly catalogued, have never been fully assessed. It is impossible to tell from the crude copy of Kimberley's memoirs which Rosebery jotted down, and which is accessible in Edinburgh, whether Kimberley provided a record of what passed in the 1886 cabinet. The memoirs, compiled by Kimberley late in life on the basis of other journals, were said by Rosebery to be 'feeble', showing 'the signs of age and confusion'. Campbell-Bannerman's diary for 1886[151] gave only the briefest indication of his activities and cannot be used for elucidating cabinet business. The diaries of Lord Ripon cover 1878–80 only. This lack of a good cabinet diary matters greatly. It means the history of 1886 must be written to an unusual degree from clues, inferences, and gossip. The historian has no spy in the cabinet room. The method used below, of bringing together in chronicle form minute incidents from a wide variety of sources, must be seen largely as a response to this difficulty.

There are also shortcoming in the diaries of those who, at other times, were almost professional eavesdroppers on cabinet proceedings. Edward Hamilton, no longer Gladstone's secretary, had ceased to be a classic source. The journal of Lewis Harcourt, Harcourt's son, though splendid so far as it goes, is available only in a tantalisingly abridged typescript copy prepared for A. G. Gardiner's use as biographer.[152] This typescript is excellent on the formation of the 1886 ministry, but thereafter contains little. The twelve volumes of Dilke's 'memoirs', written in 1891 by Henry K. Hudson, Dilke's secretary, with corrections by Dilke, cover the period 1843–1910 in a fragmentary way, but its account of 1885–1886 is based on some of Dilke's diaries written at the time, and now apparently nowhere to be found. Other, very thin diaries by Dilke for 1885–86 have survived, much lacerated, but these were not the foundation on which the memoirs were based. By 1886 Dilke's papers have ceased to be particularly informative about high politics.

The main sources for the activities of the 1886 cabinet itself are therefore the obvious ones. The first are Gladstone's so-called cabinet minutes (notes taken by him in cabinet, chiefly as a basis for his subsequent letter to the Queen) in the Gladstone MSS.[153] The second is the class PRO Cab in the Public Record Office, which contains facsimiles of Gladstone's letters to the Queen reporting on cabinet meetings (no meetings being omitted in 1886 except that of 8 March when Gladstone was away ill). The originals are in the Royal Archives at Windsor. The third is the reports in *The Times* of attendance, place, and time of meeting, revised in the light of much information found elsewhere on this aspect of cabinet meetings.

These, the official records, are obstinately uninteresting, not by accident. What is accidental is that there was no relatively humble figure in Gladstone's immediate entourage who wrote down what was going on. None of the private secretaries in 1886 'Boswellised' Gladstone as Edward Hamilton did in 1880–85: none of them, indeed, are known to have left any body of significant papers. Herbert Gladstone, always an irregular diarist, finally allowed his journal to peter out in December 1885, while the rest of his papers are uninformative as regards this administration. Mary Gladstone, the GOM's daughter, made no entry in her diary between 18

December 1885 and 24 January 1886, and then there is a gap until after her wedding on 2 February 1886, when naturally she turned aside from the political world and went to live in the country. Had she been living in London, her assessments would certainly have carried weight. Mrs Gladstone's largely undated letters do not help much, since during the session of 1886 she was almost uninterruptedly in or near London in the company of her nearest and dearest, and hence had little occasion to put pen to paper. Two other personages not greatly in the public eye, but who kept a close watch upon Gladstone, were Wolverton and Ponsonby. Wolverton's papers have almost certainly not existed for a very long time, probably for the innocent reason that successive holders of the title had no children. The Ponsonby MSS in the British Museum contain only two volumes of unimportant correspondence, and obviously bear no relation to the 117 boxes of material which Ponsonby's son claimed to have used for his father's biography.

The Rosebery MSS, some still unavailable, others available in the National Library of Scotland, have little or nothing in the way of correspondence between Rosebery and his principal colleagues and political intimates like Brett and Edward Hamilton, that throws light on cabinet proceedings. Rosebery kept a diary at this time, but it by no means constitutes either a report on high politics or an inquiry into his inner feelings. Only on the subject of his conversations with Gladstone does Rosebery consistently take pains to be illuminating rather than perfunctory.

Two of the recalcitrant trio of ministers who left the government in March and April 1886, must also remain shadowy figures on archival grounds, their standing having to be inferred almost entirely from the contemptuous comments of others. The G.O. Trevelyan MSS in Newcastle University Library lack political information relating to the period of this ministry. In particular, Trevelyan's correspondence with his wife is lacking at this time. Other letters from G.O. Trevelyan to his sisters, which might have supplemented the rather sorry collection at Newcastle, and which were at the disposal of G.M. Trevelyan in writing his evasive memoir of his father (1932), are now unknown to present members of the family. As Trevelyan's rather calculated attempt to free himself from Chamberlain by putting himself forward as the most violent Liberal critic of home rule ceased with humiliating abruptness the day he lost his seat at the 1886 general election to a Gladstonian, it is highly probable that the archival deficiencies correspond to an attempted act of wisdom aimed at safeguarding Trevelyan's reputation. As a result of this wisdom, it has become very difficult not to assess Trevelyan purely in terms of the derisory remarks he provoked, both when a Unionist from others of the same kind, and when a Gladstonian (he re-entered parliament in 1887 as a home ruler) from his fellow Gladstonians.

The other minister who eventually followed Chamberlain out of the government (though not till 9 April) was Heneage, Chancellor of the Duchy of Lancaster, a Whig landowner who still wrote of 'our own section of the party', a Liberal counterpart to Henry Chaplin in everything save panache, and certainly a figure of fun. His papers, in Lincolnshire County Record Office, reveal nothing, and probably there is nothing to reveal, save that the level of political competence tapers off very sharply once outside the top leadership. One letter from Heneage, written at the last moment before resignation, shows all one needs to know of his state of mind. Faced with the crisis of his career, he wrote 'what I want to know is can you give me any accurate idea of the numbers who will follow Hartington or who they are at all: I am perfectly convinced that Mr G is deceived about the feeling in the House and in the Country...' Heneage, who was ill in the crucial month of March 1886, had been kept informed by ministers of all shades, especially Gladstone, whom he praised as 'most anxious to meet the wishes of *all* or *any* of us'. All his calculations were made in the context of his 'wish to see a *real Liberal Party led by practical statesmen* to which loyal Radicals and Liberal Conservatives might be drawn'. He wanted, therefore, in a mild way, to change the Liberal party, but only so as to accommodate what he took average opinion to be: his picture of a good state of party politics was the 1860s, not the 1890s. What was lacking in his case, and he was a representative nonentity, was even a thought of moving over to the Conservatives. He was not intrinsically concerned, either, about Ireland, except in so far as British party structure was involved. His battle was to preserve that structure as he had known it in his youth, not to destroy it.[154]

The bulk of the Childers MSS, in the library of the Royal Commonwealth Institute, was destroyed by bombing, and what remains is especially thin for 1886, as is a secondary collection of his letters in the Public Record Office.[155]

Substantial disarrangement of the Harcourt MSS makes it almost impossible to say with certainty in any given case that the apparent absence of correspondence from cabinet colleagues, after search in all appropriate parts of the archive, can be taken to mean that none exists. (For instance, Spencer's letters to Harcourt in 1885 are not in the box labelled 'Spencer', but under 'Ireland, 1882'). In 1886 Harcourt's correspondence with cabinet colleagues is dominated by the estimates crisis and the differences over the retention of the Irish members which arose in cabinet in April. As one would expect, one can say with some certainty that Harcourt's correspondence with the minor members of the Liberal and Liberal Unionist leadership was very limited – it was small enough to fit in one envelope. There is a general absence of political correspondence of explanatory value for the 1886 ministry.

The Granville MSS in the Public Record Office, though the most important single source for the discussions within the Liberal leadership in December 1885–January 1886, peter out markedly when the Liberal ministry takes office, reflecting Granville's age, illness, and burden of work. In particular, he did not maintain his former habit of noting divisions of opinion within cabinet.

The papers of Lord Herschell were lost in a fire, almost certainly before any scholar had thought of consulting them, and consequently the best biographical treatment of Herschell, in R.F.V. Heuston's *Lives of the Lord Chancellors* (Oxford, 1964), is unable to shed much light on Herschell as a politician.

Yet there are fragmentary indications that Herschell was among the strongest of the weak men in the cabinet, stronger, especially in committee, than Mundella, Stansfeld, or Campbell-Bannerman for instance. Once appointed, he was in possession of an advantage unique to his office, for the lord chancellorship carried a life pension of £5,000 regardless of the length of time served. His confidence in giving Gladstone a rough ride over both Irish bills between 13 March and 14 April may reflect this silver lining, as much as his conscientious desire not to scamp the points of detail in the Irish bills in the way the cabinet was doing. Herschell's readiness to lose his temper at certain well-timed moments, and perhaps give up his office as well, certainly contrasted in a most interesting way with the tenacity of his ambition to become lord chancellor.

Not only had Herschell turned down an offer of the speakership:[156] there were, according to his colleagues, three other very senior judicial posts which Herschell had turned down in order to remain in the running for political office. His mode of achieving his political ambitions was to keep out of politics. He played no part in the party whisperings of December 1885–January 1886, spending his vacation at a non-political house-party with his friends the Williamsons, where life turned mainly on amateur theatricals: and even at the eleventh hour, a discreet Whig diarist could only note, *à propos* of Ireland, 'Herschell as usual very cautious, not committing himself to any strong opinions on the matter'.[157] Nor did his appointment kindle any optimism about Gladstone's policy, for he said 'the difficulties in the way of the new government are

immense and that its life would be a short one'.[158] Perhaps one of
his qualifications for the exercise of ecclesiastical patronage, his
churchwardenship at St Peter's, Eaton Square, earned him some
regard from Gladstone: but the indications are that Herschell was
no more basing his career plans on Gladstone, than Gladstone had
ever considered appointing him to any cabinet office before he was
brought up sharp by James' and Selborne's refusals.

The real question was who had helped Herschell to find a seat
in 1885 and 1886. In 1885, despite his eleven years as a member
for Durham City, the Durham Liberals were on redistribution disinclined to find a seat for him. 'He waited in vain for an invitation,
and eventually at the request of the Cavendishes contested the N.
Lonsdale division of Lancashire and was beaten'.[159] Then, on the
death of the Liberal M.P. for Edinburgh South, it was Henry James
who telegraphed the same day to Rosebery pressing Herschell's
claims to the vacancy.[160] When electoral misfortune threw
Herschell on the rocks, it made it clearer than before or later just
where he was felt to stand in the party. It was not, evidently, as a
Gladstonian, Radical, or home ruler: though, for many people,
the purely legal claims of this politically colourless if far from pliant
lawyer were the only point tangible enough to excite remark.
Selborne, generously, reflected that Herschell, Russell, and Davey
were the most legally distinguished set of law officers the ministry
could have, and he thoroughly approved of their appointments.
Yet a tentative political judgement is also possible. Herschell's
personal connections, and his state of mind as displayed in cabinet
are both fairly consistent with the comment of his closest friend,
Victor Williamson (a Liberal Unionist), 'I have never been able to
believe that Herschell really approved this business, but I do not
see how he could have acted otherwise than he did'.[161]

The point that the changes in the Liberal leadership early in
1886 were due at least as much to personal vicissitudes unrelated
to home rule, as to a traumatic ideological division, was especially
true of Shaw-Lefevre after he lost his seat at Reading in the general
election. This worthy figure, who combined an impeccable upper
class background with elevated Cobdenite principles and skilful
assiduity in the humbler chores of administration, had entered the
cabinet in February 1885 and, without making any personal mark
there, had generally acted as if Chamberlain and Dilke were his
leaders.

At the 1885 general election he had taken a strongly Chamberlain-
ite line, and shortly afterwards attended the Highbury meeting of
the five Radical ex-ministers (Morley, Dilke, Chamberlain,
Lefevre, and Trevelyan) on 5–7 December 1885.[162] In other ways,

he continued to treat Chamberlain (not Dilke) as his leader, for instance taking his advice on the South Edinburgh by-election, where the local radicals had wanted to run Lefevre against Childers. Yet even at the time of the Highbury meeting, Chamberlain's vigorous arguments for keeping the Conservatives in office for the time being while the Radical (rather than Liberal) party seized the initiative by offering a scheme of limited home rule all round, failed to keep Lefevre adequately in tow. As with John Morley, his native integrity, given an appropriate opportunity, was too much for him, and writing on a day when the wind was blowing hard against all kites, Lefevre expressed what was probably his central opinion. He 'should not be unprepared to go further in the direction of Federation if I could be certain of giving full satisfaction and effecting a final settlement, but in default of this it would I think be better to attempt nothing'.[163] Yet, to Gladstone, this lessening in Lefevre's adhesion to Chamberlain naturally meant little. Lefevre's swing towards ethical idealism over Ireland made it possible for Gladstone to drop him in a way that contrasted sharply with the fate of other defeated ex-ministers like Herschell and Childers.

Thus, though predictably 'anxious to get back' into parliament (which he did not do till returned for Bradford Central on 21 April 1886), and at a very early stage 'personally in favour of going a long way in the direction of Federation with a local and subordinate legislature as sketched out by Childers',[164] Lefevre's ideological soundness on the Irish question (rooted in a rather obsessive aversion to coercion, much more than in a positive belief in a separate legislature) won him scant attention from Gladstone.

Moreover, the home rule bee in Lefevre's bonnet was not of quite the right kind from the point of view of a party leadership determined to avoid detailed commitments. Lefevre made known his sense of an overwhelming obligation to safeguard the property of Irish landlords, and his inability to accept any transfer of police powers without prior settlement of the land question. On 10 January he sent Gladstone a detailed scheme of land purchase which conflicted with Gladstone's later views at fundamental points. These characteristic hints of tenacious rigidity hardly made Lefevre look the right man to take on what the Liberal court expected to be a journey of exceptional sinuousness.

The present state of the Shaw-Lefevre MSS makes it impossible to be categorical about his position in 1886. His papers now form part of the archives of the first Marquess of Aberdeen, at Haddo House in Aberdeenshire, but only a part of the entire collection has as yet been sorted and made generally available. However, Shaw-Lefevre seems to have kept his correspondence with Gladstone carefully together (Haddo MSS box 9). One letter, of 13 January 1886, shows Shaw-Lefevre's uncertainty about his future, following his exclusion from the consultations of 11 and 12 January. Gladstone made no effort to reassure him and bluntly rejected his request for a formal meeting of the shadow cabinet to discuss tactics. This was despite an explicit admission by Gladstone at that time that Shaw-Lefevre's views were in the main stream of Liberal policy on Ireland. Moreover, Shaw-Lefevre after 1886 came to represent the purest strain of moral ardour in the party on Irish questions, particularly on coercion, as his speeches, pamphlets, and correspondence with Morley (Haddo MSS box 8) showed. In the absence of available correspondence, however, such questions as Shaw-Lefevre's efforts to regain office, and the degree to which the opportunity to drop him was welcomed by the party leadership, must remain matters for conjecture. What is clear from this and other cases is that Gladstone in 1886 showed little inclination to behave with warmth or even civility to those true Gladstonians who were moved primarily by simple moral considerations of justice to Ireland. When one turns to look at Gladstone's relations with Stansfeld, the other main representative of the ethical spirit in the cabinet, one finds the same coolness and distance, but in a more reciprocal form.

Stansfeld was neither an uncritical Gladstonian nor an unequivocal home ruler: for his idiosyncratic position on the latter subject, see the entry for 4 May 1886 below. Gladstone's omission of Stansfeld from office in 1880 probably left scars. The few surviving remarks by Stansfeld in the year preceding his return to office show no especial commitment to Gladstone. In June 1885 he expressed pleasure at the fall of the government, and assumed that Gladstone had chosen to be defeated. In November 1885, he interpreted the Liberal losses in the towns as 'mainly Gladstone's fault' and commented 'my present impression is that the end has come for the GOM.' When offered office in March 1886, he was reluctant to take it, and made his doubts about Gladstone's Irish plans clear both then and later in May. He regarded it as his honest duty not just to support home rule, but to transform it into something else. The fullest evidence for Stansfeld's beliefs in 1885–86 is to be found in his article on future Liberal policy in the *Contemporary Review*, October 1885, where he shows himself nearer to Chamberlain than to Gladstone in tone and temper. Stansfeld had an adventitious interest in the success of the home rule ministry, in that on 16 March he had carried a resolution in favour of the repeal of the

Contagious Diseases Act, against which he had spent the best years of his life campaigning.

There is little more that can be said about Stansfeld's position in the 1886 cabinet. Only on 4 May did he make a solitary attempt to influence policy, and it is not clear that his ideas were ever put forward at an actual cabinet. Moreover, there are virtually no records relating to the small change of personal contact with him. No one noticed his presence, or spoke to him, so far as available evidence indicates: it is possible to be very lonely on the front bench, in a way that bore no relation to Stansfeld's obvious competence and sense over a wide range of subjects. So much may be gauged from the absence of reference to him in the more leisurely contemporary jottings on the social and political scene: it is not just a consequence of the point, clearly made in the Hammonds' authorised biography, that little material relating to high politics survives in Stansfeld's papers for any period of his life. The number of letters in his papers bearing on 1885–86 is only about five, and these are quite cursory. The Stansfeld MSS contain correspondence from Barbara Hammond in 1933 dealing with her unsuccessful search for further Stansfeld material, and stating her conclusion that nearly everthing had been destroyed.[165]

The Mundella MSS and Leader MSS fail to illuminate Mundella's experiences in the cabinet. Mundella, quite apart from being ill in May and June, played virtually no part in cabinet, despite his generally pushing manner. One simple reason was a heavy departmental programme. On going to the Board of Trade, he found there 'the sixth and final draft of a revised Railway Bill' as circulated to the previous cabinet, and he introduced this railway and canal traffic bill on 12 March, while at the same time launching an important reorganisation within the Board of Trade itself, involving setting up sections for labour, fisheries, and commercial intelligence. The railway bill occasioned deep and minute controversy, and together with his illness in May and June, kept Mundella quiescent in matters of general concern.[166]

However, Mundella's speeches and correspondence show that, far from evading the whole Irish question on the grounds of his own insignificance or preoccupations, as he might well have done, he was in fact at pains to form his own judgement on the broad merits of the case. His judgement, once formed, was happily on the best party lines: but in a real sense it was his own, and solid in a way that the positions of most of his colleagues were not. He had advantages of a peculiar kind to help him remain true to himself: an Anglican, and clearly labelled as the decent man's alternative to Chamberlain among the commercial Radicals, he had considerable antipathy to Joe, whom he described as 'implacable in his *hatreds*, and unceasing in his intrigues'.[167] When Chamberlain and Dilke, in December 1885, were pushing the idea of retaining the Tories in office for the time being in order to radicalise the Liberals in opposition, Mundella wrote to Gladstone dissociating himself from their policy, just as in January and February 1886, when the Radicals wanted the Tories out fairly quickly on a non-Irish issue, Mundella came out in favour of keeping the Tories in for the moment.

At least as important, however, was Mundella's visit to Ireland in November–December 1885, where he met representative men of all parties, including Lord Chief Justice Morris and Sir Robert Hamilton. His notes[168] taken at the time record his impression that Carnarvon had been 'a lamentable failure', having let effective control fall into the hands of the National League. But he also considered that the Hawarden kite had seriously aggravated the situation. Probably the most important influence on him was Spencer, with whom he became engaged in a lengthy correspondence. Spencer wrote very frankly, confiding his fears about the future, and concluding 'there seems nothing but a big measure of home rule with proper safeguards'. Mundella replied 'There is not a word of yours which does not command my hearty assent'.[169]

Mundella did not speak on the Irish government bill in parliament, but his views as explained on occasion outdoors were less idiosyncratic than those of most other minor members of the cabinet. Speaking on 8 February at Sheffield on his unopposed re-election after taking office, he stressed that home rule was the opposite of separation, that he would have preferred to keep the Salisbury ministry in office, and that his regard for Hartington was unbroken ('there was no colleague for whom he had greater respect... He was satisfied that his lordship would give an independent, although discriminating support to Mr Gladstone's government'). On 28 April Mundella was the main speaker at a Sheffield rally in support of Gladstone's Irish policy. As in his previous speech, he showed marked enthusiasm for an early and sweeping land purchase bill. He also hinted at a personal bias in favour of exclusion of the Irish members. Mundella emphasised the importance of the opinions of Spencer and Campbell-Bannerman in drawing him to home rule, claiming that 'the first thing he (Mundella) did on his return from Ireland was to compare notes with Lord Spencer...', and thus playing down the Gladstonian origins of home rule. This account of the evolution of his opinions was in fact true as well as tactically adept.

Campell-Bannerman's attempts to affect the Irish policy of the

Liberal party were confined to the period before he joined the cabinet for the first time in February 1886. Once at the War Office, an appointment he owed chiefly to the Queen, the complete absence of any evidence to the contrary strongly suggests not only his pliability but also his non-participation, not only in cabinet proper but also in private discussions.[170] With a few others like Mundella, Ripon, Kimberley, and Granville, he belonged to that minority of the home rule cabinet which neither objected strongly to particular features of the draft bill, nor had an ideal scheme of its own in mind. This should not be taken to mean that he was considered as a loyal supporter of the bills in their successive shapes: rather, that no one thought it necessary to ascertain or record his opinion, and that he regarded this view of his position as appropriate. His only important speech on Ireland in parliament, on 13 May 1886, was flat and defensive in tone, placing its emphasis on the practical difficulties of governing Ireland, and the undiminished supremacy of Westminster, rather than on giving enthusiastic endorsement to the national claims of Ireland. The strength of his speech lay in its exposure of the great weakness of the Tory coercion scheme* of January 1886: that in putting down the National League, they were far exceeding coercion as practised by Spencer, extending its meaning from the suppression of ordinary crimes by special means, to the suppression of political opinions. This kind of apologetic for home rule, cogent enough when the Liberals took office, meant very little by May when the central issue appeared to be impending separation. His speech of 13 May was technically only important as being the occasion of a definite Liberal promise to allow Irish members back to Westminster for tax purposes. His few other interventions in debates on Ireland were in response to baiting about his attitude to home rule before he took office, a subject on which he was made to cut a poor figure. Though his single public indiscretion was not itself important, it did no real injustice to the frame of mind in which he had embarked on the great adventure.

On 12 November 1885 Campbell-Bannerman made a speech at a meeting, twice quoted against him in debate in May 1886, which was reported as follows:

'But when we come to the question of giving them a separate

---

* Campbell-Bannerman's derogatory remarks about home rule in Jan. 1886 must be considered in the context of his expectation at the time, that the Tories would not introduce any scheme of coercion, let alone the exceptionally drastic one they did eventually produce (Campbell-Bannerman to Spencer, 8 Jan. 1886, Spencer MSS). Even when most disinclined to concession, he was always clear that a sustained policy of coercion was impossible.

Parliament and a separate Government, then I confess I see great difficulty, and I do not think that this is likely to be conceded them by any Government, either Whig or Tory, because it would not be consistent with the maintenance of the Empire or our duty to the Crown'.

That this was in harmony with his private views appears in a letter from him to Spencer on 8 January 1886 opposing home rule in general on the ground that:

'It is not as if any of us thought it a good thing in itself, or beneficial either to Ireland or England. On the contrary, if the Irish people would only be quiet and reasonable, they have very few grievances and these would be readily removed, leaving to the country the immense advantage of close connection with England. We regard home rule only as a dangerous and damaging *pis aller*.'

Further confirmation of the fact that he was, on balance, a good liberal Unionist in the making in the month before he joined the home rule ministry is to be found in Northbrook's letters to Spencer. On 1 January 1886, Northbrook found Campbell-Bannerman 'very doubtful in his views'. A week later, Northbrook found him still 'very doubtful' and against concessions to the Irish under current circumstances, though covering himself with the statement that it would require 'very strong reasons indeed to induce him to take a course different from yours [sc. Spencer's] on the question of Ireland',[171] and expressing a pious wish that if Gladstone could produce a home rule scheme 'free from all the defects and guarding against all the evils', this would be a triumph.[172] For middle class Liberal administrators who wished above all things to remain in the mainstream of the party, the path of greatest safety, in January 1886, clearly lay in coming under the umbrella of Spencer's (not Gladstone's) reputation.

The total picture was a little more patchy than the above suggests, and was not one of unrelieved Unionism. In a hardly noticed interview in the *Daily News* on 23 December 1885, Campbell-Bannerman advocated a bipartisan solution,* with a Tory ministry taking the initiative, and the Liberals confining themselves to offering constructive support. This was, however, an isolated effort, and on a

---

* The *arrière-pensée* here was much more to keep the Liberal party uninvolved, than to effect a solution. This is made clear in a letter to Spencer, 2 Jan. 1886, urging that there should be no premature disclosure of any kind by any Liberals, and that party action should be confined to challenging the Conservatives and Parnell to show their hands.

strict interpretation leaves a high probability that Campbell-Bannerman had nothing good to say of home rule between the Hawarden kite and the Tory announcement of coercion.

At this time he was a close associate of Northbrook, and the two of them, together with Trevelyan, also a former Irish secretary, spent three days at Stratton in conclave in the hope of finding an Irish policy which would unite the Liberal party. Campbell-Bannerman was, as much as the others, imbued with dread of home rule. On their failure to agree on a compromise scheme, he moved into Spencer's orbit, and his 'conversion', like that of Mundella, owed nearly everything to Spencer and nothing to Gladstone. His genuine sense of the administrative absurdity of the Tory plan to suppress the National League alone removed any suspicion of opportunism from his decision to join Gladstone's ministry.

He was relatively honest in his subsequent admissions of perplexity, stressing that he was 'plain and unvarnished' in his approach to problems, but some varnishing nevertheless went on. In April 1886, he claimed that he had made up his mind for home rule by Christmas 1885,[173] 'with the assistance of the most competent men in Ireland' and this 'after protracted deliberation so anxious as to be painful'.[174] Under the pressure of national sentiment among his constituents[174] at Stirling, support for a federal home rule scheme repeatedly crept into his speeches in the summer of 1886: but such enthusiasms lay outside his natural inclinations,* and, unlike Rosebery, he could not claim to have appreciated the claims of Scotland to home rule before he came out in support of a measure for Ireland.

As Irish secretary in 1884–85, Campbell-Bannerman had been completely overshadowed by Spencer, acting chiefly as the latter's mouthpiece in parliament: and he had limited his role to that of an official and man of good will. In 1886, Spencer was more than ever regarded as the voice of experience on Irish affairs, and in fact Spencer was in infinitely more intimate contact with the Irish administration during the latter months of the Tory interregnum. In the early months of the home rule ministry, Spencer took up where he had left off in June 1885, in all but name: while Trevelyan and Campbell-Bannerman, with departments to administer, were not even included in the working groups of ministers handling the details of Irish policy. It was only in December 1885 that Spencer

---

* Appreciating Scottish claims was a purely passive process with him. He wrote to the temperamentally energetic Bryce 'I hardly take your view of Home Rule for Scotland. It is difficult to set it aside, as the case for it is logically strong; but I do not think the volcano is in so active a state as might be judged from the noise it sometimes makes' (Campbell-Bannerman to Bryce, 16 Dec. 1886, B.M. Add. MSS 41211 f. 1).

showed craft and solicitude in eliciting Campbell-Bannerman's views, presumably because of the high value, polemically, of keeping all the Liberals with official Irish experience on the same side.

Campbell-Bannerman's correspondence with colleagues, rich enough in 1885, showed in 1886 a not uncommon tendency to take cover in his department, to avoid general political discussion, and to make it clear to the party that he stood apart from the politicians in the cabinet. Departmental detail apart, very little indeed remains that can be called political correspondence for 1886. His great principle of action was, already, to find out what was the minimum that needed doing: his principle of communication, that if he had anything to say, to say it only to his wife. Entering the cabinet essentially as a step in an administrative career, he achieved a respectable neutrality towards its policies which initially he was far from feeling. His real achievement was that in a cabinet where there was so much competition to be inconspicuous, his decision to be politically invisible was so entirely successful.

There were an unusual number of distinguished Scots associated with the 1886 ministry, and there was, too, for those who cared to face up to it, the weighty problem of devising ways of putting home rule into the language of Scottish politics. On the whole, the leading Scottish Liberals – Rosebery, Dalhousie, J. B. Balfour, Marjoribanks, Bryce, Aberdeen, Elgin, Campbell-Bannerman, Playfair – preferred just to let Scottish matters drift: yet it is exceptionally difficult, for archival reasons, even to pin down that much about the Scottish policy of the Liberals in 1886. One cannot hear them talking, least of all to each other. For instance, Bryce and Rosebery, fellow Scots intellectuals, each with a fine feeling for the nuances of home rule, left no hint of intellectual ferment going on while they were working together at the Foreign Office. There is nothing interesting to be said about their relationship or communications in 1886; and this although they had a feast of possible discourse spread out before them. While the reason Rosebery left Scottish politics behind in 1886 was clear enough, the choice which faced Bryce between being a party intellectual and being a Scottish politician hardly appeared to him as a choice at all.

Bryce approached the Irish question both as a man with personal ties with Ulster, and as a student of law. Before the home rule bill came out, he had urged the case of liberal protestant Ulster, with some alarm, to the Liberal leaders. 'I have strongly urged the case of Ulster with him (Gladstone) and Lord Spencer and they would I believe ... agree to some plan were any proposed by Ulstermen. But the latter, in spite of my repeated entreaties, will evolve nothing.'[175] By May 1886, however, Bryce had become an apologist for the bill in his letters to Ulster, urging that it was 'dictated by those Christian principles which ought to underlie all statesmanship.'[176] As a party intellectual, he spoke cleverly in debate on the bill, and also sent in a memorandum of fifteen pages (27 April) aimed at anticipating legal criticisms of loose ends in the bill. This paper was reported on by Morley to Gladstone, after having been worked through by Herschell and Thring. From the point of view of estimating Bryce's standing, his activities in 1886 show that despite his being well-placed to do so, he did not succeed in acting as spokesman for either Ulster or Scottish opinion.

Another case of archival deficiency only underlining a basic political insignificance, relates to the secretaries for Scotland. As with his predecessor Trevelyan, so with the thirteenth earl of Dalhousie, who succeeded Trevelyan as secretary for Scotland in March 1886: all his papers, except perhaps for personal diaries which are not open to inspection, have unaccountably disappeared, and are unlikely ever to come to light. Dalhousie is therefore a cypher in the story on archival grounds alone, but he was in any case nothing more than a pleasant nonentity in terms of political weight. (He was only appointed after Playfair had turned down an offer of the post because it was outside the cabinet).[177] Quite simply he was too open and trusting to succeed in the ruthless world of parliamentary politics, his chief defect being a tendency to believe 'everything anybody told him'. In the judgement of a close friend Lord Derby, his credulity was his 'main characteristic'.[178] It was not that, being a junior minister, he lacked the chance to get the ear of power. On the contrary, Dalhousie and his wife were family friends of the Gladstones, and saw a fair amount of them in private life. Dalhousie was also, surprisingly, an intimate of John Morley,[179] who would have liked to see him as his lord-lieutenant in February 1886 if he had not then been absent on a sea voyage.[180] His omission from the cabinet, in which both previous Scottish secretaries had sat, was due to what Granville called Gladstone's 'very wrong' but 'irremoveable idea that he was bound not to give a second sanction to making another office necessarily a cabinet post',[181] and owed nothing to personal tensions or doctrinal unsoundness. Dalhousie accepted his exclusion from the cabinet with a good grace. The ministers who appointed him were chiefly concerned about his poor health, for which there is ample evidence, even the unexacting Granville thinking him 'not what he was for purposes of business'.[182] Dalhousie in fact was to die in November 1887, though in March 1886 following his return from abroad he seemed 'fresh, vigorous, and well'.[183] The most striking thing about him was that he was really more deeply in sympathy with

Irish national feeling than any other minister. As an unsuccessful candidate at Liverpool in 1880, sponsored by Derby, he had come out boldly on the Irish side, and it was as a man of principle that he deplored the way Gladstone forced Liberals to be 'always looking out for the cat to jump before we commit ourselves'.[184]

It was of no interest to anyone that Dalhousie was a genuine home ruler, any more than it was noticed whether the Scottish secretary was in London or in Scotland: but his views, written when unpopular, deserve record if only because of their rarity:

'I am inclined to feel thankful that the Irish have recourse to parliamentary and constitutional methods of warfare... We ought to encourage them in that and not say at every turn that parliament won't do what they want... I always feel that the Irish people are a nation by themselves, different in race, temperament and religion from our own... I don't blame them wishing to govern themselves'.[185]

Dalhousie wanted Ireland given a status similar to that of Canada, and he did so writing at the zenith of Liberal hostility to the Irish.

A further difficulty in tracing developments regarding Scotland at this time is that, although a few political papers concerning lord advocate Balfour,* Dalhousie's coadjutor in the lower house, have survived in the care of his grandson Lord Kinross, none of them relate to 1885–86, nor indeed to the whole of his period in parliament. The main problem facing any lord advocate at this period was the purely administrative one of sorting out his relationship with the newly created Scottish Office, and this probably took what time Balfour could spare from his fashionable legal practice in Edinburgh and his involuntary absorption in crofter affairs. Certainly it never occurred to cabinet ministers that Balfour might be worth consulting about matters, such as Protestant sentiment and the maintenance of party unity in Scotland, which fell outside his departmental brief.

However, by 1886 probably neither Dalhousie nor Balfour were as important in articulating relations between Liberal leaders and Scottish opinion as was the rapidly rising Edward Marjoribanks, nominally only a junior whip, but in reality making the most of

---

* J.B.Balfour (1837–1905): M.P. (Lib.) Clackmannan and Kinross 1880–99: solicitor-general for Scotland 1880–81: lord advocate 1881–85, 1886, 1892: appointed lord justice-general (head of the Scottish judiciary), 1899, and cr. Baron Kinross, 1902, by Conservative ministries: not related to any of the Balfours on the Conservative side: a member of the Episcopal Church in Scotland: a much respected party lawyer who did not take political initiatives.

the much wider opportunities created by Rosebery's literal disappearance into the Foreign Office, and by Bryce's and Campbell-Bannerman's unqualified preference for departmental rather than Scottish national roles. As early as March, Gladstone was suggesting that he might be given the Duchy of Lancaster on Heneage's resignation,[186] though in the event Marjoribanks had to wait till 1892 for formal promotion. He epitomised the pliable young patricians who were never more sought after, especially by Gladstone, than in 1886. A very even temperament and a lack of ardour in presenting his own opinions made him a fit companion for both Whigs and Radicals, and he never became identified with any particular group within the Liberal party. On home rule he was 'a staunch follower of his leader'[187] but this did not prevent him from sympathising with those who differed from Gladstone on certain important points. Nature in giving him a 'superfluity of physical and mental energy'[188] clearly intended that he should be a whip; but it was primarily his flexibility on burning questions which brought him office as comptroller of the household.

Over the next decade Marjoribanks was chiefly concerned with Scotland 'of which he took practically complete control'.[189] Here his non-committal position on home rule and other matters meant that he was well equipped to deal with the difficult situation left by Rosebery's withdrawal from active management. His basic problem was to prevent a collision between the remaining aristocratic elements in the party and the radicals who were increasingly restive from 1885 onwards. His method was to reassure the Whigs by buying off the Radicals – on paper. At meetings of the Scottish Liberal Association he supported the Radicals in their attempt to impose an extreme programme on the party, and in exchange for this obtained their passive support at Westminster.[190] Unfortunately however it is impossible fully to document his activities as Scottish party manager because he was too busy to build up his files and destroyed each day's correspondence as soon as he had dealt with it.[191] Moreover, Rosebery in later life cordially disliked Marjoribanks, and even at this time there is no evidence in Rosebery's papers of anything like his grooming him for the work of Scottish party management.

The John Morley MSS are in private hands and are not directly accessible to students. As a result of inquiries, however, it is understood that they contain nothing that throws any light on the workings of the cabinet in 1886. We are indebted for this information to the present custodian of these papers.

Relatively little of John Morley's activities shows up in books[192] or in archives elsewhere. He was something of a stranger to his colleagues, and found half of them 'sceptical and cynical at bottom: especially Harcourt'.[193] He was, above all, a go-between with the Irish in negotiations where very little was put down on paper at any stage. Whether, besides being a go-between, he was also an important contributor to the essential discussions of Irish policy which centred on Gladstone's colloquies with Spencer, cannot be satisfactorily determined, at least for the initial two months of the ministry. His correspondence with Spencer is bare and brief, and compatible with the view that Morley, overshadowed by Spencer till April, took advantage of Spencer's row with Gladstone over the relative timing of the two Irish bills to correct the position and become the person generally most in agreement with Gladstone. At any rate, the bulk of Morley's correspondence with Gladstone in the Gladstone MSS is in May, while Spencer's correspondence with the premier was almost exclusively before May.

Little of Morley's mind, or of his job, comes out in his letters to Gladstone and Spencer, his two key colleagues in Irish matters. The same reticence is displayed in his letters to Aberdeen, which volunteer economical quantities of guidance and general comment without ever suggesting that Aberdeen had any serious part to play either in the government of Ireland, or in the government's Irish legislation. The less the lord-lieutenant thought or knew of matters of high policy, the better – Morley's letters to Aberdeen in 1886 suggest this as clearly as do his letters to Houghton in 1892–95.[194]

The only Liberal backbencher's diary to come to light which is of any value is that of Arthur Elliot, M.P. for Roxburghshire from 1880 to 1892, when he was defeated. The value of the diary for high politics lies in its reporting of chance conversations with the great, rather than in its accounts of Elliot's own considerable activities as a Liberal Unionist organiser. Such conversations were few, because Elliot, though no mere lawyer, had to make an income from the bar and could not afford the time to be anyone's confidant. A blue-blooded Whig in the classic tradition, son of the third Earl of Minto, a nephew of Earl Russell, and a frequent contributor to and eventually editor of the *Edinburgh Review*, he moved socially and politically rather outside the mainstream of Liberal politics. Among the leaders he was probably closest to Goschen, whose biographer he became. Like Goschen, he was distinguished by his unfaltering opposition to home rule, in the sense of legislative devolution, at all stages. (He was prepared, however, for further measures of administrative devolution in Scotland). In April 1886, his hour of destiny struck, and he became heavily involved in the work of organising the embryonic Liberal Unionist party throughout the country, from a party headquarters at Spring Gardens, London. There is a gap in his diary, which is in family hands, from 21 September 1885 to 12 January 1886.

Two other Liberal backbench diarists are known. Neither are of use. The parliamentary diary of A. E. Pease, the young M.P. for York, interesting passages from which are printed in his *Elections and Recollections* (1932), still exists in family hands but is not open to inspection by scholars. Another new entrant to parliament at the 1885 elections, Sir Edward Grey, left a fragment of autobiography, an early political diary, and a regular flow of correspondence to his wife which itself must almost have amounted to a diary. All these appear to have been irretrievably lost just after the second War, though they were known to G. M. Trevelyan, who however made little use of them in his official biography of Grey.[195]

Besides those who held office on either side, there were certain individuals who were regarded, at least in some quarters, as potential saviours of the nation. A case in point was the aged, crusty, morbidly alarmist, and contentious eighth Duke of Argyll, regarded by the public as a relic of the past and by many politicians as a leading politician, even a potential premier. The Duke, being unemployed, was a prolific correspondent, and was often able to draw out the finer tissues of Gladstone's thought, while at the same time he was probably in touch with, perhaps even acting in concert with, Goschen, Salisbury, and some other traditionalist Tories. Both Goschen (in September 1885), travelling incognito, and Salisbury, thought it worth their while to make the not very easy pilgrimage to Inverary to consult the 'Cross-bench Duke', but why they thought it worth while is not known. It was Salisbury and his friends, too, who chiefly floated the idea of an Argyll premiership in 1885–86, chiefly perhaps because, while serving to block a Hartington coalition, it highlighted Salisbury's merits. The details of his activities, however, are far from clear. Inverary Castle may well contain abundant material of high value for 1885–86, but though letters have been found in a suitcase and a number of boxes, these have not been properly sorted and are thought to be of little interest. The bulk of the Duke's papers probably lie untouched in a Castle attic, but since no archivist has so far been able to make a survey, it is impossible to make any firm statement on this point.

All one can say for sure about Argyll is what others said about him, although he played some part in forming Tory policy on crofters. While Whigs like Granville and Carlingford treated Argyll as a humorous figure quite without influence, some Tories set out to promote him as the leading moderate statesman. In February 1886, when Argyll was crippled with gout and could scarcely hold a pen, his name was advanced by Gerald Balfour and St John Brodrick as a premier under whom Hartington and Salisbury could take office. Salisbury on resigning told the Queen that Argyll, if available, would have been the best person for her to consult, and in July 1886 the Queen's mind strayed gently towards an Argyll premiership. Argyll, of all the contenders for power in 1885–86, is the most difficult to take seriously, yet, whatever the *arrière-pensée* of his backers, he was the only person apart from established party leaders to be considered a possible premier at this time.

Throughout 1885–86 the Irish law officers of both parties were, properly and necessarily, lawyers first, and politicians second: but in so ordering their position, they made no attempt to develop their unprecedented chance to act as spokesmen for their parties and for Irish opinion. On the Conservative side, the Irish attorney-general Hugh Holmes did emerge into high politics when and if Churchill wished him so to emerge: but he took no independent initiatives. His junior colleagues, John Monroe[196] and J. G. Gibson, who served in succession as Irish solicitors-general during Salisbury's caretaker ministry, did not intrude upon London politics. Monroe was a quiet man and thorough lawyer, a relative of Holmes by marriage, but hardly a politician at all: Gibson, who succeeded him in November 1885, was a Liverpool M.P. who, as Lord Ashbourne's brother, could not expect to be seen as an independent politician at that time, despite his own native sharpness.

On the Liberal side, their Irish administration afforded equally little in the way of political activity worth recording. Aberdeen was categorically and by intent a cypher. The lord chancellor, John Naish, was not a parliamentarian by background, like Ashbourne, but an administrator bred to the Dublin Castle machine, in which he had risen rung by rung from law adviser to lord chancellor during the 1880–85 administration. The shadowy picture of him that emerges is of an over-conscientious, overworked, over-anxious official without political inclinations, who through the accidents of the *cursus honorum* and of his position as a Catholic Liberal, found himself in a home rule administration, with which he had hardly any sympathy. When shown a draft of the home rule bill by Sir R. Hamilton, Naish said that if it passed, he could no longer live in Ireland.[197]

The Liberal solicitor-general for Ireland, The MacDermot, 'Prince of Coolavin', served in rather the same spirit, chiefly because of the personal admiration for Gladstone which eventually led him to come forward as a Liberal candidate in a hopeless

English seat in 1892. In 1886, however, he had no parliamentary ambitions, probably because he was too poor, having to support a large family entirely from his earnings at the bar. Only a home ruler in a very mild sense, he felt absolutely no sympathy with agitation designed to remove the landlord class from the country. In later life he seemed to relatives to have forgotten his experiences as a member of the 1886 administration: he certainly never mentioned them while reminiscing to the family circle. He left no journals, letters, or papers relating to his term of office.[198]

This deficiency also impairs our knowledge of a much more ambitious figure, Sir Charles Russell, later Lord Russell of Killowen, who was never an Irish law officer, but whose position in 1886 as attorney-general for England offered much the same scope because of his personal background. A Catholic Irishman, Russell had sat as a Liberal for Dundalk in the parliament of 1880–85, with explicit help from Parnell and Biggar at the time of his election, and enjoyed good relations with such Nationalists as R. Barry O'Brien, who later became his biographer. On the constituency of Dundalk being abolished, Russell secured a safe Liberal seat in Hackney. His address there in 1885, though sober in tone, showed him as a home ruler by strategy,* even if tactically he envisaged, and might have preferred, a slow and winding road to that end leading through local self-government. In early January 1886 he thought home rule could not be carried by a *coup de main*, but once in office spoke wholeheartedly in the debates. That he was ever present at a single significant political conversation during the 1886 ministry, let alone that he undertook more arcane tasks, such as framing the legal minutiae of the bills, or maintaining liaison with the Irish party, does not appear from the meagre evidence. Neither his biographer nor his present descendants have found any political papers, and there are no letters from Russell in the main Gladstone MSS relating to the Irish bill in 1886.

The one memorandum on Irish policy by Russell that has come to light, was simply a riposte (dated 17 March 1886) to a paper drafted by Bryce on 12 March 1886, which put the case for Ulster, the Ulster Liberals, and Ulster autonomy. Bryce had made two recent visits to the Liberals of Ulster, whom he 'had long known well' and whom he called 'the best element in the island', and he lent his countenance to a surprising degree to their more alarmist arguments about home rule meaning bloodshed and the suppres-

---

* Cf. Russell to Chamberlain, 25 Dec. 1885, Chamberlain MSS JC 8/6/3M/2, calling for an inter-party committee to consider 'what powers of self-government may be given to Ireland consistently with the supremacy of parliament'.

sion of the Ulster economy by the South.[199] Russell disliked Bryce's tone and substance, said some sharp things, as a Newry man might, about Protestant Liberals and their demands that Catholic co-operation be always given on their own terms, and concluded by opposing autonomy for Ulster, either as a whole or for its most Protestant areas. Russell's view was that religious prejudice, among Protestants could not be bought off, but that the Ulster farmers could at best be partly neutralised by a good land bill clearly tied to home rule. As to the Parnellites, Russell warned that the Irish, primarily concerned in any case with home rule, would 'require to see very clearly the gain to the Irish Authority' before taking on the job of collecting redemption payments for the English exchequer, especially as they expected that the Conservatives could deal adequately with the land question.[200]

Russell had his reasons for being, as it seems, on the outside of a situation which he was apparently born to be inside; the burden of the Dilke case, exhaustion and perhaps illness following the 1885 elections, and his labours at the bar which produced an income of £17,957 in 1886.[201] Russell, indeed, is perhaps the best of many examples of important secondary figures in the public eye who on closer scrutiny turn out to have no political significance at all.

Of Gladstone's Irish law officers in 1886, Naish and MacDermot were apolitical 'Castle Catholics', without seats in either house of parliament. Sir Charles Russell, a good Irish Catholic with useful Nationalist contacts, had a seat in parliament, spoke usefully in debate, but generally and in all good faith stuck to his legal last. Russell's junior, Horace Davey, the solicitor-general for England and Wales, had lost his seat at Bournemouth in the 1885 elections, and then was defeated at Ipswich in April 1886, and at Stockport in July 1886. Davey eventually returned to parliament only briefly, as member for Stockton in 1888–92, when he proceeded to destroy any hopes that had been formed of him as a parliamentarian. It was a matter of general surprise that one of the most successful barristers in England, who about this time was earning over £20,000 a year, could perform so poorly in the Commons. His speeches were merely those of the ordinary backbencher: a carefully prepared attack on coercion in 1888 was greeted with amused contempt by John Morley. In 1886 there was little criticism of Davey's appointment, given his legal distinction, but Gladstone was overheard confessing his disappointment with him, on what grounds was not clear. It is possible that he was not even a success technically as solicitor-general. Davey's failure in politics was often cited by contemporaries as a classic instance of the specialised character of the political world which prevented distinguished outsiders from succeeding in it.[202]

A solicitor-general must, if outside parliament, be outside politics, and this Davey was. Thus, of Gladstone's six Irish and English legal appointments, four (Davey, Walker, MacDermot, and Naish) were not in parliament: Russell, with the glamorous part of his legal career still to come, was a sound professional appointment and little more: Herschell was sometimes effective in cabinet discussion, but otherwise distinguished himself, as in his earlier career, by remaining outside party manoeuvres in a way that Ashbourne and Halsbury in the previous ministry had not. The one natural politician among Gladstone's lawyers was Samuel Walker, Q.C., the Irish attorney-general, and he neither represented a political force nor had a seat in parliament.

Walker had been returned unopposed for Londonderry county in 1884. He had seen Ulster Liberalism at its zenith, with the Liberals winning Antrim (on a pledge of coercion) in the summer of 1885: and its equally sudden collapse, as his protestant agrarian and Nationalist supporters refused to co-operate in the 1885 elections. His thoughts were of farms and fields and how these become votes. In 1886 he wanted a land bill, rather on Spencer's lines, but to save his kind of protestant Liberalism in Ulster rather than to succour the landlords. This led him indirectly to favour home rule, on the grounds that no English state authority could take over from the landlords under existing conditions without 'an agitation greater than any preceding one'. Ulster in one way, and the congested districts of the west in another, would not accept either a purely English, or a purely Nationalist, management of land purchase as fair. On the other hand, an Ireland of peasant owners, with the land question 'settled in all its aspects' under English auspices, and an agitation which had always been basically agrarian allayed, could and probably should then move towards autonomy, apparently chiefly, in Walker's mind, to enhance the credibility of the land settlement. Walker's memorandum to Spencer[203] on these lines, our only evidence for his wishes prior to the announcement of the Irish bills, confined itself to this partly logical, partly confused analysis based on knowledge of agricultural sentiment in rural Ulster. That Walker was not more worried about being wiped out by home rule, was no doubt related to the fact that he had already been wiped out in 1885 by the Tory-Irish alliance, and was in fact never to get back to parliament, though he stood again as a loyal Gladstonian in rural Ulster. Though it is interesting to know the lines on which Walker thought, consideration of his position is useful only because it directs attention to the helplessly peripheral situation of Ulster Liberalism, even at its ablest, when it came to forming policy.

The Gladstone ministry, in fact, got along and was happy to get along without informed private discussion of Ulster. It listened from habits of official prudence to those who wished to discourse on the subject – Walker, C.Russell, Bryce, and Dickson – but in order to engender silence rather than construct policy. Walker's opinions commanded more respect than attention: Bryce's long letters failed to stimulate ministerial interest in Ulster. A further neglected adviser, also of considerable ability, was T.A.Dickson,* the unofficial leader of grass roots Liberal opinion in Ulster, and formerly an impressive parliamentary exponent of agrarian radicalism. At the 1885 election, Dickson had urged Irish Liberals to avoid a simple Loyalist line, and he had sufficient standing for the 1886 ministry to encourage him to exert influence in Ulster. Nevertheless, he and Gladstone were not in correspondence in 1885–86, and his relative neglect bore out two main points – that the Gladstonians, with parliamentary not Irish needs uppermost, did not seek even sympathetic Irish advice (as Churchill had done) in order to construct an Irish policy: and that the only way in which Liberal ministers expected Ulster to become central, in debate or reality, was as a tactical embarrassment to Liberal Unionists who would find themselves tarred with the Orange brush. In the debates on the bill, the Ulster Tories did indeed take an unduly large part which must have gratified anyone wishing to unite moderate Liberal opinion (Gladstone's great introductory speech was followed by speeches from three Ulster Tories, for instance), and have removed any tactical desire on the part of Liberal strategists to 'do something' for Ulster.

In their wish not to have to think about Ulster, the Liberal and Conservative front benches were in cordial agreement. So far as the small number of surviving collections of papers of Ulster politicians in the Public Record Office of Northern Ireland is concerned, there is no trace of contact between them and English Tory leaders in 1886, even where, as in the case of Lord Crichton and Northcote, such contact had previously existed. Had the English leaders been seriously concerned to promote a crisis in Ulster in 1886 (a matter on which their own papers are entirely silent), they had a convenient agent to hand in Lord Arthur Hill, M.P. for a Down seat, who as a chief Orangeman in Ulster was both

---

* M.P. (Lib.) Dungannon 1874–80, Tyrone 1881–85: M.P. (Nat.) Dublin St Stephen's Green 1888–92: P.C. (I.) 1893: fought three unsuccessful elections, 1885–86. There is no memoir, but Dickson published *An Irish Policy for a Liberal Government* (London, Committee on Irish Affairs, 1885, 37 pp.)

respectable and had access to firebrands like William Johnston of Ballykilbeg. In fact the diary of the latter shows fairly conclusively that there were no Tory interventions from England in Ulster politics in 1886, with the single exception of Churchill's lightning visit to Belfast on 22 February, when he was the guest of Johnston. It is, however, clear from his papers that Churchill did not see his visit as requiring him to keep up sustained political contact with 'those abominable Ulster Tories who are playing the devil in the North of Ireland.'[204]

Churchill's aspersions were not untypical. Tory leaders usually refer to Ulster Tories only to disparage them. Thus Salisbury himself wrote 'I am afraid I am not competent to quell the Irish Orangemen... Their loyalty to the party is not a very fierce passion just now: and if I tried to interfere, I should be told to mind my own business. They are troublesome and unreliable allies. I remember the last letter I ever had from Beaconsfield he denounced them for having sold the pass about the Irish land legislation.'[205]

Despite the great change in party alignments between November 1885 and 1886, the Ulster Tories were, even in the new circumstances, left to fend for themselves. Their frequent conferences* in London during the 1886 session were never graced by the presence of a party leader. Their rabid speeches brought them ridicule in the English press, and made English Tories see them as a cross the party had to bear.

It is still not clear how many Ulstermen, if any, were prepared to resort to violence if necessary in 1886. What is clear is that a committee of the Orange Order was set up on 28 April to coordinate resistance (liberally interpreted), that Johnston was a member of it, and that it held at least two meetings (11 and 17 May) in the Carlton Club in London. The committee disbanded on 11 June, having decided 'to stop drilling for the present.'[206] There is no suggestion that leading English Tories in any way sanctioned this enterprise. For them, as for the Liberals, the Irish question was not one into which practical Irish considerations entered in any detail.

'To lose one parent may be regarded as a misfortune: to lose both looks like carelessness.' The lack of interesting political papers left by the lesser gods of politics is too widespread to be either misfortune or carelessness. There are no interesting papers, except at the top, because there was nothing of much interest, except at the top, to put on paper. It is not just the truism that junior minis-

---

* In the first two months of 1886, the Ulster M.Ps six times assembled to hold what Johnston called 'meetings of our party' (Johnston's diary, 1886, passim, PRONI D880/2/38).

ters are the helots of politics: it is that the amount of authentic information, and accurate perception of motive, reaching the lower depths of the parliamentary ocean, is little better than complete darkness.

It is easy for the mind to grasp the idea of a structure of politics, without questioning the implications and the conventional wisdom enshrined in the phrase. It seems (but is not) obvious that the political arrangements of a society exist in ascending tiers which connect the greatest in the land to the least. If this assumption (for it is no more) about mutual interaction through a great chain of being is taken as the basis of political society, then academic explanation becomes easy. For, on this view, what can be formally described, constitutes a real system of relationships. Against this approach, historical investigation of the structure of politics suggests that, at least in a parliamentary system where high politics is an arcane and esoteric craft whose meaning is not even intelligible to many members of the cabinet, the idea of a 'structure' is an unhelpful metaphor drawn from Meccano and fluid dynamics. It is also untrue, in that it implies that different areas of political activity are united by sharing in a common system of information and mutual response, rather than separated by concealment, dissimulation, and mutual inattention. The presentation of political practice as aspects of a connected wholeness is a dogma to be questioned.

Where mutual response most gravely lapsed, was in the case of the junior ministers, whose failure to form a link in the chain between the public and the party leaders gave the latter much of their sense of insulation. True, party leaders had their own abstract views of what society was like and what people wanted, but these conceptions were formed, on a very small factual basis, by interpreting what they read in the newspapers in the light of the opportunities they saw in high politics. All eyes looked to the front benches, and accepted what they saw there as evidence as to the state of public opinion.

161

7

Conclusion

Englishmen want their history to be agreeable. By this they mean that problems should have solutions and that liberals should be in power. If these conditions do not obtain, they wish to know why. They wish to pin the source of the fault in order to establish that, at any rate, a liberal solution was in sight if not achieved. In the case of 1885–86, the English mind particularly would like to be reassured that the Irish question could have been disposed of for good on Gladstonian lines, and that the split in the Liberal party need not have taken place. All would have been well, that is to say, but for the actions of a small number of selfishly motivated men, quite unrepresentative of the mainstream in English politics, whose divisive actions need only be indignantly repudiated. In all of this, the English mind is unprepared to admit that the working of the Irish question in English politics was quite extraordinarily difficult. All the major politicians involved, however, did understand that the Irish problem had two right solutions, home rule and repression, both highly unattractive in themselves and in terms of British domestic politics.

There are strong reasons for thinking a solution was almost impossible in 1886. The difficulty did not lie mainly with Ulster, recalcitrant though it was. Ulster failed to make any impact on events in 1886, not for lack of grass-roots Carsonism, but because it had no Carson. British politicians did not think about Ulster, and even if they had there was no means of estimating the potential seriousness of protestant revolt. The difficulty about a settlement lay in the mechanics of passing the measure. It was not a case where

winning back a few dissidents would have made much of a difference. Even if the bill had passed the second reading, it would have
stood in greater peril in committee, and even if it had emerged from
the Commons, it would never have passed the Lords unless the
Tories had felt unable to face an election. By the time the bill had
reached a stage where it could have been defeated, however, the
Tories were rightly sanguine about their election prospects. Even
had the Liberals won an election on the home rule issue, they
would only have been in the far from comfortable position of
Asquith after the election of January 1910, and with a less demagogic cry to maintain them. On a purely tactical view of the situation, then, 1886 was, and had to be, a trial run whose genuinely
Irish purpose, lay at most in forging a link of expediency between
Gladstone and the Parnellites. The latter viewed the situation in
1886 as provisional anyway: interesting while it lasted, but bound
to be replaced by some further situation in which new and unpredictable roles would emerge.

Experienced politicians only expected a successful Irish policy
to emerge when all other alternatives had been tried and been seen
to have failed. In this sense, Gladstone's attempt was a non-starter,
for it did not follow as a violent reaction against a period of unsuccessful repression. Again, until coercion had been eliminated,
it was not possible to execute the sequence found often in nine-
teenth-century politics, where the Liberals have their try and fail,
and are succeeded by a government ostensibly to their right. This
incoming ministry then would produce a bill on similar but
stronger lines, and thereby create a sense of inevitability which
settled the question. The only opportunity for this covert biparti-
sanship in 1886 lay in the chance of Hartington forming a centre
government, verbally uncommitted to, or committed against, both
home rule and coercion, in May 1886. Coming in with a free hand,
conditional Irish support, and a reactionary aura, such a ministry
could then have had the authority to give parliament its marching
orders as the Duke of Wellington had once done. Once Hartington
had actually entered power, it would have been convincingly
represented that he was the only man capable of being prime
minister. As Gladstone's conduct when forming his 1886 ministry
showed, no one could hope to pass a home rule measure unless
they could depict their ministry as representing the silent majority
of the country and its conventional prudence. Gladstone's sudden
decision to revert to radical rhetoric after the Easter recess showed
his immediate object by then was control of the party, and not a
marathon constitutional contest. This lack of unqualified intention
to do something about Ireland was a major reason why an Irish

settlement was not possible. Even the Parnellites remained luke-warm about the bill, certainly not campaigning for it with the passion that might have been expected for a substantive historical crisis. Irish politicians, of course, were not asked to discuss any but the most necessary points of business in 1886, for conversation with them was so far from respectable that if it became public, the government could have been broken. The unreality of Gladstone's Irish crusade of 1886 was increased because Irish politicians could compare his endeavours with those of Churchill, who kept his bargaining closely tied to what the realities of party considerations would allow him to deliver. What was really in the Parnellites' minds was best shown by their decision to break Carnarvon and leave Churchill unharmed, at the critical last moment before the vote on the second reading. Most convincingly, no trace exists of anyone troubling their minds over contingency plans for the new Irish state.

It is naive to think that the Liberals were bound to split because they were always quarrelling. Commentators who themselves lead the lives of church mice, note and are shocked by cabinet dissensions and tend to magnify the normal hurly-burly of poli-tics as the end of the world. In fact, quarrelling was one of the party's greatest strengths, and the Tories' refusal to argue with each other led to an unenviable torpor. The question is whether the quarrel in 1886 was somehow different from previous quarrels.

In fact it was not, because all Liberal leaders except Goschen hoped the outcome would be a united Liberal party covering all shades of opinion. Goschen wanted the Liberals to be a reactionary sect, and Labouchere wanted a doctrinal radical party. But few wished to join these prophets in their caves. The rest of the Liberal leaders wanted their party to represent, not something called Liberalism, but average British opinion as they imagined it to be. In order to gain control of such a party, they were willing to fight hard, and they put personal supremacy before party unity. What happened in 1886 shows not that disagreement over policies is a dangerous thing, but that parallel ambitions among highly talented men are much less negotiable than policy disagreements. Deter-mined in their several ways to capitalise on Tory weakness as shown in the 1885–86 ministry, traditional competition between the Liberal leaders to find a winning anti-Tory formula ended in eclipse for a generation.

This exposition should not be taken to mean that politicians are disagreeable men behaving in a disagreeable way, and that things would be much better if they were to behave according to standards professed in other walks of life. In the first place, close investigation shows that politicians maintained standards of their own which were quite high. Despite some lapses (did Hartington's mistress really play the Stock Exchange with cabinet secrets?), personal and political scandal appears rare. To some extent this reflects pure ignorance of Victorian life for which the relevant documents are still unavailable, and in ten years' time when certain Pandora's boxes of dark secrets expressly designed to shock have been opened, the picture will certainly be rather different. The Pandora's boxes, however, will at most demonstrate that politicians who at present appear without a human side, were in fact normal flesh and blood. At present, for instance, Churchill looks like a reprobate in a gallery of plaster saints. This impression will probably not survive, but the effect on politics will probably be negligible. Historically it is probably perfectly satisfactory to deal with the political world of 1885–86 as one now does, as it if were largely without stain, despite strong oral tradition among certain aristocratic families to the contrary. It is not politically interesting to know that Churchill spent the Easter recess in 1886 with his Parisian mistress, when all politicians treated that recess as a holiday anyway. What is missing from the story is colour and the human touch and no more.

Many of the most active politicians were on the most intimate terms, regardless of party, a fact which the public never suspected and would have found it hard to accept. There are two problems here. One is how far party conflict is a collusive, even conspiratorial activity arranged over dinner. The other is how far it was a life chosen by those who, whether married or not, whether homosexual or not, wished to live a bachelor life for part of the year as men without women. Most leading politicians were hardly uxorious. Wedded to their profession and its peculiar hours and West End locale, politicians whose mind was on their career were strongly pressed to forego a normal family life. Churchill's semi-separation from his wife in 1885–86 was not particularly unusual. The political career was for those drawn to it an affirmation of the insufficiency of hearth and home as a source of interest and stimulus. The male cohesion of politics was not, however, linked to, but rather apart from those young men of all ages who sought a continuation of public school life by other means. We have found only a solitary billet-doux addressed to a young secretary of state by a ministerial colleague. Whatever the ancillary attractions of political friendship, the point to be understood is that the camaraderie of London political life was not a conspiracy to delude the public, but a device to prevent excessive competition and ruthlessness among practitioners of an amateur sport. The exception here was the series of meetings *à deux* throughout 1885–86 between Churchill and Chamberlain, about which everything has been hidden except the bare fact of their existence. Their probable object was to promote a joint strategy which would enable two politicians not publicly associated to control English politics in an iron grip. The success with which the reform issue had been' fixed' in autumn 1884, led ambitious men in 1885–86 to look around for a degree of control over events which was quite unrealistic.

In a situation like 1885–86, one would expect to find plenty of secret meetings, and one does. How far these are the most important of their kind, or merely the tip of the iceberg, cannot be satisfactorily established. For instance, Hartington's meetings with Gladstone in January 1886 can be traced very exactly, whereas his meetings with Salisbury escaped observation or documentary record. Chance survivals of evidence bring to light areas of political discussion whose existence could not have been inferred from events. Rosebery's journal presents walks round the racecourse as a focus for the government of England. Again, the well-informed radical journalist, T. H. S. Escott, in his *Society in the Country House* (1907) reported an alleged meeting between Churchill and Hartington at Eastbourne in spring 1886, and also a rapprochement between the two men at a Rothschild house-party in December 1885, in both cases at times when their correspondence showed no trace of contact, and when none was suspected by the informed political public. Our exceptional knowledge of Gladstone's movements and occupations leads us to forget how little evidence there is on which to build an itinerary for the other leading politicians of the day. It is for this reason that we have recorded below even those meetings of which nothing useful can be said except that they happened.

The real problem is not that some of politics was conducted behind closed doors. It is that political activity, whether reported in *The Times* and *Hansard* or not, did not mean what those untrained to the exercise of power thought it meant. This is the crucial area where deception, if it is deception, takes place: in full light of day. The fault lay, in the first place, not with politicians, but with the series of concentric and differing audiences whom they considered themselves to be addressing. These audiences irremediably lacked two capacities needed to appreciate politics. The first was an inability to accept or even allow for the calculations about personal competition which shaped political action: the second was the lack of a sense of the inadvertence with which situations arise, cease, and unforeseeably develop into new situations. These mental disabilities were compounded by the fact that they existed in different forms at different levels of society. Politicians were under no temptation to explain things sensibly.

By the 1880s the British public imposed on its politicians standards of moral judgement which, if accepted, would have prevented them doing their job at all. It expected them to be more unselfish than the public. This religious demand by a secular society in fact enforced deception on the politicians, who felt obliged to talk about everything in moral tones, except that acquisition of power by which alone the perfectly reputable objects most of them wanted power for could be realised. Even today, people are reluctant to recognise that the maintenance of a party in being is a worthwhile task in itself unlinked to any higher end, though no higher end is likely to prosper without it.

If politicians had attempted to explain their own working assumptions about party structure and about government, they would have had to bridge a gap created not only by unfamiliarity but by a destructive public revulsion against the seeking of power itself. The resulting enforced evasion and deception, though it made any but formal democracy impossible, was mitigated by being traditional and far from deliberate. It had been going on for as long as anybody remembered, and certainly had preceded even formal democracy. It was not a new invention of the 1880s for politicians to present incidentals of personality and political atmosphere as the reality of public life, and to keep quiet about power and government. One thinks of Canning. Evasion and concealment were traditional and not a response to the working classes, and indeed a glance at the papers of ordinary members of the Upper Ten Thousand shows that political awareness hardly rose in proportion to income. Concealment is the totalitarianism of a non-coercive society.

What really went on in 1886 behind the forays into public relations no one will ever know (or knew at the time for certain). The best that can be achieved, is that people should think of the episode as a testing-ground for several competing, or even radically opposed, versions of the meaning of the same events. After the most thorough investigation in known history, that of the Warren Commission into the death of President Kennedy, equally weighty cases could be made for and against the orthodox identification of the assassin. We cannot therefore hope to narrow the range of alternatives in 1886, but should be willing to admit that evidence is unlikely to contradict any side in a continuing debate. Since what is believed about the roles of people like Gladstone, Churchill,

Salisbury, and Parnell in 1886 will be determined by prejudice as much as by anything else, the assembly of much of the relevant evidence in the following chronicle without seeking to relate it directly to our conclusions and prejudices, may be of help to all parties.

Book Two:
Diary

Part One

Government by Dispute : The Breakup of the Liberal Ministry, January–June 1885

'We are none of us very deadly weapons, we live on sham fights' (Spencer to Harcourt, 17 May 1885, Spencer MSS).

'As to all the later history of this ministry ... it has been a wild romance of politics with a continual succession of hairbreadth escapes and strange accidents pressing upon one another' (Gladstone to his wife, 1 May 1885, Glynne-Gladstone MSS).

Dates of Cabinet Meetings, January–June 1885

January
2 Friday
3 Saturday
7 Wednesday
20 Tuesday
21 Wednesday

February
6 Friday
7 Saturday
9 Monday
11 Wednesday
16 Monday
17 Tuesday
20 Friday
28 Saturday

March
7 Saturday
12 Thursday
13 Friday
20 Friday
24 Tuesday
27 Friday

April
4 Saturday
9 Thursday
11 Saturday
13 Monday
14 Tuesday
15 Wednesday
20 Monday

April
21 Tuesday
25 Saturday
28 Tuesday

May
2 Saturday
7 Thursday
9 Saturday
15 Friday
16 Saturday

June
5 Friday
8 Monday
9 Tuesday

The Liberal Cabinet in 1885

Prime Minister	W. E. Gladstone
Lord President of the Council	Lord Carlingford*
Lord Chancellor	Earl of Selborne
Foreign Secretary	Earl Granville
Home Secretary	Sir W. V. Harcourt
Colonial Secretary	Earl of Derby
Secretary of State for India	Earl of Kimberley
Secretary of State for War	Marquess of Hartington
First Lord of the Admiralty	Earl of Northbrook
Chancellor of the Exchequer	H. C. E. Childers
Lord Lieutenant of Ireland	Earl Spencer
President of the Board of Trade	J. Chamberlain
President of the Local Government Board	Sir C. W. Dilke
Chancellor of the Duchy of Lancaster	G. O. Trevelyan
First Commissioner of Works ⎱ Lord Privy Seal ⎰	Earl of Rosebery†
Postmaster-General	G. J. Shaw-Lefevre‡

* Also Lord Privy Seal until Feb. 1885.

† Appointment and admission to the cabinet announced 12 Feb 1885.

‡ Lefevre's admission to the cabinet was announced 12 Feb. 1885. It involved no change of office.

Diary

January 1 (Thursday). Gladstone told his private secretary, Edward Hamilton, that he considered France had behaved 'vilely' in the matter of the Egyptian financial negotiations, and that he was for putting all possible pressure on France to hasten a settlement. 'The mischief has been that France knew Lord Northbrook's proposals: and her knowledge of them must be due to himself. They leaked out through the Rothschilds and Blum to whom it appears Lord N. confided everything. ... Mr G does not often make use of strong language – but I fear he did not characterise Lord N.'s conduct of the business too strongly when he said "He (Lord N.) has 'bitched' the whole concern from beginning to end".'[1]

Northbrook in turn was deeply dissatisfied with Gladstone and the state of Egyptian affairs, and was considering resignation.[2]

January 2 (Friday). The cabinet met from 4 to 7 at Downing St, with Spencer and Dilke absent, the latter being in Paris on his way back from Antibes. The meeting was called primarily to discuss the French delay in dealing with the British proposals on Egyptian finance made a month earlier, and the intimated intention of the French government to submit counter-proposals about 15 January. Gloomy letters were read from Lyons and Malet, the ambassadors in Paris and Berlin, the latter suggesting there was a danger that a combination of powers, led by Bismarck, might force Britain out of Egypt. Selborne asked whether the fleet was ready.

Gladstone, looking unwell and weak, referred first to his insomnia and his misgivings as to what his doctor might order,[3] and then directed the discussion fairly firmly. He produced a memorandum, stiff in tone, insisting that if France did not open negotiations upon the British proposals soon, Britain would go its own way. On being asked what this threatened new departure would be, Gladstone said that it was not the time to go into a question certain to divide the cabinet. It seemed, however, as if his course would be to solve the difficulties by 'scuttling', for several ministers including Carlingford made it clear they could not accept the abandonment of Egypt. Gladstone's memorandum included concessions which Lord Lyons could offer the French, but these did not include payment of the interest on the Egyptian debt without reduction. When pressed, Gladstone was adamant for reduction of the interest.

The discussion was long and hopeless, with Northbrook objecting frequently, and Gladstone remarking that in the whole of his career he had never known so difficult a business. Nevertheless, it was Gladstone's memorandum on which it was agreed that despatches should be based.

The cabinet agreed not to acquiesce in the French handling of the situation, and instructed Lord Lyons to impress upon France the necessity of basing negotiations upon the British proposals, while in effect leaving France free to put forward whatever case it wished. This decision appeared in private correspondence with variations of emphasis. To Chamberlain, the decision was 'to send a pious but courteous letter to France requiring immediate consideration of our proposals failing which we shall "take our own course" '.[4] To Hamilton, 'no two ministers could agree what to do: and, in the absence of agreement, Mr G's proposal for "hurrying up" France was accepted in principle'.[5]

The cabinet also agreed to Granville's views respecting the representation of Russia and Germany upon the Egyptian Caisse de la Dette.[6]

There may have been some abortive discussion of New Guinea and Zululand, though the sources do not distinguish satisfactorily between this meeting and that of the following day. Gladstone and Trevelyan spoke, whether at this time or on the next day, against taking the Zulu coast, while Chamberlain supported the annexation of Pondoland.[7]

During the cabinet a telegram arrived from Baring giving Wolseley's opinion on the question of undertaking a campaign from Suakin, on the Red Sea coast of the Sudan, with a view to drawing off some of the Mahdist forces from the Nile front. It was decided that the Suakin operation should not be undertaken for the present.[8]

The cabinet also decided to send instructions to Wolseley that a repulse of an insufficient force attempting to march on Khartoum would be an even greater disaster than the fall of Khartoum, and should not be risked.[9]

After the cabinet, Gladstone again went to see his doctor,[10] who must have persuaded him to get away from London, for that evening, while dining at the Reays, Gladstone had said half to himself 'Rest will not come to me, but I shall go to it.'[11] Gladstone was not only ill, but was also worried about his illness. The doctor had on 1 January given him 'a composing draught which all but made me sick, and which he said I was only to take in case of need, but I took without waiting to see. I did very well. Whether it was the bad night before, the draught, a walk home of half an hour, or a passage in the Psalms, or all combined, or whatever else; I slept from say $11\frac{1}{4}$ to $1\frac{3}{4}$: then lay awake, and partly read until 4, when

I had a grand sleep till 8.34. Clark however is preaching rest and I know not what it will come to. Cannes is already (in a degree) in the air.

I am meantime surviving the best I can with all my arms and legs in the business of the day (which I shorten by not getting up till 11).' Gladstone had other troubles. 'You did not I think give me any pills. A certain department seems rather to require them. In some way I am rheumatic today.'[12] Gladstone was indeed forcing on his colleagues the consideration of his premature and imminent retirement on grounds of health, by showing no inclination to minimise or conceal his infirmity.

January 3 (Saturday). Rosebery called at Downing St in the morning and talked very briefly with Gladstone, who struck him as 'weary and unhinged',[13] 'weak and languid and quite unlike himself'.[14] Rosebery learnt that if Hawarden should not suffice to mend Gladstone's health, then he would go on to Cannes.[15] In the event, Gladstone found the country air of Hawarden a sufficient tonic (3–20 January) for him to go on without a further break before June.

The cabinet met at Downing St from 12 till 5, with Spencer and Dilke absent, the latter on his way back from France. Gladstone had to leave at 2.15 for Euston, to catch the 2.45 to Hawarden where he was to rest on doctor's orders. Derby left shortly afterwards, and then Granville went too. Trevelyan left at 3.30, and Chamberlain at 4.0. Soon after, Selborne got up and said he must go away as he had people staying in the country, but Harcourt refused to let him leave.[16] Harcourt, Northbrook, Carlingford, Selborne, and perhaps others, remained till the end, Carlingford just catching the 5 o'clock train from Paddington.

The cabinet had to consider the Egyptian finance, German annexations in New Guinea, and British expansion in south east Africa. It was almost certainly on the Egyptian issue that Chamberlain wrote 'after Mr G left, it was evident that not a single member agreed with him ... we continue to drift',[17] and there are no signs that any real progress was made towards a definition of policy, though certain despatches to France were agreed.

The Egyptian despatches would probably have played a small part in a cabinet called chiefly to deal with Derby's colonial problems, had Northbrook not raised objections to some of the concessions to France proposed by Gladstone the previous day. Northbrook especially found fault with the idea of a joint guarantee of a new loan. To Northbrook, this led straight back to the odious system of dual or multiple control: to Gladstone, it had no such meaning. The antagonism between the two men was evident. After

Gladstone left for Hawarden, the cabinet spent another two hours going over the drafts of the despatches to Lyons. Gladstone's original draft was greatly toned down, Carlingford even suspecting that it had been meant to bring the whole of Egyptian policy to a head.[18]

The cabinet agreed to send a despatch taking exception to German annexations in New Guinea, and inviting the Germans to offer an explanation of their conduct, more because it was in breach of assurances given by Germany on 15 December 1884 that no such action would be taken without consultation, than because of what they considered exaggerated colonial feeling, or because of any intrinsic objection to the annexations themselves. The colonies were to be informed that Britain was in no way a party to the German action.

The cabinet also decided to annex the littoral between Cape Colony and Natal ('from the Cape continuously up to St Lucia bay'[19]), where the hinterland was in practice already under British control.[20] Gladstone protested against the principle of opposing the settlement of other powers in areas not in our possession, and applied this principle to the Zulu coast. Derby, Kimberley, Carlingford, and other protested against the coast being left open to the Germans. The question was left open.*

---

* C.J. The question of British expansion in this area was first raised by Derby, following Liberal backbench agitation, in a letter to Granville of 25 Dec. 1884. Derby definitely wanted expansion: 'Would it not be well for us at once to secure the coast of Zululand, and perhaps also that which lies on the south, between the Cape Colony and Natal? ... the coastline is not ours, and a German settlement anywhere upon it would be a nuisance if not a danger. I am inclined to assume the protectorate of the coast. We virtually exercise it already. Tell me if you agree, and would you consult the premier?' Granville's reply gave little encouragement, so Derby wrote further letters to Gladstone (26 Dec.) and to Granville (28 Dec.), agreeing with the latter that 'there is something absurd in the scramble for colonies, and I am as little disposed to join in it as you can be: but there is a difference between wanting new acquisitions and keeping what we have. As to not being jealous of the Germans, surely their practice in both Africa and New Guinea has been very sharp?' Gladstone had fewer misgivings than Granville and thought Derby 'right in wishing to have a continuous line of coast in South Africa: but as to extending the terminus northwards, and (I presume) assuming the responsibility for Zululand outside the region which we have steadily disclaimed, I see great objection to it; and generally, considering what we have got, I am against entering into a scramble for the remainder.' Also at some time in Dec. 1884, a specific proposal to annex St Lucia Bay was circulated to the cabinet, receiving favourable minutes from all ministers save Gladstone (see below, Feb. 9, n.). In cabinet discussions on 3 and 7 Jan., annexation northward was turned down principally because of Gladstone's hostility, and this remained the position despite quite serious support for Derby's views. Kimberley, who wished to annex right up to the Portuguese border, wrote 'the presence of the Germans anywhere on that coast could hardly fail to bring

Finally Hartington raised the question of sending a force to Suakin to engage Osman Digna and so relieve the pressure on Wolseley.[21]

January 7 (Wednesday). The cabinet met at Downing St from about 1 till 4, Spencer and Gladstone being absent, the latter under doctor's orders. The cabinet had been called by Hartington, 'to decide whether a force should be sent to Suakin, which Wolseley recommends, not very positively, and Baring presses for.'[22]

The question of opening a second front at Suakin (where there was only an inactive British garrison) had been raised originally by Baring in Cairo. On 1 January he had telegraphed a proposal to Wolseley, who replied (2 January) that operations at Suakin could not be in time to help his advance on Khartoum, but 'that it would do much towards the final settlement of the country'. Baring then communicated Wolseley's opinion to Granville (2 January), who brought it at once before the cabinet, then sitting. The cabinet, not surprisingly, either pigeonholed or rejected what was essentially Baring's proposal for a fresh land war: it was to Baring that Granville sent the telegram embodying the decision of the cabinet against taking action.

When the matter came before the cabinet again, it was because of a much less ambitious proposal which was entirely of Wolseley's concoction. Wolseley requested (6 January, tel.) that 'all available men of war should be sent to Suakin. Men should be landed frequently and exercise with guns outside the works as much as possible. Admiral alone to be in the secret. Everyone else to believe that an attack upon Osman Digna is contemplated.' It was hoped 'news, when it reaches Khartoum, might help us'.[23] This reopened the whole question. Gladstone, while dismissing Wolseley's arguments as 'unsatisfactory', told Hartington (6 January) that he was not prepared to turn down anything Wolseley 'on his own responsibility' felt 'requisite for the ... success of his own expedition'.[24] Accordingly, the issue was brought before the cabinet again (7 January), Gladstone however having taken covering action by

serious trouble', and Chamberlain wanted to see British retaliation against German action in New Guinea. Dilke was also dissatisfied with British inaction, writing to Derby on 25 Feb. 1885 for an explanation of the delay. Derby explained (26 Feb.) that he had consulted the cabinet twice without obtaining any decision from it: 'In face of the German protest against our claim to St Lucia Bay it seems scarcely possible [to annex the Zulu coast], unless we wish to provoke a *fresh annexation* in the same district. But I agree that it is a question that ought to come before the cabinet again when we are out of our immediate parliamentary difficulties.' The question again came up in cabinet on 7 Mar. See Derby MSS 920 DER/21: Ramm, ii 304: memoranda by Kimberley and Chamberlain of 28 and 30 Dec. 1884, Derby MSS, unsorted: Dilke-Derby letters, in packet marked 'W.E.Gladstone', Derby MSS 920 DER/20.

sending Granville for cabinet use a copy of his letter to Hartington, with the clear intention of opposing any new expedition.

Discussion in cabinet did not really settle anything. There was probably no sympathy for Wolseley's naval proposal, but on the other hand the cabinet was clearly willing to revise its decision of 2 January if so advised, so far as land forces went. It was therefore left that Hartington and Wolseley should sort out between themselves what was to be done. It was certainly considered probable that an expedition of sorts would be launched: 'troops enough will be sent, at all events, to keep Osman Digna employed, and prevent him from interfering with Wolseley's operations on the Nile'.[25] Following the cabinet, Hartington was to have a free hand, but it was understood as a free hand to take positive action.

Even such a qualified decision constituted a defeat for Gladstone and for Childers. Childers' difficulties were on a different level. 'Stung by some recent reflections on himself by Mr G, [he] tried to induce the cabinet to take into consideration among other things the question of expense connected with the Suakin proposal: but he got no support from anyone but Trevelyan' and got 'flung into his face remarks about making the Soudan expedition "cheap and nasty" '.*

However, nothing at all came of the general agreement of Wolseley, Hartington, Baring, and most of the cabinet, that something, even if not very much, should be done. After the cabinet, Hartington sent a long telegram to Wolseley[26] offering to send two infantry battalions, a cavalry regiment, and an artillery battery as reinforcements to Suakin, where they would act as a demonstration without actually being used to fight a campaign. No mention was made of a naval demonstration. (Hartington must have been fairly clear that this offer was precisely what Wolseley did not want: what is uncertain is whether Hartington's highly specific offer bore any recognisable relation to the apparently simple wish of the cabinet the previous day to help Wolseley at Suakin. Hartington's own real wishes are also entirely obscure). Wolseley naturally replied (8 January) rejecting Hartington's proposals as 'an expensive luxury' and privately bemoaned the navy's unwillingness to cooperate.[27] Wolseley's real fear, however, was that any land force sent to Suakin would be used as the thin edge of the wedge by those in the War Office who wished to relieve Khartoum by an expedi-

---

* E. H. J. That Childers was indeed moved by a desire to win back Gladstone's regard by being a tight-fisted chancellor, is shown by Childers' subsequent letter to Gladstone, preening himself on not having 'let the question of charge drop out of view', and in return receiving warm thanks from Hawarden (Gladstone to Childers, 9 Jan., 44547 f. 161).

tion across the desert from the Red Sea – a project he loathed equally because it was bound to fail, and, worse, because if it did succeed, it would turn his efforts on the Nile into a sideshow. These were the considerations which had led him to ask for naval forces only: there was method in his madness.

Hartington, however, who had reported to the Queen (7 January) a cabinet decision to send a force to Suakin at once on receipt of Wolseley's approval,[28] was probably unprepared for Wolseley's flat rejection of 8 January, however well it may have suited him. He did not at any rate take the matter further. On 9 January he wrote to Gladstone, presuming that 'under these circumstances you and the cabinet will not be disposed to allow any expedition to be sent to Suakin'.[29] The subject was thereafter laid to rest (without the demise of the plan even being reported to the cabinet) and did not reappear in cabinet in the period 7 January–9 February. Gladstone replied to Hartington (10 January), saying he was 'greatly relieved' to know that Wolseley had backed down. The final criticism of Wolseley's predilection for naval action came when Hartington pointed out (15 January) that ships had already been at Suakin for months without apparent effect.[30]

The next point was Egyptian finance. Ferry's refusal to consider the British proposals on Egyptian finance was announced, as was his promise to present counter-proposals shortly.* The cabinet discussed what could be done in the event of these counter-proposals proving unacceptable. Gladstone's suggestion, made by letter, was that Egyptian finance should be left to the Egyptian government, and that Britain should declare that its occupation of Egypt was purely provisional. Gladstone had made no show of objection to the way that the cabinet, in his absence, had at their previous meeting on 4 January seriously altered his proposed despatches before they were sent.

In what was quite a new departure for him, Harcourt changed his tune to a policy whose epitome was 'Pay and stay': he broached a scheme by which Britain was to make good the deficiency caused by a reduction in the rate of interest paid on the Egyptian debt. Carlingford supported Harcourt, a rare event, in urging that Britain was bound to pay to make Egypt viable, and that this applied as much to debts as to defence.[31]

Chamberlain and Dilke opposed Harcourt's plan, Chamberlain putting forward his alternative plan of "scuttle without paying" at some length. What Chamberlain wanted was 'immediate bankruptcy, communication to the powers of our fixed intention to

---

* They were presented by M. Waddington on 17 Jan., though expected 'on or before the 15th' (C.J., 7 Jan.).

leave, declaration that we would not allow intervention by other powers in our place, and conference to settle details of neutralisation.'[32] One minister was left with the impression that Chamberlain wanted 'to announce that we would leave it at the earliest possible moment'.[33] In advance of the promised French counter-proposals, these discussions were of course purely academic, and no decisions could be taken.

Dilke, just back from the south of France, raised the question of unfriendly German activity in various distant parts. The previous night a telegram had arrived from the Governor of New Zealand giving details of the German annexation of Samoa. The cabinet were prepared to see Samoa go to Germany, with England taking Tonga. The next subject was Zanzibar, where it was agreed that Granville should warn Bismarck that Britain would not brook any interference there. Then Derby urged a declaration of British sovereignty over the Pondo coast of Zululand as far as the Portuguese frontier, but on account of Gladstone's doctrines on this subject in the cabinet of 3 January his proposal was not passed. According to Dilke, however, Gladstone alone had opposed annexation.[34]

Granville had arranged to catch the 4.30 from Waterloo for Osborne but missed the train.

January 17 (*Saturday*). On Waddington presenting officially the long-awaited French proposals on Egyptian finance, Hamilton foresaw, correctly, that there would be great difficulty in preventing a breakup of the cabinet on this question.

Hartington took the unusual step of sending for Goschen to consult him as to what alternative scheme could be offered in cabinet to the French proposals: but he found that by this stage Goschen had little to recommend.[35] When Hartington went to the cabinets of 20 and 21 January, therefore, it was in the knowledge that expert opinion sympathetic to him had no real policy to advance in place of the Gladstonian one of working along the lines of the French proposals.

January 20 (*Tuesday*). The cabinet met at 3, Gladstone arriving straight from Hawarden, and sat for over four hours. Spencer was absent in Ireland and Chamberlain was away with an abscessed jaw. Granville was very shaken and upset following the death of his younger sister, Lady Georgiana Fullerton, the previous day. The meeting was held to consider the French counter-proposals on Egyptian finance presented officially by Waddington on 17 January, though there was first some talk about New Guinea which was held over till the following day, and also a discussion as to whether a protectorate in Africa entailed undertaking to secure some government in the area. One minister noted that the meeting began with a discourse from Childers 'on the doctrine laid down at the Berlin Conference on the subject of protectorates'.*

Gladstone's report to the Queen,[36] correct as far as it went, that the cabinet were happy to find no suggestion in the French scheme of general international control, and some tendency to concede in principle a reduction in interest paid to bondholders, and that the cabinet wished to proceed along the lines opened up by the French proposals as a whole, concealed a heated disagreement which almost broke up the government. This was over the proposed *enquête* into Egyptian revenues by some international authority.

Derby began the discussion of the French proposals by asking whether an international guarantee of a loan implied international control of, or interference in, the borrowing country. Gladstone was certain that it did not, and quoted some such loans. By degrees the discussion came to centre on the *enquête*. This was strongly opposed by Hartington, Northbrook, and Childers, the last disagreeing sharply with Gladstone in a way most unusual for him: 'The truth is, Mr Gladstone, that if we had really taken the control of Egyptian finance into our hands, there would have been no necessity for cutting the coupon or for a conference'. Childers also furnished chapter and verse to show that he had long been in favour of having an English finance minister in charge in Egypt.[37] Northbrook thought that an inquiry after two years might be allowed, but done at once would have a very bad effect on Egypt.[38] The wider issue involved for all the dissident ministers was the degree of English involvement in Egypt, and 'Palmerstonian' willingness to stand up to French displeasure.

Gladstone and Harcourt argued strongly for taking the French proposals, including the *enquête*, as a groundwork, a course that seemed necessary if unattractive to most of their colleagues. Northbrook and Carlingford, according to Dilke,† were 'very

---

* Dilke MSS, 43939 f. 39. As regards the intrusion of colonial business into a major meeting, note the pious hope expressed by Granville to Derby, 19 Jan. 1885, Derby MSS, unsorted: 'It would be right (and also important for you and me) to get decisions from the Cabinet on all questions which require it in colonial matters.'

† Dilke to Chamberlain, 20 Jan., Chamberlain MSS JC 5/24/93. During this cabinet Dilke passed a note to Selborne saying 'The great advantage of the French proposal is that it reforms a majority in the cabinet by uniting two of the three parties, yours and mine' (Dilke MSS, 43913 f. 95). The meaning here is that Dilke wanted the true little Englanders (his party) to combine with the true expansionists (Selborne's party) against those who sought accommodation with France in a general Egyptian arrangement. Under Dilke's plan, the excluded middle would have been Gladstone, Granville, etc: i.e. precisely those whom Dilke wished to see removed by a Hartington ministry (see above, ch. 2).

cross and very bitter': Gladstone, according to Carlingford, 'grew very impatient, lost his temper, and put the question in a very perverse way'. The voting on whether to accept the French proposals as a basis (including the *enquête*) was predictable, the majority group of eight ministers being opposed by Hartington, Northbrook, Carlingford, and Childers. Gladstone made no attempt to soften the blow to the dissidents, and later in the evening talked with confident anger of his determination to go on without them. This was not altogether surprising, as he had been dissatisfied with Northbrook, Carlingford and Childers for several months, to a degree altogether unusual with him, and their voluntary departure would have been manna from heaven to him.

After the vote, though resignations were in the air, the cabinet drifted into a long discussion about what kind of *enquête* to have, and how to lessen the objections to it. Northbrook argued that any such inquiry must mean the postponement of the reduction of the land tax in upper Egypt, which he had strongly recommended for the sake of the fellaheen. Gladstone, though expecting the inquiry to take a year at least, thought that this could be met by making such over-taxation the first item for the commission to investigate.

After the cabinet, Gladstone and Carlingford went to dine with Harcourt. While there, a box arrived containing the resignations of Hartington[39] and Northbrook. Carlingford told Harcourt (but not Gladstone) that he was quite ready to share the fate of those with whom he had voted, though it is unlikely that he had any definite foreknowledge of the resignations. Carlingford and Harcourt stayed up talking till 1.30 a.m.[40]

Hartington's position was really very close to that of his cabinet opponents, as to facts and aims. He, like them, had 'no doubt that the alternative of rejecting the French proposal is very serious': like them, he thought the French themselves were anxious to settle: but unlike them, felt the way to achieve this lay in appearing tough: 'if the Govt would only insist on rejecting or postponing the *Enquête* they would give way.'[41]

Some comments may be made on the way the cabinet divided. Northbrook's threat of resignation was no surprise, as he had written to Gladstone on 22 November 1884 saying that 'the time is rapidly approaching when I shall be unable any longer to share in the responsibility' for the government's policy.* That Carlingford, whose only close friend in the cabinet was Northbrook, and who

* Northbrook to Selborne, 22 Dec. 1884, Selborne MSS 1869 f. 5: 44267 f. 170. Northbrook and Gladstone were not in correspondence, except for routine admiralty business, throughout 1885, this reflecting the enduring character of their differences in the autumn of 1884.

consistently stood out for a hard line in Egypt and the Sudan in 1885, went with him was also to be expected. What must have been disappointing for Northbrook was his failure to carry Selborne with him.* In December 1884, he had treated Selborne as a committed partisan of a spirited policy in Egypt, a position, indeed, which Selborne generally maintained throughout the rest of 1885. But Selborne, unlike Northbrook and Carlingford, had not been involved in a personal row with Gladstone, and in the context of the imminent fragmentation of the cabinet and party on 20–21 January, nothing emerged of his quite deep feelings about the need for a tough policy, and he allowed himself to be counted in with the 'quietist' majority. Nevertheless, the implication of his previous correspondence was that at heart he accepted Northbrook's arguments for bringing the powers to heel by a total rupture of negotiations on Egyptian finance.

Spencer and Chamberlain, absent both on 20 and 21 January, were still able to express clear opinions. Spencer wrote that 'the request on the part of the powers was not unreasonable ... at the same time it was a serious concession for us to make as it practically gave up the attitude we took at the conference and still worse threw Northbrook over.'[42] Spencer, who on 28 February was to be among those in favour of resignation, was at this time relieved to hear that a compromise had been reached which allowed the ministry to continue in office. The probable explanation of Spencer's wish to remain in power at this time, but not later, is that his ambitious package of reform proposals for Ireland had not yet been pigeonholed by Gladstone.

Chamberlain, unlike Dilke, was bellicose, angry, and nationalistic (despite or because of serious trouble with an abscessed jaw), writing to Harcourt that he did 'not expect to attend your cabinet tomorrow – so the Peace at any Price party will have it nearly all their own way. If I were there, I should be for telling the French to go to the Devil – in other words for courteously informing them that their propositions are inadmissible and that if they don't agree to ours ... we will settle the business ourselves and if Mounseer does not like it why he may lump it. We have come to the end of our concessions.'[43]

January 21 (Wednesday). The cabinet met at Downing St from 12 till 2.50, with Chamberlain (with whom Dilke had spent half an

---

* Though no letters between Northbrook and Selborne have survived for Jan. 1885, it is clear from Northbrook's letters to Selborne in Dec. 1884, that the two men had been in the closest agreement on Egyptian policy, Northbrook paying tribute to Selborne's 'calm judgment and great experience' (Selborne MSS 1869 f. 9).

hour that morning) and Spencer again absent. As ministers entered the meeting, the position was that Carlingford, after a bad night and under Granville's persuasion, was now much less likely to resign himself, and most anxious that his fellow dissidents should not do so either. Carlingford therefore spent the morning on a round of visits to the three ministers who had resigned, in each case without avail. Northbrook, on the other hand, had not proved amenable to persuasion by Granville, and was set on resigning whether or not Hartington did so too.[44] Childers had told Carlingford during the morning that he was against Hartington's resigning, but that if he did, he would follow. Hartington was uncertain but thought he would probably resign. As he told Childers and Carlingford at Devonshire House before the cabinet, he was willing to run the risk of telling the French that Britain would stay in Egypt as long as was thought necessary, settling its affairs unilaterally. He considered that submission to the *enquête* was humiliating. Then Harcourt arrived at Devonshire House, presumably as a further peacemaker, and Hartington protested that he did not want to see him. It was after this unpropitious morning that the cabinet settled down to discuss certain items of routine business.[45]

In a long discussion as to whether England should claim sovereignty or a protectorate in New Guinea, Gladstone and Selborne pressed for the latter, but gave way gracefully to Derby, Kimberley, and Harcourt, who argued strongly for sovereignty. At first sight it may appear surprising that an expansionist like Selborne should want an apparently more limited degree of control than a Little Englander like Harcourt, but in fact both were acting in character. Ministerial thinking was that, if Australia wanted the full protection of British sovereignty over New Guinea, they must in return administer and meet the costs of the territory: whereas if only a protectorate were declared, Britain would retain a much more direct responsibility.[46]

The cabinet gave further attention to the form of words to be used at the Berlin conference on the question of the nature of protectorates in West Africa.

According to one source only, Dilke, two minor topics were then raised. Firstly, there was an insubstantial proposal from the governor of Victoria, acting solely on his own authority, that an approach be made to the Dutch government concerning a possible British purchase, with Australian financial assistance, of Dutch New Guinea – a transaction there was no reason to suppose the Dutch wished to make. This curious proposal, dated 7 January, had drawn an immediately unfavourable reaction from Derby (10

January) and from Gladstone (13 January),[47] and it was perhaps only because of the Queen's interest that the matter was reported to the cabinet. The second minor point concerned the grant of a charter to the Niger Company. There is no record of any discussion or decisions relating to these points. *

Granville asked for views as to what should be put to the special envoy, Hassan Fehmi Pasha, recently arrived from Turkey, but no decision emerged.[48] There was talk of a Turkish occupation of Suakin.

Granville then re-opened the Egyptian discussion by proposing that England should strongly oppose the French demand for an *enquête*, while generally accepting the other French proposals as a working basis. Granville had mentioned to Carlingford before the meeting began that he had Gladstone's assent to this face-saving compromise, which the dissidents at once accepted.

For their part, the dissidents explicitly conceded a point raised by Harcourt, that the objections to the *enquête* should not be pressed to such lengths as to jeopardise the existence of the negotiations as a whole. This took the tension out of the situation, and an academic discussion followed as to whether the Conservatives would take office, supposing the government were to resign. Derby thought they would: Harcourt, Selborne and others believed not.

Granville, Hartington and Northbrook remained after the meeting to draft the reply to France.† Most ministers considered the ministry had escaped breaking up by a very small margin. Hartington, for instance, wrote with evident surprise 'So I am still in, I am sorry to say; but I don't think I could have done anything when considering the concession they made, which I did not in the least expect last night.'[49]

At some point during this cabinet, Trevelyan found occasion to state that he had come over to the side of the dissidents. The previous day Gladstone had recorded him as voting with the majority,[50] and the impression left on other ministers was of a largely unexplained *volte-face.* ‡

* Dilke MSS, 43939 f. 40. For attitudes on the former point, note Derby to Granville, 18 Jan. 1885, Derby MSS, 920 DER/21: 'What I suppose we really want, in regard to Dutch New Guinea, is an assurance that if the Dutch do not sell to us, they will at least not sell to anybody else.' See P. Knaplund, 'Gladstone on a Proposal To Buy Dutch New Guinea, January 1885', *Journal of Modern History*, vol. xi, (1939).

† 'As regards the French proposal of an international loan, we don't refuse in principle the idea of an international guarantee, so long as this entails no external interference in the administration of Egypt' (*E. H. J.*).

‡ Within a few days Carlingford also turned round again and began to

January 22 (Thursday). In the morning Hartington talked over his position at length with Gladstone, in what the latter described afterwards as the most satisfactory talk they had had for a long time. To Hartington it seemed that the break up of the Liberal party was inevitable: Gladstone concurred, or rather thought there was too much reason to fear it. Gladstone's conclusion, however, was to advise Hartington not to resign, if he must resign, on the Egyptian question, 'a question no one cared a button about'. Rupture, if it came, should take place 'on a matter of principle, known and understood by the country, and not in connection with a question like Egypt, which lies outside the proper business of government'. Both men passed on this conversation, in almost identical terms, to their respective political confidants.[51]

Hartington continued to smart over the way he had given ground to Gladstone on Egyptian policy. Drummond Wolff, driving back from the theatre with Hartington just after the cabinet crisis, noticed 'he is evidently furious with the GOM', and when asked if Bismarck disliked Gladstone for some specific diplomatic reason, Hartington exploded 'No. It is because Bismarck thinks Mr G is a man without any sense of responsibility and a man of damnable ideas.'[52]

In the afternoon the 'man of damnable ideas' returned to Hawarden, accompanied by his son Herbert, where he remained until 28 January, when he went to Liverpool for his son Stephen's wedding. He then left for Holker in north Lancashire, where he was the guest of the Duke of Devonshire, and had Hartington for company. While at Hawarden, he was under close police guard following the dynamite explosions at Westminster. Gladstone thus spent only four and a half days in London between his departure for Hawarden on 6 December 1884, and his hearing of the fall of Khartoum (5 February).

January 25 (Sunday). The important cabinets held on 20 and 21 January to consider the French counter-proposals on Egyptian finance of 17 January were reported at length and quite accurately in the *Observer* of Sunday, 25 January. The paper, which in its leading article took a strongly 'Palmerstonian' line on Egypt similar to that of the ministers who had threatened resignation, divulged information about proceedings in cabinet of which, as Edward Hamilton wrote, 'nobody but ministers and myself could rightly have had any cognisance'. The *Observer* of the previous

regret his mildness on 20–21 Jan.: 'The more I think about the proposals of the Powers, the more I hate them ... I ought to have opposed the *enquête* more decidedly than I did' (*C.J.*, 25 Jan.) Cf. Carlingford to Edward Lear, 24 Jan. 1885: '... in foreign affairs I sigh for Palmerston'.

week had displayed an uncanny command of almost equally confidential information, printing on 18 January the proposals presented by Waddington only the previous day. The details given of the schism in the cabinet on 20–21 January were quite full, even including the declaration of support for the dissidents by a previously neutral minister (i.e. Trevelyan) at the second meeting. The purpose of the leaks was transparently to arouse opposition to the alleged flaccid internationalism of the majority in the cabinet: ministers by their decision of 21 January, it was claimed, had handed over Egypt to an international commission under which the country would be 'bound hand and foot'. Hence it was the Radicals who, both on political grounds and with some hope of discrediting Hartington's entourage, reacted most strongly to the leaks. Dilke raised the matter* generally with other ministers on 26 January, and specifically with Harcourt on 28 January, the two men meeting in the evening to discuss the issue. Dilke at first insisted that a private secretary must have been the source; writing in retrospect, he indicated a wider range of hypothetical misconduct, referring to this storm 'which never burst but threatened greatly for some time, as to stock jobbing ... one great lady (the duchess of Manchester) was perhaps guilty and one leading private secretary (Edward Hamilton) wrongly suspected: but there was no doubt about another private secretary (Reginald Brett) not stock jobbing but telling the newspapers everything'.† There is, in fact, also no doubt that Hartington kept the Duchess of Manchester (a Tory) informed of what went on in the cabinet, for his letters to her, in the Devonshire MSS, though not numerous, make it clear that he treated her as a political intimate.

Cabinet leakages, at least to selected persons, were sanctioned by custom. For instance, when Horace Seymour, one of Gladstone's junior secretaries, gave up his post at the end of 1884,

* 'Oughtn't somebody to make a row about the enclosed? We have never had so bad a case.' (Dilke MSS, unaddressed note dated 26 Jan. in Dilke's hand, 43913 f. 96).

† Based on *E. H. J.* Dilke MSS, 43939 f. 47: *Observer*, 25 Jan., p. 5. Brett finally relinquished his position under Hartington at the War Office, in late March or early April of 1885, in mysterious circumstances which perhaps involved a similar though separate indiscretion. The published *Journals* (1934) of Lord Esher rather fail to establish a legitimate alternative explanation to that which reached Wolseley: 'I hear Brett is in disgrace about some papers in connection with Russia: I am not sorry, for I think him a most uppish Gentleman that did Hartington no good: I am glad he is no longer in any way connected with the War Office...' (Wolseley's journal, 18 May 1885, in A. Preston ed., *In Relief of Gordon* (1967) 214). Happily Wolseley did not know that Brett had a cabinet key (see Hartington to Brett, 3 May, asking for its return, Devonshire MSS 340/1763).

his superior, Edward Hamilton, continued to send him news of cabinet business for a time, just as a matter of private friendship.[53] The professional heads of the civil service also gossiped freely about their political masters' shortcomings and secrets. There was no code of conduct, save avoidance of publicity.[54] The *Observer* leak came to matter unduly because it came as an ideal diversionary issue for the Radical ministers at a time when they were about to be carpeted for Chamberlain's speeches, not because high standards of confidentiality were in fact normally maintained.

January 28 (*Wednesday*). Gladstone received from Spencer a letter outlining what Hamilton called an 'excellent and well-reasoned' package of Irish measures, although 'a large programme and one difficult to carry into effect in an expiring parliament'. Here Hamilton was almost certainly echoing his master, for on 30 January Hamilton wrote that Gladstone thought it premature to submit Spencer's Irish programme to the cabinet, 'though he views with favour the remedial measures'.* This very large, or flagrant, exercise of prime ministerial discretion occurred before the worsening of the situation in Central Asia or on the Nile.

February 4 (*Wednesday*). A meeting of all the ministers who were in town was held during the morning at the Admiralty, and lasted two hours. Those attending were Granville, Northbrook, Derby, Dilke, Childers, Trevelyan, and Chamberlain. The Congo and New Guinea were discussed, Childers and Dilke standing alone in support of Portugal's claims in the Congo. Dilke expressed strongly his belief that Britain had behaved shamefully to Portugal.[55]

This meeting, which by coincidence is the most poorly recorded ministerial discussion in January–June 1885, was almost certainly the only one at which there was an opportunity to give more than perfunctory attention to the Berlin West Africa Conference (15 November 1884–26 February 1885), and the highly significant decisions which were being taken in connection with it. There is an obvious case here for talk of settling imperial questions through absence of mind. Yet the absence of mind (entirely true where

---

* For Spencer's proposals for decentralising Irish government and substituting a secretary of state for the lord-lieutenant, while arguing that certain clauses of the Crimes Act were indispensable, see Spencer to Gladstone 26 Jan., 44312 f. 2: for Gladstone's reply, 29 Jan., urging that time until Easter would be taken up by Egypt, redistribution, and estimates, see ibid., f. 10. For further reforming pressure from Spencer ('I feel very strongly the importance of settling the purchase question'), see Spencer to Gladstone, 28 Mar., ibid., f. 36: and for Spencer's printed cabinet paper, 25 Mar., urging remedial measures dealing with land purchase, local government, and abolition of the lord-lieutenant and the creation of a royal residence, while making the Crimes Act less invidious by applying it uniformly to the whole of the U.K., see ibid. f. 38.

West Africa and the Congo were concerned) was itself due to intense imperial anxieties elsewhere. The five cabinets held in January (2, 3, 7, 20, and 21 January) were overwhelmingly focussed on Egypt and the Sudan. These topics left little time, and more important, little emotional interest, for any other issue. Yet some time was available at each meeting for residual imperial questions. This residual time was, however, principally used for reacting against what was peripheral in Bismarck's colonial policy, in the areas of New Guinea, Zanzibar, Samoa, and (on 2, 3, and 7 January) by attempting to develop a forward policy on the coasts of south-east Africa. The centre of Bismarck's colonial policy, i.e. the distinctly pro-British line he was taking concerning Franco-British conflict on the Congo, on the Niger, and in West Africa, went largely undiscussed and probably even unnoticed, precisely because it did not cause pique or apprehension in the cabinet.

It is true that the cabinets of 20 and 21 January did discuss the question of protectorates, and by inference the general question of how effective occupation in Africa was to be defined. It is probable, though it cannot be established, that little time was allowed for discussion on either day. It is certain that the discussion went almost unnoticed by those present, and that all those present were really interested in was whether the ministry would break up over Egypt. The next two occasions when the cabinet dealt with African subjects (9 February and 7 March) were limited to minor reports on Anglo-German negotiations over limited areas, and if they engendered discussion at all, which is far from clear, it was not at the level of a general review of the Berlin Conference or of the partition of Africa, a subject that one can safely say was never discussed by a full cabinet in 1885.

There was no clear criterion except perhaps the form of summons itself, which has rarely survived, to determine what constituted a cabinet meeting: and whether this gathering, with half the cabinet absent, passes muster is a matter of taste and of degree, illustrating the flexibility with which an apparently formally defined body actually worked.

February 5 (Thursday). The news of the fall of Khartoum reached the War Office in the small hours, unaccompanied by any news of Gordon. Brett came bounding into E. Hamilton's bedroom at 2.30 a.m., then at 3 a.m. Dilke and Brett went together to awaken Granville. All ministers were in London except Gladstone, Hartington, Selborne, Carlingford, and Kimberley (and Spencer in Ireland).

A telegram was immediately sent to Hartington at Holker, where the Gladstones were also still staying. However, no one thought of disturbing the ministers with the message, which was in code, and since Hartington overslept it was not until nearly midday that the catastrophe was known. Within minutes a second telegram arrived from Hamilton, addressed to Mrs Gladstone, to urge her to persuade her husband to return to London.[56] Half an hour later all three were on their way south, Gladstone having telegraphed a summons for a cabinet before leaving. Gordon's fate at this time and for several days to come was entirely problematical, and hopes that he was alive were strong.

In the train, Gladstone slept almost uninterruptedly with his wife and Hartington stretched out on either side of him. 'Having done all he can he shuts it out' Mrs Gladstone wrote, 'this saves his life or rather his head.'[57] During the evening he was in excellent form at a small dinner party given by Lord Dalhousie, appearing '*wonderful* telling old stories political and home' while Mrs Gladstone showed great curiosity over their hostess' pregnancy. Critics who thought the only permissible reaction to Khartoum was profound anguish, had grounds for their bitter attacks on Gladstone's complete detachment, which were not diminished by his visit to the theatre with the Dalhousies on 10 February.

During the day there was a meeting of ministers on central Asia, which approved a reply to Russia drafted by Kimberley and Dilke, from which Granville and Northbrook somewhat dissented.[58]

February 6 (Friday). The cabinet met at Downing St at 11, with only Spencer absent. Carlingford however was nearly two hours late.

Wolseley's announcement of the fall of Khartoum and request for fresh instructions were considered. The cabinet held strongly that all military questions should be left to Wolseley's discretion. Hartington submitted a draft of a telegram to him, which was adopted with some modifications. (The rough draft had been drawn up by Hartington in consultation with Granville the previous day, both agreeing that military instructions should be avoided as far as possible).[59] Wolseley was instructed to ensure the safety of Gordon if alive, and to check the advance of the Mahdi into districts as yet undisturbed. Gladstone and Granville wanted to refer in the telegram to the possible necessity of negotiating with the Mahdi, but it was thought that Wolseley would do this without prompting if appropriate. The cabinet also considered what announcement should be made to the public.

Gladstone read a ciphered telegram received that morning from the Queen.

Some general but indecisive conversation took place on Granville's interviews with the Turkish envoys.[60]

February 7 (*Saturday*). The cabinet met at Downing St at 12, with Spencer the only minister absent. Dilke meticulously listed eight topics touched upon, though as usual he generally gave no indication as to any decisions taken upon them.

A request from the British Museum for a small vote (£300) to enable them to open their Natural History section on Sundays was held over till the new parliament, since the existing House had already shown itself against such measures.

The second topic was the question of instructions to Wolseley.

The third topic was the proposed visit of the Prince and Princess of Wales to Ireland. Gladstone referred to his colleagues what he had heard from the Queen as to this, and the cabinet thought the visit highly desirable on public grounds. A sum of £1,200 Secret Service money was allocated in connection with the visit.

Fourthly, according to Dilke, it was decided that Gordon should be bought from the Mahdi.

Fifthly, there was discussion of the purchase of Egyptian railways, on which Harcourt talked volubly to Dilke's evident annoyance.[61]

There was no enthusiasm for the idea of using Indian troops in the Sudan, presumably initially around Suakin, this point being raised separately from the main issue of instructions to Wolseley.

The last two points noted by Dilke were a treaty between the USA and the West Indies, and trouble over Fiji, where German land claims were a problem,[62] but these escaped the attention of other observers, and Dilke himself left no hint as to the view taken by the cabinet on these points.

The main question facing the cabinet was the second topic, military policy on the Nile: indeed, this was the only subject of discussion recorded by Carlingford in his journal. Hartington began by reading a telegram from Wolseley asking the cabinet to say whether, *irrespective of Gordon*, his object should be to destroy the power of the Mahdi at Khartoum, either at once (which Wolseley considered most unlikely) or in the next cold season. Harcourt began to speak against this, but Selborne intervened strongly on the other side, saying he could not be a party to a negative policy, and Kimberley and Derby then both came out firmly for the overthrow of the Mahdi. It became clear that they had the cabinet with them, and Harcourt quickly found reasons for reversing his previous views. Gladstone raised no objection, though Carlingford suspected he had probably not made up his mind before the meeting, except in the negative sense that he was willing at this stage to leave it to the cabinet to work out what they wanted. A long discussion followed the decision in principle, over the wording of the telegram to Wolseley,[63] 'giving him almost complete discretion to do what he thinks best...'[64] The account of the discussion above as given by Carlingford can only be supplemented by one very minor aside, Dilke's censure of Wolseley 'who had confused us by greatly varying his statement'.

Edward Hamilton in his diary for 1 April 1885 asserted that 'The main consideration in the decision to overthrow the Mahdi was the Muslims in India' but this lacks corroboration beyond the fact that Kimberley, the minister responsible for India, was a strong and early supporter of the policy.

The lack of firm criteria for deciding what kinds of business were to come before the cabinet at its meeting is illustrated by a question which was settled by members of the cabinet on 7 February through the circulation of opinions in cabinet boxes. Dilke had proposed to consult the Tories about finding ways of speeding up the operation of the new electoral arrangements, so that an election under them would be possible as early as November. Gladstone saw no objection. Harcourt saw no advantage, while Chamberlain, Trevelyan and Childers agreed with Dilke. For Dilke's purpose this expression of views was probably as valuable as anything he would have obtained from cabinet discussion, and, given the very trivial nature of much cabinet business even at times of great crisis, suggests there was no clear boundary in anyone's mind between business suitable for bringing up at cabinet meetings, and business only needing settlement through the circulation of papers.[65]

February 9 (Monday). The cabinet met at Downing St at 2, with only Spencer absent. Gladstone began by announcing that Shaw-Lefevre* and Rosebery were to join the cabinet, though they were not actually to attend a cabinet meeting till 16 February.

An offer of military help by the Italian government was discussed and in effect rejected, because the cabinet wished Britain at least to appear to triumph unaided in the Sudan. On the other hand, ostensibly independent Italian action, perhaps around Kassala, aimed at distracting the attention of the Mahdists from the Nile front, was by no means excluded. Dilke noted cryptically that an initial decision 'Italians to be allowed to go to Kassala' was 'afterwards reversed'.

Granville referred to the possibility that some of the Powers might not share in guaranteeing an Egyptian loan, but this was

---

* Shaw-Lefevre was attending the deathbed of his mother, who died on 10 Feb. He first heard of his appointment through a private letter from Selborne congratulating him on his promotion to the cabinet (Shaw–Lefevre to Selborne, 11 Feb., Selborne MSS 1869 f. 13).

felt not to be a serious difficulty. Rather, opinion was that a tripartite guarantee by England, France, and Italy would be admirable.

Chamberlain proposed that the Canadians should be invited to send a force to Suakin, and Hartington stated the composition of the British force which was to be sent there. There was also an argument as to which of various officers should be given the command at Suakin, the question being left to stand over till Wednesday so Wolseley could be consulted further.

Then Childers was allowed to mention finance, 'the object for which the cabinet was called', according to Dilke. The navy estimates were first discussed, then those of the army. The proposed increases were considerably reduced. Hartington's request for a scheme of fortifications for British ports was dropped, though similar schemes for overseas coaling stations were allowed to continue.[66] Gladstone said that 'with his intentions' (of retirement) he felt bound to acquiesce in expenditure which he could not otherwise have accepted.[67] It was decided that two committees of the House of Commons should be set up to consider the estimates: the increase in the defence estimates alone was variously put at £2m. or £2.75m.[68]

The cabinet considered Wolseley's demands for Indian and other troops, and approved the proposals made in relation to them by Hartington and Kimberley, subject to the proviso that Britain should make good any charges falling on India because of the expedition. Hartington stated that it would be necessary to call out a portion of the reserves to carry through the measures already agreed.

The consequences of the cabinet decision to use Indian troops at Suakin were instructive, if obscure. The tale is as told by Lord R. Churchill, who happened to be staying with the viceroy in Calcutta at the time: 'Yesterday the government telegraphed to Dufferin to despatch a brigade of Indian troops and thirty miles of railway plant to Suakin. Great preparations were at once made. Late at night comes an order from London countermanding the whole thing. Dufferin, diplomatist as he is, could not conceal his disgust at this vacillation when they handed him the telegram on our return from dinner. I telegraphed to Borthwick, and I hope put the fat in the fire.'[69]

Granville mentioned that a difficulty had arisen with Germany over St Lucia Bay, which would require further discussion.[70] The question of letting the Turks go to the Red Sea coast was raised. A meeting of the colonial committee of the cabinet was fixed for the next day.[71]

Thanks to the Mahdi, this cabinet could be called 'the most

satisfactory one there has been for a long time – and even Mr G makes no difficulty about Khartoum or anything else.'[72]

The way in which the Radical leaders reacted to their two new colleagues is interesting. To Dilke, here as elsewhere the more militant in his relationships behind the scenes, it was clear that 'Rosebery and Lefevre will greatly help to strengthen the cabinet to the public at this moment. But, it will weaken *us*.'[73] Dilke's relations with Rosebery were always reserved:* in the 1885 cabinet, his communications with Rosebery were limited to a congratulatory note and a letter on 14 February about Canadian troops. Dilke, indeed, made no attempt to cultivate Rosebery, while Chamberlain made it clear from the start that he regarded Rosebery as a potential collaborator: 'I fancy that we agree about most things of importance in politics and we can be content to differ about details if necessary. I have always looked forward hopefully to the prospect of more active cooperation with you.'[74] It was on this assumption of inherent like-mindedness that he told the Whig aristocrat his views on Childers, expletively, on 20 April, and unfolded his Irish schemes on 17 May.

February 11 (*Wednesday*). A meeting of the cabinet was hurriedly called for 11 a.m. at Downing St, taking many ministers by surprise. Selborne, Spencer, Carlingford, Trevelyan and Chamberlain were absent.[75] The business of the meeting was confined to the choice of a commander for the Suakin expedition, a matter already talked over on Monday but postponed in order to obtain Wolseley's opinion. On Monday the choice had appeared to lie between Greaves, a relatively junior officer and a known Wolseley protégé, whom Wolseley had suggested, and Alison, a senior officer whom Hartington appeared to want. The Duke of Cambridge was strongly against Greaves, and Gladstone and Childers were strongly against the Duke. Hartington regarded Greaves as raising the issue, not of merit versus seniority, but of Wolseley's notorious tendency to favouritism. The cabinet then adjourned, believing, according to Gladstone's minutes, that Wolseley was to be sounded as to his preference between Greaves and Alison.

In fact on Tuesday Wolseley had received a telegram from the Duke of Cambridge offering him a choice between three senior officers, Graham, Alison, and Stephenson, with whichever one was selected taking Greaves as his chief of staff. Wolseley had replied that of the choices offered, he liked Graham and Greaves

---

* 'Rosebery's sense is nil. He's full of talent' (Dilke to Grant Duff, 2 Jan. 1885, Dilke MSS 43894 f. 161). Cf. the opinion of Rosebery's friend and backer, Edward Hamilton: 'Rosebery practically declines. I give him up as hopeless for political service' (Hamilton to H. Seymour, 3 Feb., Glynne–Gladstone MSS).

best.[76] It was presumably this answer which the cabinet were summoned to consider on Wednesday.

Hartington urged acceptance of Wolseley's somewhat constrained reply, and was supported by Dilke (who admitted to his journal 'I do not know why'). Gladstone however made a very obstinate stand against this and on behalf of Greaves.[77] Gladstone said he thought that the cabinet were departing from a general principle of importance, but that since he was overruled, the question was settled. The vote taken on the question whether Wolseley should be further consulted, went against Gladstone by five votes (Hartington, Dilke, Harcourt, Northbrook, Kimberley) to four (Gladstone, Childers, Granville, and Derby).[78] Presumably what particularly exercised Gladstone was that the War Office and the Duke of Cambridge had so put the question to Wolseley, that neither the cabinet nor the commander in the field had a free choice in the matter.

Graham, then in London, was called to the War Office the same day, at once beginning detailed discussions of operations. Born in 1831, he had already commanded at Suakin with success in 1884, and did so again in 1885. Given that he was known to be at least relatively acceptable to Wolseley, the vote in cabinet which came near to rejecting him on Gladstone's advice was a surprising result, coming at a time when Gladstone's standing in military matters had never been lower. Gladstone's unwonted military zeal arose from an apparently simple desire for a prestige victory, however irrelevant – another Tel-el-Kebir. A curious instance of this was Hartington's parting message to Graham when he saw him off on 20 February: the prime minister, so the General was told, was very anxious that Osman Digna should be captured and that bribes should be used if necessary to get him.[79] Gladstone had already at an earlier stage (8 January) wished to kidnap Osman Digna.[80]

Gladstone here appeared to be playing the part of a war minister. In fact he was probably only involving himself in what was, after all, intended to be the lesser of the two campaigns in the Sudan, because of his concern with the management of opinion. It is inherently unlikely that he approved of the advance on Khartoum as authorised, yet he maintained complete silence in cabinet as to his real views. To his son, however, he had said of the British successes in the Nile war at just this stage, 'It is torture.'*

---

* Herbert Gladstone's diary, 9 May 1885, Glynne–Gladstone MSS. His Cabinet colleagues almost certainly did not suspect such intensity of feeling. However, on 2 Mar. Gladstone spoke to Bright of having 'suffered torture' over Egypt, and disavowed Gordon, whom he had never seen, as 'a man totally

The distinction to draw attention to here, is that while Gladstone gave to the Nile war no more than a cryptic acquiescence requiring no personal involvement, in the case of the Suakin front he manifested both personal interest and something like eagerness for results. One explanation could be, of course, that he was taken by strategic fancies about the safe and easy route to Khartoum lying across hundreds of miles of unexplored desert. There is no evidence, however, that he did think on these lines, or that he questioned Wolseley's 'river war' policy. Moreover, till very recently, Gladstone had set his face firmly against any activities, or perhaps even any British presence, in the eastern Sudan.

Gladstone's opposition only a month earlier to any campaign at Suakin had been unequivocal. He could then only have assented to it at Wolseley's express demand, and 'with great repugnance',[81] and it 'would have been with much pain that I should have seen the Osman Digna episode acted over again, with the escape of that worthy for its probable if not certain end'.[82] Even the retention of Suakin as a garrison port for some years, without necessarily campaigning in the area, was not obviously reasonable to Gladstone, who attached 'very little weight' to Wolseley's view that the port should be thus retained. Nor did Gladstone, prior to the fall of Khartoum, believe that it mattered much either way what occurred militarily near Suakin: 'We can defeat, but can we catch him [Osman Digna]? ... After all he does not seem able to do us much harm.'[83] And, in conclusion, it was necessary to remember that the 'country would shudder at a new war'[84] around Suakin. Accordingly, Gladstone and Hartington (the former 'astonished' at 'the levity' shown in Baring's eagerness[85] for activity at Suakin) sent a deliberate reminder to Cairo, emphasising that Wolseley's 'full discretion as to his present military operations' should not be taken as allowing any commitment to 'lengthened occupation' of the Sudan,[86] a pinprick probably aimed partly (in view of the date) against any assumption that the Suakin pale should grow into a permanent military colony, as in fact it did in the period 1885–98.

Gladstone, therefore, had in January set up to his own satisfaction arguments that military activity at Suakin was inherently foolish, even for local purposes, and irrelevant to the issue of the war on the Nile. In February he found himself with a much expanded Nile war on his hands, which for the time being he could not directly oppose. If one is to look for any wrecking activities on his part, it must be in the function he had in mind for opera-

unsuited for the work he undertook' (R.A.J.Walling ed., *The Diaries of John Bright*, 1930, 524).

tions on the eastern front. The suspicion that Gladstone was finessing here, hoping to use an innocuous and early success on the Suakin front (where victory could not lead to a significant territorial annexation) to weaken the public demand for an advance along the Nile, must be very strong. When in later months the Suakin front ceased to have this function of drawing patriotic emotion in a harmless direction, Gladstone had no use for it whatever.

After the cabinet, Gladstone wrote to the Queen that press reports of Gordon's death, now generally believed, still lacked official confirmation. The previous night, contrary to advice from his private secretary, Gladstone had obstinately insisted on fulfilling a long-standing theatre engagement with the Dalhousies. This provoked a storm of adverse comment, though it took place prior to the bad news of the 11th, the high point of national anguish over Gordon and the evening selected by Hartington, without incurring censure, to take his mistress to the Prince's Theatre to see Lily Langtry in *A School for Scandal*. The accusation that Gladstone was fiddling while Rome burned, which was widely made, had substance in some odd ways: three days later Gladstone composed a thoughtful and lengthy letter on a recent pamphlet, *The Unicorn: A Mythological Investigation*.[87]

February 13 (Friday). Hartington, at this time pressing strongly for a railroad from Suakin, invited Dilke to be a member of a cabinet committee he was setting up to consider it.* The invitation to Dilke is not recorded as having any connection with a cabinet decision, nor is there any evidence as to whether or when a committee on this question was set up by the cabinet.

February 16 (Monday). The cabinet met from 2 till 5.30[88] at Downing St, with only Spencer absent. It was the first meeting attended by Shaw-Lefevre and Rosebery, the latter jesting to Granville that the attendance was 'more numerous than the House of Lords and not quite so united'. Northbrook passed a note to Rosebery saying 'I think you have joined a very short-lived cabinet.'[89]

Granville, at the instance of Kimberley, undertook to give grave warning to Turkey against continued encroachment on a British-protected Arab state near Aden.

The cabinet discussed the manner in which their policy in the Sudan should be put before parliament, but postponed conclusions

---

* For the free hand given to a senior minister in forming a cabinet committee, see Gladstone to Hartington, 12 Feb. 1885, on this same committee: 'I should think of yourself, Childers, Chamberlain, and Kimberley and Northbrook and such others as you may think fit to associate yourself' (44547 f. 177).

till the following day. Hartington stated his views on questions of military manpower: there was to be no compulsory calling out of reserves. Hartington also reported Wolseley's approval of the acceptance of the offer of Australian troops. According to Dilke, Hartington asked for £5m. for the Suakin-Berber railway. This provoked Chamberlain into asking whether the construction of the railway committed Britain to staying at Khartoum: if so, he protested, it was not fair to pre-empt the latter question in this way. This led to long discussion, which Gladstone had to adjourn.[90]

A preliminary discussion on crofting legislation had already been held at the Home Office on the previous Friday at 2 p.m.; with Harcourt, Rosebery, the lord advocate, and possibly Gladstone present.[91] Carlingford, despite his expertise in the intricacies of land legislation, was conspicuous by his absence, but took part in the discussion in cabinet. Harcourt adopted the most fulsome tone in seeking Rosebery's advice on the question, an attitude which was redundant at best, since he had been a consistent backer of Rosebery since 1884.

The question of the crofters was discussed further, at considerable length, during this cabinet, in view of the expected parliamentary necessity of making an announcement on Thursday of their intention to introduce a bill dealing with the subject. The lord advocate attended the discussion. A good deal of reference was made to the Irish Land Acts. Gladstone referred to the proposed bill as one whose 'details will require to be very carefully weighed'. The plan put forward by Harcourt roused Hartington to object. Chamberlain also objected strongly to Harcourt's proposals.[92]

Dilke's notes also listed several other items of business not referred to by other sources, *viz.* 1) the Russian proposal to guarantee one sixth only of the Egyptian loan; 2) committees on the estimates; 3) that the recommendation of a committee on the labourers (Ireland) bill as to taking compulsory powers should be adopted; and 4) whether to make Scottish education come under the wing of the proposed Scottish secretary, the decision on this point being postponed.[93] On the Scottish issue, Carlingford as on previous occasions insisted there were no educational reasons for separating the Scottish educational administration from the English, the demand for a change being purely on home rule grounds. Rosebery advised that the decision should be put off until the Scottish members could be consulted.[94]

Bills in connection with the following subjects were to be introduced into the House of Lords: Australian federal council, lunacy law amendment, extradition, and Scottish secretaryship.[95]

February 17 (*Tuesday*). The cabinet met at 2.30 at Downing St, with only Spencer absent.

The first item taken was the financial situation of New Guinea. It was agreed to inquire into the cost of civil expenditure there, to which Britain would contribute. Gladstone, Harcourt, Chamberlain, and Trevelyan were for making the Australian colonies meet the whole expense, but were overruled. Gladstone said bitterly 'I wish there was some fund at the disposal of the House of Lords for these purposes'. *

Further consideration was given to the question of what parliament should be told about British policy in the Sudan. Gladstone read from notes a proposed statement of policy, which was in the main approved. This was intended as a draft of a despatch to Baring, but it was settled that Gladstone should present it as a statement in the House instead.[96] Trevelyan and Chamberlain found grounds for uneasiness because not enough was made of the safety of the troops as an inhibiting factor.[97] Since by usage military telegrams were not among the papers presented to parliament, it was left to Gladstone in his statement on Thursday to indicate their contents. The cabinet were unaware whether the opposition would propose any vote of censure.

---

* R.J., 17 Feb. Most ministers had already aired their views on New Guinea finance in minutes on a draft telegram to the Australian governors circulated by Derby. Derby's initial draft stated that H.M.G. was quite unprepared to contribute to territories 'not essential for Imperial purposes' and acquired solely 'in Australian interests'. Derby's draft caused sharp division among his colleagues. Nobody proposed that Britain should bear the whole cost. Five ministers (Northbrook, Selborne, Hartington, Carlingford, Lefevre) objected to Derby's draft and supported a British contribution. Northbrook and Selborne felt that it was Britain's duty to safeguard native interests from the Australians, and this was their main reason for demanding a British contribution. Selborne, a devout High Churchman, wrote 'I feel very strongly on this point', meaning 'we ought not to abdicate our duties' for 'a comparatively trifling expenditure', while Northbrook, a deeply evangelical Christian, was principally concerned about the labour traffic and the use of spirits. Five ministers (Chamberlain, Dilke, Trevelyan, Gladstone, with Harcourt as leader) thought, as Harcourt said, that 'we should adhere strictly to the principle that the colony should pay all the cost of annexation and that the British taxpayer should not be called upon to contribute to a measure which is certainly not to his advantage'. Childers and Rosebery were neutral. Gladstone saw scope for compromise: 'A reasonable arrangement for protecting natives seems to be all we want. Cannot this be had by a reasonable and friendly arrangement ...?' Because of this division of opinion, Derby on 12 Feb. asked Gladstone if it should be brought before the cabinet, to which Gladstone agreed without comment. For above, see envelope labelled 'Cost of New Guinea. Cabinet Minutes Feb. 1885', Derby MSS 920 DER/23.

It was decided to lump the whole prospective increase in taxation for 1885–86 into one vote of credit, the time for laying this before parliament to be later rather than earlier.

Without wishing entirely to decline the offer of untrained Canadian troops for the Sudan, it was felt to be too little and too late, especially when compared with the Australian offer of a fully equipped force. Even so, it was resolved to make acceptance of the latter dependent on the war lasting until the autumn.[98] This was almost certainly a nominal cabinet decision following an agreement between the ministers concerned (Derby, Hartington, and Gladstone) to this effect on 12 February. Hartington had then written 'We might say that the Suakin operation must on account of climate be undertaken within the shortest possible time, and they could scarcely reach Suakin soon enough; but in the event of operations continuing next autumn, the offer should be considered.'[99]

The question of Italian activity in Africa was mentioned.[100]

February 18 (Wednesday). The Central Asian committee of the cabinet met at the Foreign Office to discuss the Russian advance.[101]

February 19 (Thursday). Dilke had an interview with Gladstone, and found him longing to be turned out on the coming vote of censure, 'in the firm belief that if turned out he would come back after the dissolution in November'.[102]

February 20 (Friday). The full cabinet met at 2 at Downing St, chiefly to consider what parliamentary tactics to adopt in face of Northcote's impending vote of censure and Morley's critical amendment. The cabinet decided to meet both with a direct negative. Chamberlain was strongly against any public suggestion that Britain might set up a government at Khartoum, and was even bitter at Hartington's plea that the government should not commit itself against that policy. Trevelyan and Lefevre were anxious about the reactions of their radical constituents, unless, as Trevelyan proposed, the military plans were justified principally as a means of assuring the safety of the British troops concerned.[103]

Granville reported progress in the negotiations on Egyptian finance, and stated how he proposed to deal with suggested new arrangements for the Suez canal. It was probable that the Suez Canal Commission would be given up in the form proposed.

The question of military aid from the colonies again arose *à propos* of an impending parliamentary question. Derby was attacked for a 'stupid and ungracious' telegram sent by the Colonial Office.[104] Far from wishing to snub the colonies, Derby had originally been in favour of accepting the Australian offer 'for the sake of the moral effect it will produce, both here and in

Australia' but had been overruled by Hartington and Gladstone, the discredit for their decision as always rubbing off on Derby.[105] The cabinet decided that Gladstone should acknowledge the colonial offers and their historical significance in terms of great warmth, especially in the case of New South Wales: or as Dilke put it in more personal terms, 'Hartington and Derby had snubbed the colonists and were snubbed by the cabinet in consequence.'[106] Hartington accused Chamberlain of being 'sentimental' about the colonies, and the two men became pugnacious.[107] As a result of cabinet pressure, Derby later that day announced that the offer of troops by New South Wales was 'absolutely accepted',[108] while Gladstone made a rather fine speech that afternoon in the Commons welcoming in his best manner a development that until a few hours earlier he had intended to ignore. As Rosebery rightly said 'we succeeded in impressing upon Mr G the necessity of putting strongly what he had to say about their offers, and he afterwards did it very well.'[109]

Dilke learned that Chamberlain had settled with Childers that the latter should see Gladstone and propose the appointment of a committee to examine the civil list, an interesting example of typical cabinet business being dealt with entirely outside the cabinet without any apparent awareness of infringing sound usage.[110]

In view of the close bearing of the Afghan situation on ministerial willingness to take effective action on the Nile, it is important to note when the first indications of serious concern in Whitehall about Russian intentions occurred. The first tremor recorded by E. Hamilton was on 20 February, when he mentioned a strong telegram having been sent remonstrating with Russia against its reported advance on the Afghan frontier. On 25 February Hamilton described the Afghan situation as threatening to become very serious, one of the dangers being the apparent tendency of Lumsden to instigate the Afghans to occupy territory not previously in their hands. The departments involved had never taken their eyes off the problem – for instance a secret memorandum[111] on the Afghan frontier was printed by the India Office on 24 January 1885.

February 28 (*Saturday*). The full cabinet met at Downing St from 2 till 6.30. The following points were taken:[112]

1. Following its low majority at 1 a.m. that morning in the vote of censure on its Sudan policy, the cabinet after protracted argument decided not to resign.
2. The cabinet asked Wolseley to comment on the *Daily Chronicle* report of 28 February that the Mahdi had proposed a truce, and that Gen. Buller had offered to begin negotiations.

3. The cabinet approved Granville's draft of a friendly reply to a menacing letter from Bismarck.
4. A plan by Sir J.Pauncefote for settling border difficulties in New Guinea* was favourably received as a possible basis for a solution.
5. The cabinet sent instructions to Lumsden, the British agent on the Afghan border, to report home, before giving advice in any case where an armed collision of Russians and Afghans was probable.
6. Wolseley's desire to be proclaimed governor-general of the Sudan was raised, but a decision was held over till the next meeting. †
7. A decision was taken to go ahead with building the Berber-Suakin railway, but it was to be only made 'as far as necessary for purely military purposes'.[113] It is quite clear that the Suakin railway was at least discussed at this meeting, for it was on this item that Childers uttered his *cri de coeur* 'Kimberley has spoken nineteen times and won't let me speak once.' ‡
8. The question of giving a grant to Gordon's family was considered.

In the final vote on resignation, the numbers were equal. Rosebery abstained, and gave no hint as to his leanings: Gladstone gave his casting vote against resignation, which was readily accepted as decisive. Granville, Derby, Hartington, Selborne, Spencer,[114] Northbrook and Childers voted for resignation. Kimberley, Lefevre, Trevelyan, Harcourt, Dilke, Chamberlain and Carlingford were for continuing in office.

In the preceding discussion, Harcourt, who the night before had been against resigning, was initially in favour of resigning, and spoke 'solemnly and at length' in that sense,[115] but in the course

* After the cabinet, the colonial committee met at the Colonial Office to discuss New Guinea. Rosebery attended (*R.J.*, 28 Feb.). The colonial committee consisted of an unknown group of ministers appointed in an unknown way, even to the colonial secretary: cf. Childers to Derby 19 Feb. 1885, 'Did you take a note of my appointment to the Colonial Committee of the Cabinet?' (Derby MSS, 920 DER/20).

† Gladstone's cabinet papers include at this point a memorandum, of not quite certain date, written by him advancing ten reasons why Wolseley should not take the title. Dilke had the impression that the sense of the meeting was against Wolseley's suggestion: 'Wolseley not to be g-g' he noted.

‡ R.R.James, *Rosebery* (1963), 166. Gladstone once spoke of Kimberley as the most long-winded man he had ever known in a cabinet (F.E.Hamer, ed., *The Personal Papers of Lord Rendel* (1931), 57). Cf. also E.Hamilton diary, 18 Nov. 1884: 'No one talks more lengthily or writes more succinctly than Lord Kimberley, while no one writes more lengthily and talks more succinctly than Mr Childers.'

of the argument changed his mind. At some point Harcourt said they could get through the session with Tory support. He was followed by Chamberlain, who argued in favour of getting out of office while the party was still united. Granville was 'tremendously strong'[116] for resignation. Dilke may at first have agreed with Chamberlain, but both changed their attitude after Gladstone had spoken vehemently against departing. Kimberley, Dilke and Trevelyan spoke strongly against resignation. The initial speakers, Granville, Harcourt, Derby and Chamberlain, were all in favour of resigning,* and at one point Gladstone appeared to have been the only advocate of holding on, giving a personal sense to his argument by saying the decision was 'one for those who in the future will have the responsibility. For me it is evident that my retirement would mean something – definite.'[117] Yet even 'Mr G had been rather inclined to resign the night before'[118] and most of those who had talked to him thought that was what he would recommend. Gladstone may also have cited his chief whip as an authority against resignation.[119]

Gladstone put forward, or left record of, his reasons for staying in office. There was the lack of precedent for resigning over a successful vote. There was the likelihood of resigning with greater credit later on. There was the question of the still unsettled finance for the year. There would be a feeling of astonishment at resignation. He summed up the case thus: 'I am for staying with the hope and expectation of being able after Easter to go, when we come to finance for war.'[120]

Those, who in the end, voted for resignation, included virtually all those who were finding their departments, their colleagues, public opinion (and Bismarck's pinpricks) too much for them. Granville, Derby, Hartington, Childers and Spencer all had strong departmental reasons for wishing to escape: within a matter of months, indeed, Hartington, Derby, and (perhaps) Spencer were talking of leaving politics altogether. Hartington's private view was 'of course ... rather in favour of it' though 'not sure it would have been the right thing: it would have looked too much like running away ...'[121] From the start, however, Hartington had been eager that the vote of censure should overthrow the government,

---

* Derby and Granville had found themselves in complete agreement earlier in the day. Derby had written 'I wish the majority had been larger or smaller. But looking to the future, to the fact that Gladstone must soon resign in any case, to the difficulties attending reconstruction, to the divisions amongst ourselves, and the certainty of alienating a section of the party whatever we do about the Sudan, I think we had better throw it up. What do you say?' Granville replied '*J'abonde dans votre sens.* And I think the majority is small enough' (Derby MSS 920 DER/20).

finding it 'a great disappointment' that its drafting was such 'that there is not much chance of its being carried ... No one can scarcely see how we can carry on much longer even if we are not turned out on this vote'.[122] Granville, who had understood from Gladstone that he would resign, was annoyed and disappointed at the result, and was visibly very sulky at dinner that evening. Spencer, who had come from Dublin specially, possibly at Granville's instigation, also went back to Ireland disappointed. Selborne and Northbrook were perhaps a different matter, and in Selborne's case subtler calculations may have been at work, since he took the view around this time that the Conservatives would not in any case want to take office. Broadly, however, the ministers who wanted to resign were those who needed a rest: those who wished to stay, were those who were on top of their work, or had very little to do. The difference was not one of political appraisal.

Those against resignation had little in common, except to a minor extent that they were particularly unwilling to see Gladstone disappear from the scene. Carlingford, whose career would almost certainly have terminated with resignation, and who believed that he needed his official salary to keep afloat, might be accused of acting on interested grounds, but in fact, as he gave his vote, said 'I suppose it is too late to change so I must vote No',[123] and explained his action in his diary as a reluctant act of deference to Gladstone. Lefevre, Trevelyan and Kimberley were perhaps consistently and strongly in favour of remaining in office, but the evidence for this is not a shadow of the evidence, borne out by all observers, that at the meeting Gladstone was entirely clear that he wanted to carry on. Gladstone, that is, got the cabinet to decide the vital question of its own existence in exactly the way that he wanted and in a way that perhaps no one else actively would have worked to secure, without even leaving them with any clear picture of why he wanted to remain in office. *

March 7 (Saturday). The cabinet met at Downing St from 2 till 5.30, with only Spencer absent. At 3.15 Rosebery stole away and

---

* Hartington, for instance, interpreted Gladstone's desire to remain for the present as being based on a conviction 'that we shall be beaten soon and have a better case for resignation' (Hartington to Duchess of Manchester, 1 Mar.). For the inability of a Conservative backbencher to conceive of his party except as an opposition, see C. Dalrymple's diary, 28 Feb.: 'I think no one anticipates that the government will resign.' For Gladstone's ability to convince his wife that he acted with good reason, see Mrs Gladstone to her daughter Mary, n.d. but 28 Feb., (misdated in B.M. 28 Mar.), 46223 f. 199: 'The division Lord Rosebery and Papa expected to be larger but it will look well for the country and after all it is satisfactory to be without the Irish... Papa is saying again and again "No one not even Goschen knows the hopeless situation if we had not got through." '

unveiled the Burns bust in Westminster Abbey, returning to the meeting later on.

The cabinet decided there was no reason to oppose a curious motion by Lord Wemyss giving thanks for the offer of troops by New South Wales.

Kimberley summarised the latest reports from the Afghan frontier in the light of the important coming visit of the Ameer to Lord Dufferin.

The cabinet agreed to Wolseley's request for 47 miles of light railway up the Nile valley from Wadi Halfa, to be rapidly completed as essential for any autumn campaign. It was not however possible to gather from his telegrams whether he still really required a railway from Suakin to Berber for the purposes of the contemplated autumn campaign. A telegram was framed to obtain from him clear views on this issue. Some ministers expostulated against both campaigns, treating them as one. According to Dilke, he, Northbrook, Harcourt and Chamberlain were in favour of stopping the campaign in the Sudan.[124] Harcourt laid it down that there would never be an expedition either to Berber or Khartoum, and that within three months Wolseley would himself advise the abandonment of the whole enterprise. Chamberlain said sharply that he could no longer support the Berber-Suakin railway. Dilke expressed the same view. The Radicals appeared to be ready to call off the Sudan campaign as a whole without delay.[125] Their attitude was in sharp conflict with that of Hartington, who had only just asserted that the cabinet was committed to a forward policy in the Sudan, and that Wolseley should be given no grounds for doubting their intentions.[126]

Granville reported on his dealings with Herbert Bismarck on colonial matters, especially concerning New Guinea, St Lucia Bay,[127] and the Cameroons. It appeared that all outstanding matters of controversy were settled. Nevertheless, Bismarck *père* was still not definitely committed to signing the proposals on Egyptian finance. The questions of Pondoland, and of the Niger Company, were also raised.

Fehmi Pasha, the Turkish envoy, had asked Granville whether he should advise the Sultan to send troops to Suakin. Turkey had appeared to be interested of late both in having some share in the reorganisation of the Egyptian army, and in the neutralisation of Egypt. Granville was aware also of the need to prevent the Sultan moving closer to Russia. At the suggestion of Turkish troops joining the British forces at Suakin, however, Harcourt burst out that admission of the Turks to Egypt or the Sudan would be intolerable, and was for him a vital question. He continued at length in a declamatory vein, till compromise emerged.[128] It was left to Granville to suggest that in view of 'congestion' at Suakin Turkish intervention elsewhere on the Red Sea littoral might have advantages; also that, while showing some deference to ostensible Turkish wishes for neutralisation, Britain should press for Turkish assent to the Egyptian financial scheme, 'the early settlement of which is a matter of some importance'.[129]

Finally, Harcourt also began to pronounce against the Charter for the National African Company, but Chamberlain broke in upon him, and said the commerce of the country would never forgive them if they did not secure the Niger.[130]

The Turkish ambassador had an audience with Granville just after the cabinet.

In the evening Hartington and Rosebery dined with Herbert Bismarck, the former getting the impression that despite the current tendency to drop Anglo-German controversy, the Germans would not be satisfied till they had got rid of Derby.[131]

March 11 (*Wednesday*). A despatch arrived in the evening from Wolseley which in effect ran (in Dilke's paraphrase) 'Please tell Lord Granville that I cannot wait any longer and I must issue proclamation and will do so on my own authority if I do not receive answer to this by the 14th. I hope I may be able to issue it as governor-general.'[132]

The following day, Granville said that he had received from Waddington the welcome news that Egyptian finance was finally settled, so far as France was concerned.

March 12 (*Thursday*). The cabinet met at Downing St at noon, with only Spencer absent.

The lease of Dover House having fallen in, Rosebery raised the question whether it should be converted, at large expense, into the official residence of the premier. Kimberley, Chamberlain and Gladstone were all against the idea, Gladstone decidedly so because it would lead to the premier being expected to entertain. Gladstone took the opportunity to stress once again the imminence and certainty of his retirement. Granville, Rosebery and Lefevre were in favour of the proposed change in use.[133] The question was laid aside till three ministers unacquainted with the building had time to visit it.

This gave Childers an opportunity to put forward his cherished idea that the office of prime minister should be joined to that of lord president of the council, since the latter post would be largely honorific 'as it was now decided to take away Education from the President' to create a ministry of education. This last recommendation had in fact never been brought before the cabinet. No decision was reached on Childers' idea, which either from insensitivity or otherwise was an expression of disregard for Carlingford.[134]

At Lumsden's request, Kimberley undertook to arrange that British troops could if necessary be safely moved into Herat without risk of friction with Afghan regiments.

The idea of liberating the slaves in the Sudan was not considered 'to be available at this time for any useful purpose'.

The cabinet were willing to overlook the florid phraseology in the draft proclamation forwarded by Baring concerning Wolseley's governor-generalship, had it not been for the ideas of policy underlying it. They therefore vetoed it, despite Hartington's vigour in support of Wolseley. Their main reason for doing so was the Asian crisis. As Hamilton put it, 'the possible necessity of a rapid reinforcement of the British army in India' made it 'imprudent to extend our obligations into the Sudan'. The cabinet saw clearly that Indian necessities might come to override existing intentions in the Sudan, and at very least it was felt to be important not to tempt Russia to aggression by explicitly extending British commitments in Africa. Harcourt, repeating what he had said at the last cabinet, asserted that there never would be a Sudan campaign. Even Hartington raised the question of how the diversionary attack at Suakin could be justified, if there was a chance that the main campaign might never materialise. (Hartington's remark was not lost on Gladstone, who on 15 March introduced to the Queen the 'remote possibility' that the Russian quarrel might lead to the calling off of operations in the eastern Sudan).[135] Gladstone was already waiting for Penjdeh. Gladstone, Dilke and Chamberlain also poured cold water on Wolseley's hopes of legitimising his position in the Sudan.

The cabinet therefore agreed that Wolseley should be sent a telegram, to be drafted subsequently by Hartington, supplying him with the statement of policy in the Sudan which Gladstone and Granville were to make to parliament on 19 March. The telegram also instructed Wolseley to confine his public declarations to matters relating to tribes in his immediate neighbourhood and to obligations already contracted.

The possible arrest of Zobehr and of two other less important Egyptians was considered at the urgent request of Wolseley and Baring. It was thought that while the two others might be allowed to escape, Zobehr should be arrested and his papers seized as an act of military necessity, the Khedive for his own sake not being brought into the matter. Zobehr should be held in a ship off Alexandria, rather than sent to Cyprus.[136]

There followed a long discussion of relations with Russia, with Harcourt again in full voice as a critic of his colleagues' blindness, until Hartington punctuated his flow with 'Now I bet you a 100 to 1 you haven't read any of the papers.' An answer to Russia which had been prepared by Kimberley and a committee was mentioned, and consideration of it was adjourned till the following day.

The questions of arrests in Egypt and of Wolseley's title had already been worked over thoroughly before the cabinet met, and practice on this occasion may be cited as a particularly clear example of how discussions in cabinet were only one part, and not necessarily the most critical one, of continuous discussions by the cabinet when not in session. Opinions had already been taken on these Egyptian questions through the circulation boxes, the resulting 'division list' indicating the consistency of the composition of those wanting a strong policy on the Nile regardless of the specific matter immediately under discussion. On the arrest, Trevelyan was adverse, and Gladstone very hesitant, while Rosebery, Dilke, Selborne and Carlingford were in favour, Carlingford minuting 'I can't see why we should scruple to do in Egypt in time of war what we do in Ireland in time of peace.'[137] On the question of Wolseley's title, Selborne had wanted the proposed title to be approved on military grounds, irrespective of feeling in the Liberal party: Rosebery thought the proposal absurd, but would concede it simply because Wolseley so greatly desired it: Carlingford was against overruling Wolseley, and could 'not see that his temporary assumption of the title wd. commit the Govt. to anything': Chamberlain did not see much harm in it, and did not like to refuse any of Wolseley's recommendations without absolute necessity. Dilke, on the other hand, understood the cabinet to have already decided against both Egyptian proposals. *March 13 (Friday).* The cabinet met from 5.30 to 7.50[138] in Gladstone's room at the House of Commons, with only Spencer absent.

The cabinet went over a despatch to Russia declaring its proposals on the Afghan frontier to be inadmissible, and setting out British counter-proposals. The proposed despatch was read out by Kimberley, not by Granville.[139] The cabinet took the view that the territory between the English and Russian lines of demarcation should be treated as a distinct zone for the purposes of the inquiry to be made.

Granville reported the disagreeable news that Bismarck's confidently expected signature to the Egyptian financial agreement was now delayed by a proposal involving an unwelcome major change[140] which had been put forward by the German Ambassador on uncertain authority. Granville went out of the cabinet room to press Count Münster to clarify the status of his proposal, and to declare whether, if acceded to by Britain, German signature of the financial agreement would immediately follow. Münster, ashamed of the hitch, put forward (jointly with the other ambassadors) an alternative proposal which proved acceptable to the cabinet, and which it was hoped Bismarck would adopt.

Granville returned, and it was left that Münster should be told to inform Bismarck of the British disposition to accept.[141]

March 20 (Friday). The cabinet met at Downing St at 2, with only Spencer absent.

It was decided to refuse the demand by the opposition for a considerable interval before debating the agreement on Egyptian finance, on the grounds that delay would produce confusion in that country.

Childers indicated that it might be necessary to ask parliament for a vote of credit to the extent of £7½m.; and that even without reducing the expected current deficit of £2m., it would still be necessary to raise £9³⁄₁₀m. of additional taxation in the coming financial year (1885–86). Gladstone groaned.[142]

At Dufferin's request, sanction was given for the movement of 25,000 men to Quetta.[143]

In the light of the impending conference between Dufferin and the Ameer, attention was given to the defence of Herat. On a different point, it was felt that, as regards the Afghan-Russian boundary, the Ameer should place himself entirely in the hands of the British government, which in return would stand pledged to act as if Afghanistan were British territory. Gladstone also suggested that both the north-east and the north-west frontiers of Afghanistan should be considered together.

Granville reported on his negotiations with Fehmi Pasha. 'The cabinet saw no objection to the issue of a Turkish firman confirming recent Egyptian legislation'[144] but turned down the idea of proclaiming Ottoman law as being the law of Egypt. The question of Turkish reunion with Egypt was discussed in a general way, especially in the context of the eventual neutralisation of Egypt.

The cabinet agreed to ask for further information concerning reports on Zobehr.

A recent alarmist telegram from Wolseley about prospects for the Nile campaign was discussed, and it was felt that it would be best to keep quiet about his views. Hartington felt badly let down by Wolseley's sudden shift of opinion, and even suggested that Wolseley had expressed readiness to advance on Khartoum in the first place, because he was quite certain that the government would order his retreat: so that the resolute policy of the government had taken him by surprise.[145] Selborne privately agreed: 'We seem to be fighting three enemies at once – 1. the Mahdi, 2. certain of our people here, 3. Wolseley.'[146]

The publication of Gordon's diary was considered.

The timetable for the budget and the vote of credit was decided.[147]

The cabinet considered telegrams from Sir Hercules Robinson, high commissioner in South Africa, relative to Sir C. Warren's position in Bechuanaland. The cabinet wished to appear to stand firmly behind both men, but also wished especially not to disturb Warren's work in Bechuanaland. Warren was however to be instructed to address his communications to the home government through Robinson, his official superior, and to act in concert with him.[148]

March 24 (Thursday).[149] The cabinet met at 5.30 in Gladstone's room at the House of Commons with only Spencer absent.

A last minute delay had been caused by Turkey about the signing of the Egyptian financial convention. Musurus Pasha, the Turkish ambassador, had announced that full powers to sign were on the way, and the government had, on the strength of this, laid the convention before parliament, and fixed a day for its early discussion. The Sultan had then refused to authorise Musurus to sign.[150] There is no evidence of dissent within the cabinet about the strong line adopted in retaliation. It was agreed that Granville should threaten the cessation of the annual Egyptian tribute to Turkey, the breaking off of diplomatic relations between Britain and Turkey, and the adoption of the separation of Egypt from Turkey as the basis of British policy, if the Turkish representatives had not received powers to sign within twenty-four hours.[151]

The cabinet discussed Russian designs on Herat, the resulting decisions being embodied in telegrams to Dufferin. Granville was asked to inform Russia, without unfriendliness, that any attempt upon Herat would be a *casus belli*. 'All are agreed that any design on Herat must mean war.'[152]

What war would mean, rather baffled the cabinet, for they went on to turn over such questions as the powerlessness of the navy against Russia, the impregnability of Kronstadt, the shutting off of the Black Sea unless Turkey became an ally, and the ineffectiveness of any blockade while Russia had the use of German ports. Selborne was particularly morose on these grounds.[153] Gladstone privately held that Russia would refrain from attacking Australia because 'civilisation would forbid it'.[154]

The Liberal Cabinet in Downing Street in early 1884: 'For the last time, it was shown that the best political

The members of Salisbury's first cabinet, 1885–86. They had 'all been picked and trained by Disraeli to be

The Queen was to be asked to declare a state of emergency before she went abroad, so that the reserves could at once be called out if it became necessary to send reinforcements to India.[155] *March 27 (Friday)*. The cabinet met at Downing St at 2 with only Spencer absent, though Dilke arrived quite late.

Chamberlain pressed that Britain should urge both sides to withdraw from the disputed areas on the Afghan frontier, pointing out that a Russian refusal would unite the country and the Liberal party. Full consideration of this was postponed till Dufferin could sound out the Ameer at their impending meeting on his willingness to adopt the plan of reciprocal withdrawal.

The cabinet considered a telegram to Thornton for considera-tion by M. de Giers, informing Russia that Britain felt bound to regard as an act hostile to herself any aggression upon the Ameer's territories. Herat was the locality chiefly in mind.

A decision was taken to call out the reserves.*

The operations at Suakin were discussed. Trevelyan proposed that the troops should be withdrawn at once from there, and Harcourt interpolated a wish to withdraw altogether from Egypt. Trevelyan's proposal was felt to be impossible.[156]

The draft of Harcourt's crofters' bill was considered, the lord advocate being invited in during this part of the meeting. In Harcourt's subsequent account to his son, the bill received unani-mous assent, all the ministers who understood it saying it was an excellent bill. Hartington only asked 'Is it very bad?', meaning very radical.[157] Carlingford, who took a good deal of part in the discussion, described it as the Irish Land Act without free sale, and thought it a good bill,[158] a view later privately shared by a leading Scottish Tory, who described it as a 'fair enough attempt to deal with a very troublesome question'.[159]

On the same day, and probably at the cabinet, Gladstone talked over with Derby problems relating to Robinson and Warren in Bechuanaland, and saw the relevant telegrams.[160]

April 2 (Thursday). According to Dilke, Dufferin met the Ameer on this date and assured him that a Russian advance on Herat 'would be met by war all over the world'.[161]

April 4 (Saturday). The cabinet met at Downing St at 12, with Spencer, Childers and Dilke absent, to consider the Russian proposals which had been previously circulated, but had not yet reached all members of the cabinet. Dilke was in Edinburgh in

---

* Mentioned only by Dilke: but plausible in the light of Hartington's letter the following day: 'I don't think that things look much better with Russia. They have not actually advanced, but keep sending in more troops ... very difficult to avoid war' (Hartington to Duchess of Manchester, 28 Mar.).

connection with the Royal Commission on the Housing of the Working Classes. Gladstone introduced the subject and was emphatic that he did not think there could be any disagreement as to the Russian reply being wholly unsatisfactory. The course agreed on, of making no counter-proposal to Russia for the moment, but simply expressing incredulity that their answer accurately represented their considered policy, was opposed only by Harcourt, who denounced this as rushing into war. Harcourt offered specific proposals for a buffer zone, but did not attempt to persuade his colleagues by an offer of resignation, and received no support, Chamberlain saying 'I wish, Harcourt, you would not think it necessary to address us as if we were a bunch of Jingoes'.[162] The following decisions were reported to the Queen:

1. The cabinet felt that Kimberley and Hartington already had full authorisation to go ahead with whatever military measures the situation and the needs of the Indian government might demand.
2. The cabinet considered M. de Giers' proposal of 15 March for a unilateral Russian definition of the frontier subject only to subsequent modification in detail by a commission. Given the underlying assumption behind de Giers' civil language that Russia need not treat Britain as an equal in the matter, the cabinet felt bound to reject the Russian proposal, though Harcourt advised acceptance of the Russian scheme as a basis.
3. Granville left at 2 to fulfil an appointment with the Russian ambassador, returning before 3 with an explanatory memorandum from M. de Staal which in Granville's view did not alter the situation. The cabinet concurring in this view, Granville therefore returned to M. de Staal to express the hope that the proposal of 15 March would soon be superseded by further communications from his government.

In a letter to Childers describing the cabinet, Gladstone referred to the Sudan without making it quite clear whether this was actually brought before the meeting. Wolseley had asked for reinforcements, and at Suakin hopes of defeating Osman Digna were vanishing. Gladstone remarked that Wolseley's demands had continuously expanded as his promises of success had contracted, and thought that the limit of his wants might not yet have been reached. Gladstone told the cabinet that Wolseley had described prospects in the Sudan to Hartington as 'the most serious affair since 1815'.[163]

After the meeting Chamberlain said and wrote various points which betrayed his perplexity and relative ineffectiveness in cabinet when confronted with an international crisis. He said that it would not be difficult to hint to Wolseley at an impending change of policy and withdrawal of troops from the Sudan: and also, that Britain must offer Russia the alternative of arbitration before resorting to war. Chamberlain also wrote to Dilke describing the cabinet, arguing that the nature of the Russian answer left no alternative to rejection, but adding 'I am very uncomfortable about it because the more I study the matter the more I think the Russians are right'. Harcourt, wrote Chamberlain, had been more impracticable than ever, being inclined to accept the alternative of the Russian zone which had already been refused.[164]

April 6 (Monday). Hamilton made a note which clarifies Gladstone's position on the Sudan as it was on the eve of the Penjdeh crisis. Gladstone was described as 'aghast' at Wolseley's demands and pessimism, but 'he showed no signs yet of actually admitting that the policy in the Sudan must be reversed'. This statement qualifies the value of earlier remarks by Hamilton, a strong partisan of withdrawal, that a very strong feeling was mounting against the Sudan campaign (26 March) which would enable the government to abandon its decision to defeat the Mahdi, and that Gladstone had come to think the Sudan expedition could not be justified any longer (28 March).[165]

April 9 (Thursday). The cabinet met at 2 to review telegrams from Lumsden, British representative in Afghanistan, and from Thornton, envoy in Russia, giving news of a Russian attack upon the Afghans at Penjdeh (the 'Penjdeh incident'). The attack took place on 30 March, but word of it did not reach Downing St till the morning of 9 April.

As the cabinet meeting escaped the attention of *The Times*, and the diarists Dilke, Rosebery* and Carlingford were absent, one cannot be certain who attended. However, Selborne was absent nursing his sick wife, Carlingford was at Aix-les-Bains with the Queen, and Dilke was on his way back from Edinburgh. Gladstone had returned in the morning from Holmsbury, admitting himself to be very well, but striking his secretary with the thought 'he broke his voice last autumn in Midlothian, and it will never be what it was'.

The cabinet considered the Penjdeh incident and the best means of presenting such information to parliament, their conclusions

---

* Rosebery's brother Everard had died of typhoid in the Sudan the previous day, but Rosebery would certainly have attended the cabinet, had he heard in time of the Penjdeh incident (*R.J.*, 9 Apr..). His brother's illness had caused Rosebery to postpone a private but diplomatically intended visit to Berlin due to have started 6 Apr.

being embodied in the later statement by Gladstone in the House of Commons.

The cabinet were however 'inclined to a favourable view of the negotiations concerning the frontier, after the concessions which Russia has now been induced to make' provided that the 'catastrophe of Penjdeh' could be so dealt with as not to prevent the wider negotiations moving ahead.* In the private secretary's office, the incident appeared less final than it did to the outside world, Hamilton noting that 'Mr G by no means despairs of an amicable settlement', and (writing on 10 April) that Lumsden's telegrams left the question of the technical responsibility for the Penjdeh incident in doubt.†

During the day, but not in connection with the meeting itself, Gladstone drew up a memorandum admitting that policy in the Sudan required reappraisal, and arguing against further operations there, although 'he is not clear if the government should resign if policy is reversed'.[166] In another, more secret memorandum, Gladstone set out the arguments in favour of abandoning the Sudan.[167]

April 11 (*Saturday*). The cabinet met at short notice at noon to consider the now related problems of Russia and the Sudan, the meeting lasting three and a half hours. Four ministers were absent. Spencer was in Ireland, and Carlingford in attendance upon the Queen at Aix-les-Bains. Selborne's absence was due to the death of his wife on the previous day. Rosebery, despite his brother's death on 8 April, was only too eager to attend the meeting, and thereby missed it. Convinced that a cabinet would be called, he set off for London without receiving a summons, and not finding any trace of one there, he returned home, where a misdirected notice of the meeting eventually reached him by third post at 7.30 p.m. The method by which Rosebery was informed of proceedings is interesting: the same day Hamilton sent him Gladstone's cabinet report (now missing, but presumably as composed for the Queen) with a gloss by Hamilton to the effect that 'The decision

---

* Cf. Gladstone to his wife, 9 Apr., Glynne–Gladstone MSS, showing genuine horror at the Penjdeh incident, but retaining considerable optimism about the peaceful intentions of the Russian government: 'we have reason to hope that the negotiations on the frontier may go well'.

† Cf. Gladstone to his wife, 10 Apr., loc. cit.: '... Lumsden, on whom we depend for information, gives it extremely ill'; also Herbert to Henry Gladstone, 10 Apr., loc. cit., calling Lumsden 'opinionated, impulsive, and not very discreet'. When the sensible Sir Algernon West met Lumsden in London on 8 July 1885, he formed an impression of him as a 'real Russophobist' (A. West, *Recollections 1832–1886* (1899), ii, 243). On Lumsden's return, he was treated with indifference by Liberals, then conspicuously honoured by Conservatives.

will probably have to be taken on Monday. Meanwhile a lengthy memo of Mr G's is being circulated which will explain more fully his personal views.'[168] Hamilton and Rosebery were, of course, on intimate terms politically, and had known each other at Eton.

Gladstone's notes on this cabinet began cryptically 'Rothschild advances – agreed to.'[169]

According to Dilke,[170] Egyptian finance was the second item on the agenda, but no record of what was said or decided remains.

A telegram from Dufferin was read, raising the question of Lumsden's position. Kimberley returned instructions that Lumsden should remain where he then was, near the Persian border but still within Afghanistan.

The cabinet was pleased with Kimberley's reports on what the Ameer had told Dufferin. What the cabinet were not told, from deliberate mistrust, was secret information that the Ameer was decidedly suffering from disease of the kidneys though his life might well be substantially prolonged. Gladstone and Kimberley, while withholding this information from their colleagues, reported it to the Queen.

The cabinet thought that in view of the possibility of war with Russia, Granville should try to make arrangements with China and Japan which would give Britain the use of Port Hamilton in Korea if needed. Granville however later described this as 'academic talk'.[171] In the same spirit, the cabinet examined the legality of employing Indian troops in Afghanistan.

The cabinet considered the timing of parliamentary business in relation to the vote of credit, the budget, and discussion on the calling out of the reserves. It was settled that the vote of credit was to be the occasion for unfolding future policy.

A preliminary discussion took place upon how far military action was still possible in the Sudan given the threat from Russia.[172] After this cabinet, but before the next one, a lengthy memorandum by Gladstone was circulated on this question.

The elaborately slow discussion was chiefly for the purpose of allowing Hartington time to back down. Other ministers who had formerly been strongly for an active policy in the Sudan and Egypt, were finding much less difficulty in reversing their views. Selborne wrote to Gladstone agreeing in effect to such a change as regards military operations in the Sudan, admitting 'the embarrassment caused by Lord Wolseley's despatches' and taking the view that if Russian proceedings led to war ('and I can hardly see what else can be their issue'), then the whole resources of the country would be required for that purpose. In any case, Selborne agreed that 'a suspension of active operations' in the Sudan might become necessary. Selborne, in making this admission, did not at all lend his support to a policy of evacuation of territories already held.[173] Granville's account of the meeting conveyed well this sense of a tide having turned:

'We had a long conversation yesterday at the cabinet – chiefly about the Sudan. No decision taken. No one argued for the expedition against Khartoum next autumn, excepting Harcourt, who says we must go there, if we do not altogether retire which he warmly advocates.

The current was in favour of the latter.

Hartington raising many objections – Chamberlain wishing to maintain the Railway in order to show that we had some dividend for our late investment.'[174]

Politically, however, it was clear enough that, now Gladstone had made it clear which way he wanted to go,[175] the cabinet generally would follow, and the central question at issue was no longer the merits of certain policies, but finding a way of keeping Hartington in the government. Hartington's own statement after the cabinet, made the difficulties of his position plain:

'Although I admit that if we go to war with Russia it may be impossible for us to carry on two such enterprises at once, or at least unwise to attempt it, I feel the strongest dislike to abandoning the Sudan expedition until it is absolutely certain that we shall have to fight Russia, and on that ground alone.

If it were now necessary to send more troops to the Sudan which might be wanted for Russia, it might be urgent that we should come to a decision: but that is not the case. The urgency is a parliamentary one & consists in the necessity of telling parliament in a week or so whether the expedition is to proceed or not. There is no doubt that Wolseley's demands have greatly increased & that to go to Khartoum will now in his opinion be a much bigger affair than he had led us to expect in February, but I cannot admit that it is a sufficient reason for a complete change of policy, that it is rather more difficult than we had supposed. Mr Gladstone, I believe, thinks that the reasons for the expedition have become weaker as the difficulties have increased: but I can see no strong arguments in support of this.

I have got a short memo. of Mr. Gladstone wh. he did not read, but most of wh. he stated, in wh. he gives his view of the question. If you are coming up for the cabinet at 12 on Monday I could show it to you... I can't send it to you now, as I want to go over the points carefully and see whether I can make up my mind to take his view, or on what grounds I can definitely decline to accept it.'[176]

The difficulty of bringing Hartington into line was compounded by the fact that he knew exactly why he wanted to resign. 'He thinks his resignation will not injure him, and if he is to be PM, would like to have breathing space before Mr G retires'.[177] He spent the greater part of Sunday consulting Rosebery about whether to go, treating him as his political conscience; and dined with him again on Monday after cabinet for the same reasons. Rosebery, as fresh as Hartington was tired, was an unwearying partisan of Hartington holding on for the present. Rosebery's relations with Hartington at this point, based on confidentiality rather than the pursuit of any policy, closely resemble his relations with Gladstone later in the year, and tell much of the kind of relations Rosebery needed to have with senior colleagues.

April 13 (*Monday*). The cabinet met at Downing St from 12 to 4.30. Spencer, Selborne and Carlingford were absent, the last en route from France.

The cabinet first considered the French demand for an immediate reversal of the decision to suppress the *Bosphore Egyptien*, an Egyptian newspaper hostile to the British presence. The order for suppression had been issued on 29 February, but had not been executed till 10 April.[178] In view of the curt tone used by France with its implied exploitation of British preoccupation elsewhere,[179] the cabinet decided to reply by expressing surprise and asking what legal grounds there were for the French demand.

The cabinet then discussed a suggested settlement in Afghanistan, put forward in a private capacity by M. de Staal and passed to Gladstone in a letter[180] from Reginald Brett, Hartington's secretary at the War Office until very recently. Brett's letter enclosed a memorandum from M. Lessar. M. de Staal undertook to recommend his plan to his government if it found favour with Britain.

The plan proposed that the Penjdeh incident should stand over pending inquiry: that both sides should withdraw their forces from the disputed territory: and that the commission to establish the frontier should meet at once, on a basis which was not made quite clear. Rosebery criticised the document as ambiguous and intentionally obscure throughout, a quite unauthorised attempt to find out whether Britain was in earnest.[181] The cabinet, however, attached great value to de Staal's second proposal, and it was left to Granville to see what could be built upon the basis of his offer.

Over the weekend ministers had been circulated with Gladstone's long memorandum[182] on the Sudan. This, though balanced, ended decidedly in favour of withdrawal. In the light of this and of Saturday's inconclusive discussion, ministers resumed their examination of the bearing of the international situation on policy in the Sudan. In particular they considered whether to abandon the proposed offensive operations, and whether such an abandonment of the offensive should be followed by evacuation qualified only in minor ways and by the general need to defend Egypt. Ministers were not able to reach agreement on this question.[183] Hartington declared himself absolutely unable to agree to such a change of policy,[184] not on simple expansionist grounds, but because, in the parliamentary context, Gladstone's 'mainly negative' memorandum 'does not give me sufficient materials on which to frame the vote of credit' and so fund the Egyptian war. On the one hand, 'the bent of the cabinet was clearly in favour of abandoning further offensive operations', but this 'may very likely involve the resignation of Lord Hartington, and likewise possibly of Childers and the Lord Chancellor'.[185]

At 4.30, Gladstone was writing his letter to the Queen, and the cabinet were getting up to go, the air heavy with resignation, when Rosebery spoke up and insisted that there should be another cabinet held on the question.[186]

April 14 (*Tuesday*). The cabinet met at Downing St at 2, with Selborne and Spencer absent.

Granville reported on his negotiations with Russia. He and Kimberley had met Staal and Lessar, and possible boundaries had been reviewed. Granville undertook to impress on Russia the impolity of its announcement that it was increasing its forces on the frontier, though he was to some extent restrained in doing so by a fear that the Afghans were doing the same thing at Zulficar.

Spencer sent his views on the Sudan, saying that immediate withdrawal 'would be an immense advantage' provided (and to him this was crucial) that 'something like a settled government was left behind'.[187]

The cabinet postponed coming to a decision on the abandonment of the Khartoum expedition,[188] 'though it is pretty evident what that decision will be'.[189] This postponement, for the third cabinet in succession, was to allow Hartington more time to come round, chiefly under Harcourt's persuasion, to a reversal of policy which fell short of an immediate announcement to abandon the autumn expedition. To Gladstone at least, things looked well: he 'was very benign, and showed a kind of senile cheerfulness'.[190] To others, however, the chances of losing Hartington still seemed rather high,[191] though there was a consideration which favoured his retention of office. This was his satisfaction at the firm tone taken by Britain with Russia.[192]

April 15 (*Wednesday*). The cabinet met at Downing St from 2.30 to 5, with Spencer and Dilke absent, the latter steering the seats bill through committee.

An unsatisfactory communication from France about the *Bosphore Egyptien* was discussed, and telegrams to and from Lord Lyons and Sir E. Baring were considered. The message that Lyons was to give to Freycinet, was 'of civil regret that he was misinformed' about the case.[193] This was a strong line for the cabinet to take and it owed more to anger and ignorance than to prudence or to the legal issues involved. Gladstone had reported Freycinet's view as being 'unless he has full and immediate satisfaction he must proceed to all extremities. (He has, says Granville, 50,000 men ready for China, who will not now be wanted).'[194] It was decided to seek a firm opinion on the legal issues involved from the law officers.

Hartington read a telegram from Wolseley protesting against abandonment of Dongola, in the event of the Khartoum campaign being called off. A telegram on future military policy, drawn up by Hartington, was accepted by the cabinet for sending to Wolseley.[195] It expressed an intention to withdraw, though not precipitately, to Wadi Halfa.[196]

According to only one source, Gladstone's cabinet notes, the third item on the agenda was a plan for improving the security of the Suez Canal. After only a short and inconclusive discussion it was decided to ask Baring, the author of the plan, for further details.

In view of impending changes of policy in the Sudan, the officer commanding at Suakin (Gen. Graham) was instructed not to sign any alliances with the surrounding tribes, the clear implication of this being that an active British presence in that area could no longer be assumed.[197]

A telegram reporting that the Ameer thought Penjdeh an insult he must wipe out, was left to Dufferin to handle.[198]

The approaching vote of credit requiring definition of policy, Gladstone read out the substance of the statement he proposed to make in parliament, much of it composed by Hartington. The cabinet agreed that the vote asked for 'does not include any provision for military preparations for an early advance on Khartoum. As to ulterior steps, we reserve entire liberty of action subject to the approval of parliament.' The troops set free in Egypt and the Sudan would be held as a reserve, while the Indian army would be reinforced from home.[199]

219

The form of this decision was adopted to save Hartington's face, and to a lesser extent to mollify the Queen who was still intensely active in pressing for conquest and occupation. No 'definitive reversal of the policy of February' was to be announced, and liberty of future action was, ostensibly, reserved. The Wadi Halfa railway from Suakin was to be completed up to a certain point, while its further continuation would be decided later on military grounds. This was the price exacted by Hartington for his assent to dropping preparations for an autumn offensive on the Nile.[200]

April 16 (*Thursday*). 'Baring has changed front and telegraphs against withdrawing from Dongola.'[201]

April 20 (*Monday*). The cabinet met from 2 to 4.30 at Downing St, with only Spencer absent. Though the budget was the main topic, owing to sharp differences the cabinet were unable to dispose of it and adjourned consideration of it indefinitely.

Besides financial measures, the cabinet seems only to have considered a despatch about Penjdeh from Sir P. Lumsden. The meeting was however overshadowed by de Giers' note to Staal seeking to shift the blame for Penjdeh on to the Afghans and the English officers, a communication which in the circumstances spelt a willingness to risk war, and which put Gladstone into his gravest mood.[202]

It was decided to ask for a vote of credit the following day for £11m., divided into £8m. for the Army, and £3m. for the Navy: or into £4½m. for the Sudan and, £6½m. on account of the Russian threat. £115,000 of the special expenditure for the Sudan was for railways. In addition to this sum of £11m., it was found that £4m. was required to meet the increased recurrent charges, principally in respect of defence. Childers proposed to raise the requisite £15m. as follows: £6m. from new taxation within the year, £7m. by suspending the reduction of the National Debt, and to meet £2¼m. by borrowing if necessary. Childers also proposed to keep income tax at 7d. for three years.[203]

Controversy centred on the proposed raising of the beer duties. By also increasing taxes on landed property and on middle class incomes, Childers had attempted to spread the costs of the emergency as widely and as fairly as possible. Derby, Childers, and probably also Gladstone were clear that some of the extra revenue ought to come from the working classes by indirect taxation.

At least, Childers' case was much stronger than his handling of it. Rosebery thought 'he stated his case wretchedly... It was a Childers bait (as we should have said at Eton) for 2 hours': he 'bitched it', said Gladstone.[204] The fact of Childers' recent success in the important Egyptian financial negotiations at Paris counted for nothing, partly because their very success had made them unnoticed, partly because they had left Childers flat and unimpressive. Nor did the imminence of war in any way reduce the propensity to argue.

Dilke's objections on party and electioneering grounds to the increases were shared by Harcourt and Chamberlain: but it is hard not to see Dilke as the prime mover in making the dispute into a major one. The row about the beer duties had been impending for some time and was well known to the prime minister. On 2 March Dilke had warned Gladstone of the political dangers involved, and in early April he presented Gladstone with a memorandum on the budget, arguing that the real wages of the working class were falling.[205] After the cabinet on 20 April a brisk exchange of letters followed, Dilke beginning 'I did not wish to say anything likely to cause unpleasantness at the cabinet, but I meant what I said, and I could not agree to the additional tax on beer under the present circumstances.' Further letters on 20 and 21 April made it clear that both sides regarded this as an offer of resignation, which Dilke could not be persuaded to withdraw.[206] The letters were mild in tone, and Dilke was able to employ courtesies which were noticeably absent when he next attempted to break up the ministry in May. Dilke, as in May, appeared to be at first going beyond what was common ground between him and Chamberlain, and then drawing back as Chamberlain showed signs of proving amenable to Gladstone's persuasions. While there was probably more to Dilke's action than the genuine Radical objection to electorally damaging taxation, the natural consequences of his behaviour were likely to extend only to his leaving the ministry, rather than putting the party in opposition in one bound. The episode is interesting not for what it established of the scope of Dilke's intentions at this moment, but as showing that Dilke, on grounds of pure calculation, was willing to give a much more ruthless precedence to the future (i.e. the political situation under the new franchise) over the present, than was Chamberlain. *

April 21 (Tuesday). The cabinet met at 2 at Downing St, with only Spencer absent.

The parliamentary timetable for the vote of credit and the budget was settled. The question of whether to ask for two votes

---

* Dilke almost certainly had constituency grounds for opposing increased beer duties; 'I once had to fight the publicans and Lawsonites combined against me, but I had rather not have to do it again' (Dilke to Chamberlain, 13 Nov. 1884, Chamberlain MSS JC 5/24/74). Chamberlain, on the other hand, had to take into account the temperance element among his supporters. We owe this point to Dr M. Barker.

of credit or one was resolved, and it was decided to take them on Monday. The budget was fixed for 30 April, although settlement of disputed points in it was held over till the cabinet of 25 April.[207]

The cabinet agreed that Lumsden's very full telegram, received that day, should be presented to parliament at once.

Granville then laid before the cabinet the reply received at 1 p.m. from M. de Staal to his letter on Sunday, 19 April. An answer to the Russian reply, which was unsatisfactory as regards past and future military action, could not be devised owing to the meeting of the House of Lords, but the cabinet felt that weight should primarily be given to their belief that no vital differences of opinion separated Britain and Russia as regards the delimitation of the frontier. Granville was absent from the latter part of the discussion on this subject,[208] which in any case was very heated, confused, and unproductive, principally because Harcourt attempted to hold the stage with a lecture, violently delivered, on peace. Kimberley showed anger: Chamberlain said he preached the doctrine of eating dirt offensively: Hartington said '*Your* way is easy enough – to give way in everything.' Harcourt replied that he would regard a Russian attack on Herat as a *casus belli*. Chamberlain commented 'He'd find some way out of that when the time came.'

Later, over tea in the House of Lords, Northbrook, Kimberley and Carlingford talked over the situation, Northbrook saying that Harcourt's absence made it possible to talk rationally. Kimberley came up with the idea of isolating the Penjdeh incident from the general frontier negotiations, by referring it to a third power.[209]

The discussion on the budget was highly acrimonious, with the Radicals trying to impose their ideas of a popular electioneering budget on measures brought forward to meet an international crisis. Gladstone in turn could not agree to not putting any of the fresh taxation on indirect taxes. 'Mr G felt that in present circumstances the great thing was to gain time. At present Chamberlain and Dilke show no sign of yielding...'.[210] Indeed, Chamberlain himself had just written:

'Childers is ——!
I will speak to him and if he maintains his position, Mr Gladstone must choose between his Chancellor of the Exchequer and *two* of his colleagues.'[211]

Rosebery's summary of the two cabinets of 20 and 21 April was correct: 'Discussion on budget and Russia. Two hours today and two hours yesterday with no result.'[212]

April 24 (Friday). In the evening, Gladstone had a satisfactory interview with Chamberlain and removed the possibility of his departure over the budget, Gladstone's casuistry being to stress that Childers' increased death duties on real property were a triumph for Chamberlain's policies.[213] Dilke had earlier in the day consented to the increased beer duties, at Chamberlain's wish,* so that the way lay clear for the cabinet on the budget the following day.

Another preparatory meeting went less smoothly. A draft despatch to Russia proposing arbitration had been circulated and had been criticised by Hartington, Harcourt and Rosebery, all being chiefly concerned with what the next step would be if Russia rejected arbitration. To iron out the differences, the above three ministers met with Granville, Northbrook, Kimberley and Gladstone in Gladstone's room at 6.30. There was a long wrangle. Harcourt, because Kimberley once interrupted him, said he had better leave the government at once, never having been so insulted. On some other point he said he must resign. Granville protested against resignation perpetually being used to replace argument.[214]

April 25 (Saturday). The cabinet met at Downing St at 12, with only Spencer absent.

'Chamberlain and Dilke having given way about the beer duty',[215] the details of the budget were to all appearances finally agreed. The main points were i) income tax at 8d.; ii) higher duties on beer and spirits; iii) an increase in the death duties, virtually assimilating the duties on real and on personal property; iv) the virtual suspension of the repayment of the Debt. Specific attention was given to the question of how the clergy would pay on their lands.[216]

The attorney-general, Henry James, and the solicitor-general, Herschell, attended in order to advise on the case of the *Bosphore Egyptien*, about which Granville had just been talking to Waddington. The complaints of M. de Freycinet in this case, which he had contrived to link to the satisfactory execution of the Egyptian financial convention, appeared to turn on the manner of the suppression rather than the suppression itself. The law officers were

---

* Dilke, op. cit., f. 132: allegedly 'in view of Chamberlain's local government scheme for Ireland [having been] accepted as final by the R.C. bishops, and offering in my mind the only chance of the pacification of Ireland and my own strong hopes of obtaining it from the wisdom and liberality of the cabinet' (undated memorandum in Dilke's hand, Dilke MSS, 43913 f. 131). Also on 24 Apr., Dilke wrote to his future wife 'even Croke, the most extreme of the great bishops, will denounce an Irish Parliament' (ibid., 43906, f. 58). Some or much of this 'Irish' explanation of Dilke's backing down on the beer issue must be taken as a *fable convenable* covering the simple point that Chamberlain was much less interested in the issue, and was not prepared to give him full backing.

quite clear that the closure of the printing office had been an illegal method of exercising censorship.

The cabinet did not wish to throw responsibility on to Nubar Pasha, which might turn out properly to lie with Baring. At the same time, wishing to close the issue quickly, they instructed Granville to admit illegality in the manner of suppression, and to advise the Egyptian government to express regret for the incident, while allowing the printing office to be at once reopened.[217] However, the paper (presumably as distinct from the printing office) was not to be allowed to reappear. In Hartington's view, the 'horrid mess' over the *Bosphore Egyptien* was due to the Foreign Office trying to manage Egypt without legal advice: 'Nothing therefore for it but to apologise... How Granville can go on making apologies for his blunders without proposing his resignation I can't imagine: but it seems never to occur to him'.[218]

Chamberlain then proposed that Britain should take the opportunity offered by recent French harassments to get out of Egypt altogether. Britain should tell France that the position was intolerable, that it could not go on acting as agents for Europe there, and that Egypt would have to go bankrupt. Britain should simply leave as soon as possible, insisting only on the freedom of the Suez Canal. This strange proposal was not supported by anyone, not even by Dilke or Harcourt. Gladstone and Granville, ironically, did the work of quietly expressing the collective sense of the fatuity of Chamberlain's proposal.

The cabinet discussed the progress of the bills for the session.

'A despatch was sent to de Staal inviting further examination of the facts about the Penjdeh incident and suggesting reference to a friendly power'.[219] Hartington, Rosebery and Harcourt were against this offer of arbitration to Russia, the two former because it smacked of appeasement, the last because it was a further step on the road to war. Hartington, who thought that things were getting worse and worse, and that a breach of diplomatic relations with Russia would soon come, naturally found the arbitration proposals 'rather absurd'.[220] Harcourt and Kimberley disputed the terms of the despatch to de Staal, the words 'as a final effort to preserve friendly relations' being modified to satisfy Harcourt, by leaving out 'final'.[221]

April 28 (*Tuesday*). The cabinet met at 2 at Downing St, with all members present.

Granville reported on his conversation with M. Waddington about the *Bosphore Egyptien*, and on his negotiations with Russia, who continued to offer amicable support for an inquiry into the recent skirmish.

The programme of legislation for the session was reviewed. The cabinet, after hearing of discussions between the Queen and Gladstone, decided to give precedence over all other legislation (except the seats bill), to the bill to make provision for Princess Beatrice. According to Dilke, the progress of the registration bill in particular came under scrutiny.

A committee[222] of the cabinet was appointed to consider in what way the Crimes Act (Ireland) ought to be renewed, and also what would be the proper proposals to incorporate in an Irish local government bill. The committee might also proceed to frame recommendations relating to land purchase in Ireland.

In the initial discussion on Ireland, Spencer said that renewal of much of the Crimes Act was necessary. To balance this, he wanted also a land purchase bill, a local government bill, and the announcement of the abolition of the lord-lieutenant, and of the institution of a royal residence in Ireland.* Gladstone backed him up, stressing that these proposals must be treated as a single package. Chamberlain said he could not consent to a crimes bill unless the local government bill was very far-reaching. Carlingford said a crimes bill was imperative and that he wanted a liberal scheme of county government as its main accompaniment.[223]

The cabinet thought it would be advisable to introduce and if possible carry a crofters' bill, a Scottish secretary bill, and a bill for intermediate education in Wales. The Scottish secretary bill was to be introduced by Rosebery into the House of Lords, and was to assign Scottish education to the Scottish Office, though this was not to be made a vital point. Carlingford again protested that there were no educational grounds for splitting off Scottish education, an argument which was not impugned.

Hartington raised anew the subject of the publication of the *Journals* of General Gordon. The cabinet would on no account undertake their expurgation, leaving the matter in the hands of Sir Henry Gordon and expressing only a desire for the publication of the whole text.[224]

April 29 (Wednesday). Gladstone gave a long interview in the morning to Spencer and Chamberlain to discuss Irish local government on which Hamilton declared 'Mr G feels very strongly.'[225]

---

* The plan for stronger royal links with Ireland was something of an *idée fixe* with Spencer and figured in most of his sketches of an Irish reform programme in 1885. The Irish tour of the Prince of Wales in Apr. 1885 had been very much his doing. Nevertheless the proposal does not seem to have been taken up at all in cabinet or cabinet committee, and despite initial friendliness on some points in an interview with Spencer on 6 May, the Queen changed front sharply and by 11 May had imposed a virtual veto on the whole project. See Sir Sidney Lee, *King Edward VII, A Biography* (1925), i, 223.

The Irish committee appointed by the cabinet the previous day met at 2 in Campbell-Bannerman's room in the House of Commons. Spencer, Trevelyan, Chamberlain, Harcourt, Carlingford, and (though not in the cabinet) Campbell-Bannerman attended. By way of overture, Harcourt protested against dropping any section of the existing Crimes Act – a position much more extreme than that of Spencer or any other member of the cabinet – and Chamberlain protested against having a new crimes bill at all. The committee then went through the expiring Act clause by clause, accepting Spencer's proposals to drop certain unnecessary or counter-productive clauses, and to renew the rest. How many ministers accepted this revision is not clear. Trevelyan, for instance, who had recently assured Spencer of his support, said at this meeting that he 'almost entirely agreed with Chamberlain'. The latter, who made a show of reluctance about even attending the committee, had not been made more conciliatory by having been led to think that Gladstone was strongly behind him on the central board scheme. Spencer and Chamberlain had already spent a long time discussing this privately with Gladstone. Spencer had been sent the scheme by Chamberlain on 13 April.[226]

May 1 (*Friday*). The Irish committee of the cabinet met at Spencer House from 11 to 2.30 to discuss Chamberlain's central board proposals, details of which had previously been circulated to most or all of those on the committee. Those present were Spencer, Campbell-Bannerman (although not a cabinet minister), Carlingford, Trevelyan, Hartington, Harcourt, Childers, Lefevre, and Chamberlain. Discussion revolved entirely round Chamberlain's scheme, no attention being given to the alternative of a county government bill. On Chamberlain's scheme, the committee was divided without chance of agreement.

Chamberlain formally explained his plans: how they had been long in his mind; how he had 'discovered' that Parnell had a similar plan, which would satisfy most home rulers; and that Manning had promised it the support of the church. Chamberlain said he was convinced that his plan was the only way of avoiding home rule.

Carlingford and Harcourt violently attacked Chamberlain's central board scheme, though on different grounds: Carlingford because it appeared to him to involve nationalist control over the Irish administration, being 'a virtual acceptance of home rule, and in the worst form': Harcourt because the central board, though otherwise acceptable, would be abused for ulterior purposes. As ever, Harcourt's arguments struck Carlingford as absurd. Hartington said little, but was evidently against the scheme, though less

226

violently so than Harcourt and Carlingford. Spencer declared against it, but apparently not in any forcible way: Campbell-Bannerman, who said nothing at this meeting, had in fact the previous day circulated an adverse memorandum on the scheme. Campbell-Bannerman had argued that any viable solution would either have to be much larger or much smaller than the scheme proposed. Childers, Trevelyan, and Lefevre declared for the scheme, Trevelyan having minuted his approval of it at length the previous day.

Because Hartington and Spencer did not play a prominent part at this meeting, the Radicals may have left under the impression that the resistance to their Irish scheme was really not too formidable. Dilke wrote an account of the meeting (which he did not attend) which uses two points, not mentioned elsewhere, to support this interpretation. Firstly, he claimed that at a certain point in the meeting, Spencer seemed to waver, whereon Harcourt began to change his line: secondly, that after the meeting Gladstone told Chamberlain that Carlingford's opposition did not matter.

Dilke occupied himself with a further meeting with Manning.[227] *May 2 (Saturday)*. On the Russian reply to the British proposals for arbitration being received, a cabinet was at once summoned, meeting at Downing St at 5 p.m. Those absent were Carlingford, Chamberlain, Harcourt, and Spencer. Rosebery arrived late, at 6.15, just as the meeting was finishing.

The Russian acceptance of the suggestions lately made in despatches by Granville had arrived early in the afternoon. In particular they agreed to submit to arbitration the incident at Penjdeh, which had just been the subject of a telegram from Dufferin warning of the doubtfulness of the British case. The cabinet regarded the Russian proposal as 'sufficient and satisfactory', or in E. Hamilton's report, 'they agreed to shake hands' with Russia and recommended the immediate resumption of proceedings for delimiting the Afghan frontier. Granville was to see the Queen the following day to put before her the terms of the British reply.[228]

According to Dilke's notes, the course of discussion preceding the above decision was as follows. Those for acceptance were Kimberley, Selborne, Northbrook, Derby, and Dilke. Hartington was against arbitration, and Granville was undecided. Trevelyan and Shaw-Lefevre were silent. Gladstone wavered, then came down on the side of the majority.

The only minor business recorded relating to this meeting was that Childers, with Dilke's approval, drew up the form of words to be used as regards the Select Committee on the Civil List.[229]

After the meeting, Gladstone asked Rosebery to talk with him

227

about Ireland, principally because Gladstone 'considered that any Local Govt. scheme for Ireland has so important a bearing on Scottish affairs: what Ireland has, to that Scotland is entitled'. Besides this idea (never followed up) that Scotland 'should have a kindred measure', Gladstone was also looking for a political heir, and talked to Rosebery 'because as youngest member of cabinet, he had most interest in future'.[230]

Hamilton, presumably on the basis of information from Gladstone, also noted at this point that Chamberlain's scheme of Irish reforms was supported by Childers, Trevelyan, Harcourt, and Hartington, among others, while Spencer and Carlingford 'alone hold out'. Hamilton's analysis should be regarded sceptically.[231] Rosebery noted opinions on Chamberlain's scheme as being Carlingford hostile, Harcourt and Hartington dubious, while Spencer had gone to Althorp to consider. Spencer would have been hostile but was much surprised by Harcourt and Hartington not being so.[232]

The apparent solution of the Russian crisis, and the presence of hopeful signs about Ireland, filled Gladstone with an exalted joy which he expressed by quoting his favourite hymn:

'How is it possible to be sufficiently thankful.
>   Praise to the Holiest in the Height,
>   And in the depth be praise
>   In all His works how wonderful
>   How just in all his ways'.[233]

The sense of exceptional inner strength, hope, and energy that filled Gladstone at times in May and June 1885 must be used to elucidate his apparently negative tactical moves over the same period, the two things taken together creating a strong presumption that he was interested in resignation only as another way by which he would shape history to his ends.

May 5 (Tuesday). 'Mr G does not see how he can assent to a Crimes Bill without a remedial measure.'[234]

May 7 (Thursday).[235] The cabinet met at Downing St at noon, with all ministers[236] present. Lord R. Grosvenor, the chief whip, attended the meeting.[237]

The cabinet considered recent telegrams from Egypt which did not accord in policy either with each other or with previous cabinet decisions. Hartington was asked to impress upon Wolseley that he must arrange to evacuate the province of Dongola, as previously instructed.

The cabinet agreed with Kimberley that frontier negotiations with Russia should proceed at once, especially since such a policy had been expressly approved by the council of the viceroy.

The cabinet accepted the preference of Gladstone and Granville for the Kaiser as arbitrator in the Afghan dispute, and failing him the King of Denmark.

The main purpose of the meeting was to discuss the desirability of a resignation over a contrived defeat in the near future, following the recent narrow division about Irish registration expenses. While Gladstone was more inclined than in a conversation with Ponsonby the previous day, to think that on balance difficulties internal to the cabinet might be resolved, he expected the management of the House of Commons to become increasingly difficult. Gladstone argued that the ministry had held on after the Gordon debate because, in large measure, of passing the seats bill and carrying out their agreement with the opposition. The recent hostility shown by the opposition on such questions as the Sudan, Russia, and taxation, made firm and effective government by the Liberals exceptionally difficult in Gladstone's view. He anticipated concerted action by the Conservatives and the Irish, which would greatly diminish the chances of passing a war budget in conditions of relative tranquillity.

The cabinet agreed to resign if they were again beaten on the question of registration payments. 'It was announced we should certainly be beaten on the budget and if not, would break up on Ireland.'[238] On the whole, however, the cabinet were only vaguely envisaging a defeat, and were not specifically enjoining Grosvenor to procure one for them, even on registration. There was no direct decision to ride for a fall over such impending questions as local taxation.

Consideration of the budget was again put off because of disagreement.

Gladstone was at this time highly attracted by the idea of terminating his career,* a mood which lasted four days, terminated with his packing his bags on Sunday at Downing St, and did a great deal to secure that the question of his continued leadership of the party never became an openly debated issue after the fall of the ministry. Gladstone, after the cabinet, took Rosebery back to his room:

'in great spirits at the prospect of escape. Thought he wd. go abroad. If he re-entered the H. of C. it must be understood that he

* 'Almost every individual minister is madly keen to get out. The person who has this desire most strongly upon him is Mr G' (E. H. J.). The optimistic tone of Gladstone's letters to his wife in early May belie the latter statement, in so far as they point to the great problems sorting themselves out.

should only attend when desired by his friends.* But he did not think of standing again. Nor of a peerage. His wife had an ancient barony in the family which he thought she might have revived, and Sir B. Burke had drawn out the pedigree for her but she had lost it.' †

May 9 (Saturday). Conversation in the private secretaries' office in the morning was gloomy. Gladstone said that he was with neither side on the crimes bill and would therefore retire. Rosebery said the cabinet could not go on.[239] And Dilke's views returned to the proposal of a contrived defeat already canvassed on 7 May. 'His argument was that it would be far better to be beaten on a side issue like that of registration expenses than on a main question like the budget.'[240]

The cabinet met at Downing St, with all ministers present. The meeting was called unexpectedly to settle what announcement should be made about policy in the Sudan. It was noted that already there had been as many cabinets that year 'as there are in a year in normal quiet times'.[241]

It was agreed to postpone consideration of the budget until after Whitsuntide. Childers announced what Dilke saw as a declaration of commercial war against Spain, by means of a large increase in the wine duties. Dilke's opposition was expressed in terms of the bad effect the change could have on relations with France.[242]

Hartington rehearsed a statement to be made to the House of Commons on Monday regarding the new policy of concentrating British military strength. This would involve *inter alia* the abandonment of any expedition to Khartoum. Hartington proposed to reserve his judgement on the question of the extension of the Suakin railway, and the question of retaining some loose and indirect control over Dongola was to remain open.[243] Selborne wanted to resign over what he saw as a weak policy in the Sudan.[244]

Gladstone raised afresh the idea of an inquiry by committee into the financial provision for members of the royal family. The cabinet approved the idea, but felt it was too late in the session to take any immediate action.

Kimberley reported satisfactorily on the Afghan frontier negotiations. The cabinet felt that a treaty with Russia would be of great value, Hartington wanting a special pledge about Herat.[245]

Granville mentioned the King of Saxony as a possible frontier

---

* Rosebery's comment shows how belatedly he became a Gladstonian in 1885: 'This wd. never do, he shd. not stand again for H. of C.'

† R.J., 7 May. But, Rosebery went on, Mrs Gladstone had told him she had not really lost it, but just hated the idea (ibid.).

arbitrator, but the suggestion was dismissed, and the cabinet adhered to its previous preference for the Kaiser. The Queen had raised objections to the King of Denmark. Asked how the Turkish negotiations were proceeding, Granville complained of the difficulty of dealing with a man of oriental reticence who spoke no French. 'I have no doubt' said Hartington, 'that you spoke to him in excellent French, but I expect your reticence was quite as oriental as his.'[246]

At the close of the cabinet, a discussion was opened on Irish legislation 'in which however no progress was made. The subject must be resumed in a few days, by Friday at latest, but today some members of the cabinet left the room before the subject was opened.'[247]

Those who had left, Harcourt, Dilke and Trevelyan, had certainly heard all the arguments before. Chamberlain again expounded his central board scheme, and said that without it he could not be a party to a crimes bill. Chamberlain offered to turn his scheme into a bill in a week if he were given the English local government bill, Sir John Lambert, and an Irish official.[248] Derby, Carlingford and Selborne spoke out against the scheme, Carlingford strongly so. Then Spencer denounced it: 'it would be a *Convention* sitting in Dublin'. Kimberley supported his views. Childers and Lefevre were with Chamberlain: Gladstone described Chamberlain's plan as the 'only hope for Ireland' but said it was quite useless to go into the argument.[249] 'Eventually Spencer and Chamberlain both pinned themselves down – S not to swallow C's bill, C not to swallow S's crimes bill.'[250]

May 10 (*Sunday*). Gladstone responded to the divisions shown in the cabinet the previous day by a quite unwonted show of determination to resign. Mrs Gladstone began to pack, and Gladstone himself talked of retirement from politics, these actions together with Harcourt's activities as peacemaker successfully bringing the warring factions to heel for the time being by the evening.

After the cabinet on Saturday, Gladstone had written to Spencer saying he must resign, as no agreement could be come to about Ireland. Rosebery and Hamilton both refer to Sunday at Downing St being spent in packing up, Gladstone being entirely passive in Harcourt's attempts to reach a settlement. By 7 Harcourt was able to report that 'the ox had been pulled out of the pit', the crimes bill was settled, and 'that the great object to which all have sacrificed their own prepossessions is that of keeping you as our Chief *for the time* and not breaking up the party at this critical moment.' Dilke ironically described Harcourt's formula of conciliation as 'no home rule, no coercion, no remedial legislation, no Ireland at all', which may have been correct in that Harcourt had achieved momentary agreement on the basis of simply dropping all Irish topics except a greatly weakened crimes bill. Rosebery's view was that it was Chamberlain's wing which had given most ground in order to retain Gladstone.[251] The most detailed account of the deal was that reported by Carlingford on the basis of a conversation with Harcourt on Monday, 11 May. In return for Spencer giving up those sections of the Crimes Act dealing with public meetings and powers of search, Chamberlain was supposed to have agreed not to raise the question of Irish local government until after the elections. Harcourt had achieved his temporary success simply by threatening each party to the split with the loss of Gladstone's mantle. Harcourt's motives are not easy to explain, since he had been aggressively for resignation, forced or contrived, in the cabinet of 7 May, but can best be understood as an intelligent attempt to maintain a situation where, with no faction able to win, he and Gladstone were the indispensable men in the middle.

May 12 (*Tuesday*). It became common knowledge that Chamberlain could only consent to the new crimes bill being operative for one year,[252] while Gladstone wanted two years.

A meeting of the Commons ministers took place to discuss the situation created by the refusal of Russia to accept the Kaiser as arbitrator on Penjdeh, and the Queen's refusal to accept the King of Denmark as an alternative. The Queen ultimately gave in, but the arbitration never took place.[253]

The Irish committee of the cabinet met at Spencer House, attended by Spencer, Harcourt, Chamberlain, Trevelyan, Campbell-Bannerman, Carlingford, and Walker, the Irish solicitor-general. The committee first went through the surviving sections of the Crimes Act without much contention, and it appeared that the compromise arranged by Harcourt on Sunday had indeed gained acceptance. Then Chamberlain brought up the question of the duration for which the new Crimes Act should operate. On Sunday Chamberlain had been taken to accept that the bill could be a permanent measure, since it was by this stage more a measure of administrative reform than an emergency measure. Since then, however, Chamberlain had said that conversations with Dilke, Collings and John Morley had led him to think that he could only accept the bill if it were limited to one year, though he added that Gladstone did not agree with him about this. This *volte-face* disturbed Spencer and Harcourt, for whom the permanence of the new, weakened bill had been a great inducement to make concessions in other ways. To exonerate himself from any suggestions of bad faith, Chamberlain therefore came forward with a proposal that if Spencer conceded a limitation to one year, Chamberlain would withdraw his opposition to those other clauses of the bill which he had just made Spencer give up. Spencer declined this further bargain.[254] Later, Spencer told Harcourt that he could not swallow limitation to one year at any price: Harcourt was very sarcastic and said no great party had ever broken up over such a trifle.[255]

May 13 (Wednesday). Chamberlain told E.Hamilton at a party that his predominant feeling was eagerness to quit office and be free again. Chamberlain also urged that the renewal of coercion was unnecessary.

May 15 (Friday). At Gladstone's instance, Spencer called a meeting at 11 a.m. at Devonshire House of the ministers who agreed with him about the crimes bill. Those attending were Granville, Derby, Hartington, Spencer, Kimberley, Northbrook, Rosebery, and Carlingford. It was however left to Hartington to inform Rosebery of the meeting and to invite him to attend. The immediate problem to be decided was whether Spencer, who it was believed had already made great concessions as to the contents of the bill in order to obtain a permanent measure, should now submit to accepting a bill limited to two years, which Gladstone now proposed as a further compromise. Chamberlain seemed willing to let the cabinet proceed on a basis of two years, while hinting at reserving his right to resign in favour of a measure limited to one year. Spencer's adherents were probably ignorant of how keen Spencer himself was on administrative grounds to reduce the new crimes bill to a bare minimum as compared with the expiring Act of 1882. Spencer's resignation in view of the further demands now made hung in the balance: had he resigned, Carlingford at least would have followed him. What moved Spencer and the sense of the meeting generally against resignation were two considerations: the importance of associating Chamberlain and Dilke with some kind of crimes bill, however weakened, and the danger, if the ministry broke up on the question, of open warfare between the moderate Liberals and the Parnellite-Radical alliance. Hartington was especially strong on the importance of committing the Radicals to some form of coercion.[256] Rosebery was likewise anxious to avoid a rupture, and said the thing to do was for Spencer to write down the irreducible minimum with which he could govern Ireland.[257]

The cabinet met in Downing St at 2, with only Trevelyan absent (ill).

Kimberley reported inconclusively on the negotiations with Russia.

The cabinet considered what further important bills could

reasonably be brought forward that session. As regards Scotland, it was felt that no addition need be made to the two bills (crofters and Scottish ministry) already before parliament: while as regards Wales, it was proposed to introduce an intermediate education bill in the following week, its claim being felt to be very strong. Gladstone was to announce these arrangements that night.

The cabinet decided to remain silent on the subject of the viceroyalty in Ireland, 'which Lord Spencer so much wished to see abolished', partly because the subject involved the Queen and had not been put before her, but probably more because no one was interested.

On the main problems of Irish legislation, Gladstone sent the Queen a formal account which was wildly at variance with the political realities of cabinet life. Gladstone's statement ran: 'the cabinet have agreed upon the provisions which it is necessary to select from the Crimes Act of 1882 and to embody in a fresh bill of a far milder character. This is to be introduced shortly after Whitsuntide. There are three other subjects on which the government desire to legislate for Ireland. They are local government, land purchase, and abolition of the viceroyalty. As regards the first two, it was felt that Mr Gladstone should acknowledge their importance, and the duty of the government to deal with them', but should add that it was too late in the session to do other than postpone them.

In fact very serious disagreements arose during the cabinet, and Gladstone's report on proceedings represented a precarious compromise which it is not clear was accepted by most ministers. A purchase bill and a coercion bill were presented to the cabinet. The former had apparently been generally agreed to, and discussion had turned to its details, when, after a conversation on paper with Chamberlain, Dilke expressed strong opposition to it unless it were accompanied by Chamberlain's local government scheme. Upon this Harcourt at once threw over Spencer and said purchase must be given up, at which Carlingford protested strongly. Chamberlain, Dilke, and Lefevre protested against the coercion bill, while declaring that they might accept some parts of it provided the land purchase bill were dropped, or the local government measure introduced. These complicated conditions naturally left doubt as to whether the purchase bill had or had not been finally shelved.

The position about the coercion bill was also ambiguous. It would seem from accounts given by Gladstone and Hamilton that, putting on one side the position taken up by the Radical ministers, good progress had been made in determining what clauses should be contained in any future bill. Gladstone described the provisions as 'recited and settled' and Hamilton wrote simply 'at a cabinet today, the provisions of the crimes bill were settled'. Hamilton's interpretation of the Radicals' refusal to let Spencer sweeten the pill with reforming legislation was that 'Chamberlain & Co. want the coercive legislation to stand out in all its nakedness', while Carlingford supplied a further motive, that the Radicals opposed purchase in the present, because they regarded it as a desirable garnishing for their home rule schemes in the new parliament. In all the controversy in May, there was no specific mention of what was supposedly the traditional Radical objection to land purchase, that it placed needlessly large sums of public money in the pockets of undeserving landlords. Such cries were heard enough in 1886, but appear not to have been resorted to in 1885. It is therefore likely that the crux of the opposition to a purchase bill, was that any such bill would be taken as a sign that the Radical ministers were prepared to accept some degree of coercion.

It is probable that the draft coercion bill was examined clause by clause for the last time at this cabinet: for instance there is a record of Selborne's protest against the dropping of the public meetings clause of the Crimes Act. Gladstone's optimistic interpretation of this cabinet as having settled the future coercion bill, applied to most of its provisions, but not at all to whether the bill after scrutiny commanded the politically requisite degree of support within the cabinet. The behaviour of the Radicals in no way suggested that they would either easily assent to the bill, or that they had as yet decided explicitly to resist it. But their victory over purchase, won without a vote, gave them some idea of their strength: for most of the cabinet, including their opponents, considered purchase as dead.[258]

May 16 (*Saturday*).[259] All members of the cabinet, except Trevelyan, met at 12 to receive Childers' amended proposals for the budget. Childers had shifted the emphasis of his increased taxation of liquor in a democratic direction, by raising the wine duties, and making a corresponding reduction in the duties on beer and spirits. This hasty rearrangement of the wine duties was laid by Childers at the door of the breakdown of the commercial negotiations with Spain. As a concession to party requirements, Childers' new proposals failed to satisfy either Harcourt, who claimed that they would not pass parliament now the imminent possibility of war had passed away, or Dilke and Chamberlain, who held it to be a fatal budget for the elections.

Gladstone and most members of the cabinet agreed in wanting to emasculate what had only been accepted as a war measure, but were still more anxious to give no overt sign to Russia that Britain regarded the central Asian crisis as over. Childers, however, wanted his revised proposals announced before Whitsuntide, while his colleagues on diplomatic grounds wished to do nothing* till the Russian negotiations had proved successful.

Childers, looking very ill, therefore said he must resign, despite no decision having been taken against him beyond postponing the announcement of any changes for three weeks, the main body of his critics simply wishing to temporise. Some colleagues pressed him strongly against going, Carlingford writing to him after the meeting on those lines.

Others, however, regarded the merits of the case and of Childers as entirely secondary to the continuing quest for an advantageous contrived defeat. Thus, after Childers' statement, Harcourt simply said 'So far as I know, the budget is as good a question to resign on as any other, and Tuesday as good a day', Tuesday being the day Childers had hoped to announce his amended scheme to parliament. Rosebery was also particularly offhand about Childers, whom he regarded as the type of the dull official, saying that Childers would not in fact resign and that it would not matter if he did.[260]

Kimberley reported that the Russian negotiations appeared to be going well.

The request made by Nubar Pasha and Baring for the retention of English troops in Dongola was turned down with finality, though it was not denied that such a retention would serve purely Egyptian interests as well. But as parliament had already been informed that the evacuation of Dongola would be governed by military considerations alone, the Egyptian argument could not affect ministers' previous decision. Before the cabinet began, Hartington, Gladstone and Harcourt had circulated opinions against reopening the Dongola question, while the 'hawks' on the other side were Selborne, Northbrook and Carlingford, the latter pointing out that even Buller could no longer be cited as an authority for immediate evacuation.[261]

The evacuation of Dongola did not come before the cabinet again before the fall of the ministry, though the town of Dongola was not completely evacuated till 5 July 1885. Yet despite the finality of the decision of 16 May, further minutes attacking the speed of the evacuation went round in the cabinet boxes. The

* For Childers' view of the delay, see Childers to Granville, 15 May, PRO 30/29/22 A, arguing that without immediate settlement, 'the present agitation will gain such strength ... as inevitably to defeat the Budget proposal. This is Chamberlain's and Dilke's wish'.

occasion for these further rumblings may have been a communication dated 16 May from Wolseley to Hartington, arguing strongly against the folly of the retreat, and asking if it was too late to reconsider handing over the province to the Mahdi. Wolseley's communication of 16 May was probably circulated only after the cabinet. Carlingford took the strongest line in support of Wolseley, saying 'I have been opposed to immediate retirement from Dongola, and I greatly regret it. I hope at all events it may not have immediate effect with the haste which seems to be intended.' Rosebery had accepted the principle of leisurely withdrawal as final, but was alarmed that the Generals were turning this into a discreditable flight. Granville surprisingly agreed with Rosebery and Carlingford, the two latter having taken a firm line in favour of the temporary retention of Dongola since the controversy on the subject opened in mid-April.[262]

E. Hamilton, after talking with Rosebery of the restiveness shown at this meeting, wrote that apart from Gladstone, 'all ministers individually want it to break up', Hamilton estimating on 18 May that within the last month at least ten ministers out of sixteen had threatened resignation. Gladstone himself made a tentative list[263] of ministers 'who within the last month have on one ground or another appeared to contemplate resignation', these being named as Selborne, Northbrook, Hartington, Chamberlain, Dilke, Lefevre, Spencer, Harcourt and Trevelyan. Neither Hamilton's nor Gladstone's estimates should be taken literally except in their evocation of the general situation, Gladstone for instance omitting the clear case of Childers. *

May 17 (*Sunday*). Churchill at a dinner party told Dilke that the Conservative leaders had decided that they would not attempt to renew the crimes bill if they took office in the near future. It appears that from this date the Radical ministers no longer felt able to regard Irish policy as negotiable, though there is no direct evidence for the effect on their views of the Tory *volte-face*.

May 18 (*Monday*). Hamilton noted that 'Gladstone will attempt to pass Purchase Bill', probably basing his observation on the fact that Gladstone had sent for Campbell-Bannerman during the day about such a bill. The Irish secretary urged it as strongly as

---

* The information that Childers 'had volunteered to alter his budget and remit the increased tax on beer, but that it was decided not to do so' was passed to that arch-enemy of the ministry, Lord Wolseley, on 10 June by Childers' son, who was serving on Wolseley's staff in Egypt. This probably referred to the events of the cabinet of 15 May, though it might be just postally possible for the cabinet of 5 June to be the one in question. This leak was probably slightly garbled, but it illustrated how easily confidential matters got out. Source: A. Preston ed., *In Relief of Gordon* (1967), 225.

possible, and claimed that it would be parliamentarily successful despite Parnellite lukewarmness. After seeing Gladstone, Campbell-Bannerman saw Thring about producing a draft bill.[264]

Hamilton wrote to Rosebery that Childers had agreed, with an ill grace, to remain in office at any rate for a further three weeks.

The supposed change in Tory attitudes to coercion, revealed the previous day, was leading the Radicals into strange thoughts as to their future course. 'If the Tories were through Northcote to move in favour of "remedial legislation", they would fetch out Chamberlain and self. We should strike for the promise of Chamberlain's big scheme next year, and this we should not get from our colleagues.'[265] But this relatively prosaic version of a Tory-Irish-Radical entente was not all that presented itself. The Radical ministers now also had to consider an even more than usually idiosyncratic scheme put forward by Churchill, though they do not appear even momentarily to have regarded it as significant:

> 'Chamberlain also wrote to me after his interview with Mr Gladstone on the Monday afternoon telling me that Randolph Churchill was going to give notice of a committee to inquire into the state of Ireland, that Churchill thought that we should be out by that time and supporting him, and that he contemplated a separation from his own leaders, and a union, on a Radical Irish policy for local government and against coercion, of the two sides below the gangway.'[266]

This sounds visionary: and in a sense it was, since Churchill did not succeed in involving anyone else in the dream. That the dream meant something not quite fleeting to him, may be perhaps hinted at in a curious (undated) talk Churchill had with Goschen. Goschen, that meticulous destroyer of parties, told Churchill he was very dangerous. Churchill, deferring to the elder statesman, then consulted Goschen as to the sources of his own popularity – was it political or personal? Goschen said 'Largely personal'. Churchill said 'That decides me.' Hearing this story from Goschen, Rosebery made the strange comment 'His decision was of course to leave the Conservatives.'[267] Nothing could be more gnomic, but the only context to which this jotting can be plausibly attached is the period in May when Churchill was still liable to assume that the Tory 'Old Guard' would not readily abandon coercion.

There is further evidence which suggests that, at a level of reflection where they were rarely visible, the possibilities of leaving the old Tory party were present in Churchill's mind over perhaps quite a long period. In January 1887, just after he resigned,

Churchill got Labouchere to sound out Gladstone on the prospects for concerted action to overthrow the Tories. On 16 January 1887, Churchill called on Labouchere, and asked the latter to put before Gladstone hints for concerting parliamentary action, 'but in such a way that it should not appear to come from him'. On 22 January, Labouchere again saw Churchill, and passed on to him Gladstone's views of the inexpediency of being precipitate. 'I asked him', Labouchere wrote, 'whether it would not be more simple to declare himself a home ruler. This, however, he is not prepared to do, but would, on speaking on a finance resolution, say that, if he has to choose between home rule and bad finance, he ought to accept the former as the lesser of two evils.'[268] One can take Churchill's aberrations of May 1885 and January 1887 as momentary speculations of an over-active mind, and no more: or one can see them, as Rosebery to some extent implied in his study of Churchill, as evidence that Churchill understood well enough that he could only lead a parliamentary majority by acting in a Liberal manner, and in the end, in a Liberal context.

The resignations over the land purchase bill announcement, 20–21 May 1885. On 20 May Gladstone told Dilke in the course of ordinary conversation that he would continue till the end of the session and then hand over to Hartington.[269] At their meeting Gladstone made no mention of a land purchase bill, but at 3 that afternoon he rose in the commons and announced that a bill would be introduced on the subject. Gladstone did this believing that Chamberlain had agreed to a coercion bill limited to one year, in which case the prior announcement of a purchase bill was an appropriate douceur. For the Radicals, then, Gladstone's announcement of a purchase bill implied that they had finally agreed to concede a new, if limited, coercion bill.

The other possible implication, equally distasteful, was that the purchase bill meant publicly shelving the central board scheme. Either implication could only serve to catalyse the Tory-Irish entente which the Radicals knew to be rapidly developing. Whether or not at some point in the private negotiations of previous days they had really conceded, and meant to concede, a limited coercion bill, they had not, and the cabinet had not, technically conceded a land purchase bill. Though the land purchase bill was on the merits neither attractive nor unattractive to the Radicals (or Irish), the cry against it on financial grounds being hardly heard, its technically improper announcement gave Dilke the opportunity he wanted to delete from the record any past tendency to compromise on the coercion issue. A probable factor is that Dilke was interested in imposing his own tactics on

Chamberlain, whom he saw as erring in the direction of decency and 'timidity'* as Dilke called it. The running at any rate in the May resignations was made by Dilke, naturally enough since the announcement pointed to a developing understanding between Gladstone and Chamberlain which was certainly of great potential importance from early May and which threatened Dilke's position grievously. To prevent Gladstone becoming increasingly necessary to the *amour propre* invested by Chamberlain in Irish schemes with which Dilke had had little to do, Dilke had to take decisive action to prevent Chamberlain seeing positive action in Ireland as offering more scope, than unremitting concentration on forcing the breakup of the ministry. Chamberlain's interview with Gladstone which had led to the 'misunderstanding' had probably taken place on 16 May after the cabinet, and had led Gladstone to look forward with buoyancy to an Irish programme in the intervening days. What was at stake in these few days was whether the Radical wing, if given Gladstone's support, were sufficiently interested in closing ranks around a positive Irish programme to make it worthwhile for the ministry to stay in office during the summer and until the elections. This involved a choice of priorities between the achievement of substantive Radical objectives on the Irish front (which was possible, but involved staying in office in an unreconstructed cabinet) and the attainment of effective control of the Liberal party under the new franchise (which in their eyes meant breaking up the cabinet and going into opposition). After 20 May the Radicals gave priority to breaking up the ministry over achieving Radical objectives within it: but had Chamberlain been left to his own devices, he might well have gone the other way.

Dilke opened fire[270] on 20 May with an immediate and formal request for his resignation to be tendered to the Queen. His letter was felt to be, and indeed was, rude. He followed with a further assertion that the land purchase bill had been discussed and

* Dilke's actions were governed by thoughts of a possible replacement of Gladstone by Hartington, coupled with doubts as to whether Chamberlain might not rat on him. 'Mr G keeps on saying he is going at once. Therefore we have to court Hartington. Now we doubt if we can form part of a Hartington govt and we *certainly* can't do if we do not threaten and impose our terms by threats. If we were to join a Hartington govt without making our own terms we should be lost... This is why I have been forcing the pace of late, with much help from Lefevre. Chamberlain is a little timid just now, in view of the elections and the fury of the *Pall Mall*. I could not drive Chamberlain out without his consent, so I am rather tied' (Dilke to Grant Duff, 3 June 1885, Dilke MSS, 43894 f. 181). Dilke's edginess stemmed in part from fatigue: 'all creative energy has been driven out of me by overwork' he wrote to Mrs Pattison on 9 May, referring specifically to the seats bill (Dilke MSS, 43906 f. 70). Chamberlain on the other hand, was in good spirits and not feeling any pressure from his work.

rejected by the cabinet. On 21 May he was even more the picture of outraged propriety: 'I consider that a deliberate opinion of the cabinet has been reversed without any warrant and the only two members of the cabinet [Hartington and Northbrook] to whom Chamberlain and I have spoken agree with me in this though they differed on the main question'. Dilke refused to withdraw his resignation unless the incident was explained to the whole cabinet, as indeed it eventually was on 5 June, and put his grounds for rejecting compromise openly enough by making his dissent virtually all-embracing. 'We differ so completely on the questions which will occupy the time of parliament for the remainder of the session that I feel the cabinet cannot hold together with advantage to the country'. Irrespective of specific issues, Dilke was giving notice that the cabinet must be broken up, presumably because the potentially effective centre-left ruling group which Gladstone had been offering to provide since late April and which probably interested Chamberlain, with his atavistic interest in substantive issues as apart from political relationships, would have made it less necessary to oust Gladstone by direct confrontation in the future, and might make Dilke unimportant to Chamberlain.

Dilke did not at once achieve all he wanted. He fatally disturbed whatever prospect there was of Gladstone combining with the Radical wing to force on the Whigs a Radical-Irish programme, though this possibility was glimpsed again before 8 June, for the good reason that the objections to it related more to calculations about power in the party, than misgivings about how to rule Ireland. But he did not carry through all he seemed to have in mind when he started operations on 20 May. Though Chamberlain and Shaw-Lefevre offered their resignations on 20 and 21 May respectively, they were in a different tone, and Lefevre's was based on different grounds:[271] and Gladstone, using as bait the prospect of giving further attention to Irish local government, was able on 21 May to face Dilke with the news 'Chamberlain is quite willing that his letter should stand until after the recess'. Dilke had in fact acted on 20 May quite on his own, sending in his resignation first at once on hearing the news and only then setting off in search of Chamberlain, Trevelyan and Lefevre. Chamberlain probably wished to give a lesser meaning to the episode, viz. that, having demonstrated that Gladstone had been caught off balance, one could then return to hard bargaining over Irish policy in a cabinet which was intended to continue for some time. So far as one can tell from the swift succession of notes, it was only after Chamberlain's interpretation of the episode as not an occasion for immediate breakup, that Dilke called on Gladstone at 3 on 21 May and dropped matters for the time being. The face-saving formula was that Dilke was to try to negotiate a compromise Irish policy with Spencer while on a Boundary Commission visit to Dublin: in fact Dilke had called off a major operation and given Gladstone further time to feel his way towards winning that left of centre position from which the Liberal party would have to be led after the next elections. The more successful Gladstone was in helping the Radicals to achieve what they ostensibly wanted, the less need there would be to replace him.[272]

On 21 May Lefevre sent in a tentative and reluctant offer of resignation, which was never accepted. Lefevre resigned on quite different grounds from Dilke, for he agreed with the land purchase bill, but thought the time had come for him to demur to the prospect of a new coercion bill, which the announcement of the land bill appeared to bring within sight. Lefevre had turned down the Irish secretaryship in autumn 1884 over the issue of coercion – he had then proposed the immediate suspension of its operation to test its necessity – and in later years as a home ruler, he showed much energy as a pamphleteer in ventilating its wrongs. For Lefevre, what was involved was his standing in his own mind as an austere administrator sworn to Cobdenite principles, not connivance with the manoeuvres of Dilke and Chamberlain. (Dilke had described Lefevre's accession to the cabinet as 'weakening *us*').[273] There is very little mention made at this time of what Lefevre thought or said: but it is probably significant that there is none of the usual evidence that he took a strongly critical view of some colleague or colleagues. Arguing *ex silentio*, it is also probable that he was not on close personal or political terms with any other member of the cabinet.

Trevelyan on the other hand was thought to act under fear of Chamberlain and Dilke, and of the new situation created by a franchise reform which he had been the first to advocate, *i.e.* a radicalisation of politics to a point where a House of Commons minister could no longer safely be simply a loyal subordinate of Spencer. Trevelyan in 1885 had no wishes beyond trimming till a new ruling group emerged in the cabinet, and he had the sense not to offer his resignation on paper at any time during the year. He had no objection to being counted as one of a group of four Radical ministers, provided he took no risks thereby. That such a Radical group took form in Dilke's mind as something that should be conjured with and wielded, is true, but it was a most fragile construction. At the fall of the cabinet, Dilke and Chamberlain had still failed to find a third cabinet minister willing to throw in his fortune with theirs, to act with them as they acted with each

A scene in the Commons division lobby, June 1885: 'Explanations of Westminster should centre not on its being at the top of a coherently organised pyramid whose bottom layer was the people, but in its character as a highly specialised community, like the City or Whitehall, whose primary interest was inevitably its own very private institutional life.'

Hartington in later life in his robes as mayor of Eastbourne: 'He was trusted, respected, and did not make mistakes. He was the only politician able to impress himself upon the public as strong and resolute.'

other, rather than giving them transient support under specific circumstances. Trevelyan's position was much more like Harcourt's in that both, sensing their isolation between the two wings of the party, looked to Gladstone to provide a safe balance in which their careers could thrive. Chamberlain and Dilke, while looking at times to a reconstructed ministry under Gladstone, were also interested in one under Hartington: and in any event the day of Gladstone's final departure was the red letter day on which their eyes were hopefully fixed. For Harcourt and Trevelyan, on the other hand, prosperity required a further long period of Gladstone's rule, following a reconstruction to improve their own position. At the dinner table Trevelyan's casual conversation on 10 May 1885 was very enthusiastic in favour of Gladstone, though 'his admiration for Gladstone did not extend to other old members of the cabinet – he would like a clean sweep of senilities, and the young people between 40 and 50 to have their hands free'.[274] The absence of any Trevelyan MSS, and the incompleteness of the Chamberlain and Dilke MSS, make assessment of Trevelyan's standing with the Radicals difficult, but the general bearing of what survives, especially the inattention shown to Trevelyan in Dilke's diary, strongly suggests that Trevelyan had only very limited contacts with Chamberlain and Dilke in 1885: even, perhaps, that they were little interested in canvassing his support.

May 21 (Thursday). Rosebery called on Gladstone at 10.30 a.m. and found the old man harassed by the discourtesies involved in his dealings with the Radical ministers. He said that he could not face the election, but that on the other hand Chamberlain and Dilke should not break up the government. His eyesight, voice, and hearing were failing, he confided to Rosebery, and he had just been asked by the Queen whether it would not relieve him very much to be a peer. Rosebery was leaving for Berlin that evening, but Gladstone had nothing to say of Bismarck except that he was a liar, as he had discovered in the Danish affair of 1864.[275]

'An informal meeting of the cabinet in Mr G's room, H. of C., about the Russian negotiations'[276] took place during the late afternoon. The meeting, hastily called, refused Russian demands on two important points, the Zulficar Pass and Meruchah.

May 23 (Saturday). A long letter[277] from Gladstone to the Queen, dated 23 May 1885, took the very exceptional course of describing divisions in the cabinet on Irish policy, principally as regards coercion. The letter is in part printed,[278] and was freely shown by the Queen to visiting politicians as evidence against Gladstone. It affords the best explanation of the state of feeling in the cabinet on

Ireland in the long interval between the meetings of 16 May and 5 June, and is especially useful as indicating the very definite nature of Gladstone's objectives.

What Hamilton gleaned[279] was that Gladstone's purpose in writing to the Queen was 'to prepare her for Irish Local Govt', and that Gladstone was advocating Chamberlain's scheme. The Irish central board was to be municipal, not political, with education, poor law, sanitary matters and public works entrusted to it, and also police under certain conditions.

A better idea of the excitement and hopes which Chamberlain's scheme had aroused in Gladstone, and of his complete openness in communicating his feelings, may be found in something he wrote to Hartington at this time:

'I go rather further than they [the Radicals] do: for I would undoubtedly make a beginning with the Irish police. Secondly, as to the ground: here I differ seriously. I do not reckon with any confidence upon Manning or Parnell: I have never looked much in Irish matters at negotiation or the conciliation of leaders. I look at the question in itself, and I am deeply convinced that the measure in itself will (especially if accompanied with similar measures elsewhere e.g. in Scotland) be for the good of the country.'[280]

June 2 (Tuesday). Rosebery walked home with Hartington, who, 'gloomy and ill, talked of an impending revolution he feared'.[281] The following day he was at the Derby with Rosebery, and afterwards they drove out into the country, Hartington being amazed and delighted by Box Hill and Betchworth. Hartington stayed overnight at The Durdans, and returned to London on 4 June.

There is a political point to make about this Derby Day idyll. It is that there were the strongest social and personal reasons why Rosebery should have become Hartington's follower and confidant, whereas as late as June 1885, no strong personal or political reasons had emerged as a basis for a strong allegiance to Gladstone. His ties to Gladstone only became strong, in the ensuing months in opposition, partly simply because Rosebery was Gladstone's Scottish host. Because of that transposition of context, brought about by the general election, Rosebery was able to establish himself as Gladstone's intimate and to forget all that he had been doing when in office – that is, making himself agreeable to all those who mattered, ignoring the politically irrelevant (like Childers) and keeping close to both Hartington and Chamberlain as probable successors in the leadership.

June 4 (Thursday). Dilke had a long talk with Gladstone and agreed to support the proposal, associated variously with Heneage, Lefevre, and O'Shea, for bringing in coercion by proclamation. On this basis Dilke consented to attend the cabinet of the following day, though without withdrawing his resignation.[282] It is not clear that his cabinet colleagues were generally aware of his suspended resignation: they showed no sign of considering it important in itself, as opposed to his general stance of dissidence.

June 5 (Friday). The cabinet met at Downing St from 11 to 2.30, with only Spencer absent.

At this cabinet Gladstone showed the first signs of a much firmer tone and a new determination to master the elements of strife: or rather, and more markedly, he gave no further sign of the readiness to stage a personal collapse and disappearance which had marked his talk in May. One explanation may be that Wolverton had recently been to Hawarden, putting before Mrs Gladstone the case for her husband staying on into the new era of democracy: arguments not unwelcome to his hearer. It is not really possible to say what function Wolverton had for Gladstone, there being virtually no papers surviving, but it is certainly clear that Wolverton was on hand at the great moments and that he was suspected of having great influence. Talking to E. Hamilton after cabinet on 5 June, Rosebery learned that it now looked as though Gladstone, if pressed, would lead for another session.[283] Gladstone's report written to Spencer just after the cabinet was also confident and buoyant.[284]

The first point dealt with was the budget. It was decided that the increase in beer duty should last for only about a year, and (on Childers' proposal) that the increase in spirit duties should be one shilling, not two. Childers also proposed to increase the wine duty, but Dilke made a statement against this, and was supported by Granville on account of the already difficult relations between Britain and France. Chamberlain pointed out that it was not necessary on social grounds to raise the wine duties as a counterpoise to the increase in beer duty, as the wine drinking classes were already hit by increased direct taxation. Gladstone supported Childers at first, but afterwards advised to make no change in taxation of wine. With the whole cabinet against him on this single point, Childers said he could not consent and left the room. He was pursued by Harcourt, the official pacifier, and then by Gladstone, amid general mirth. They came back in twenty minutes, saying he required an hour's thought. Then Granville and Selborne were sent off to see him: and shortly after the cabinet, he withdrew his resignation. Childers did not return, but Granville came back and said all would be well, and that 'Childers had gone to consult a high authority on indirect taxation.'[285] The decision of the cabinet to raise the beer duty without raising the duty on wine was the question on which the cabinet fell on 9 June: there is no actual evidence that considerations of this kind came into play when Childers' policy was overruled on 5 June, but it is highly likely that the Radicals at least wished the beer duties to be as inequitable as possible so as to ensure defeat.

Gladstone made a statement about the leakage of cabinet matters to the press, which he said was a disgrace and of bad augury for future governments. This referred to an account of the ministerial crisis in the *Birmingham Daily Post* for 22 May.[286]

The relative priority of the budget, the crimes bill, and the crofters bill was discussed, and it was decided that Gladstone should give notice that he would introduce on Thursday a 'bill to replace the Crimes Act'.

Conversation followed on some minor Egyptian matters.

The cabinet then turned to Irish affairs. At some point, and rather outside the main flow of the discussion, Dilke reported on his recent talks with Spencer in Dublin, asserting that Spencer would agree to provincial administrative bodies, a central board for legislation, and some special arrangements for dealing with Irish private bills. Little account was taken of this Spencer-Dilke compromise and the large vistas of agreement and action it opened up.[287] The cabinet did not want to be saddled with a large Irish programme, however promising: it simply wanted to concoct a coercion bill that would attract as little attention as possible.

Instead, Gladstone began by referring to his mistake in thinking Dilke and Chamberlain had consented to the purchase bill. Upon this Chamberlain stated where the Radical ministers now stood. They held that, as a purchase bill had now been promised, it could not be now withdrawn. On the other hand, since the purchase bill had been promised improperly, he and Dilke were relieved of any obligation it might have imposed to support any measure of coercion. The Radicals were therefore free to define afresh the terms on which they could accept coercion.

According to several sources, the three Radical ministers 'would all disappear unless one of three points were conceded'[288] regarding the crimes bill. The points were 1) limitation to one year, a possibility which Gladstone described as having 'been put on one side by the cabinet, and in all likelihood will not be seriously renewed'; 2) a bill not so restricted to be accompanied by an announcement about local government; 3) the operation of the bill to be at the discretion of the executive.

There was little or no discussion of the first two alternatives.[289] The third alternative had been put forward in different ways by Heneage, O'Shea, and Lefevre, but was generally labelled Lefevre's proposal. It had already been referred to Spencer, who not unnaturally protested against a concession which, in an extreme reading, could mean that the Radical ministers would in practice be able to veto the coercion act ever operating at all. Gladstone, in introducing the subject, read out Spencer's objections as sent in his letter of 4 June.

Selborne, however, while not wishing to move without Spencer, saw Lefevre's proposal as providing a possible solution, and was supported by Gladstone, Kimberley, and Trevelyan. A further question opened up, as to whether discretion as to the operation of the bill should lie with the cabinet or with the lord-lieutenant. Harcourt and Carlingford were vehemently against the original plan, but may have hinted at willingness to make the bill operative by viceregal proclamation. Chamberlain, suddenly amenable again, even suggested that if Lefevre's concession went through, he would accept extension of the bill to a term of three years.

Chamberlain passed a piece of paper across to Rosebery, asking 'Can you not give us a lift in this matter? I fancy you agree with us though I have not liked to ask your opinions.' Rosebery replied that he was in favour of a strong local government measure, but could not throw over anything which Spencer declared to be the least possible special provisions for governing Ireland.[290] In general, however, ministers obviously hoped that Spencer would come to see Lefevre's proposal, if not in its original form then in a variant, as the answer to their perplexities.

In view of the apparent consensus, Gladstone expressed regret over Spencer's attitude, and adjourned the discussion to allow ministers to write to him. The idea of balancing the new coercion bill with a generous announcement on Irish local government remained in Gladstone's mind, though probably in no one else's, as something that the cabinet might look at further, and the Spencer-Dilke conversations had shown the possibilities of this approach. However the meeting of 5 June made clear that what really interested the cabinet was eroding the coercion bill itself by the device of making it subject to executive discretion, and it was this issue which went forward to the next meeting.

Following the cabinet, Gladstone wrote to Spencer appealing to him to accept 'Lefevre's proposal' and saying with some economy of truth 'no one actually spoke in positive condemnation' of the general idea of executive discretion, disregarding the fact that Lefevre's proposal was only one form of this general idea, and one which two ministers had hotly attacked. Spencer sent an unfavourable reply on 6 June.[291]

Pending any decision on permanent occupation, it was decided to offer some kind of temporary rent to Korea for Port Hamilton, a naval base occupied earlier in the year for use against Russia.[292]

During the cabinet Dilke pushed a note across to Gladstone saying 'I'm very sorry. I fear this looks like a break up.'[293] But the quality of his regret must be assessed in the light of his explanation to Grant Duff the same day that his tactics were to force the pace, in view of the probable imminence of Hartington's leadership, and because Chamberlain was 'a little timid'.[294]

The behaviour of Selborne, as the representative man of principle on the right wing of the cabinet and a future Liberal Unionist, showed the same failure to live up to his public image as did his attitudes in January 1886. Instead of leading a party for the continuation of strong government in Ireland, he came out noticeably for Lefevre's proposal for weakening the Irish administration in the cabinet of 5 June knowing Spencer was opposed to the plan. His strongly reactionary tendencies when thinking in terms of years were rendered inoperative by his wish to behave effectively on a day-to-day basis. Yet even so the pure opportunism of one who was considered one of the most straightforward ministers comes out in a letter from him to Gladstone the following day, saying that, at the premier's suggestion, he has put his first thoughts on coercion before Spencer, but was waiting to hear from him before coming to any final conclusion on the matter.[295]

June 8 (Monday). The full cabinet met at Downing St at 2. The previous day a letter had been circulated from a representative Liberal M.P, Hussey Vivian, predicting a formidable division in the party (quite apart from the cabinet) if the new Coercion Act were not made dependent on executive discretion.

Spencer, though still objecting, agreed to making the operation of the next Crimes Act dependent on proclamation, except for the clause on intimidation, which was to come into force automatically. Spencer said that intimidation was increasing and even with the existing provision was hardly being dealt with properly. Gladstone acknowledged Spencer's generosity and recommended acceptance of the bill on the terms now offered, evidently hoping to carry Chamberlain and Dilke with him. However, Chamberlain would not hear of it and said it was no concession at all. Trevelyan said he would have supported Spencer if he had insisted on bringing any clauses other than intimidation into automatic operation. Dilke and Lefevre were clearly also behind Chamberlain.

There was more to Radical dissidence on this occasion than

mere ruthless perversity. Spencer had offered a major concession, but according to Dilke, not the concession the Radicals wanted, viz. operation of the new Crimes Act to be subject to Order in Council (i.e. the cabinet), rather than by viceregal proclamation, as in Spencer's concession. The importance of this difference was brought home by a remark from Spencer that, if things remained as they were, he should be obliged to proclaim a large part of Ireland, as soon as the new Act came into force, a needless provocation which Gladstone tried to reduce to an admission that all would depend on the circumstances at the time.

After 'long and confused and simultaneous discussion ending in nothing',[296] the cabinet decided to defer the subject to the following day, it being clear that Spencer was in no mood to give any ground.[297] Chamberlain, for his part, was talking of beginning entirely new negotiations, and forgetting everything so far agreed and disagreed. However, Gladstone had opened the cabinet by mentioning that the whips were less optimistic about the division that night, and that the solution of resignation might be available almost at once. Gladstone in his report to the Queen on the cabinet expected that the opposition, with the aid of the Irish, would put an end to the ministry.

Granville reported the recent Russian answer, commenting that their intentions about the Zulficar Pass remained equivocal. The conduct of Sir P. Lumsden was discussed.[298]

In the evening debate began on Beach's motion attacking the way the government had distributed the increased taxation on various kinds of drink. The debate culminated in a vote, taken at 1.45 a.m. the following morning, in which the government were defeated 264–252. Politically it was probably possible for the government to have had the vote reversed and constitutionally it was probably feasible to have disregarded it as trivial. There was, however, never any question in any Liberal minister's mind that this opportunity to resign should not be lost. Even Gladstone, whose inclination for office was manifest to everybody, did not actually urge his views on anyone.

The problem here is to form judgements as to who was trying to achieve what. The senior Conservative leaders were clearly lukewarm at most about taking office: Churchill was generally determined to break up the existing situation in any way possible and also specifically, at this stage, wanted his party to be in office. The party, in the sense of opinion at the Carlton, instinctively needed office (and perhaps in many cases the cash that went therewith). The motion that defeated the ministry was not an official frontbench one, but the last plot dreamed up by the Fourth Party.

Because Churchill was a party to it, one cannot rule out the possibility of an attempted partial arrangement between Churchill and Chamberlain. There is no evidence of this; and the strongest criticism of such a view would be that there was no need for overt inter-party contact. Chamberlain and Dilke took the initiative, in the cabinet of 5 June, by ensuring that the proposed taxation would excite the maximum opposition. By glibly manufacturing a case for taxing beer and not wine, contrary to all their previous deepest views about fiscal policy in a democracy, they manoeuvred the cabinet into riding for a fall. The readiness with which the cabinet overruled Childers and accepted the Radicals' tuition suggests that they sensed roughly what was afoot. The possibility of defeat was mentioned in cabinet on 8 June, wistfully perhaps but without real involvement or apprehension.

What is fairly clear, is that whatever his earlier views, Gladstone during the day hardened in his view that because there were still things he wished to see done, therefore there would be no defeat. On coming out of the cabinet, he gave E. Hamilton the impression that all the problems would come right. His mind was firmly and narrowly on the work that lay ahead of him, not, as on several previous occasions, on the quickest way of moving out of No. 10. His family were emphatic as to his temper at the time. His son wrote:

'Defeat at last. Some appear to have expected this. I did not & the first doubt I had was when dividing, as Duff told me that they had counted enough men in the House to give us a majority of four, and this was not enough for safety. It appears that 16 men went away without telling Grosvenor. Father I am sure knew nothing of the probability of defeat until the last moment. Tories taken aback, except Randolph who danced madly about like a Cherokee on the war path... When I got back to D. St. I found the P.M. walking up & down the pavement & I went up & told Mother & then we had tea.'[299]

Since Gladstone talked openly enough at home, it is hard to think that he acted the part of one bruised by fate to his family, while inwardly rejoicing over the successful execution of an elaborate plot (the opening move of which he had in effect opposed on 5 June). To Mrs Gladstone the matter was simple:

'Today began by Lord R. Grosvenor expressing some anxiety as to the votes on the Budget, it left a mark on my mind. My husband came home to dinner late, he looked *so tired*, for his mind had been absorbed in two anxious questions, Russia and Ireland. ... Soon he perceived midst the absorbing and gt. questions, he must give himself to the Budget. It was only past nine when Lord R.G. told him he must speak... The speech was very great. He had had little or no fear of *real defeat*. Sitting down while the fervour of that speech was yet ringing in the House, Ld. R. whispered we should lose. "I should not wonder whether they wd. achieve the victory". I believe this came as a shock.

I had left the House before 12 ... Herbert was the first to open my door: "we are beat by 12" – "How is Father? where is he?" "Quite well & a splendid speech! He is walking up & down in Downing St."

He came in, it had been a blow, he had gone in to win.'[300]

Then, Mrs Gladstone added, 'before he fell asleep, came the lovely calm, the words coming from his lips "All praise to God for his mercies." '[301]

As regards the wishes of the other Liberals, it is important to realise the difficulty of envisaging the Tories forming a ministry at all, or if they did, only doing so under duress. On the walk home from the House after the vote, Hartington thought that 'the wilder Conservatives, Randolph Churchill & Co., will insist on the Tories forming a government however little at the present moment the more steady going members of their party may wish to come in.'[302] Apart from the pressures of Churchill's ambition, both party leaderships concurred in believing the manifest destiny of the Conservatives lay in being a party of opposition.

Chamberlain and Dilke, therefore, might wish their party out of office* on electioneering grounds, and in order to regain their freedom of manoeuvre: they also hoped to capture Gladstone for their section with the bait of an advanced Irish policy. If their party were forced back into office, they stood to gain in any reconstruction. They could well be happy with their defeat, however it was interpreted. For the main body of Liberals, however, a reconstructed Liberal ministry was as likely to emerge from the defeat as any other situation. Harcourt and Rosebery, who had marked themselves for promotion, took this view most strongly. The question of whether some ministers, independently of the Radicals and despite Gladstone, put their leanings to the whip and persuaded him to relax his rigours, cannot be answered, since

---

* Cf. Herbert to Henry Gladstone, 9 June 1885, Glynne–Gladstone MSS: 'Chamberlain, to whom I spoke this afternoon, is well satisfied and thinks the defeat fortunate.'

Grosvenor's papers were all destroyed and nothing but circum-stantial evidence remains. But if there was a plot of some sort, this was the kind of plot that might be expected: *reculer pour mieux sauter* rather than *felo de se*, keeping Gladstone in the dark, not definitely wanting a Tory ministry, and perhaps using the Fourth Party as a ready instrument.

Interpretations of the division varied widely. One school of thought looked hopefully (in the case of Salisbury) or angrily (in the case of Liberal loyalists), for some incipient cave of Whig or other dissidents. The *Pall Mall Gazette* published a black list of Liberal abstainers, and the *Daily News* belaboured these unfor-tunates.[303] Salisbury in turn tried to find out from his chief whip the names of those who had walked out to avoid voting, only to learn the disappointing truth that not one person was seen to leave within quarter of an hour of the division, and no Liberal had been seen hanging around during the division, though sixteen Liberals who had been in the house earlier had simply gone home.[304] In truth there was no specifiable political group at work.

Another school of thought held that Gladstone had engineered the incident. Stansfeld, who devoutly hoped for Gladstone's dis-appearance wrote 'I am glad this government has come to an end. Gladstone chose to be beaten. He could easily have adjourned the debate and avoided defeat.'[305] In this view, the fact that Gladstone abruptly brought his speech to a halt just after his chief whip had come and whispered something to him, ending on a challenging note and making it a question of confidence, was proof enough that the premier was simply timing his speech to fit in with a momentary minority in the house.[306] This view does not tally with other accounts of Gladstone's mood, and if he did indeed act on prompting from the chief whip, it may have been on faulty advice as to his having a temporary majority in the house.

A more realistic view is that neither party was behaving very competently. Liberals and Tories alike mostly failed to sense that anything was going on, and there was little tension in the air prior to the result. As Herbert Gladstone remarked, 'our whips were slack and a little more energy would have given us a majority of ten. People had no opportunity to realise that the government were going to make it a vital question till yesterday evening.'[307] Similarly, Giffard, a Tory backbencher, commented on going into the lobby ... 'we know the numbers in the house, and there are not quite enough of us.'[308]

June 9 (Tuesday). The cabinet met briefly from 12 till 1 at Downing St, with all ministers present.

Gladstone began by referring to the intended Irish legislation, saying he would be glad to make an announcement of the decision of the cabinet as to the crimes bill, but he supposed he could not. There was an awkward silence which at once made it clear that the four main objectors to coercion refused to agree to any such thing, even in the light of a concession made by Spencer overnight, and there was virtually no discussion. Dilke could not understand, in view of this, how Gladstone later felt able to assert that the cabinet was agreed on its Irish policy.[309]

It was then agreed to resign. Resignation 'did not take a minute',[310] there being 'no difference of opinion among us as to resignation'.[311] Rosebery's inquiry whether the cabinet could not resign by telegraph 'horrified Mr G'.[312] Gladstone also announced that he would act as leader during the remainder of the session but that afterwards he would retire from active leadership.[313]

Arrangements were then made concerning a number of minor points: the adjournment of the House of Commons, Princess Beatrice's jointure, the beer and spirits duties, and that Granville should write informing Salisbury that a letter of resignation had been sent, and putting him *au fait* with consequential changes in the order of parliamentary business.[314] In casual conversation at the end much play was made with the comparison with Disraeli's abortive resignation in June 1868.[315]

E. Hamilton noted the visible delight of Harcourt and Dilke at the resignation: and Derby and Granville, that the only exception to the happy faces round the cabinet table was that of Gladstone. Rosebery wrote in his diary 'All in high spirits except Mr G who was depressed.'[316]

The cabinet sent Algernon West of the Board of Inland Revenue to consult with Erskine May as to how far they were in honour bound to respect the House of Commons resolution on spirits duties. The oracle pronounced in favour of respecting the resolution, but by the time his views were reported, the cabinet had decided to act in a contrary direction and give up the extra two shillings on spirits. Their decision was superfluous in that no definite announcement could be made by the outgoing ministry, despite prodding from the Inland Revenue.[317]

At Balmoral, where there had been six degrees of frost that morning, the events of 9 June were lucidly recorded by the Queen: '... Heard by telegram, that the Govt were defeated by 12 on the Budget. When we were at breakfast, heard from Mr Gladstone, that a cabinet was summoned. This sounded serious. ... After luncheon, received a telegram from Mr Gladstone resigning. Sent for Capt. Bigge: think the difficulty great, and telegraphed to Mr Gladstone, I would await his letter, but would be ready to receive him, to expedite matters. Had previously cyphered to Sir H. Ponsonby that one or other of the Ministers should come here to explain matters. ... Had a telegram from Mr Gladstone, saying he had not much more to say, and wished to avoid the journey – his opinion best given from London: time and attention required in evacuating his house! My early return anxiously desired. Bertie telegraphed through Sir H. Ponsonby, he hoped I would not accept the resignation, as it would ruin the Conservatives to come in now...'[318]

June 10 (*Wednesday*). A long conference about honours was held at Downing St in the morning, those who came to Gladstone's room being Granville, Hartington, Cork, Wolverton, R. Grosvenor, and E. Hamilton. The list was not finally decided, but peerages were to be offered to N. Rothschild, Samuel Morley, and E. Baring, in order to give an addition of the commercial element to the upper House. Garters were to go to Kimberley, Sefton, and St Albans. R. Grosvenor, the chief whip, was asked if he would like a peerage, which he at first accepted, but he then decided to continue as whip till the end of the current parliament. There is no evidence that the cabinet collectively had any say in the distribution of honours in 1885.

The message containing the resignation of ministers reached Balmoral on the afternoon of 10 June. The Queen in reply expressed her disquiet at being faced with a political crisis and asked that Hartington or Carlingford should be sent to explain matters to her. The Queen made it clear that she could not suddenly leave Balmoral. Hartington prepared to set off that evening, then was suddenly stopped at the last moment.[319]

Ministerial reactions continued on predictable lines. W.H. Smith wrote of having seen 'some of the Ministers walking and driving, and they all appear to be in roaring spirits at their escape from the intolerable position in which they found themselves'.

June 11 (*Thursday*). In the afternoon the Queen accepted the resignation of the ministry, and sent for Salisbury.

In the evening Gladstone, Sir H. Ponsonby, Wolverton, and others dined with Rosebery, Gladstone opening up about himself and past times, telling how he was now fifth among prime ministers in duration of office, just beating Pelham.[320]

Part Two

The Conservatives in Office, June 1885–February 1886

'Nothing was ever settled satisfactorily in the cabinet' (Salisbury in an interview with the Queen, *Queen Victoria's Journal*, 5 Feb. 1886).

'While I don't believe a cabinet would be of any assistance to you, I think for appearance's sake you should summon one' (Lord John Manners to Salisbury, 17 Oct. 1885, Salisbury MSS).

'Though all were entitled to speak on every subject, as a rule no one spoke unless departmentally or personally he was seized of the question in hand' (Ashbourne's autobiographical notes on Tory cabinets, n.d., Ashbourne MSS).

Meetings of the Conservative Cabinet, 1885–86

June
26 Friday

July
1 Wednesday
4 Saturday
8 Wednesday
11 Saturday
14 Tuesday
18 Saturday
20 Monday
22 Wednesday
24 Friday
29 Wednesday

August
3 Monday
6 Thursday
11 Tuesday

October
6 Tuesday
9 Friday
23 Friday

November
10 Tuesday

December
14 Monday
15 Tuesday

January
2 Saturday
9 Saturday
12 Tuesday
15 Friday
16 Saturday
18 Monday
23 Saturday
26 Tuesday
27 Wednesday

The Conservative Cabinet in 1885–86

Prime Minister	Marquess of Salisbury
First Lord of the Treasury	Sir Stafford Northcote, *cr.* Earl of Iddesleigh, 3 July 1885
Lord President of the Council	Viscount Cranbrook*
Lord Chancellor	Lord Halsbury
Foreign Secretary	Marquess of Salisbury
Home Secretary	Sir R. A. Cross
Colonial Secretary	Col. F. A. Stanley
Secretary of State for India	Lord Randolph Churchill
Secretary of State for War	W. H. Smith
First Lord of the Admiralty	Lord George Hamilton
Chancellor of the Exchequer	Sir M. Hicks Beach
Lord Lieutenant of Ireland	Earl of Carnarvon
President of the Board of Trade	E. Stanhope†
Postmaster-General	Lord John Manners
Secretary for Scotland	Duke of Richmond‡
Lord Privy Seal	Earl of Harrowby
Lord Chancellor of Ireland	Edward Gibson, *cr.* Lord Ashbourne, 4 July 1885

* In January 1886 arrangements were made for Cranbrook to take over the War Office from Smith, who on 17 January accepted office as Irish Secretary. At the same time Carnarvon took steps towards resigning, but these changes were speedily overtaken by events.

† Vice-President of the Council till Aug. 1885.

‡ President of the Board of Trade till Aug. 1885.

Sources

There are three excellent sources for the Salisbury ministry: the Salisbury MSS, the Churchill MSS, and the Carnarvon MSS. These collections are abundant, many-sided, carefully preserved and arranged, and in general their qualities may be left to speak for themselves. The Carnarvon MSS, incidentally, have an importance not confined to Irish matters, since during Carnarvon's visits to Ireland, his colleagues competed in informing him of cabinet proceedings. The history of the ministry could virtually be written from these three sources alone.

This is not to say that further efforts have not been made. On the contrary, with a single exception, the archives of all members of the cabinet have been located and nearly always profitably consulted. The collections left by Northcote, Manners, Richmond, Cross, Halsbury, Beach, Smith, Harrowby, Cranbrook, and Ashbourne, are all interesting minor sources for the period, and most of them provide rich detail on one or more points. Though they vary considerably in size, what they have in common is that one cannot find in them a sense of the central political narrative at that time. The same applies to the papers of the successive Tory chief whips of the period, Rowland Winn and Aretas Akers-Douglas, which were found to be unimpressive in bulk and quality for high politics at this time, while another small man in a big (though non-cabinet) job, Sir W. Hart Dyke, the Irish secretary, left neither biography nor papers. With three members of the cabinet, however, archival problems have been encountered which require further explanation.

Col. Stanley (1841–1908), who succeeded his brother as sixteenth Earl of Derby in 1893, embodied the virtues of the squirearchy rather than of the nobility. Home-loving and uxorious, he was the model of a solid party man who, lacking his brother's wide intellectual interests and genuine finesse, lacked also his instability of character. He grudged each minute away from the family hearth, and his wife, although Clarendon's daughter, showed no ambition on his behalf. The couple corresponded daily when apart, but largely about trivial family matters and not politics. If he had an absorbing interest outside his family, it was the management of the Derby estates generally, rather than politics.

These sober virtues were appropriately rewarded by his appointments to junior office in 1868, to the financial secretaryship to the war office, 1874–77, and then to the financial secretaryship to the

Treasury in 1877–78. The turning-point in his career was his brother's resignation from the Foreign Office in 1878. Determined to have the Stanley influence in the cabinet, Beaconsfield appointed him to the War Office, where he made no particular mark. More surprising than his promotion to the front bench was his emergence in 1885 in Salisbury's eyes as a central figure in any Tory ministry, a view soon altered by his lack of grasp of quite minor issues while colonial secretary in the late summer of 1885. This innate unimpressiveness, together with his aversion to Lord Randolph, rapidly led to an enforced peerage (August 1886) and to oblivion of the fact that he had very nearly become the representative man of Tory orthodoxy. There is no sign that he contributed anything to the discussion of policy, or that he effectively expressed his strong repugnance for opportunism. When in 1888 he left the cabinet to govern Canada, he at last found a suitable berth for his staunch simplicity.

Those papers of Col. Stanley that have so far come to light, are divided into two portions. Firstly, there is a small collection of letters to him from his family and close friends, containing marginal political references, in Liverpool Record Office. These papers, which lie unsorted in a tin box, deal to a very limited extent with the years 1885–86. Secondly, a number of his routine official papers as a minister and governor-general of Canada have found their way into private hands in Essex. A very full index to this second group of papers may be found in the National Register of Archives. It is clear that neither collection contains a diary. However, those best able to judge, can well envisage further papers coming to light. Nevertheless, there is no reason to suppose that such discoveries would modify our picture of Stanley as a man lacking the qualities necessary for a politician, and recognising himself as such.

The Stanhope MSS, which do exist, were at the time of writing not fully sorted, but at first sight appeared to be a thin source for 1885–86. The most difficult case is that of Lord George Hamilton. Extensive checking of wills, correspondence with family solicitors and descendants, and inquiry in Ireland, by ourselves and others, have failed to turn up even a hint that his general political papers might somewhere exist. Hamilton's published memoirs made virtually no use of correspondence relating to 1885–86, so it may well be that he rarely kept letters in the first place. In any case, Hamilton's own letters in his colleagues' archives, do not suggest that his papers, if found, would show any broad interest in problems confronting the party or the cabinet as a whole. Though an Ulsterman, he shared with his colleagues a distaste for the discussion of Irish affairs, a point which, as the only member of the cabinet to publish his memoirs, he himself later confirmed.

There is no regular cabinet journal for the 1885–86 ministry. Carnarvon's diaries have altogether disappeared. All other ministers except Cranbrook, Iddesleigh and Manners definitely left no surviving journal, and very probably never wrote one. There is, alas, no reason to believe Churchill's remark (made, when very sick, in 1895 to the journalist H. W. Lucy) that he had kept one of the greatest political journals of all time.[1] All we have is Cranbrook's diary, which, though continuous and copious, is dull, discreet, and a major source for the weather: and intermittent though politically lively fragments from Manners and Iddesleigh.

Iddesleigh kept two distinct journals. One, covering July–August 1886[2] dealt solely with foreign business: and, quite apart from this, Iddesleigh left political notes in diary form for 1885–86.[3] These latter cover in detail only June 1885 and January 1886: they give adequate accounts of no more than two or three cabinet meetings, and are virtually silent as to the course of events between July and December 1885. Nevertheless they are an important source for the internal structure of the ministry, for Iddesleigh's views, and for the development of Irish policy in January 1886. Manners' account, in diary form, of the formation of Salisbury's first cabinet, is printed as an appendix to Charles Whibley's *Lord John Manners and his Friends* (1925). The diary does not continue after 25 June 1885.

When one turns to the cabinet papers themselves, the position is even more unsatisfactory. During the Salisbury ministry, twenty-nine cabinet meetings were held. Only eleven of these were reported by Salisbury to the Queen in special cabinet letters now extant at Windsor. (Copies of these are in the cabinet papers in the Public Record Office). It is likely that a larger number of accounts of cabinet discussions written by Salisbury once existed, and were destroyed at some time in unknown circumstances. The eleven meetings, accounts of which survive in the cabinet papers, were those held on 26 June, 4, 8, 14, and 20 July, 3, 6, and 11 August, 14 December, and 16 and 23 January. There are no letters from Salisbury to the Queen covering the four important pre-election cabinets held in October and November.

To some extent, these gaps can be filled from typescript copies in the Salisbury MSS of Salisbury's general correspondence with the Queen. These include incidental comments on several cabinets, in marked distinction to Gladstone's practice.* These comments

---

* Gladstone claimed that his reports to the Queen were never delayed for as much as twelve hours after a cabinet meeting (Gladstone to Earl Grey, 17 June

are used in the synoptic account below. It is fairly clear, however, that Salisbury's practice of mingling cabinet news with other topics is not even mainly responsible for the absence of direct reports on cabinets. For instance, on 9 October, Salisbury wrote a letter to the Queen pointing out an omission 'in his account of the cabinet this morning': that account is not, as one would expect, to be found in the cabinet papers. Again, an unknown hand has inserted the note 'ff 132–6 struck out' against the section in the cabinet papers where Salisbury's accounts of the cabinets of early January might be expected to be found.

The papers of Conservatives outside the cabinet require little comment. Most holders of junior office left to posterity only negative information. The shining exception was Hugh Holmes, the Irish attorney-general, whose memoirs throw much light on Tory moods and practice. The unprinted diaries of Lady Knightley continue through 1885–86 and give a rich aroma of rustic Toryism: how representative they were of feeling among the squires one cannot possibly say. They are interesting because Lady Knightley was ill-informed and credulous, and therefore recorded feelings under-represented in sophisticated sources.

One substantial backbench diary has however come to light, and as it is cited below as a guide to party feeling, it is best to give here some account of its author, Charles Dalrymple, (M.P. Bute 1868–85, Ipswich 1886–1905), who in 1885–86 reached the peak of his career. Already recognised as head of the Scottish Conservatives in the Commons while in opposition, he was appointed as Scottish whip in June 1885, with full authority over Scottish affairs in the House of Commons. His appointment was not a success, partly because he publicly opposed party policy in handing over Scottish education to the Scottish office. In all other respects, however, he fitted the part of a Tory junior whip very well. His elder brother was Sir James Fergusson of Kilkerran, returned as a Manchester Tory M.P. in 1885, and he had changed his own name to Dalrymple on succeeding to a small landed estate in Midlothian. Though he had practised briefly at the English bar, his main source of income was probably directorships, especially of investment trusts. He continued to attend board meetings frequently, both in London and Edinburgh, while junior whip. His faith in the Church of England and the Auld Kirk was also a very important part of his life, the more so as the death of his wife in September 1884 left him broken in spirit. Quixotically, he agreed

1884, 44486 f. 246). Gladstone favoured more formal cabinet minutes signed by each minister (ibid.) and condemned some existing methods of cabinet business as 'slipshod'. We owe this point to Dr A.Jones.

to stand against Gladstone in Midlothian in November 1885, and was without a seat until he got in at Ipswich in April 1886. This absence apart, his diaries are a useful record of average backbench opinion, with a few jottings of conversation with ministers.

Following the defeat of the ministry at 1.45 a.m.[4] on Tuesday, June 9, by 264–252, the Commons at once adjourned. The cabinet met at noon and decided to resign. The defeat took members rather by surprise, though Northcote had been reckoning his side would win by 3 or 4 votes.[5] Conservative backbenchers were probably not under any particular pressure to vote. Charles Dalrymple wrote 'There was a debate on an amendment of Sir M.H.Beach's ... I did not much care for the amendment or the speech (which however was able enough) and went away at 8 to the Athenaeum, not intending to vote. I returned at 11.30, still undecided, but finally made up my mind to vote.'[6] At the Carlton, *God Save The Queen* was sung, but jubilation was far from universal: that elder statesman of the country gentlemen, Sir R.Knightley, for instance went home and told his wife at 2 a.m. that if Salisbury 'accepts office now, he is no statesman'.[7]

Salisbury, Beach and Northcote met to discuss the situation, Beach being much disinclined to accept office, Salisbury hesitating, and Northcote being strongly in favour, chiefly to avoid appearing to shirk responsibility. Northcote later went the rounds of the Carlton, where opinions were divided but on balance in favour of taking office. Meeting Harcourt and Gladstone, he asked them for news, which surprised them as they had informed Salisbury of their resignation – Salisbury having left Northcote in ignorance. Later that evening, perhaps still considering himself tomorrow's premier, Northcote was giving out to casual inquirers that it had been decided to take office.[8]

On the following day, the Tory 'Old Guard' began reluctantly to face the prospect of office. Thus Cranbrook could 'see no way out from the acceptance of office if the government resignation is persevered in and accepted.' Manners thought his party would probably have to take over, whatever manoeuvres the Queen or the Liberals might engage in. He added that Northcote 'was in very feeble health, and, in my opinion, not equal physically to the strain of the House of Commons' and welcomed the emergence of Beach as the obvious successor to Northcote, a development to which Manners had long looked forward. Chaplin and Churchill were putting it about that they did not personally want office: Cross and Stanhope were anxious that the party should form a government.[9]

With Salisbury still not invited to form a government, Thursday
the 11th was another quiet day on the Tory side, the third such
since the defeat of the ministry. Salisbury lunched with Manners
and talked jobs. Salisbury wanted the Foreign Office as well as the
premiership: Iddesleigh to be First Lord, with a peerage: Cross to
take the Exchequer, Gibson the Home Office, Churchill India,
Beach the Colonies, and Carnarvon Ireland. Salisbury also asked
Manners to consider whether Ireland could be divided for local
and private bill purposes into its four provinces, with a central
court of appeal.

The Queen having accepted Gladstone's resignation,[10] Salisbury
at last received a summons and started almost at once for Balmoral,
leaving Arlington St at 7.45 p.m. to catch the night train for Scotland. Before leaving he had visits from Ponsonby and Churchill.[11]
It is likely that Churchill was offered India at this very early stage,[12]
but nevertheless made it clear that he would not join a cabinet of
which Northcote was a member.[13]

Salisbury had also talked to Beach and Northcote before leaving.
Vague discussion arose about dissolving on the old franchise: it
was felt they were taking office almost entirely because there was
no alternative. This reluctance among the 'Old Guard' contrasted
with the euphoria felt by most younger men at the Carlton at the
thought of office. 'Our friends seem quite cock-a-hoop about
coming in.'[14]

Northcote recorded extensive discussion of appointments,
Churchill incidentally not being considered as having any part to
play in allocating jobs. Northcote suggested Cross for home
secretary, but Salisbury, as before, wanted Gibson (to whom it
was duly offered and who turned it down on pecuniary grounds).
Salisbury, again as before, proposed to take the Foreign Office,
with Northcote as first lord of the Treasury – a proposal which was
not contested but was received with grave misgivings. Northcote
privately resolved to insist on seeing all foreign despatches as if he
were premier. Northcote objected strongly to Salisbury's wish to
give the Exchequer to Cross – 'I could not stand Cross's fussiness,
and constant desire to push himself forward' – though Smith
would be 'charming', and 'I should much like Fred Stanley, who
is modest, zealous, and devoted to myself.' Salisbury wanted
Carnarvon as Irish viceroy ('not a good choice in my humble
judgement' wrote Northcote, a persistent enemy of unorthodoxy
in Irish policy) but rejected Beach's suggestion that Arthur Balfour
become Irish secretary. 'I want him for the Local Government
Board: when we come to our local government legislation, I must
have someone there with whom I can be in close relations' said

Salisbury. (Though this was in fact where Balfour ended up, Salisbury in the meantime spoke of him probably becoming secretary to the Treasury).[15] Salisbury wanted Churchill for the India Office, Beach for Colonies, and Esher as lord chancellor, and was shaken by Northcote suggesting Giffard, later Lord Halsbury, for the latter post.[16]

By the time Salisbury set out for Balmoral on the evening of the 11th, a clear picture of a possible government was emerging. It was one in which Churchill's place at the India Office was not contested, though this meant anything but acceptance by the party power structure. (As Salisbury remarked, Churchill would be prevented from doing much mischief by the India Council at one end and the viceroy at the other). Northcote and Salisbury agreed to the central idea of their relative roles, however much Northcote disliked it privately. It is unlikely, however, that Northcote at this stage envisaged giving up the leadership of the lower house and taking a peerage, the issue that dominated subsequent discussion, and it is probable that Salisbury had not told Northcote, what he had told Manners, that he wanted him to take a peerage. Otherwise, Salisbury, Northcote and Beach were in general harmony about appointments. Churchill's objections to this kind of readily agreed 'Old Guard' ministry, though probably privately voiced to Salisbury, had not yet impinged on discussion as something that could not be neglected.

While Salisbury was away at Balmoral on 12 June, Northcote, still oblivious of Churchill's supposed refusal to serve with him,[17] asked for a 'scientific frontier' between his responsibilities and those of Salisbury.[18] A flattering reply from Salisbury on 14 June asked him to call that morning, and agreed to show him all despatches. Salisbury added, going to extremes of amenity, that he had only taken the Foreign Office because he did not think 'Lytton – the only obvious alternative – could have been acceptable to the party and to you... I, of course, told the Queen as I had previously told Ponsonby, that if she preferred that you should form the government, I should acquiesce very willingly in that arrangement: but that was a matter purely for her independent decision.'[19] Up to the 15th, then, Northcote was given to feel a partner in a condominium. The only sign of the storm brewing against him was when, on the evening of the 14th, he was told of a strong feeling in the Carlton that he should go to the upper House.[20]

On Monday the 15th, just before the House adjourned till Friday, Churchill's faction inflicted what was taken to be a serious blow at Northcote, designed to remove him from effective leadership. A motion by Wolff, Churchill's Fourth Party ally, to delay the seats bill (thereby implicitly challenging Northcote's exposed position as a loyal upholder of bipartisan arrangements, which had grated on backbench nerves for months past), was defeated 333–35, thus having technically no significance. The division could have been taken to show the fewness of Churchill's host, especially as some of his support came from 'chiefly old and independent members' like Sir R. Knightley, who were simply very averse to taking office, yet thought of Churchill as 'an unprincipled political adventurer copying Dizzy'. (Knightley had written to Salisbury on the 13th saying how strongly the 'older and more experienced' M.Ps felt against taking office, and later was the first to sign, on the 19th, a projected memorial having the same object). Perhaps thanks to this support from bitter opponents, Churchill was able to establish a convincing picture of his independent power: at the same time, he annoyed the orthodox so much that in subsequent days he felt the need to play for lower stakes than at first intended, and to drop the wider project he perhaps had in mind originally, of engineering a discreditable failure by the official Tory leaders either to form a government, or to refuse clearly to do so.

Churchill's action on the 15th was not confined to the above parliamentary exercise. Refusing an invitation to attend a meeting of leaders at Salisbury's house 'saying he did not like some of Lord Salisbury's friends', he laid down his terms for joining. These, as understood by Northcote, involved a peerage for the latter, and the exclusion from the cabinet of Richmond, Cross, Carnarvon, and Manners.[21] His opposition to Carnarvon is especially noteworthy. All those he sought to exclude were old or anti-Churchill or both: Richmond, for instance, coming away from church with Northcote the previous day, had burst out against Churchill, 'and did not see why so much was to be made of him'. The Queen was told by Salisbury that Churchill refused to serve with Cross (whom the Queen much liked) 'and stipulated that Sir S. Northcote be deposed from the leadership'.[22] As to the meeting of leaders on the 15th, it was not an important affair, though it was attended by all future members of the cabinet except Stanley (away in Lancashire), Halsbury, Stanhope, Ashbourne, and Churchill. Salisbury put the question as to taking office, all agreeing except Beach and Hamilton (and, in his absence, Churchill). This looked on the surface as peaceful as could be, but, like the parliamentary incident and Churchill's orally circulated ultimatum, it pointed once again to an attempt by Churchill to break the older generation of leadership, even though the India Office suited his taste. Beach's known willingness to confront Northcote, and his links with Churchill added to the threat of party convulsion.

Party reaction to Churchill's *démarche* was rapid. Churchill's remark, known to Tory leaders, that 'the chances of a Salisbury ministry were now at an end' inspired salutary energy. In the evening, for instance, Harrowby spent an hour with Salisbury 'to tell him how strongly I felt' that Northcote should take a peerage at once.[23] Manners, always close to Salisbury, fully supported the replacement of Northcote by Beach (if only because 'I have not now the physical strength for such a task').[24] Churchill's opponents in the 'Old Guard' were only too glad to dish Northcote for him, and the following day Manners was sent to tell him that Salisbury had settled on a peerage and the Colonies for him.

That evening Northcote struck back by becoming very depressed. He had, indeed, been willing if necessary to go to the Lords as Indian secretary (knowing Salisbury would not make that offer): but the colonies were not enough for his position. More generally, 'the Queen's passing me over without a word of sympathy or regret is not pleasant'. He therefore called on Salisbury, returned home, and wrote proposing to leave the Commons without taking office 'which would be infinitely more agreeable to myself'. He could 'not but feel that the position assigned to me is not what I might fairly have expected'. Salisbury, replying on 16 June, acted rapidly to prevent overt controversy. He would never have pressed the subject of a peerage, had not Northcote himself raised it. Moreover, 'if you think the Colonial Office irksome, take the Presidency of the Council... But do not leave us altogether.'[25] Salisbury also hastened to ask the Queen to make Northcote not only first lord of the Treasury, but also to give him as high a rank in the peerage as possible: the Queen agreed readily to an Earldom. The arrangement as put to the Queen was that Northcote would exercise a general superintendence over money matters, and would control the smaller appointments and patronage.[26] Salisbury thus showed himself as determined to retain Northcote in office as he was to exclude him from authority.

Northcote on 17 June replied with deep dissatisfaction. He observed that, agreement having been reached about 14 June that he was to be first lord of the Treasury and second member of the government, Salisbury had then abruptly and without consultation altered his plans and taken up out of context a suggestion originally made by Northcote that he would be willing to go to the upper House. Northcote only came to hear of this switch through Manners, its timing being such as to make it appear entirely due to Churchill's demands, and not in part to his own earlier offers. Further objections were that Northcote had particularly wanted the India Office, which went to Churchill, and that Beach was now to be the first lord in place of Northcote. Salisbury replied at once offering the first lordship again to Northcote.[27] On this being well received, the pieces were at last fitted into place, with Northcote taking a peerage as first lord, Beach taking the Exchequer (an office for which nobody had originally considered him) and leading the House, and Stanley the Colonies. These arrangements, made on the 18th and not afterwards questioned, turned on the removal of Stanley from the Exchequer, where he had seemed for two or three days past to have been securely established. His removal from this post turned solely on the need to accommodate Northcote and Beach, just as his appointment to it had been out of all proportion to his intrinsic competence or to his seniority in the party. The Conservatives simply accepted their patent inability to make fitting major appointments.

As the Northcote imbroglio subsided, it became clear that the distribution of offices was not a major problem: in fact it went peculiarly easily. By the 17th, for instance, Salisbury could comment 'Churchill has made it up with us',[28] and there were few personal difficulties. However, whether to take office at all was more uncertain on the 18th than on the 9th, and this dominated discussion between the 15th and the 22nd, with the outcome entirely uncertain until the end. Ostensibly, all turned on whether Gladstone could be trusted to give the Tories a fair run: the real issues were more internecine. Beach and Churchill, having broken up any incipient partnership between Northcote and Salisbury now had at least one eye on bringing about a discreditable failure on Salisbury's part. Electoral reasons may have had their part in this, but were not prominent. Salisbury wished to hesitate until he saw which way the wind was blowing, to detach Beach from Churchill, and to guard against the remote chance of a Northcote comeback if he gave up. Apart from this, however, one matter of policy had to be despatched, and this was done at a meeting at Arlington St at noon on the 17th, with Gibson (Ashbourne), Churchill, and F. Stanley attending in addition to those present on the 15th.

The main question was the extortion of adequate pledges from Gladstone, but renewal of the Crimes Act was touched on and those present appeared unanimous against. Many Irish Conservatives were known to take the view that they could get on without it. Thus, to an honest man like Manners, no question of appeasing the Irish was involved in dropping coercion, and certainly no understanding with them entered the matter for a moment. Honest men use honest rationalisations: 'we shall have to study the confidential advice of the Irish executive', 'it may be necessary to take extra precautions ... between October and the meeting of the new parliament' and above all 'no coercion bill is possible now'.[29] The tone of discussion excluded intrigue and assumed as the basis of action, an unaltered wish to maximise order in Ireland.

The following day, however, the ministerial crisis was again dominant. All the moves made were apparently conventional and impersonal in character, and some at least were primarily about the substantive business of pledges: but underneath, wrecking was going on. On the 18th, the leaders met again at Arlington St[30] to consider Gladstone's assurances. Gladstone's answer was unanimously considered satisfactory, and Northcote made the bearer of this message of unanimity to the Queen, through whom all negotiations were conducted. Northcote learned at Paddington that Gladstone had just left for Windsor by special train; and on arrival Northcote learnt from Ponsonby that Gladstone, somehow told by the Queen that his previous answer did not satisfy the Conservatives, was producing a new formula. His new answer was very involved but Northcote was inclined to accept it. Not so Salisbury, and still less so Beach, the two men sitting far into the night drawing up a rejoinder, in the form of a private letter taken to Gladstone by Balfour the following day. Gladstone refused to accept this and insisted on negotiations through the Queen. Salisbury then put the same proposals in more formal shape via the Queen.

These setbacks were generally known and were considered as serious. At the Carlton on the 18th, Churchill said that all arrangements were in an acute state of uncertainty,[31] and later the venerable Sir R. Knightley, according to his wife's diary, 'came in and danced a literal hornpipe in my room at 1.30 a.m. saying the whole thing was busted up'.

On the 20th, the future cabinet met to consider Gladstone's refusal of the previous day, with only Giffard absent. Northcote thought Gladstone's pledges might safely be accepted. Beach took the opposite view, arguing that they could not go on as things stood. Churchill and Gibson found themselves agreeing with Northcote, but most of the others, including especially Salisbury, held to the line that honour was involved, and that having demanded pledges, however unwisely, they were bound to adhere to that demand. The views of Cranbrook and Richmond closely followed those of Salisbury.[32] Despite Churchill's urging a speedy settlement, Northcote suspected 'that all this is playing Randolph's game. He has practically got rid of me: and now he will prove a thorn in the side of Salisbury and Beach...'[33] In general conversation, Churchill concealed his real aims by remarking that 'the worst was that Gladstone would score most from the correspondence that had taken place'.[34]

Until Churchill's sudden conversion to taking office on the 20th, the ministerial crisis had really been going rather well for Salisbury. He had achieved two major objectives, the complete humiliation of Northcote and the partial separation of Beach from Churchill, with ease. If he had any views on the subject of taking office, no one knew of them, and he had left himself free to come down on either side throughout the crisis. Northcote's wish to take office could be treated as what it probably was, the eccentric act of honestly expressing an opinion, so long as it was balanced by opposition to taking office on the part of Beach and Churchill. Most of Salisbury's colleagues were quite happy not to take office, and increased desire on the part of the Liberals to resume office in the second week of the crisis, opened the door to collusive disagreement between the parties over the small print. Both parties would resume the status quo of June 8th, the function of the ministerial crisis having been to permit an intra-party purge by both leaderships. On the 20th, therefore, the time was ripe for Salisbury to try to unite the party by riding for a fall in the negotiations with the Liberals. He felt able to do this because he had Beach with him. Churchill, faced with isolation, blocked this by going over to Northcote's side, with the implied threat of leading a clamorous backbench section against Salisbury. Since there was now a real hope that the Liberals might block Salisbury taking office even if he really wanted it, Churchill had caught Salisbury seriously off balance. He (and Beach?) had induced Salisbury to come forward as the embodiment of an opposition mentality, by leading him to believe that was where party unity lay and by threatening to disrupt any positive plans on Salisbury's part, thus permitting Churchill to turn round and come forward, perhaps using Northcote, as the representative of an undoubtedly substantial rank-and-file desire for office. What Churchill had perhaps not allowed for was the speed with which Salisbury could turn round too.

The potential fluidity of the situation was brought out on Sunday when Winn, the chief whip, called on Northcote to report party feeling at the Carlton. There was great fear the party would not take office: 'in that case the party would really be broken up'. Winn said that many now thought that if Salisbury gave up the attempt, Northcote should try. Northcote replied expressing his abhorrence of intrigue, while indicating that he would not be afraid to try his hand. Winn added that Churchill was furious, and that the whole thing was going not only to break down, but to break down discreditably. Churchill was now openly pinning the discredit firmly on Salisbury alone. 'Randolph went about saying that Gorst had always warned him that Lord Salisbury was a coward, and that he wished he had followed Gorst's advice and gone for Northcote as leader.'[35]

Some Tory M.Ps were almost certain of failure on the 21st: thus over breakfast, Sir J. Fergusson talked of how his brother 'should have got something if the Conservative government had gone on'.[36]

On Monday, 22 June, at 12.30 p.m., Salisbury met with Beach, Richmond, Manners and Cranbrook to discuss the letter from the Queen strongly urging them to accept Gladstone's assurances. It was decided that such a royal request could not be resisted, though Salisbury remarked that he personally would be glad enough to retire almost entirely from politics. Beach held out longest against acceptance of the Queen's wishes, but finally agreed with the other four leaders.[37] According to Northcote, a reference by Gladstone to new difficulties with Russia provided Beach with an invaluable bridge across which to retreat. Northcote played no part in the final settlement: Smith and Manners simply called to tell him that all was virtually settled.[38] The following day, 23 June the cabinet met at 1 to confirm the arrangement,[39] and Salisbury went to Windsor to kiss hands. Other ministers were sworn in next day, Northcote nervously omitting to kiss hands in the requisite manner:[40] Richmond was absent with a bad foot.[41] In the Commons, which adjourned till July 6 for the re-election of ministers, the Conservatives sat on the government side for the first time.[42] Last and least, on 25 June Salisbury spoke successfully to a party meeting at the Carlton about the general situation, with support from Northcote who spoke briefly but well, and from the Duke of Northumberland who was inaudible. Talking privately to a backbencher who had been prominent in opposition to taking office, Salisbury said 'the pressure the Queen put upon him had been such as he could not resist', his unsuspicious hearer going off flattered that he had received, as he thought, a hint of unrevealed dangers in international affairs.[43]

June 26 (Friday). The first cabinet[44] met 12–1.30 p.m. at 10 Downing St, Northcote's official residence, with Stanhope absent.*

The first business was to protest against Harcourt's practice of employing detectives to guard cabinet ministers. Cross agreed to try to dispense with them.

---

* Stanhope had probably entered the cabinet by a narrower margin than any other minister: Salisbury had expected him to be no more than under-secretary for India (*Q.V.J.*, 16 June). Northcote became Earl of Iddesleigh on 3 July.

The main topics were Egypt and Afghanistan: regarding the latter, no decision was taken, but the feeling was that Liberal concessions had deprived the proposed frontier of much of its value, and that Zulficar was unimportant except as the subject of a promise to the Amir. A decoration for Lumsden was thought very desirable, and it was felt that the frontier arbitration scheme of the previous ministry could well be dropped.

Wolseley was asked to state his views on the possibility of arresting the evacuation of Dongola, and on the general military situation. Until Wolseley had reported,* it was felt it would not be wise to let him return home. He was also told that he could send the Guards from the Delta to Cyprus at once, unless he wished to recommend otherwise. According to Cranbrook, it was in particular the risk to the health of the Guards arising from their being kept for no good reason in Egypt that was discussed. Cranbrook noted that Irish business 'stood over for more knowledge', and that Northcote showed 'pallor and general physical feebleness, and I am afraid that he must have been for some time in very bad health'. Wolseley's wish to attack Khartoum was probably never discussed by the new cabinet, for Smith had by Saturday made it clear to Wolseley that it was only the retention of Dongola, without regard to any larger campaign, which was under consideration. Cranbrook thought a return to Khartoum in the autumn virtually impossible.[45]

A suggestion that the government should announce a Commission on depression of trade was cut short by Churchill, who pointed to the urgency of ministers gaining control of the days needed for government business at once, if they were to be gained at all. This insight, such as it was, wrung from Northcote the judgement 'He is about the shrewdest member of the cabinet.'

Coming away from the cabinet, Harrowby told Northcote of his dismay about the terms attached to his position as lord privy seal, an office he had accepted under the impression it was salaried. In fact, not only was there no salary, but he was horrified to find

---

* Wolseley replied by telegram on 27 June 'telling the Government emphatically that the true policy is to carry out the Autumn Campaign as originally contemplated and approved of', the only other alternative in his eyes being to pay Turkey well to take over the Sudan. A further exchange of telegrams between Smith and Wolseley followed on 28 and 29 June on the military case for and against retention of Dongola: A. Preston ed., *In Relief of Gordon: Lord Wolseley's Campaign Journal of the Khartoum Relief Expedition, 1884–85* (1967), 229. The cabinet learnt on the evening of the 26th that the British rearguard was still at Dongola pending orders (Northcote's diary, f. 435). Wolseley, in a state of temporary elation at the prospect of a reversal of policy, had halted the retreat on the first sign that the cabinet might possibly believe its own imperial rhetoric.

that he could not get an allowance for a private secretary, nor for a messenger, stationery, etc.[46]

July 1 (Wednesday). A cabinet was held at Downing St, with only Carnarvon and Ashbourne absent. Smith had an interim report on army matters, and a discussion was opened as to whether there should be a budget, and if so, what its contents should be.[47]

It was unanimously agreed not to suspend further the withdrawal from Dongola, but to hold the head of the railway and to consider further what should be the boundaries to be defended. In the meantime Wolseley was summoned home for consultations. (In the event Dongola was finally evacuated on 5 July, and Wolseley reached London on the 13th).

There was much division of opinion as to the budget, some holding (with Churchill) that all the proposed new taxes should be abandoned, others (a slight majority) desiring to maintain the 2d. increase in income tax proposed by Childers. The ultimate decision was postponed to Saturday. A good many other things were discussed, but no important decision emerged.[48]

July 4 (Saturday). The full cabinet met at Downing St at noon, with the intention of disposing of all Irish questions so that Carnarvon could get away to Dublin.

On the advice of Carnarvon and Ashbourne, fortified by that of the Irish law officers, it was unanimously decided not to attempt a renewal of the Crimes Act, which was due to expire at the end of the session. Though boycotting and intimidation were known to be on the increase, they took forms that fell outside the scope of the existing Crimes Act. It was pointed out that the Crimes Act could if necessary be continued practically up till the time of the elections, by deferring the formal prorogation as long as possible.

It was decided to introduce a land purchase bill, for the sake of loyalists, and to refuse Parnell's motion to reopen the case of the Maamtrasna murders, which most of the cabinet thought would be a most dangerous precedent. Carnarvon, Gibson, and Dyke had all agreed beforehand that 'we are bound to uphold Spencer'.[49] Churchill dissented from this last view.

The cabinet also resolved to bring in a bill to prevent the disfranchisement of persons in receipt of purely medical poor relief. They decided to support, as they had already done in opposition, the Scotch secretary bill.

There was fairly sharp division of opinion within the ministry as to whether the Scottish Office should take over education. Stanhope was against this, while Dalrymple, who had accepted office as Scottish whip on condition that he had a general overlordship of Scottish affairs in the Commons, felt very strongly against the transfer on educational grounds. Dalrymple even spoke in the House against the government on the issue. Dalrymple's supposed subordinate, the lord advocate J. H. A. Macdonald, was however equally strong for transferring education to the Scottish Office. (The final cabinet decision in favour of transfer was given on 8 July).

Though not mentioned in Salisbury's report to the Queen, the labourers (Ireland) bill was probably selected from the bills already before the House for passage this session, following a letter from Carnarvon to Salisbury on 1 July recommending this. Power, the Irish whip, had offered Parnellite support for the Conservatives on condition they introduced an extension of the existing Labourers' Act, and a bill to eliminate sheriff's expenses in uncontested elections.[50] It is not clear that this deal was either ever clinched or that it was known to the cabinet. Cranbrook commented that Carnarvon's 'views were clear as to what we must do – not so clear as to what may be needed'.

The Egyptian and Afghan questions were held over for a future meeting, the former in expectation of Wolseley's arrival and in the hope that the money needed might be found.[51]

July 6 (Monday). In the afternoon Carnarvon made a major statement on Irish policy in the Lords, announcing that the Crimes Act would not be renewed, and that a land purchase bill and a bill to amend the Labourers' Act of 1883 would be introduced. Carnarvon then left for Dublin where he launched a major attempt to win over catholic opinion.

In the morning Carnarvon had met Justin McCarthy M.P, the Parnellite leader.[52] They met at 1 Grosvenor Square, the house of Howard Vincent, first Director of the C.I.D. (1878–84) and at this time Tory candidate for Sheffield Central, which he held from 1885 to 1908. Vincent was not present at the meeting, but Carnarvon later told him that it had given him great pleasure, and that he was to meet Parnell. Vincent appeared to play no further part in the matter, though his tour of Ireland in August and September 1885 must have appeared to informed Irishmen that of Carnarvon's emissary. The fact that Vincent had tried to get into parliament as a home ruler in 1873 (and had been cut dead by Spencer before the hunting field for his pains) is simply an amusing sidelight.

This interview between McCarthy and Carnarvon had its origins no further back than a dinner in late June, when Vincent, talking to Carnarvon in a restrained home rule vein, urged contact with the Parnellites. On this occasion and at subsequent meetings, Carnarvon asked Vincent to arrange a meeting with Parnell. On 28 June, Vincent had tried without effect to arrange a meeting between Carnarvon and Gray, owner of the *Freeman's Journal*. Vincent then approached McCarthy telling him of Carnarvon's wish. Parnell was not then in town, and McCarthy was uncertain of his wishes, but the latter agreed to try to arrange a meeting and to begin by seeing Carnarvon himself. A preliminary exchange of letters between McCarthy and Carnarvon, then just about to leave Dublin, speedily arranged this initial meeting.[53] These letters were probably passed on almost at once by McCarthy to a friendly lady novelist.

At this preliminary interview, McCarthy afterwards wrote, Carnarvon and he 'had a very friendly talk about the condition of things in Ireland, and the possibility of some policy being adopted by the government which might meet the wishes of the Irish national representatives and the Irish people. Lord Carnarvon distinctly told me that for his own part he was prepared to go as far in the direction of home rule as either Parnell or I could desire. But he did not convey to me, and I am sure did not intend to convey, the idea that he was speaking on behalf of Lord Salisbury's government. What I understood was that he had some hope of being able to bring over his colleagues to his own views on the subject, if Parnell and he could agree upon some course of policy which would be approved of by the Irish people, and which could safely be recommended to the consideration of the Conservative government.'[54]

In a letter written at the time to non-political friends (the lady novelist, with whom he was collaborating on a political novel about an 'ambitious man who is willing in the end to sacrifice everything to the sweet wild-flower girl', and her husband), McCarthy was rather less sanguine:

'I don't think that much more will come of our talk with "our mutual friend". He is willing and anxious to go as far, he says, as I could wish to go, but he fears that his party would not be prepared just at present to go so far, and I fear the result will be that the Grand Old Man will come in... We had a long talk.'

Despite secrecy as to details, it rapidly became well known in political circles that something was afoot. At a political luncheon on 12 July, with McCarthy present, the talk was of Carnarvon being the last viceroy and 'Prince Eddie of Wales' taking up residence in Ireland. To this idea, McCarthy said 'We shall be quite indifferent.' Mrs Jeune, the hostess, had little doubt that 'there is some sort of bargain between the Conservatives and the Parnellites, and that Lord Carnarvon has a great deal to do with it.'[55]

The interview, however, was an unqualified success is so far as it led McCarthy to undertake to persuade Parnell to meet the viceroy. McCarthy later claimed that he had difficulty in persuading Parnell to agree to a private meeting, and in particular that Parnell refused to meet Carnarvon at Vincent's house.[56] It was nevertheless soon arranged that Carnarvon and Parnell should meet on 4 or 5 August. An initial intention by Carnarvon to have Ashbourne present at the interview was not adhered to, to Salisbury's disquiet, and Salisbury in general showed some apparent reluctance about agreeing to the meeting.[57] Had his reluctance been real or weighty, the meeting would of course never have been allowed to take place.

July 8 (*Wednesday*). Ashbourne received a cipher wire in the evening from Beach asking (if possible) for a draft land purchase bill by Saturday.[58] Ashbourne, believing that there was no draft Liberal bill available as a model, felt: 'By throwing over as much contentious matter as possible, abandoning all thought of turning out an ideal measure, and applying myself to produce a few clauses introducing improvements which may work if fairly administered, I think I should have done as much as can be fairly expected *in the time...* '[59] Carnarvon urged him to incorporate into his draft of the bill, some suggestions made by Archbishop Walsh.[60]

The cabinet met in Beach's room in the Commons at 11 a.m., Carnarvon and Ashbourne not attending.

The cabinet discussed the Queen's wish to confer the rank of Royal Highness on Prince Henry of Battenberg, and her fear of objections abroad. The cabinet were unanimous that the matter was for the Queen alone, and that no foreign objections would be admissible.

It was decided to proceed with an income tax of 8d. as proposed by the late ministry, and to make up the deficit by some form of loan.

It was decided to bring in a bill exempting from disfranchisement those who obtained medicine or medical attendance from parish doctors: to include education among the functions of the Scottish secretary: to pass that portion of the criminal law amendment bill which provided for the protection of young girls up to the age of 15: and to set up a Royal Commission on the depression of trade and industry.

The position regarding the criminal law amendment bill is difficult to sum up. Stead's revelations in the *Pall Mall Gazette* had begun two days before this cabinet, and it might be held that the cabinet was moved by his revelations to take swift action. Indeed, Stead's action was prompted by the opinion of a Tory leader, given soon after taking office, that the moribund bill 'hadn't the slightest chance of passing', though whether this opinion was based on discussion in an early cabinet one cannot tell. Also, Stead's daily offerings on white slavery, which continued to 12 July, were at first received with execration, and were singularly unlikely to carry the cabinet into a course it did not otherwise wish to take. It may be that the chronology suggests that the cabinet, despite Stead, wished to see the bill through as a purely independent decision on their part.

July 11 (Saturday). The cabinet met at Downing St with only Carnarvon absent. The main topics were Ashbourne's land purchase bill, Afghanistan, the troops at Suakin, Admiralty finance, and the rate of interest on Treasury loans. Some other minor matters were considered.

Firstly, Salisbury briefly outlined Russian evasiveness over the Afghan border issue. The second problem was whether the Treasury should lend money for labourers' dwellings at $3\frac{1}{8}$ per cent, a rate adequate to secure against loss but liable to be a dangerous precedent: Beach feared Irish farmers would want to borrow at that rate. Thirdly, mismanagement at the Admiralty (by Northbrook) was, at Churchill's suggestion, put before a small Commons committee so as to produce an early report. Fourthly, in view of ill health among the English forces at Suakin, Smith agreed to consider using black or Turkish troops paid if not officered by England. On Irish land, the cabinet looked at Ashbourne's draft bill,[61] and appointed a committee on its details which were to be considered at Tuesday's cabinet.[62]

July 14 (Tuesday). The cabinet met at Downing St at noon, with Carnarvon, Halsbury, and Ashbourne absent. It was agreed to pass those parts of the criminal law amendment bill concerning a higher age of consent for girls, a proposal of which the cabinet had been 'very shy' according to its main supporter, Harrowby. Cross stated police objections to parts of the bill, which would probably be difficult to pass. Harcourt subsequently refused Cross's request to steer this bill through parliament.[63]

As for Ashbourne's land bill, it was decided, subject to the opinion of the Speaker as to its being a money bill, to introduce it into the Lords: that purchase should be encouraged by offering the lowest possible interest: and that the Church Fund residue should be guarantee against any loss incurred.[64]

Harrowby gave a full account of the meeting: '... The most important question pending in the cabinet is Bechuanaland, about which Stanley promises a full memo tomorrow, and the policy will probably be settled at Saturday's cabinet. Sir H. Robinson telegraphed that if Warren's troops, numbering 4,000, were to remain, an immediate provision must be made of food etc. for 2 months. Smith was directed to telegraph that no step must be taken of this kind, and that full, final directions would be sent next week.

'I suspect Stanley can hardly make up his mind what to do. Beach and Randolph press him to decide at once. The former expresses himself as very hostile to the annexation in any form. being much alarmed at the general prospect of our finances. Stanley seemed inclined to the same view, and I suspect Salisbury. Personally I should much regret our desertion of the native Chiefs again and doubt the wisdom of making over this important territory to the Cape. It is said that a mounted police of 500 could hold the country, but Stanley fears reverses if we try this experiment. Salisbury and others hope you may send your opinion by Saturday...

'I see no signs whatever of disagreement in our cabinet – even the Scotch secretary's affair has gone off smoothly – the Admiralty financial scandal can only do us good... It was a bitter pill for the Treasury to swallow the scheme of advances for workmen's dwellings in England, and for the purposes of your Irish land purchase bill, at $3\frac{1}{8}$ per cent, but as the success of both affairs seemed to depend on this, Northcote and Beach had to give way.'[65]
July 17 (Friday). In the debate on Parnell's motion for the reopening of the Maamtrasna and other cases, apparent ministerial sympathy with the Irish combined with the throwing over of Lord Spencer, led to deep disquiet among average Tory opinion. A representative junior minister, Dalrymple, wrote in his diary that there 'were many things one does not like', while the worthy figure of Lord G. Hamilton, meeting someone for business after the debate, was so sick he could not bring himself to speak.

The breach of propriety on this occasion was virtually absolute. The cabinet had, at the behest of all its Irish team, made a perfectly clear decision at its meeting on 4 July to stand by Spencer's decisions, and had not since discussed the matter. In the days prior to the debate, however, word had somehow got around that a *volte-face* was in the air. Carnarvon, who was at all stages entirely opposed to this form of appeasement, wrote on 15 July to Beach, stressing 'the extreme difficulties of my position' especially if it were made possible for any convict to appeal, and urging that any concession would raise difficulties 'infinitely more formidable' than 'any mere refusal to reopen this case'. What Carnarvon emphatically did not want to occur during his absence in Dublin, were 'a few kind and generous words' towards the Parnellites in their struggles with Dublin Castle.[66] Carnarvon also expressed his anxieties to the premier, who wrote to Beach just before the debate 'I gather ... you are disposed to go back on the decision which the cabinet took on the Maamtrasna case. I think you ought to consult the cabinet before doing so.'[67] The cabinet was of course not consulted. In the face of the opposition of the premier, the cabinet, and the Irish government, the Beach-Churchill-Gorst group seized the opportunity to proclaim an entente with the nationalists which still really existed only in their own minds.

The consequences of this studied insolence were largely ironic and unfortunate. Carnarvon, whose opposition to the episode was not known, found they included an agreeable letter from the catholic archbishop of Dublin listing the things he had done to create a better feeling.[68] In general, however, the repercussions for Carnarvon were far less agreeable. Carnarvon's immediate object at this time was to govern Ireland through the bishops by being pleasant to them on educational questions. This meant principally money, but also a temporary suspension of traditional suspicions about catholics, the latter concession being one that the cabinet by itself might have swallowed had the country not known about it, but which after the Maamtrasna affair had to be considered in the light of public opinion and not just in terms of the delicacies of administration. As regards Carnarvon's need for money to sweeten official Irish catholic opinion, the key man here was Beach, who though obviously sympathetic on a purely Irish plane to such an entente, at another level did not see eye to eye at all with Carnarvon. Beach was also, as chancellor, rather short of money to hand out for any purpose, since his own motion which put the Tories in office had at the same time cut away necessary taxation. In crude terms, because Carnarvon took an anti-Irish line and Beach a pro-Irish one over Maamtrasna, it was natural that Beach should take an anti-Irish, and Carnarvon a pro-Irish line, over the other Irish issues before the cabinet in July, viz., a reconstruction of Irish education in favour of the catholics, and paternalist support for the Irish banking system. The two pro-Irish groups in the cabinet acted as much in opposition to each other, as to the silent majority of ministers who as honest self-deceiving men wished only to be sure that they heard and saw no evil.

After Maamtrasna, the silent majority was sufficiently alert to something undefined being afoot, to reassert certain fundamental negations in a way that made it impossible to use the cabinet as a major constructive instrument for building up a known and agreed Irish policy, as had been done at the exemplary cabinet of 4 July. The way in which Maamtrasna nipped in the bud precisely the non-traditional developments which it sought to put firmly into public view, by awakening the basic party instinct for survival, was best put by Harrowby. His reaction is all the more valuable because he was a decent, average, unprejudiced crypto-liberal minister, and a personal friend of Carnarvon,* whom he only wished to help:

> 'The Roman catholic vote of money is, I fear, really impossible. I have no doubt it would ruin our prospects at the general election. Already there is a growing distaste in the country for our supposed Irish alliance and distrust has been excited by Randolph's and Gorst's speeches on the Maamtrasna affair. The vote in question would be considered as showing that the compact was signed, sealed, and delivered, and ... we should awaken the whole Protestant feeling which is only slumbering and turn both dissenters, evangelicals, Scotchmen, middle class artisans, who are just joining us, into disappointed friends.'[69]

July 18 (*Saturday*). The cabinet met at Downing St, with only Carnarvon absent.

Gorst's speech on Maamtrasna the previous night was criticised, especially by Cranbrook, and Beach was instructed to remonstrate with Gorst.[70] Even Churchill repudiated Gorst.[71]

The other main topics were Bechuanaland, and the failure of the Munster Bank in Ireland. In Cranbrook's view, the information on Bechuanaland was inadequate, and Stanley, the minister responsible, less lucid than he might have been. Cranbrook felt that Warren's ambition, despite the admirable work he had done, had in any case outrun public money if not also going beyond what public opinion would ratify. The larger question of what to do with Khama's Land, which Cranbrook thought was unacceptable as offered, was left for the time being.

On the advice of Sir H. Robinson, the cabinet decided to annex Stellaland and Goschen, and, on the same advice, gave instructions for the gradual withdrawal of Warren's force, and the substitution of a strong body of police, Warren himself to be warmly thanked.[72]

Carnarvon's proposal to guarantee Irish bank deposits, involving quite unknown liabilities to the Exchequer, caused consternation but had to be accepted because no one wanted to risk Carnarvon's resignation.

Ashbourne had promised Dyke that he would raise the subject of Irish education at this meeting:[73] it is not clear that he found an opportunity to do so.

---

* To Carnarvon, Harrowby was a friend 'from whom as you know I really have no secrets' (Carnarvon to Cranbrook, 5 Aug. 1885, Carnarvon MSS). There is no firm evidence, however, that Harrowby knew of such secrets as the Parnell interview.

July 20 (*Monday*). The cabinet met at Downing St at 2, with only Carnarvon absent. Little is known of what took place beyond that there was probably some retrospective discussion of the Maamtrasna debate.[74] The only business recorded by Cranbrook was that the cabinet heard a somewhat less alarming account of things in Ireland, so far as the danger of a run on the banks was concerned. Similarly Salisbury wrote:

> 'At the cabinet today reports were received concerning Lord Carnarvon's action in respect of the Munster Bank. Considerable alarm had been created in the cabinet by the reports received on Saturday: and it was feared that the viceroy had pledged himself to make advances to save the Munster Bank to an imprudent extent. But there appears to be no serious danger now.'*

There is hearsay evidence, not of contemporary date, of an important split occurring at this cabinet. The story, as told by the respected young Tory peer Cadogan to Rosebery a year later, cannot quite be ruled out. 'Salisbury was outvoted on the question of suspending the National League by Churchill, Ashbourne, Beach, and Halsbury, which he then declared he would not forgive.'[75] It is highly implausible that such a repressive measure should have been under discussion at this time, still more that it should have left no trace in ministerial papers. There is however one piece of evidence which may point to some subterranean disturbance of the kind to which Cadogan alluded. The Tory party paper, the *Standard*, came out on 31 July with a blistering first leader attacking Churchill. The *Standard* was often and probably rightly taken to reflect the views of Salisbury (or perhaps of his wife), and Churchill himself believed that the article had been officially inspired. Despite smoothing over by Beach, this episode continued to affect relations between Churchill and Salisbury during August, when Churchill for the first time threatened resignation, doing so over quite minor departmental issues in a way that was inexplicable without reference to the general tension that had built up at the end of July. The origins of this tension may lie in the Maamtrasna debate itself, or in some

---

* Salisbury to the Queen, 20 July 1885, Salisbury MSS D/86/148. Carnarvon however writing on the same day to Richmond was not sanguine. 'I do not believe from what I hear, in the power of recovery of the Munster; and I feel uneasy as to the existence of the Hibernian. It is a terrible blow to the prospects of peace and order in the autumn' (Richmond MSS 871/D 43). Carnarvon's colleagues were probably unaware that the viceroy himself 'had the misfortune to lose a considerable portion of my outfit money in the Munster Bank' (Carnarvon to Spencer, 8 Jan. 1886, Spencer MSS).

hidden cabinet debate corresponding to Cadogan's story, or in the *Standard* article taken by itself, but whatever the cause, an era of good feeling which had apparently existed in the Tory cabinet up to 20 July, came rather sharply to an end, and perhaps never recovered.

July 22 (Wednesday). The cabinet met at Downing St at 11, with Carnarvon and Hamilton absent. The main topics were Irish: the run on the Irish banks, and Carnarvon's plans for Irish university education. The cabinet rejected a proposal by Carnarvon to grant £6,000 to the Queen's Colleges, only Churchill and Ashbourne speaking in his support.[76] However agreement was reached on holding an inquiry into Irish higher education in the autumn.

On the Munster Bank failure, the cabinet heard a letter from Carnarvon and explanations in person from Sir George Kellner, an Irish high court official. Carnarvon's letter 'threw the cabinet into terrible disarray'.[77] The view taken by the cabinet was that the Bank of Ireland, acting strictly as a private concern, had lent to the distressed banks only on complete security, and that hence the Government was only called on to adjust its balances in the Bank of Ireland in ratio to the public spirit of that body.[78] The cabinet was in general reacting strongly against paternalist proposals put forward by its Irish administration: Cranbrook not only described the university policy as dangerous, but saw the bank question as another 'scrape' just averted. More light on the sensed danger of impending unorthodoxy is shown by Salisbury's report to Carnarvon after the cabinet, 'one of the financial members of the government said that he must resign if it came to asking the House of Commons to guarantee half the deposits of the Munster Bank: and others held language tending in a similar direction ... there was a belief in the minds of most of the cabinet that such a proposal would be rejected by a large majority of the House of Commons'.[79]

July 24 (Friday). The cabinet met at 3 at Downing St with Carnarvon absent. It was agreed to accept the medical relief bill, though Cranbrook and some others wanted a wider measure covering outdoor relief generally.[80] Salisbury described the issue over Collings' clause as 'not a large one':[81] 'it was decided that in some form or other, the Bill should pass'. News was received that the run on the Irish banks was waning, with the banks still unbroken likely to hold out.[82]

At one or other of the cabinets of 22 and 24 July, Ashbourne spoke with near idolatry of Carnarvon's personal gifts in dealing with Ireland. Similarly the Irish secretary, Dyke, who later did not get on at all well with Carnarvon, wrote to tell him 'you have done wonders as to this education question'.[83] On this last, Ashbourne wrote 'The cabinet were glad to learn that the immediate consideration of the £6,000 Education vote was no longer necessary. I think that the R.C. authorities, who so informed you, were prudent. The feeling of our friends was one, not of antagonism of principle, but of doubt.'[84]

July 29 (Wednesday). A cabinet was held at Downing St, with Carnarvon, Halsbury, Ashbourne, and Richmond absent. The Criminal Law Amendment Act and Afghan affairs were discussed.[85]

August 1 (Saturday). Parnell and Carnarvon met secretly at an empty house at 15 Hill St several days earlier than previously arranged. The meeting had possibly been brought forward from the later date (4 or 5 August) originally arranged for it, in order to facilitate the holding of a cabinet on 3 August specially devoted to Irish affairs, an arrangement which ministers were expecting over the weekend and which must have been revoked, presumably by Salisbury, probably at the last moment, and quite possibly as a result of what passed at the interview with Parnell. The conversation lasted an hour and a quarter, according to a letter[86] written by Carnarvon to Ashbourne later the same day which made no mention of the contents of the interview, although it was made clear that Ashbourne would be told verbally of what had happened. Carnarvon had originally intended Ashbourne to be present, and his departure from this intention had somewhat alarmed Salisbury.[87]

After the meeting, Carnarvon went at once to Hatfield, where he drew up a long memorandum[88] recording what had taken place. According to this, 'there was no sort of bond or engagement' but merely an 'interchange of opinion on a most difficult question.' Parnell allegedly referred at length to his fears of a radical land movement led by Davitt, at the head of 'an extreme party'. He agreed to leave the responsibility for Irish land under home rule with the British government, if necessary. As to the precise shape of home rule, Parnell was elusive, stressing only that there must be a central parliament and not regional bodies. In Carnarvon's view, the great point was that Parnell seemed to accept a gradual development of devolution from small beginnings. 'He was in fact', Carnarvon wrote, 'singularly moderate throughout the whole discussion, and not so absolutely cold as I had expected. He met every objection with perfect fairness, admitting every difficulty, and apparently anxious to find common ground.' As an ultimate aim, Parnell looked to the encouragement of Irish industry by protectionist legislation under home rule. To obtain this, Parnell offered to accept the removal of the Irish M.Ps from Westminster.

In discussion between Salisbury and Carnarvon, it was agreed that neither the Queen nor the cabinet should be informed of the interview. This was probably contrary to Carnarvon's advice, at least where the Queen was concerned. The cabinet as such was clearly never informed even of the fact of the interview having taken place.

Justin McCarthy was told by Parnell that the meeting offered some hope of a satisfactory understanding, without there being any talk of a pledge or promise.[89]

This is the best point at which to set out how the interview became public knowledge. Despite widespread suspicion that something was afoot, well-informed Tory, Liberal, and Irish parliamentary circles showed no specific knowledge of the 'empty house' meeting in the winter of 1885 and spring of 1886. It was not until May 1886 that an evident belief can be found among Tory leaders, in Carnarvon's own mind, and probably among leading Parnellites, that the matter could not be concealed. Parnell on 7 June asserted that a Tory majority would have granted home rule. On Beach arising to deny this, Parnell revealed his meeting with an unnamed cabinet minister. Carnarvon, on 10 June, confirmed that he was the minister referred to by Parnell. The substance of his statement was that the meeting was held solely to elicit Parnell's demands, and that the cabinet was in no way involved. Carnarvon made no mention of Salisbury's prior sanction, nor of his own visit to Hatfield immediately after the interview.[90] Despite partisan embroideries, the matter rested there until the publication of Hardinge's biography of Carnarvon in 1925. The main historical consequence of the interview was that though in fact a non-event, it was such an excellent parody of a historically significant fact that it enabled Churchill to escape uninjured from his more diffuse but more systematic Parnellite entanglements.

August 3 (Monday). The cabinet met at Downing St, with Richmond and Ashbourne absent. It was decided to proceed with four of the remaining bills (Scottish secretaryship, housing of the poor, Irish land, and criminal law amendment bills), and if possible also to pass the Irish labourers and police enfranchisement bills.

Important telegrams from India were read in reference to the Amir's unaccountable delay in fortifying Herat. The viceroy and his council strongly upheld the fidelity of the Amir, and the necessity of standing by him. The cabinet resolved to adhere to the viceroy's opinion.

French intrigues for commercial concessions in the kingdom of Upper Burma were reported, telegrams from the viceroy being read on the subject. The complaint of the viceroy was not against action by the French government, but against a private attempt by a French capitalist, aided by the perhaps unofficial exertions of the local French consul, to gain control of a large part of the Burmese economy. Further telegrams from the viceroy, dated 29 July and 2 August, insisted that France must not be allowed to dominate the Burmese economy, and proposed to send to the Burmese court a British agent 'to whose advice in all matters of foreign policy the Burmese Government should submit'. By 3 August, it was clear there was no reliable information as to what was going on, though the existence in the background of a still unratified commercial treaty between France and Burma, made in January 1885 but not recorded as ever having been discussed in cabinet, led to the worst suppositions. It was therefore resolved that, in the first instance, Salisbury should see the French ambassador, which he duly did on 7 August, the ambassador disowning all knowledge of the alleged activities. Subsequent developments, such as the French government's removal of the consul in question, tended to prove that Paris was less than deeply interested in the Franco-Burmese intrigues that were undoubtedly going on, and after this episode the centre of irritation in Anglo-Burmese relations became a fine imposed by the Burmese on an English company, a matter which first engaged Churchill's attention in the latter half of August, and subsequently became the most specific *casus belli*. The Burmese question next came before the cabinet at its meeting on 9 October.[91]

It struck Cranbrook at this cabinet that in some way Churchill was working with Parnell and Healy, and Cranbrook spoke in protest to Salisbury about it.[92] Some letters also record Cranbrook's considerable annoyance with suggestions made by Churchill at this cabinet that he (Churchill) was in 'intimate relations' with Parnell and Healy.[93]

Although virtually no Irish business was dealt with, Salisbury had asked Carnarvon to attend for that very reason, and Smith had understood the meeting was 'to talk about Ireland'.* This rather abrupt and unexplained change in the agenda is the only hint that Salisbury reacted positively to the Parnell interview.

August 6 (Thursday). The cabinet met at 2.30 at Downing St, Carnarvon, Ashbourne, and Richmond not attending.

* Carnarvon to Harrowby, 3 Aug., Harrowby MSS lii 136; 'Our friend, the P.M., is essentially a strange being! He as good as brings me to London, he certainly keeps me here two days and as I understand summons a cabinet in order to talk over any Irish question ... and then never asks me to say a word.' Cf. Smith to Stanhope, 2 Aug., Stanhope MSS: 'We shall meet tomorrow to talk about Ireland, but I am very anxious something should be settled about Afghanistan before parliament rises.'

Sir H. Wolff's instructions were carefully considered and some modifications made, not for the purpose of altering the substance of them, but in order to prevent misconstruction if they ever should be published. Russia was also discussed: despite a great wish to bring the Anglo-Russian negotiations to a conclusion, this was not immediately possible without unacceptable concessions. It was resolved that the naval and military preparations might now be somewhat relaxed.[94]

The 'conspiracy' by the Liberals to refuse to serve on the Royal Commission on the depression of trade was considered.[95]

August 11 (*Tuesday*). The cabinet met at Downing St 12–2.30, with Carnarvon and Richmond absent. A gloomy letter[96] from Carnarvon was read, warning the cabinet against too confident language about Ireland, as there were many anxious symptoms there together with much that was encouraging. It was agreed to do as Carnarvon advised, and to avoid what Salisbury called 'language of extravagant hopefulness'.[97]

Ashbourne said that he concurred in every syllable of Carnarvon's letter, and that Carnarvon was carrying on his work with great resource, courage, and success, and that he had made himself most acceptable to all.[98]

The Queen's Speech was the main topic. In Cranbrook's view, it was settled rather well, though the parts of it dealing with Ireland were left unwritten for the time being.*

The service ministers explained their requirements. It was agreed that all ships already estimated for by the late ministry should be built with all speed, and that specifications for two large ironclads should be prepared at once: whether they should be built by contractors or in naval dockyards was held open till the specifications were known.

It was resolved to bring home from Egypt those superfluous battalions which had only remained there on account of the Russian difficulty. The cabinet thought the money saved would be well expended on artillery etc. Churchill was anxious for the battalions to remain in Egypt but the rest of the cabinet without exception adopted the opposite view.[99] The changes were to be presented as measures for efficiency, not of demobilisation.†

* As Salisbury wrote to Carnarvon on 12 Aug. 'We thought all the matters connected with Ireland so difficult that we have made no mention whatever of her in the Queen's Speech' (PRO 30/6/55/12).

† Cranbrook's diary, 11 Aug. 1885. Shortly afterwards Cranbrook withdrew to his Highland estate for the vacation. Parliament was prorogued on the 14th, Salisbury gave an end of season dinner for the cabinet on the 18th, and on the 19th Salisbury, Stanhope, and the lord advocate attended a Council at Osborne, thus winding up the year's routine business.

Warren's differences with Robinson in Bechuanaland again came up, following previous cabinet discussion on 18 July. Cranbrook expressed doubts about Stanley's policy there.

August 14 (*Friday*). The Secretary for Scotland Act having come into force on this day, Richmond became the first Scottish secretary. Richmond, who for medical reasons had been at Homburg for some time, was offered the Scottish Office by Salisbury on 7 August, and wrote back accepting it on 9 August 1885.[100] Richmond explained to Rosebery, who was also taking a prolonged cure at Homburg, that it had come on him as a great surprise: that he had always thought the office unnecessary and been opposed to it (though never publicly) but that now he was in charge, he should do his best to push it.[101] He had earlier told the Queen that 'he had not at all wished to take office, but had thought it his duty to serve in any capacity – that he would have liked the War Office, but if that could not be, was content to take the Board of Trade'.[102] Stanhope succeeded Richmond at the Board of Trade.

During the vacation, ministers became increasingly anxious to settle their party line on Ireland. Ashbourne and Carnarvon wanted the policy of the 'muted voice' to continue[103] and most ministers accepted this to some extent. Harrowby, who may have wanted home rule by stealth, was alarmed that Parnell's strong speeches 'will overthrow all hope'. His words are ambiguous, but he clearly feared a premature Unionist declaration by the Tories.[104] Churchill was not at all alarmed about Parnell's speeches and thought 'the English press is making a most foolish fuss about them. His programme is studiously vague...'[105] Manners, looking back to his youth, pronounced that Ireland must 'have the power of the purse, and lay aside the doctrines of political economy': Ireland, Manners thought, had been ruined by English mercantilism, and should be saved, he implied, by a tariff wall.[106] Iddesleigh, whose strength in Irish matters normally consisted in his resolute avoidance of imagination, so far forgot himself as to feel 'full of hope'[107] about Ireland, and urged a policy of 'treating Irish ideas with great tenderness'. Home rule had to be avoided, he said, but nevertheless the party should have a clear Irish programme, and not leave the matter 'to be fiddled with, and treated with Parnell in one way and with the British electorate in another way'. A 'conciliatory but firm programme' would win 'the best class of Irish support'.[108] Thus ministers (with the conspicuous exception of Salisbury) poured upon Carnarvon various strands of advice and appraisal which, though not exactly in conflict, did not easily fit together in the absence of more formal discussion. All the letters, too, can be read equally in two quite different ways: as manifestations of a naive helpfulness, or as discreet symptoms of an unmentioned conspiracy.

Carnarvon had written to Salisbury on 18 September, with Ashbourne's moral support, putting forward the idea of an early cabinet devoted to the co-ordination of ministerial election speeches. 'I hardly think it is very safe to leave us all to make speeches, in which Ireland must form more or less a topic of debate, in the face of bitter and unscrupulous critics without an attempt at some common understanding.' Salisbury delayed replying till 24 September, when he wrote saying it was impracticable to have another cabinet before his speech at Newport on 7 October. On 25 September however, perhaps immediately on receiving Salisbury's letter, Carnarvon wrote to his closest ministerial friend saying he was coming to London the following day,[109] and on the same day it had become clear in London that, whatever Salisbury had said the previous day, it was practicable to have a cabinet on 6 October, just before Salisbury's keynote speech. Beach may well have intervened to secure this, as he wrote specially pressing Carnarvon to attend the meeting, 'as it is quite time we knew what to say about Ireland'.[110]

October 1 (Thursday). Churchill arrived in Dublin for a brief visit, going on landing in the morning to the house of Holmes, the Irish attorney-general, from whom he got the impression, confirming his own previous views, that 'there is nothing alarming in the state of Ireland at all'.[111] Going into the library after breakfast, Churchill relieved Holmes' mind over his attitude to home rule. Churchill said that he had many understandings with Irish members which were faithfully adhered to on both sides but that he had never either directly or indirectly countenanced home rule.[112] Churchill probably continued his visit by spending two nights with his old friend, the brilliant and sensible opportunist Lord Justice Fitzgibbon, at Howth.[113] (Churchill's impatience with conventional Tories arose from his measuring people by the high standard of his Irish friendships).

October 6 (Tuesday). The full cabinet met at Downing St at noon. Carnarvon's report on Ireland was followed by discussion of an Irish parliament.[114] Carnarvon's picture of the situation was in the gloomiest colours[115] and was confirmed by Ashbourne and Hamilton. He had no remedies to offer other than the more intensive application of the ordinary law. Something, he thought, might be done as regards reducing boycotting: but practically the separatists had got complete command.[116] According to Northcote,

'His views seemed to point to our setting up an Irish Parliament. Gibson seemed not quite clear on that point. Beach simply said that if we went in for that policy, we should have our enemies for us and our friends against us. Cranbrook and I held that it was impossible for the Conservative Party to go in for a separate Irish Parliament.'[117]

Cranbrook's account of the discussion on Ireland is very guarded: 'I made my protest against certain methods as I thought that was needed though the time for them if ever is not yet. But I am bound to say I feel dissatisfied and fear Carnarvon's nature. It is too sentimental. We talked of many points and no doubt Salisbury's speech tomorrow will reproduce some.'

During this cabinet, Churchill pencilled a note to Ashbourne 'I think Cross a bigger fool than ever.'[118]

There was a short discussion on South Africa which left much untouched, and Turkey was mentioned and then held over till Friday. The cabinet were also told of the declaration to be submitted by the ambassadors at Constantinople to both parties, condemning the illegal presence of Bulgarian troops in Eastern Rumelia. The 'cabinet have approved this declaration if approved by other powers'.[119]

October 7 (Wednesday). Salisbury spoke at Newport, referring incidentally to the Irish question in a highly ambiguous way. To the eye of faith, it appeared that Salisbury had 'made a great speech ... which ought to be a source of much confidence in the party'.[120] Though later the Newport speech came to look like a notorious effort at masterly ambiguity on Salisbury's part, in fact at the time it simply reflected cabinet thinking. Carnarvon had written to Salisbury summing up the situation as to law and order in a very balanced way, stressing that little beyond ordinary measures could or need be done, although the amount of disturbance was still 'very large'. Churchill, for his part, could genially say (and with little motive as regards swaying his auditor): 'Boycotting will in time cure itself. No law can deal with it, but everybody will get so bored with the practice that it will disappear.'* Salisbury at Newport was saying what leading ministers had already come to regard it as normal to think.

October 9 (Friday). The cabinet met at Downing St, 12–2.45, with

---

* Churchill to Carnarvon, 27 Sept., Carnarvon MSS (i.e. just before his visit to Dublin). Carnarvon was at this time worried by the landlord problem, e.g. 'I apprehend serious disturbances later in the autumn unless they [landlords] can be induced to take a moderate view of their rights' (Carnarvon to Beach, 25 Sept., Carnarvon MSS): and in an earlier letter (23 Sept.) in the same correspondence, Carnarvon stressed that landlords' conduct was often bad.

all ministers present. Cranbrook listed the topics dealt with as Wolff's convention: Ireland: the Scottish Office: the Bombay command: and the crofters.[121]

The cabinet unanimously came to the conclusion that the political position of the commander-in-chief of an Indian presidency could not be filled by a son of the Queen, and that therefore the Duke of Connaught could not go to Bombay in that capacity.[122]

The Burmese question had made its appearance at cabinet only once previously during the calendar year, and that was at the meeting of 3 August when the cabinet had to consider it in the light of an allegedly imminent French coup there. Unfortunately, there is no evidence as to why Burma appeared on the agenda on 9 October, or what views were taken. The only clear point that can be made, is that when allowance is made for other business, little time can have been spent on deciding the future of Burma for the next sixty years. There was no pressing Burmese business before the cabinet, and it is not known whether ministers were aware that, before they met again, the government of India would have drafted, and Churchill would have approved, on 16 and 17 October respectively, an ultimatum to Burma which in all probability meant war followed by annexation. Ministers did not, at all events, think the matter worthy of recording on paper, in contrast to the rather minor officials whose views in all their lack of nuance are printed in the Blue Books. Out of sixteen ministers, we can make no comment on the attitudes of fourteen or so: we do not even know whether there was a political situation created by its handling in cabinet. (A measure which tied up 30,000 men in remote country over a long period could not be without its implications for general diplomatic, financial, and even Irish policy, implications which probably by coincidence tended to favour Churchill's general line). The papers as printed in the Blue Book of 1886 tend, by their arrangement, to show pacific attitudes on the part of Salisbury matched by a peremptory spirit towards Burma on the part of Churchill and the Indian authorities. During the period of the drafting and execution of the ultimatum, Salisbury in particular was producing evidence establishing the unreality of the French danger in Burma at the same time as Churchill was looking forward with relish to hurrying on an invasion designed to thwart that very risk. Churchill was well aware, no doubt, from urgent entreaties from commercial quarters which poured in upon him, of a certain latent commercial Toryism which his policy could stimulate: but what is surprising is the incongruity between his carefully stage-managed Burmese policy, and his image as a central, moderate figure seeking to appeal to a wide range of urban ex-liberal opinion of a still basically Gladstonian kind. It is not clear, that is to say, that Churchill's Burmese policy arose from his policy for his own career in any other sense than that he was inevitably deeply conscious of the implicit comparison between himself and Salisbury as Indian statesmen. *

Another substantial piece of policy that was dealt with, probably en passant and certainly without leaving adequate record of views expressed, during this meeting of under three hours, was that of native unrest in the Scottish Highlands. So far as one can tell, unrecorded and probably perfunctory discussion on this occasion determined ministerial policy on crofters. As far as is known, the question did not come before the Conservative cabinet again. Yet two months later, Cross was able to write 'I am afraid that it is absolutely necessary to name a crofters' bill in the Queen's Speech. The cabinet certainly gave orders to have it drawn.' If such a decision was taken at this meeting by the cabinet, the records suggest that it might just as well not have been.

What, if anything, was done to turn the discussion of 9 October into legislation is hard to say. One crucial factor in blocking developments was that further progress depended, once the matter had left the cabinet, on Richmond. Now Richmond was well able to get what he wanted, since he was not only the leading party figure in agricultural matters, but had conferred an obligation on his colleagues by taking on the Scottish Office. His wishes at this stage were inscrutable, but he showed no desire to legislate. In later years he reacted with fear and anger to Gladstonian threats to his enormous Highland estates, though indignation on this score during the caretaker ministry does not stand out. At any rate, Richmond's inertia, self-interest, and unusual departmental autonomy, all worked against the emergence of a policy for the Highlands. It is impossible, however, to know whether or not Richmond ever set to drafting a crofters' bill in January 1886. His correspondence with cabinet colleagues omits all reference to legislative preparations, and the departmental files for this period in the Scottish Record Office for the three departments concerned (the Scottish, Home, and Lord Advocate's Offices) are a broken reed for the purpose of tracing the formulation of policy within the office. The preparation of legislation was treated as a matter for

* For developments in Burma 1878–86, see Parl. P 1886, C. 4614, and also above, entry for 3 Aug. 1885. For the apparent lack of further cabinet discussion of Burma, cf. Salisbury to Churchill, 24 Nov. 1885, Churchill MSS ix 1087 a, arguing that since 'our interest in Burma is entirely Indian and our interest in China nearly so', it followed that 'the India Office should therefore prevail' as the questions involved were 'not worthy of reference to cabinet'.

private correspondence at ministerial level, and surviving records are for routine administrative matters relating to people outside the government. Neither the two volumes of reminiscences, nor the papers in family hands, left by the lord advocate, J. H. A. Macdonald, contain anything bearing on the topic.

An intervention by Argyll, and a speech at Inverness by Chamberlain, did however draw ministerial attention again to the subject in December. Argyll wrote to Cross on 16 December, in his usual vein bristling with objections to all proposals, and predicting that any crofters' bill would endanger landed property generally. Argyll however did propose fixing of rents on the basis of free market value. Richmond, whose vacation reading included the report of Napier's Commission of 1883 and the bill drafted by the Liberals in 1885, wrote to Salisbury, agreeing with Argyll's point that any radical remedies would soon be applied to all tenants. His tone was unpromising, 'I am afraid it will be very difficult to draw a bill but I shall try. I see the bill of the late Gov. set up a court to fix the rent which I should not like to do at all.'[123] Salisbury agreed with Richmond on this, objecting to judicial rents in any form, even as proposed by Argyll. With such views, it was predictable that Richmond by 25 December had not yet attempted to draft a bill, and doubted if the Queen's Speech should promise one. Perhaps partially converted by Cross's letter cited above, Richmond arranged to meet Cross to discuss crofters on 7 January.[124] Thereafter Richmond's coolness increased. On 26 December he could not see how any Tory bill could satisfy the crofters: 'as I understand it, they complain of their rents and want a tribunal to fix them'. On 1 January he told Salisbury that he did not see much difficulty in putting the crofters' bill in the Queen's Speech in the manner Salisbury proposed, 'but what most puzzles me is how we are to legislate for them in a safe and prudent manner'. At this point, with an implicit divergence in policy established between presentation and intention, Richmond's efforts ceased to leave any trace.[125] The Queen's Speech simply said that a bill would be introduced to improve conditions.

The cabinet decided that Carnarvon's return to Ireland was very expedient, thereby enabling him to escape a visit to Balmoral.[126]

Carnarvon passed an inquiry to Smith about the level of the army in Ireland, Smith later replying that no reduction in strength had yet been made (as Carnarvon implied), and that none would be made without Carnarvon's knowledge.[127]

October 23 (Friday). The cabinet met at Downing St, 2.30–4.30. Carnarvon, Stanhope, Churchill and Richmond did not attend. Richmond was in Scotland, and Churchill had a speaking engagement in Birmingham. The subject was the international conference on the Balkan situation: the cabinet decided to enter negotiations on the basis of qualified support for Prince Alexander.[128]

The date of the dissolution was fixed for 18 November.

Before the cabinet, Ashbourne saw Harrowby and told him Carnarvon's views on the rebel Riel, who was about to be executed for treason by the Canadian government. Harrowby raised the subject in cabinet, but the 'feeling was against interference, and against our right to interfere'.[129]

In the latter part of October 1885, Richmond became involved in disagreement with the Treasury over salaries and staffing at the newly formed Scottish Office, and at one point he even told Cross 'I have written to Salisbury to say that under the circs I do not see how I can continue to hold the office.' Obviously a row took place, but since none of Richmond's three letters of October 1885 in the Salisbury MSS mention either resignation or Scotland, it must be doubted whether Richmond ever really aimed his bolt at the premier, or made his disquiet known to the cabinet.[130]

November 10 (Tuesday). The cabinet met at Downing St at noon. Carnarvon, Ashbourne and Harrowby were absent, the last, who was at Balmoral, having been told by Salisbury that this cabinet was not for any important business.[131]

Owing to the absence of the Irish ministers, discussion on Ireland hardly went beyond mention of the prevalence of the worst forms of boycotting. The meeting was chiefly devoted to foreign affairs, and especially to Russian aims in the Balkans. Egypt was thought in danger of attack and needing more troops.

The cabinet then adjourned till after the elections, in which its prospects were generally felt to be improving.

Later the same day, at 4.30–5, there was a meeting of ministers in the lord chancellor's room, attended by Salisbury, Halsbury, Iddesleigh, Beach, Stanley, and Smith.

December 13 (Sunday). The election results, beginning on 25 November, were still in doubt as late as 3 December. There was no haste shown in calling together the cabinet, and it was not till Thursday the 10th that Carnarvon came over from Dublin, arriving early for the cabinet announced for the next Monday so as to give himself time to lobby for his home rule ideas beforehand. On Sunday the 13th he met Justin McCarthy at dinner with Mrs Jeune.[132] Carnarvon said he had not been able to win over all his colleagues and that negotiations were at an end. He thought the cabinet had been influenced by a speech by Parnell saying little was to be expected from the Conservatives.[133]

McCarthy said Gladstone was making overtures, but that he

would disappoint the Irish, and a rising would take place. McCarthy said he and others would greatly prefer the Conservatives, who could deal better with all three aspects of the question, viz. land, education, and parliament. McCarthy accepted the principle of securities and safeguards for religion and property, the retention of the imperial connection, and a parliament in name with comparatively few powers. Carnarvon pointed out that whatever might be agreed to later on must be a result of political education, and expressed the fear that because the Conservatives were not ready at present, Gladstone would step in and the matter would be closed. McCarthy 'agreed and deplored it', and would have liked a small meeting or committee of the three parties. Carnarvon distinctly stated that he spoke only for himself.[134]

December 14 (*Monday*).[135] Ashbourne returned to London from Ireland in the morning.

The cabinet met at Downing St, 3–5.30, with all ministers present. More than thirty telegrams arrived during the meeting. After much discussion, it was resolved that the ministry ought to meet parliament, subject to the condition of an early vote of confidence being sought.

Statements on Ireland were made by Carnarvon and Ashbourne, and the question of home rule and Irish local government discussed. The discussion on Ireland took as its point of departure Carnarvon's memorandum[136] of 7 December recommending 'a Committee of both Houses to consider the relations of Ireland and England'. 'It was resolved that though in some form or other the legislation in regard to local government which was passed for England would necessarily be extended to Ireland, it was not possible for the Conservative party to tamper with the question of home rule.' Carnarvon expressed his earnest desire to retire from his office, in accordance with an understanding entered into with him when he took it. 'The feeling of the cabinet however was that at this moment such a retirement would be misunderstood; and he was very strongly pressed to remain for the sake of the peace of Ireland.'

The first lord of the admiralty brought before the cabinet his proposed appointment, on professional grounds, of the Duke of Edinburgh to the command of the Mediterranean fleet, and it was decided there was no political objection. In obedience to a letter from the Queen, the Cabinet again considered the question of the appointment of the Duke of Connaught to the Bombay command, but again felt it preferable that he should be appointed for the present to Rawalpindi rather than Bombay. The appointment of the Duke of Edinburgh was considered a very strong additional reason for this view.[137]

Churchill's plans for reforming parliamentary procedure were discussed. They were sweeping, involving a regular autumn session, alteration in hours, closure at midnight, reform of private bill procedure, and enlarged powers for committees.[138]

Cranbrook recorded with reference to the question of a future vote of confidence, that 'Beach, Churchill, and others forgot the rules and wanted to break them which was impossible as I thought and not wise if possible. Facts brought all to the same mind, which in substance had always been the same – not to submit to be a Govt under direction.'

December 15 (Tuesday). The full cabinet met at Downing St 2.30–4.30. Carnarvon, Ashbourne, Stanley and Beach remained in conference for twenty minutes after the end of the meeting.

Discussion on Ireland was resumed. Carnarvon outlined, in what he himself called 'a rough sketch', his highly secret Irish university bill.[139] It was no doubt because of this that Churchill wrote to Carnarvon agreeing 'entirely and absolutely with all you put forward on Tuesday ... (though perhaps) the bribe should be higher.'[140] Carnarvon, it appeared, had previously had only tenuous knowledge of Churchill's views on the Irish university question, and had not worked with him in preparing his draft. Carnarvon's university bill was actually printed, in six copies, on 19 December, the type being at once broken up. Copies went to Salisbury, Carnarvon, Churchill, Ashbourne and Dyke. Its proposals, similar to those eventually achieved in 1908, appeared in early drafts of the Queen's Speech, but the topic henceforth disappeared from recorded discussion. No specific decision to shelve it was reported.

Churchill's proposals for new rules of procedure were again considered. Churchill thought they had been rejected and offered to resign, but Salisbury assured him they had only been postponed.[141] This contretemps was probably the occasion of a wounding rebuke from Manners to Churchill about his vanity in making such threats, a rebuke which apparently struck home.[142]

Carnarvon informed Cranbrook at the meeting that he had arranged to continue in office until decisive action was taken, which was to be before the end of January. Cranbrook observed the threatening language used by Churchill at the close of the meeting as a possible indication that he was seeking a pretext to break up the government without meeting parliament.[143] Churchill tried to insist on the absolute necessity of procedural reform taking precedence over all other business, an insistence which on further reflection confirmed Cranbrook in the view that Churchill was insincere in agreeing to meet parliament.[144]

It was on this day that Gladstone met Balfour at Eaton Hall, the Duke of Westminster's home in Cheshire, and expressed the hope that he would be able to support the Conservative ministry in a settlement of the Irish question. The date is established *inter alia* by a letter from Gladstone to Hartington written on 20 December 1885 referring to this meeting as on the previous Tuesday.

December 15–January 2. Beach wrote to Churchill on 15 December earnestly rejecting the idea that he was in honour bound to have supported Churchill on procedure,[145] but Churchill on 16 December was still unappeased: 'worried, vexed, and personally embarrassed by a certain decision of the cabinet yesterday. Beach was most treacherous to me.'[146] On the same day Churchill informed Salisbury that he ought to resign, but did not want to increase difficulties. Salisbury returned an emollient reply at once on the lines that procedure had only not been given full consideration because of want of time, and that Salisbury himself favoured Churchill's plan.[147] The vagueness of Churchill's position may partly be gathered from the fact that Carnarvon did not even hear Churchill's original threat of resignation, until Ashbourne, who was sitting near, told him.[148]

Beach and Churchill were soon working hand in glove again on the tactics to adopt for meeting the new parliament. Despite the fairly clear decision taken by the cabinet on 14 December, the unorthodox views then aired by Beach and noted in Cranbrook's diary were revived by Churchill and Beach in letters to Salisbury. Churchill wrote on 22 December[149] suggesting procedure by address framed to suggest general approval of the ministry in a way Liberals could support, while Beach, in letters of 23, 24, and 28 December, suggested, before the Address, an immediate vote of confidence 'in the form of an adjournment say to 9 or 11 February as the expression of assent by the House to our continuing to conduct the affairs of the country'. However, before the end of December, the Speaker had replied to an inquiry from Beach, that a vote of confidence before the Address was impossible.[150] The ghost of the proposal was finally laid at the cabinet of 2 January, where it was decided to reject Beach's suggestions and proceed in the ordinary way by treating a Liberal failure to carry an amendment as an expression of confidence.[151] Harrowby elaborated the causes of Beach's failure in a letter to Carnarvon on 3 January.[152]

Beach was firmly opposed by Iddesleigh, who, 'although very much in the dark' was consistently against any tactical experiment, and hence, by implication, against plans for eliciting Liberal support. Iddesleigh's fatalistic preference for 'going quietly on our way, proposing our own measures, and resigning if we found ourselves defeated'[153] was a reassertion, important if only because Salisbury agreed, of the primacy of questions of party structure over questions of Irish government – or of tenure of office in the short term. Beach's campaign may have enrolled Smith and Ashbourne, at least in so far as both gave way before this most recent interlocutor, though the references to their conspiratorial meeting in late December are too cryptic to establish this.[154]

December 17 (*Thursday*). The 'Hawarden Kite', a press report alleging Gladstone was about to commit himself to home rule, appeared in the *Leeds Mercury* and the *Standard*. Gladstone's repudiation reached the evening papers the same day, and the following morning news of the Kite first appeared in the major London papers, including *The Times*. Whatever their point of view, ministers welcomed the news. Cranbrook remarked of Gladstone 'I am all for letting him try his hand if he will', while Carnarvon, for very different reasons, hoped Gladstone would deal with the question.[155] Dismayed reactions to the Kite were far stronger in Liberal than in Tory circles. Churchill, for his part, despite his keen interest in using procedure as a gambit in case the ministry should continue, was also immediately attracted by the thought of abandoning ship, as Justin McCarthy wrote at this time:

'I had some talk with Lord Randolph last night, and infer from what he said that his party thought they had no chance about home rule after Gladstone had taken it up and that they had better therefore drop it and take to the British Philistine view... Lord Randolph says that his strong wish is that the Conservatives should be turned out at once. They cannot govern, he says, under present conditions. And he wants to have them out of the responsibility.'

December 24 (*Thursday*). Churchill ordered the viceroy to prepare a proclamation annexing the newly conquered state of Upper Burma to the British empire. The proclamation was duly issued, by Dufferin, on 1 January 1886. The question that arises here, is whether the annexation was a mere formality involving no issue of policy, or whether it was an instance of a major decision taken with little or no reference to the preceding cabinets of 14 and 15 December, at which Churchill, to say the least, was a world away from Burmese matters. It is not only that there is no record of Burma having come before the cabinet on 14–15 December, but there is also an obvious inference to be drawn from the ten days' gap between those cabinets and the first move towards annexation on Churchill's part, and the fact that the whole business of annexation was completed in the depths of the vacation before the cabinet could meet again.

The decision to annex did not, at any rate, arise from any crisis in Burma. Churchill's information at this time, as sent by the viceroy, was that 'there is no national resistance anywhere' (22 December) and 'that the provisional (native) government is working satisfactorily, a revenue beginning to come in' (17 December). Annexation did mean a rejection of the solution of a protected state on the lines of Afghanistan or Nepal, at a time when official opinion had only recently been pressing for such arrangements, and when they still appeared workable in Burmese military and political terms. To this extent annexation did involve a deep political decision which the cabinet may never have had fully put to it. On the other hand, the question of whether to retain a native Burmese government was not directly affected by annexation, and was left to be settled, against the Burmese, by the Liberals in February 1886, in the context of a swiftly deteriorating situation on the spot.

December 28–January 1. Churchill went to Ireland to join the light-hearted house-party of his old and confidential friend Lord Justice Fitzgibbon at Howth near Dublin, as he had often done previously at this time of year. On the day of his arrival, he breakfasted with Holmes, the Irish attorney-general, and talked exultantly of the home rule tendencies shown by Gladstone's approaches to Balfour: 'Surely the Lord has delivered him into our hands.' Holmes, an Ulsterman known publicly only for sound protestant sentiments, had Churchill round for the day later in his visit and introduced him to Col. Saunderson, leader of the Ulster Unionists between whom and Churchill so much rancour had existed. Their discussions ended with their arranging the rough outlines of Churchill's 'Orange' campaign in Ulster. The occasion showed Churchill at his most impeccably partisan.

Yet it was not so. It was of this visit that Churchill had just written to Salisbury 'If I get a chance may I intrigue with Archbishop Walsh while I am in Dublin? I don't think Carnarvon understood that worthy person.' Churchill would, it seems, have been as happy seeing a papist prelate as an Orange bigot, so long as it afforded relief to his activity of mind: and on his return to England, he plunged into a policy of douceurs towards the Irish in the field of local government and education which suggested that his feint towards Orangeism had nothing much to do with his general strategy for the weeks each side of Christmas. This was a period when he was in very close contact with Carnarvon, was in general holding out against the drift towards coercion, and still capable of dreaming up 'a bribe ... higher than yet proposed ; an endowment of a Catholic College in Ulster might be considered'.[156] This was not the voice of a man who could throw himself whole-heartedly into vulgar Unionism.

December 30 (*Wednesday*). Gen. Stephenson gained a substantial victory over Mahdist forces at Giniss on the Nile frontier, in which the newly trained Khedivial army under English officers for the first time showed itself to be militarily effective. Had the cabinet been at all interested, the victory could have been taken as opening the way to the reoccupation of Dongola during the cool season: as it was, its only practical result was to make it feasible to withdraw English forces from the Wadi Halfa frontier and replace them with Egyptians, thereby committing Britain more firmly than ever to that purely defensive policy on the Nile which had been the bane of the Conservative party in opposition.

January 1 (*Friday*). A meeting of the committee of cabinet on local government took place at the local government board office and lasted several hours. Those present were Beach, Stanhope and Balfour (who was president of the local government board but not in the cabinet). Churchill was at this time 'impressing upon the Irish authorities the extreme importance' of having a local government bill for Ireland ready,[157] but it is not clear that the matter was discussed by ministers in London.

January 2 (*Saturday*). The cabinet met at Downing St. Richmond, whose third son had died the previous day, and Carnarvon, who was in Ireland,[158] were absent.

The business dealt with included the discussion of the form of the Address in reply to the Queen's Speech: the local government bill for England, which was approved in principle: Churchill's procedural reforms: and the Sudan.

It was reported that the Speaker had written to Beach refusing to allow a vote of confidence to be taken before the Address, and hence it finally became clear that the ministry would have to meet parliament in a perfectly normal way. In view of this, machinery was set up to tackle the most urgent parliamentary tasks.

Committees were appointed to deal with the Bradlaugh case, and with changes in House of Commons procedure, in the latter case on the understanding that whatever the committee decided on (the cabinet having reached no definite conclusion) should have precedence when brought before parliament.[159]

Salisbury produced Gladstone's two letters to Balfour[160] and raised the question of a possible reply.[161] Cranbrook favoured returning an emphatic answer, but it was decided to reserve any such statement till the Queen's Speech.[162]

Cranbrook, having received a long letter from Carnarvon urging him to press Salisbury for a replacement, raised the matter some time near the cabinet meeting, only to be told by Salisbury that it was clearly impossible to find a new man in present circumstances, but that Carnarvon would as promised be set free on 25 January.[163]

Carnarvon's pet Irish university bill, which ('though it will need revision') he had posted to Ashbourne and to Salisbury the previous day presumably for cabinet purposes, was not discussed in cabinet at this meeting, nor so far as can be seen at any later one, this being a fine example of prime ministerial pigeonholing. The bill had actually been promised in one of the earlier drafts of the Queen's Speech.[164]

January 5 (Tuesday). An informal meeting of ministers (whether a cabinet committee proper is not clear) took place at Downing St, 3.30–5.30. Those attending were Iddesleigh and all ministers in the lower house. Press speculation on the objects of the meeting differed; *The Times* of 11 January suggested it was devoted to discussion of the drafting of various bills,* while the usually well-informed *Standard* (6 January) speculated that it concerned 'the duties of the popular Chamber', which might imply a consideration of Churchill's proposals on procedural reform.

January 6 (Wednesday). A committee of the cabinet met with Balfour at the office of the Local Government Board to continue the drafting of the local government bill. The committee sat for 2 hours. Those present were Beach, Stanhope and Balfour.

That the committee managed to produce a draft bill of 88 pages dated 8 January,[165] setting up elective county councils for England and Wales exercising the administrative functions of quarter sessions, was certainly not due to the original leanings of some important members of the cabinet. Iddesleigh wrote to Beach at length pressing home every conceivable objection to county councils,[166] and Beach wrote to Balfour on 23 December, 14 and 15 January, expressing misgivings over the powers given to the councils, especially over finance.[167]

January 8 (Friday). Another meeting of all cabinet ministers in the House of Commons, and Iddesleigh, took place at Downing St 3–5.[168]

January 9 (Saturday). A cabinet lasting about two hours was held at Downing St, Carnarvon being the only minister absent. The

---

* Drafting of quite major measures was making rapid progress, e.g. Churchill on 3 Jan. could say definitely 'The Irish Education Bill is drawn ...' (Churchill to Smith, Hambleden MSS).

'sitting was occupied almost entirely with local government in England'.[169]

Ashbourne made 'vague and indefinite remarks'[170] in favour of coercion, saying that Ireland was going from bad to worse and that in a few weeks at latest, whatever government was in office, some measure of coercion was inevitable. This was music in Cranbrook's ears,* but it earned Ashbourne a private reprimand from Churchill after the meeting. Churchill appeared to Cranbrook to be not at all friendly to the idea of resolute action in Ireland, another indication that his recent contact with Ulster loyalists had not affected his line in cabinet.

A measure for local government in England was the main business, for which purpose Balfour was called in, but no decision was reached. 'It was clearly one for which our members were not eager. They recognise the necessity of a move in the democratic direction but I expect will try limitation which will fail.'[171] As Churchill commented, 'the majority of the cabinet in their hearts hate the thing'.[172]

The *Standard* (11 January) reported that the cabinet discussed measures framed by the large committee of ministers which had met on 5 and 8 January and further that Richmond had drafted a crofters' bill:[173] both items however lack documentary confirmation.

Ashbourne wrote to Carnarvon after the meeting '... I gather *the* Speech will not be fully dealt with and disposed of until Saturday the 16th...'[174]

January 12 (*Tuesday*). The cabinet met at Downing St, with Carnarvon, who was 'far from well',[175] and Ashbourne absent. Ireland was nevertheless a major topic, being probably first raised by Cranbrook who raised serious questions connected with it. Then 'Churchill threw out suggestions which I confess made me think with a view to effective action.' Cranbrook then secured that the next meeting of the cabinet should take place on Friday instead of on Saturday as previously intended, in view of the amount of discussion he felt Irish policy would require. Salisbury's absence at Osborne in the middle of the week made any earlier cabinet impossible.[176]

Parliament was opened and a Speaker elected. Parliament met

---

* Cranbrook had just begun to emerge, belatedly, as a tough Tory who wanted no compromise with disorder. Writing to Carnarvon the previous day, he denounced the National League as making a 'triumph of treason' which was 'intolerable'. 'The same lawlessness is being reproduced in the Highlands and impunity will increase the evil in both countries and possibly extend it to England.' (Cranbrook to Carnarvon, 8 Jan., Carnarvon MSS, PRO 30/6/55/67). Cranbrook had spent a long summer holiday in the Highlands in 1885.

for formal business and the swearing in of members on 12–15 January, adjourning on 15 January until Wednesday, 20 January. Beach held a two hour meeting of ministers in his room in the Commons.[177]

January 13 (Wednesday). Salisbury went to Osborne for two nights. Carnarvon left Ireland by the mail steamer in the evening and read unauthorised press reports of his retirement en route.

The speaker, acting on his own initiative and without cabinet assent, permitted Bradlaugh to take the oath and thus to become fully a member. The speaker refused to permit any motion opposing this course, this refusal being aimed chiefly at Beach who had been trying hard to revive the issue (a former focus of Tory-Irish cooperation, incidentally) in previous weeks.

January 15 (Friday). The cabinet met at Downing St, 2.30, with all ministers present, Ashbourne having arrived in London that morning.

In discussion on the problem of law and order in Ireland, wide disagreements on questions of method were revealed. Manners and Carnarvon were for no action beyond the enforcement of the ordinary law: Salisbury was for procedure by a secret committee of the House of Commons, following a precedent set in the case of Westmeath: Iddesleigh and others, including probably Salisbury to some extent, and eventually Cranbrook, wanted the immediate introduction of a bill to suppress the National League: while Churchill, Beach, and Hamilton, in view of the parliamentary impracticality of such courses, with Cranbrook as an ally in the earlier part of the discussion only, wanted an illegal executive suppression of the League, to be followed by a parliamentary indemnity.

Hugh Holmes, Irish attorney-general, was called in, at Churchill's instance, to supply evidence on unrest in Ireland, but in Cranbrook's view failed to supply satisfactory evidence on essential questions such as payment of rents, existence of treasonable conspiracy, etc.

Cranbrook was ready to take 'a somewhat risky responsibility' in which 'I was backed by some strong and sober members and warmly by Churchill, but the steps proposed needed union and force and became impracticable unless all were of one mind. Much discourse followed and there was a general feeling that the Irish government was ill informed, irresolute, and wanting to make our standing ground a shifting quicksand, by simply waiting for the end of the ministry to arrive, speaking ambiguously in the meantime and proposing nothing.'[178]

No account makes it clear how far Cranbrook and Churchill had already brought forward their proposals for an active policy during the discussion on Ireland in the cabinet of Tuesday, January 12. An account in Northcote's diary, however, gives a plausible version of the development of the argument, without being specific as to time. 'On the first reading of the original Speech [which at that stage chiefly reflected Salisbury's and Carnarvon's views] Cranbrook declared himself wholly dissatisfied and proposed that we should at once act against the National League, declare it illegal, close its offices, and examine its records, which would probably disclose treasonable matter. We might then come to parliament for an indemnity. This proposal was warmly approved by Randolph Churchill: but the general feeling was that the course was too violent for us to take so immediately before the opening of the session: that we should probably not find any compromising matter in the offices of the League: and that force would probably have to be used, which might lead to bloodshed: and might place our officers in a serious position: they might be tried for murder.' Iddesleigh then suggested that another way of giving effect to Cranbrook's intentions might be to amend the Queen's Speech by including a promise to deal with the League by legislation. Iddesleigh explained that by this he understood giving notice on the first night of the session that a bill declaring the National League illegal would be introduced next day, the debate on the Address being suspended for this purpose. Cranbrook then accepted Iddesleigh's proposal as preferable to his own, while Churchill immediately expressed great contempt for it, urging the lack of evidence to present to parliament. The meeting adjourned with nothing settled, except that Salisbury was to put Iddesleigh's proposal forward at the following day's cabinet.[179]

January 16 (*Saturday*).[180] The morning post brought a letter from Salisbury to Cranbrook urging him to take Ireland. The full cabinet met at Downing St. Opinion on Irish measures had polarised further, with twelve ministers in favour of statutory suppression of the National League, and four opposed.[181] Since the dissidents were Churchill (the most strongly opposed), Beach, Hamilton, and Carnarvon, the large majority for Iddesleigh's proposal did not signify a decision so much as a deadlock, which remained unresolved till the following week-end.

Cranbrook had no hesitation about refusing Ireland, partly because of what it would mean for his wife, but also because he was vividly aware of the political difficulties. Cranbrook consulted only Richmond, who confirmed his view, but Beach, despite his own views, offered unsolicited support for a presumably repressive Cranbrook regime in Ireland.

The cabinet agreed on the first of the two paragraphs in the Queen's Speech dealing with Ireland. It had before it an abortive coercion bill drawn up by Ashbourne.[182]

Of the cabinet meeting proper Cranbrook wrote: 'all but one or two were ready to act, and all see that action is not far off. Ashbourne had been convinced and had prepared at once an account of the reports of resident magistrates received last night'. This appeared to Cranbrook to show enough evidence existed for a case to present to parliament justifying coercion, if not to secure conviction in individual cases. 'Salisbury would have been content to begin with inquiry, but this could not be satisfactory without witnesses directed to some object. I should have no objection if both were combined though I prefer, as I think he does, legislation. We agreed to a strong pronouncement on the Union [the wording of which was left to Salisbury] and I have strong hopes that we shall be unanimous on all on Monday as even Carnarvon was not very strong in his opposition. Beach was more so but only on account of the stickiness of Irish officials and this is passing away. Those who were anxious to fall are those who hesitate and yet how could we stand or fall better than by supporting law and overthrowing the League against it.'[183]

Cross however saw the question of evidence as still the major difficulty. Writing to Salisbury after the cabinet, he said 'we are all determined to put down the Land League if we have evidence of its *overt* treasonable acts' but that quite clearly the Irish administration had failed to provide a statement of facts to warrant the kind of bill Cross wanted.[184] Cross's view that the government were weaker on evidence than anything else was substantially more correct than that of those ministers who thought simple honest commitment (in the case of Cranbrook) or a straightforward *volte-face* (as with Ashbourne) a sufficient basis on which to put up a good showing in the House of Commons.

Salisbury and Churchill continued their debate about Irish strategy in an exchange of letters following the cabinet. Their difference was due to their thinking on different levels: Salisbury was essentially concerned with identifying his party in the public mind with the cause of firm government in Ireland, whereas Churchill was concerned to defer raising the issue, until there was greater promise of its purely parliamentary success. Churchill later admitted that he feared the House of Commons till he had seen it.[185] 'At present there is no sufficient parliamentary case for a Bill, estimated by the weight of facts adduced ... I am certain that you know that none of us could sustain a case for coercion. Yet you press it on us – for we could have come to an agreement on Lord Cranbrook's suggestion, only that evidently it was not acceptable or good in your eyes.'[186] Churchill, being persuasive rather than truculent, assured Salisbury that it was only a question of introducing the bill a month hence rather than at once: curiously, Churchill was still thinking seriously in terms of the ministry surviving the debate on the Address.

Churchill's anxiety not to play the 'Orange' card won a dusty answer from Salisbury, which Churchill acknowledged in a further letter that day with due subservience: 'But *after all*, you are the head of the Government, and have had a very long experience of public affairs; and if you think it absolutely incumbent to go further, – well, then, further we must go.'[187] Throughout the January crisis on Irish policy it is remarkable that it is Salisbury, playing a winning hand, who engenders talk of resignation, while Churchill, getting rather rough treatment from the Cabinet, showed virtually none of his usual signs of temperament.[188]

Beach wrote on Sunday chiding Churchill for going so far in accepting Salisbury's point of view, and reiterating his opposition to coercion, especially coercion justified by the spurious argument that Salisbury had apparently used in his final dealings with Churchill. This, which can have had no reality for Salisbury, was the danger of a hostile amendment in favour of coercion being proposed in the debate on the Address. It was therefore probably Beach's obstinacy which prevented the cabinet from making full use of Churchill's apparent capitulation, in his letters of 16 January, and led it the following day to a weak compromise formula which delayed effective action for a week, Beach and Churchill only hauling down their flag finally on Saturday 23 January.

The position was further complicated by the unexpected and inexplicable resignation of Dyke from the Irish secretaryship. On the Saturday night, Dyke went to Beach and afterwards to Salisbury, explaining that he did not want to go on, 'that Carnarvon had never let him know anything that was going on, and that for that and other reasons more special to himself, he did not feel equal to doing the work in the House of Commons'.[189] It would be pleasant to think that Dyke had been prompted into creating a slot for someone else (the obvious candidate is Churchill),* but he was not an easy man to prompt into subtleties, and his motive was probably merely to evade the responsibility of running Ireland on his own in view of Carnarvon's impending retirement. Dyke's broad agreement with Carnarvon's appeasement policy may have

---

* Churchill wrote at once to Salisbury on the day of Dyke's resignation (which appears to have emerged suddenly in the evening) to put forward his own name, as well as those of Smith and Cranbrook, as candidates for the vacancy.

led him to be uneasy about proposing coercion, but the cause of his resignation, which excited no attention, cannot really be established. Dyke's post was offered by Salisbury to Smith without further ado the following day, Carnarvon not being consulted or even informed of the offer to Smith till nearly a week later, and then only after it had been announced in parliament. Carnarvon in fact thought Smith's appointment 'a very good one. I do not think you could have made a better selection.'[190]

January 18 (*Monday*). The cabinet met in Salisbury's room at the Foreign Office, 2.30–5, with all ministers present. Carnarvon and Lord G. Hamilton left shortly after 4 en route for Ireland and Osborne respectively, Hamilton taking the Speech to the Queen. The other ministers sat on until nearly 5. Cranbrook associated Carnarvon's departure for Ireland with the illness of his child, but there is no confirmation of this in other main sources.

The cabinet's main achievement was to reach full agreement on the Irish section of the Queen's Speech, an agreement which was limited to how the probability of coercion should be presented to parliament, and did not remove the deadlock about what action the executive should take.

Salisbury began by saying that he had modified the section on coercion to meet what he thought the general wish. This involved throwing over Iddesleigh's suggestion of immediate statutory suppression of the National League, which twelve ministers had supported on Saturday, in favour of the rather colourless version ultimately presented to parliament. Iddesleigh was much annoyed by this sacrifice to cabinet unity, though Cranbrook, who had been an equally consistent upholder of a tough policy, took it very calmly. Salisbury excused his backing down by sending a note to Iddesleigh arguing that a more vigorous policy would have risked the disruption of the cabinet.[191]

The cabinet also talked over local government: British action in the event of a Greek naval attack upon Turkey: and bimetallism.

In the evening Cranbrook entered in his diary: 'Our cabinet was unanimous and I am satisfied with a somewhat weaker expression of the same thing as I wanted [coercion] because it meets the views of the weaker kind. ...Smith divulged to me that on Dyke's resignation Salisbury offered the [Irish] secretaryship to him and his strong feeling of duty will I fancy make him take it. He said he had told no one but I heard Salisbury whisper it to Iddesleigh.'

January 19 (*Tuesday*). Iddesleigh threatened resignation because Irish policy was insufficiently vigorous,[192] telling Salisbury of his 'great doubt whether I am justified in acquiescing in what seems to me such fatal policy',[193] and demanding suppression of the

National League. Salisbury replied soothingly, indicating sympathy but pointing out that the other hard-liners, Smith, Cross, and Cranbrook, were satisfied with a compromise. Salisbury added 'we shall not bring in our Irish County Reform Bill until circumstances are favourable'.[194]

January 20 (Wednesday). Beach wrote to Gladstone,[195] giving notice that he would the following day propose that the Conservative scheme for procedural reform (essentially Churchill's work) be taken immediately after the debate on the Address, with facilities for continuous discussion in order to reach an early settlement. Beach sent a copy of the government's proposals, which he offered to delay laying on the table the following day if Gladstone wanted private inter-party discussions. While Beach's request for Gladstone's cooperation was partly a formal courtesy, the whole gambit of prodecural reform, with its implied temporary suspension of party warfare, necessarily looked towards an understanding between the English parties about asserting their joint interests against the Parnellites. On Thursday, the Queen's Speech was read.

January 23 (Saturday). A cabinet lasting about an hour and a half was held in Salisbury's room at the Foreign Office, Carnarvon (in Ireland) being the only minister absent. Afterwards, Ashbourne and Smith left for Ireland (probably at different times but on the same day), Smith's mission being in the first place simply to be sworn in, something which could not be done in England, and secondly to prepare a coercion bill for early introduction.

Salisbury reported German pressure for a quick settlement of the Bulgarian negotiations, and stated that he had warned Greece of the danger of any hurried act of war.

This cabinet in its discussion on Ireland clearly registered a marked shift of opinion towards effective early commitment to a policy of legislative coercion, but probably left the process to be completed in private conversations later that or the following day. At any rate, on Sunday Salisbury was writing to the Queen: 'The recalcitrant members of the cabinet have changed their minds about coercion, under party pressure, and a bill will probably be introduced in two or three days.'[196] Cranbrook wrote:

'Our cabinet on Saturday was on many important topics, mainly Irish. Smith preparing to start for his unwelcome post, the discussion turned on Irish subjects and I think the feeling that we had not been bold enough in our announcement (the reason explained before) was universal and today R.C. [Churchill] acknowledged the mistaken course in which he had joined. Land Purchase on the Tithe Rent charge precedent talked of and abandoned. – O'Brien's motion on evictions – how cd. we stop them... Then to Railway Commission on which we thought Stanhope infringing parliamentary rights. The glebe bill – proposal of rent charges thought good. Thence to the unhealthy atmosphere of Sierra Leone and native raids and their punishment.'

After the cabinet Salisbury and Beach tried to decide whether Dyke or Sir James Fergusson should be appointed under-secretary for war. Though 'the former has claims and Carnarvon thinks highly of him', he was held to know nothing while Fergusson knew a good deal.[197]

Henry James in a published entry in his journal made on 15 February 1886 suggested that Churchill and Beach came round to Salisbury's views on Sunday 24 January, having been reassured by strong speeches from A. Grey and A. Elliot that the wind, among Whigs at any rate, was blowing in the direction of coercion. Though James' source was Churchill himself, James' dating of events is consistently askew and his version cannot be relied on. In James' account, two points not explicitly stated elsewhere stand out: that Smith left for Ireland on Saturday with no precise policy, and was instructed by telegram to go ahead with coercion on Sunday as a result of Churchill's capitulation some time after the cabinet of Saturday: and that 'Salisbury very nearly resigned, but was prevailed upon to continue in office' over Churchill's veto on parliamentary action against the National League.[198] This dramatic version of events, as told by Churchill to James, was probably designed to cover up the speed and completeness of Churchill's surrender. It can only be said that neither point ties in easily with what is known from other sources, though something of Salisbury's mood over the weekend can be seen in his words to a confidante 'Oh! for a good adverse division! It will not be long coming if all tales be true. We have had great troubles, and our internal condition is unsatisfactory.'[199]

January 25 (Monday). Ministers were again engaged in inconclusive discussions. Salisbury and Beach telegraphed to Smith pressing for 'prompt action'.[200] Smith wrote to Churchill that he would be unwilling to ask for large repressive powers 'unless I had authority to promise a large scheme', that 'so big a question cannot be decided offhand', and that he was not to be hurried. He suggested returning to London in 3 or 4 days (from Monday). Smith wrote on the same day to Salisbury, 'I must take a day or two to determine in my own mind how far it [coercion] ought to go' and suggesting sweetening it with land purchase. Churchill replied by telegram to Smith on 26 January that the government had to state its Irish policy at once as 'the only method of averting defeat on Jesse Collings'.[201] Smith's telegram in reply,[202] insisting there was 'no excessive urgency' and that he would prefer to provide against intimidation rather than directly suppress the league, arrived half an hour later after the cabinet meeting on Tuesday. Churchill telegraphed from the Commons that Beach had just given notice that Smith would introduce a bill on Thursday.

January 26 (Thursday). The cabinet met at the Foreign Office. Carnarvon, Ashbourne, and Smith were absent in Ireland, and Richmond and Harrowby also did not attend, the latter on account of the death of a cousin.

Salisbury obtained the formal assent of the cabinet to the immediate announcement of coercive legislation for Ireland, though he expected at the time that the ministry would fall that or the following night. The decision to announce coercion had however been settled in private discussions between ministers over the preceding three days.

Cranbrook recorded 'At the cabinet we resolved (why not earlier) to announce our repression for Thursday adopting Smith's language in his letters. Beach did it and we shall die the death tomorrow. Rumours are rife that Hartington, Goschen and even Harcourt support us against Collings.' In the evening, but before the vote was taken, Cranbrook wrote that he had done nothing yet about his War Office arrangements and probably never would. 'There was a general impression last night and today that our innings were nearly over as they ought to be.'

Immediately parliament resumed business, Beach accordingly gave notice that an extensive coercion bill would be introduced by Smith on Thursday, 28 January, taking precedence of all other business, and that it would be followed by a land purchase bill extending Ashbourne's measure of the previous session.

Later Beach, by the direction of the cabinet, announced that Collings' amendment would be treated as a vital question. Gladstone for his part had required his chief whip to issue a three line whip in favour of the amendment.[203]

January 27 (Wednesday). At about 1 a.m. the House divided on Collings' amendment on agricultural policy, ministers being defeated 329–250. The House at once adjourned till Thursday. The division was followed by an impromptu supper of about a hundred M.Ps at the Carlton, where Churchill, who was in high spirits, said he hoped to have another such occasion soon.

The division on Collings left no happy feelings among Tories. Many Tory members, still believing in the unity of the rural community, were furious at having to go into the lobbies in apparent opposition to the social welfare of the labourers. Knightley, the old-fashioned country gentleman who sat for Northamptonshire, refused to come up to town to vote against Collings, whose principles he had been strongly advocating in every speech of his election campaign. Also annoyed, but on the other side, were the dogmatic economic Liberals, who had hoped for a Tory stand on the principle of market forces, thereby drawing together a new party of resistance, and had instead got an accommodating speech from Balfour which threw over Goschen and his principles in an all too visibly intended manner.

Ashbourne and Smith[204] arrived at Euston from Ireland at 6.30 a.m., expecting to be called on to introduce a coercion bill, and finding instead the news of the defeat of the ministry. They consulted with Churchill at the Carlton before going to the cabinet.

A telegram arrived from Osborne in the course of the day. 'H.M. telegraphed not to be precipitate and resign on ''a triviality''.'[205]

The cabinet met at the Foreign Office, 2.30–3.30, attended by all ministers except Carnarvon, who was still in Ireland, and Harrowby, who did not arrive in London from Staffordshire till the evening.

Cranbrook's account was 'But Beach by direction of the cabinet pledged us and though R.C. doubted today, he was one of us yesterday and stood alone today so that eventually he decided not to impair the unanimity of our decision wh. Salisbury wd. at once send H.M. by Rowton, whom she had summoned. Our cabinet was not long for we were all of one mind except as above.'[206] Salisbury informed the Queen that the cabinet were unanimous in their decision to tender their resignation.

Manners wrote to Salisbury some time during the day suggesting the formation of a Hartington ministry committed to a policy of coercion.[207] That such ideas were in the air among ministers at this juncture is shown by a letter from Hartington to the Duchess of Manchester, written on 27 January, reporting a conversation with A. Rothschild. Rothschild had been told by Churchill, on the government's resignation, that the Queen would send for Gladstone but would require assurances. Churchill thought that the Queen might therefore end up sending for Hartington, in which case Salisbury would be prepared to serve under him as Foreign Secretary.[208]

Cranbrook's reaction was: 'Out! joyfully do I record our defeat in the Commons last night... I have done nothing but laugh over our defeat as if it were a triumph and feel enormous relief.' Manners wrote in the same vein 'the lookout is gloomy in the extreme, for he [Gladstone] is half mad and quite reckless. All my colleagues are delighted at their release from an untenable position.'[209] As an epitaph for the ministry, none was more representative of Conservative opinion than that written by a junior whip, 'Lord Salisbury has done wonders in the time':[210] as comment on their manner of departure, Lady Knightley sum ed up rank-and-file feeling: 'Anything so bad as the way they have played their cards cannot be imagined!'[211]

January 28 (Thursday). Both Houses adjourned till Monday, 1 February.

Lord Rowton reached Osborne at 2 p.m. and tendered the resignation of the cabinet to the Queen. Salisbury was at once summoned by a telegram received just after 3 p.m., and left Waterloo at 3.40 p.m. He saw the Queen at 7.30 p.m. By his advice, the Queen asked Goschen to come to Osborne the following day (Friday).

January 29 (Friday). Salisbury left Osborne just after 8 p.m. and returned to London, where Balfour and Beach later called upon him.

Goschen saw Salisbury as soon as the latter returned: Salisbury said he had advised the Queen to send for Gladstone. On the Queen making objection, Salisbury said he had then suggested she send for Goschen as an 'independent man'. Salisbury agreed with Goschen that coalition was at present impossible.[212]

Goschen also saw Hartington in the course of the morning, apparently to no purpose other than to speculate upon events. Goschen, for instance, mentioned but did not show his correspondence with the Queen to Hartington.[213] Goschen declined the royal invitation to Osborne. Upon Goschen's refusal, Sir Henry Ponsonby was sent to London to see Salisbury, Goschen, 'and then, if necessary, Mr Gladstone',[214] all three of whom he saw later that night.

Salisbury wrote further to the Queen some time on 29 January, presumably in the evening, advising the Queen against dissolving, because 'a dissolution *now* would not favour the Constitutional sections of the House of Commons'.[215]

January 30 (Saturday). Gladstone accepted at once Ponsonby's oral and qualified invitation to form a government, in the early hours of Saturday morning.

February 6 (Saturday). The Conservative ministers travelled to Osborne to surrender their seals.

Part Three

Gladstone's Recapture of the Liberal Party, December 1885–June 1886

'It is impossible to conceal the fact that Mr Gladstone is more completely master of the country and of his cabinet than he has ever yet been' (R.Brett to Chamberlain, 9 February 1886, Esher MSS).

'If the Tories had resigned in December last after the Election ... what chance would a "Parliament in Dublin" ... have had in a Cabinet containing Hartington, Chamberlain, Goschen, James, Trevelyan, Bright, or Dilke!! to say nothing of Lord Derby and Lord Northbrook' (E.Heneage to A.Grey, 21 March 1886, Grey MSS).

'But his (Gladstone's) voice is clear and ringing as he said "for the last thirty years I have felt in me the desire and determination to fight with old age"' (Lady Monkswell, *A Victorian Diarist* ... *1873–95*, p. 180, referring to conversation in 1891).

'For the interests of landlords I think that the best solution might probably be a Home Rule scheme combined with a fair land purchase measure' (Hartington to Lansdowne, 4 January 1886).

Meetings of the Liberal Cabinet, 1886

February	March	May
15 Monday	29 Monday	4 Tuesday
16 Tuesday		8 Saturday
22 Monday	April	25 Tuesday
25 Thursday	1 Thursday	
	6 Tuesday	
March	9 Friday	June
8 Monday	14 Wednesday	8 Tuesday
13 Saturday		
26 Friday		July*
		20 Tuesday

The Liberal Cabinet in 1886

Prime Minister	W. E. Gladstone
Lord President of the Council	Earl Spencer
Lord Chancellor	Lord Herschell
Foreign Secretary	Earl of Rosebery
Home Secretary	H. C. E. Childers
Colonial Secretary	Earl Granville
Secretary of State for India	Earl of Kimberley
Secretary of State for War	H. Campbell-Bannerman
First Lord of the Admiralty	Marquess of Ripon
Chancellor of the Exchequer	Sir W. V. Harcourt
Chief Secretary for Ireland	J. Morley
President of the Board of Trade	J. Chamberlain †
	J. Stansfeld
Secretary for Scotland	G. O. Trevelyan ‡

* The meeting of Liberal leaders on 28 July was in one sense not a cabinet, in that their resignations had been accepted, and Salisbury had kissed hands as premier. On the other hand, more technically, the Liberals did not surrender their seals of office till 3 Aug., and Gladstone described the discussion to the Queen in the manner customary for cabinet meetings.

† Chamberlain's resignation was accepted on 27 Mar. 1886 and he was succeeded by Stansfeld whose appointment was announced on 29 Mar.

‡ Trevelyan's resignation was accepted on 27 Mar. 1886, and his successor, the Earl of Dalhousie, was not a member of the cabinet.

Diary

So far as public appearances went, 1885 was a quiet year for Gladstone, especially for an election year. This, of course, is partly to say that his main employment consisted of writing letters,* but it is also to stress his gift for being inactive when he wanted to be. He did not make a public speech between autumn 1884 and November 1885. He did not speak on any Irish topic, in or out of parliament, at any length during the year preceding his Midlothian campaign of November 1885. Between 7 July and 9 November 1885, he spoke not at all, inside or outside parliament. This economy of effort was indeed the basis of the substantial exertion he made in November, when he gave six campaign speeches in fifteen days. (These were his last extra-parliamentary speeches until the general election of the following June). While Gladstone's total load of work was remarkable, in some very obvious ways he did only a fraction of what a modern politician is expected to do. Nevertheless, his manifesto and his election speeches worked well in reassuring an anxious party that the Liberal party would continue to be something that ordinary opinion could believe in, and at the beginning of December 1885 the point which a non-partisan observer would most have stressed about the tone of his leadership was its calm reasonableness.

After the Midlothian election, Gladstone and his party left Edinburgh by the limited mail at 6.5 p.m. on 28 November, passing through great demonstrations at stations en route, and reaching Chester about midnight.[1] Once back home, Gladstone settled happily to his special combination of rural leisure and the full life, with some politics, and despite some outings in the locality he did not spend a night away from his own roof till he returned to London on 11 January. As Gladstone had just spent much time at Dalmeny discussing the political future in depth with Rosebery, he kept his consultations on his return to a minimum, and three weeks after his return could write that Granville, Rosebery and Spencer were 'the only colleagues I have seen'.[2] All three had an openness towards home rule lacking in the rest of the ex-cabinet. Granville was at Hawarden on 5–8 December, then travelled via London to Chatsworth on the 8th, whence he returned to town on the 12th. Rosebery arrived at Hawarden from Scotland on the 8th and departed for London just after noon on

---

* At this time, although out of office, he received 3,000 letters a month (*The Times*, 14 Dec. 1885).

the 9th, after he and Spencer had spent the morning in joint discussion with Gladstone. (It is not clear when Spencer had arrived).
These visits led to no action, and there is no evidence that they
had any particular significance.

On the 10th, Sir Thomas Acland and Lord Wolverton arrived,
the latter not till evening. Wolverton stayed till the 12th, but
Acland remained at hand till the 14th. These people came into the
category of those whom Gladstone liked to see, as did his chief
whip and neighbour, Lord R. Grosvenor, who paid a visit on
2 December and again called for three hours' talk on the 21st.

Some idea of the conversation can be gleaned from Acland's
letters. On the morning of the 11th, while Wolverton talked
electoral worldliness 'about Hodge and how to keep him', Acland
had a long walk in the park with his host, who at first talked highly
confidentially on Ireland (in what sense is not known), then
turned to the problem of the book of Genesis in its relation to
science. On the 12th and 13th Gladstone continued to talk freely
to Acland, again to unknown effect, on current politics, Acland
trying without much confidence to be a useful listener. On Sunday
the 13th, Gladstone's sycophantic high churchman Canon MacColl
preached the sermon and stayed overnight.[3]

On the morning of Monday the 14th, MacColl had an interview on political subjects with Gladstone. (Nothing of consequence
appears to have passed between them the previous day.) Gladstone
certainly spoke of Ireland and of its bearing upon parties. He had,
MacColl learnt, lately been working out and testing every scheme
which fell short of separation, and he was deep in Burke.[4] He also
put forward some of the ideas that he put to Balfour the following
morning about the desirability of the Tories settling the Irish
question with Liberal support. So far, Gladstone's talk was predictable. What was not predictable was the impression (possibly
only semantic, possibly only guileful, but perhaps expressing a
real feeling) given by Gladstone regarding home rule. 'Certainly
the impression I brought away with me from Hawarden was that
Mr Gladstone was not in favour of a Parliament in Dublin',[5]
MacColl later wrote of their talk this morning. Even after the Kite,
MacColl could tell Gladstone 'the impression you left on my
mind was that you were *not* in favour of a Parliament in Dublin:
but you said nothing to justify me in drawing a positive conclusion
either way'.[6] MacColl, a compulsive polemicist and intriguer,
would hardly have Gladstone's full confidence, but his impressions,
precisely because they were what Gladstone wanted to be passed
on, may indicate that at this moment Gladstone was willing (whatever his private opinions) to lay aside a parliament in Dublin for

the sake of an Irish settlement under Tory auspices. Gladstone's conversation with MacColl had a public function far beyond chat, for MacColl had a long-standing appointment to see Salisbury, presumably in London, that same evening. There is nothing to show that MacColl's visit to both leaders in one day was a carefully pre-arranged means of liaison, any more than there is anything to suggest Balfour's presence at Eaton the following morning was not accidental. Gladstone later went to unusual pains to establish that MacColl was not his emissary,[7] but this was probably the backwash from the Kite. MacColl of course agreed (as did Salisbury) that 'I did not intend to carry any message' from Gladstone. Nevertheless, MacColl told Salisbury in the evening all that Gladstone had said in the morning: and he wrote to Gladstone, though not till the 22nd, reporting Salisbury's conversation that evening. Moreover, MacColl sent on to Gladstone two letters he had received from Salisbury. MacColl's self-importance created the semblance of a negotiation despite the least possible encouragement from either leader, and his report on Salisbury's latent sympathy with home rule may have been one source of Gladstone's persistent belief that the Tory-Irish alliance would not necessarily break up.

Though his visitors sound a substantial prior charge on Gladstone's energies, in fact they were probably not so. For one thing, his daughter's coming wedding to the local curate loomed large. For another, his combative instincts were involved in refuting Huxley's heresies. Underneath all this, his mind was seeking the bedrock of unassailable truth and moral inspiration on the Irish question. At this level of reflection he was entirely alone, whatever the company around him, in an isolation which the drudgery of repudiating the Kite led him to emphasise ever more strongly. By the 23rd he could cut down to size all his previous very open discussions of Ireland thus: 'Of the conditions of any measure for Ireland, or of my own intentions about one, I have not given to any human being any binding indication...'[8] Gladstone had said much in December about Ireland, but at the two levels most meaningful to himself, moral right and parliamentary tactics, he had said nothing.

Ironically, it was largely upon the neighbouring ducal seat of Eaton, where the Grosvenors were rabidly anti-Parnellite in principle and practice, that Gladstone depended for society. It was at Eaton that he met Arthur Balfour on the 15th and offered him Liberal support on the Irish question, an opening which continued to occasion correspondence and even cabinet discussion into early January without ever looking like meaning something.

When Gladstone received casual visitors from his great neighbours, such as Lady Brownlow and Lady Cowper on the 14th, or when he went into Cheshire society, as on the occasion of a Chester funeral on the 19th, all turned on the fact of his living in the shadow of Eaton.

At the time of the Hawarden Kite (17–18 December) Gladstone was however without company at Hawarden except for his family. Gladstone was aware from the beginning how far from serious, in parliamentary essentials, the incident was. Moreover, his disclaimer had reached the evening papers on 17 December, before the major London dailies, including *The Times*, had even printed the initial reports. The Kite enabled colleagues to claim to be irritated, which was no great matter. Less immediately, it led politicians of both parties to realise more quickly than they would otherwise have done, that they could not provide any alternative to Gladstone, nor was it in their interests to do so. The Kite also created unwise hopes that Gladstone would make some disastrous mistake, which, since he did not do so, again only strengthened his hand. Where Gladstone did lose through the Kite, was by the excessive reaction of that extra-parliamentary public which followed politics as an entertainment, and which believed it had witnessed an event. The campaign initiated in *The Times*, for instance, was undoubtedly very damaging, and was on the same lines as if the Kite had been a substantive action. The parties, however, stood still. The Irish did not switch to the Liberals in succeeding weeks. The Conservatives considered virtually all possible Irish policies in succeeding weeks, and did so without reference to Gladstone's supposed position.

After Grosvenor's visit on the 21st, life at Hawarden became very quiet, with no political visitors at all during the rest of his vacation.[9] The time gained was largely devoted to high political meditation, and to local cares and interests. On his birthday, 29 December, he suffered a servants' ball and 700 items of mail. He continued his usual relaxations: he attended a lecture on healthful exercises, illustrated by members of the Liverpool Gymnasium, on 31 December, he gave tea for 500 young people and received non-political friends from Eaton on 2 January, read the lessons in church on 3 January, attended morning prayers and cut down a tree assisted by his two sons on 4 January, attended morning service again and cut down two trees on 6 January. His heart, however, lay not in these activities, nor in the writing of numerous non-committal letters, but in 'doing what little the pressure of correspondence permits to prepare myself by study and reflection'.[10] This certainly involved brooding over Burke and the inner meaning of the history of the Irish question. It probably also led him to contemplate the far from pressing problem of Anglo-Irish financial relations.

As regards his correspondence, two themes may be discerned: a willingness to suggest, and to let it be suggested to him, that something might yet come of the Tory-Irish alliance: and a promulgation of the doctrine that a party in opposition ought not to discuss Ireland, the real meaning of this (apart from intrinsic good sense) being that Hartington and others had to realise that Gladstone while out of office would simply refuse to say anything which might give malcontents a chance to question his leadership.

There is no reason to suppose that Gladstone had any reliable knowledge, direct or second-hand, of Tory or Irish intentions at this time. He wrote to Balfour[11] on 5 January disclaiming any wish that might have been read into his previous notes, for inter-party consultation on Salisbury's Irish policy, and the short and totally inconsequential chapter of Gladstone's attempt to float, or to be seen to be floating, a bipartisan policy would seem to stop there. He did, however, differ from most of his Liberal colleagues in believing the Tory-Irish alliance could and might continue. His grounds for this belief are certainly obscure, but at any rate it was not until the Parnellites made clear their new frame of mind when parliament sat, that he saw in them an intention to be his allies. There was no real decrease in his grim distrust of the Parnellites in the month after the Hawarden Kite, no increase in contacts or understanding of Irish intentions, and little change in his belief that an effective Liberal-Irish alliance was on the outer margins of practical politics. Thus on 2 January he asserted, as against Hartington who took the opposite view, '... nor do I know whether you are right in supposing there is a breach, by which I mean a breach to become public on the Address, between Tories and Nationalists. The imperfect information which I possess rather looks to the opposite conclusion.'[12]

Five days later, in an important letter to his chief whip,[13] we find Gladstone in much the same frame of mind. The whips' intelligence had got wind of two contradictory plans on the part of the Irish: one, that of Parnell, by implication leaned to the Liberals, while what Gladstone mysteriously called 'the Randolph–Healy concordat' was obviously in accord with Gladstone's own 'impression (not conviction) that there will be no ostensible breach between Tories and Nationalists on the day of the Address', something not unwelcome to Gladstone as affording 'momentary relief'.

It is reasonably clear that Gladstone was not in consultation with the Irish. He did not regard the Hawarden Kite as having in any way secured Irish support or clarified the situation. He thought a temporarily continued Tory-Irish alliance at least as likely as its break-up in the short term. He thought some wild and intolerable action by the Parnellites, such as withdrawing to set up a national assembly in Dublin, had to be allowed for. In this context, one can take *au pied de la lettre* his words to Grosvenor 'I am not quite certain how long we ought to persist in the system of making no spontaneous communication to Parnell: this is a matter for consideration.'[14] In fact, Gladstone chose the more cautious path when the question actually arose. On 9 January he replied to a letter from Mrs O'Shea,[15] who had suggested that he should 'advise', by saying that 'advice from me would be negotiation, and negotiation by me in the present position of the case, would be fatal to any prospect of being useful which may, I am far from saying does, lie before me'.[16] At a tactical level, Gladstone for most of January held the door firmly closed to any development of an understanding between the Parnellites and the Liberals. Knowing what he knew from Grosvenor of the two minds the Irish were in, Gladstone's letter to Mrs O'Shea can be taken as a thrust against Parnell's wish for a Gladstonian orientation for his party.

Only a few Liberal leaders were in London in the first few days of January: Childers, because he was trying to re-establish himself after losing his seat, Dilke because he was trying unconvincingly to behave as if nothing had happened, and Harcourt because he was as visibly hungry for the formation of any Liberal ministry, not least on financial grounds since he had a new house to pay for, as he was eager to berate Gladstone's wild folly. On 4 January Chamberlain returned to town from Birmingham, and Hartington arrived in Devonshire House from the country, but their arrival did not affect the dearth of political activity in London, where no significant political moves were made before Gladstone's return on 11 January. This was exactly what the old man calculated the effect of his absence would be.

The absence of any link or compact between the Irish and Liberals is a major point, but one peculiarly hard to establish. The Irish kept their secrets all too well, while the Liberal chief whips of the day, Grosvenor and A. Morley, both left nothing on paper. All that is reasonably clear is that in late March or early April 1886, John Morley rapidly became the trusted sole medium of communication, while before that there is a good deal of negative evidence to suggest there were no secrets behind the public face of things.

Of Gladstone's Whig confidants, Spencer could not talk to

Irishmen at this time, Granville was too busy cajoling other Whigs, and Rosebery was fully under-occupied passing on spasmodic gossip from Labouchere to Gladstone. There is no sign that John Morley was used to negotiate with the Irish before late March. The only letter of any significance from Morley to Gladstone between his appointment and the end of March was dated March and suggested minor changes to the home rule bill. Communication between Morley and Parnell began at the end of March over the question of Irish tariffs. Chamberlain's attempt to negotiate in January was glacially received by Parnell. The Irish and English officials who assisted with the Irish bills sounded out other officials about the land question, but no one appears to have consulted Irish politicians about either bill. Mrs O'Shea's letters to Gladstone in spring 1886 met a brick wall: her husband was occupied with the Galway by-election. Herbert Gladstone passed on Labouchere's views of Parnell's and Chamberlain's minds in a somewhat innocent way. Brett, whom Churchill had suspected in December of being Gladstone's prime negotiator with Parnell, was playing little part in affairs. In short, none of the usual intermediaries were seriously employed in Irish-Liberal liaison in the phase between the Hawarden Kite and Chamberlain's definitive resignation. Gladstone knew roughly what the pool of intermediaries had to pass on, which was very little, and he probably also received sensitive reports from his whip as to the diversity and ambiguity of Irish intentions.

While Gladstone was actively and successfully managing to impose inactivity on large sections of the Liberal and Irish parties, his lieutenants occasionally attempted to take a purposeful initiative. The most important instance of this was the meeting of Liberal leaders at Devonshire House on 1 January to discuss what to do about Gladstone. Harcourt had been to see Hartington at Devonshire House the previous Wednesday morning to arrange about the holding of this conclave.[17] Chamberlain came up specially from Birmingham, and Hartington, Harcourt and Dilke were also there. Granville[18] and Rosebery[19] had refused invitations to the meeting. Dilke wrote, 'I did not see my way clearly and did not say much. The other three argued strongly against Mr G's course and conduct in sending Herbert Gladstone to let out his views... [but] neither Hartington nor Chamberlain saw their way to opposing Mr G though they both hate his scheme... The principal conclusion come to is to write to Mr G to urge him to come up to consult us.'[20] The lieutenants, in the space of one short discussion, saw they were powerless to do other than let the situation develop, and then went their separate ways out of town, having only decided that Hartington should write pressing Gladstone for early consultations (i.e. before the 12th).[21] Hartington rightly thought that nothing would hurry Gladstone down to London earlier than he intended, but went through the motions of urging the proposal. As for his colleagues, Hartington told Granville that Chamberlain and Harcourt were 'as much opposed to home rule as I am' but both were 'more impressed than I am with the hopelessness of resistance ... or of governing Ireland by repression'. Hartington in passing reaffirmed 'the impossibility of my being able to agree to any policy in the home rule direction.'[22]

Gladstone replied to Hartington saying he would be in London about 4 on 11 January, thus only rendering more definite his earlier suggestion on 23 December that consultations should be left until 12 January or so, a view that Hartington had himself echoed on 30 December before his conclave came out for urgency.[23] Gladstone added that on 17 December 'I communicated to you all the opinions I had formed on the Irish question' and that he had not a word to add. Though stressing that there was no question of converting the private opinions expressed in his letter of the 17th into explicit intentions, Gladstone emphasised that Hartington and others had since then known his 'opinions en bloc'.[24] The demand for party discussion put forward on 1 January only clarified Gladstone's unbending refusal to be drawn into Irish discussions with his colleagues at large, which he maintained without lapse throughout January 1886, thus rendering the apparent strength on paper of his dissident lieutenants almost meaningless, not least in their own eyes.

The importance of the meeting lay not in what it did, but in what it failed to do. It simply confirmed Gladstone in his refusal to discuss substantive policy. On the other hand, it showed the impossibility of forming an overtly home rule ministry, by demonstrating how isolated the supporters of home rule would be if it came to forming a government. As Spencer wrote to Rosebery:

'you and I, and I know not whether you still hold the views you did at Hawarden – you might well have gone back from them – will stand alone among Mr G's colleagues. Possibly Lord G will follow Mr G, but I know of no one else inclined to do so. We three peers and John Morley could not form a Gladstone government, and at present I see no prospect of Mr G getting a following enough to justify his going on.'[25]

Succeeding weeks were to show that what Gladstone could not possibly have achieved by attempting to convert his colleagues, could readily be effected by his policy of refusing to attempt to convert anyone.

January 2 (Saturday). Rosebery made quite clear in private conversation what his feelings were, not about Ireland as such, which he never discussed, but about what was required by English public opinion, and about which party he wanted to see in office. Rosebery argued strongly for turning out the Tories, and held that public opinion would not permit an Irish policy based on coercion. His case for home rule was not that the Liberals should lead English public opinion, but that they must accept the decision of public opinion against coercion. 'Home rule ideas may be perilous; but are they attended with the same amount of peril as must attach to the other alternative – a despotic rule?'[26] Rosebery maintained a fairly sanguine feeling in favour of a Liberal government pledged against coercion (and therefore in effect pledged to some constructive scheme for meeting Irish demands) throughout January. His views carried little weight with others, and were only important in that his explicit dissent from any possible future Liberal premier, if one can imagine Rosebery dissenting from any future premier at this juncture, would have much diminished the number of straightforwardly loyal Liberal ministers who were also political assets. Rosebery was straightforwardly loyal throughout this period to both Gladstone and Hartington, in the sense that both men could count on him taking any office, if senior enough, under them without any ado. He did not much mind which of the two succeeded. Rosebery could be loyal to both leaders, because he genuinely liked, understood, and appreciated the qualities of both leaders, and because he expected the Irish policies of both to fall within the same genre. (Why Rosebery had been in a position to be the close friend of both possible Liberal leaders, with a side-bet in the form of an agreeably chummy relationship with Chamberlain, is a more interesting question). Rosebery was on the whole a Gladstonian at this time, but then he had long expected Gladstone both to form the next ministry (a prediction he was rather clear about) and to elevate his own political status in public eyes to the point, perhaps, where he could go into any future Hartington government right at the top. Rosebery had already undergone a status change in the inner world of politics, but to give full public recognition to this, something like a short Gladstone ministry, with a drastic upheaval among the old gang, offered an ideal stepping stone. In the circumstances, it is not surprising that Rosebery found it expedient as well as congenial not to play the active politician during January 1886, and spent most of his days in diligent idleness.

January 4 (*Monday*). Harcourt, still in the bitterly anti-Gladstone mood which had gripped him since the Hawarden Kite, shot what was virtually his last bolt in that direction. He wrote to Chamberlain, the 'rising sun' to whom he had tried to commit himself during previous months, as the sands ran out for Dilke, in the belief that Chamberlain needed a new political ally. It was not clear that Chamberlain felt any compelling urge in return to rescue Harcourt from the paths of wayward eccentricity to a well-planned career: and Harcourt's subsequent lust to dish Chamberlain, must be seen in the light of his self-abasement before him at the previous stage of the game. Harcourt wished Chamberlain to give a clear lead, on the basis of ideas supplied by Harcourt: and Harcourt was now urging that the Liberal chiefs should meet Gladstone as a 'posse comitatus' on 11 January, rather than reporting individually to the G.O.M. and being out-manoeuvred in detail. Harcourt's proposal probably fell flat almost at once: his colleagues did report individually to Gladstone, and were individually out-manoeuvred. Harcourt's plan demonstrated, even to his obstinate temper the inability of the leadership to do more than paddle their own canoes. Harcourt ended up agreeing to take counsel with Chamberlain: and from that point the two great conspirators appear to lose heart for joint conspiracy. (They are not reported as having met in January 1886 for non-social purposes.) When one wonders, as one must, why Harcourt, given his Irish opinions, did not act with Chamberlain in destroying Gladstone's Irish policy from inside the cabinet, one must remember that Harcourt had been quite sharply jilted by Chamberlain over the general question of a personal alliance, that he had found Chamberlain a broken reed when he had proposed a raiding party against Gladstone's Irish policy in January, and hence did not wish to try again paths that had badly failed in the immediate past.[27]

During the rest of the month, Harcourt found little outlet for intrigue. It was more from habit than hope that he turned again to Hartington on 9 January,[28] suggesting a second cabal at Devonshire House. This proposal, which fell flat, may have been his only attempt to assert himself in the period before Gladstone's return to office, apart from his share in the not very arduous task of devising Collings' motion on allotments.

January 5 (*Tuesday*). Chamberlain spent his second night back in London convivially with John Morley, who wrote 'Chamberlain and I went to the French play on Tuesday, after a snug meal at the Athenaeum. We are going again on Wednesday. So you need not believe the stories of the London correspondents that we have quarrelled.'[29] There is vast evidence that Morley and Chamberlain had, with much self-dramatisation, reached the parting of the ways either in autumn 1885, over collectivism, or in December 1885, over Ireland. Certainly Morley was reaching towards a more equal position, certainly they found it easy to reach substantive disagreements, and certainly Morley needed to make it look publicly as though (as Gladstone said the day before offering him office), he were 'no friend of Mr Chamberlain's'.[30] However, men in fundamental disagreement do not have long confidential discussions and seek out each other's company: and Chamberlain and Morley throughout January really only had each other to talk to about that engrossing subject, themselves.

January 8 (Friday). Trevelyan, Northbrook and Campbell-Bannerman concluded three days of discussions on Ireland at Northbrook's home at Stratton in Hampshire. All were agreed that home rule was undesirable. Only Trevelyan, however, thought that 'a sustained policy of coercion is possible', and was clearly in favour of a hard line. As Northbrook said, Trevelyan was more strongly 'in favour of resisting the Parnellites than any of us', and approved of Hartington's published letter. On the other hand, Campbell-Bannerman, while seeing no way of 'preventing the spoliation of the landlord under home rule', was not prepared to dismiss out of hand the possibility of Gladstone producing an adequate scheme, 'a task almost more than human'. Northbrook's view was that the Conservatives would introduce a coercion bill (an expectation not shared by Campbell-Bannerman), but otherwise Campbell-Bannerman wrote, 'I think I can say that Lord Northbrook and myself take an identical view of the position...'[31] The Stratton meeting showed in the case of junior ex-ministers what the Devonshire House meeting had seven days earlier established for their seniors – a fatalistic acceptance that only Gladstone could now make a significant move.

January 9 (Saturday). Rosebery had a visit from Harcourt, whom he found in a good humour, and whose arrival enabled Rosebery to refuse an invitation to go up to Hawarden. Apart from casual chat with E. Hamilton and some of the Rothschilds, Rosebery had not seen any politicians since 30 December.

Gladstone read and made many extracts from Burke, presumably on Ireland and America, and commented, '*sometimes almost divine*'.[32] He had earlier regretted that pressure of routine business was preventing him from making the 'full historical study' of the Irish question that he wished.[33]

January 10 (Sunday). Rosebery, Harcourt, and E. Hamilton, immured in one of Rosebery's many country houses, continued to meditate on political prospects, and moved towards Hamilton's view that 'it certainly looks as if Hartington's moment may be at hand', a view which Rosebery partially accepted despite his claim the day before that the Liberal ex-cabinet would 'fall into Mr G's ranks in due course'. Harcourt appeared to be still sitting on the fence, but again, like Rosebery, to be inclined by preference and vanity of prediction to jump down on the side of Gladstone. The party at Mentmore was joined in the afternoon by H.James, who urged that 'every nerve must be strained to keep the present Govt in their saddle',[34] advice which was rather wasted on two ministers expecting the major promotions of their career within a month. James was quite simply strongly anti-home rule, but had not matured any political plan for dealing with the situation, beyond an implied proposal for a Whig-Tory entente in the very short term, a project which had already been stamped into the ground in the first fortnight of the previous December. This project appealed to James in a not quite austere way: it made him the indispensable intermediary, through his close links with Churchill, in operating a hypothetical Whig-Tory alliance, and would have turned him into the central figure in politics. This distorted his appreciation of the realities, which were that Salisbury and Hartington had clear reasons of their own for accepting a Gladstone home rule ministry, even if Churchill had not.

January 11 (*Monday*). Parnell left London for a party conference in Dublin, but owing to an 'accidental' missed connection found himself unable to keep his engagement, and instead found himself, at 11.35 a.m., waiting for ten minutes at Chester station with Gladstone. However, Gladstone stayed in his saloon, while Parnell went to the refreshment room. The G.O.M., perhaps unaware of the coincidence, was travelling from Hawarden to London, where he arrived about 4 p.m., accompanied by his wife.

On their arrival in London the Gladstones went to 21 Carlton House Terrace, as guests of Lady Frederick Cavendish, but at this time they expected to be able to return to Hawarden by the end of the week. Soon afterwards Gladstone received calls from Granville (who found him 'looking a little pale and his voice husky'),[35] Harcourt, Dilke, Godley, E.Hamilton, and Lord R.Grosvenor, the chief whip. Dilke's visit was an 'unexpected and unwelcome appearance',[36] as he realised when he heard Gladstone whisper to Harcourt 'this is very awkward'.[37]

Chamberlain addressed a meeting of the Allotments and Small Holdings Association in the Westminster Palace Hotel, announcing that he had in readiness a bill giving local authorities compulsory powers to acquire land for allotments. He promised 'a strenuous and unrelenting resistance' to any Tory local government bill, used very strong language against the landlords, and abused the Duke of Richmond. What he did not refer to, naturally enough, was Ireland, but the tone and tactics of his speech made it clear that, in order to maintain a following in the party, he could not any longer afford to think of joining any Whig proposal to keep the Tories in office for the time being on Irish considerations. Chamberlain's speech of 11 January was an important step towards Collings' motion and a Gladstone ministry: it showed that Chamberlain, pricked on by Morley's speech four days earlier, and unsure of his support, felt more need to re-establish himself as a leading Liberal than as a leading anti-home ruler.

January 12 (*Tuesday*). Gladstone continued to receive visits from former cabinet colleagues. Spencer, just back from the country, called at 11 a.m., and half an hour later the two men were joined by Chamberlain,[38] followed by Granville. The four had a long meeting. At 1.55 Gladstone arrived at the Commons, and when Hartington appeared there on his return from Hardwicke, Gladstone was seen to greet him heartily. When Gladstone returned home from the House, he received a visit from Hartington for nearly an hour.[39]

Just before dinner E. Hamilton called on Gladstone and found him 'remarkably well and essentially calm', working up the Irish question energetically, and still reading Burke. Gladstone gave the impression of being in no hurry to turn the Tories out.[40]

In the evening Labouchere gave a private dinner, arranged about a week before with some deliberateness, at which Churchill and Chamberlain were the only guests. The dinner, like most aspects of Chamberlain's relationship with Churchill, was not recorded by Chamberlain in his *A Political Memoir*, but fortunately Churchill sent a report of Chamberlain's remarks to Salisbury as follows:

'... Joe told me a lot of things. 1) He had been with Gladstone in the morning, but could not make him out. Nothing had been decided on, but he was almost sure Mr G would abandon his home rule plan. Joe hinted that some independent member would move an amendment to the Address regretting that no announcement was made of provision for the wants of the agricultural population. This he was very vague about: he said it might fail, or it might get the whole Liberal support. This would not be known until it was moved. I think they are preparing some coup of this kind, from Joe's manner. He was evidently letting out a secret. Then Joe was very bitter about John Morley, who, he said, was trying to run alone. They were, he said, great friends still, but would never be political friends again. He never mentioned Dilke's name. ... Joe did not conceal at all his hatred of Hartington and Goschen, and snarled awfully at both many times... I told him we should go out on the first creditable opportunity, and should be on the lookout for such an opportunity. He said, if he could have his own way, he would keep us in, making it pretty easy for us... Summing it all up... I am of opinion that the Liberals guided by Harcourt, Granville and the GOM are going to try conclusions with us immediately.'[41]

January 13 (*Wednesday*). Gladstone's visitors were Bright, Mundella, H. Primrose (a private secretary) and Spencer, who stayed to have some mutton broth. As far as Mrs Gladstone could tell, 'Uncle William keeps his hopeful and trustful spirit and quite coincides with the others as to its being right to be in a waiting condition.'[42] Bright did not have much talk with Gladstone, but the two men walked down to the House together. Kimberley, after a long visit to Granville in the morning, also saw Gladstone.

John Morley and Chamberlain dined together, with only Collings present, and went on to the French play (where they shook hands with Hartington on leaving), their evening being given a certain significance in that Morley had just (7 January) 'shot my bolt for removal of Irish members from Westminster,' in a speech at Chelmsford.* (What Morley had taken up, indeed, had its opportunist aspects, being not so much an altruistic recognition of Irish nationality, as a much more widely acceptable cry for disenfranchising the Irish at Westminster).† The question arising was whether Morley's public avowal of home rule principles cut him off from being Chamberlain's adviser. As Dilke was already only a shadowy figure in Chamberlain's future calculations, Chamberlain had to think twice before he terminated his political alliance with Morley. Morley himself plainly hoped that he could both be the Radical who stood to gain most by any swing to home rule, and that he could retain a special relationship with Chamberlain as his major political alliance. In this he very nearly succeeded: Morley had no reason whatever to expect the special status that Gladstone offered him at their second (but not first!) interview

* There is no correspondence in the Chamberlain MSS between Morley and Chamberlain in the crucial period between 9 Jan. and 3 Feb. 1886.

† 'I can well believe what you say about the anti-Irish sentiment. John Bull *won't have* it at present... My way of putting it may tempt him, by and by – namely, that we won't have Irish members at Westminster' (Morley to R. Spence Watson, 8 Jan. 1886, Spence Watson MSS).

on 31 January, and he was conspicuously absent from those whom Gladstone consulted during January. In the circumstances, Morley was wisely irresolute in taking a leap in the dark and then returning whither he had leapt: and Chamberlain could only grumble in a way that made it clear that their relationship would continue to have some kind of existence.

Chamberlain's unusually inactive role in January, when he made no major speech, must be seen in the light of Morley's categorical defection in his Chelmsford speech of 7 January, about which Chamberlain showed unconcealed annoyance.[43] Thereafter he could not stop Morley joining a Gladstone ministry, and thus giving it the necessary Radical minister: nor could he easily risk not joining himself, for fear that Morley wrest a portion of the Radical leadership from his hands. Indeed, it never seemed really likely at any time during January that Chamberlain would stay out of office, whatever his or Gladstone's Irish views, and in the end he went like a lamb, saving his objections for the dinner table which was now, as with any other territorial politician, his favourite arena. From early in January, Chamberlain ceased to be actively interested in preventing a Gladstone ministry.

January 14 (Thursday). At noon Ripon and Granville called on Gladstone and remained for more than an hour, Granville then walking to Devonshire House for a long interview with Hartington. Although there is no direct evidence as to what passed between Ripon and Gladstone either during their long interview, or at dinner that evening, Ripon had at the least an adequate opportunity to gain an impression of the way Gladstone's mind was moving. His sense of what Gladstone might be inclined to, is all the more important, as Ripon was considered a discreet man, and he had of his own volition probably come round to home rule views by this time, so Gladstone had no reason to dissimulate with him. Yet what Ripon felt it necessary to impress upon Gladstone in a subsequent letter had a quite opposite implication: 'I earnestly trust that you will give no countenance to any return to coercion under present circumstances.'[44]

In connexion both with Ripon's apparent impressions of what Gladstone might possibly countenance, and with Mrs Gladstone's observations below, a letter which probably reached Gladstone on this day may be significant. From Sir R. Hamilton, in Dublin, it stressed 'we are in the throes of a revolution ... face to face with the serious alternatives of letting Ireland govern herself, or of ruling her with a rod of iron involving disfranchisement in one shape or other, and coercion legislation'.[45]

In the afternoon Gladstone received visits from Grosvenor,

Kimberley and Rosebery. The last, who had travelled down from Edinburgh overnight, spent an hour with Gladstone in what was their first meeting since Rosebery's fleeting visit to Hawarden on 8–9 December. Rosebery found Gladstone highly satisfied with Spencer, and was shown the letter written by Hartington to Gladstone in the name of the Devonshire House malcontents of 1 January, together with Gladstone's own reply.[46]

Mrs Gladstone in private conversation gave her own summary of the position. Gladstone, she said, was entirely uncommitted and simply waited upon events. 'He would aid and abet the Govt if they took up a right line on the Irish question.' She added that there were other possibilities. 'If the Irishmen were deaf to reason or if they took up a threatening attitude, he might very possibly appeal to his own unbroken record of attempts to do justice to Ireland and, their failure being proved, he would resort to strong alternatives which might even include disenfranchisement.'[47]

That Mrs Gladstone was not just rattling recklessly on in her talk of a possible worsening of Irish affairs, but was simply saying what was in the air at home, can be confirmed by considering a letter written by Gladstone to his chief whip a week earlier. In it Gladstone, still inclining to regard the Irish as opponents rather than allies, had mentioned the possible adoption of abstentionism, on Sinn Fein lines, 'as by far the most formidable thing that can happen. It will be followed by an assembling in Dublin, which brings into view very violent alternatives. If Parnell is wise, he will keep to the game he has been upon heretofore, viz. the ejecting of governments. He must of course begin with the present one. Then a Liberal government *not* prepared to deal with him. Or if there were a Liberal government prepared to *try* dealing with him, their ejectment would be soon provided for by others.'[48] Gladstone not only had not seen any sign that the Irish were ready to co-operate with the Liberals, but he took a gloomier view of Irish developments than most people had in mind at this time. This was the non-tactical element in his reiterated view that 'we ought on no account ... to join issue with ministers on the government of Ireland'.*

The Gladstones attended a dinner party given by Harcourt, the other guests including Hartington, Ripon, Granville, and John Morley.

Chamberlain dined with the Francis Buxtons and declared against home rule in the most outspoken manner.[49]

---

* Later repeated in same context, Gladstone to Granville, 18 Jan., 'we ought not to join issue with the government on what is called home rule (which indeed the social state of Ireland may effectually thrust aside for the time)...'

January 15 (*Friday*). Gladstone's son Henry left for India with his friend Spencer Lyttelton, and Gladstone walked to the station to see them off. During the rest of the day, Granville and Gladstone spent much time closeted together at Carlton House Terrace.

E. Hamilton called on Gladstone with details of civil expenditure in Ireland, and a letter from Sir R. Hamilton in favour of home rule which earned high praise from the old man. Gladstone said that if home rule were granted, he intended to fix Irish civil charges at their present level and appoint an English receiver to see that they were paid.[50]

Gladstone dined with the journalist Knowles and others, and talked at length about manners and customs in parliament. Beards came in, he said, with the militia in '52. He then went on to speak of the sacred duty of keeping up all the old forms and traditions. 'I notice with alarm the growing irreverence and not in the House alone, but throughout society. I say with alarm because the decline of reverence means the decline of liberty ... such an attitude and style was unknown, not indeed to be imagined until quite lately.' Gladstone added 'The Irish in the House are all quite devoid of wit or humour. There is not a witty man amongst them excepting perhaps Callan, a drunken fellow, who shows however flashes of wit, real Irish wit. The others are gloomy, monotonous, and vulgar.'[51]

January 16 (*Saturday*). Hartington called on Granville, who then called on Gladstone. Both interviews were lengthy. Gladstone had by now abandoned all earlier hopes of returning to Hawarden. In the evening the Gladstones dined with Alfred Lyttelton and his father-in-law, Sir Charles Tennant, in Upper Brook St.

Gladstone wrote a letter refusing to see a Unionist deputation from Belfast, as Irish policy was entirely a matter for the government.

Joseph Arch, just returned as the first rural labourer ever to enter parliament, was the guest of honour at a dinner at the National Liberal Club, attended by a large number of M.Ps. Chamberlain as president proposed the toast to 'The newly enfranchised labourers and their first direct representative in parliament' and also spoke out strongly against any measure regarding Ireland such as Gladstone was supposed to have in mind.

While out hunting in the shires, Spencer told Lady Knightley that Carnarvon 'was set to do impossibilities – e.g. govern Ireland without the Crimes Act and that irreparable mischief had been done: he didn't know how it was ever to be remedied'. Asked why renewal of coercion had been left so late, Spencer said 'Ah! that was not my fault' and fell back on the usual answer about passing the seats bill first.[52]

January 18 (*Monday*). Ponsonby called on Gladstone in the morning with a letter from the Queen. Then Gladstone went with Grosvenor to consult Sir Erskine May, Gladstone walking home through St James's Park. Hartington visited Gladstone at 4.15, followed after quarter of an hour by Granville, both men staying a long time. Their discussions were almost certainly highly critical ones, concerned with whether Hartington should declare against Irish autonomy on Thursday.

Northbrook returned to town to take part in the discussions of the Liberal leadership, from which he had virtually withdrawn in the six months before the Hawarden Kite. He had sworn often enough never to serve under Gladstone again, yet when it came to the point, he made sure that he did not miss the meeting of Gladstone's ex-cabinet or allow himself to be seen as out of the running for the next ministry.

Granville had a long and intimate conversation with Dilke, who had been very much out of things since his unsolicited visit to Gladstone on 11 January. Granville may have been sent to smooth things over, or even to capitalise on the fact that it was now possible to point out to Dilke brighter prospects as a backbench loyalist, than as anything Chamberlain had in mind for him. What Granville certainly did not intend, any more than anyone else, was to consider Dilke as a still significant politician. It was no longer necessary, in anyone's calculations, to assess what Dilke might do. Granville took a bold line on Ireland in the course of his talk, for he praised John Morley's speech at Chelmsford on 7 January.[53]

January 19 (*Tuesday*). Gladstone saw Spencer and Grosvenor for a long time in the morning, and did not leave the house all day.

Great commotion was caused at Carlton House Terrace by Hartington's threat to make a strong statement in parliament on Thursday denouncing Irish demands, and thus publicly going against Gladstone's policy of silence and reserve. Word of this rift was going round the London clubs on 19 and 20 January. If Hartington did speak, Herbert Gladstone said, there would be a split in the party and 'Mr G will abdicate'.[54] This amounted to a clear ultimatum, and probably not an unauthorised one, that if Hartington prevented Gladstone from forming a government, then it was hardly likely that Gladstone would make it possible for Hartington to form one.

The timetable of Gladstone's successful confrontation with

Hartington is slightly uncertain, but it was certainly concentrated on the days 18–19 January. On 18 January, Gladstone wrote angrily to Granville of having had a letter from Hartington announcing his intention to challenge Gladstone's Irish tactics in debate. Gladstone retorted that 'in a week's time Hartington will have to consider whether he will lead the Liberal party himself or leave it to chaos. He will make my position impossible.'[55] Any Hartington leadership, or even coalition ministry, would clearly have to face so many caves and schisms to left and to right that it would not be worth having. By the end of the week Hartington, his Unionism put out of operation, was seriously turning over the possibilities of competing with Gladstone as a home ruler. As early as the evening of 19 January, indeed while the confrontation was supposedly at its height, Goschen ran into Hartington at Brooks' and had a highly significant talk with him, in which he entirely failed to convince Hartington that it 'would be disastrous' if he abandoned his proposed 'firm' statement on Ireland. Goschen actually argued 'that we must not think of party' to a man who might within the week have become leader of a permanent majority for the rest of his life.

Earlier in the day Goschen had met John Morley at the Athenaeum and talked freely with him about the Hartington-Gladstone rift, and about Morley's differences with Chamberlain. Morley reported that Gladstone was talking of 'the mad passion which is rising in England against Ireland'.[56]

January 20 (Wednesday). Rosebery called early on Gladstone, and again later on, and found him 'subdued, but manly and firm in tone'. On the other hand, when Goschen saw Gladstone at the House, he thought he looked 'tired, excitable, unhappy, and irritable'. Gladstone's voice continued to be weak, and he dined at home.

Granville gave a large parliamentary dinner at his house which was attended by future Unionists like Derby and Northbrook as well as by Rosebery, John Morley, and Spencer.

At some point during the day a number of Liberal leaders, including Hartington, Grosvenor and Harcourt assembled at 21 Carlton House Terrace where Gladstone was staying. The chief topic of discussion was the passage in the Queen's Speech which appeared to indicate that the Tories intended to bring in a crimes bill. Later the G.O.M. told his wife 'It is God's will, the break and the difficulties.'[57]

After their discussion with Gladstone about the Queen's Speech, members of the former Liberal cabinet met Harcourt and Hartington, both of whom showed considerable perplexity as to Gladstone's intentions. The meeting was held in Gladstone's room, and was entirely unproductive.

Just after 11 at night, Hartington and Lord R. Grosvenor caught up with Goschen at Brooks', where they held a 'tremendous séance' which lasted till 1. The meeting, or cabal, at which Hartington had recently been, had been attended by Harcourt, Chamberlain, Grosvenor and Hartington only. (Dilke was by now firmly excluded even from informal counsels.) Hartington had also just had a private meeting with Granville.

Hartington handled Goschen's importunities admirably, saying with firm dignity that he would certainly rise to challenge Gladstone if the latter attacked the passage about the maintenance of the Union in the Queen's Speech (a mistake Gladstone could be counted on not to make). Beyond this Goschen failed to pin down Hartington to anything: 'Hartington *may* speak tomorrow, and the split is there: if he doesn't there may be a row among the Liberals. I have urged him very strongly.' Goschen of course told Hartington that he 'wished the lead to remain' his, but threatened to act independently 'with a great following' if Hartington showed undue caution.

Grosvenor interposed to point out that Gladstone 'may possibly make a backing down speech', while Henry James massaged Goschen's wilting optimism to the point where, on leaving Brooks', he believed it 'quite within the range of possibility that by Monday, Hartington will be the leader'.[58] Goschen had indeed been handled well.

January 21 (*Thursday*). The Queen opened parliament in state. A meeting of the former Liberal cabinet was held at Granville's house at 11 a.m., twelve of the former ministers, including Hartington, being present. The meeting broke up after about an hour and a half, with little decided.[59] Carlingford (ill in Italy), Selborne, Shaw-Lefevre and Childers were absent. Childers was absent fighting an election in Edinburgh, and Shaw-Lefevre, having lost his seat at Reading, was probably considered *hors de combat*.[60] Only Selborne stayed away voluntarily.[61] Dilke sat 'morose in a corner' at this, his last appearance at a meeting of the Liberal leadership.

According to Dilke, it was at this meeting that it was agreed to support Collings' amendment to the Address, though this decision was perhaps only a provisional one requiring activation by later contingencies. According to the same source,[62] the terms of what was to be known as Collings' amendment were in fact drawn up by Chamberlain and Dilke just before the meeting, though this claim lacks confirmation.

Gladstone's note on the meeting has just a cryptic heading 'Ireland'. Gladstone refused, 'with great eloquence and vigour', to be pinned down precisely, declaring 'I may resign my seat, but I will not part with my liberty... When in obedience to the wishes of a majority of my party and colleagues – at the last moment before the dissolution I consented to stand, it was in the hope of being able to contribute to the settlement of this question.' Gladstone was taking the line that he should not allow the reference to coercion in the Queen's Speech to draw him into a premature declaration of opinion. Hartington demurred, and said that the Queen's Speech did not force his hand more than he wished it to be forced (i.e. presumably, that he was ready to state his position on coercion and perhaps generally on Ireland). Inconclusive bickering about Ireland followed. Gladstone's main aim remained, not to commit the party leadership to home rule, but to commit them to parliamentary silence – a strategy in which he almost totally succeeded in the most masterly way.

The meeting of 21 January finally demolished any hopes that a collective party leadership might impose its policy on Gladstone. Gladstone quite clearly was not going to give an inch, and Mrs Gladstone was talking of how she was looking forward to Downing St. What was still entirely open was whether, as Rosebery thought gloomily after the meeting, Gladstone would now or very soon have to hand over the leadership to Hartington (a view in which E. Hamilton concurred). Gladstone had given up no ground, which was in itself an achievement, but he could not convince his senior colleagues of his ability to form a ministry, and the question remained entirely uncertain until the crisis actually arose.

In the afternoon Rosebery called upon Gladstone.

January 22 (Friday). Granville had another long interview with Gladstone. Wolverton and Spencer both called on the premier and congratulated him on his speech of the previous day.[63]

An undated memorandum[64] by Chamberlain was sent on this day to Parnell via O'Shea. A second copy of the memorandum was read to Parnell by Labouchere.[65] Chamberlain argued that Salisbury should be left in office pending more complete evidence of failure to deal with the Irish crisis, and that if the ministry had to be defeated, it should be on Collings' motion not on Ireland. Chamberlain stated that home rule proposals would split the Liberals, and as an alternative asked for Irish co-operation in passing 'some large operation of land purchase, without pressing for an immediate consideration of home rule proposals'. Parnell, according to Labouchere, at once returned a frank negative.[66]

January 23 (Saturday). Rosebery called on Gladstone and found him 'cock-a-hoop – never so pleased' as he said when congratulated on his speech. Chamberlain had told him he agreed with every word of it, though Hartington had kept his own counsel.

Sir H. Ponsonby, the Queen's private secretary, went to stay with Rosebery at Mentmore for the weekend. While on a sleigh ride the following day, they discussed the Queen's wish to send for Hartington, and her anxiety to keep Granville out of the Foreign Office. Rosebery was told, if coalition was ruled out, then the Queen had fixed on him for the Foreign Office. Rosebery told Ponsonby that it would be 'a great calamity' if the Queen sent for Hartington, adding that it 'would defeat Hartington's object as I explained'.[67] It was perfectly clear throughout January that Rosebery, despite some wobbling, wanted Gladstone to be called upon to form the next ministry: but the question whether, in wishing this, he placed Gladstone's or Hartington's long term interests higher, is imponderable rather than obvious.

Spencer and Granville spent the weekend (22–25 January) as guests of the Duke of Westminster at Eaton, both returning to town on the Monday.

On the Saturday afternoon, a conference of a strictly private nature was held at Devonshire House to consider how to use procedural reform to crush the Parnellites in parliament. Those present at the meeting included Hartington, Chamberlain, Courtney, Playfair, Herschell, Whitbread, and others, presence being obviously partly connected with sagacity as to procedure. Nothing is known of the discussions. However, Hartington spoke in significant vein to Courtney before the others came. 'His difficulty', Courtney reported, 'about opposing Home Rule is that he cannot see how the House of Commons is to go on with the Irish members in it, however stringent the new rules of procedure may be.'[68]

January 24 (Sunday). A. Grey 'had some talk with Hartington… He seems to have an idea of some plan which will repeal the Union, by getting rid of the Irish Members from the H. of C., and converting Ireland into a subject province.'[69]

January 25 (Monday). Hartington's brother, Lord E. Cavendish, M.P, a future Unionist, speaking at Lancaster in reply to a toast to his brother, flew a kite that was just as significant as, and probably more authorised than, that flown by Herbert Gladstone. Cavendish lauded the Parnellites for their conciliatory temper, urged the leaders to speak out on the Irish question, and even went on to claim that his brother would meet Parnellite reasonableness with unspecified legislation. Cavendish's words were nebulous, but any contemporary politician would have read them as a hint that Hartington wanted to form a government to deal with the

Irish question, that he wanted to do so on moderate home rule lines, and that he was looking to coming in with Irish rather than with Tory support (since support there must be).

Harcourt talked very bitterly of those Whigs like A. Elliot who not only held views on Ireland similar to his own, but ventured to express them. Harcourt called Goschen 'a poisonous intriguer', [70] and since Harcourt's aim was a broad-based Liberal ministry committed to nothing, he had good reason to vilify those who wished to precipitate conflict.

Harcourt and Gladstone talked over the difficulty of finding Liberal cabinet ministers in the Commons. [71]

January 26 (Tuesday). Spencer called on Granville, who later visited Gladstone, as did Grosvenor and Wolverton.

Gladstone replied to Mrs O'Shea's offer of Parnellite support in the lobbies (provided Gladstone himself formed the new government), informing her that he would speak and vote for Collings' motion that evening, but otherwise brushing aside her leading questions. [72] In an earlier and explicitly interim reply he had refused to commit himself at all in advance. [73]

Mr and Mrs Gladstone, Arnold Morley, F. Leveson-Gower, and Wolverton dined at the Wests, Gladstone arriving belatedly at 9 p.m. after speaking on Collings' amendment, and soon leaving again for the House. He looked very tired, and told Mrs West that he had had a *mauvaise dizaine de jours.* [74]

January 27 (Wednesday). At about 1 a.m. Lord Salisbury's ministry was defeated 329–250 on Collings' amendment to the Address. The House of Commons adjourned till Thursday, when both Houses adjourned till 1 February. In the morning, the cabinet unanimously agreed on resignation.

Gladstone wrote buoyantly to the Duke of Argyll, minimising the difficulties raised by Collings' motion, [75] and seeking to treat the Duke as an incipient home ruler on the basis of a letter by Argyll to *The Times* about American federalism. Gladstone can hardly have been insensitive to the reactionary feelings of the Duke on land and Ireland (though Rosebery, who found him writing to Argyll, thought he was being naive). It was an instance of how determinedly (and instinctively) Gladstone sought support on the right.

Gladstone, still a guest of Lady Frederick Cavendish, began his day with a visit at 10.30 from Godley, his former private secretary. At 11 Granville arrived, remaining till about 12.30, when he was followed by Herbert Gladstone. At 1 Mrs Gladstone and Lady Frederick Cavendish drove to Devonshire House. Meanwhile, Henry James called and spent 1.30–2 with Gladstone. Shortly after,

Hartington arrived from the Reform Club and stayed with Gladstone probably for over two hours, after which he felt that Gladstone had told him a good deal more about his Irish opinions than he had done before.[76] For his part Gladstone was 'greatly pleased' and told his wife 'it had been one of the nicest talks he had had'.[77]

On leaving, Hartington called on Granville, and, after walking some way with him, turned back and encountered Rosebery, who had also just visited Gladstone.

Later in the afternoon Gladstone and his wife drove in the park, returning to receive a call from Derby, and to have a long discussion with Spencer and Granville in the early evening.

When at 1.30 Henry James called on Gladstone at the latter's request, he was offered the lord chancellorship or any other office he might wish for; a flattering offer, this, to one who had never yet sat in cabinet. James was assured that Selborne was no longer in the running for the Woolsack. Following an inconclusive interview, Gladstone wrote of James 'This most loyal man ... will do his best to reconsider and examine.'[78]

In the evening the Gladstones dined with the Speaker, who afterwards enlisted the sergeant-at-arms into playing three rubbers of bridge against Gladstone and Sir John Mowbray. Gladstone struck his partner as wonderfully cordial and pleasant, and in great spirits.[79] After returning from the Speaker's dinner, Gladstone resumed work, and probably had further discussions with Spencer and Granville.

That night at his house, Gladstone talked over with West the reasons leading him to form a ministry. The first was that the weight attaching to his age might make him the most likely man to settle the Irish question: the second, that he wished to defer the inevitable split in the Liberal party as long as possible. He added, that Chamberlain was now cordially in agreement with him.[80]

January 28 (*Thursday*). Lord Rowton reached Osborne at 2 p.m. and tendered to the Queen the letter of resignation agreed the previous day.

Afterwards Rowton talked to Ponsonby,[81] who told him that the Queen abominated the idea of sending for Gladstone and was angry with him for saying that this was inevitable.[82] On Rowton asking why the Queen did not send for Hartington, Ponsonby said that Hartington himself would not like that, as he must decline to form a government unless Gladstone had already failed.[83] Rowton and Ponsonby agreed, like everyone else, that Goschen would not do.[84]

In the morning, Gladstone received visits from Granville, Lord

R. Grosvenor, Wolverton, Spencer, and Rosebery, the two last arriving together at 1 by arrangement in order to save Gladstone's voice and energy. Granville then left to visit Hartington, and their deliberations were joined by Goschen. Wolverton, Rosebery and Gladstone became involved in a discussion on how to get Granville out of the Foreign Office.[85] Gladstone's standing opinion, as given to Rosebery for instance on 9 December 1885 was that Granville's reappointment would be inexpedient: in this conversation 'Mr G said Kimberley would do.' Rosebery was himself anxious enough to shift Granville from the Foreign Office, as he had told Ponsonby a few days before, 'but could not remonstrate as I should be countered with the demand "Whom would you suggest instead?" which I could not answer.'[86] On the following day, 29 January, the Queen made it clear, through Ponsonby, that Kimberley would not do, and proposed Rosebery. Again, as with Gladstone, Rosebery was a second choice: Ponsonby had had to tell her that she could not have Goschen. 'Her idea is Goschen as F. Sec.'[87] Granville only relinquished his claims, in a private interview with Spencer, on 30 January.[88]

The conversation then turned to Harcourt, who earlier in the day told Wolverton and E. Hamilton that 'nothing would induce him to go back to the Home Office. He was sick to death of the House of Commons and would gladly be quit of the whole business.'[89] When Wolverton passed on Harcourt's intention not to serve again in the lower house, Gladstone replied 'But I am determined he shall.'[90] Harcourt's remark was a staple of his conversation at this time. Cursing home rule as 'insane folly' in late December, he had been asked by Rosebery if he would not find it rather awkward to sit beside Gladstone defending the policy. 'Oh, but I should not go back to the Home Office' Harcourt had said, which Rosebery took to mean 'that he would also leave the House of Commons, but he would not get the Woolsack for all that'.[91]

Later, after the adjournment, a group of Liberals, including Gladstone, James, Chamberlain, Harcourt and Hartington gathered in discussion. Then Hartington and Gladstone were observed in deep conversation alone on the frontbench for fifteen minutes, afterwards leaving the House of Commons together.

In the evening, Gladstone and his wife dined with Sir Charles Forster, M.P. (Lib., Walsall 1852–91) and others. A guest noted that everything in Gladstone's tone and manner made her think he was now willing to accede to Parnell's demands. The general drift of his conversation on this occasion formed a sharp contrast to the highly disparaging comments he had made about the Irish

M.Ps earlier in the month.[92] Gladstone indeed said of Ireland: 'What that country requires is a great *Arrears* Bill. We must efface our past and so must the Irish... There is, I think very little difference of opinion regarding Davitt, he is an honest earnest man...' He laughingly alluded to the present deferential attitude of the Irish party to him. 'Healy is so very civil and considerate that he seems another man.' Gladstone advised a reading of Burke on America for principles applicable to Ireland. Later he said to T.Burt, M.P, 'There is one thing wanting in all of you. None of you are economists ... as for me I glory in the appellation of Skin Flint...'[93]

Hartington's state of mind on this day is clearly set out in his letter to the Duchess of Manchester (28 January):

'There is no news today at all. I have seen a good many people at the House, Reform Club, and Brooks's. I don't think there could be the slightest chance of my being able to form a Govt with Lord S if the Queen asked me. ... [James and Goschen] both agree that my people would not join the Tories: at least not yet, and I should have only a very small following. It may come afterwards but not now. I hope the Queen won't ask me but I am afraid she may. I don't think however that I shall under any circumstances join Mr G.'[94]

January 29 (Friday). In the morning Grosvenor, the Liberal whip, saw Gladstone for an hour, and paid a further short visit in the afternoon. Grosvenor was also with Granville for forty-five minutes in the morning. Wolverton and Rosebery also called on Gladstone.

During the morning Gladstone learned of Parnell's anxiety that, if Gladstone were to take office, he would continue his fixed policy of not negotiating with Parnell, and indeed of not letting Parnell know any more of his intentions than the public at large knew. To satisfy Parnell, Gladstone wrote to Mrs O'Shea, assuring her that, broadly, this would not be the case, 'full interchange of ideas' being in his opinion 'an indispensable condition' of any government inquiry into Irish autonomy.[95]

At Devonshire House, Harcourt called just after noon and remained a long time with Hartington, who had previously been engaged with his brother, Lord E.Cavendish. Derby also called but soon left on finding Hartington engaged. After Harcourt's departure, Hartington received a long visit from Goschen, who then called on other prominent Whigs before returning to Devonshire House at about 4. It is possible that at some period of the day there was a meeting of Hartington, Granville, Derby and Goschen at Devonshire House, but the reports are not clear on this point and a series of *tête-à-têtes* is more likely.

It was probably on this day that Hartington convinced another Liberal backbencer, Buchanan, that the Whig opponents of Gladstone should bide their time. Opposition might be tactically correct 'if Mr G were to come forward with a home rule programme', but to make any move in the present situation 'could be interpreted to be a revolt and an attempt to wrest the lead from Mr G. Those who are opposed to a separate parliament for Ireland' should not waste their strength in trying to prevent Gladstone forming a ministry.[96]

Although on Saturday Gladstone went through the motions of inviting Hartington to join the ministry, it was already clear on Friday that for Gladstone and his confidants 'all hope of Hartington is at an end' though 'he has parted company with Mr G the best of friends. Mr G was much pleased and even touched by Hartington's behaviour.'[97] The intensive negotiations of the previous fortnight had been successful, from both men's points of view, in preserving a united, dominant Liberal party available for the unrevealed purposes of both leaders.

John Morley dined with Chamberlain, the only other guest being the Parnellite M.P. for Dublin, Gray, owner of the leading nationalist newspaper, the *Freeman's Journal*. Naturally Ireland was the only topic. 'Gray thought Home Rule might die down, if land question were settled... After I was gone, Gray told C. he thought his people would be content with land plus Local Government. Well, I don't believe it: no more does Gray.' Chamberlain, as usual, stuck to proposing a massive settlement of the land question, and a measure of local government.[98]

In the afternoon Rosebery called upon Gladstone, whom he found worried about not being sent for, but resting himself by reading a book on *The Court of Louis XIV*. He had tired himself drafting an answer to possible objections the Queen might make.[99] Gladstone had even, rather fussily, sent off his chief whip to ask E. Hamilton, who was after all only one Treasury civil servant among many, whether he thought it likely that the Queen might stipulate for an election or a renunciation of home rule as a condition of his taking office.

Gladstone did not leave the house all day, but entertained a large party to dinner, in a household preoccupied with rumours of some unusual move by the Queen. Among the guests were Arnold Morley and G. W. E. Russell, the latter having left behind his recollections of Gladstone on that evening. 'All day long he had been expecting a summons from the Queen, and it had not arrived. "It begins to look", he said, "as if the Government meant after all to ignore the vote of the House of Commons, and go on. All I can say is that, if they do, the Crown will be placed in a worse position than it has ever occupied in my lifetime".'[100]

After receiving Salisbury's resignation in the morning, the Queen had sent Ponsonby up to London for further consultations. On reaching Salisbury, Ponsonby found a telegram from the Queen telling him to call on Goschen. Salisbury's comment on this was that, as Gladstone had announced no definite plan, the Queen would have to send for him. Goschen was not at home, so Ponsonby sat chatting to Mrs Goschen until midnight when her husband at last returned. Goschen summed up the situation by saying that the delay in sending for Gladstone was becoming very serious. On this, exercising the considerable degree of discretion open to him, Ponsonby went to see Gladstone, whom he found on the point of retiring to bed.[101] The Queen, guided by Goschen, Ponsonby, and Salisbury (and to a lesser degree by Hartington, Rosebery and Rowton) had been diverted from her ideas of a (tactically premature) anti-Gladstone coup, by enemies of Gladstone convinced of the tactical benefits of putting him in power.*

January 30 (Saturday). About 12.15 a.m. Ponsonby called on Gladstone, found him still up, and gave him the Queen's invitation to form a government, which he at once accepted. Ponsonby explained that the Queen had not sent for him earlier because 'he had so often expressed the wish to retire'. Gladstone, equally straight-faced, said he would indeed have retired if the Liberals had not resigned in June 1885. But, he added, 'matters have changed since then. In Lord Spencer's time Parnell would have accepted Local Government. Now that policy had been discredited, and Parnell wanted independent Parliament.' Gladstone gave no indication of his policy, beyond claiming that his age and standing would have special value. Finally Gladstone asked if the Queen had sent a letter, but was 'satisfied with this verbal summons'.[102] Ponsonby reported Gladstone's acceptance in a telegram which reached Osborne at 9.30 a.m.: shortly afterwards another arrived

---

* Cf. Goschen to the Queen, 29 Jan. 1886, Royal Archives RA C/37/192, on the need for Gladstone to try and fail, stressing the danger that any major crisis might create immense sympathy for Gladstone: and Salisbury to the Queen, 29 Jan. 1886, loc. cit. C/37/192, arguing 'A dissolution *now* would not favour the Constitutional sections of the House of Commons. It would probably be better at the end of the session: and better still next year when the agricultural labourer has to some extent found out the hollowness of the promises made to him. There is a fear that a dissolution at the moment might expose us to the extreme hostility of the Irishmen without having gained to us any other class.'

from Gladstone, expressing optimism about his chances of forming a government.[103]

Both Ponsonby and Gladstone must have been profoundly relieved that Gladstone had at last been called upon, and entirely without strings too. The only inhibiting royal demands made on Saturday were for the removal of Granville from the Foreign Office, a demand which was entirely superorogatory, and a rather less obvious stipulation that Kimberley was also entirely unacceptable as foreign minister: the Queen wanted Rosebery.[104] The royal proscription of Kimberley may have played a small part in steering the post in Rosebery's direction, but as so often, the Queen was only repeating with emphasis what average political opinion thought. After Ponsonby's brief call, Gladstone went upstairs, turned to Mrs Gladstone, and said 'Not a word now: off to sleep.'[105]

Gladstone left copious but not very clear notes on his activities during the day.[106] The first note was dated 10.30 a.m. One of his first actions must have been to send a telegram to his former private secretary, E. Hamilton, at this time a principal clerk in the Treasury, who was staying at Mentmore with Rosebery, summoning him at once to his side. (Rosebery, not summoned at all by Gladstone till Tuesday, was left to continue shooting alone in the rain on Saturday, while on Sunday he played lawn tennis and rode, seeing no politicians till Monday afternoon, and taking no part in the formation of the ministry at any stage, in sharp contrast to his closeness to Gladstone over preceding months.)[107] Hamilton, assisted at times by Herbert Gladstone, acted as Gladstone's main aide during the formation of the government, though early on Saturday morning a Queen's Messenger and a foreign office messenger arrived with despatches and remained at his disposal all day. Hamilton, who until recently had been keenly hawking round the idea of a Hartington government as 'the best way out of the difficulty',[108] and who three days earlier had sent a memorandum for the Queen's consideration urging that Rosebery should be sent for if others failed,[109] had the composition of Gladstone's secretariat placed in his hands. Gladstone also told him of his perplexity about Granville, and then sent him on his rounds, where the first person he met was Henry James, just outside Brooks's, where they went for a short talk.

The course of Gladstone's work during the day is fairly clear. Shortly after rising, he drew up a draft memorandum formulating the Irish policy of the ministry (if he had not done this before, for which there is no evidence), wrote to Granville[110] enclosing it and enlisting his aid generally, and began to summon his less accessible colleagues. Just after 10, Granville walked across to see him, leaving before 10.30, and was subsequently in and out of the house throughout the day. Soon after 10.30, Gladstone summoned Spencer from Althorp, and wrote to Selborne and Lord Sydney. Grosvenor came in, was shown a list, probably of a conjectural ministry, and was sent on his way with a message to Freddy Leveson-Gower, Granville's brother. Hartington was with Gladstone from 11.30–12, and then went to call on Granville, James entering just as he was leaving and remaining with Gladstone till 12.30. On departing, James joined Hartington as he was coming away from Granville's, and they strolled in St. James's Park. Wolverton was then called in to discuss finding another seat for James. Herbert Gladstone was also an early caller.

During the afternoon, official business unconnected with his main labours also led Gladstone to communicate with Salisbury during the afternoon, and later he received a visit from Pauncefote, the permanent under-secretary at the Foreign Office, who told him of the position concerning the Greek fleet. Lord Derby then called to give what Gladstone described as 'a friendly negative', presumably to an offer of office, saying he was 'too much committed by declarations heretofore', although Gladstone showed him his emollient memorandum on Ireland in an attempt to persuade him to change his mind.[111] Derby's visit followed fairly urgent attempts by Gladstone to locate him and to ascertain his frame of mind, made at the very beginning of the day's work.[112]

Childers arrived from Edinburgh following a summons by telegram, and saw Gladstone at 7.20 for half an hour. Later still, Spencer arrived from Althorp and visited Gladstone, to say that he was 'at my disposal for any office or none. I said "Some, absolutely"'. The matter stands over.' Spencer was then sent off to see Granville's brother to go over the question of demoting Granville.

By Saturday evening Gladstone's notes show him to have regarded Hartington, Derby, Selborne, Carlingford, Shaw-Lefevre and Dilke to be definitely exluded from the cabinet.

Hard on Derby's heels arrived Ponsonby, to whom Gladstone reported that, of the sixteen members of his last cabinet, he had lost five, counted on nine, and had doubts about two other names. Among those he had in mind to fill the vacancies, he mentioned Ripon, John Morley, Mundella, Campbell-Bannerman, and Courtney. In view of Gladstone's obvious confidence in his ability to form a ministry, it was arranged that he should go down to Osborne to kiss hands on the following Monday.

Wolverton then returned, with a favourable report on his efforts to find a safe seat for James, information which probably was never passed on to James before the latter's final refusal of office on Sunday. Granville then returned to help in the negotiations, and shortly afterwards Gladstone found a moment to settle that Henry Primrose, a cousin of Rosebery, should be one of his private secretaries, Edward Hamilton being then sent off to check on Primrose's suitability. Chamberlain then called for a major interview with Gladstone, not leaving for two hours.

Lord R. Grosvenor then returned with the results of his interview with Granville's brother about excluding Granville from the Foreign Office, Granville being probably occupied elsewhere. Selborne then came in for a brief interview at which his final refusal of office was settled. Chamberlain later returned for further discussions.

Gladstone's conversations with Selborne and H. James about, among other things, the Woolsack, deserve explanation. In the first place, it is somewhat odd that Gladstone should be worrying about filling the lord chancellorship, at a time when the Exchequer and the Foreign Office were unallocated, and Rosebery and Harcourt had not even been summoned. A minor reason for this haste, no doubt, was the necessity to dispose of Selborne one way or the other, but with courtesy, before the real bargaining with others could begin. More important was the need to secure James, for whose merits and lack of political coloration Gladstone had enormous respect. James was wanted, of course, as chief lieutenant in the Commons (Gladstone seeing correctly that he was a born subaltern), taking the role which Harcourt was later to fill – which is why Harcourt was not summoned or offered any post until James had refused. On the other hand, it was essential to keep Harcourt in play in case James fell through: and he would in any case be a valuable support, though there is no real sign that Gladstone wished to advance him to a central position. Harcourt, however, wanted to be lord chancellor, and Gladstone was not prepared to confer a post of high value and no political consequence on a person whom he only tolerated as a political asset, if thereby the person ceased even to be an asset to him. It was reasonable to offer James the Woolsack, because though not a politically strong arrangement, it had justifications in that James was Hartington's right hand, that he was a pleasant person, and that if he accepted the Woolsack, he might the following day be edged into accepting a central place in the Commons instead. It was therefore important both to fill the lord chancellorship with great speed to block Harcourt's claims and retain him as a workhorse in the Commons, and, concurrently, not to provoke Harcourt's temper by letting him know he had been passed over for the Woolsack.

The speed with which Gladstone acted on Saturday over this appointment, does fit the view that he wished to close this door much more rapidly than in any other case. After he had dealt with Selborne and James, he moved quickly to make his final choice, despite lingering elements of uncertainty about James. He chose Herschell, an austere and legally very distinguished man who was neither Whig nor Radical, and was indeed not really so much a politician as an official. Herschell, who had failed to win a seat at the general election and who was strictly next in line for promotion after James among the Liberal lawyers, brought non-political respectability to the ministry without detracting from its political strength in the Commons. He proved a wise choice. The note offering him the Woolsack reached him while at the dinner table on Saturday evening,[113] and the following day Herschell called on Gladstone at 1 p.m. and accepted office.[114] The new lord chancellor had the previous Wednesday expressed much distrust of home rule, saying 'his main objection is not so much the measure, as the men to whom you would have to entrust the working of it'.[115]

Hartington's visit early in the day produced a definite refusal, reported in Monday's *Times* before anything else was known of the new ministry. The interesting feature of his visit, however, was not his refusal, but his promising to write a letter to Gladstone which could be shown to the Queen, stating that he would try to give general support to the ministry, and would offer no opposition to a fair consideration of its Irish proposals.[116]

The essential point made by Hartington in his letter was that, whether coercion or concession were the end ultimately in view, nothing could be done in either direction until an English ministry brought forward a practical scheme and sought for it the support of parliament and of the Irish party.[117] While remaining wholly uncommitted, Hartington hoped 'that it may be possible for me, as a private member, to do something to prevent obstacles being placed in the way of a fair trial being given to the policy of the new government'. He was 'fully convinced that the alternative policy of governing Ireland without large concessions to the national sentiment, presents difficulties of a tremendous character which, in my opinion, could now only be faced by the support of a nation united by the consciousness that the fullest opportunity had been given for the production and consideration of a conciliatory policy'.[118]

Hartington's letter, designed to be passed round, led inevitably to considerable uncertainty as to his real position, as he must have known it would. It was also open to abuse. Its real deceptiveness, however, lay simply in the fact that Hartington wrote it when he was more favourable to concessions to Ireland than he ever was to be again. Thus, on 5 February Hartington complained to Gladstone that his letter of 30 January had been misrepresented by third parties to give the impression he had refused office solely because bound by declarations to his constituents, and that he intended not to oppose ministers even on home rule.[119] Hartington may here have been referring to the cajolery exercised upon Heneage (see 4 February below). Nevertheless Mundella speaking at Sheffield on 8 February felt it safe to declare of Hartington. 'There was no colleague for whom he had greater respect... He was satisfied that his lordship would give an independent, although discriminating support to Mr Gladstone's government.'

Later in the day Hartington wrote two letters, almost identical in spirit and in form of words used, to his father, the Duke, and his mistress, the Duchess. To the latter, he explained that Gladstone

'asked me to come and see him this morning and asked me if there was any hope of my joining him. I told him that I would not, giving as my principal reason that I had committed myself too deeply against a Legislature for Ireland, whether independent or not, to be able to join a government, which is going to *examine* after certain preliminary conditions into the practicality of something of the kind. He didn't argue much with me, and said that no man could decide for another how far he was bound by such previous declarations; and we parted in a very friendly way... I think now he has gone as far as he has, it is necessary that he should have a fair trial and should show his hand. If he fails, and if either the English or Irish won't have his plan, there may be some chance of governing Ireland in some other way; but if he is prevented from having a fair chance by premature opposition or obstruction then I don't believe that the country will be governable at all... I wish I felt certain that he would succeed in making a government but I expect his difficulties will be great. He pressed H. James tremendously... if he and one or two more refuse, Mr G may give it up.'[120]

Before seeing Gladstone, James had talked, by chance, to E. Hamilton, whom he must have understood to be acting as Gladstone's ears. James pulled out of his pocket a newspaper cutting containing the report of an anti-home rule speech he had given to his constituents at Bury. 'Do you think', he said, 'I can join Mr G's government in view of that speech? You know how I revere Mr G, and how great is the effort I would make for him.

Can I in order to avoid deserting him explain what I said by calling a special meeting of my constituents?' Constituency commitments, rather than the current political situation, were consistently represented by James as the decisive factor in his calculations. There is really no way of telling how far constituency difficulties were simply used as a pretext, or even how far they were cold-bloodedly arranged. What is much more clear is that James had sensibly decided to bank on Hartington inheriting the earth: that he had not anticipated an offer of major promotion from Gladstone, (indeed, something like an invitation to be the second man in the government), and quite naturally, when such an offer came out of the blue, he found great difficulty in revising his calculations.

James went in to see Gladstone as Hartington was coming out, and was offered anything he wanted (including, if necessary, a seat other than Bury). The interview was inconclusive, James waiting for information about Hartington and about his constituents. Gladstone made a note about getting Wolverton to see about finding another seat for James, which implied that something could still come of the negotiations.

On Sunday, following a telegram the previous day, the chairman of James' election committee in Bury came down to London and saw James in the morning. He made it plain that James would not be re-elected if he took office in a home rule ministry. If there was a by-election at Bury, the chairman said, he personally would oppose James, who would be defeated ignominiously.[121] The chairman further obliged James, by putting his sense of the local situation in a letter which was then passed on to Gladstone. James then also wrote to Herbert Gladstone,[122] presenting his case for staying out, and asked whether he could avoid the further inter-view with Gladstone that he regarded as already arranged. In fact, his discussion with Gladstone the previous day was probably their last political conversation for some time.[123]

That James was conscious of the obvious weakness of his citing constituency problems as his reason for refusing office, at a time when the Liberals were eager to search out alternative seats for him, came out in a letter he wrote to Mundella on 4 February, adding to his previous apologetics the quite new argument that 'there was no one to keep the Chancellor of the Exchequer in order',[124] an appointment, of course, that was quite undecided at the time he took his decision. In later years, his opponents found it difficult to recall James as having made any kind of moral stand in 1886. During one attack in the 1890s by James on Trevelyan, Gladstone said 'To think of this man attacking you like this, when he came to me in '86, and only refused office because he said his

345

constituents at Bury wished him to vote against Home Rule and that he had promised them he would do so'.[125]

To go over the main points about James again: he was profoundly averse to home rule, as were many who took office in 1886. Gladstone made little progress in his first two interviews with him (on 27 and 30 January), but the same applies to other senior ministers who later accepted office. He had at any rate agreed to further negotiations, much as the others did. There is no really good evidence that James made up his mind to stay out of the ministry, at any time before the promise by his constituency chairman that he would lose his seat ignominiously if he joined. He himself wrote just after this news 'nothing now can alter my determination'.[126] It was perfectly clear that he did not wish to be the first to commit himself to Gladstone: what his position would have been, had it become clear, as it did on Monday and Tuesday, that Gladstone would succeed, is a different matter. He alone among frontbenchers stood to lose his seat: he alone among frontbenchers in the Commons refused specific office. He had been vaguely offered an alternative seat, but such things often fell through or involved undue loss of reputation.

When Chamberlain called on Gladstone for their first political conversation for some time, he had in his mind a discussion with John Morley, who had called on him at noon, in effect both to ask permission to join Gladstone's government and also to plead that Chamberlain should act jointly with him, either in taking office or in staying out. Morley made it plain that he was looking for a reason for not joining, but that if Gladstone formed a government on the lines of Morley's speeches, it would be his painful duty (after only three years in parliament) to enter the cabinet. Chamberlain was quite clear that Morley would be offered a cabinet place: and this calculation, which was of great importance to him, must have affected his behaviour on Saturday. Chamberlain had good-naturedly warned Morley that if he entered the cabinet alone, he would 'be smashed', without mentioning who was to do the smashing. Morley did not take the hint, and so Chamberlain had to shift his ground, though he brushed aside Morley's solicitations that they should hunt as a pair, overlooking without repudiating Morley's home rule principles, and effectively campaigning as Dilke and Chamberlain had done the previous year, the common adversary being necessarily Gladstone.

Chamberlain then went on to spell out the conditions without which he would refuse to join Gladstone, this meaning, of course, that his imperfect control over Morley meant that he realised he could not afford the risk of turning down office. He would require

Granville to leave the F.O., and promised to make his English land proposals a *sine qua non* (they were hardly heard of again: the topics of the unauthorised programme of the previous autumn had ceased to be topics, and Chamberlain knew it). He could not join if Gladstone had cut-and-dried schemes for home rule and/or coercion (Morley noted at the time 'I said the same as to that') but thought home rule might be left as an open question for the cabinet to settle. All this meant that Chamberlain had decided to give in all along the line, but meant to go through the motions of tough bargaining to satisfy his self-esteem.[127]

When Chamberlain saw Gladstone, therefore, he first stipulated that he 'could not agree to the Irish programme without modification', but then, according to Gladstone, 'this he practically withdrew', and with the help of Granville, a formula was produced which allowed Chamberlain to take office without committing himself to anything. He then asked for a few hours to consider. He also talked on the question of Dilke and the Foreign Office.

Later in the day Chamberlain returned bringing a draft of his acceptance.[128] At this stage Gladstone made a tentative note that he might prefer the Colonies to the Admiralty; and that he wished Collings to have office. Chamberlain wrote a further note bearing this date, declining the offer of the Admiralty.[129]

Childers arrived at 7.20 and without much ado accepted the War Office. He was told the tale of the latest developments, and shown Gladstone's memorandum[130] proposing 'examination and inquiry' into home rule.

Gladstone's notes show the following appointments to have passed under consideration: Hartington, Goschen, Mundella or Campbell-Bannerman for the Exchequer: Northbrook or Ripon for Ireland: Dalhousie or Rosebery for Scotland.

Chamberlain dined at home with Harcourt, E. Hamilton, the historian Froude, and others. The host explained at length why he had 'no belief' in anything Gladstone might produce, and why his central board scheme coupled with a land bill (which the Irish 'would not dare to refuse'), was still the path of wisdom. Less tiresomely earnest was Harcourt, who was dramatically sore at not having been sent for, and 'would prefer standing out', if he were to be slighted simply because of his known loyalty. Harcourt's bad temper had been made known to suitable emissaries since Thursday, when the ministerial crisis began, and continued till Monday morning, when the news that the lord chancellorship was no longer available and that he was to be chief lieutenant in the Commons completely cured him: indeed he became positively benign within the hour. But on Saturday, the only silver lining in sight was that he would have the pleasure of seeing Childers make up his mind, which he had never been able to, Harcourt said, in his experience. The conversation at Chamberlain's dinner table was duly reported by E. Hamilton to Gladstone the following morning.[131]

January 31 (*Sunday*). Gladstone went to church twice, walking there and back for the morning service, and therefore received fewer visitors than the previous day.[132] E. Hamilton arrived early, and remained at Gladstone's beck and call throughout the day. As regards colleagues, Gladstone began by inviting Herschell to call at 1 p.m., but it is likely that Herschell simply delivered his letter of acceptance instead of remaining in discussion. He had a major interview with John Morley at 2. At 2.30, Arnold Morley called to accept the post of chief whip, though Grosvenor continued to be active in his old role during the following week. Grosvenor also visited Gladstone. Later in the afternoon, Gladstone saw Granville, who was 'grave' and 'did not name the subject' of his own demotion, but left after talking over the cases of Chamberlain and Herschell. Then Wolverton came in and considered the idea that Granville might become first lord of the treasury while Gladstone became chancellor of the exchequer (perhaps concurrently with the premiership). Gladstone noted 'I did not exclude this at once but wrote to him on it.'*

The worst of the day was yet to come. Harcourt had his first interview, though he had been sounded by Granville the previous day, and was far from amenable. Then Childers was with Gladstone 6–7, partly to report on a conversation he had had with Hartington. The arrival of Spencer signified that the problem of Granville remained unsolved, Spencer having talked to Granville that afternoon. All indirect pressure having failed, Gladstone now as a last resort asked Spencer to convey that Granville could not again be foreign secretary. E. Hamilton, who was on his way to dine with Granville's brother, was asked to convey a similar message. These blunt messages produced a reply from Granville by about 11.30, which, together with an ominous letter from Harcourt received about 10.30, suddenly placed the existence of the ministry in jeopardy. These letters, together with the major interviews of the day, are dealt with more fully below. While in the morning a Gladstone ministry seemed almost certain, by the evening it looked as though Hartington would be the next prime minister, a result which Hartington had taken no positive action to achieve, however closely it corresponded to his calculations.

At 1 John Morley, who was at home working on an article, was

* See below, Thurs. 4 Feb.

interrupted by a telegram from Gladstone asking him to call at 2. 'I got there to the moment, and found him at his writing table with no fuss or hurry', Morley noted:[133] Gladstone had just returned from his second church service of the day. It is important to remember that the two men were virtually strangers where political co-operation was concerned: probably the only time Gladstone had encountered Morley since the elections was at a large dinner on 14 January. It is likely that Gladstone had had little contact with Morley prior to this Sunday. It was as strangers, then, that they began their talk.

Gladstone at once invited Morley to be Irish secretary. (There was never any hint, on either side, of any other proposal). 'Nothing could have taken me more by surprise, after my two speeches at Newcastle and Chelmsford', wrote Morley in his diary, showing that it was still appropriate to claim that the Hawarden Kite meant nothing.

'I asked what was to be the Irish policy, or at least the base of it. He drew a paper from a drawer and read it to me. I took it, behind all the words about future examination and so forth, to point pretty definitely to Home Rule in some shape or other, but I told him that before accepting I should like to have some talk with Chamberlain... He seemed a little taken aback at the delay, but could not refuse. I asked only a couple of hours to consider. Our conversation had lasted little more than twenty minutes.'

Gladstone for his part regarded this first interview, like the second one, as satisfactory, and wrote of it 'John Morley 2 p.m. All in the right sense. Asks until near 6... [Later] stated objections to himself but accepted.'[134] In thinking that Morley's case was all plain sailing, Gladstone did rather gloss over the ambiguities of Morley's position and the extent to which he left open loopholes, which were not finally dealt with till Tuesday.

There was one good reason why it was difficult for Morley and Gladstone to clinch a deal on Sunday, and that was the lord-lieutenancy. It was impossible to predict whether it would go to a major, or to a minor politician, and to guess at the political temper of its holder. One can assume that Morley was offered cabinet rank from the start, simply on the ground that the absence of such an offer would have left a very noticeable mark on Morley's temper.* What one cannot discover is whether he would have

---

* Cf. Morley in conversation with Chamberlain on Saturday 'I should certainly not take office out of cabinet' (Morley, loc. cit.) and a correspondingly categorical statement to Brett on Friday (Brett's journal, 29 Jan.).

been the only cabinet minister dealing with Ireland. Since Gladstone could at this time still have hoped to land a big fish (Northbrook, for instance) with an offer of the viceroyalty and cabinet rank, it is necessary to make every allowance for the tentativeness shown by both Gladstone and Morley at this stage: they were two people discussing an arrangement which necessarily concerned three people. However, on these points there is no information, and this important point seems to have been the one thing with which neither Morley nor anyone else concerned themselves.

On leaving Gladstone at 2.20, Morley drove to Chamberlain's house, but found that the British Robespierre had gone to lunch with Mrs Jeune, the leading Tory hostess. Morley set off after him, and found the meal over and Chamberlain in the drawing-room when he arrived. Chamberlain came down and saw Morley in the empty dining-room. 'For an instant he changed colour, and no wonder. My going to Ireland was the sudden arrival of long-apprehended peril to a cherished private intimacy, and of mischief to the commonwealth. "Well", he said, "it is just what I expected. I thought that was what he would do. I suppose you have accepted".'

Morley replied 'No, I have not. It is no trifle for a man who has never been in office and who has been less than three years in the House of Commons. And if the cabinet should in the end decide on a narrow Irish policy, I should be left isolated in the lurch, if that matters. I told Mr G I should not decide without seeing you.' Chamberlain said 'I don't see how you could keep your self-respect if you were to refuse' and became sombre in looks and words, inveighing against Gladstone.

The encounter took a quarter of an hour: then Morley left, walked slowly down to the Athenaeum, had tea, finished his article, wrote down seven separate reasons against his fitness to be Irish secretary, and then went back to Gladstone for his second interview. 'I steadily recited my seven objections. He swept them aside wholesale, made me a cordial speech about confidence in my loyalty, and evidently means me for a special ally...'

It was probably at this second interview that detailed discussion on Irish policy took place. Gladstone inquired whether Morley had gone further than himself on the Irish question. Without giving anything away himself, he drew Morley into proposing the creation of a statutory legislative body, and (prior to the creation of that body) a settlement of the land question so as to prevent confiscation. Gladstone appeared in agreement with this, but was not able to commit himself to Morley's other major proposal, the exclusion of the Irish from Westminster. On this latter point,

Morley was to write on Tuesday, presumably referring to the interviews described here, 'as you told me some days ago, you are not, as yet at any rate, able to assent'.[135]

How Morley left matters with Gladstone is made clear by a letter he wrote later that evening to his constituency chairman in Newcastle: '*Prepare.* I have had two interviews today. I have accepted the post of danger – much, much against my wish. The burden is too heavy for an untried man. It is hardly fair to lay it on me. He would not have a No...' However, Morley's further dealings with Gladstone on Tuesday concerning his appointment leave it to be inferred that something remained unsettled even after the second interview. It is clear that Morley wanted the job, and had probably spoken out at Chelmsford with a view to getting it. However, he wanted the job without risks or penalties, and he had no confidence in the prospects for a Gladstone ministry, nor any assurance that a Gladstone cabinet would follow a home rule policy. Chamberlain's menaces made him write out seven reasons for refusal: the countervailing impression that Gladstone 'evidently means me for a special ally' made him turn round again. Morley, the great man of principle whose parliamentary education had been as apprentice to Chamberlain and Dilke, was treating the crisis of his life as a tactical situation to be played by ear, attempting to gain time, to keep his options open, and to multiply the possible issues of principle involved.

On leaving Gladstone for the second time, Morley went off to consult Reginald Brett, later Lord Esher, who had been Hartington's private secretary until the arrangement was abruptly terminated in spring 1885 in rather suspicious circumstances. Morley probably considered Brett his link with the Hartington world, and the interest of his going to consult Brett did not lie in the advice he was given, namely, that he should accept office. It lies in the company Morley was keeping, and in those to whom he turned when planning his next move. Brett was well known for his view that Gladstone, and still more Granville, were not fit to govern: what he wanted was a strong Hartington government carrying out advanced social policies and as much of concession to Ireland as was necessary to extinguish Gladstone. Brett had given his views wider currency in a peculiarly sour letter published in *The Times* (4 January), in which he had turned down a request to stand as an advanced Liberal against Childers, the official Liberal, in the Edinburgh by-election, while making it plain that he thought Childers and the Gladstonians were indeed ripe for the axe. It was to this failed yet still ambitious *éminence grise* that Morley was wont to open his heart, as he had done the previous

Friday, when Brett noted 'J.M. expects to be offered some subordinate place. I said of course you will refuse it. He said certainly. I said no doubt a subordinate place is not worth the unpopularity which the new government must incur. He spoke in strong praise of Hartington's speech',[136] this last view no doubt being intended to be passed on in case of an imminent Hartington ministry. It must be remembered that Morley's prospects would probably have looked brighter under Hartington, in that the latter would have had much greater need than Gladstone of a minister who would symbolise to the Irish the end of Tory-Irish alliance. Morley in January may well have been setting his cap primarily at a Hartington ministry, immediate or eventual, in which he could achieve his main objects of working with Chamberlain, being a man of principle, and blocking 'socialist' tendencies, all at the same time.

What the chronology of Morley's negotiations and utterances at this time means, is that he was not going to allow his avowals of home rule principles to drag him inside a home rule government, till he could be quite sure that such a government would be formed, and in particular that it would include Harcourt and Chamberlain. By Tuesday, with the latter safe inside and all element of personal risk removed, Morley was anxiously taking the initiative in seeking office. On Sunday, he was, among other things, leaving some room open for gaining moral advantage by backing out of the home rule ministry, really through cold feet, but ostensibly because it did not go far enough in principle.

After seeing Brett, Morley dressed for dinner and went to a large party given by Chamberlain, who was pleasant enough to him and arranged for him to call on the following day. It was only when Morley called on Monday, that Chamberlain showed how sore he felt by giving his guest an hour of stale argument on Ireland, but even this tirade indicated in a way that some kind of relationship was felt to continue.

Lord R. Grosvenor called about the Duke of Westminster, who in the course of the day wrote to Granville declining the mastership of the horse and withdrawing his support from Gladstone.[137]

In the afternoon Gladstone, who knew from Hamilton that Harcourt had not taken kindly to being treated as non-existent,[138] sent Hamilton over to smooth the way for a visit from Gladstone at teatime. A comment on the oddity of Chamberlain's position in a ministry which he might have to leave within weeks provoked Harcourt to lecture: 'But we are all in the same boat. We none of us believe in Mr G's plan; but we have no alternative policy to support. It is just as if Mr G had declared that he had a scheme for moving traffic by balloons. Some of us, like Hartington and H. James don't believe, and have publicly declared disbelief in balloons. Those have to stand aside altogether. Others like Chamberlain and myself recognise the existence of balloons: and though we do not believe they can be turned to account as a motive power, we feel bound to approach the consideration of Mr G's boasted invention and to see if it can be worked out practically. If the invention proves, as we expect, to prove unworkable or unsafe, we must then give it up and take our own line.' This kind of Olympian talk on Harcourt's part was well suited to a man who believed the Woolsack within his grasp: ministries may come and go, but the incomes of ex-lord chancellors go on for ever. No one had yet told Harcourt of Herschell's appointment, though Gladstone had intended Hamilton to break this news, and Gladstone confined himself to an offer of high office, not particularised, but (perhaps innocently) leaving it to be thought that the Woolsack was available. It was not till later, when Harcourt wrote a letter bristling with difficulties, that Gladstone dashed his hopes. The bad news overnight turned Harcourt from a highly successful career lawyer who had never been quite at home in cabinet politics, into a major Liberal statesman.

In a momentous interview with Harcourt, Gladstone secured his assent to taking office at the same time as drawing from him the most rigid commitment against home rule pronounced by any official Liberal at this stage. Since, by Tuesday morning, Harcourt looked like becoming Gladstone's leading lieutenant in the Commons, and the only Commons minister who had a hand in the allocation of offices, his emotions at the point of no return are worth considering. Gladstone noted, 'Saw Harcourt – previously seen by Hamilton at my desire. He despaired and made difficulties – agreed with Chamberlain and with Hartington – hoped cabinet would be free to consider question of an Irish legislative body either way. But came in and would not refuse office.'[139] The last sentence was unequivocally true, the rest a rather optimistic gloss when set beside Harcourt's later letter to Gladstone of that evening:

'I have not, either from any reflections of my own or from the slight indications I have received of your views on the subject been able to arrive at the conclusion that there is any possibility of devising a scheme of home rule, by which I mean a plan involving *a legislative body sitting in Ireland*. ... If therefore your Govt. was about to be formed on the basis of the adoption of a separate legislative body in Ireland, I could not conscientiously join it. But I understand this is a question to be examined by the cabinet with perfect freedom.'[140]

And, if any doubt remained, Harcourt went on to remove it by mentioning his grave misgivings about John Morley being offered the Irish secretaryship.

During the day there appeared a statement by Hartington denying rumours that he had joined the government. This, with the absence of any positive announcement from the Gladstonian camp, only spotlighted the fact that in two days, Saturday and Sunday, filled with hard interviewing, Gladstone had been able to fill only four offices, the War Office (Childers), Ireland (Morley), the Woolsack (Herschell), and the Admiralty (Chamberlain). Of these appointments, those of Childers and Chamberlain were soon unmade. Those who had believed Gladstone could not form a ministry were proving good prophets.

In the morning, E. Hamilton had gone around to make himself useful to Gladstone, and even then he found that the question of Granville was assuming intolerable dimensions. Spencer had already been over the ground with Granville, but to no avail. Gladstone was willing to disregard the press outcry against Granville's reappointment, except where the Foreign Office was concerned: 'he would gladly give up the Premiership and serve under Lord G' but yet could not consent to his returning as foreign minister. When Granville came across in the afternoon, 'looking very haggard and troubled', neither man 'could summon up courage to allude to it. So no way was made.' Turning to indirect expedients, Hamilton, who happened to be dining with Granville's brother, was commissioned to use new arguments about age and infirmity in the hope that the brother would make use of them. Freddy Leveson-Gower accepted the unhappy task of talking to Granville, and arranged that he would call on Gladstone with the results. Instead of Leveson-Gower calling, however, there only arrived after much waiting a letter from Granville refusing all office. Gladstone, in despair, sent Hamilton across the road with another letter, the prime object now being to keep Granville inside the ministry. Haggard and perplexed, Granville when pressed for a message in reply would only say that he would sleep on it.

The worsening prospects for the ministry late on Sunday evening were well rendered in an account given by Herbert Gladstone, who had been round to 21 Carlton House Terrace, at 10.30 p.m. and had found there H. James' definitive refusal:

'...in comes a long letter from Harcourt marked Conf. and Priv. Inside were 8 sides quarto raising every kind of difficulty *à la* Chamberlain. Enclosed was another more Conf. So I went up to Father in the Drawing Room...

He told me to open the Encl. This was to the effect that he (H) wanted the Chancellorship and wd. not serve in the Commons: but that he wd say no more as he understood Mr G wd not fill any big post till Tuesday.

Herschell had accepted at midday! Lower and lower fell his poor face, for he told E. W. H. [amilton] to tell H. [arcourt] about the Lord Chancellorship. Eddie [Hamilton] who fortunately turned up at this moment had made a mistake and had not done this. So Father set to work to answer H[arcourt] and told E[dward Hamilton] and me to copy his letter and take the correspondence to Lord G[ranville].

Now Lord G[ranville] was in a most critical state over the F.O. and every minute we were expecting news through Freddy Leveson. At 11.30 comes a long letter from Lord G to say (very kindly and generously) that he must finally decline office as he cd not have the F.O. You may imagine how hard it was to take this up seeing that he looked to Lord G more than anyone except perhaps Spencer, to help him through his difficulties. Remember also that we could not shelve these letters as he was to leave for Osborne at 9 next morning with a proposed basis of the new Admin.

So there was no help for it and I gave him the letter wh. he read through. I never [saw] him so depressed for the minute. His arms fell all limp from the table. But he grappled with it, told us to take over H[arcourt's] correspondence wh. we had held back and began a letter to Lord G. E[dward Hamilton] and I went over and Lord G approved the answer to H[arcourt].*

Then we came back and E[dward] Hamilton left with instructions to see Harcourt early and I went over with the letter to Lord G who read it and told me he wd write in the morning.

I came to breakfast and a rather hopeful letter came from Lord G. Then I drove to Waterloo with him [i.e. W. E. Gladstone]. He said "From what Ponsonby has told me I think the Queen will bowl me over". But so great were these difficulties

---

* This is presumably the letter from W.E.Gladstone to Harcourt, dated 31 Jan. 1886 (copy), 56447, mollifying Harcourt as follows: '... I have not in any way considered the question of when and how as to communication with the Irish party.' As to examination and inquiry, 'unquestionably they commit no one to the advocacy of a separate parliament. Nor can the appointment of John Morley have any such effect.'

that he was not depressed at this – in fact it could make no difference and he went off gallantly though he had had an almost sleepless night.*

Then the clouds rolled by. E[dward Hamilton] cleverly settled with Sir W.H[arcourt] who consented to take the Home Office again. Lord G came to 21 [Carlton House Terrace] and I telegraphed to O[sborne] his acceptance of the Colonial Office; and finally H.M. was very kind and Father came back at 7.30 tired but in good heart. Since then there have not been any special difficulties.'[141]

February 1 (Monday). Both Houses met to hear statements on the change of ministry, then adjourned till Tuesday, when a further adjournment took place.

Gladstone went to Osborne to kiss hands, leaving Waterloo at 9.30 a.m., and taking a special steamer from Portsmouth to Cowes, where he arrived just after 1. He spent about two and a half hours at Osborne, and returned, after two audiences divided by lunch, to reach Waterloo about 7.45. When the Queen saw him, before lunch, he 'looked very pale, when he first came in, and there was a momentary pause, and he sighed deeply. I remarked that he had undertaken a great deal, to which he replied he had, and felt the seriousness of it.' Throughout their conversation he struck the Queen as 'dreadfully agitated and nervous'. The substance of their talk was about cabinet appointments and about Ireland. Gladstone dealt with the case of Hartington by reading the latter's note of explanation and leaving it with the Queen (who showed it to Salisbury four days later). As to Granville, Gladstone explained the painful negotiations which had led to Granville's consenting at last to take the Colonial Office.[142] Gladstone told the Queen that he had purposely kept her name entirely out of the question, 'but the feeling was so strong among all those he had consulted, that it would have been impossible for Lord Granville to have returned to the Foreign Office'. On Ireland itself, Gladstone's most significant comment was 'he might fail, it was 49 to 1, that he would, but he intended to try'.

Gladstone stayed to lunch, and resumed political discussion afterwards. He thought it would be best to give office to Chamberlain, 'though he is not quite certain of him'. At any rate,

---

* Cf. W.E.Gladstone's diary, printed Morley, iii, 291: 'except church, my day from one to eight was given to business. I got only fragmentary reading of the life of the admirable Mr Suckling and other books. At night came a painful and harassing succession of letters, and my sleep for once gave way: yet for the soul it was profitable, driving me to the hope that the strength of God might be made manifest in my weakness.'

Gladstone felt 'he would not be dangerous, and his land plan would be discussed, if it came forward'. Dilke he spoke of as impossible, an attitude from which neither he nor anyone else departed during this period.

Gladstone thought that proposals on Ireland were a matter quite independent of other radical views: thought that his present ministry would be less radical than the previous Liberal government: and himself struck the Queen as being less radical than formerly, though 'intensely in earnest, almost fanatically so, in his belief that he is almost sacrificing himself for Ireland'.[143] After Gladstone left, the Queen sent a telegram about the latest developments to Salisbury, as she had done on the previous day.[144]

He returned to London weary and harassed, had a late dinner, and spent most of the rest of the evening in interviews.[145] Spencer and Granville were waiting to see him at his house when he returned, Spencer having earlier visited Granville.

After dinner, however, Gladstone seemed none the worse for his sleepless night and strenuous day. In a long talk with E. Hamilton, 'he was in the most charming of humours and in good spirits. What had really cheered him up was Lord Granville's change of mood', though Gladstone wished Granville had taken the lord presidency rather than the colonies. Gladstone was quite satisfied with his audience at Osborne, and talked freely of the men available for his cabinet. He was outspoken about Chamberlain. 'Chamberlain was wanting in straightforwardness. He was not to be trusted. He sadly lacked public spirit. Contrast Chamberlain with a man like James.' Gladstone enlarged on the merits of James. 'That is indeed a splendid fellow and I do not see how I am to get on without him to help me in the House of Commons.' Gladstone then talked a little on the question of an autonomous Ireland making a fixed contribution to the imperial exchequer, a matter on which Gladstone had already stated some quite firm intentions in a conversation with Hamilton on 15 January. It is characteristic that Gladstone should have formed a definite financial plan for Irish autonomy, at a time when he had no definite political plan for Ireland in mind.[146]

During the day Harcourt, having been disabused of any idea that bad behaviour might win him the Woolsack by Gladstone's letter of the previous evening, returned to his normal role of everyone's friend. A visit by E. Hamilton first thing in the morning found him 'more reasonable and more complaisant': a visit a little later from John Morley found him brimming with good will. Harcourt was even ready to return to the detested Home Office, news which Hamilton telegraphed to Gladstone at Osborne. The change of mood was complete, and largely unaccountable, but it had made a Gladstone ministry possible. What the change of mood did not mean, was any conversion of Harcourt to home rule.

Late in the evening Harcourt received a note from Granville, asking him to come with Spencer to Granville's house at 11 a.m. the following day to decide appointments: Gladstone was to join them immediately after his daughter's wedding, at which the three of them were not expected to be present.[147] It was probably at this point that Harcourt definitely joined the ruling group within the party leadership.

February 2 (Tuesday). Soon after 11, Harcourt called on Granville, remaining there, with two short absences, until 6. Gladstone also called at Granville's for ten minutes, just before going to the wedding of his daughter Mary to the Rev. Harry Drew. Gladstone told the triumvirate of Granville, Spencer and Harcourt to start work on allotting cabinet places, and he would come in and consider their plans after the ceremony.[148] As he wished to keep his house free for the wedding reception, the deliberations were to take place at Granville's. Gladstone then went to the wedding, arriving with the bride at the church at 11.30. One fruit of their consultations was a note sent by Granville to Gladstone during the wedding service, that 'Harcourt, Spencer, and D. [*sc.* Lord Richard] Grosvenor agree with me in choosing Rosebery'.[149] Two points arise from this note. Firstly, Grosvenor, already a committed Unionist, was taking part, and not only momentarily, in discussions on key appointments to a cabinet committed to considering home rule. Grosvenor was indeed in constant attendance on Gladstone throughout the day. His position was unusually clear-cut: he had told Gladstone as early as late December that he could not support his Irish policy and tried to intimate that it was very unpopular in the country, but Gladstone thereupon, it was said, had turned him out of the room.[150] Secondly, Granville's relinquishment of the Foreign Office on 30 January had clearly not involved a definite decision at that time to appoint Rosebery instead. Indeed, over the weekend Gladstone had been talking of Rosebery being young for the job, and had seemed to be thinking instead of Spencer.[151]

On leaving the church after the wedding, (where he 'looked as if he had nothing in the world to do but give away a daughter')[152] Gladstone went round for ten minutes to Granville's, and then went home for the wedding breakfast. There he took the opportunity of asking West, as chairman of the inland revenue, whom he should propose as chancellor of the exchequer. West suggested Chamberlain, urging that a few weeks of official experience would soften the crudeness of his views, but Gladstone thought that the City would be terrified by his views of ransom.[153] Gladstone's query probably indicated that Harcourt, though accepted as a principal lieutenant, was not yet allotted to a particular office.

It was probably at this stage that the new collective leadership, which had been formed specifically to handle ministerial appointments (as opposed to handling Irish policy, which Gladstone in preceding days had either kept in his own hands or worked out bilaterally with Granville or Spencer) produced an early draft which ran into interesting difficulties. Ripon was to take the presidency of the council, and Spencer was to go to the Admiralty, the department he particularly coveted. But as the impossibility of making a catholic responsible for education dawned on the junta, it became a question of someone making way for Ripon: and Spencer reluctantly agreed to change places.[154]

Rosebery, who had attended Mary Gladstone's wedding, afterwards called at Carlton House Terrace and there found that Gladstone had sent for him. Gladstone was recalled from Granville's, and when he came in, at once offered Rosebery the Foreign Office. It was made clear to him that there was no alternative office available to him, apart from the Scottish Office. Rosebery asked for an hour or two to consider the offer, and Lewis Harcourt, with uncanny accuracy, reported that he had pretended to be much taken aback. Rosebery had indeed said 'it was too big a thing for me'. Later, at 3 p.m., he wrote a straightforward letter of acceptance to the premier, not saying a word about Ireland, and requesting only that he should be consulted as to the choice of under-secretary in the lower house.[155]

Rosebery dined at Brooks's with Arnold Morley, the new whip, and Munro Ferguson, all three later going with James to Covent Garden circus. At 11 p.m. Rosebery was sent for by the Prince of Wales, who knew of his appointment[156] and had lobbied for it, and then at 11.55 took the train home to Epsom.[157] Since the previous Thursday, Rosebery had seen no colleagues apart from Gladstone and Spencer, both perfunctorily, and had played no part in what was going on.

Kimberley, who had been talked of as a possible candidate for the Foreign Office, later wrote 'Rosebery I hoped would be the man. He would be the best choice that could be made... My appointment would have been received with a chorus of newspaper denunciation.'[158]

At about 4 p.m., Gladstone drove to the Foreign Office and spent quarter of an hour with Salisbury talking about the affairs of Greece and related European problems.[159] According to Salisbury's letter to the Queen, Gladstone 'questioned him minutely, carefully writing down Lord Salisbury's answers.' Afterwards Gladstone returned once more to Granville's, remaining there till 6 when the conclave finally ended, and Ponsonby arrived to collect a list of appointments for the Queen's scrutiny, and to discuss the Queen's objections to Childers. Rosebery and Ripon briefly put in an appearance during the latter part of the meeting, for what reason is not known.

Northbrook was summoned and told by Spencer that 'Mr Gladstone wished me to join'. Several positions were mentioned as available. The post that was especially pressed on him was that of lord lieutenant of Ireland: '...Northbrook is to be Viceroy, if he wants it.'[160] His was almost the first name put forward for this post, the only other suggestion traceable at this stage having been Ripon, whose appointment (as a Catholic) would have required special legislation.[161] Northbrook, in refusing, left no doubt that at this time he was relatively sympathetic to the new ministry: 'it seems inevitable that we should see whether any tolerable terms can be made with the home rulers, and I am not going into opposition to any such proposals ... I feel pretty sure Mr G has a plan in his head.'[162]

John Morley's appointment was virtually settled by correspondence during the day. Morley began by writing, summarising his own position and enclosing a speech he had made at Chelmsford on 7 January, 'the high water mark of my Irish deliverances,' with the operative sentences underlined. Morley referred to the broad agreement revealed in their conversation on Sunday, and then proposed that if his views as expressed at Chelmsford were too strong, 'I will very cheerfully lend such help as I can' without taking office.

Morley received a reply which in the circumstances amounted virtually to an acceptance by Gladstone of Morley's proposal to take office. Its interest lay rather in its determined attempt to be totally opaque:

'... I do not anticipate any difficulties of a serious nature from what you have said. In the spirit and in the main I agree. It would be too much to say I have a design to propose an Irish legislative body: for I do not sufficiently see my way as to what it would be reasonable to recommend... On the removal total or partial of the Irish members my mind is quite open... About land, I think it has a logical priority but that practically it is one with the other great members of the trilogy, social order and autonomy.'[163]

The appointment of Campbell-Bannerman to the War Office, reversing a decision of three days standing to appoint Childers, represented the most significant royal intervention in the formation of the ministry. The Prince of Wales, the Queen, and the Duke of Cambridge were all determined to stop Childers, and only to a lesser extent did they positively want Campbell-Bannerman, who was nevertheless well regarded as an administrator, an influence for sanity, and a Scot.[164] Following earlier protests from Osborne, Ponsonby was sent to see Gladstone on Tuesday evening, and reported that 'on hearing that Your Majesty would not hear of' Childers, Gladstone had given way. Arriving in London late in the evening, Ponsonby talked of little but Childers, explaining that the Queen could not now consent to his taking either of the service departments, owing to the dislike felt for him there. Gladstone 'at a great sacrifice' thereupon agreed 'to select the gentleman named by Your Majesty, Mr Campbell-Bannerman, for the War Office'. With this matter decided, they then talked about Ireland, Gladstone being emphatically negative and stressing his complete lack of commitment to any scheme.[165]

Chamberlain's appointment to the Local Government Board was settled during the day by correspondence.[166] John Morley's appointment had been settled in the same way, following one interview, so there is no reason to take the manner of the transaction, which followed two personal interviews (and a letter) with Gladstone on the previous Saturday and Sunday, as unduly slighting or neglectful. The two interviews, both on Saturday, had defined the basis on which Chamberlain was to enter the government, without settling the office he should hold. The letter, written by Chamberlain on Sunday, formally committed him to joining the ministry, in any post save that of the Admiralty. It was not till Chamberlain saw Harcourt on Monday that Chamberlain suggested the Local Government Board 'as it would give me the opportunity of preparing the measure for local government which I assumed would be the first work of the ministry'.[167]

Granville later came to regret his insistence on taking the Colonial Office on the 31st, as removing the most attractive inducement which could be offered to keep Chamberlain tied to the ministry.[168] There is no doubt that Chamberlain quite naturally and spontaneously had strong sentiments about the colonies by 1885, which were not incompatible with a routine Radical aversion to extensions of the empire of conquest. All the same, had he set his heart upon that office before February 1886, it is likely that at least his immediate circle would have known of it, and this was not the case. There is no evidence to indicate that Chamberlain wanted the Colonial Office strongly in itself, as opposed to its merits as a way of escape from the Admiralty. The Admiralty was a prison for a Radical leader: but the Colonial Office was hardly less so. In the context of Gladstone's attempt to make the consideration of home rule appear an inevitable next step to moderate propertied opinion, Chamberlain, as the most distrusted man in the country, could only expect to be given a small part to play.

Compared with most other ministers, however, Chamberlain did receive a fair amount of attention from Gladstone, when the latter's absorption in other tasks permitted. On his second Monday in office, in what was his first free moment after the formation of the ministry, Gladstone invited Chamberlain to give him 'a long exposition' of his views on Ireland on the following Saturday.[169] This was an attention which certainly set Chamberlain above other ministers.

February 3 (Wednesday). Gladstone saw Trevelyan at 10.30, Grosvenor at 11, Childers at about the same time, Ponsonby at 11.15–11.25, Wolverton 12–12.45, with Campbell-Bannerman calling for twenty minutes during Wolverton's visit, and Goschen, at about 12.45–1 p.m. Then Gladstone went on to a conclave of senior ministers at Granville's, attended by Spencer, Grosvenor, Harcourt, and Granville, which probably lasted, with fluctuating membership,[170] from 1–7.30. During the meeting, Gladstone had to leave to see Mundella very briefly, and again to talk to Ponsonby for five minutes. At 3.30, Spencer left the meeting, at which Wolverton and Shaw-Lefevre arrived a little later. It was perhaps on this occasion that Lefevre 'kindly volunteered his services to go to Ireland as a working Lord Lieutenant – a useful, not ornamental one'.[171] At 4.45 Gladstone left to see Ripon briefly, and to receive visits from the Turkish and French ambassadors. In the evening a dinner given by the Prince of Wales was attended by virtually the whole political world,[172] including Gladstone, Granville, Chamberlain, Hartington, Spencer, Churchill, Rosebery, and Salisbury.

Trevelyan called on Gladstone at 10.30 a.m., following an engagement made the previous day,[173] and accepted the Scottish Office on the spot, no letter of acceptance being written. It is impossible to trace what people were saying or thinking about Trevelyan and what office he should hold at this time, and he was probably given very little thought. He wore no particular badge: it was Morley, not Trevelyan, who had been Chamberlain's close counsellor over the previous weekend and month. However, Rosebery's reported comment that Gladstone had 'the poorest opinion' of Trevelyan, was probably soundly based.[174]

During January, Trevelyan had been engaged in a clownish

362

version of playing his cards close to his chest. He had privately taken a very hard line against the Irish in the Stratton conclave on 8 January: he had then eulogised Gladstone in a speech at Croydon in which he urged all good Liberals to sit on the fence. On 24 January he allegedly told a junior colleague that he would feel able to take office and to co-operate with Gladstone's Irish plans.[175]

Goschen called on Gladstone, for a meeting described by Morley as short, courteous, and negative. According to Morley, Goschen was actually offered office;[176] but evidence bearing on this point is scanty, though Gladstone had earlier jotted his name down as a possible chancellor of the exchequer. According to notes taken at the time, the subjects of the interview were Collings' motion and Ireland,[177] and no mention was made of taking office. Goschen was shown Hartington's letter.

A conclave of Liberal leaders met at Granville's, Harcourt again being among the inner group which dealt with appointments. Harcourt went to Granville's at 1, stayed till 5, returned to see his son for tea, and then went back to Granville's and continued work till 7.30. Grosvenor, still acting as an intermediary, reported that Wolverton did not wish to take office, although Gladstone was set on it.

The appointments of Mundella, Childers, Ripon, Kimberley, Spencer, and Lord Morley were arranged. Campbell-Bannerman accepted the War Office.[178] Sir C. Russell accepted the attorney-generalship, and Kay-Shuttleworth, in January an active opponent of home rule, took junior office[179] without demur.

Gladstone's categorical indistinctness in talking to those invited to take office came out also in his words to Lord Morley on 3 February, that 'he could not state what his scheme now was especially as to whether there should or should not be anything in the form of an independent parliament ... Many of the cabinet went no further than I did – especially Trevelyan. That complete freedom of action had been accorded to them to resign...'[180]

The lord-lieutenancy of Ireland continued to give trouble. Following tentative consideration of Ripon, and a firm refusal by Northbrook, the names of Lords Aberdeen, Camperdown, and Dalhousie were considered.[181] According to Harcourt's son, Camperdown was offered the place, but refused. There was some idea of sending Lorne and the Princess Louise, which was not assisted by Lorne's reply 'that he would be glad to do so later on if the Government went on well and a place could be found for him'.[182]

At the large dinner given by the Prince of Wales, as mentioned above, Churchill told Rosebery that he would never again assist or so far as he was able allow the Irish party to turn another ministry out. Churchill complained of being weary of work and fighting, and compared the smoothness of Rosebery's career with his own – 'all fighting, first against the Prince, then Salisbury, then Iddesleigh'. Churchill thought Gladstone as mad as a March hare, adding that the Liberals were probably in for ten years.[183]

February 4 (Thursday). Gladstone's first caller was Grosvenor, followed by Rosebery. During the morning Gladstone was feeling ill effects from the dinner of the previous evening, and Mrs Gladstone insisted on his staying indoors. The meeting of ministers at Granville's house to discuss the lord-lieutenancy was accordingly rearranged.[184] From 2.30 to about 4.30 a conference of leaders met at Gladstone's house, those present being Gladstone, Granville, Harcourt, Spencer, and Grosvenor. The meeting was clearly not just a casual one, and it is therefore the more remarkable to find that R. Grosvenor, a convinced Unionist, was present, while Rosebery and the incoming chief whip A. Morley were absent. After the meeting, Herbert Gladstone and Grosvenor left and walked across the park together.

Then Mr and Mrs Gladstone drove in an open carriage in the park for an hour. On their return, Granville arrived for a long interview. In the evening, looking very tired and worn, Gladstone dined at Algernon West's. On being told of Granville's sore feelings at being passed over for the Foreign Office, Gladstone expressed his regret in the most unguarded way: 'I am quite ready to let Lord Granville be Prime Minister, and I will be Chancellor of the Exchequer, and you may tell him so from me.' This idea had been mooted the previous Sunday by Wolverton.[185]

Certain minor appointments were arranged during the day, including those of Heneage, Marjoribanks, Flower (as junior whip)[186] and Playfair. The case of Playfair was instructive. On 3 February, he received and rapidly refused an offer of the vice-presidency of the council (i.e. of education minister for England), a post for which he was especially well fitted, not least in his own eyes. His refusal was based solely on Ireland, in which he was 'intensely interested'. Given his 'advanced views', he wished to be free to act as a 'friendly critic', rather than be restrained by the ties of office from taking part in the Irish debates.[187] Whether from guileful motives, or because at the time it was a sensible view to take, Playfair was really saying that he could not join the ministry because of his home rule inclinations. Later in the day, however, after having already been asked to call at Downing St on Thursday morning for explanations, Playfair happened to meet Gladstone at dinner at Marlborough House, where he was strongly pressed to reconsider. Granville and Spencer also pressed Playfair to change his mind. Accordingly, Playfair called on Gladstone the following day. Mrs Gladstone received him first, telling him that Playfair's refusal had made her husband 'very poorly'. Gladstone then renewed his persuasions, saying that owing to Playfair's lack of previous interest in party controversy, he could not be put in the cabinet, but 'that anyone who stood by him in this emergency had a right to look to that soon'.[188] (In the event it was Gladstone who, two months later, absolutely declined to admit Playfair to the cabinet when he was offered the Scottish Office.) Under these importunities Playfair accepted the office he had refused the previous day. Not the least remarkable feature of the episode was that Gladstone had sought to allot political responsibility for education, an area where major changes were pending and in which the electorate and House of Commons took all too much interest, by means of a purely formal two-sentence letter unaccompanied by any suggestion of an interview or any discussion of policy.

The case of Heneage showed different artifices being used to overcome the same widespread unwillingness to take office. On being offered the Duchy of Lancaster, Heneage 'demurred and proposed to go to see Lord Hartington, and Primrose [Gladstone's secretary] left the room and on coming back said that he had seen Grosvenor and he wished him to tell me that Lord Hartington had advised all his friends to join the government'.[189] As Heneage had allegedly declared against home rule the day before taking office,[190] his presence in the ministry was the best possible evidence that appointments were being made not on the basis of what men thought, but of what they might be persuaded not to say in public.

Ripon, Lorne, Cork, St Albans, Acton, Dalhousie, Carlingford, Aberdeen and Wolverton were talked of as possible viceroys of Ireland.[191] Gladstone and Granville wanted Wolverton, but Harcourt said he would leave the government at once if this were done. Spencer said pretty much the same and the office was to be pressed on Lorne again.[192] Accordingly Gladstone at once sent a telegram to the Queen seeking her approval for an offer to Lorne. The Queen replied signifying her disapproval, really on political grounds. West's impression at the time, that Wolverton had been seriously offered the post, looks unfounded in the light of other evidence.

At this point the curious case of Craig Sellar may be introduced. Sellar, an influential Whig backbencher, had written to the chief whip after the Hawarden Kite, threatening to resign the whip if a home rule bill was proposed, partly because he feared Rosebery's influence would extend it to Scotland.[193] Subsequently Sellar abstained on Collings' motion. He was then sent for by the premier (4 February) and offered a post as junior whip.[194] He was also given the refusal of the surveyorship of the ordnance. Neither offer secured him, but led to his having 'close and confidential talk with several important and influential people', from which he concluded 'the best informed people … have made up their minds that some form of home rule has become inevitable'. As an exercise in the use of inducements, the story requires no comment beyond Sellar's own after having been offered two jobs and many confidences: 'My views, I must tell you, are somewhat modified.'[195] What is far more problematical is what it meant at the level of general policy for Gladstone personally to offer a job as whip to a supposedly stalwart anti-home ruler (a position Sellar in fact returned to later in the year).

February 5 (Friday). In the morning, Harcourt, Childers and Campbell-Bannerman made early calls on Gladstone, but left almost at once for a conference at Granville's house at 11, where Gladstone joined them. Those present were Gladstone, Harcourt, Campbell-Bannerman, Childers, Fowler and Grosvenor. All left after half an hour except Harcourt, Grosvenor and Gladstone (and possibly Granville). Mundella joined them briefly, as did Wolverton who arrived at 12.30 for a few minutes. At 2.40 the conference began to break up, and Gladstone went for a drive with Granville. A special messenger left for Osborne. When Gladstone returned home, he received Fowler, Broadhurst and C. Peel, and discussed the preparation of the estimates with his whips Grosvenor and A. Morley.

It is impossible to tell what led to the appointment of Broadhurst, the first working man ever to hold office. His appointment was very well received, especially in the provincial press, and may even have assisted the initially satisfactory by-election record of the ministry. Gladstone called him an 'excellent man' and did good by stealth in smoothing over the difficulties caused for him by court dress.[196] On the other hand Gladstone indicated that 'as a matter of course' Broadhurst must let his many exertions in journalism 'fall to the ground' on taking office. Salisbury's comment was: 'The most peculiar appointment is that of Mr Henry Broadhurst… Some years ago he was a working mason. He is a man of fair, but not conspicuous ability: but he can do no harm at the Home Office.'[197]

Broadhurst, an experienced trade union administrator, did in fact match up to his job, and also worked well with his chief, Childers. Gladstone, while virtually commanding Broadhurst to take up office without time for second thoughts, placed stress on the help Broadhurst had given him in the metropolis during the Bulgarian atrocities agitation of 1876–78, when the two men had first collaborated. This version of what lay behind his appointment, given in Broadhurst's autobiography, must be regarded sceptically in view of Broadhurst's subsequent silence about his relations with Chamberlain in 1885, when he first sat for a Birmingham seat. The problem of Broadhurst has to be related to the wider problem of the sources of exceptional Liberal sensitivity to working class and social issues in early 1886. It is probable, however, that Broadhurst got this particular job because a Whig to whom it had been offered the previous day, had turned it down, and not because there was a premeditated policy about appointments for working class leaders.

Although home rule views were no passport to office (as Lefevre and Dalhousie found), Broadhurst was in fact that extreme rarity, a man who had welcomed the Hawarden Kite:

'I certainly approve of your supposed determination to settle the question of home rule... It appears that no effective public work can be done while the Irish question remains before the country... No one living is so well fitted for the task as yourself and I pray you will undertake it... Should any measure of home rule be produced I hope it may, after due safeguards, be a bold and thorough one.'[198]

After again consulting Granville, Gladstone decided to make Aberdeen lord-lieutenant. Aberdeen, a 'very charming gentle fellow' who 'called Mr G Sir and spoke to him so reverently and nicely as if he were his own grandfather',[199] accepted on the spot at an interview that very day, although he 'would very very much have preferred an undersecretaryship in the hope of earning a character'.[200] The story that Lady Aberdeen received the offer first,[201] reflected her standing as frequent hostess to the G.O.M. at Dollis Hill, just outside London, and her belief in being agreeable to Gladstone and Rosebery. Perhaps because of this, smart opinion in town looked upon the appointment as a 'feeble jest',[202] while in Scotland it 'was painful to hear with what contempt' ministers of the kirk spoke of it.[203] Spencer in effect admitted the Queen's objection that Aberdeen was 'weak, nervous, not clever' by saying this was better, as it allowed all to be left to John Morley.[204]

Edmond Wodehouse, Whig member for Bath and a cousin of Kimberley, 'ruined his political career' by rejecting offers of a junior post at the Foreign or the Colonial Office. He had already refused an appointment at the Home Office the previous day: Gladstone was 'very indignant' with him, and his Whig friends were astounded by his obstinacy. This was perhaps the only clear case in which opposition to home rule, unallied to any ulterior motive, led to someone refusing office in 1886.[205]

Salisbury went down to Osborne, where in the evening the Queen told him 'all that happened since we met last Wednesday', showed him Hartington's memorandum on Ireland written the previous Saturday, and went over the Bulgarian crisis in great detail. Salisbury took good care to make the point that the change of ministry had been 'hastened and even brought on' by Beach and Churchill, through their refusal to announce 'a decided measure of repression' in the Queen's speech.[206]

February 6 (Saturday). The Queen saw Salisbury, who said they must force the new government to speak out at once on Irish policy and that they would have to organise and encourage meetings of the loyal Irish in Ireland and England.[207] This synthetic activism in fact defined all that Salisbury studiously neglected to do in spring 1886.

The Liberal ministry, other than Gladstone, went to Osborne to take office. A courtier-like performance by Rosebery, in a long audience devoted to Balkan affairs, won him golden opinions, Rosebery having taken as his theme the need for continuity in foreign policy. The Queen, indeed, virtually offered to join in alliance with him. The House of Commons adjourned till February 18.

Gladstone wrote to Harcourt suggesting advantages in taking up the reforms of parliamentary procedure drafted by the previous ministry. If this were to be done by committee, Gladstone thought Hartington should be put in charge of the work. Gladstone also wanted Trevelyan and the lord advocate to set to work at once on the crofters' bill so that it might be dealt with before any Irish measure.[208] Before leaving London, Gladstone had also seen Grosvenor, A. Morley and Granville, with a view to settling the household offices and the surveyorship of the ordnance.

Mr and Mrs Gladstone went down to Mentmore on Saturday afternoon 'for a little rest' and remained there till Tuesday or Wednesday, though Rosebery, their host, was away on business much of the time. Their absence assisted the business of moving into Downing St, where Gladstone took up his official residence on his return.

Two of the most principled new ministers, Ripon and John Morley, dined with two or their most versatile opponents, James and Brett: the social character of politics had not been in the least affected at this time by home rule hysteria.

February 7 (Sunday). Salisbury asked Rosebery to call on him at

6 p.m. on unspecified business.[209] Rosebery had himself arranged
for the Greek ambassador to be at Mentmore on Sunday so that
he could hear at first hand that Gladstone was as strongly opposed
to Greek policy as his Conservative predecessors had been.[210]
These particular arrangements may have fallen through, for
Rosebery's diary for Sunday only noted a satisfactory conversation with Gladstone on foreign affairs. However, Rosebery and
Salisbury had already succeeded in capturing Gladstone for a
'traditionalist' policy of stability in the Balkans, maintained if
necessary principally by the employment of British naval force
against a Christian power. By 8 February the Greek government
had received Gladstone's letter announcing his adhesion to the
note sent by Salisbury, defining British action in the event of a
Greek attack on Turkey. All this was settled without the cabinet
meeting.

February 8 (*Monday*).* The work of filling up the household
appointments did not really begin till the government's second
week in office, and was left very largely to Granville, who emerged
in this context, as still a highly knowledgeable party manager where
titled nonentities were concerned. Suffield, for instance, a friend
of Spencer's, was offered the mastership of the buckhounds on
9 February by Granville, not by Gladstone, and accepted the
following day in a letter to Granville stressing his freedom to resign
at his discretion.[211] The Queen's private secretary had previously
formed the impression that the household officers generally
'accept office on the supposition that a Repeal of the Union will
not be proposed',[212] but though this indicates something of the
atmosphere at the time, it cannot be taken as a clue to Granville's
line with his flock in the Lords in February/March 1886, which is
almost entirely unascertainable.

In their second week in office, with ministers busy seeking
re-election, even friends of home rule could only define what the
ministry thought about Ireland in purely negative terms. One
extraordinary case of this was Gladstone's conversation with the
Duke of St Albans on 12 February (see below): a more authoritative
statement of uncertainty was Spencer's explanation to the Queen:

'...Mr Gladstone never had declared for Home Rule (!!?), that
it might never come to that – that the time for coercion was
past – and that he feared concessions must be made – but that

---

* During this afternoon parts of the West End were sacked by a mob: for
cabinet discussion of matters relating to this, see below, 16 and 22 Feb. For an
interesting press account of the riots, see George W. Smalley, 'The London
Riots', in his *London Letters and Some Others* (2 vols, 1890), 369–87.

it was only intended to examine into the *state* of Ireland to see what could be done... He said he [Spencer] knew nothing about him [John Morley] and the Chancellor for Ireland.'[213]

February 9 (*Tuesday*). Goschen called, apparently at his own request, to see Salisbury, to discuss, among other things, the possibility of a treaty to protect the seats of dissident Liberals from Conservative attack. Salisbury was affable enough and undertook to put the matter to his chief whip, but said that a definite break with Gladstone would be required, which Goschen admitted. Goschen himself limited the scope of his proposal to those seats where, without a Liberal split, the Conservatives had no chance. Even at this early stage, Salisbury was able to sum up the interview by saying 'Without pledging myself I gave him general hopes of an understanding.'[214] There had been little or nothing in Salisbury's immediate past to suggest that he would react relatively warmly to the idea of building a bridge for the Liberal right to cross over: after the last election he had written 'I wish our friends in Edinburgh had taken my advice and run a candidate against Goschen: they might have got a seat.'[215]

Unionist militants, as opposed to those Conservatives who thought in party terms, were, for subjective reasons, greatly over-estimating the need for specific and urgent activity, although it was obvious that no developments could take place for some time. It was in this mood of exaltation that the Queen had told the infirm and aged Lord Cranbrook at the weekend 'We must agitate – I do not like agitation but we must agitate every place small as well as large and make people understand.'[216]

February 12 (*Friday*). The Duke of St Albans called on Gladstone at 3.30 to discuss the offer of a court appointment to his wife. He declined the appointment, ostensibly on non-political, but really on Irish grounds:[217] but the conversation at the interview was really how Gladstone rationalised his Irish policy at that time. Gladstone's account of the discussion ran 'I ... said all would be free to accept or reject our results, but said we had a moral claim on persons interested in Ireland and desirous of an amendment there. This he rather admitted.'[218] Less predictable was the Duke's impression of what had passed, in a letter to Goschen:

'Your arguments would have more force with me if it were not that I have still ringing in my ears a conversation I had last week with Mr Gladstone in which he assured me there was no question of Home Rule. That he did not believe it could be carried in the cabinet, and that as regards himself though he had never been against home rule, which it is difficult to define, yet he had never made up his mind to propose it, and he doubted it being carried in the cabinet. He added "I wish everyone to know this. Pray make no secret" (in reply to my saying that, of course, I should not mention the matter) ... I believe at this moment Gladstone is quite likely to go to the country on an anti-home rule cry as on a home rule one...'[219]

St Albans felt himself ill used by fate, because at heart he was 'as strong a Liberal or even Radical[220] as ever' and had nothing but contempt for the Tories, especially Churchill, under whom 'the law of the League reigned in Ireland'. Yet he was not impressed by Gladstone's citation of Spencer as an authority: 'as a politician and a man he is weakness of the weak'.[221] His own panacea for Ireland was government studs for stallions, bulls, and rams!

February 13 (*Saturday*). Chamberlain saw Gladstone at Downing St[222] following the latter's request on Monday for a 'long exposition' of Chamberlain's views on Ireland. Chamberlain urged him to deal first with Irish land, and then with education and municipal and county government. Gladstone then asked how the land question should be solved. Chamberlain never having given exact form to his thoughts on the subject, Gladstone urged him to draw up a memorandum for circulation to the cabinet.

Chamberlain's plan, into which he threw himself with some enthusiasm, was shelved without ever having been discussed. The essence of Chamberlain's scheme was to make available a sum of at most £40m. for the purchase of holdings under thirty acres, with the civil police being placed under the control of elected county councils. The Royal Irish Constabulary would become a para-military garrison, taking the place of units of the army then stationed in Ireland, which could be withdrawn.[223]

Harcourt called on Rosebery at noon to announce his impending resignation,[224] presumably over budgetary differences with the service departments. Despite lack of direct evidence on the point, it must be assumed that Chamberlain knew of this, and that his rapprochement with Gladstone in mid-February probably owed something to hopes of replacing Harcourt as Gladstone's indispensable ally in the Commons. It is also likely that Gladstone's wooing of Chamberlain, soon to be abruptly discontinued as the Harcourt crisis subsided, owed something to the need to isolate Harcourt. It should be noted that had Chamberlain made common cause with Harcourt at this time, the two in alliance could at least have brought Gladstone's ministry to a sharp end, with unforeseeable consequences, had that been what they wanted. They could have stopped home rule in its Gladstonian form, without committing themselves to any view on Ireland. What prevented this happening, apart from the difficulty of seeing where it ultimately led, was almost certainly that Chamberlain wanted Harcourt's job, and was prepared, just as Harcourt was, to swallow the unpalatable provided it gave him the lieutenancy in the Commons.

In the evening Rosebery gave a dinner at Greenwich for the new 'Labour' M.Ps in the Liberal party. Gladstone, John Morley, and Chamberlain were among the guests invited to meet the working men M.Ps. Rosebery sat at the head of the table, between Broadhurst and Chamberlain. Gladstone sat next to Broadhurst. 'The dinner was the most jovial I ever remember', wrote Broadhurst, 'politics were abandoned and the feature of the evening was the telling of good stories by our host, Mr Gladstone, and Mr Morley.' The miners' M.P, W. Abraham, contributed to the entertainment by singing *Men of Harlech*, and another song in Welsh. Chamberlain, in good humour after his interview with Gladstone, spoke very freely to Rosebery about his wish to take the Exchequer, but said that he had only asked Gladstone for the Colonies. Chamberlain said he had advised Dilke 'to go through the session quietly, and in two years all will be forgot', but Rosebery thought Dilke's failure to go into the witness box gave grounds for objection.

Gladstone was in sparkling form, reminiscing as always of the parliamentary scene of earlier days. He recalled how when Palmerston became a practised sleeper on the frontbench, his head would move backwards and forwards to such a degree as to distract and even alarm the Speaker. At the close of the session, therefore, the Speaker privately gave orders for the reconstruction of the two frontbenches to a height which gave adequate rest for dozing heads, a luxury which the rest of the House did not enjoy.[225]

February 15 (*Monday*). The first cabinet council of the new ministry took place at Downing St, 2.30-5-45, all its members being present. Before the meeting, Morley had an interview lasting about an hour with Gladstone. The questions considered included the handling of the adjourned debate on the Address, due to recommence on Thursday: the appointment of a committee of both Houses, as contemplated by the previous ministry, to consider the working of the India Government Act; the possible setting up of a committee of the House of Commons on procedure; the choice of chairmen for these committes: a new crofters' bill, which it was decided Trevelyan should introduce; and the naval and military estimates.

As regards the Address, the cabinet decided to present so much of it as had already been considered, while simply waiving its original closing paragraphs as inapplicable to the changed situation.

The cabinet decided to try to prevent the defence estimates exceeding £30m.: as Harcourt understood it, they should be 'brought down to the level of those of 1885–86 or thereabouts'.[226]

Lewis Harcourt interpreted this as a decision not to exceed the expenditure of the previous year on defence. According to his journal, Campbell-Bannerman took this well, but Ripon was 'rather cross'. In the middle of the discussion Harcourt threw a note across the table to Chamberlain, 'Why the devil don't you support me in this?' Chamberlain wrote back, 'I saw you were getting on swimmingly so I seized the opportunity to take a short but refreshing nap.' Lewis Harcourt also reported a remark by Rosebery to the effect that he hoped to keep Gladstone fully occupied with Irish affairs, and was not consulting him at all in what he did in foreign affairs.[227]

According to *The Times*, British policy in eastern Europe was explained by Rosebery. Gladstone in his somewhat bare report to the Queen did not refer to this, but an item in his cabinet jottings for this day runs, '5. Greece and the Balkans'. *The Times* also reported that a committee of the cabinet was set up to frame legislation on Ireland, but this point figured neither in Gladstone's report to the Queen nor in his notes, and nothing so definite as a formal Irish committee of the cabinet can be traced in February 1886.

The very early introduction of several other bills was considered. These probably concerned Welsh intermediate education, railway rates, Scottish universities, and Osborne Morgan's bill on burials.

Other subjects which figure in Gladstone's notes for this Cabinet, but are not confirmed elsewhere, are the future of the title of lord privy seal: the state of the facts as to order in Ireland:* a decision to go into committee of supply at the earliest moment; that Gladstone should propose a committee on procedure, and ask Whitbread or Goschen to be its chairman: and the need to make some pronouncement on Burma. Some of these topics may have been partly or wholly held over for future consideration.

Rosebery gave dinner to Chamberlain, along with some other, rather minor figures. Chamberlain 'talked for two hours about

---

* That this item was on the agenda is indirectly confirmed by a letter from Gladstone to Spencer of 13 Feb., asking him and Morley 'to have the most salient facts as to the social state of Ireland ready for notice in the cabinet on Monday' (44313 f. 33). Morley spent all afternoon on 13 Feb. going over the details of Irish unrest with the law advisers (Morley to Spence Watson, 13 Feb., Spence Watson MSS).

peace, and China, and getting contracts for £500 millions of railways there'.[228]

February 16 (*Tuesday*). The full cabinet met at Downing St from 12 to 2.30. The first item was Burma, on which Dufferin had sent telegrams requiring prompt reply. Kimberley and Ripon spoke for recognising the annexation (made 1 January), Ripon doing so against his earlier opinion. The cabinet agreed, and notice was sent to Dufferin and to the foreign powers accordingly. Though there is no direct evidence as to the cabinet having been consulted, it is probable that this meeting also took an important new decision in Burmese policy, presumably without much time for discussion, as well as ratifying the status quo of formal annexation. The viceroy had proposed (13 February) the assumption of direct rule in Burma in view of the power vacuum there, this being somewhat against his own and Churchill's professed earlier leanings to maintaining some form of indirect rule. The viceroy was on the spot in Burma at the time and his advice must have appeared incontrovertible, for on 16 February Kimberley sent a telegram sanctioning the viceroy's proposals. Apart from the usual point that the cabinet, if it settled this matter at all, must have settled it in very few minutes and with little debate, the political point to be made is that those politicians in the cabinet who might have exploited Little England issues (gunboat diplomacy in Greece, military rule in Burma, and the budget controversy) to escape honourably and ambiguously from a sinking ship in February 1886, did not in fact use these issues as they might have used them a year earlier. With Hartington not in the ministry, there was now no scope for a dissident Little England cave to the left of the Gladstonian régime: any challenge to Gladstone had to gain its support from the right alone. Gladstone and his followers, without being very left or very impressive, had nevertheless in early 1886 managed to accommodate the new Radicalism under their aegis in a way which had escaped them in 1880–85.

Rosebery informed the cabinet of developments since 30 January with respect to Greece and the Greek fleet. Rosebery's statement was accepted by the cabinet, Chamberlain and Morley dissenting but acquiescing. According to one source 'Chamberlain protested and said that nothing but the extreme importance of other affairs would have prevented him from resigning.'[229] Gladstone thought that his cabinet would in any case have adopted Salisbury's policy, independently of any question of past commitments.

The cabinet considered Egyptian frontier defence and the views on Egypt of Wolseley and Wolff, but the papers available being still incomplete, and Baring's opinion not yet known, the discussion was closed without a decision being reached. The whole question of policy in the Nile valley was still so open that Harcourt for instance, found it necessary on 17 and 19 February to press Campbell-Bannerman to 'put an end to the cherished project of reoccupying Dongola and the Sudan' and thus hold the Egyptian frontier with 5,000 rather than 20,000 troops.[230] Harcourt was not simply pressing economies *in vacuo*, but was resisting clear cut proposals[231] put forward by Wolseley and other officers for using the victory at Ginniss to reoccupy the province of Dongola with a semi-autonomous Muslim army under Djawdat Bey.

The cabinet decided that the office of lord privy seal, which no longer carried a salary, should be held by the first lord of the treasury, rather than, as Gladstone wished, by the senior secretary of state.

Gladstone made a note that 'Chamberlain mentioned his evidence of a cheque of Lord Salisbury for £25 to Peters [word illegible] of Kelly.' Peters and Kelly were spurious working class agitators who had served the Conservatives at previous general elections, especially in connexion with the sugar bounties question.[232] Chamberlain was trying to establish a Tory connexion with the West End riots of 8 February.

In the evening Granville entertained some colonial premiers and other worthies. When all were gone, he drew Rosebery aside and asked 'Now tell me, who *are* my guests?'

February 17 (*Wednesday*). Gladstone and Spencer saw the Queen. The former, whom the Queen thought looked ill, expressed himself against any great alteration in the metropolitan police as a consequence of the West End riots.

At a private dinner of the Devonshire Club, Chamberlain 'made a strong speech in favour of Heneage's formula – "One Law, One Administration, One Parliament"!'[233] This new slogan neatly encapsulated Radical aversion to coercion, to Dublin Castle, and to the Parnellites.

The Irish hierarchy met in Dublin to consider Gladstone's appeal to Ireland for an expression of its views, made in a letter to Lord de Vesci, president of the Irish Loyal and Patriotic Union, published in *The Times* on 16 February. They passed a series of resolutions which Spencer called 'an important document ... moderate and conciliatory in tone'. The bishops called for home rule, while stressing that this meant devolution rather than separation: for the buying out of the landlords as a whole, with re-letting at a much reduced rent: and, in the short term, a public works programme in the poorest districts, and an interim suspension of evictions. Similar resolutions, received from Dublin corporation, were also moderate by previous standards.[234]

At some point during the day Chamberlain and Spencer called on Gladstone. The subject of their discussion is not recorded.[235]

February 18 (*Thursday*). Both Houses resumed sitting.

February 22 (*Monday*). The full cabinet met at Downing St at 2. On Wolff's mission, the first item, Gladstone noted that 'waiting information, we do not interfere'.

The cabinet accepted Rosebery's proposal issued by the Italians to blockade the Greek fleet if necessary to prevent it attacking Turkey. Rosebery added that the Sultan, mainly in response to British views, had dropped the mutual aid clause of his agreement with Bulgaria. The cabinet also considered that the Prince of Bulgaria should be nominated, without any limit of time, governor of Eastern Rumelia.

The cabinet decided to bring in a bill to allow compensation for the West End riots to be met from the metropolitan police rate.

The new crofters' bill prepared by Trevelyan and the lord advocate was accepted in general, including important additions to the Liberal bill of the previous year, but some details stood over for further consideration. The work had probably been already largely done outside the cabinet, for on Saturday Trevelyan had asked Rosebery, on behalf of himself and the lord advocate, for a meeting at the Scottish Office any time on Sunday or Monday before the cabinet, urging that 'Mr Gladstone wants those of us who are interested to settle it as far as possible beforehand.'[236]

The background to the urgency of ministers lay in backbench pressure. On 12 January the crofter M.Ps had met and decided on an amendment to the Address urging the government to suspend rents in the Highlands until land legislation had been passed. This threat did not disappear when the Liberals came in, and indeed the inconvenience of such a divisive amendment, obliging ministers to appear to be against immediate remedies, was felt all the more sharply as it could, as a side effect, divide the Irish from the ministry. On 15 February Harcourt wrote to Gladstone of the danger that Macfarlane, a crofters' leader, and William O'Brien, for the Irish, might insist on going ahead with their amendments, already on the paper, on the Scottish and Irish land questions,[237] and thus start a possible 'peasants' revolt' on the left of the Liberal-Irish alliance. It was probably Harcourt's prompting of Gladstone on tactical and procedural grounds that led the latter to write hurrying up Trevelyan and Rosebery. On the other hand, it is of note that Gladstone was showing no signs of unwillingness to be politically identified with, and to give substantive help to, the collectivist social reforms the new parliament was supposed to want.

These accidents of business gave Rosebery a much clearer picture of Trevelyan than before, and deeply impressed him with the latter's vanity, which he had never suspected. When a question came up in cabinet, Trevelyan said about three sentences, then added 'This is a subject upon which no one knows more, or to which no one has directed more attention than I have.' A little later on the same day, on another perfectly different matter, he used the same phrase, though Rosebery was sure that in both cases Trevelyan knew no more about it than he did himself.[238]

During the cabinet of 22 February, notes passed between Gladstone and Harcourt on a matter apparently not under discussion, namely the reduction of the service estimates as supposedly settled in cabinet on 15 February. Asked by Gladstone to settle the details outside the cabinet in conference with the service ministers, Harcourt replied that they had already met and disagreed,[239] and that Gladstone's authoritative intervention was needed. Gladstone thought Childers should mediate[240] and this was in fact what happened. The following day Childers wrote to Harcourt to point out that no threat of resignation could secure cuts in estimates of £2m.[241] The question was eventually settled in a routine manner, by a compromise announced at the next cabinet,[242] but it left Harcourt at this early stage bereft of an independent role as a great economising chancellor, and with no other part to play but that of party gladiator.

At Belfast, Churchill addressed a large Unionist meeting with restraint and responsibility. His message was that Ulster need not fight, but should leave matters to the policitians. *

February 24 (Wednesday). In the evening, Gladstone called on Rosebery to reveal the state of his mind on Ireland. 'Gladstone began to expand his Irish plan, with which he said he did not trouble me as he knew how busy I was, and that he was acting within the scope of what he knew to be my ideas. I implored him to spare me. But when he sketched a vast skeleton, I could not resist saying slyly "Is it six or seven years since you told me you had lost all power of constructive legislation?" Mr G could not help chuckling.'

Also after dinner, Rosebery received a call from Harcourt, who again announced his resignation.[243]

February 25 (Thursday). The full cabinet met at Downing St from

---

* On 27 Jan. Churchill had gone to Saunderson, the leader of the Ulster Unionists, and placed himself at his disposal for a meeting in Belfast whenever Saunderson thought necessary (Saunderson MSS).

2 to 3.30: Rosebery called it 'good-humoured and short for the first time in his experience'.[244]

The cabinet agreed to the leading proposals of the crofters' bill, including one restricting the compulsory provision of leases for hill pastures to a landlord's existing tenants. The bill finally became law on 3 June (the first legislation ever to deal with the subject) after being given a rough ride by the crofters' M.P.s, who voted against its third reading.

The women's suffrage bill, expected the following week, was to be treated as an open question, though most ministers as individuals were probably against it.

The vote for the expenses of Wolff's mission in the east was also imminent. The cabinet therefore agreed to support the vote while reserving judgement on his policy.

Despite cuts, Harcourt had still to report a £1m. increase in the defence estimates, which the cabinet reluctantly accepted as unavoidable.

February 28 (*Sunday*). Bryce, talking to Sidgwick at an Oxford dinner, gave the impression of enjoying his work at the Foreign Office, where the arrangement was that he had special responsibility for commercial affairs, as well as being free to make suggestions on anything else that interested him. (In fact Rosebery had assured the Queen that he would make Bryce write down every word he was to say, and say nothing on his own account.)[245] In a further conversation on 3 April, Sidgwick found Bryce looking forward cheerfully to a life of literary leisure. His detachment followed from his view of the case for home rule, as he presented it to Sidgwick on 7 May. His chief argument then was that the Democracy would not coerce, and therefore home rule must come in the end: so it was better to give it at once quickly.[246]

March 1 (*Monday*). Gladstone published a letter to Lord de Vesci, chairman of the Irish Loyal and Patriotic Union, inviting opinions from everybody interested in the Irish problem. At this point there was a strong feeling in certain Liberal circles that he intended to proceed by resolutions and not a bill.[247]

March 4 (*Thursday*). The former Irish attorney-general, Hugh Holmes, was, in his own later words, 'obliged against my will to move an absurd and absolutely futile amendment on going into committee of supply, in the hope of inducing the Prime Minister to show his hand'. All that was shown, in fact, was how far Gladstone, who dominated the debate and pleased his followers without giving any clues as to his policy, had regained the parliamentary supremacy he had lost during the previous year. The motion, a refusal of supply on the grounds of the disturbed state of

378

Ireland, which had been drafted by Beach, Smith, Churchill, and Holmes, gained little more than neutrality from Salisbury: but Churchill's eagerness for conflict forced it forward, despite growing misgivings on the part of Beach* and Holmes. The effect of Holmes' intervention was to enable Gladstone to demonstrate, by a vote of 364 to 204, that the Liberals could act as a united party.[248]

Holmes' motion gave Hartington the pleasure of attacking Churchill's wanton partisanship: 'I will not be a party to any attempt to prejudge the policy of the government by agitation of a political or sectarian character.'[249] Hartington's loftiness of principle was very necessary, as his immediate object was to come to an understanding with Bright.[250] In so far as Tory blundering on this occasion made the dissident Liberals realise that their only hope lay in their remaining a party of strong Liberal principle, the fiasco ultimately assisted the Unionist cause.

March 5 (Friday). Gladstone and Granville went to Windsor, the latter to present the Sultan of Johore, the former to talk 'of various things'. The Queen, inevitably, felt that Gladstone looked very worn.[251]

Gladstone had no sooner arrived back from Windsor, after what he described as a pleasant audience, than an angry letter arrived from the Queen about Labouchere's resolution attacking the House of Lords, which had been defeated by only 36 votes earlier that afternoon. Though on the point of going to lie down (at 6 p.m.!) Gladstone immediately set to work and wrote four and a half pages pacifying his sovereign.[252]

Gladstone circulated a minute to the cabinet, in which he entirely denied an appended news agency report that his policy on Ireland was now virtually settled, and that rough drafts of it had been shown to certain ministers. Gladstone wrote '...I hope we shall first consider the question of Irish land. I have circulated a paper on this subject by Chamberlain. Another paper has been prepared and on Wednesday [3 March] was placed in the hands of Sir Henry Thring to consider the method of shaping it into a bill...' In corroboration of this, Morley wrote on 7 March to

---

* Beach wrote 'I do not like reversals of policy', but reversed policy none the less on the ground that Churchill was 'wild for an Irish row'. Churchill afterwards tried to argue, unconvincingly, 'that what is called "our tactical blunder" was perfectly right'. The attitude of the Tory leadership to the debate showed that a belief in lying low for so long as possible had become the central piece of conventional wisdom in the party's thinking on home rule. Goschen, in bed with a cold at the time, was 'extremely uneasy' about the motion, hoping 'there will be no division for I do not think any Liberal will vote with Holmes' (Goschen to Salisbury, 4 Mar., Salisbury MSS).

Chamberlain 'It is impossible that I should have said that "a scheme had been prepared" for I know it had not.'[253]

Mrs Tennant, widow of a former Liberal M.P. for Glamorgan, and her daughter Dorothy attended a dinner party for the Gladstones given by Sir Charles Forster. Other guests included Childers, Sir Charles Russell, and Dr Vaughan, the former headmaster of Harrow. Miss Tennant, who had not seen Gladstone for over a month, thought he seemed 'more full of life and energy' than ever, and in truly magnificent form, as she recorded in her diary. Gladstone spoke first of Disraeli's early speeches for which he professed to have a high regard, and then of the Act of Union. On this latter subject he became very heated, saying 'I will not make a speech on the Union' and he brought his fist down on the table. 'No! I never will, for it is too terrible an indictment against England.' 'But you *will have* to speak on the Union', interposed the attorney-general. 'I may be obliged to allude to it,' replied Gladstone, 'to say a word or two on the subject, but I will *never* make a speech on the Union. *Never!*' Following this outburst, Gladstone derided the Conservatives, in equally vehement terms, for treating Ireland solely from the point of party advantage. 'He talked with amusement of Lord Randolph Churchill and his "convictions". He said Lord Randolph cared nothing for Ireland, or for the Empire, that he only talked and felt nothing. He then said that he happened to *know* as a fact that Lord Randolph, Lord Ashbourne, and Lord Carnarvon had prepared a scheme of home rule, that Lord Salisbury knew of the scheme, and that those Conservatives who now will, in all probability, make the greatest outcry against home rule, were prepared to go to great lengths in that direction themselves.' On a calmer note, Gladstone mentioned that he would like to find some way of paying a salary to certain working-class M.Ps though without carrying the principle very far. He said: 'I object to the general payment of all members. It would alter the whole tone of the House of Commons, but one might make exceptions – make a kind of test, that if a man's income was as low, say as Mr Burt's, he should have a sufficient grant from the state.'[254]

March 6 (Saturday). Spencer entertained all his cabinet colleagues to dinner, except for Trevelyan. Gladstone sat between his host and Rosebery, and declared the fog 'did him no harm'.

March 7 (Sunday). After returning from St Margaret's, Westminster, in the fog, Gladstone felt unwell. Sir A. Clark was summoned and ordered him to bed, but diagnosed nothing worse than a cough and cold. Mrs Gladstone was jubilant at the prospect of nursing her husband.[255]

In the afternoon Chamberlain visited the Courtneys. He made it clear that he was biding his time pending Gladstone's proposals, and gave as an additional sign the absence of any sign of what the electorate wanted. 'The caucus is public opinion' he said, and 'if you ask me what public opinion will do, I tell you frankly that for once I don't know'. Referring to the newly elected parliament, he said it was 'thoroughly good, businesslike, as well as immensely Radical'.[256] Chamberlain's mood of apparent indecision in this conversation must be seen as in strange contrast to his intransigence on the same question in cabinet on 13 March.

March 8 (Monday). The cabinet met at Downing St, 2.30–4: Spencer and Childers were absent at Windsor, and Gladstone was in bed with a cold, which troubled him until the end of the week. (The cold went to his chest and even on Wednesday, when he appeared much better and tackled 'some headwork with figures', he remained in his bedroom and had lunch on a tray).[257] Granville visited Gladstone before the meeting. During the meeting, Rosebery went to the Foreign Office for a short time, then returned.

The cabinet dealt first with military problems in Egypt. It was decided not to attempt to reoccupy Dongola: that the Egyptians should hold Wadi Halfa: that Aswan was to be strongly held by British forces, and the Nile controlled by steamer. Six battalions were to be brought home as quickly as possible. Despite the onset of the hot season, this order to withdraw did not reach the officer commanding at Wadi Halfa, till 23 March. The decision marked a final settlement in favour of a purely defensive policy on the Nile.[258]

Rosebery raised the question of Greece, whose fleet, according to the Greek minister, was under orders not to act against Turkey. There remained the question of Greek land action, which Rosebery suggested might be met either by breaking off diplomatic relations, or by a declaration of neutrality. Without information on Greek mobilisation, the cabinet thought a decision premature, and agreed that Rosebery should telegraph Bismarck.

The cabinet agreed with Gladstone's suggestion that Harcourt should speak for him in the Welsh Church disestablishment debate. Some discussion arose as to the line to be taken, and Harcourt was asked to consult Gladstone. Some House of Commons ministers said that they could not vote against disestablishment and must be allowed to abstain.[259]

March 10 (Wednesday). The Queen received from Gladstone 'a sketch of his home rule and land measures'.[260] This was an advance copy of his memorandum of 11 March.[261]

Bright went to see Hartington at the latter's request and talked for an hour on Ireland, on which Bright thought him 'very reasonable'. Hartington wished Bright to see Goschen as to their common difficulties.

Thirty-three Scottish M.Ps met in the Commons at 4 as a result of an invitation from the crofters' party, who, together with several Radicals, proposed the setting up of an independent Scottish party with its own whip and a strict code of discipline. The majority of those present, including some Whigs, would however only agree to occasional meetings to which all Scottish members should be asked, to discuss only Scottish questions. A committee of five was appointed to urge Trevelyan to consult Scottish M.Ps about contemplated Scottish measures.[262]

Trevelyan asked Albert Grey, M.P, 'to walk away with him from the House yesterday ... I have not exchanged a single word with him since he took office. He spoke to me with great freedom and absence of reserve... He denounced in the strongest language those Liberals who had turned round on their former convictions and become home rulers, denied that there was any reason to suppose that the leaders of the Liberal party were in favour of home rule, pointed out that all his colleagues were last July strongly opposed to home rule, that nothing had as yet taken place to justify us in the supposition that they had changed their opinions, that he did not know of any home ruler in the cabinet except John Morley, and that he knew no more than I know of Gladstone's plans, etc. etc.'[263]

March 12 (*Friday*). Gladstone asked Spencer and Morley to call, which they proposed to do at 2.30, to work over points preliminary to Saturday's cabinet. According to Gladstone's notes, the points for deliberation were:[264]

'1. As to confining Bill to first option.
2. As to communication with Nationalists.
3. As to cabinet committee on Irish govt – agree or no.'

Gladstone gave a dinner attended by Lord Northbourne and his son, by Admiral Egerton, by Sir Charles Forster (one of the premier's regular dinner-table choices) and by John Bright, who noted that Gladstone now looked 'much better'. Gladstone took Bright on one side to test his reaction to his Irish proposals. As he put it, his main concern was to settle the land question, a matter that at one time had been close to Bright's heart. On this occasion, however, the roles of 1870 were reversed, and Bright merely said that Irish land 'ought *now* to be considered as settled'. On home rule, Gladstone found Bright entirely in favour of removing the Irish from Westminster.

Northbourne took Bright home and expounded his pet theory of turning Belfast into a Free City, a notion with which Bright had little patience.[265]

March 13 (Saturday). The cabinet met at Downing St, 2–5.30. Though Gladstone was visited by his doctor before the meeting in order to get permission to leave the sickroom he found that after the cabinet he had to cancel his engagement to dine with the French ambassador.

The idea of a Royal Commission on currency and banking, to review *inter alia* the working of the Bank Charter Act of 1844 and the question of bimetallism, was favourably considered.

The subject of the Channel tunnel arose, the only evidence being a note by Gladstone, 'continue on previous tunnel'.[266]

The third item was a new measure of Irish land purchase. Here Gladstone's letter to the Queen diverges in emphasis from his cabinet notes. The letter states:

'Mr Gladstone introduced to the notice of the cabinet the printed suggestions with regard to land in Ireland of which a copy has been sent to Your Majesty; with some further development in particulars. The cabinet considered to some extent the nature and bearing of these proposals, and also the nature of the authority in Ireland required and qualified to work them with a view to the relief of the landlords, the extended creation of a small proprietary, and the general benefit of Ireland. But the subject was too large and fresh to admit of being at once decisively handled, and, after some days for reflection, it is proposed to resume it on Tuesday next.'[267]

According to Gladstone's rough notes, Gladstone, while explaining his views on Irish land purchase, was criticised by Chamberlain, who was the first to open the subject of home rule. The latter said 'he did not object to an Irish parliament provided it did not legislate, nor to coercion if necessary and H. of C. had sufficient persistence'.[268] Kimberley and others then entered the discussion. Gladstone stated his view that there should be an Irish authority for legislative purposes.

Spencer, Morley, Granville, Campbell-Bannerman, Mundella, Rosebery, Ripon and Childers were all in turn favourable to this view.

Gladstone noted that 'the Chancellor' expressed reservations. By this, Harcourt rather than Herschell is probably intended, though both were unenthusiastic about Gladstone's Irish policy.

Harcourt had written to Gladstone on 7 March outlining his misgivings about the Irish government proposals, especially about the possible occasional readmission of Irish members to Westminster,[269] calling exclusion of the Irish a *sine qua non*. On 20 March he endorsed a memorandum criticising the land proposals.[270] During the cabinet, Gladstone slipped a note across the table to Harcourt saying 'I will tell you afterwards my reasons as to silence on the machinery.'

Gladstone announced two points to be considered at the next cabinet:

'1. Years' purchase, and 84–5 rental as basis.
2. How far to press duality.'[271]

Sir Henry James was told at the time by one who was present at this meeting 'that Chamberlain's manner was almost brutal, and that before [Gladstone] could make any statement Chamberlain demanded a prefatory declaration against any scheme of independent legislature. This [Gladstone] of course objected to, and said that his plans must be considered in succession as he submitted them for consideration. Through the rest of the cabinet meeting [Chamberlain] remained almost in silence. An adjournment took place till Tuesday the 16th, but on the Sunday Chamberlain wrote a long letter (with, I believe, the concurrence of Trevelyan) informing [Gladstone] that he dissented from his proposals and tendering his resignation.'*

March 14 (Sunday). Gladstone postponed the cabinet arranged for Tuesday the 16th, to give further time for the drafting of the land bill and to consider possibilities for the nature of the authority in Ireland.

Gladstone had recovered sufficiently from his cold and bronchial catarrh of the previous week to attend the Chapel Royal, but later in the day his doctor again visited him.

March 15 (Monday). Trevelyan sent in his letter of resignation. Gladstone replied that when the Irish proposals became 'definite ...

---

* Lord Askwith, *Lord James of Hereford* (1930), 171–2. James misdated the cabinet of the 13th as occurring on Saturday the 10th. Dilke's possibly contemporary account ran 'On the 13th Mar. there was a cabinet, an account of which I had from Chamberlain who was consulting me daily as to his position. Mr Gladstone expounded his land proposals which ran to 120 millions of loan, and on which Chamberlain wrote "As a result of yesterday's Council I think Trevelyan and I will be out on Tuesday"' (43940 f. 128). The letters of resignation were actually dated Monday, 15 Mar. After the Saturday cabinet Chamberlain went home to Birmingham, returning to London on the Monday after having talked to a large number of local Liberal leaders, and having leaked his resignation to the *Birmingham Post*.

realities', not 'views and leanings', then he might be justified in resigning. 'But I am confident that the time has not come for such a step.' Trevelyan replied, very late on the same day, agreeing to delay his resignation.[272]

Chamberlain's letter of resignation[273] drew Gladstone to expostulate:

'Of what I may propose on Irish Govt you know little but shreds and patches: even the paper on land was not definite... It has been absolutely beyond my powers, though I have worked as hard as my age permits, to fashion a plan of Irish government.'[274]

The box containing the two resignations was brought in to Gladstone at 8 p.m. and 'a great consultation' then took place, those attending not being named. Afterwards the Gladstones dined with Donald Currie, a Scottish M.P. who as usual had not invited any other guests, much to Mrs Gladstone's disgust. According to the same authority, Trevelyan was cracking under the strain of running the Scottish Office, as he had before as Irish secretary. Unable to sleep, he was 'wretched, quite wretched'.[275]

March 16 (*Tuesday*). George Howard entertained John Morley, John Bright, Wilfrid Blunt, Henry James the novelist, Lady Airlie, and Ponsonby. Inevitably there was 'much talk on Ireland and Mr Gladstone's supposed plans',[276] and the dinner may well have been an inspired one designed to capture Bright for the Gladstonians. If so, the plan misfired. Bright inveighed against the bombardment of Alexandria in 1882, then took Blunt aside for an hour to talk about the Parnellites, whom he thought 'scoundrels who ought to be strung up'. He had not forgotten Irish abuse of him in 1880–82, especially that of T.P.O'Connor 'who had contradicted him flatly, called him names and jeered at him when he spoke'. Morley talked to Blunt of Gladstone's determination to stand or fall by his land bill. He described the old man as he had seen him that morning, figuring up the sums of his Irish arithmetic just like a boy at school, his grandchildren making a hideous noise on the piano in the neighbouring room, but himself all serene and cheerful.[277]

March 17 (*Wednesday*). A letter of this date showed that Gladstone had placed in the hands of Spencer and Granville the task of mediating with Chamberlain, although Spencer thought Gladstone himself ought to see Chamberlain.[278]

In the evening Gladstone went to a party given by Stuart Rendel, the self-appointed leader of the Welsh Liberals who was soon to become Gladstone's bosom friend. The party, held at 4 Whitehall Gardens at 8, was chiefly for Gladstone to meet the Welsh Liberal members, but he also made himself agreeable to a newly elected young English backbencher, Alfred Pease. Two Welsh harpers in national costume entertained the guests.[279]

At the same time Rosebery gave a male dinner to thirty guests of very varied political opinions. Derby was there, 'very frank in his disapproval of the government', as was John Bright, who insisted that if he were in Chamberlain's place he would resign. Bright and Chamberlain in a long conversation on this issue earlier in the day had found themselves of one mind. Other guests included C. Villiers, the aged Anti-Corn Law leader, still an M.P, and the young Milner, but the party really centred on the Scottish M.Ps who were present. For much of the evening conversation revolved around a bill unsuccessfully introduced into parliament by R. B. Finlay, the Liberal member for the Inverness Burghs and later a lord chancellor. He was 'rather the hero of the evening', everyone praising his speech on the second reading earlier in the day. Finlay's bill had aimed to reconstruct the Established Church of Scotland so that Presbyterians outside it could return to the fold. The government was supposed to be neutral on the issue, but Trevelyan, perhaps for constituency reasons, had rallied opponents to the bill, led by Scottish Radicals, with a fighting speech which was felt to have turned the day, the voting being 202 to 177. Significantly, the Parnellites voted against the bill, not from any strong views on Scottish church reunion, but as a calculated attempt to win good will for home rule. As Milner said, 'the nationalists are already setting up a claim to the gratitude of Scotch radicals on the strength of the help given them' on this occasion.[280]

March 18 (*Thursday*). Granville, John Morley and Spencer were asked to Gladstone's room in the House of Commons at 5.30 for a discussion.[281] They were probably well aware that Chamberlain was putting it about that if Gladstone did not accept his resignation, then he would stay and 'would be master in the cabinet': this is the other side of the coin to the view often put that Gladstone and his allies could have had Chamberlain's loyalty, but for their maladroitness at a personal level. Hartington, probably stimulated by Chamberlain's now dangerously mobile energies, was himself putting it about that 'it probably will be necessary' for himself and not Salisbury to lead opposition to the bill. Hartington thus sought to pre-empt Chamberlain from making the running, while leaving himself fundamentally uncommitted.[282]

March 19 (*Friday*). Sir Charles Forster gave a dinner, not beginning till nearly 9, for Gladstone, Mundella, Lubbock, Erskine May, Dr Vaughan, Lord Kilcoursie, and Frank Lockwood. (Gladstone, although 'drowned in business', had during the day been unable to resist reading a learned paper on Chaldaean astronomy, finding 'the passage from Diodorus ... extremely valuable'.) 'The old man was full of talk: he was very pleasant and spoke kindly to me about York. He was speaking about sleeping, and said he always drank tea after midnight – what a stomach he must have. The night before he had what he called "solid sleep" from 12.30 to 9.15! He reads some light work before going to bed. Dr Vaughan mildly asked whether he read Greek at night. The old 'un returned a "Certainly not" which took the wind out of the doctor... We had just finished dinner when one of the whips sent for us to go back for a division... The G.O.M. lamented the departure of the east wind – he says it suits him – another instance of a wonderful stomach.'[283]

March 20 (Sunday). Arnold Morley, Lord Spencer, and A. West gathered at Wolverton's house at Coombe Wood, and talked over Irish affairs at great length.[284]

Meanwhile, Gladstone remained in London and had an interview lasting two hours with Bright. According to the latter, the meeting was 'very free and open. Mr Gladstone was cheerful and earnest ... and said how much he relied on such assistance as I could render him.' Before getting down to business, Bright was asked to read a memorandum, dealing mainly with Irish history, which he found less than fair to the protestant minority. Ensuing discussion showed that Bright held firm to the view that the 1881 land act contained a definitive settlement of the question. He therefore 'objected to the land policy as unnecessary'. On home rule, Bright's attitude was harder than in his previous talk with Gladstone on 12 March, perhaps because of Chamberlain's actions since that date. While still seeing removal of the Irish M.Ps as a benefit, he thought Gladstone's policy involved 'surrender all along the line'. Bright used the standard arguments against home rule for most of the rest of the interview, giving no ground at all. Gladstone's parting words were intended for more ears than Bright's alone: 'This question should not be made a great party question involving a struggle in the constituencies, and that if he failed he should retire and leave others who thought themselves capable of doing it to undertake the settlement of the Irish difficulty.'[285]

Gladstone's cunning here in letting it be understood that he would do the exact opposite of what he eventually and unwaveringly did, must be seen as follows. By hinting that the Liberal party would soon quite likely be delivered into the hands of the anti-Gladstonian leaders, he made it that much more difficult for the anti-Gladstonians to attack the Liberal party and its official policy. Still less could possible future leaders wish to commit themselves definitely to future policies. In March and April, the threat of resignation was the right card to play, and it was not until May that it became right to publicise the threat of a penal dissolution instead. The main tactical intent on Gladstone's part at this time was to inhibit the institutionalisation of Liberal dissidence by emphasising the fluidity of the situation.

March 22 (Monday). Rosebery saw Gladstone on business, and was startled with 'an astounding and unprecedented eulogy stating that if this Govt had existed for no other reason it would have made him happy because of the administration of the F.O., etc.... He made an admission that he began to think it possible there *was* something tricky in Russian diplomacy as compared with that of other nations!'[286]

Granville, John Morley, Spencer and Gladstone again met at 5.30, to discuss 1) Irish land; 2) whether Chamberlain should see Gladstone's home rule plan; 3) the position of Trevelyan; 4) Gladstone's plan for introducing a home rule resolution, which was much approved.[287]

Reginald Brett entertained to dinner A. Grey, Arthur Balfour, N. Rothschild, and Chamberlain, the talk of the last being at once reported to Hatfield.[288]

March 23 (Tuesday). A conclave of Granville, Morley, Spencer and Gladstone, this time with the addition of Harcourt, met at 5.30 in the House of Commons. The question of whether to stand or fall on Irish land was discussed. Then the disposal of offices came up, the names of Whitbread, Illingworth, Dalhousie, Stansfeld, Bright and Forster being considered. It was agreed to proceed with Irish government first, and to get the cabinet on Friday to ratify these decisions.[289] This group of ministers may also have met Trevelyan.[290]

A memorandum by Gladstone, misdated 23 April but presumably 23 March, stated that communications with the Queen made it impossible to hold a cabinet before Friday (i.e. 26 March) but that he wanted to state in the House on 24 March that Irish policy would be brought forward on 8 April. Ten ministers endorsed this including Trevelyan and Chamberlain.[291]

Goschen talked with the Queen at Buckingham Palace. She spoke very warmly of the speeches of Brand and other unionists: Goschen in turn specifically praised the work done for the cause by the Whigs, Ebrington, Lymington, and Albert Grey, and, rather curiously, that other professional representative of 'moderate' business opinion, W.H.Smith, whom he had found very friendly. Smith, indeed, was to be one of the very few Tories who had a good word to say for coalition when the moment came in July 1886.

Goschen then gave the Queen a lecture on the general situation. He said that Hartington was very determined to oppose the bill. Goschen had lately come to think the bill would be defeated in the House of Commons. Dissolution immediately would be very bad for the Unionists: on the other hand, Goschen was anxious to see the Irish legislation brought forward well before Easter, rather than delayed while the ministry consolidated its position. He could not understand why Chamberlain and Trevelyan, but especially the latter, should ever have joined the ministry, but he feared that Chamberlain's opposition to home rule might be counter-productive through its vehemence. Goschen explained Chamberlain's attitude on Ireland as entirely natural in view of his dictatorial temper and dislike of disorder.

Goschen and the Queen brooded over Hartington's letter to Gladstone defining his position, and lamented his inclusion of a conciliatory paragraph. This led them to more crying over spilt milk, in this case a reiteration of Goschen's view that had Salisbury not shaken moderate Liberal opinion by omitting coercion from the Queen's Speech, everything would have been all right.[292]

March 24 (Wednesday). The Queen saw Gladstone at Buckingham Palace to discuss the Irish question. He told her he believed Chamberlain would resign immediately.[293]

At a dinner, Henry James told Cranbrook that he was nervous about Hartington's position, and that he did not see the possibility of a Hartington cabinet until Salisbury had tried first.[294]

March 25 (Thursday). For the first time there was a hint of a deeply unscrupulous tactician operating against Gladstone. The prime minister received a letter, on Mrs O'Shea's notepaper and apparently signed by her, marked secret. Mrs O'Shea wanted to discuss the possibility of arranging a meeting between Gladstone and Parnell, the implication of her words being, no doubt correctly, that no such meeting had yet taken place. The letter mentioned a talk between Morley and the writer, in which Morley had envisaged such a meeting. It was suggested the meeting should be in Morley's room 'as being less likely to be noticed'. It is not known what, if anything, was Gladstone's reaction on receipt of this letter.

The following day Gladstone received a telegram, sent that

morning (26 March) from the post office in the high street at Eltham, where Mrs O'Shea lived. The telegram read 'I understand that a communication was sent to you yesterday from Albert Mansions in my name. I do not know anything whatever about it and have not even seen it. I have not been in London for some days.'[295] 1, Albert Mansions, S.W., was of course the town address of her husband, Capt. O'Shea.

The problems raised by these documents cannot be solved without further evidence. One conjecture, and perhaps the most likely one, is that Capt. O'Shea forged a letter in his wife's name in order to compromise Gladstone by an ill-judged furtive meeting with Parnell, which would find its way into the papers just as the home rule bill was announced. The suspicions later held by Parnell, that O'Shea had forged the Pigott letters, lend incidental support to this view. Quite other and far more innocent readings of the documents are possible: but the hint of forgery related to political tactics provides a clue to be borne in mind.

March 26 (*Friday*). The Queen discussed general politics with Goschen at Windsor. Goschen said that an election must be avoided, that any fusion of Liberal and Conservative elements must be limited to the issue of home rule, that both unionist sections should stand simply as Loyalists in the coming election, and that Gladstone might still be beaten by the Irish members not accepting his bill as adequate. The Queen spoke to Goschen of the draft legislation received by her from Gladstone on 10 March.[296]

The cabinet met at Downing St, 2.00–3.10, with all ministers, including Chamberlain and Trevelyan, present. Harcourt, Granville and Rosebery remained in conference with Gladstone for about half an hour after the end of the meeting. Following the meeting, a letter was sent to the Queen advising her that Chamberlain and Trevelyan wished to tender their resignations,[297] and recommending Stansfeld and Dalhousie as their successors. (Playfair had turned down the Scottish Office, probably earlier the same day, because it was not to be continued as a cabinet office.)[298]

The first point concerned Churchill's objections to the size of the Commons' representation on the joint Indian Committee of both Houses. It was resolved to persevere with the project.

The following form of words was then accepted by the cabinet, Trevelyan and Chamberlain dissenting: 'That it is expedient to ask Parliament to establish by Statute, under carefully framed provisions, a Legislative Body in Dublin.'[299]

According to Gladstone's letter to the Queen, Trevelyan was disposed to make large changes in Irish administration,[300] but could not agree to putting the care of law and order through the magistracy and police under the control of an Irish body. Chamberlain, however, according to Gladstone's notes, did not object to Irish control of the police, but stood firm on the questions of removal of the Irish members from Westminster, Irish control over finance, and the appointment of judges. According to Rosebery, however, the items which Chamberlain demurred to were rather different – being the exclusion of the Irish members from Westminster, the grant of powers of taxation to the new Irish régime, the grant of powers over trade, and the power to enrol a volunteer force.[301] In Gladstone's view, Chamberlain was willing to see some kind of body established in Dublin, and he did not object to calling it a parliament, but he did object to giving it what to Gladstone were powers essential to a parliament.[302]

Gladstone later gave notice in the House of Commons that he would bring in a bill for the future government of Ireland on Thursday, April 8.

Gladstone's readiness to see Chamberlain and Trevelyan go by this stage was noted by John Morley.[303] Gladstone had his own very clear picture of the situation, 'With men like most of my colleagues it is safe to go to an extreme of concession. But my experience in Chamberlain's case is that such concession is treated mainly as an acknowledgment of his superior greatness and wisdom, and as a fresh point of departure accordingly.'[304]

March 27 (Saturday). There was much miscellaneous activity in Downing St during the day. Spencer called on Gladstone before noon, followed shortly afterwards by Dalhousie, the incoming Secretary for Scotland, who remained a considerable time with the premier. (Only three days earlier Dalhousie had told Gladstone 'I would not exchange my freedom for any office in your gift even if a seat in the cabinet were attached to it.') At some time during the day Gladstone was visited by Sir A. Clark, if only for the purpose of impressing upon his physician that he had fully re-gained his health. Early in the afternoon Ponsonby, the Queen's private secretary, arrived from Windsor with communications from the Queen concerning the pending ministerial resignations.

Almost immediately afterwards, as a result of a notice sent out earlier the same day, an informal meeting of ministers took place at Downing St, lasting from about 2.30 to somewhat after 4.30. Those attending were Gladstone, Granville, Herschell, Morley, and Kimberley. Ripon also called during the meeting, but was unable to remain long. After the meeting, Morley and Herschell walked away together in conversation, but about five minutes later a special messenger was sent to retrieve Morley, who then had a further interview alone with Gladstone for twenty minutes. Later in the afternoon Ponsonby again called for an interview with Gladstone.

At some point, Professor Stuart, a devoted Gladstonian, called on the premier with reassuring news about the impact of Chamberlain's resignation on backbench sentiment. He said it would probably have the effect of uniting the party behind Gladstone.[305]

In the evening Gladstone dined with Lord Tweedmouth in company with several leading politicians.[306] Mrs Gladstone talked to Dalhousie, who expressed no disappointment at being left out of the cabinet.[307]

A deputation of Ulster Liberals waited upon Bright who 'tried to console them as far as I could'. In the evening Bright dined with Trevelyan, Mundella, and Campbell-Bannerman. Trevelyan bitterly attacked Gladstone, while the two ministers warmly supported him.[308]

March 28 (*Sunday*). Trevelyan visited Hartington for an hour and a half during the afternoon, his second visit since resigning.

Chamberlain talked with Churchill in the evening about his resignation. Chamberlain's line was that he had separated from Gladstone on the question of keeping Irish M.Ps at Westminster, Chamberlain wanting the Irish at Westminster 'as they are now' with 'little more than a kind of central vestry' in Dublin. 'Joe is very anxious, and cannot count for certain on Radical support. He is rather drawing his bow at a venture...'[309] The two men arranged to dine alone at Chamberlain's house the following night.

March 29 (*Monday*). The news of the resignation of Chamberlain and Trevelyan, and the names of the new appointments, had appeared in the morning papers, and on entering the chamber, both ex-ministers for the first time left the government bench and sat as ordinary members below the gangway, thereby intimating 'that they are not any longer pledged to support the government in anything'.[310]

Shortly after noon a cabinet was hastily summoned for 2 at Downing St. So unexpected was the summons that Kimberley, hearing it rumoured while in the clubs, drove to Downing St to ascertain what had been arranged, while Rosebery did not hear there was to be a meeting till 1.25. Before the meeting, Childers had a short interview with Gladstone, then left briefly to make a call at the Home Office. Ripon arrived in company with Trevelyan, who had walked with him from the Admiralty, where they had been talking for some time, as far as the door of 10 Downing St. Owing to late arrivals, the meeting effectively began about 2.15, and lasted till 4. Stansfeld remained with Gladstone for a short time after the meeting broke up. All ministers were present, including Stansfeld, whose first cabinet it was since 1874.

Stansfeld's presence was mildly surprising, as only the previous Friday he had warned Gladstone 'your home rule scheme goes further than my mind had so far travelled' and concluded that 'I should best avoid all possibility of embarrassing you ... by not taking office.' Exclusion of Irish members was his 'most serious difficulty', which 'startled me so much that I had to take time to think'. Apart from that, he wanted Ulster to be left alone: landlords to be paid less: protective tariffs to be banned, and much else. In short, agreeing with Gladstone on little except on party unity, the importance of Progress, and a sense of what was justly due to him, he took office in the hope of remedying Gladstone's frailties. As he told a confidante on 30 March, '... I was needed and there was a kind of amende honorable implied rather than expressed.'

The cabinet agreed that Gladstone should at once make known his intention to proceed with a plan relating to Irish land almost immediately after the plan for Irish government, probably on 15 April.*

On the Irish government bill, a general decision was taken in favour of the exclusion of Irish representatives from Westminster, but without closing the door against consideration of methods for Irish participation in discussion on foreign policy, or against exceptional treatment for Ulster. It was however agreed that no plan of separate treatment for Ulster could at present be prepared by the cabinet.

Gladstone's notes indicate that the only non-Irish topic entered upon was the question of new ministerial appointments.

In the evening, John Morley sought out McCarthy, because he particularly wanted to arrange a meeting with Parnell for that night. McCarthy arranged the meeting at once, and had the impression that it was 'momentous'.[311]

Chamberlain, dining alone with Churchill, told him Gladstone planned to propose a one-chamber Irish parliament with full fiscal and economic powers, subject only to a vague veto but otherwise without guarantees, and that Gladstone's land bill involved the issue of £220m. for purchase. What Chamberlain told Churchill

---

* On the night of 29 Mar., Gladstone announced in the House of Commons that on 8 Apr. he would move for leave to bring in 'A Bill to amend the provision for the future government of Ireland', and on the following Thursday, 15 Apr., he would further ask leave to introduce a bill 'to make amended provision for the sale and purchase of land in Ireland'. Just after the announcement, McCarthy found himself talking to Parnell, who was well pleased with the way things were going, being sure that Gladstone's scheme would be acceptable as a complete settlement of the home rule question (McCarthy and Praed, loc. cit.).

was, probably in all innocence, a wildly inaccurate account of Gladstone's schemes. On tactics, Chamberlain said he could not oppose the introduction of the bill: 'it was everything that the country should see the GOM had had the fairest of fair play'.

Beach and Hartington had a long talk, which, as passed on by Beach, appeared to Churchill to have been much too helpful in giving assurances 'as to what the Tory party would do under certain circumstances'.[312] This probably meant that Beach had proffered Tory support for a Hartington Whig ministry, if Gladstone resigned without dissolving.

March 30 (Tuesday). Gladstone dined with Ripon, the company including Lubbock, Millais, Dalhousie, MacColl, Houghton, and Bickersteth.

March 31 (Wednesday). A meeting of the cabinet committee on Irish finance, summoned by Gladstone the previous day, was held at 2 and lasted for nearly two hours. The ministers present were Gladstone, Kimberley, Spencer, Childers, Morley, and Harcourt:[313] E. Hamilton and Welby represented the officials of the Inland Revenue and the Treasury respectively. The committee was faced with the decision as to whether control of the Customs was to be handed over to the Irish. Gladstone was very firm on this point, seeing endless difficulties if the power were retained by the imperial government. It is important to be quite clear as to what Gladstone had in mind here, as the spectre of a protectionist Ireland was being freely used at this time by tender consciences as a highly convenient stumbling-block. Gladstone, and Morley with him, thought as early as 31 March – in effect from the start of detailed discussions on the subject – that no power of imposing protective duties should be given.* Tariffs should be confined to those needed for revenue purposes, a distinction that was accepted as a 'capital point' by the cabinet on 1 April, before Parnell's surrender of all claims to the Customs. There is little explicit evidence as to whether it was also initially proposed that the routine administration of the Customs service in Ireland should be in local rather than imperial hands. It was against this very diluted form of fiscal autonomy that Childers ran amok in the week preceding 5 April, when Parnell relinquished all such claims.

---

* 'With reference to a rather menacing article in the *Scotsman*, I may say that Morley and I think no power of imposing protective duties should be given' (Gladstone to Rosebery, 31 Mar. 1886, Rosebery MSS box 19). Gladstone here was rebutting the initial *Scotsman* leak of 29 Mar., which stressed that the proposed Irish legislature would have control in financial and fiscal matters, and of which its editor later wrote 'Every word that had been printed – even the comments I have quoted – had been sent to me by Mr Childers...' (Cooper, *An Editor's Retrospect* (1896), 406).

Hamilton added 'Harcourt was not in an amiable mood. He was bent on fault finding and hole picking, taunted Mr G with converting Ireland into a colony *pur et simple*: and hinted (before Welby and myself) that he might have to reconsider his position.'[314] At this meeting the basis for the future Irish contribution to imperial expenditure was fixed at one fourteenth.

April 1 (Thursday). The cabinet met, first in Downing St 2–4, and then in Gladstone's room at the House of Commons from 5.15 till 8 or 8.15. In fact various delays, especially questions in the lower house, prevented proper resumption of business till about 6.15. Rosebery was absent from the adjourned meeting,[315] but otherwise the cabinet was fully attended.

Rosebery reported on the Balkan crisis, and the cabinet agreed that further pressure might be exerted on Greece should she not comply with an anticipated demand of the Powers to disarm. The nature of the pressure to be exerted – possibly a partial embargo on Greek merchant shipping, combined with an effectual stoppage of naval movements – was discussed, but not settled. Harcourt raised objections to Rosebery's policy, but acquiesced.

Nearly the whole of the cabinet was spent on the Irish government bill,[316] most of whose provisions had by the end been disposed of. The cabinet agreed on the following six 'capital points':
1) The list of subjects reserved to the Imperial Parliament, viz. the monarchy, defence, foreign and colonial matters, certain contracts, and trade and navigation. The Irish parliament was to have the power of raising revenue duties, but not protective or differential duties. Other minor subjects were also reserved to Westminster.
2) The Imperial contribution was to be one fourteenth of the whole Imperial charge. 'It is expected that the Irish will claim to pay still less: but under this arrangement each inhabitant of Ireland will pay less than half what is to be paid, on the average, by each inhabitant of Great Britain...'
3) 'The Cabinet also considered at much length the proper composition of the Legislative Body. They think it should be subject, like Parliament, to all the prerogatives of the Crown: should consist of two orders, sitting together, but with a power of separate vote, giving each a vote on the proceedings of the other: the veto however to be limited to a term of years: each order to depend as a rule upon election, but the 28 Irish representative peers to be members thereof for life if they shall think fit. The election of the two orders would be by different constituencies.'
4) 'The civil government generally, it is proposed, should continue as it is, until altered by arrangement.'

5) Arrangements were brought forward to protect the independence of the judiciary and the interests of existing officials especially those charged with the suppression of crime.

6) 'Lastly the cabinet consider that, although the word parliament is applied by statute to the Legislative Houses of Canada (perhaps to distinguish them from the provincial bodies) it ought not to be applied in the statute to the Irish Legislative Body.'

According to Lewis Harcourt, Gladstone said at the end of the meeting 'I do not think we shall want to have another meeting as the [Irish] Bill is practically settled.' At this Harcourt *père* was furious* and said he would not remain in the cabinet if they were not to be allowed fuller discussion. Herschell, John Morley, and one or two others agreed and said it was 'too bad' of Gladstone to treat them in the way he was doing. At a party later in the evening, Spencer 'in a great fright lest W.V.H. should resign' encountered Lewis Harcourt, sought his good offices in the matter, assured him that Gladstone would probably hold another cabinet on the question, adding 'Your father is very difficult to deal with on this question for first of all he refuses to discuss it at all and then he makes a bother because he has not been allowed "enough time to discuss it".'[317]

In the evening Gladstone dined with Knowles, editor of the *Nineteenth Century*, the company including Holman Hunt, the Duke of St Albans, Ponsonby, and the French and American ambassadors. Gladstone was full of Eton and of flogging. A whisper went round as to whether he had ever been flogged. 'Yes, indeed, once and only once – for good nature in not reminding Keate as I ought to have done that there were three friends of mine awaiting punishment.' Turning to novels, he defended those of Sir Walter Scott but also praised *Middlemarch*.

Ponsonby found a moment to press upon Gladstone an invitation to dine at Windsor, but Gladstone 'could do nothing' until the bill was introduced. 'His work was enormous and he had to do in the midst of the session in four or five weeks what ought to occupy four or five months out of the session.'[318]

April 2 (Friday). Gladstone asked Granville, Spencer, Kimberley and Morley to confer with him at Downing St during the day to review arrangements for the home rule bill. According to a subsequent press report, however, the ministers actually attending

---

* Cf. 'I hear Harcourt made it very stormy and harassed Mr G much' (R.J., 1 Apr.) Although Gladstone resented being treated (as he said) like a clerk by Harcourt, he did not believe that Harcourt would resign and was not therefore unduly alarmed by his outbursts (Mrs Gladstone to Mrs Drew n.d. but Friday, 46223 f. 279).

this meeting, (2.30–4), were Gladstone, Spencer, Kimberley, Morley and Childers.[319]

Childers' position at this time (and at this time only) requires close attention. Unlike his colleagues, he had in his own eyes long been a supporter of some form of home rule, perhaps since 1880. Certainly his private view before the 1885 election was that 'devolution is in my opinion most necessary'.[320] A Dublin parliament should have imposed no strain on his integrity. Moreover, Childers had never been known to engage in far-reaching cabinet intrigue, and least of all could he have been expected to do so against Gladstone. Childers was in the Liberal leadership, and perhaps always had been, because Gladstone had so decided, and for no other reason. Childers was normally quite without other political allies. It is all the more strange, therefore, that he should have run a press campaign against aspects of Gladstone's home rule bill. Two things cannot be settled: why he did it, and whether he did it alone (the obvious possibility being that he was put up to it by Chamberlain).

Despite his advanced views on Irish autonomy, Childers had shown no signs of joy when his dreams materialised in 1886. As a financial expert, he found it hard that he was not, initially, consulted about the financial aspects of the scheme; and harder still that his objections to the customs and excise provisions cut no ice with Gladstone. On 2 April, he felt his position was almost intolerable, and that it must end in his resigning either his seat in the cabinet or his seat at Edinburgh, all because the converts in their zeal had gone so far beyond his own moderate ideas.[321] The terms of his protests to Gladstone on 2–3 April bore a curious resemblance to ideas put forward in letters[322] he had received from Charles Cooper, editor of the *Scotsman*, on 28–30 March, objecting to the customs and excise proposals as likely to cost Childers and Gladstone their seats, and suggesting that Childers should resign in order to save Gladstone from ruin. Childers' misery deepened as discussions continued and the prospect of his exerting leverage on policy decreased: 'I've already told Mr G that my seat in Edinburgh is gone, if the Irish are turned out of Westminster, and the control of the customs and excise are given to them.'[323]

Childers had indeed just lost his long-held seat at Pontefract, in his own locality, and was understandably concerned over the novel difficulties of keeping in accord with the unfamiliar factions of Edinburgh. His constituency committee did in fact later come to pass a resolution condemning Gladstone's bill, by 27 votes to 18,[324] whether with or despite Childers' guidance it is impossible to say. His opposition to home rule, however, was out of all proportion to these constituency troubles, though his official biographer by no means revealed its extent.

According to its editor, the *Scotsman* of 29 March 1886 published the crucial details of the home rule plans as they then were, as sent by Childers. The *Scotsman's* leader of that date revealed that home rule would involve exclusion of the Irish from Westminster, and would give Dublin control over finance, customs, and excise. Leakages of the same kind were prominent again in the paper of 31 March,[325] special stress being laid on Childers' *bête noire*, the Irish control of the customs. (The leakages were unusual in that they immediately preceded ministerial meetings called to discuss the subjects leaked. The inference must be that Childers was confident that he knew what was in the wind before Irish proposals were brought forward for discussion.) Another *éminence grise* of Edinburgh Liberalism, Ivory, wrote:

'C. [Cooper] told me at the time of the split in '86 he received directly from a member of the cabinet a copy (or summary) of the Home Rule Bill. That this was sent by the cabinet minister with the concurrence of *other members of the cabinet* in order that he might rouse public opinion before the bill was made public, and by strengthening the hands of the moderate section of the cabinet, force Mr Gladstone into so modifying the bill as to make it acceptable to all sections of the Liberal Party.'[326]

Cooper and Childers were perhaps acting on less sophisticated grounds. Cooper had very recently become a political intimate of Childers when the latter was fighting the S. Edinburgh by-election, and had indeed played a large part in arranging his candidacy. It so happened that both men had a very clear conception of what form home rule should take; Childers having taken his stand at the election on the principle of 'home rule all round', and were in very close agreement. The leak therefore represented their joint attempt in the long term to enforce their own conceptions on Gladstone, while in the short term forcing him to remove from his bill features they both agreed were objectionable. Cooper had been accustomed to this kind of work, by having co-operated closely with Rosebery in 1880–85; but Rosebery had by 1886 effectively dropped him. It is unlikely that any other minister was involved in direct contact with Cooper over this episode.[327]

In the evening the Gladstones, the Dalhousies, and John Morley met at a dinner given by Rosebery. Throughout dinner Rosebery could talk of nothing but his work at the Foreign Office and, in particular, of the Greek crisis.[328]

April 3 (Saturday). Bright called on Childers at the Home Office on business, and found him thoroughly upset and worried on Irish questions. At Childers' request Bright went round to Downing St to see Gladstone, where he only stayed a short time. The interview was predictably unproductive. Bright said the bill would not pass the Commons. Gladstone 'insisted upon it that there was no cabinet difficulty, only the ordinary differences as to details', a statement which Bright 'knew not to be accurate',[329] suggesting perhaps that Childers had leaked cabinet divisions to him also. Bright thought Gladstone looked 'weary and not so brisk and eager' as when he last saw him on 20 March.

At this late stage of the proceedings, Gladstone asked John Morley, now as always during this ministry his only negotiator with the Irish, to sound them out on the essentials of the Irish financial arrangements. The question at root was whether the power of raising revenue duties should be committed to the Irish legislature *tout simple*, as in the existing draft bill, or whether to retain at Westminster a limited power of taxation over Ireland in this respect, retaining 40 Irish members (i.e. in proportion to their financial contribution) for the purpose ('the plan which Childers so strongly prefers').

Gladstone, though he 'had no doubt of the superiority of the plan we have selected' wanted to be free to state in his opening exposition that the choice between the two methods was still open. To make this statement, he wanted Morley to get the assent of the Irish to this method of forestalling parliamentary attack. The Irish were by no means Gladstone's greatest difficulty in achieving total tactical flexibility in this respect: 'I am however by no means sure that the cabinet will assent to the retention of Irish members on any terms.'[330]

April 4 (Sunday). Lewis Harcourt made the following interesting survey of the Liberal dissidents:

'Goschen is said to be trying very hard to make Hartington join the Tories, but James is working hard the other way and an offensive and defensive alliance with Chamberlain on the Irish Question may save him from it. Trevelyan says Chamberlain is much dissatisfied with the small amount of support he has received and complains that his letter bag is empty and Birmingham in revolt. He has told John Morley that he has made a mistake and wishes to be taken back – not into the government but into the Liberal fold, and holds out hope that he may be able to extend a sort of independent support to the Home Rule bill.'[331]

April 5 (Monday).[332] Parnell and Gladstone met at 10.30 p.m. in Morley's room at Westminster[333] to discuss financial arrangements, Parnell giving up the claim to tariff autonomy in return for an expected substantial reduction in Ireland's contribution to imperial taxation.

In view of the apparently large role sometimes played by civil servants in the formation of Irish policy in 1886, it is interesting to note that the decision not to give tariff powers to an Irish legislature, reached on 5 April, was probably purely political. At any rate, the chairman of the inland revenue, West, found that the matter had already settled itself before he could give his opinion on it.[334]

Herschell wrote two letters, one eight pages long, to Gladstone during the day demurring at certain features of the Irish government scheme. He particularly felt the lack of safeguards given to the propertied classes and to Crown servants such as policemen, and also argued that the bill did not provide for increased Irish contributions to defence costs in the event of war. Herschell's conclusion was that he could not support the measure as it stood.[335] Had Herschell's *démarche* come a day or two earlier, when Childers was also parading his just fury and his desire to resign, it could have seriously shaken the ministry. As it was, it coincided so exactly with Childers' return to the fold, that its impact was largely lost.

Also on 5 April Salisbury wrote to Hartington proposing to call and discuss the situation. The meeting took place at Devonshire House the same day, but no record of the conversation has survived. From the dearth of correspondence between the two leaders after this, it is probable that this visit initiated a series of little-noticed or unnoticed personal meetings.[336]

April 6 (Tuesday). The full cabinet met at Downing St, 12–2. The meeting appears to have been wholly devoted to the contents of the Irish government bill.

Gladstone described the situation to the Queen thus:

'It was only yesterday that there appeared to be reason to believe that the Irish Representatives would consent to be removed from Westminster and yet to let the taxation of Ireland through the present system of Customs and Excise Duties remain in the hands of parliament. This materially simplifies the projected plan and also improves the prospect of its passing. At the same time they have felt much anxiety lest parliament when rid of their presence should alter the measure and withdraw the boons it gives.

'The cabinet think this jealousy, not unnatural under the circumstances, may be met by providing in the new law that its provisions may not be changed except either in conformity with an Address presented by the Irish Legislative Body, or else after recalling to the two Houses the Peers and Commons representative of Ireland in conformity with the provisions of the Act of Union and subsequent Acts.'[337]

Gladstone's notes on the meeting[338] add considerable information not in his letter to the Queen. They show that the proportion of the Irish contribution was decreased from one fourteenth to one fifteenth: that Gladstone's plan for the constitution and powers of the Irish legislative body was passed, Harcourt being probably the only critic: that membership of the second order in the Irish legislative body was to be by election subject to a property qualification for members, similar to that existing in British law until 1858: that the establishment of religion should be prohibited: that further questions of drafting were to be referred to Spencer, Morley, and Herschell: and that communications with the Irish were to proceed.

Childers described the main features of this cabinet to his wife with apparent relief or triumph, his account agreeing closely with that given above by Gladstone. Childers however mentioned explicitly a decision to reserve currency, posts, and patents to Westminster. Childers added that 'Harcourt was in a state of resignation from beginning to end', though he did not expect this dissidence to endure.[339] Rosebery, too, did not worry that Harcourt was 'very captious and cross', for 'otherwise things went well'.[340] As Childers' particular bugbear of Irish control of the customs had now suddenly and finally disappeared, the tendency he had shown in the previous few weeks to emerge as an emotional and unscrupulous opponent of home rule, cannot be traced in the evidence subsequent to this date. However, his underlying disapproval remained, for throughout the general election campaign of 1886 Childers in private agreed with his confidant Cooper that home rule in effect meant separation, and separation was the most pejorative word in both men's vocabulary. Childers 'expressed his regret that Mr Gladstone had brought forward the Home Rule Bill, or that he made it what it was ... he thought the bill bad and Mr Gladstone wrong...'[341]

When Morley told Parnell of the cabinet's decision to fix Irish taxation at one fifteenth, the latter accepted it reluctantly after 'much obstinacy' making it clear that the correct figure should have been only one twentieth.

April 7 (*Wednesday*). In the evening Spencer called to see Harcourt, and found not a word of resignation or reference to the quarrels in cabinet the preceding day. At midnight Spencer looked in on Rosebery to report this good news.[342]

Chamberlain and Hartington conferred together about the handling of the coming debate, at an interview which began uneasily but 'ended amicably'. Chamberlain, who had previously intended to speak immediately in reply to Gladstone, agreed to stand aside at first while the Tories and Trevelyan kept the debate going. Chamberlain urged Hartington in turn not to speak in the first few days, so that Chamberlain could make the first major attack on the bill. Hartington was not convinced of the wisdom of this.[343]

April 8 (*Thursday*). Gladstone introduced the Irish government bill in the House of Commons.

Morley had an interview with Parnell, whom he found much exercised by the three columns which had appeared in *The Times* that morning on the financial resources of Ireland. Parnell, Morley reported, now pressed harder than ever for an Irish contribution to the imperial budget of only one twentieth. Morley had urged moderation, and the matter was left undecided.[344] The interestingly timed financial article in *The Times* might be considered in relation to Goschen's view, expressed to the Queen as recently as 26 March, that the bill might be beaten by the Irish objecting to it as inadequate.

April 9 (*Friday*). At W. E. Forster's funeral service in Westminster Abbey, Rosebery met Gladstone, who said that his reception the previous day had exceeded all his expectations, adding 'This Home Rule question will control and put aside all other political questions in England till it is settled.'[345]

The full cabinet met at Downing St at 2. The cabinet first discussed the arrangement of business in parliament, so far as the relative positions of the Easter recess, the budget, and the Irish government bill were concerned.

The principal item was the budget, which was very simple. Harcourt proposed to retain income tax at 8d. and to suspend only a small portion of the Sinking Fund, expecting thereby to achieve a small surplus.

The cabinet also considered Kenrick's motion for free education, then pending, which in Gladstone's view would have meant the virtual extinction of the Voluntary Schools of the elementary class. It was determined instead to support Cross's amendment, and to reserve judgement until after the Report of the Commission on the Education Act.

The ex-cabinet, with the exception of Carnarvon, met at Arlington St at 12 to consider Gladstone's speech of the previous day.[346] Akers-Douglas, the chief whip, was among those whom Salisbury invited.[347] 'There was nothing particular to decide on.'[348]

April 10 (Saturday). In the afternoon Gladstone talked to Rosebery with great confidence, although the debate had gone against him on Friday night, and although he admitted that next month he might have to consider a dissolution. 'Resignations pour in, but his *mot d'ordre* is to close the ranks at once.'

For his part Chamberlain appeared 'very much excited' by what he saw as his successful confrontation with Gladstone in debate, but also declared, over dinner at the Athenaeum, 'that his feelings of admiration and wonder for the power of the G.O.M. over the minds of men was greater than ever'.[349]

April 12 (Monday). The appointment of a new chancellor of the duchy of Lancaster, *vice* Heneage, was at last settled by a definite acceptance from Kay-Shuttleworth,* who had earlier demurred on non-political grounds. The office had initially been offered to Lord Hampden, the former Speaker and Liberal chief whip, who turned it down on health grounds despite political agreement. Hampden was in fact remarkably full of home rule principles.[350]

Morley and Spencer consulted with Gladstone at Downing St at 2 p.m. on the draft of the Irish government bill.[351] Parnell for some unexplained reason failed to turn up for an appointment with Morley.

Gladstone dined in Downing St with his sister Miss Helen Gladstone, his daughter Mrs Drew, Lady Frederick Cavendish, Lord Kilcoursie, Lewis Harcourt, Algernon West (who had been busy all day on the revenue clauses of the Irish bill), and John Bright, the last sitting next to Gladstone. Bright was 'very querulous, and Mr Gladstone was rather short with his querulousness, so altogether the dinner was not as pleasant as usual'.[352] Talking of the annexation of Burma, Bright described it as an atrocity and said there was nobody in these degenerate days to protest against wars and annexations. This provoked Gladstone, who said: 'I should like to know what I was doing between 1878 and 1880 but protesting against war and annexation. Nobody ever protested more vehemently than I did at that time. I believe you had some hand in protesting against the Corn Laws, but I tell you, you never protested to the extent I did in 78–80.' Gladstone raised the question of the strong opposition being shown to the exclusion of the Irish members: Bright said it was the only good point in the

---

* Cf. Shuttleworth to Hartington, 11 Jan. 1886, Devonshire MSS 340/1891, urging Hartington and Trevelyan to give a strong lead against home rule.

bill.[353] The dinner ended more happily with Kilcoursie and the premier capping each other's anecdotes.[354]

April 13 (Tuesday). Mr and Mrs Gladstone dined at the Wests with Lord Wolverton, Lady Fannie Marjoribanks, Charles Guthrie, and Frank Mildmay, all later going back to the House with Mr Gladstone. Harcourt's brilliant fighting speech earlier on had proved very reassuring, though Harcourt had himself told Gladstone that very morning that the bill was 'as dead as mutton'. Gladstone found Harcourt's embarrassed position highly amusing, and the premier seemed 'very, very pleased' about the results of a by-election.[355]

April 14 (Wednesday). The full cabinet met at Downing St at 2 to consider the proposals on Irish land which Gladstone was due to announce in the House of Commons the following day, according to a timetable virtually settled at the cabinet of 29 March. That the Irish land proposals re-emerged at cabinet level at this late moment may have been due to pressure from Herschell, who wrote to Spencer during the day 'I cannot be a party to such a measure without thorough discussion as to its leading points. We were hustled into a corner about the Government Bill. It seems to promise to be worse still about the Land Bill.'[356] Spencer and Morley had on 10 April asked Gladstone to call the 'Purchase Bill Cabinet' on Monday or Tuesday.[357]

The meeting began with conversation on a possible local government bill and a registration bill, the latter to have priority over the former.

The second subject was Irish land purchase. It was agreed *inter alia* that landlords should have the option of being bought out, that parliament should be asked to authorise for this purpose the issue of £50m. if required, in one of the great public stocks, asking more later if necessary: and that the basis of the transaction should be the net rental after all deductions, at twenty years' purchase. It was proposed that tenants should become proprietors at a net charge 20 per cent below the present rental.

Harcourt then raised the question of the exclusion of the Irish members, which he considered a vital topic and requiring recognition as such. Harcourt was very offensive to Gladstone about this.[358] He was perhaps the sole objector to Gladstone's language on this topic of the preceding night, when the premier had said that the general exclusion of all Irish members was not a vital point in the bill, and came near to inviting parliament to suggest alternative ways of dealing with the difficulty. Both Morley and Harcourt were said that evening to be furious at what to them was an outrageous breach of faith, as exclusion had been settled on by the cabinet as a vital point. Harcourt suggested to his son on the evening of 13 April that he, Spencer, and Morley were likely to resign. In fact, on the following day Harcourt told his son that Herschell, Morley and himself had announced in cabinet that they would resign if Gladstone gave way on this issue.

At a party on the evening of 14 April, Spencer told Lewis Harcourt that after a most painful scene, Harcourt had given way: but on getting home, Harcourt found his father denied this, saying that both Spencer and Gladstone understood that he would resign if the point was conceded. Spencer indeed had afterwards to write that he had not meant to imply that Harcourt had backed down over the retention of Irish members, but that his remark to Harcourt's son simply meant that he (Spencer) expected differences to be settled without resignations.[359] On the following day, Morley said that he and Harcourt were 'in the same boat and shall go together'.[360] Putting matters beyond doubt, Harcourt wrote to Gladstone that 'I strictly adhere to the view stated by J. Morley at the cabinet yesterday that this is a "vital and essential" condition of the bill.'[361] While Morley's pointing a gun at Gladstone's head is as interesting as his probable inability to pull the trigger, great caution must be exercised about connecting his absolute stand in April against retention of Irish members (i.e. against reconciliation with Chamberlain) with the pressure he exerted on Gladstone in May. The intervening Easter recess created a sharp break between acts, and events after 4 May were a virtually new situation.

The cabinet accepted Rosebery's proposal that the Greeks should be asked to disarm by an allied fleet sent to the Piraeus for that purpose, and that failing their compliance a blockade based on that of the Scheldt in 1832 should be put into force.[362]

The burials bill, formerly in Harcourt's hands, was to be brought in by Osborne Morgan, with slight alterations.

It was noted that the Irish Arms Act[363] would expire on June 1.

The Liberal dissidents also had a full day. In the morning, Goschen held a breakfast party for them at his house in Portland Place, which was attended by such Whigs as Sellar, Lymington, A. Grey, Elliot, Sir R. Blennerhassett, and others. After the meal, some of these stayed behind to discuss arrangements for a series of demonstrations at carefully selected places up and down the country. The point of interest here is that it was Goschen who was leading, convening, and organising what is often taken to be a Whig group tied to Hartington.[364]

In the evening, a packed meeting organised by the Irish Loyal and Patriotic Union to protest against home rule was held at Her

Majesty's Theatre, Haymarket. The chairman was Earl Cowper, accompanied on the platform by Hartington, Salisbury, Fife, P. Rylands, Goschen, Cranbrook, and W.H.Smith. Sympathetic apologies were received from Argyll, Derby, and Churchill, the last however, privately calling the meeting 'a piece of premature gush'.[365] The names of such Unionists as Selborne, James, Northbrook, and Carlingford were not mentioned in connection with the meeting in *The Times* report. As befitted a moderate home ruler, Chamberlain naturally did not attend.

April 15 (Thursday). A meeting of Liberal unionist peers took place at Lord Derby's house, with 48 peers present and 16 sending letters of sympathy. According to Lord Morley, those present included Derby, Northbrook, Selborne, Coleridge, Hobhouse, Lingen, Stalbridge (lately Lord Richard Grosvenor), Camperdown, Belper, Romilly, Fife, Aylesbury, Ribblesdale, Ebury, Morley, Argyll, Alcester, Annaly, Grafton, St Albans, Normanby, Clarendon, Cowper, Fortescue, Minto, Sherbrooke, Bramwell, Clifford, Crewe, De Vesci, Foley, Lovat, Lyttelton, Monk Bretton, Monteagle, Revelstoke, Robartes, Rothschild, Sefton, Stratheden, Arran, and Truro. Lord Randolph Churchill was also present.

Derby spoke first, and was followed by Hartington, Argyll, Camperdown, De Vesci, Ribblesdale, and Selborne, the last speaking very strongly against Gladstone. Derby characteristically expected that the bill would reach the House of Lords and it would become their duty to throw it out and force an appeal to the country. Hartington however thought that the bill would not pass the Commons, and that the efforts of peers were best directed by their acting as individuals to secure its defeat in the lower house. Hartington went on to disclaim any ideas of coalition, but said that all Unionist candidates would be loyally supported by the Conservatives. According to Lord Morley, he went on to express himself sanguine as to the possibility of his forming an administration. Hartington was full of fight and optimism, and his views as to tactics were generally accepted. Two days later, however, Hartington thought the degree of coalition shown by having a joint meeting was 'a great blunder'.[366]

Rosebery walked with Derby for over an hour.[367]

April 16 (Friday). Gladstone received a letter written on this date from Eltham by Mrs O'Shea. We know that the letter was viewed as authentic, for it was docketed 'Mrs O'Shea – Asks for colonial appt for her husband, who is on verge of bankruptcy. He would go *anywhere*.'[368] Claiming to write on behalf of her husband, whose imminent bankruptcy she feared, she asked for an allegedly half-promised colonial job anywhere, or the prospect of one. 'My

Aunt, with whom I had been living for many years, and who although she is in her ninety-eighth, is as keen and far-sighted as ever, will, she says, assist my husband out of his present difficulties, for my sake, if she can see any hope of his getting any lucrative occupation, – *but* if not, she will not help him, so you will understand how important your answer is to us in every way.'

On 17 April Gladstone replied to Mrs O'Shea, simply referring her to his invariable rule of never attempting to interfere with the patronage of his colleagues. He did not actually refuse her request in so many words. The most curious feature of his reply, partly illegible though it is in the copy, was an apparent offer to lend O'Shea money in view of his political services.

This episode, which had no aftermath, must be viewed, coming when it did, as a possible attempt by a hidden enemy to compromise Gladstone. Had O'Shea been given a colonial appointment, newspaper criticism could well have been arranged, at very least on the grounds that Gladstone was buying off an opponent of home rule, but if necessary on the lines that Gladstone had been forced by political considerations to assist Parnell remove an injured husband. On the other hand, the episode could be almost innocent of all but purely financial implications.

At this point reference may be made to what little information was available to the public about the Irish land legislation. On 16 April, just before the recess, Gladstone introduced his sale and purchase of land (Ireland) bill. The occasion provided little drama. There was no division: Gladstone avoided detail: and the bill was not physically available to members. (Morley hoped it would be ready in a few days.) Gladstone's task was to present the bill as a boon to landlords, while at the same time pronouncing on the evils of landlordism in a way that warmed all Radical hearts. History was called in, with a comparison being made with negro emancipation in 1833. The peculiarity of Gladstone's measure was its reliance on an official called the receiver-general, who was to be appointed by the Irish parliament to channel peasant repayments to London. The assumption Gladstone made about Irish peasants (and here he criticised Ashbourne's Act of 1885) was that they could not be trusted to pay money to England except through an Irish intermediary. Gladstone had in fact settled in his own mind for a receiver-general in mid-January. This made it all the more interesting that Parnell condemned it as 'a very unnecessary, strange, and absurd proposal' in view of other Irish revenues remaining in British hands as security. Parnell's willingness to embarrass Gladstone on this occasion is a major piece of evidence for the fragility of Irish-Liberal relations at this stage, and perhaps also evidence of sheer lack of contact between the two sides; unless, of course, one chooses to view it as a calculated gesture of independence by Parnell for Irish consumption, an inconvenient row that had to be staged in order to make his connivance at a rather tame home rule bill credible to his supporters. Parnell's reaction apart, the debate was dull. There was no flood of Radical criticism about expense. Only one of the five Liberal speakers attacked on this ground, and he was a Whig. The debate took a major detour to include Chamberlain's resignation speech. Gladstone's request for a suspension of judgement pending production of the bill was more than met, for parliament did not discuss the matter again, and the bill was next heard of in the autumn when Gladstone denounced it as an albatross round the neck of home rule.

April 17 (Saturday). Kimberley wrote: 'Gladstone sent up a note to the House of Lords to ask if I could agree to a possible retention of the Irish members at Westminster. With great misgivings I gave way. I have never ceased to regret my weakness on this occasion.'[369] However, three days earlier he had sent Gladstone a memorandum in which he said that it might be expedient 'not absolutely to close the door' on the Irish.[370]

April 19–May 3. Political activity slackened during the period of the Easter recess. A round of creditable ministerial speeches in the provinces, by Morley, Spencer, Ripon, Childers, and Campbell-Bannerman, no more formed part of the thread of political manœuvre than did a performance by Hartington and Goschen at Edinburgh (1 May). Gladstone, Rosebery, and Harcourt were quiet, and the general position at the end of the recess was very much what it had been at the beginning. There was no conclave or country house-party of any political importance: while Gladstone and Granville only exchanged two letters during the period. The normal process of jockeying for position was, by tacit agreement of all concerned, virtually suspended.

The importance of this was that no better moment for reuniting the Liberal party could have presented itself than this lull between the two readings. Ministers who did not want the bill were free to join with ministers who wanted modifications, to create a wall of resistance to Gladstone's apparent heedlessness. Instead, ministers bowed to the convention that they were on holiday, without even trying to do anything to affect a situation they already saw as fugitive. When they returned in May, the pace of events was too fast for them: the April recess was really the latest date at which an effective initiative from within the cabinet was possible.

Within a few days, London was empty. By the 19th, Salisbury was at Hatfield 'to recruit his health' and had no engagements for the next fortnight. Halsbury and W. H. Smith went abroad, and Harrowby to Staffordshire, on the 17th. On the 19th, Herschell went to Dorset and Ripon to Yorkshire. Harcourt, Kimberley and Goschen retired to their country retreats on the 20th, while Churchill went to Paris without his wife. Granville went abroad, returning via Guernsey in Wolverton's steam yacht. Campbell-Bannerman went abroad. Childers withdrew to Wales. Politicians, generally speaking, were out of touch with each other for ten days or more, and it was not until about 2 May that most frontbenchers were back in town.

Gladstone had taken the 4 p.m. train from Euston for Hawarden on Saturday the 17th. At Chester, in reply to an invitation from the Chester Liberal Club, he declined to speak there the following week, saying 'I am really greatly fatigued, and I require a few days recreation at Hawarden. I am much worn.' After exchanging a joke about Ireland with a member of the crowd, Gladstone left for Hawarden, arriving at 9.30 p.m. and intending to stay put, as he succeeded in doing, till the end of the recess. A notice in the press asked his correspondents to write to Downing St, meaning he had left his secretaries there and he was leaving his letters to look after themselves.

His vacation passed without incident, except at Easter weekend. When the premier arrived at Hawarden church halfway through the three-hour Good Friday service, crowds flooding the church began to stand on the seats to catch a glimpse of him at prayer. His son, who was officiating, had to stop the service. On Easter Saturday 3,500 people visited Hawarden. Gladstone refused to speak, as requested, being in mourning for Laura Lyttelton (née Tennant), but later drove rapidly about his park. Herbert Gladstone did briefly address the enthusiastic crowd, who appeared to be warm supporters of home rule.

April 22 (Thursday). Henry Brand, one of the leading Whig backbenchers, wrote to acquaint Chamberlain with the fact that he and a few other militants had set up an office in Spring Gardens to organise the Liberal Unionists, and asked for support.[371] Chamberlain's reply was cordial in tone but he refused to join the committee.[372]

Though no public announcement was made, this may be taken as the day on which the Liberal Unionist party came into existence. Previous activity by anti-Gladstonian backbenchers had been fitful and chiefly confined to corridor and parliamentary politics, rather than formal organisation. The first action of the committee, its circulars to the eminent, including all Liberal M.Ps, seeking support, received many unsatisfactory replies. Many recipients, especially peers, asked uncomprehendingly, in effect, 'Who are you?' Both Goschen and Hartington at first refused to be publicly identified with the Liberal Unionist Committee, preferring to cling to the shadows regardless of the reproaches of the partisan young. But they were probably sensitive to pressure even from a determined and bossy underling like Milner who condemned Goschen's 'perfectly worthless secrecy' as hampering a cause which could not 'in the face of such terrible odds, afford to submit to any handicapping'.[373] Thus Hartington's refusal to join on 25 April, was followed by his sending James round to the Liberal Unionist office on 26 April to say that the committee might in fact make public use of his name. This brought the strength of the committee up to about seventeen, excluding some minor peers. Such senior Unionists as Selborne and Derby, however, had remained silent in face of the approaches from the committee.[374]

April 24 (Saturday). The Liberal Unionist Committee held a satisfactory meeting at Craig Sellar's house in the morning. 'Sellar was in capital form and much encouraged by his experience in Scotland', where he had been making arrangements to start a separate Liberal Unionist office (which actually opened on 10 May). The committee formally decided to circulate a large collection of leaflets, etc., which had just come back from the printer.[375]

April 28 (Wednesday). Chamberlain dined with Edwin Arnold, Hutton of the *Spectator*, Courtney, and others as a guest of Miss Dorothy Tennant. Chamberlain spoke bitterly:

> 'Two bad winters and we shall see the people taking the bit between their teeth. ... I don't know what I *can* do. I don't see what I am to do', and, with a very savage expression, added 'What can be done with a madman as leader! And you have helped to make him mad – yes, you, you, and all the others! Why, he is going to destroy Ireland and we are helpless. It is all very well saying prevent this and that. The mischief is already done. The evil has taken root.'

> Courtney whispered later: 'Chamberlain has pledged himself to vote for the second reading, if clause 24 (relating to the banishment of Irish members from Westminster) is abolished, or so far modified as to do away with Chamberlain's objections. It was supposed that Gladstone was quite *determined* to keep that clause intact. John Morley has declared he will never consent to its withdrawal. If however Gladstone *were* to change his mind, Chamberlain would be obliged however reluctantly to accept the second reading...'[376]

May 1 (Saturday). Gladstone published a manifesto[377] addressed to the electors of Midlothian, appealing to their class sense, their party loyalty, their Scottish particularism, and their supposed dislike of Conservative opportunism. Gladstone drew a sharp contrast between the clear intentions of the government ('you have before you a cabinet determined in its purpose; and an intelligible plan'), and the division of its opponents between a number of alternative policies. The Conservatives could not be trusted to maintain a policy of resistance: they were liable to surrender to the Irish 'without conditions and without thanks'. Moreover, the Liberal attitude towards Irish home rule offered to Scotland and Wales the prospect that the question of devolution there could also be shaped by public opinion in time to come.

Gladstone attacked his opponents as embodying 'the spirit and power of class' as well as for not being truly reactionary. 'The adverse host, then, consists of class and the dependants of class. But this formidable army is ... the same ... that has fought in every one of the great political battles of the last sixty years, and has been defeated... The classes have fought uniformly on the wrong side, and have uniformly been beaten, by a power more difficult to marshal, but resistless when marshalled, by the upright sense of the nation.'

On the status and prospects of the land bill, Gladstone hedged consummately ('... I leave the Irish Land Purchase Bill to stand on the declarations we have already made...') and simply chided the landlords for giving no hint of approval to a plan which went very far in catering for their interests.

Where Gladstone did rather break new ground was in his avowal of unconcern about detail. 'We are not now debating the amount of Irish contribution to the Empire, or the composition of the Legislative Body, or the maintenance of a representative connection with Westminster' but simply the principle of Irish management of local affairs. This meant two things from the point of view of Gladstone's general strategy: firstly, that in his campaign for ascendancy in opinion outside parliament, he was in effect proceeding by way of resolution upon the general principle of autonomy, a strategy he had repeatedly refused to adopt for parliamentary use. Secondly, he was throwing into the melting pot all the points on which senior ministers thought they had pinned him down in the preceding four months.

May 4 (Tuesday). The Gladstones left Hawarden in the morning for London, to attend a cabinet held at 5, with all ministers present, in Gladstone's room in the Commons.

The meeting began with conversation at large on the question of excluding Irish members, or admitting them only in much reduced numbers, all members of the cabinet according to Gladstone's notes being against any retention which was not restrictive in numbers and subjects. However, they reserved their freedom to reverse the clause excluding Irish representation, to some extent, if this would win support. It was left open whether such Irish representation should be on grounds of assent to taxation, or simply as a symbol of Imperial unity.

The idea of holding a party meeting was canvassed but dismissed as impracticable in the circumstances.

Rosebery reported developments concerning Greece.

It was at this stage of the discussions that Stansfeld made his most determined attempt to influence legislation on Ireland. On 4 May he wrote to Gladstone, mentioning his original hope that the ministry would deal with the Irish question by a development of the system of grand committees, as outlined in an article he had written in the *Contemporary Review* for October 1885. He added that he thought a very simple plan of federation along related lines might solve the objections to exclusion of the Irish members from Westminster.

On 5 May he wrote to Gladstone sketching plans on which he hoped to speak at the next cabinet, to avert 'the absolute exclusion of Irish members, to which I, in common, I believe with Childers,[378] am opposed. My notion of the way to deal with the subject, on the second reading, would be to leave it *not quite closed*.

'If not now, I cannot help thinking that at some time after a legislative body shall have been established in Dublin, we might ... have essentially the same thing for England, Scotland, and Wales severally, if we wished, by a further development of the system of grand committees in the House of Commons here: giving [them] ... which would consist respectively of all the members for England, and for Scotland, and for Wales, similar powers to those conferred upon the proposed legislative body.

'If we could open out the prospect of "Federation" thus simplified, without appearance of doing so at any one's dictation, my belief is that we should gain, compared with our present prospects, on any appeal to the country.'[379] It is not possible to tell how far, if at all, Stansfeld in fact brought his ideas before the cabinet. At all events, his speech on the second reading on 17 May was a vigorous effort on orthodox party lines, with only a passing glance at the possibility of a wider federal scheme. Gladstone considered it the best speech he had ever heard from Stansfeld.[380]

After the cabinet Rosebery dined alone with F. Rothschild, then

walked with him to the Turf Club, and from there walked home-
wards with Lord Randolph Churchill.[381]

May 5 (Wednesday). The committee of the National Liberal
Federation met at the Westminster Palace Hotel and passed an
overwhelming vote of confidence in Gladstone. The effect of this
in ministerial circles was to produce a sharp reduction in the
estimated number of members that Chamberlain could carry with
him, perhaps even from fifty down to ten. According to one eye-
witness, the meeting 'was almost terrible in its merry ferocity
against J.C. When Illingworth slipped out the word traitor, the
meeting caught it and there was loud and long-continued
cheering'.[382]

In the morning, Gladstone wrote a memorandum on the Irish
government bill, and sent it at once to Morley,[383] though the
latter had the impression that it was actually circulated on Thursday.[384] The memorandum suggested conditions on which the
Irish could be retained. Initially, Morley gave limited support:

> 'If it is pretty clear that opposition to the second reading would
> be lessened by the two proposals, a) return of Irish members to
> vote on alteration of taxation, b) standing committee, I for one
> should cheerfully concur. To get the principle of a Dublin
> legislature (*in a real sense*) once affirmed, is the all important
> aim.'[385]

Gladstone's memorandum, however, also evoked Stansfeld's
federal scheme, which Childers supported, and which Morley
probably opposed, backing his objections with his supposed
knowledge of Parnell's views. This sense of opening the doors to
the disintegration of the bill within the cabinet coincided with a
negative move on Chamberlain's part to harden Morley's feelings
against making rearrangement a substantive object of policy:

> 'Chamberlain's letter in the newspapers seems to me to make it
> useless for us to propose any such compromising expedients as
> those in your memorandum... They will give an impression of
> weakness on our part, without conciliating the little section
> who work with Chamberlain. With a view to an election, we
> should be stronger if we had stuck to the text of your last
> manifesto...'[386]

(As in January, Morley wished to use English chauvinism about
'getting rid of the Irish' as the emotional fuel for a home rule
campaign.)

Moreover, Parnell's opinion on retention had hardened,
curiously in harmony with Morley's views: 'he is much more stiff

against retention than he was before'. Parnell argued, plausibly, that retention of the Irish members would afford opportunities for altering the imperial contribution to Ireland's disadvantage.[387] Gladstone agreed that Chamberlain's letter made real conciliation impossible, yet wanted nevertheless to go ahead with the presentation, at least, of a modified scheme: 'I am sure you will not stereotype any idea *against* qualifications.'[388] What was only just left unsaid here, was a feeling shared by Gladstone and Morley that the nominal conciliation of, or capitulation to Chamberlain implicit in any scheme of modifications, was in fact to be done very much more with the intention of putting Chamberlain at a disadvantage, rather than restoring the position prior to his resignation.

Rosebery dined with Alfred Rothschild, sitting between Ferdinand Rothschild and H. Chaplin. Afterwards he had a long talk with Lord Randolph Churchill, finding him all for absolute non-intervention in foreign politics, an agreement with Russia, and a foreign policy hinging entirely on India.[389]

May 6 (Thursday). Gladstone and Rosebery went to Windsor and talked with the Queen after lunch. After condemning the Greeks for refusing to disarm, and praising Alexander of Bulgaria, Gladstone enlarged upon Ireland. The Queen tried to persuade him to alter course and put forward a scheme of purely local or regional government covering England as well as Ireland: Gladstone simply said this would not be accepted, and went on to discuss the issue of exclusion *v.* retention of the Irish members. This was the first time that her journal recorded the Queen as giving any attention to this issue.

Gladstone said Parnell 'had become better than he had been, since Kilmainham – that the Irish would not be nearly so dangerous in an Irish parliament as in the British, but that there was a good deal to be said for retaining them in the latter. That, however, they had been a great trouble in it, always going with the extreme Radicals. It was Mr Chamberlain's wish to retain them. Mr Gladstone went on at great length about this, I saying but little.'

The Queen also saw Goschen briefly on his return from a campaign in the north.[390]

At a dinner given by Rosebery, E. Hamilton had the chance to draw John Morley on the subject of Parnell. Morley remarked on his extraordinary elusiveness which made him seem never available for consultation, but confessed to being impressed by 'qualities of statesmanship' which exceeded those of just 'an acute tactician'. Morley also expressed great surprise that none of his meetings with Parnell had got into the press, although 'the draft of the bill was shown to some besides Parnell himself, all more or less connected with the press'.[391]

May 7 (Friday). According to *The Times*, a cabinet was summoned for this day, then postponed at very short notice till Saturday. The delay was in order to give Granville time to return from Manchester, where he had to give a speech.

A note in the Gladstone papers indicates that Gladstone had an engagement with Parnell at 2 p.m. on this day.[392]

After dinner Spencer called on Rosebery to discuss the cabinet due the following day.

May 8 (Saturday). The cabinet met at Downing St at 2.30, with all ministers except Rosebery present, but Herschell had to leave town before the end.

This cabinet was called in preparation for the debate on the Irish government bill due to begin the following Monday. Gladstone was 'authorised to offer provision for the continued attendance of the Irish members in cases involving taxation, and to speak with favour of more than one suggestion having for its aim a continued exhibition of legislative unity on all Imperial matters'.[393]

A note by Gladstone records a decision that Herschell was not to confer with Chamberlain. The suggestion had been made by Chamberlain himself through Labouchere.[394]

Rosebery was absent owing to diplomatic and court engagements. Some time during Saturday afternoon, Rosebery arrived at Windsor to act as minister in attendance and had an audience of the Queen. He had warned Gladstone of his forthcoming absence at Windsor in a letter[395] of 6 May, adding a protest against allowing a delegation of Irish members to sit at Westminster when foreign and colonial affairs were under consideration. Rosebery argued: 'In foreign affairs it would be mischievous, and in colonial affairs derisory, unless you admitted a colonial element. You could not have a special arrangement in order to enable Irishmen to discuss colonial affairs from which you excluded colonists.' Gladstone replied on Friday that he was sorry to have made Rosebery's hair stand on end, but only denied in the most indirect manner that he was moving in the direction which Rosebery feared. Gladstone would only say that 'the idea of a joint Commission' need not at that stage require any rigid definition of its powers or scope. Gladstone added 'I hope you will get back from Windsor as soon as you can. Though Chamberlain is rather in the dust, Hartingtonism is on its high horse, and I am sorry to say that though things are said to be moving in the right direction, and I have much faith in the country, the parliamentary outlook is at this moment very far indeed from being clear.'[396] On 8 May,

Gladstone wrote to reassure Rosebery: 'Cabinet is over but nothing has been done or will be said by me on Monday to raise your sympathetic apprehensions.'

It is not to be thought that Rosebery strongly objected to retention either on principle, or because it would rescue Chamberlain. In fact Gladstone always regarded Rosebery as an unenthusiastic retentionist, prepared to modify as circumstances and the premier dictated. On this occasion, however, the thought of the Irish meddling in foreign policy was too much for him.

May 9 (Sunday). Churchill was clearly well informed at this juncture as to Chamberlain's negotiations with the ministry, and possibly even as to the tendency of cabinet discussion. At any rate, it is curious that on Saturday he should have written anxiously 'Joe has been "cornered" ', pressing W. H. Smith to call on the Sunday morning to see what could be done about this.[397] Labouchere, for his part, was also perfectly clear on Saturday that the Unionists understood that great pressure had to be brought to bear on Chamberlain. The situation was sufficiently critical for a little group consisting of Beach, Churchill, W. H. Smith, and Akers-Douglas to have to go to Hatfield by special train at 3.30 on Sunday afternoon.[398] It was there decided that, should Gladstone announce changes which retained Irish members, a motion for adjournment would be put on the ground that the bill was not the same as that which passed the first reading.[399]

The Liberal chief whip, working even on a Sunday, calculated the position as follows. Some 65 Liberals he considered to be certain opponents. A considerable number of further potential dissidents would be satisfied with recognition of the principle of Irish representation. Even some two or three of the 65 determined opponents might be brought over by such a concession. Others, however, would more or less wait to see what Chamberlain did. The chief whip concluded: 'I still think it all important to secure his support'[400] and on the whole he thought the prospects for doing so were good. He expressed no doubts as to whether the leadership really wanted to win back Chamberlain.

May 7–9: the abortive reunion with Chamberlain. The negotiations between Gladstone and Chamberlain which had been proceeding by fits and starts since 17 April[401] when Arnold Morley worked out that the Radical dissidents could defeat the bill, finally came to a head over the weekend of 7–9 May. A great deal of hectic activity took place, involving Gladstone and Chamberlain and their principal intermediaries, Labouchere and Arnold Morley. The main question at issue was not whether some of the Irish M.Ps should be retained at Westminster – this was accepted in general terms – but the precise conditions on which they would be retained. At two points agreement appeared to have been reached. On 8 May a memorandum authorised by Chamberlain was delivered to Downing St during the cabinet meeting by Labouchere, who was afterwards told by Stansfeld that 'all went right' with regard to the proposed bargain.[402] On 9 May Gladstone, who was staying with Wolverton at Sheen, sent a messenger on horseback with a satisfactory reply to a second memorandum[403] ('the best thing I have ever seen')[404] drafted jointly by Labouchere and A. Morley in London. By the second of these arrangements Chamberlain was given to understand that about 90 Irish M.Ps would be admitted to Westminster when Imperial taxation was under discussion and on all other occasions relating to Imperial questions when the Irish themselves wished to be admitted, while a special body would be set up to transmit the opinion of Ireland on all subjects to the Westminster government.[405] Yet much to the surprise of the press and several cabinet ministers the carefully prepared rapprochement came to nothing.

It is not at all clear that the negotiations were meant to succeed. Their ultimate failure was due to something more than plain misunderstanding. On both sides the will to create a genuine reconciliation was absent, and the decision to employ Labouchere, whose word no one could rely on, as intermediary may have been deliberately designed to ensure that distrust continued. No sooner had the terms been settled on 8 May than Chamberlain set out to sabotage them by putting it about that the cabinet had made an 'absolute surrender' to him,[406] news which quickly reached O'Shea and Parnell who then got Gladstone to issue a public denial. For his part, Gladstone took a highly sceptical view of the proceedings from the beginning: a violent attack on the bill root and branch by Chamberlain in *The Times* of 8 May convinced him that it was 'hopeless to frame a measure of conciliation for him'.[407] John Morley became more adamant against reconciliation:* and even if he were expendable, the confidence of the Irish might be shattered by his departure.

Under cover of the shadow-boxing, Chamberlain and Gladstone sought to improve their respective positions. Chamberlain made a (partially) convincing display of sweet reasonableness to satisfy his supporters that Gladstone's inflexibility made reconciliation

---

* 'J.C. must be taught that a leader is one thing, and a tyrant another. We will not give way to J.C. one further inch. I will certainly, for my poor part, resign rather. Mr G went almost too far last night, and things are worse rather than better in consequence' (John Morley to Spence Watson, 11 May 1886, Spence Watson MSS).

impossible.[408] He may also have acted in collusion with Gladstone's opponents inside the cabinet: significantly his relations with Harcourt improved dramatically at this time, after several months of coolness. Gladstone, who started from the assumption that Chamberlain was implacable, eventually made a nearly adequate offer in the hope of detaching Chamberlain's following and leaving him isolated, a strategy relished by Mrs Gladstone a fortnight later: 'what I should like would be our gaining over many of what are called Chamberlain's men without him'.[409] In fact however the effect of the negotiations was to leave the prospects of the bill essentially unchanged.

May 10 (*Monday*). Gladstone moved the second reading of the Irish government bill. As regards the expected concessions, the comment 'proposals very little cheered: can scarcely prove satisfactory'[410] summed up all views. As one loyal Gladstonian backbencher put it, the premier's speech 'closed with a feeling that he had yielded nothing',[411] which may account for Gladstone's own statement that he was 'well satisfied' with his performance.[412]

In his speech Gladstone promised that the Irish M.Ps would be allowed at Westminster when the taxation of their country was under discussion, and he also alluded vaguely to a possible Commission of representatives of both parliaments. Gestures from Chamberlain during Gladstone's speech made it clear that he was not satisfied. Herbert Gladstone tried vainly to mend the damage, explaining that the problem was not 'a want of good will to meet their fair objections, but because father had not sufficiently mastered the difficulties'.[413] Chamberlain immediately broke off the negotiations which, he believed, had served the useful purpose of showing Gladstone's inflexibility. Chamberlain had not necessarily expected anything of the sort, for earlier in the day he had guarded against the danger of a humiliating reconciliation, by sending Caine and O'Shea round the lobbies to give out that Gladstone had given in to his terms.[414]

On the following day Gladstone set down in detail for the first time the modifications he was prepared to make to the bill. As it happened, his list of proposed amendments (probably never seen by the cabinet) met in full all the demands made by Chamberlain on 8–10 May.[415]

May 12 (*Wednesday*).[416] Chamberlain held a meeting at his house in South Kensington attended by 52 M.Ps,[417] about 12 others sending expressions of sympathy. The meeting lasted nearly two hours. It was agreed that unless the Irish members were retained at Westminster, the bill should be opposed. Chamberlain announced that any further negotiations with Gladstone must be done publicly.[418]

Chamberlain was the main speaker. He began by referring to the hope that had been entertained over the weekend that Gladstone would, in his speech on Monday, offer an acceptable solution concerning the retention of Irish members. For the disappointment caused when Gladstone spoke, Chamberlain held the intermediary (Labouchere, as everyone understood) to be responsible. Chamberlain carefully avoided any direct attack on the premier, but insisted that any further attempts at an understanding must be made on the floor of the House. His other demands were enumerated, and hardly fell short of an entire redrafting of the scheme. Besides making retention of the Irish members an essential point, saying retention was 'not a technical point, but the symbol and flag of the controversy', he urged further steps to protect the Irish Unionists, if necessary by the separate treatment of Ulster, and that the taxation clauses should be entirely remodelled.

Trevelyan followed, saying that 'though in the cabinet he had thought there were serious differences between Mr Chamberlain's position and his own, he had now come to the opinion that on certain points his rt. hon. friend was right'.* Caine, Meysey-Thompson, and Goldsmid also spoke. Caine, Chamberlain's unofficial whip, said that 102 Liberal M.Ps had promised to vote against the second reading if the bill were not amended, and that another 30 or 40 were undecided. No resolution was passed at Chamberlain's meeting, but retention was in effect made more than ever the vital point.[419] An interesting feature of the meeting was the warmth with which mentions of Hartington were greeted.

At midnight, a body of 50 staunch Gladstonians, with Alfred Illingworth as chairman, held their own meeting in the conference room of the House. It was resolved to express their unanimous determination to carry the second reading, and to suggest that a private meeting of the party might do great good.[420] A suggestion that Chamberlain should also be approached led to a violent clash and only found three supporters.

Chamberlain's strength of purpose corresponded with, or produced, an equal loss of nerve on the part of Hartington's principal adviser, Henry James. Algernon West, invited to call on the Gladstones to help socially after what they expected to be a 'stiff dinner',[421] found himself talking there to James 'who told me that he had come to the conclusion that this Irish question must be

---

* 'Trevelyan is unthought of, and his impotence more than manifest. He would have done better to stick to his biographical studies, rather than to attempt to make history' (Esher's journal, May 1886).

settled one way or another: Lord Hartington did not want to take office, and they could not trust the Tories to deal with so fearful a subject. All the Liberals at Mr Chamberlain's meeting, 49 or 52, had settled to attend the Hartington meeting, and the result would be a complete disruption of the Liberal party. ... if in some way or another the principle of autonomy could be put forward, the majority, possibly including Hartington, would vote for it, and on it a Bill could be introduced and considered in the autumn session.' Gladstone, talking to West about this later in the evening, stressed his hopes of a *modus vivendi* being found, especially by Whitbread, and left West with the impression that he might agree to postpone to another session the details of the bill.[422]

James' anxiety was strategic in origin, rather than a momentary aberration. A clear sign of his determination to leave the way open for eventual reconciliation, was his letter of reinsurance to Mundella confiding that 'my heart is all with Mr G':[423] another was his attempt to sell to the Tory leadership the idea of walking out of the House on the second reading.[424] Behind this *volte-face* was the collapse of James' personal position as honest broker between Hartington and Churchill, the latter having quarrelled with James and declared that he 'would never speak to him again'.[425] Churchill had, naturally, taken some remarks by James denouncing those who incited Ulster to resist by force, as aimed at himself.[426] The rift between the two men lasted till about 6 June, when James told E. Hamilton that good feeling had been restored, though he still insisted that he had no real belief in Churchill, whom he compared to a batsman habitually prone to running out his own side.

A few days later James showed another facet of his *crise de nerfs* by calling, with Hussey Vivian, on E. Hamilton to ask for abandonment of the bill, and procedure by resolution which might include anything not actually called a parliament in Dublin.[427] There is nothing to show that James' various attempts at reunion left any mark on the main protagonists, though they certainly allowed him to retreat far and fast himself. By early June he was saying 'Home Rule of some kind ... must be faced.'[428]

James' abortive manoeuvres roughly coincided with a largely independent campaign led by three highly respected backbenchers, Joseph Pease, Illingworth and Whitbread who, for quite unselfish reasons, were anxious to save the unity of the party. Their concern was to ensure that the vast majority of Liberals supported the government's home rule policy, and they were not particular about the means used to achieve it. The bill might be withdrawn or amended at once or proceeded with on the understanding that amendments would follow after the second reading. Alternatively a resolution might be substituted: this was the course of action which all these honourable men ultimately found to be the best for their purpose. It was also the one that Gladstone ruled out with the utmost firmness, for if the government adopted it ministers would be 'fatally damaged in [their] authority'.[429] In letters to these backbench well-wishers Gladstone made a point of stressing the impracticality of their suggestions. At the same time he made sure that the hard-line exclusionists in the cabinet (Harcourt and Morley) were kept fully informed of the pressure building up in the party which was making the announcement of major concessions inevitable.[430] Gladstone's strategy was not to prevent the bill being modified, but to ensure that he appeared to control the content and the timing of the amendments which could no longer be avoided. The backbench movement finally ground to a halt around 19 May. Significantly however all the compromises which Gladstone later toyed with were foreshadowed in the efforts of a group of honest men in the middle of the party to find a bridge by which the dissident Liberals could return to the party.

May 14 (*Friday*). At question time, Chamberlain sat down next to Harcourt on the Treasury bench and they talked for several minutes. Later Hartington came across and talked to Harcourt.

Hartington's meeting at Devonshire House was held at noon and lasted about two hours. Prior to the meeting, Sellar and Trevelyan (who 'has got his spirits back again') had breakfasted with Goschen, who then suddenly became too unwell to attend.[431] Out of 130 M.Ps invited, 64 attended, including 20 who had been at Chamberlain's meeting on Wednesday. Hartington said he would vote against the second reading, even if it were announced that it would be treated as no more than an abstract resolution, and that he could not 'believe that Liberal statesmanship was not capable of dealing with the difficulties of the Irish question in the event of the government bills being defeated'.

Chamberlain followed, attacking Gladstone's concessions as inadequate, and refusing to accept that withdrawal of the bill after the second reading would be a satisfactory compromise. The bill should be withdrawn at once: if not, it would be rejected by 70. Trevelyan spoke briefly, and then a general discussion ensued whose tone was set against compromise. Speakers included R. B. Finlay, Mitchell Henry, W. Saunders, H. Meysey-Thompson, H. Wiggin, P. Rylands, and H. Vivian. After the meeting, Chamberlain and Hartington remained in discussion.[432]

Morley had an important talk with Parnell.[433] Afterwards Gladstone wrote a short memorandum for Morley's benefit 'in connection with the points so well put by Mr P.'. In it he touched on the importance, for the Parnellites, of delaying an election in order to produce a clear majority for home rule 'in the next parliament'. This strategy would embarrass critics, and might even produce a small majority for the second reading.[434]

A group of earnest Liberal backbenchers, led by Samuel Whitbread, who were anxious to prevent a party split, attempted to enlist Bright's aid. Meeting him by appointment at the Reform Club, Whitbread told Bright that his aim was to secure a solid vote for the second reading, to be followed by immediate withdrawal of the bill. Bright was unimpressed, writing 'no solution possible at the moment'. Caine, the unofficial whip for Chamberlain, was working on him the other way round, assuring him the bill was as good as dead, in a series of meetings designed to get Bright to vote against the bill and not merely abstain.[435]

The shadow cabinet met at Arlington St at 12: at 2.30 the Tory whip met Henry Brand and Alexander Craig Sellar, the unofficial Liberal Unionist whips.[436]

May 15 (Saturday). Gladstone went down to stay with Algernon West and his wife at Coombe, where on Sunday they were joined by Harcourt.[437] John Morley and Granville also joined the company. West described the GOM as being 'in one of his frivolous, provoking moods, making a cabinet for Hartington, which on the 17th appeared, as he had written it, in the *Pall Mall Gazette*, and we could not imagine how it got there'. When pressed by West to proceed with home rule by tactics of general resolutions and deferment of details, Gladstone replied that it was too late for conciliation, and that proceeding by resolution was proper for an opposition, as in 1868, but not for a government.

Gladstone returned thoroughly refreshed from his visit. During the night, however, he had a bilious attack and got little sleep, though by Monday morning he had largely recovered.[438]

Salisbury addressed the National Union of Conservative Associations (the party conference) at St James's Hall, making a highly reactionary speech intended to destroy Hartington's attempted creation of a moderate consensus in his speech of the previous day. Salisbury's cunning identification of opposition to Gladstone's scheme, with some choice diehard slogans, brought immediate joy to the Gladstonians and depression to the non-opportunist Unionists.

May 17 (Monday). Ponsonby called on Gladstone to discuss the bill and to scotch persistent rumours (instigated, Gladstone believed, by Churchill) that the Queen would refuse to dissolve if the bill was defeated. Gladstone told him at the moment the bill appeared doomed, but that any one of several possible compromises might carry it through the second reading. Limited admission of the Irish, Gladstone continued, was already decided in principle and would present no difficulties. The suggestion 'by a friend ... (and) some of the opponents' that the bill be abandoned after the second reading, a new bill being introduced in the autumn, was still being weighed by the cabinet. [439]

At the House Bright talked to Chamberlain 'whose anxiety is very apparent' and to Harcourt, who said Gladstone would dissolve if defeated.

Gladstone returned to his wife after 'a capital night' in the Commons feeling extremely satisfied with the progress of the debate. He had also some hope that Chamberlain, who had asked to meet Herbert Gladstone, was on the verge of capitulation.

After the House had risen Chamberlain took Herbert Gladstone on one side and talked at length about his desire to reach an agreement with the government, speaking with impressive earnestness and sincerity. He showed quite uncharacteristic signs of humility: 'he blamed nobody for last Monday's misunderstanding except perhaps himself, for he may not have made it clearly known what he wanted'. He went on to express his satisfaction at several of Gladstone's assurances, notably as regards Ulster, and although nothing new was said about the retention of the Irish M.Ps, Chamberlain linked that difficulty to the general question of retaining the supremacy of the Imperial Parliament which, he suggested, might be done in other ways. He then came to the heart of the matter which consisted of a conditional undertaking that 'he might see his way to the affirmation of the principle of a Parliament if more time was given for the reconsideration and working out of details'. [440] There was, he implied, a distinct possibility that Hartington could be made to see the wisdom of such a compromise.

Chamberlain's conduct was absolutely consistent at this time. He accepted as true the false rumours that Gladstone was about to substitute a resolution for the bill: in those circumstances he believed that revolt within the Liberal party was no longer possible. Consequently the most serious attempt by Chamberlain to encourage reunion occurs at this time. To members of his family he said for the first and last time that he and Gladstone 'might come together again'. [441]

May 18 (*Tuesday*). Chamberlain walked down to the House from the Athenaeum, accompanied by Goschen, Lord George Hamilton, and C. Dalrymple, a former Tory junior whip. On reaching the

House they broke up, and Chamberlain walked away *tête-à-tête* with Goschen.[442]

May 19 (Wednesday). Goschen saw the Queen and explained to her his plans for preventing any compromise between the government and its Liberal opponents. 'We thought Lord Hartington and Mr Chamberlain could form a government.'[443]

May 20 (Thursday). Soon after 5, some 35 dissident Liberals assembled in one of the committee rooms, on an oral summons from Chamberlain. No circular was sent out. The conference lasted well over an hour. The meeting decided against adhering *en bloc* to the Liberal Unionist Committee, though Chamberlain wished them to do so.[444] It was left as a matter for individual decision. On the other hand, the general feeling was that if the Gladstonians opposed them at elections, the dissident Liberals must retaliate actively. It was again stressed that withdrawal of the bill after the second reading would not be an adequate compromise.[445]

Schnadhorst had an interview with Gladstone and was rumoured to have given a very reassuring account of feeling in the country.[446] In fact, Schnadhorst was probably less optimistic than was made out. According to E. Hamilton who butted in on the conference (at which the chief whip, Arnold Morley, was present), Schnadhorst thought a snap election *before* the second reading would be infinitely preferable to making damaging concessions to the bill's critics. Schnadhorst doubted whether the gain of the Irish vote in British seats would offset defections elsewhere.[447] Whether the idea of a snap election held simply to reunite the party was ever more than a fleeting thought considered only as a local possibility, cannot be established. What is clear is that the cabinet never considered the issue formally.

A full meeting of the month-old Liberal Unionist Committee, until this date simply an ad hoc committee of individuals recruited by solicitation, was held at the Westminster Palace Hotel. A general committee of 59 was appointed, including 19 M.Ps and 13 Peers,[448] to act as the governing body of what was to become a nation-wide association. Hartington urged the need for organisation to resist pressure being brought to bear on the dissidents by the constituencies. Goschen, Rylands, and Argyll spoke in support of Hartington. Derby and H. R. Grenfell moved a vote of thanks to Hartington.[449]

The meeting probably gave special consideration to the financial arrangements required in the event of a dissolution on the Irish question. At any rate, the rumour among Gladstonian back-benchers the following day was that the 'great Hartington meeting' had been held 'to raise £100,000 to fight Liberal candidates',[450] while Nathaniel de Rothschild ('Natty') told Brett 'that Albert Grey's committee have unlimited funds, and that this circumstance, and the poverty of the ministerialists, procures the seceders adherents',[451] a view which Brett thought much exaggerated. In fact, however, A. Grey had just been given the task of raising funds, and had received an initial £2,000 from one individual towards a target of £50,000, which he hoped to collect by the end of May.[452]

May 23 (*Sunday*). Harcourt wrote to Gladstone, agreeing with Granville that a mooted negotiation with Hartington would be inexpedient.[453]

May 25 (*Tuesday*). The cabinet met 12–1.20 at Downing St, from which Mundella was absent. Herschell was also absent when the meeting began, hearing a case in the court of appeal, but on his being sent for, the hearing was suspended.[454]

Mundella had been reported off work with a sore throat as early as 11 May, [455] his illness probably developing into bronchitis. Even at the end of the month colleagues were writing to him as to an invalid.[456] Mundella had had a similar prolonged bronchial attack in spring 1885. For purposes of political analysis, he must be regarded as being outside the political situation during the most critical period of May 1886, and probably for a good deal longer. How long he remained an invalid is uncertain. He managed to vote on 8 June, but took no part in parliamentary business before the elections. *The Times* of 22 June carried a report that he had just ceased to be confined to his London house, and had left for Hertfordshire on his way to take part in his election at Sheffield Brightside.

It was decided that a party meeting should be held on Thursday, at which Gladstone should explain that the vote on the second reading was simply one of principle and would not imply acceptance of details. Moreover, it was decided that if the bill were read a second time, 'there should be no further proceeding on it ... until an early date in the autumn...'[457] The discussion which led to this decision was for once very harmonious.[458] Immediately after the cabinet, Gladstone left for Windsor,[459] which started rumours of a dissolution. A circular was issued later the same day announcing a party meeting on Thursday.[460]

The prospect of a resounding statement affirming imperial supremacy being made at the coming party meeting caused some alarm. Parnell 'was very anxious that we should on no account say a word to harden the doctrine of supremacy', and Morley, concurring, duly impressed this on a sympathetic Gladstone.

Ripon probably also put the same point to Morley: while Herschell, Morley thought, probably leaned in the other direction.[461]

The Gladstones went out to dine at a party which was a 'perfect success', the guests including Professor Stuart, Mr and Mrs Buxton, Lubbock, and Mrs Dugdale. Mrs Gladstone reported 'Papa at his best talking to the table and between acts deeply interested in Maggy's stories about her child and her dolls... I never saw him more at his ease... When the gentlemen came in, Father in high glee though standing in grave talk with Stuart after which he sunk down into a lovely sofa by Mrs Dugdale taking her in, so full of Macaulay talk.'[462]

May 26 (*Wednesday*). Parliament adjourned for the Derby.

A memorandum by Gladstone bearing this date which was circulated to the cabinet described the shift in his position. Gladstone, after describing the decision of the cabinet on the previous day as to letting the bill stand over till the autumn, now sought cabinet sanction for an announcement of an entirely new bill. Kimberley, Herschell, Morley, Mundella and Campbell-Bannerman agreed to this rephrasing, only Kimberley doing so unconditionally, the rest in deference to Gladstone's views.[463]

Gladstone dined at the Austrian embassy, taking with him Marjoribanks, the junior whip.[464]

May 27 (*Thursday*). A meeting of the Liberal Party was held at noon at the Foreign Office, attended by more than 200 M.Ps.[465] Invitations had been sent, dated 25 May, to 'all members of the Liberal party who are desirous, while retaining full freedom on all the particulars of the Irish Government Bill, to vote in favour of the establishment of a Legislative Body in Dublin, for the management of affairs specifically and exclusively Irish'. Chamberlain received an invitation.[466] Gladstone spoke for more than an hour, his theme being that a vote for the second reading would be a vote for the principle only. He also offered to retain the Irish at Westminster for purposes of taxation.

The occasion was a tonic to backbench morale. One staunch loyalist wrote:

'The Prime Minister came into the big room followed by members of the Government amidst cheers, and at once addressed us. He spoke for three-quarters of an hour, was in splendid form, cheerful, clear, and sparkling, and handled the delicate and complex subjects in a most masterly manner. The effect of this speech was immediately self-evident and several prominent dissentients proclaimed their conversion, whilst those

426

who had hitherto been strong in opposition like my father came away in a better state of mind.'[467]

After the premier had finished, a number of backbenchers spoke briefly. These included Dillwyn, Whitbread, Arch, Beith, Saunders, Bradlaugh, Ruston, and Illingworth. There were some questions about the financial aspects, and Rathbone and Moulton asked how long it would take, if the second reading were passed, before it would be possible to proceed with a redrawn bill. Gladstone said that legislation would be recommenced in less than six months.[468] The meeting dispersed after giving Gladstone three hearty cheers on a motion proposed by Brunner, the M.P. for Northwich. On the way back from the meeting, Gladstone met E. Hamilton, who found the premier immensely pleased with having timed his appeal so successfully.

Following the meeting, Chamberlain attempted to muster his supporters, but only 35 or 36 M.Ps turned up. Chamberlain said the dissident Liberals should refuse all compromise, but opinion was divided on this, and several M.Ps were in favour of voting for the second reading, if the bill were then to be withdrawn. Because of these differences, and the low attendance, the meeting was adjourned to 31 May.[469]

After the Foreign Office meeting, Gladstone drew up a memorandum estimating the dissidents at 8 Chamberlainites and 66 Hartingtonians and others.[470] The implication of these figures is very similar to that of the statement by Caine, Chamberlain's whip, that following the Foreign Office meeting some thirty of Chamberlain's group were shaky or had deserted to the Gladstonians.[471] The apparent demoralisation of the Radical Unionists by Gladstone's promise to withdraw the bill, was so quickly reversed that it is almost impossible to judge whether it did, in fact, very fleetingly take place.

The sitting of the House of Commons had to be abruptly closed, the smell from the drains proving intolerable.[472]

May 28 (Friday). Childers' son, Lt. Francis Childers, died of typhoid in India.

May 29 (Saturday). Hartington presided at a meeting of the Liberal Unionist Committee at Spring Gardens which was practically unanimous in favour of opposing the bill on its second reading. This was in sharp contrast to expectations early the previous day, when it had initially appeared that the Liberal Unionist leaders would have to give way to their followers' pressure for abstention on the second reading, after a big swing in backbench opinion created by Gladstone's Foreign Office speech. On Friday evening, however, the mood had veered equally sharply back again, following an indiscreet reply by Gladstone to Beach in debate which served to cause, as it perhaps was calculated to do, a hardening of attitudes throughout the Liberal Unionist party. A suggestion that Hartington's followers should abstain on the second reading was rejected practically out of hand, perhaps because at that moment, since Whigs generally believed the Chamberlainites would abstain, the Whigs needed to muster every show of strength. Hartington himself put his support at about 60, thus giving Gladstone a majority of nine on the second reading.[473] The tone of the meeting can hardly have been confident, because Milner came away thinking for the first time that the bill might really pass.[474]

Salisbury held a small meeting of ex-ministers at Arlington St at 4. Harrowby pencilled an undated explanatory note on his invitation from Salisbury, as follows: 'to hear scheme from Sir H. James etc. that Conservatives, Hartington and his followers, and Chamberlain and his followers, should all walk out and refuse to vote on 2nd Reading ... as they feared Radicals were affected by Foreign Office speech of Gladstone. Refused unanimously.'[475] A more interesting version is that the shadow cabinet were 'practically unanimous, though R.C. did not pronounce one way or the other',[476] a typical instance of his surly and uninvolved stance at this time. Salisbury, writing earlier the same day, invited Akers-Douglas, the chief whip, to attend, but described the meeting as not worth staying in town for.[477]

May 30 (*Sunday*). Caine, Chamberlain's whip, reported to his master that everything depended on Bright. 'If Bright speaks and votes, he will rally a lot of our waverers', enough, Caine thought, to ensure a unionist majority of about 38. In the absence of action by Bright, Chamberlain could only avoid humiliating defeat by walking out at the head of his followers. Caine calculated that of 112 dissidents on Chamberlain's lists four days earlier, only 69 could still be relied on: 12 had definitely joined Gladstone, and the remainder were doubtful, even perhaps adverse.

The Gladstones gave a dinner party attended by Henry James and several other Liberal Unionists, sufficient to carry a vote of no confidence in him by three to one, as the G.O.M. genially remarked. All passed off well, and Gladstone was at his most charming, but James felt the occasion was one of 'no little sadness'.

May 31 (*Monday*). Chamberlain's supporters met in Committee Room 15 from 5 to 6.45, with from 53 to 55 M.Ps attending,[478] of whom perhaps 20 were really followers of Hartington.[479] There is probably some substance in the allegation that the meeting was 'packed so as to ensure a hostile majority'.[480] It was said that night that 'Chamberlain's meeting was a plant. There were above 20 Hartington men (at a meeting from which Hartington men were excluded). Of these 13 were on the Hartington Unionist Committee...'[481] If these allegations, from three different sources, are broadly correct (and attendance cannot actually be checked man by man), then one does reach the rather important result that an unpacked meeting would have been roughly equally divided on the question of whether to oppose the second reading, even after taking into account Bright's notorious letter which was read as though he blamed those who abstained.

Chamberlain said that the concessions outlined by Gladstone in his Foreign Office speech left the matter exactly as it stood before. Then, with an impressive air of impartiality, he discussed the pros and cons of the only two alternatives open to them – walking out on the second reading, or voting against it. He then presented his *coup de grâce*, the letter from John Bright saying he would himself vote against the second reading, almost as if it were none of his doing. Bright's letter, selectively read by Chamberlain, made a decisive impact.[482] Then Trevelyan made 'the speech that one would expect from a nervous and sensitive politician', asking for a straight vote against the second reading.

An animated discussion followed, with contributions from R. B. Finlay, David Davies, Sir Julian Goldsmid,[483] Hussey Vivian, and Powell Williams. Sir Joseph Pease begged the dissidents to abstain on the second reading, but his motion to that effect was defeated by 38 to 12, with 5 actually for the bill. On a second and final vote, 46 were for voting against the second reading, 4 for abstaining, and 3 were in favour of the bill. Reports of the numbers voting naturally vary slightly.[484]

The final vote undid any hopes that had been aroused by the Foreign Office meeting on 27 May. 'The meeting spread dismay in our ranks, and it was practically the unanimous opinion that the bill was lost by a considerable majority.'[485] Ponsonby sent a telegram of jubilation to the Queen describing the outcome of the meeting as contrary to expectation.[486]

The following day Mrs Gladstone wrote of 'the sudden collapse' of hope at Downing St when Arnold Morley came round and broke the news of the Chamberlain meeting. Herbert Gladstone thought 'it has been a real plot'. According to fresh calculations made by the whips just after Chamberlain's meeting, Gladstone expected at this stage to be defeated by thirteen.[487]

June 1 (Tuesday). At 4 p.m., Hartington held a meeting, originally called for Monday but postponed, at Devonshire House attended by 60 M.Ps, including 20 who had been at Chamberlain's meeting the previous day: 58 voted for voting against the second reading.[488] However, even at lunchtime that day one of Hartington's whips, Craig Sellar, had been confidently talking about the defeat of the bill, saying Hartington's supporters were even stiffer against it than Chamberlain's.[489]

Rosebery heard from the Greek ambassador that his government had agreed to a settlement which would allow Britain to dismantle the blockade, and in fact take the Greek question off the diplomatic agenda. After dinner Rosebery went to report this to Gladstone, noting that he had not seen the premier 'for at least six weeks' except at two cabinets when they were unable to exchange a word.[490]

June 2 (Wednesday). The Gladstones entertained to dinner Rosebery, Canon MacColl, H. Ponsonby, Hutton, and others. The G.O.M. was 'very fine and animated, but unreasonable about gratitude of Ireland'.[491] Rosebery disagreed, saying 'I agree with you in most things, Mr Gladstone, but not on that, for I think the Irish have been most ungrateful. You have passed more bills for their benefit than any other minister and they have opposed you on every occasion – and even now may probably do so again.'[492]

After dinner, Gladstone's party went on to a ball in honour of the Queen's birthday. Mrs Gladstone spoke to Bright who was upset at the effect his letter had had on Chamberlain's meeting. Ponsonby met Hartington, who said that in certain conditions he would be prepared to form a government.[493] Late that night, Gladstone's view was that the bill had a fairly good chance, even though more than fifty votes were undecided.[494]

Chamberlain, full of affability, dined with a Tory hostess, the company including the young Curzon and the ancient Lady Dorothy Neville. Chamberlain told E. Hamilton that Gladstone 'had played his game badly', and might have obtained a majority by any one of three concessions: omission of clause 24, substitution of a resolution, or a promised withdrawal of the bill. As to the future, Chamberlain looked forward, not to his own professed federal schemes, but to the prospect of firm government which would break the Irish party and cause the problem to melt away. This (probably his real view) was at odds with his concurrent creation of the Radical Unionist Committee 'to secure the extension of local government on similar principles to all parts of the United Kingdom', as he defined it to his brother on 7 June.

June 4 (Friday). Gladstone and his wife dined with the Wests, Paulton, Edward Grey, and John Morley being also there.

Gladstone was 'in great form and spirits, notwithstanding all his anxieties and troubles. Nothing seems to weigh him down.'

June 5 (Saturday). Gladstone and his wife left Downing St in the evening to stay till Monday at Dollis Hill with Lord and Lady Aberdeen, who had come over from Dublin on a brief holiday. The house-party included the Spencers, Marjoribanks, Dalhousie, Lady F. Cavendish, Sir R. Hamilton, and Herbert Gladstone.

Churchill, on the other hand, was expected to spend the week-end with Labouchere at Twickenham, Ellen Terry being of the company.[495]

June 6 (Sunday). Rosebery and his private secretary Munro Ferguson (who later, as Lord Novar, sat in Baldwin's cabinet) drove to Dollis Hill. Gladstone told Rosebery it was anybody's division, though the odds were against, adding 'I think with great comfort of the fact that in all human probability all connection between Chamberlain and myself is over for ever.'

In the evening Rosebery dined with a party of about 30 at Marlborough House, and had a long talk with Hartington with whom he walked home. Hartington said the government had no chance of winning,[496] and his confidence was also apparent to another guest, E. Hamilton. The latter was told by Rosebery that 'Mr G could not repress his satisfaction that come what might, he was rid of Chamberlain for good.'

June 7 (Monday). On the evening of the division, Wolverton, coming out of the chief whip's room, told West 'there were yet hopes of the Bill being carried'. Wolverton, a former chief whip whose opinion probably weighed with Gladstone, also wrote during the day to the premier predicting a small overall majority for the government at an election. Arnold Morley, visiting Gladstone at Downing St during the afternoon, found him immersed in a French novel and somewhat put out by the interruption.[497]

In the evening Gladstone dined at the Scottish Office with Dalhousie.[498]

The home rule debate was concluded. Goschen spoke unremarkably, but was followed by Parnell who quietly declared for the first time that he had been in communication with leading Conservatives, who had encouraged him to think they would support home rule, with power to protect Irish industries. Beach fiercely denied the revelations, though Churchill, 'rolling in excitement, tearing at his moustache and casting quick glances at the Irish benches, as if in terror of their splitting on him' was seen kicking Beach for his too emphatic denials. Pressed to give names, Parnell said 'If you procure your colleagues' consent, I will give names.'[499]

June 8 (*Tuesday*). The ministry was defeated on the second reading of the Irish Government Bill at 1 a.m. by 341–311 (excluding tellers).[500] Rosebery later told the Queen that the division was 'larger than was expected ... that Mr Gladstone had made a very fine speech, but still, all the waverers had gone against him, and it had not turned one vote'. Gladstone himself lent weight to this interpretation of the final trend of opinion, saying 'the group of the undecided, who augmented at last from 20 to 30, went almost in a mass against the bill'.[501] Almost certainly Gladstone was quite unprepared for the size of the majority, which his son called 'much more than we expected'.[502]

The Unionists, on the other hand, had for some time had an approximately accurate idea of what their majority would be. For instance, on 6 June A. Grey had expected a majority of 36 or over. Similarly, on 7 June Chamberlain joined a Tory M.P. on the terrace and told him the majority against would be 30. However, Lubbock, unlike other Unionists, thought the eventual majority 'better than we ventured to hope'.[503] On the evening of the division itself, A. Grey offered a Gladstonian M.P. odds of six to four in favour of a Unionist majority of over ten.[504] In the event he thought the majority should have been greater, and he named Rathbone, Sir J. Pease,[505] and Macinnes as men who had all told him they objected to every clause in the bill, and yet had voted for it. He was astonished that C. M. Palmer had not at least abstained, given his dislike of the bill. Though Grey reported a common impression that Gladstone's speech had been 'the most impressive piece of eloquence they ever listened to', he did not assign to it any influence over voting, and sensibly stressed his own pedestrian achievement as whip:

> '... My time during the debate being occupied with M.Ps who wished to walk out. Each one had to be spoken to separately and to be convinced that his position would be a very peculiar and exceptional one if he walked out inasmuch as nearly all the Dissentients were going to vote like men against the Bill – and I flatter myself I did more good in the lobby talking to members, than I should have done in the House listening to Gladstone.'[506]

In the lobby after the division, Hartington was on his way to telegraph the result to his mistress, when he was attacked by an elderly man and quite a brawl ensued.[507]

The cabinet met at Downing St at 2, attended by all the ministers except Granville, who was ill with gout. Granville's illness was quite severe, and even when not severe, highly disabling. First reported as ill and confined to his room on 4 June, he was still confined to bed on 6 July, without any respite in between. Not till 13 July was he even able to take a drive, though he had kept up his correspondence during his illness.

Ministers decided *nem. con.* in favour of recommending a dissolution rather than resigning, Granville expressing in writing his agreement with this decision. Gladstone's point of view at this juncture can be found in a pencilled memorandum dated 8 June concluding in favour of dissolution for the sake of 'the cause': resignation, he argued, entailed 'abandonment of the cause'.[508] There is evidence that Rosebery differed from Gladstone at this time on the question of strategy, though he only put his views privately. On 5 July 1886 Hamilton, on being shown a letter from Gladstone to Rosebery on the question of resignation, wrote 'it almost implied a wish that he had taken that course some weeks ago when Rosebery and myself urged it'.[509] Rosebery himself told the Queen that ever since April, he had been strongly in favour of resignation in the event of defeat, although 'he did not urge the question in cabinet'.[510]

The future handling of business of supply was considered, and Rosebery and Campbell-Bannerman were asked to see the Queen, who was at Balmoral. Rosebery had to go to a meeting of the Liberal Scottish M.Ps at Marjoribanks' house later in the day. He left for Balmoral at 8 the following evening, after having called on Gladstone.

In the Commons, Gladstone moved the adjournment till Thursday. The Queen received a cypher from Gladstone asking for a dissolution, which she sanctioned on condition it took place at once. The request was not unexpected, as she had heard on 6 June that Gladstone would want to dissolve if defeated,[511] and as early as May the Queen's soundings[512] had shown her that the opposition wanted her to grant any such request.

June 10 (Thursday). After question time, Gladstone announced the dissolution of parliament. Routine business was then resumed, and continued up till the prorogation of parliament on Friday, 25 June.

Rosebery arrived at Balmoral at 1 p.m. on a visit which must be reckoned one of the minor triumphs of the ministry. Before his departure at 2 p.m. on 12 June – when he impressed on the Queen his enchantment with Balmoral and his dejection at leaving it – he was the subject of the highest commendation to be found in the Queen's journal for any politician at this time: 'excessively agreeable', 'a very clever, pleasant man, and very kind', in fact warmer terms than any awarded to members of the Salisbury ministry. The Queen told him 'he had a great future before him', and advised him to keep his options open.

Rosebery in return talked freely, not only on current Foreign Office problems like the New Hebrides crisis, but on general cabinet politics. He said that the cause of Gladstone wanting to dissolve, not to resign, was his age; that Gladstone was terribly ill-advised, but would never resign without defeat in the elections and perhaps in parliament subsequently as well. Rosebery described Gladstone as pugnacious on the issue, and made his own coolness towards the cabinet decision of 8 June clear enough, without stating whether he had done anything effective to oppose it.

Rosebery said Dilke's vote for the bill was 'clearly on account of social reasons, hoping to get back into society, which he will not'.[513]

At Downing St, Gladstone, who was 'excellently well and full of go' had ten to dinner, including Aberdeen, Flower, Marjoribanks, and Wolverton.[514]

Part Four

The General Election of 1886 and its Aftermath

On Thursday, 17 June, Gladstone left London for Midlothian, stopping to greet enthusiastic crowds en route. The following day he delivered a major speech in Edinburgh, where he spoke again on the 21st. On the 22nd he spoke in Glasgow, on the 25th in Manchester, and on the 28th in Liverpool, in a campaign which in geographical range went altogether beyond anything he had attempted in 1880 or 1885.

After his Glasgow speech, Gladstone returned to Hawarden, where he was greeted by several hundred members of the Chester Liberal Association, at 1 p.m. on the 23rd. On arrival he was exhausted, but recovered rapidly enough to make his two final campaign speeches, asserting that neither of the Irish bills required more than slight modification. Apart from these excursions, however, Gladstone remained quietly at Hawarden, getting out a good deal in the fresh air, and doing nothing more exciting than read the lessons in church and attend the annual parade of the Hawarden Rifle Volunteers, until his return to London on 14 July.

Gladstone's Scottish campaign, though not on the grand scale of previous efforts, produced very respectable results. Nowhere were the Gladstonians more successful in 1886 than in Eastern Scotland, where the Tories proper won only 1 seat out of 43. In this area, where Gladstone most directly influenced popular opinion, 32 Gladstonians were returned compared with 9 Unionists of all brands. Moreover, despite the Gladstonian collapse in Glasgow and Western Scotland, where there was an anti-home rule majority of 20 M.Ps to 9, there was no perceptible defection to Conservatism at all in Scotland. In the 17 Scottish seats which the Tories fought both in 1885 and in 1886, the total Tory vote actually dropped from 52,290 to 50,800.[1] Twelve Scottish seats returned Gladstonians without a contest. Looking at the Scottish electoral scene, then, and remembering that it was Gladstone's own chief vantage-point and stamping-ground, Gladstone's buoyancy can be seen to have some basis. Supposing for the sake of argument that Gladstone had stood for all English marginal seats, in the way he came forward to crush a supposed Liberal dissident by standing at Leith,[2] the elections could have taken a very different aspect.

The position in Wales (including the Monmouth seats) at this election also showed the imperturbable solidity of regional fastnesses as a factor in party strength. Of the 30 Welsh seats, the Gladstonians won one (Montgomery District) from the Tories, while losing to them three other marginal borough seats (Pembroke, Monmouth, and Carnarvon districts). The Tories in general however were not able to use home rule to gain back the ground, or the morale, they had lost in Wales in 1885. Indeed, in the case of seats which were contested in both 1885 and 1886, the anti-Gladstonian forces improved their position in 12 cases (eight counties, four towns), as against eight cases (three counties, five towns) where the Gladstonians did better in 1886 than in 1885. Old enmities prevented any satisfactory coalition between Tory and Liberal Unionist elements.

The Liberal Unionists did badly in Wales at the election, and much worse than appears at first sight from the reference books. Seven Welsh Liberals voted against the second reading of the home rule bill, and one, Richard Davies (Anglesey) abstained (and did not again contest an election). This looked at first sight as though it might provide the basis for a substantial schism. But there was no Welsh leader of any stature deliberately seeking to widen the breach, and it was probable that several of the dissidents were honest men who, while wishing to record their opposition in principle to the bill, had in so doing no intention of splitting the party or changing its power structure. However, it was still remarkable that shortly after the 1886 election, Liberal Unionism in Wales had sunk almost without trace.

Liberal Unionists came forward in ten Welsh seats. They failed badly in five contests, and in a sixth their sitting member lost by 200. In the seventh case, that of Cardiganshire, a weak Gladstonian candidate defeated the sitting member, David Davies, 'railway king' of Wales, by nine votes. Only in the remote division of West

Denbighshire was an unequivocal Liberal Unionist returned, and here the reason seems to have been simply that the Gladstonians did not get round to finding a candidate to oppose him. When they did contest the seat, in 1892, it produced a Gladstonian majority of nearly 2,000. Apart from this one M.P, let in by default and notched for execution, the Liberal Unionists' only successes were Sir H.H.Vivian (Swansea District, unopposed) and C.R.M. Talbot (Mid-Glamorgan, unopposed), but these, though they were elected as Unionists, both returned readily to the Gladstonian fold. Welsh society was too unequivocally divided into two sides, and the Gladstonian ascendancy was too recently achieved and too charged with purely Welsh meanings, for there to be any scope for turning divisions among Welsh Liberals at Westminster into part of the structure of regional politics. The strength of the Gladstonian cause in eastern Scotland and in Wales, as well as its weakness in western Scotland, illustrated the importance of purely regional political patterns in which national politics could hardly get a foothold.[3]

In England, the pattern might be almost equally regional, if anyone knew what the true regions of England were. Liberal Unionists did well in Devon and Cornwall, where seven of their eight sitting members were returned, and in Birmingham, which remained Chamberlain's fief. In the north, and particularly in Yorkshire and Northumberland, the Gladstonian ascendancy was perhaps even clearer than before for having been challenged. The Liberal Unionists were weak in London, because they could only be strong where Liberalism had been strong. In the south and midlands the Gladstonians lost 35 county and 28 borough seats, but the meaning of this is enigmatic as one does not know how far Liberal success in the counties in the previous election should be regarded as a flash in the pan. The tendency of the suburban clerk to vote Tory, long established, became more pronounced, and the Gladstonians were left with a more working-class vote than ever before. It is very difficult to determine why that working-class vote did not prevail in 1886, as it did in 1887, and statistics do not help much, for with 152 seats uncontested, about half a million of those who voted in 1885 had to stay at home in this election. If it were clear that the working-class vote shifted to the Tories in bulk, then the 1886 election would be very important. As it is, all that can be said is that the 1886 elections did not give the Tories as many seats as they really required, and that it confirmed rather than reversed the voting patterns of previous elections.[4] Perhaps the most remarkable contrast between this election and the previous one lay not in what the electors did but in the degree of freedom with which Gladstone defined, confused, or declined to define the policy of his party. The Liberals had passed since the previous year from the extremes of collective leadership to the extremes of autocracy.

June 25 (Friday). Balfour, Chamberlain, Hartington, Hartington's mistress, and Chaplin met at the Rothschild seat of Waddesden.[5]

July 2 (Friday). The first contested elections took place. Though the Orkney result was not till 27 July, other results were in by 17 July, and the direction was clear from the start. On 2 July Gladstone was still looking forward to a very close result 'which could hardly be satisfactory to anyone, as it might point to a prolonged struggle' and expecting to pick up between 20 and 40 seats through the Irish vote.[6] On 3 July Rosebery wrote 'we are done'. The actual election results that followed were the subject of anything but intense attention among party leaders, who were far too busy trying to work out anew their sense of the general situation, if they were not simply taking a holiday. Gladstone's comment was supposedly 'again, you have the aristocracy against the working classes'.[7]

Salisbury left London for a French spa at 9.40 a.m. on 3 July, not returning till the 23rd. He had 'extreme irritation' from eczema, which had reached a point 'where he found he really could not go on working at all'. Several weeks of hot baths produced a great improvement.[8] Churchill left Hull for Norway on 2 July with a congenial male companion, it being given out that his departure was on doctor's orders.* Spencer, rather knocked up and disappointed, had gone abroad on 26 June, first to Carlsbad and then to Aix-les-Bains: the election results dashed his hopes, which had risen high in view of the enthusiasm shown at meetings in recent months. Even Harcourt, usually impossible to detach from the scene of action, went on a fishing holiday in mid-July, and then joined Wolverton on a yachting trip to the Channel Islands and Cowes. Granville remained an invalid, though on 12 July he was able to drive out for the first time in five weeks, while Gladstone continued to enjoy rural calm at Hawarden until 14 July. Hartington was at Chatsworth, or elsewhere out of town, till 13 July. For two or three weeks, because there was a general election in progress, there was abnormally little political

---

* Cf. Churchill to his mother, 16/17 June 1886, typescript, Churchill MSS xiii, 1531: 'I have arranged with Tommy Trafford to go to Norway with him for three weeks, starting on July 3rd. This will be, I think, very good for me and I shall escape those beastly elections and it will not cost me any money.' '...It is quite true I am not best pleased just now with the two Tory leaders, who seem to think that they know a great deal more about everything than I do. I therefore intend to please myself by taking a very quiet part in the coming election.'

manoeuvre, and the politicians treated themselves to a kind of summer Christmas holiday.

July 13 (*Tuesday*). The Queen talked with Goschen at Windsor on predictable lines, Goschen advising the Queen to send for Salisbury when the time came, but suggesting that a coalition was now more likely than before, and undertaking to put before Hartington the Queen's wish that he should join a unionist administration. Goschen was much struck by the thought that had Hartington lost his seat, disaster would have ensured for the unionists.[9]

Goschen's friendliness towards coalition in this conversation was little more than soft soap, for he and Hartington had, with evident contentment, just been assuring A. Grey that there was no question of any such coalition.[10] Goschen and Trevelyan had lost their seats and could not easily be found new ones, while Hartington thought that, apart from himself, any Whigs who took office would also lose their seats when seeking re-election.[11]

Derby, who was entirely content to leave active leadership to Hartington, never wavered in the view that coalition would be a 'dismal mistake', offending Chamberlain, splitting the dissident Liberals, and, most interestingly, because 'Salisbury might find or make any pretext to break up the concern, and remain in with his own people only. And he is just the sort of man who would do it.'[12]

July 14 (*Wednesday*). Gladstone and his wife returned to London from Chester by special train, arriving at Downing St about 9 p.m. Gladstone had made a speech in support of the local Liberal candidate on Chester station. Hartington, who had returned from Derbyshire the previous day, had a long talk at Devonshire House with H. James.

July 15 (*Thursday*). In the morning Gladstone saw G. W. E. Russell, then had a long call from Kimberley. Later Bryce, Broadhurst, and Schnadhorst also had interviews. In his old age Bryce described the occasion:

> 'We were alone. He was not depressed or dejected by the result – I never saw him really dejected; he had too much spirit for that – but he was rather saddened, and looked at the future with apprehension. He delivered to me, sitting in front of him, a short speech almost in his House of Commons manner, grim and emphatic, chiefly about Chamberlain. Its exact phrases escape me, but the substance was that Chamberlain was a most dangerous man, restless, ambitious, unscrupulous, and that the country would suffer from him. "It does not much affect me",

he said, "but those of you who will be in public life during the next twenty years will have experience of the mischief he can do." There was not in his words a note of personal hatred, but there was the sternest condemnation I ever heard him utter of anyone.'[13]

July 16 (*Friday*). Hartington had to leave London for Kempton Park races, but was able to see Goschen and Trevelyan before he left.

July 17 (*Saturday*). All the ministers, except for Granville who was ill and Stansfeld who had not yet returned to London, dined at Downing St with Gladstone, assembling there at 8 and departing at 10.30. This was the first ministerial gathering since Gladstone's return to London. Spencer and his wife had returned from Aix-les-Bains to Spencer House for the occasion, and other ministers also returned from abroad to attend. The only first hand evidence as to the course of discussion is a statement by Rosebery that after dinner J. Morley presented his information about Ireland.[14] According to press reports, however, the meeting was to prepare the ground for an agreement to resign, to be finally taken at the cabinet on the following Tuesday.[15] A cabinet council had earlier in the week been announced for this date, but was subsequently postponed.[16]

July 19 (*Monday*). The press contained reports suggesting that a coalition government might be formed under the Duke of Argyll. If this was no more than a canard, then it was probably an inspired canard none the less, and the question of who inspired the rumour, and why, has defied solution. The Queen had shown interest in using Argyll either as a coalition premier or as her constitutional adviser, but Rowton's objections probably laid the idea quickly to rest, and Argyll was not consulted in subsequent negotiations.[17]

July 20 (*Tuesday*). The cabinet met at Downing St, 2–3, with all ministers present, including Granville, still very weak after his serious illness, who had to be carried from his carriage in an invalid chair. Granville remained behind some time after the meeting, and an informal consultation, lasting till 4.30, took place with Lord Wolverton, Lord Monson (chief whip in the Lords) and Arnold Morley (chief whip in the Commons).

The cabinet had no difficulty in reaching a unanimous decision to resign without meeting parliament, though the pros and cons of the situation were carefully considered. The ground which Gladstone stressed to the Queen was the importance of the maintenance of social order in Ireland, (and a desire not to give their successors the excuse of lack of time for not announcing their

Irish policy till the 1887 session). In fact, there had earlier been very strongly held contrary views as to desirable tactics: Harcourt at least had called resignation without a parliamentary vote 'an immense mistake' and had urged 'the seceders ought to be *compelled to vote him out*', and Mundella had thought the 'general feeling is that we ought not to resign'.[18]

Gladstone then announced 'that if it were deemed advisable by the cabinet, he, though he could not undertake the ordinary or habitual attendance in parliament, was willing to retain the responsibility of leadership, and to place himself at the disposal of his friends to appear and take part when they might call upon him: and of course to have a special ear to the calls of the Irish question'. Following Gladstone's statement, Rosebery wrote, 'all applauded', then Stansfeld pressed for better organisation on the frontbench as necessary.[19]

In conversation on future prospects, a desire was expressed to promote co-operation with the Liberal Unionists on Liberal grounds, and it was also decided 'to maintain the character and do the work of the opposition'.

Rosebery explained 'that the Afghan Commission had reached the impossible point', and a record of this was to be left for successors.

The Queen received and accepted the resignation this day.[20]

Mr and Mrs Gladstone, having been specially pressed by their host, attended a ball for 1,000 guests given by the militantly Unionist Duke of Westminster. Gladstone, who left early, was seen wandering about rather forlornly, with not many people around he cared to speak to, and not many who cared to speak to him, but yet looking remarkably well.

Hartington told Arthur Elliot, one of his leading Whig supporters, that he had already taken the decision not to form a ministry himself or to serve with Salisbury under the Duke of Argyll. He admitted that the temptation was strong since the Conservatives were ready 'to allow almost any arrangement to be made about places to please the Liberals' but almost all his colleagues were opposed to coalition with the exception of H. Brand, Goschen, and the Duke of Westminster.[21] It must be said that Hartington here showed himself apparently more gullible than usual about the generosity of Tory intentions.

July 21 (Wednesday). Salisbury received the summons at Royat in the Auvergne during the morning. Several other Conservative leaders who were abroad had to be telegraphed to return. Beach was particularly concerned that Churchill should be summoned home from Norway. At the Carlton and among frontbenchers,

Beach found, what he wanted to find, a strong feeling that Salisbury must become premier, and that the party in the country would not stand a Hartington government, though they might just stomach him leading the Commons with Salisbury as premier.

All the soundings going on in Tory circles in London pointed the same way. Of former Tory ministers, only Webster and Smith[22] thought coalition possible. Beach thought Hartington leading the Commons was impracticable. Smith, Beach, and the Tory chief whip Akers-Douglas, meeting on 15 July, decided that Salisbury must be premier. The Tory rank and file were categorical about this. Coalition, to the Tories, was never conceived as anything more than the offer of a junior place to the Whigs. The Tory chief whip said that to make Hartington premier 'would break up the Conservative Party – they must be blooded – they have regained the position they lost in 1880 and must occupy the first place.' The 'Carlton people' thought coalition 'would never do in the country'. Before Salisbury returned, therefore, the Tories had in effect decided blankly against coalition, irrespective of their Liberal allies' views, out of pure party feeling, while the Liberal Unionists, with the dubious exceptions of Goschen and Trevelyan, had never desired coalition. (By the 23rd, however, Goschen clearly thought coalition impossible).[23] The negotiations after Salisbury's return, therefore, have a distinctly redundant character except in so far as they exhibited, for public consumption, supposed good feeling between the allies.[24]

Gladstone spent this day and those to come quietly preparing to leave Downing St and receiving few visitors of note.

July 23 (*Thursday*). Salisbury arrived in Paris. Trevelyan left for Northumberland for an indefinite period.

Hartington wrote to suggest that Goschen should seriously consider accepting office under Salisbury, so that he could be a channel of communication between the two Unionist parties. Hartington at least had little doubt that Goschen, and probably Argyll, would be asked as individuals to join Salisbury's government. The breach this would involve with the Liberals was not treated as important by Hartington: 'I don't feel very confident that I shall be able to do it [rejoin the Liberals] myself: if I do, it will be because I have a greater capacity for swallowing unpleasant morsels than you have. If as some people think, a total reconstruction of parties must come, you will only have preceded me a little.'[25]

Hartington made it clear that he saw the situation as cut-and-dried, and expected others to do likewise: 'I suppose it is quite certain that a formal offer [of coalition] will be made by Salisbury, but the Press have prepared him pretty well for a refusal',[26] and this on the simplest of grounds: 'the principal reason for my refusing would be ... I could not take the whole but only a section of the Liberal Unionists with me, and that the remainder would drift back to the Gladstonian party'.[27]

July 23 (Friday). Gladstone gave a farewell dinner at Downing St for Welby, Edward Hamilton, Earl and Countess Spencer, Lord and Lady Dalhousie, Lady Ailesbury,[28] J. M. Carmichael,[29] G. W. E. Russell, Algernon West,[30] and Professor James Stuart. They discussed the chances of Hartington joining the incoming Tory ministry.

Salisbury, accompanied by his wife and Lady G. Cecil, arrived at Charing Cross at 5.40 p.m. He then drove to Arlington St, where he saw Lord Rowton for an hour. Rowton had brought a letter from the Queen urging coalition, Salisbury's message in reply being that he felt 'as deeply as Your Majesty the paramount importance of coalition'.[31] At 7 p.m. Lord G. Hamilton arrived in London and drove straight to Arlington St. Several other leaders visited Salisbury after dinner. These probably included Beach, whom Salisbury was already pressing to serve in Ireland. Smith, Akers-Douglas, and Beach had been expressly summoned by Salisbury for a talk at 10.30, about which 'nobody else need know anything'. Churchill's absence was solely due to his still being away from town. Beach, earlier opposed to a Hartington ministry, was now 'very anxious that Hartington should join' and 'very indisposed to take office' without him.[32]

Since Salisbury was thus evidently building his Irish policy round Beach from the earliest hours of his ministry, and since Beach was subsequently largely able to determine the colour of Tory administration in Ireland, it might be supposed that Salisbury was wishing to put into effect certain ideas which Beach was known to Salisbury to embody. A premier who wanted a stern unbending Irish policy would hardly appoint a man of whom it was soon clear that he 'dislikes and despises the Irish landlords' and was opposed to a further downward revision of rents only for the time being.[33] In fact it would be rash to suppose that Salisbury much cared what Beach felt about Ireland, at the moment he pressed office on him, or even that he stopped to inquire:

'... But I think you will agree that I could not be expected to take such an office unless I saw my way to doing some *real* good in it. Without that I could not again take up the petty and irksome details which constitute much of the work of the office, and which would be quite as well done by anybody else. I have thought much on the subject of an Irish policy since we met. I

443

have not, so far, been able to see my way to do any real good. I am not even at all sure that you would approve of my ideas as to the lines on which the humbler task of "keeping things going" should be attempted. However, I can tell you what these ideas are as soon as you like to send for me.'[34]

This important letter suggests that while Beach's acceptance of Ireland (which he claimed to prefer to leading the Commons) was perhaps contingent on getting a certain degree of carte blanche, Salisbury's offer to Beach was contingent upon nothing in particular except the need to have a strong appointment in Dublin, and the unstated sense, too obvious for discussion, of not affronting Liberal Unionist sentiment. Beach was one of the very few really capable potential ministers, and moreover his communications to Salisbury had shown, besides flattery, admirable orthodoxy about the need to maintain the Tory power structure intact. Given these major qualifications, one cannot really make any inference from Beach's appointment as to the kind of Irish policy that Salisbury wanted, except that in the next few months he simply wanted nothing to happen.

Hartington spent the day at Sandown Park races, but in a long interview that evening with Salisbury refused all ideas of coalition.[35]

July 24 (Saturday). In the morning, Salisbury first (10–10.30) saw Churchill, who had just returned from his Norwegian holiday. Salisbury told Churchill that he had already asked Beach to govern Ireland.[36] Churchill, rightly, understood this to imply that in Beach's absence, he would lead in the Commons.[37] Salisbury, accompanied by his secretary, Henry Manners,[38] visited Hartington at Devonshire House for three quarters of an hour. Hartington countered Salisbury's arguments for a coalition in his usual sleepy manner, but must have already made up his mind, for he ended by reading extracts from a long paper[39] setting out the reasons why the Liberal Unionists could not take part in a coalition. Salisbury would not accept an immediate refusal, and Hartington agreed to consult his colleagues and send a formal reply that night.[40] Salisbury then left London at 11.30 for Osborne, where he struck the Queen as 'looking remarkably well'.[41]

After Salisbury had gone, H. James paid a long visit to Hartington, prior to a meeting of 12 to 15 members of the executive of the Liberal Unionist Association at 35 Spring Gardens, with Hartington in the chair. Most leading Liberal Unionists were present, and supported Hartington's decision to refuse office. A very strong letter from Chamberlain was read out urging Hartington to guarantee their support to the Tories 'not merely for one session but for several years'.[42] It was decided that the Liberal Unionist headquarters organisation must at all events be kept up, at any rate for the present, and that Chamberlain should be invited to join it. There were to be two whips, one Whig, one Radical. Subscriptions to local Liberal Associations were to be broken off. It was agreed that the Liberal Unionists should sit on the Conservative benches below the gangway, a decision which was strongly urged by Hartington but was subsequently reversed under pressure from Chamberlain and some moderate Unionists. Hartington's decision, already quite firm, not to join the ministry, was approved. 'It was however, stated that Mr Gladstone is already making advances to the Liberal Unionists ... it seemed to be agreed that we have broken with Mr G's leadership for ever.' A general meeting of the party was fixed for on or before 5 August.[43]

Later a messenger arrived at Devonshire House with messages from the Queen, and Derby also called. Hartington also consulted Northbrook[44] and Stalbridge before writing his final letter[45] of refusal to Salisbury in the evening. Writing to Goschen on the same day, Hartington said that the conclusive factor in his declining to form a government was that Salisbury had said he could not sit in a cabinet with Chamberlain,[46] a slightly curious argument since Chamberlain had been quick to let Hartington know that he could not himself join a coalition, though not against Hartington doing so.[47]

Hartington's arguments against coalition were purely and simply about losing the Radical Unionists, whom nothing would induce to act with Conservatives in general opposition to Liberals. Backbenchers as well as ex-ministers among the Liberal Unionists concurred with Hartington in seeing this as the great danger, and as leading on to one greater still, the conversion of the Liberals into a 'purely Radical and Democratic party'. Hartington concluded 'the most useful part which I can now take is to afford you an independent but friendly support. In this course I think I can rely on the assistance of Mr Chamberlain, though I have had but little conversation with him since the elections.' Hartington had left dealings with Chamberlain chiefly to Henry James. It was James, for instance, who reported to Chamberlain on Saturday's talks with Salisbury, saying that he had passed on to Hartington an (unidentified) letter from Chamberlain: that he thought Hartington 'not very firm' in his refusal of coalition: and that he believed, without a precautionary grain of salt, that Salisbury was really 'most anxious' for coalition.

Chamberlain wrote to ask Churchill to meet him for dinner that evening (i.e. 24 July),[48] though nothing more is known of this. It is however interesting that Chamberlain, as before, maintained this close link with Churchill, while having little personal contact with other leading Unionists.

July 25 (Sunday). After much discussion on appointments, Salisbury kissed hands some time after 4 p.m. The most persistent difficulty examined by Salisbury and the Queen over the weekend was not to do with Hartington, or even with Churchill, but concerned the Foreign Office. None of the Conservative leaders was considered adequate. Lord Lyons, ambassador in Paris, was seen by both as a very serious candidate, despite his being 69, and was actually offered the post in a most pressing way.[49] Another diplomat, Malet, was strongly favoured by the Queen. Cranbrook, they agreed, was both too old and unsuited to foreign affairs, while the Queen's suggestion of Lord Cadogan was turned down by Salisbury as 'not morally strong enough'. Lord Lytton was mentioned as 'very clever, but not suitable, and dangerous'. There was apparently no question of Salisbury taking on the Foreign Office again. The possibility of putting Iddesleigh there was probably in no one's mind at this stage, and startled the Queen very much when she first heard of it the following Wednesday.[50]

On other points, Salisbury 'feared' Churchill would have to take the Exchequer and lead the House (the Queen remarking 'he is so mad and odd, and has also bad health'):* suggested Balfour for Scotland; and went through the household peers with the Queen and got them more or less settled.[51]

Beach wrote to Salisbury pressing the idea that Goschen should take office at the local government board, largely because he might manage impending county council legislation well. However, Beach reported, Churchill would object to the inclusion of Goschen in the ministry.[52]

July 26 (Monday). Salisbury arrived back in London from Osborne at noon, having already taken office as first lord of the treasury. From his arrival, Salisbury was at Arlington St in consultation with colleagues. Two of his cabinet colleagues in his previous ministry, Richmond and Harrowby, had already made it plain that they genuinely did not wish to serve, on grounds of age and

---

* Churchill's doctor had just sent him an unsolicited note 'as your responsible medical adviser' warning him not to take a post like Ireland or the Foreign Office, and urging him to go back to the India Office as 'liable to be less trying to your constitution' (Dr Robson Roose to Churchill, 23 July, Churchill MSS unbound). The Duke of Marlborough, however, had just urged his son 'the F.O. is the key to the premiership and I feel sure you will know how to sit tight and not allow yourself to be humbugged out of being Foreign Minister' (loc. cit., 22 July).

health,[53] and they were absent from all ensuing discussions. Salisbury's callers included Cadogan, Akers-Douglas (the chief whip), Cranborne, Cranbrook, Smith,[54] Beach, Churchill and Manners.

Though an outline of the cabinet was expected 'by today or early tomorrow provisionally', the main unresolved question was the Irish secretaryship, for which Beach, Churchill, and Smith were all possibilities. While Beach's prior claims were not seriously contested, there was difficulty in finding terms acceptable to him as regards policy.

Hartington was visited at his house by Goschen and James, who remained a long time, and by Chamberlain,* who was at Devonshire House from 3 till 4. Then Lord Stalbridge, the former Liberal chief whip and a Unionist, called for an hour. Hartington left Victoria by a Royal special train at 5.30 to spend race week at Goodwood House, his companions including the Duchess of Manchester, Henry Chaplin, Cadogan, the Prince and Princess of Wales and the Duke of Cambridge.

Chamberlain, who had come up to town specially on Monday, dined alone with Churchill,[55] leaving London again on Tuesday morning, and not returning till 4 August, the day before the opening of parliament.

July 27 (Tuesday). The chief whip called on Salisbury at 11, and stayed for an hour. Beach arrived just before noon, followed by Churchill and Smith, this group of ministers remaining in conclave till 1.30. Discussion again centred on Irish appointments, with an increasing likelihood of Beach emerging as chief secretary, although he still refused to go to Dublin unless an Irishman was found as lord-lieutenant.[56]

The emergence of Lord Londonderry as lord-lieutenant, which was clear enough on the 27th† if not finally confirmed till the 28th, told its own tale as to the course of the discussions about Irish policy which had been going on between Salisbury, Beach, Churchill, and perhaps Hartington. It signalled that a policy of 'soft words and hard cash' would continue: that the ministry would try to please Ireland rather than crush it. In personal terms,

---

* Presumably in consequence of Henry James' advice: 'It is however *most* important that you should be in London as H[artington] is not very firm. Do if you possibly can manage it come up on Monday morning as renewed attacks from many quarters will be made on H...' (H.James to Chamberlain, n.d. but 24 July, Chamberlain MSS JC 5/46/5).

† Cf. Salisbury to P. of Wales, 27 July: 'It is important to have an Irishman ... by his private character and known opinions, as well as his family connections, [he] unites the necessary qualifications in a singular degree' (Sir Sidney Lee, *King Edward VII* (1925), 1, 243).

it meant that Beach and Churchill were settling Irish policy on their own terms, either over Salisbury's head or with his sceptical acquiescence, and before any cabinet existed to consider the alternatives. Possible repressive viceroys, like Wolseley, Plunket, or Beresford, were ruled out so readily in favour of a politically inexperienced young peer of thirty-four, who had only succeeded his father in 1884, that it was clear that the angry sharpness shown to the Irish during the home rule bill, had been superseded by a return to the diffuse goodwill of the caretaker ministry. That the appointment of Londonderry was not viewed simply as a matter of filling up an ornamental office, was shown by the fact that Beach in the course of the afternoon made it clear that his own willingness to go to Dublin, was contingent upon Londonderry accepting office. Beach's insistence on having the one lord-lieutenant who was *persona grata* to Churchill, was especially necessary in the light of Churchill's initial wish to go to Ireland himself, and his subsequent offer, later that evening, to take the lord-lieutenancy if Londonderry turned it down. There were, of course, adventitious factors behind the appointment, such as Londonderry's beautiful wife* with her social flair, his great wealth,† his devotion to sporting pursuits, his being brother-in-law to Churchill, and Churchill's wish to exclude the Duke of Abercorn, with whom he was on very strained terms: but these qualifications only reinforced the fact that Londonderry's naive and rather apolitical paternalism‡

* Besides being one of the very few ladies of rank who then frequented Newmarket, she allegedly combined omnivorous reading with gifts of conversation and of memory that made her as successful a hostess in Dublin, as she was later to be when holding a brilliant Tory salon in London (Mrs G. Cornwallis-West, *The Reminiscences of Lady Randolph Churchill* (1908), 86).

† Cf. J. A. Jamieson to Iddesleigh, 25 July 1886, Salisbury MSS: 'I have had to see a good deal of the Irish viceroy's internal arrangements during Lord Aberdeen's tenure of the office... No man can hold that office unless in addition to the allowance of £20,000 a year he is prepared to spend from £10,000 to £15,000 more... I know that at least £12,000 a year must go if the traditions of the office are to be maintained'.

‡ The collection of papers relating to various members of the Londonderry family in Durham County Record Office, which may not be complete, contains nothing bearing on Londonderry's vice-regal activities. A fairly detailed statement of his views shortly after taking office (Londonderry to Cadogan, 12 Oct. 1886, Cadogan MSS) is therefore especially helpful. The new viceroy was impressed by Buller, who 'has worked like a nigger and done wonders'; he spoke of the better conditions of the country and the weakening of the National League, citing the case of a League secretary getting stoned at Listowel; he saw as the key to good feeling, a decrease in evictions, wishing 'landlords this winter to be as easy as they can with their tenants'; and he wished any coercion act to be limited to reforms in legal procedure like change of venue and prompter trials. Further, 'the common people treat us quite differently to what I had expected'.

happened to fit the policy of the moment, as agreed by Churchill and Beach and swallowed by Salisbury. Londonderry had been elected in 1878 and 1880 as M.P. for Down, and had played the part of the liberal reformer and good landlord, in the face of a strong Liberal challenge. His platform had been tenant right, temperance, elective county government, strict economy, and class co-operation: and, as his own nostrum, he had become the first M.P. pledged to demand intermediate education, a curious background to his later post as lord president of the council in 1902–05. Thus he fully matched Churchill's view at this time that politicians must do what the public wanted, and that what the public wanted was what the Liberals thought they wanted.

Though Churchill and Beach drove together to the party meeting at the Carlton, on arrival Beach sat beside Salisbury at the table, while Churchill was in the front row of the audience. The meeting, which began at 2.30 p.m., was strictly private, and was reliably reported in the press.

Salisbury spoke for about twenty minutes, and was loudly cheered at the end by his audience of about 300 M.Ps and peers. He emphasised that he could not speak for his colleagues, as he had none, but simply wished to inform the party of his negotiations with the Liberal Unionists, and to take counsel with them as to future tactics. He thought that Hartington would have been the best Unionist leader, and explained that he had done everything to secure this. He wanted it to be known that the failure to obtain the cooperation of the Liberal Unionists was not due to the action of the Conservatives, as they were prepared either to serve under Hartington, or to support him and stand aside altogether.

Salisbury then stated that, as to tactics, his preference was for disposing of current business in August, and then not calling parliament together till early in 1887, when the government would be in a position to state its Irish policy. The speakers who followed Salisbury, namely Sir John Mowbray, Cecil Raikes, and Henry Holland, were as unanimous in their wish to dispense with an autumn session as they were in expressing support for Salisbury. Col. Tottenham pressed for some early measure of coercion, to which Salisbury gave a stonewalling reply. Then Lord Carnarvon, unexpectedly, 'expressed his intention to give his most cordial support to a Conservative government, which he thought absolutely necessary at the present time, having regard not only to home affairs, but to the general state of politics in Europe'.[57]

In short, Londonderry in office fitted Beach's and Churchill's resumption of appeasement like a glove.

After the meeting, Beach sent for Holmes, the former Tory Irish law officer, and they discussed ministerial arrangements. As things stood on the late afternoon of the 27th, Churchill was to take the exchequer and lead the house: Beach was to be Irish secretary provided Londonderry would be his viceroy: and Ashbourne would be lord chancellor of Ireland again, but would be dropped from the cabinet. Beach seemed to convey that, had he not taken Ireland, Churchill would have taken the post, and he also seemed to regret the retention of Ashbourne when Fitzgibbon might have taken his post.

On returning to the Carlton in the evening, Holmes met Churchill, who said he had offered to go to Ireland, and would still do so if arrangements with Londonderry fell through. Churchill added that in the latter case he would insist on his old friend, Fitzgibbon, becoming Irish lord chancellor, and that whatever happened, Ashbourne would not be in the cabinet. This agreement on the part of Churchill and Beach that their erstwhile collaborator must be dropped partly reflected a strong set against Ashbourne taken by general party opinion, but chiefly meant that he was rightly regarded as a rather weak appointment especially when considered beside Fitzgibbon, who was indeed a remarkable man. Fitzgibbon, who had himself conceded to Churchill that Ashbourne's reappointment was inevitable, illustrated the feeling of the few Tory policy-makers who knew Ireland when he wrote slightingly that Ashbourne's '300 magistrates, his Land Commission appointments, and something of the same sort about the Four Courts, have not left an agreeable smell', contrasting such goings-on with the rectitude of Beach ('the best official I ever met here, for he was death to jobbery and in earnest at his work')[58]. There was no question of policy involved, since Fitzgibbon represented the idea of governing Ireland by being subtle, ambiguous, and pleasant, just as Ashbourne had once done, and Beach's and Churchill's hankering to have Fitzgibbon as their right-hand man in Dublin signified a wish to return to the main themes of the caretaker government.

A few hours after seeing Beach and Churchill, Holmes was accosted by Ashbourne, who tried to elicit some news, saying he had been in London for some days and had heard absolutely nothing. Ashbourne somehow sized up the situation, for he called on Salisbury the following morning and came away a cabinet minister, to the anger of Churchill who believed that Salisbury had set aside a clear understanding (and, incidentally, brought into the cabinet yet one more minister who would not be sorry to see the last of Churchill).

July 28 (*Wednesday*). Salisbury spent all day at Arlington St settling appointments, the first of which were announced. Salisbury's callers included Ashbourne, Cross, Abercorn, Halsbury, Dyke, and Beach.

One of the main problems which Beach had arranged to see Salisbury about at 6 was what to do about Ashbourne. While Churchill simply did not want him in the cabinet, Beach's position was rather different. Because Londonderry had, with Beach's approval, made a point of having no responsibility for government before agreeing to accept office, Beach now had to find someone 'on the spot whom I can trust to tell Londonderry what to do in the event of any emergency'. Beach thought 'it may be necessary to squeeze Ashbourne', which meant that Salisbury should stipulate that, as a condition of readmission to the cabinet, Ashbourne should remain throughout the parliamentary session in Dublin as a listening-post for those who had to deal with Irish business in the Commons. Soundings had shown that Ashbourne would accept this mild indignity in order to remain in the cabinet, 'even though he would only attend the cabinet when I allowed him to go'.[59] Beach was also averse to paying an unnecessary pension to a man who could be kept at work. As a result of these considerations and Salisbury's presumed indifference, Ashbourne regained his place in cabinet despite a strong feeling that he was not the man for the job.

On Lyons refusing the Foreign Office, Cranbrook was sounded but promptly declined, and the job went almost at once to Iddesleigh. The Queen, surprised at his being put forward, objected to his appointment on health grounds.

The range of candidates who were considered, or flattered into thinking they were being considered, for the Foreign Office, in the brief interval of a few hours, between Lyons' refusal and Iddesleigh's acceptance of the post, was quite surprising. Cranbrook whom nobody had previously considered believed, as he told Smith, that 'he had refused the F.O. as he could not talk French, and with the same breath he said that Iddesleigh was very good at languages'. Stanhope was also thought of, but his 'perpetual youth, in appearance at least' made him appear 'hardly big enough or strong enough'.[60] Smith approved the final selection. 'I think Beach was too strong about Iddesleigh. He has yet the power to do very good work.'[61] Although Beach objected to Iddesleigh, Churchill did not, but was anxious to keep Stanhope out of the job. If Stanhope were appointed, it should be on condition of his being a peer: Churchill had never liked Stanhope at close quarters. Churchill added that Goschen, with a peerage, might be worth considering, but would have liked Salisbury to continue himself.[62] While Churchill's objections to Iddesleigh might be muted while it was a question of preventing Stanhope, who was much more of a potential rival, from rising in the party, they soon returned in unabated degree: 'Iddesleigh is conducting himself like a child. No settled purpose but fussy suggestions from day to day.'[63]

At 10 a.m. Halsbury saw Henry Matthews, who agreed to accept the Home Office if offered it.[64] Halsbury had earlier seen Webster, who told him that he could not afford to take a post which would mean giving up legal practice, and had been asked by Salisbury to press Macnaghten to accept this post. It is not clear which of Macnaghten[65] or Webster was Salisbury's first choice, but it was probably the former, whom the premier 'particularly wanted ... as we need a man who can speak on Irish measures as a cabinet minister'.[66] The implication of this sounding of Macnaghten and Webster, is that both were in line for the Home Office and it was only their refusal which led to the offer to Matthews. Such a version makes sense, in that Matthews, unmarried family man and apparent protégé of Churchill, had little to commend him except, in Salisbury's eyes, his decided willingness to hang people. A Catholic who, probably tongue in cheek, had first entered parliament as a home ruler, his appointment was an inexplicable embarrassment which at most filled an awkward gap, and did not become less embarrassing as time went by: once at Hatfield, when drunk, he gave the company an unsolicited rendering of Irish rebel songs.

The Queen was informed late in the evening that the appointments of Beach, Churchill and Londonderry had been finally settled.[67] Smith, humble as ever, offered to give up his place in the cabinet altogether – but Salisbury refused.[68]

The Liberal leaders met 2–3.40 on a sudden summons from Gladstone, chiefly prompted by the results of the Carlton Club meeting the previous day. Owing to Granville's continuing weakness,* the meeting took place at his house in Carlton House Terrace. All of the Liberal cabinet, except Spencer, were present, as also was A. Morley, the chief whip. Rosebery, however, was twenty minutes late, and Mundella did not arrive till 3.15. After the general meeting broke up, Gladstone, Granville, and A. Morley remained in consultation.

On the question of honours, Gladstone was advised to insist on

---

* His convalescence had not been helped by his presidential speech to the City Liberal Club on Monday, when, seated in a small invalid chair, he wheeled himself into the room and spoke with great force from that position.

the baronetcy and two knighthoods struck out by the Queen, which he was rather reluctant to do.

After a long talk, it was decided to take no action in respect of Dilke.*

The decision taken by the Conservatives the previous day to postpone Irish issues till 1887 was condemned, but the question of how their procrastination should be opposed was left open. Gladstone was evidently all for making a parliamentary fight out of the issue, while his colleagues wished to confine themselves to abusing the policy in debate, without forcing a division upon it.

July 29 (Thursday). Salisbury was immersed in arranging the distribution of offices. One of his main difficulties during the day arose from an overnight revolt at the Carlton against the rumoured appointment of Cross to the Home Office, which led to a communication being sent to Salisbury, asking him to consider Raikes, a popular and energetic party figure with a considerable following and more considerable claims upon the party, while Cross's reputation had fallen sharply since 1880. Smith, indeed, kindly suggested to Cross in the morning that he should go out to govern Madras: Cross was not unfavourable but 'doubts as to his family'.[69] In the morning, Col. Stanley was Salisbury's first caller, followed by Ashbourne, Gorst, Hamilton, and Matthews. Then Salisbury had a longer and more formal conference with Manners, Hamilton, Smith, and Churchill, after which Raikes was sent for and spent half an hour with Salisbury. Smith, and no doubt others, had objections to make to Matthews, but, as Smith said, these 'doubts and fears' were 'fairly weighed and that is enough'. The chief whip, Akers-Douglas, was present for part of the conference, then returned to the Carlton where he was interviewing leading Conservatives.

About this time, Stanley, one of the failures of the 1885–86 ministry,† expected to go to the Lords without taking a cabinet post, chiefly because his hopes of a senior ministry had been dashed. Salisbury had originally wanted Stanley to go to the Board of Trade. When Smith, on Salisbury's behalf, had sounded him on this, the previous evening, he was at first well-disposed, but

---

* Gladstone, on 24 July, had asked Herschell whether his advice now was that Dilke should be removed from the Privy Council, an act about which Gladstone expressed grave doubts. Herschell replied, 24 July, suggesting leaving all action to the next administration (44498 f. 276). The meeting of 28 July was described by Gladstone in the normal way in a letter to the Queen: another description of it is in the Spencer MSS, in a letter of that date from Granville to Spencer.

† Cf. Smith to Salisbury, 11 Sept. 1885, Salisbury MSS, on Stanley: 'he is so afraid of responsibility that I am afraid he will do himself irreparable mischief unless he is prepared to act' (i.e. on Bechuanaland).

then, on discovering that Stanhope was to have a higher post than before, said that for him to change from his previous post at the Colonial Office, to go to the Board of Trade, 'would be a descent which would be unfair'. The idea of the peerage attracted him, and when he went to see Salisbury, in the morning he had not definitely made up his mind.[70] (His formal acceptance of both peerage and office was not till 30 July). Rationalising his position, he and his wife took comfort from the great gain of his not being in a House of Commons led by Lord Randolph, which they felt would be 'most unpleasant'. Stanley had indeed been consistently averse to Lord Randolph. His return to office, as president of the board of trade (a most unusual office for a peer) was almost certainly the result of careful coaxing by Salisbury: 'you could not refuse the appeal made to you to waive your claim to the higher office' wrote his brother, Lord Derby, on 1 August.[71]

About 5, Gorst paid a second visit. He had been offered a judgeship by Salisbury and had refused it, holding out instead for a frontbench post in the Commons.[72]

The Gladstones, Mrs Drew, and Margot Tennant dined with the Roseberys.[73] Rosebery did not meet Gladstone again till 22 October, when he visited Hawarden just for the evening, returning after a visit of only five hours to Mentmore, where he was busy preparing for his departure for India on 24 October.

July 30 (*Friday*). Gladstone took his final leave of the Queen at Osborne, in an audience which did not touch on public affairs at all, the Queen's manner and cheerfulness being, to Gladstone's mind, at once courteous and wounding.* Leaving Waterloo at 9.30 a.m., Gladstone's visit to Osborne was over by 4.30, and he was back in London at 8.30. The Queen left a record of their conversation. 'After luncheon, saw Mr Gladstone, who looked pale and nervous. He began by talking of his train being late, of the weather, and of his requiring rest, which he meant to take now. He then at once began speaking of the horrible last trial of Sir Charles Dilke, and the letter he had written to me, as to the question of his being removed from the list of Privy Councillors, which Mr Gladstone thinks will have to be done, but not till after it has been seen, whether he will have to be tried for perjury or not. Many in that trial would be liable to this! Mr Gladstone said

---

* See Gladstone's memorandum of 2 Aug. 1886 on this interview, printed in Morley, *Gladstone* (1903), iii, 347. When the private secretary called to take him to the Queen, he found Gladstone absorbed in *Kidnapped*, and asked if he found time to read much. 'Why, what else could I do coming down here?' said Gladstone. 'I have no time to pick up novels but when I hear of a good one I read it'. He then spoke of reducing the 25,000 letters a year written by him and his secretaries when in office (A. Ponsonby, op. cit., 260).

it was one of the most shocking and scandalous trials in history... That he was a very clever man, and that it was most lamentable that he should have ruined himself in this way... Spoke of education, it being carried too far, and he entirely agreed, that it ruined the health of the higher classes uselessly, and rendered the working classes unfitted for good servants and labourers.'[74]

Arlington St witnessed much hasty consultation, the purpose of which was thought by the press to be to find some way of adequately rewarding Raikes in response to party feeling in his favour in the Carlton. Also still unsettled was the question of finding something for Cross. Akers-Douglas called first, followed by Cross and Stanhope. Salisbury had discussed the question of the India Office for Cross: Churchill, consistent in this at least, was still opposed to the idea. Balfour arrived next, stayed for quarter of an hour, and then went on to the Carlton. Churchill, who was pressing for the appointment of Gorst as education minister,[75] called briefly at 2.30, went on to the Carlton, and returned with Balfour to Arlington St. After an hour's conversation Balfour, Churchill and Salisbury were joined by Smith. At 4.30 Smith and Churchill left together, and Balfour returned to the Carlton.[76]

Cranbrook wrote to Salisbury accepting office. Stanley also.

July 31 (*Saturday*). Gladstone and his wife left Downing St at 5 p.m. to stay as guests of Wolverton at Coombe until Tuesday. Granville was also staying at Coombe. Rosebery went to the Foreign Office for the last time, and then retired to Durdans, where he spent the weekend without company.[77]

Salisbury had a continual flow of callers before he left for Hatfield in the afternoon, including Ritchie, 'disgusted' at not getting the Board of Trade.[78]

August 2 (*Monday*). Salisbury returned to London, 'sick to death of the whole business' of minor appointments, but hoping to finish them that day.[79]

As Gorst had at last been fitted into a political post,* Salisbury was now able to ask Edward Clarke to become solicitor-general, with Webster as his senior colleague.[80] Clarke had no problems about accepting an office where for the next six years his legal income averaged £17,500 p.a.

Rosebery invited Hartington to lunch, and afterwards they drove together. Salisbury had told Hartington that his great

* Perhaps in response to a letter to Salisbury written the previous day by his private secretary, Manners, stressing 'the cave that might be formed if Chaplin, Bartlett, Gorst, and Co. seceded would be a very mischievous thing' (Salisbury MSS).

difficulties were finding a foreign secretary and a leader of the House: that Beach was the only man for Irish secretary, which made Churchill leader of the House – 'a great risk'. Salisbury had admitted to doubts as to whether all his party would support Hartington as premier. Hartington himself thought Churchill would not. Hartington doubted whether he had been right to refuse the premiership.[81] Rosebery and Hartington met again, at thoroughly non-Gladstonian dinner tables, on 4 and 5 August, renewing an acquaintance which had lapsed virtually completely since January.*

August 3 (*Tuesday*). The outgoing ministry (except Granville, who was too ill, and Gladstone) went to Osborne to vacate office, followed later by the new cabinet. Childers struck the Queen as 'looking very ill, and very unhappy at the loss of his son', while Spencer seemed less unwell than when she last saw him on 25 June looking 'so wretchedly ill'. Spencer told her that six months earlier, he had expected a disastrous election, but that later he had been more optimistic, as he had thought the public meetings were so favourable.[82]

Salisbury travelled down alone in a first class carriage, leaving his colleagues to their own devices in a saloon. After receiving their seals, the other ministers returned to London, but Salisbury stayed the night at Osborne. Among the Conservatives, it was Iddesleigh, then 68, whom the Queen singled out as looking very ill.[83]

August 5 (*Thursday*). The newly elected parliament opened with an autumn session beginning this day and ending on 25 September.

A meeting of Hartington's supporters was held at Devonshire House at noon, with Chamberlain present and all Liberal Unionists invited. It was the first party meeting of both wings of the dissident Liberals, and the first meeting of Hartington's followers since 1 June. Trevelyan was a noticeable absentee, following his defeat at the elections.

In a lengthy speech, Hartington explained he had declined to

---

* Cf. overtures being made by Gladstone at this time to H.James; also 'Harcourt has already had Chamberlain to dinner' (Camperdown to Selborne, 1 Aug., Selborne MSS 1869 f. 205.) Similarly, Sir H.James gave a dinner party at Greenwich for both sides of the Liberal party in early August, the dozen or so guests going by boat from Westminster and dining very well. Those present included James, Collings, Chamberlain, Harcourt, Asquith, and Broadhurst; the occasion was an obvious exercise in bridge-building despite a rather strained atmosphere at first (H.Broadhurst, op. cit., 304). There was therefore perhaps a minor, very short-lived, but probably concerted attempt at reconciliation, with the initiative coming from the Gladstonians, in immediate response to the dissidents' refusal to enter the Salisbury ministry.

form a government with or without Conservative participation, and said he hoped Liberalism would soon be reunited on a Unionist platform.

Chamberlain then spoke, entirely endorsing Hartington's action, and pledging himself to follow Hartington's leadership from then on. Chamberlain went out of his way, however, to stress that Liberal reunion would be an unmixed blessing. Chamberlain undertook to unite his Radical Unionist Association with Hartington's Liberal Unionist Association.

The period between the opening of parliament on 5 August, and Churchill's resignation on 23 December 1886, was at most a phase of inconsequential recuperation. Nothing happened, or was expected to happen. Ministers administered, and put off decisions. Many actors were not on stage. Gladstone left for Munich and theology on 25 August, Granville made an autumnal round of the great country houses, and Rosebery left on 24 October for a long visit to India. Herschell left to hear Parsifal at Bayreuth on 3 August, and remained abroad several months. John Morley, who had earlier been complaining 'This August session is a cruel nuisance', managed an Italian holiday in December. As regards campaigning, Gladstone lapsed into virtual silence. During the August session, it is true, he made three speeches of some length on Ireland, and two brief interventions, but he did not address any meeting outside parliament between the election campaign in June 1886 and March 1887, apart from receiving an address from a deputation of Irish women at Hawarden in October 1886. Politics, despite its apocalyptic rhetoric, remained a very discontinuous seasonal business. Slight Tory gains in the municipal elections in November were offset by the Leeds conference of the National Liberal Federation, which managed to give the impression that the worst was over. There was, however, no flowing tide in opinion, either among politicians or among the electorate, only a determination to wait silently and see what time and the spring would bring. The policy of the ministry, especially as regards Ireland, appeared as always to hang in the balance. The cabinet remained undecided about coercion right up until the end of the year. Churchill's speech at Dartford on 2 October, with its plagiary of Liberal nostrums, added to the general confusion about party identities. On the Gladstonian side, Gladstone had completed the process, begun during the election, of making his Irish commitments as elastic, light, and indefinite as possible. Though otherwise refraining from seeking the limelight, Gladstone issued on 25 August a not quite innocent pamphlet divided into two parts called *History of an Idea* and *Lessons of the Election*, whose function was to drop the land bill and to make the details of home rule an open question within the party. It was difficult to tell whether Gladstone was backing down, quietening down, or simply consolidating his position on essentials. These remained questions for 1887. The home rule crisis of 1886 ended with a degree of latent flexibility in the situation not much less than that with which it had started. The year ended with Churchill's resignation and yet another attempt at a general realignment of parties.

Was it all a storm in a teacup? Certainly, Gladstone's forecast that it 'was 49 to 1 against' had been justified. Even on a modest definition, this was true. Both support for, and opposition to, home rule, had been greatly augmented, but the increased inflexibility of opposition was the operative point. A definitive Parnellite-Liberal alliance had not emerged. Gladstone had not created a rapport with Parnell. There were, however, areas of negative success. Prospects for law and order in Ireland had not deteriorated as much as Gladstone had feared. His home rule discussions – one can hardly call them more – contributed to this. More generally, the Irish issue kept the economy out of politics. It enabled the politicians to avoid making any response to the real aching crisis of the mid-1880s. The burning topic dowsed the fires of constituency restiveness. Otherwise, the crisis had brought Gladstone to supremacy in his party (a not infrequent occurrence) and had presented Morley and Harcourt with unexpectedly large roles. The crisis had submerged those who wanted an ideological reconstruction of parties, whether on the right or on the left. It had submerged those (Hartington, Churchill) who had wanted to establish central opinion as a dominant force in government. It had succeeded perfectly for those (Salisbury and Gladstone) who wanted to confine power within the traditional party structure of two opportunist parties presenting a spectacle of rigid polarisation. Where change had occurred, it was within the pattern of talent at the top. The tendency of most major politicians to gravitate to the Liberal party, had provided a sense among the unusual and able that their interests, and those of the country, lay in opposing each other from within the same party. After 1886 the party system was far less able to perform its basic function of enabling able and unusual people to rule, except in Ireland where Balfour solved the Irish problem on the lines laid down by Gladstone in 1881–85.

Citations

The citations given here for all numbered references in the text are in accordance
with the following rules. With books, the full title is given only at first appearance, and place of publication is London unless otherwise stated. With manuscript material, where no volume or folio numbers are cited, these were not
available. With letters, etc., of several pages, the folio reference is for the first
page of the document only. Where the reference for a manuscript involves a
five-figure volume number, this should be taken as a British Museum Additional
Manuscript. Two political diaries are referred to in abbreviated form in the
following notes. The journal of Edward Hamilton, Gladstone's principal
private secretary 1880–June 1885, is cited as *E. H. J.*, whether the source is the
original in the British Museum, or the edited version by D.W.R.Bahlman. *The
Diary of Sir Edward Walter Hamilton* (2 vols, Oxford 1972), part of which was
kindly made available to us in proof at a late stage of our work.

The journal of Lord Carlingford is cited as *C.J.*, references being to the abridged
published version, *Lord Carlingford's Journal: Reflections of a Cabinet Minister,
1885*, A.B.Cooke and J.R.Vincent eds (Oxford 1971). Agatha Ramm's edition
of *The Political Correspondence of Mr Gladstone and Lord Granville 1876–1886*
(2 vols, Oxford 1962) is cited as Ramm. Standard biographies are cited by short
titles only. Other abbreviations used in footnotes are: Cranbrook's diary is
referred to as *C.D.*; Dalrymple's as *D.D.*; L. Harcourt's as *H.J.*; Queen Victoria's
as *Q.V.J.*; and Rosebery's as *R.J.*

Book One

1 Herbert Gladstone's diary, 4 Aug. 1885, Glynne-Gladstone MSS. Similarly,
the historian can make nothing of allegations by a Parnellite leader about a
mooted Irish-American invasion of Ireland in Russian ships at the time of the
Penjdeh crisis, a project supposedly discussed with the Russian envoy by an
emissary acting for Parnell (William O'Brien, *The Parnell of Real Life*, 1926,
p. 90). Another difficulty is that the major ecclesiastical archives are closed: cf.
C.J.Woods, 'Ireland and Anglo-papal relations, 1880–85', *Irish Historical
Studies*, vol. xviii, no. 69, March 1972.
2 C.C.O'Brien, *Parnell and his Party* (1964), whose definitiveness has been

enhanced for these years by the subsequent disappearance of the first volume of the manuscript minutes of the parliamentary party. We are indebted to Professor F.S.L.Lyons for this point, and for his comments confirming the thinness of the Irish sources before autumn 1886.

3   Cf. his ambiguous Lambeth speech, *The Times*, 25 Sept. 1885.

4   Salisbury to Manners, written from Florence, 1 Feb. 1885, Rutland MSS.

5   Salisbury to Austin, 12 Sept. 1885, Alfred Austin MSS.

6   Dilke to Chamberlain, 30 Nov. 1885, Chamberlain MSS JC 5/24/147.

7   Chamberlain to Harcourt, 6 Dec. 1885, copy, loc. cit., JC 5/38/146.

8   Dilke to Chamberlain, 19 Nov. 1885, loc. cit., JC 5/24/145.

9   Mundella to Chamberlain, 4 Oct. 1885, loc. cit., JC 5/55/7.

10   Ibid. but 11 Oct., JC 5/55/8. Citations and arguments are taken, by kind permission, from Dr Michael Barker.

11   See James Stuart, *Reminiscences* (1911), 221. Stuart, acting with Stansfeld, got what he wanted by a direct approach to Gladstone, despite Arnold Morley's ruling that legislation on the subject should follow the Irish bills. The operation of the acts had been in suspension since 1883, hence repeal was at most a precaution against resuscitation. According to an anecdote by Kimberley, Gladstone had earlier taken the line of Josephine Butler. Kimberley's tenacity in opposing him on orthodox grounds had led Gladstone to say 'Well, Kimberley, you hold a pistol at my throat and I must give in.' Kimberley then wrote out certain heads for discussion and Gladstone took these point by point in the House, arguing for the C.D. Acts, 'so cleverly that everyone must have thought it was from conviction...' (memo. of Nov. 1895, Spence Watson MSS).

12   F.A.Channing, *Memories of Midland Politics 1885–1910* (1918), 50.

13   See Sir A.West, *Recollections 1832–1886* (1899), ii, 232, for Granville's contrary view of 3 Feb. 1885 that Gladstone would go on for some time after the election as a peer premier.

14   *Annual Register*, 1885, p. 2.

15   Chamberlain to Dilke, n.d. but c. 6 Jan., 43887 f. 7.

16   Carlingford to Spencer, 7 Jan., Spencer MSS.

17   From Lewis Harcourt's journal, Harcourt MSS, hereafter cited as *H.J.*

18   Ibid.

19   Chamberlain to Dilke, copy, n.d. but 5 Jan., Chamberlain MSS JC 5/24/386.

20   We owe this point to Dr Andrew Jones.

21   *H.J.*, 4 Jan.

22   *E. H.J.*, 29 Jan.: press reports: Glynne–Gladstone MSS. Mrs Gladstone and her son W.H.Gladstone had been to London on the 27th for her niece Annie's funeral. On the 28th W.E.Gladstone left Hawarden for Norris Green, West Derby, Liverpool, where he stayed with the Heywoods. On the 29th the Gladstones were at church in Liverpool for the wedding at 11.30 a.m. but did not stay to the breakfast owing to recent bereavement. The Gladstones spent a further night in Liverpool and went on to Holker by train on the 30th. No reference has been traced to the obvious possibility that well-wishers manoeuvred Gladstone out of London for security reasons following the bomb attacks of the previous month.

23   Hartington to Duchess of Manchester, 3 Feb., Devonshire MSS.

24   Chamberlain to Dilke, c. 20 Feb., 43887 f. 76: J.L.Garvin, *Chamberlain* (1933) ii, 33.

25   43887 f. 78.

26   Dilke MSS, 43939 f. 82.

27   Cairns d. 2 Apr. 1885: 'a statesman of the first order' (Manners to Duke of Rutland, 4 Apr. 1885, Rutland MSS), on whose judgment Manners and Richmond habitually relied.

28 56452.
29 *Annual Register* has 14 Liberals totally absent.
30 Hardinge, *Carnarvon* iii, 134.
31 Beach to Churchill, 10 Jan., Churchill MSS iv 537.
32 Richmond to Cairns 7 Mar. 1885: Cairns MSS PRO 30/51/3 f. 212.
33 Salisbury to Alfred Austin, 19 Feb., then writer on foreign affairs for the *Standard*, the leading Conservative daily paper, in the Alfred Austin MSS.
34 Ibid., 5 Mar.
35 Northcote to Salisbury, 12 Feb., Salisbury MSS.
36 Ibid., 6 Feb.
37 Ibid., 28 Feb.
38 Churchill to his mother, 5 Mar., typescript copy, Churchill MSS iv 575.
39 For a survey of evidence relating to Tory malaise, see *C.J.*, 57n.
40 For instance, Lady Knightley was informed by a Gladstone relative in June 1885 that 'Lord Randolph was in Downing St with the Gladstones a week ago – swearing at his party and vowing he would turn Radical' (Lady Knightley's journal, 18 June 1885). Again, Churchill in May 1885 went so far as to draw up, for nobody's eyes but his own, three draft lists of appointments in a future Conservative government, which excluded at least six of the incoming ministers of June 1885 (Churchill MSS v 600).
41 Salisbury to Churchill, 3 Dec., Churchill MSS xi 1129a.
42 Carnarvon to Salisbury, 6 Dec., Carnarvon MSS, urging early resignation purely on grounds of party expediency.
43 Maurice V. Brett ed., *Journals and Letters of Reginald Viscount Esher* (1934) i, 118: Esher to Hartington, 15 Dec.
44 Chamberlain to Labouchere, 26 Dec., in A. Thorold, *Labouchere* (1913) 272: Chamberlain to Dilke, 21 Dec., 43940 f. 97.
45 H. James to Churchill, n.d. but early Dec., Churchill MSS x 1127, 1147: Chaplin to Churchill, 8 Dec., x 1153. Churchill had only one letter (14 Jan.) at this time, indicating rapprochement at a personal level but falling outside the context of these negotiations.
46 Churchill to Salisbury, 16 Jan. 1886, Salisbury MSS class E.
47 Cranbrook's diary, 12 Dec. Cranbrook MSS T501/299.
48 Herbert Gladstone's diary, loc. cit.
49 Gladstone to Mrs O'Shea, 4 Aug. 1885, copy, Gladstone MSS new deposit, 56446.
50 Gladstone to Granville, 9 Dec. 1885, copy, loc. cit.
51 See jottings, n.d., in Gladstone's hand, Gladstone MSS new deposit, loc. cit.: also Rosebery MSS, box 28.
52 *Earl Cowper, K.G., A Memoir* by his wife (1913) 622: the date of Lady Cowper's visit was 14 Dec. 1885.
53 John Morley to R. Spence Watson, 19 Apr. 1886, Spence Watson MSS.
54 Same to same, 10 Mar. 1886, loc. cit.
55 Salisbury MSS.
56 Cf. Salisbury to MacColl, 22 Mar. 1885: 'I quite agree with you in disliking the Sudan war. It promises no good results. Our complaint is that we have been brought into such a position that retreat will be even more injurious than persistence' (G. W. E. Russell ed., *Malcolm MacColl: Memoirs and Correspondence*, 1914, p. 280).
57 Lady Knightley's diary, 13 May 1885: cf. ibid., 4 June 1886, 'nothing is talked of but politics and the innumerable stories to prove that Gladstone is mad! He *must* be more or less.'
58 Memo. in Salisbury MSS.
59 H. A. L. Fisher, *James Bryce* (1927), i 209.

60 Armitstead to Herbert Gladstone, 6 Nov. 1885, 46029 f. 1.

61 Campbell-Bannerman to Spencer, 19 Mar. 1885, Spencer MSS: Mundella to Herbert Gladstone, n.d. but mid-Nov., 46051 f. 203.

62 46051 f. 160.

63 Winn to Salisbury, 20 June 1885, Salisbury MSS.

64 According to Winn's notes of his conversation with Power on 20 June, five names were submitted to the Irish party, who chose Sir Henry Holland as first preference, with Dyke as the next best (Salisbury MSS).

65 Justin McCarthy and Mrs R. M. Praed, *Our Book of Memories* (1912), 15.

66 For Churchill's relations with Carnarvon, see A. B. Cooke and J. R. Vincent, 'Ireland and party politics, 1885-7: an unpublished Conservative Memoir', *Irish Historical Studies*, vol. xvi, Sept. 1969, 452-4.

67 Churchill to Fitzgibbon, 14 Oct. 1885, Churchill MSS viii 978.

68 Carnarvon left a number of memoranda describing these conversations in the Carnarvon MSS, PRO 30/6/67.

69 Carnarvon to Harrowby, 3 Aug. 1885, Harrowby MSS lii/136.

70 In autumn 1885 it was widely rumoured that he shared Carnarvon's leanings towards home rule. The Queen's private secretary cited them as joint advocates of 'peculiar views on Ireland' which they failed to keep 'strictly secret' (Ponsonby to the Queen, 23 Dec. 1885, Royal Archives RA B36/120). See also C.J., 128n.

71 Notes taken of Churchill's conversation c. 1890 by Henry James, James MSS: W. S. Blunt, *The Land War in Ireland* (1912) 32.

72 *Memories of Father Healy of Little Bray* (1898), 211. Churchill's letters at Blenheim from miscellaneous Irish correspondents at this period give a strong impression of a network of contacts being built up for future use.

73 Anita Leslie, *Jennie: The Life of Lady Randolph Churchill* (1969), 108.

74 Mrs G. Cornwallis-West, *The Reminiscences of Lady Randolph Churchill* (1908), 154-5.

75 Albert Grey, M.P. (hereafter cited as Grey) to Earl Grey, Grey MSS.

76 Chamberlain to Churchill, 12 May, Churchill MSS xiii 1500.

77 John Morley to Spence Watson, 19 May, Spence Watson MSS.

78 For the realities, see Neal Blewett, 'The Franchise in the United Kingdom, 1885-1918', *Past and Present*, 32, Dec. 1965, 27-56, and Grace A. Jones, 'Further Thoughts on the Franchise, 1885-1918', ibid., 34, July 1966, 134-8. Individual constituencies in Great Britain are surveyed in Henry Pelling, *Social Geography of British Elections 1885-1910* (1967), which supersedes all previous work on the subject: see also Michael Kinnear, *The British Voter: An Atlas and Survey since 1885* (1968).

79 Salisbury to Brabourne, 2 May 1886, Brabourne MSS C 174/7.

80 Goschen to Grey, 20 Dec. 1885, Grey MSS.

81 56447.

82 A. Elliot's diary, 13 Jan.

83 Ibid., 14 Jan.

84 Ibid., 17 Jan.

85 Sir A. West, op. cit. ii, 259.

86 Elliot's diary, 24 Jan.

87 Milner to Goschen, 25 Jan. 1885, Milner MSS box 182.

88 Goschen to Sir R. Morier, 10 Feb. 1886, cited in A. Elliot, *Goschen* (1911) ii, 14.

89 Grey to Stead, 11 Dec. 1884, Stead MSS. On general points, see also Harold Begbie, *Albert, Fourth Earl Grey: A Last Word* (1918).

90 Lady Knightley's diary, 23 June (husband's view) and 20 Apr. (her view) 1885: Dalrymple's diary, 5 Feb. 1885, and ibid. 20 Oct. 1886 wishing Goschen 'were not so contemptuous of our party': Smith to Northcote, 22 Feb. 1885,

cited Sir H. Maxwell, *W. H. Smith* (1893), 273, for Smith's offer: for their abhorrence of the Tories' 'socialistic' tendencies, see Milner to Goschen, 17 Oct. 1886, Milner MSS box 182.

91   Grey pamphlet no. 1678, Grey MSS. The first Unionist demonstration was on 14 Apr. 1886.

92   The proposal came from the aged third Earl Grey, and was passed on, with approval, by Grey to Goschen.

93   Grey to Earl Grey, 12 Jan. 1886, Grey MSS.

94   Ibid.

95   Churchill to Salisbury, 29 Mar. 1886, Churchill MSS xii 1438 c.

96   Grey to Earl Grey, 19 Mar., Grey MSS.

97   Churchill to Salisbury, 28 Mar., Churchill MSS xii 1438 b.

98   Grey to Earl Grey, 13 Mar., Grey MSS.

99   Ibid, 30 Mar.

100   Ibid., 13 Apr.

101   Ibid.

102   Milner to Goschen, 26 Apr., Milner MSS box 182.

103   Ibid., 25 Apr.

104   H.J.Hanham, *Elections and Party Management* (1959) 369: Grey to Earl Grey, 29 May, Grey MSS.

105   Grey, ibid., 22 Jan.

106   Ibid., 23 Jan.

107   Ibid., 25 Jan.

108   Ibid., 13 Feb.

109   Ibid., 17 Feb.

110   Ibid., 1, 2, and 3 Mar.

111   Ibid., 1 Mar.

112   Ibid., 6 and 11 Mar.

113   Memo of Oct. 1890, Stead MSS.

114   Julia Cartwright ed., *The Journals of Lady Knightley of Fawsley 1856–1884* (1915), 263.

115   Wolmer to Selborne, 29 Jan. 1886, Selborne MSS 1869 f. 143.

116   For the later retreat of the Selborne family into partisanship, see J.K. Chapman ed., *A Political Correspondence of the Gladstone Era: The Letters of Lady Sophia Palmer and Sir Arthur Gordon, 1884–1889* (Transactions of the American Philosophical Society, March 1971).

117   W.E.Gladstone, *Autobiographica*, J.Brooke and M.Sorensen eds, (1971), 111.

118   Gladstone to Selborne, 27 Jan. 1886, Selborne MSS 1869 f. 137: copy, Gladstone MSS 56447. Gladstone wrote 'it looks to me as if ... you intended to shut yourself out ... '

119   Lord Askwith, *Lord James of Hereford* (1930) 157.

120   Selborne to Gladstone, copy, 28 Jan. 1886, Selborne MSS 1869 f. 139. Lady Sophia Palmer, Selborne's daughter and amanuensis, sent copies to an old family friend, then Governor of Ceylon. She was indignant at Gladstone's misconstruction of her father's entirely innocent actions: 'Father did not dine with Lord G only because he does not wish to enter Society yet': and his letter attacking the Liberals over disestablishment at the elections had only got into the press by accident. See Lady Sophia Palmer to Sir A.Gordon, 28 Jan. 1886, Stanmore MSS 49222 f. 11.

121   Gladstone to Selborne, copy, 30 Jan. 1886, Gladstone MSS 56447.

122   Selborne to Sir A.Gordon, 3 Feb. 1886, Selborne MSS 1874 f. 63: cf. Lady Sophia Palmer to A.Elliot, 29 Jan. 1886, Elliot MSS, stating that it was Ireland, not disestablishment, which prevented her father joining Gladstone.

123 Mrs Humphry Ward, *A Writer's Recollections* (1918) 284–7.
124 The best study is in Sir Edward Russell's *That Reminds Me* – (1899), 278–290, there being no biography. See also *Speeches and Addresses of Edward Henry, XVth Earl of Derby K.G.*, Sir T.H.Sanderson and E.S.Roscoe eds, with a prefatory memoir by W.E.H.Lecky (2 vols, 1894).
125 Derby to Granville, copy, 25 Dec. 1884, Derby MSS, 920 DER/21.
126 Derby to Gladstone, 15 Jan. 1885, 44142 f. 115.
127 Granville to Derby, 13 June 1885, Derby MSS.
128 No special significance should be read into his refusal to write a personal letter of support to the Liberal candidate at Macclesfield (Derby to Brocklehurst, 7 Nov., Derby MSS).
129 Cf. Gladstone to Derby, 15 Sept. 1885, Derby MSS, declining a prior invitation from Derby, but asking Derby to Hawarden (which Derby accepted).
130 Gladstone to Derby, 17 July 1885, Derby MSS, enclosing unspecified 'letters which have been seen by three or four colleagues and which I shall be glad if you will read and return to me'. The letters related to the Irish negotiations as they stood before the Tory-Irish entente of 'two or three weeks ago'.
131 Derby got as many as 12 letters from Granville, Nov.–Jan. 1886 (Derby MSS) as well as very full and candid assessments of the position by Kimberley and Hartington.
132 Speech at Liverpool, 1 Nov. 1885.
133 Ibid.
134 Derby to Gladstone, 21 Sept. 1885, 44142 f. 145.
135 Ramm, ii 424.
136 See Derby to Gladstone, 13 Jan. 1886, 44142 f. 150, requesting a meeting on that or the following day. This is the last surviving letter between the two men during the period of cabinet making, Jan.–Feb. 1886.
137 Sir E.Russell, op. cit., 279.
138 W.H.Dunn, *James Anthony Froude, A Biography: 1857–1894* (1963), 583.
139 Derby to Col.F.Stanley, 28 Jan. 1886, Derby MSS.
140 Derby to Granville, 15 Dec. 1885, passed on to Gladstone: 44142 f. 148.
141 Sir E.Russell, op. cit., 287.
142 Derby to Gladstone, 25 July 1885, 44142 f. 140.
143 Rosebery MSS box 32.
144 Crewe, *Lord Rosebery* (1931) i, 251.
145 Gladstone to Rosebery, 13 Nov., Rosebery MSS box 18.
146 Ibid., 13 Dec.
147 Rosebery to Gladstone, 20 Dec., 44288 f. 285.
148 Same to same, 12 Dec., ibid. f. 279.
149 Rosebery to Chamberlain, 20 May 1885, Chamberlain MSS JC 5/61/1.
150 C.Dalrymple's diary, 31 May 1886, hereafter cited as D.D.
151 41249 A.
152 For suggestions as to ways in which the original and the typescript versions of the journal diverge where the 1890s are concerned, see Stephen Koss, 'Morley in the Middle', *English Historical Review*, vol. lxxxii, July 1967. Both versions are in the Harcourt MSS at Bodleian Library, except as regards the 1880s, where only the typescript version (undoubtedly an abridgment) has come to light.
153 44667.
154 Based on Heneage to Grey, 21 Mar. 1886, Grey MSS.
155 PRO 30/61/1.
156 Herschell to Gladstone, 17 Nov. 1885, 44484 f. 79.
157 A.Elliot's diary, 15 Jan. 1886.
158 Ibid., 3 Feb. 1886.

159 'Memoirs of Victor Williamson' (typescript) in the possession of Mr E. Watts Moses.

160 James to Gladstone, 29 Dec. 1885, 44219 f. 199.

161 'Memoirs of Victor Williamson'.

162 Chamberlain to Lefevre, 24 Nov. 1885, Haddo MSS box 12: Lefevre to Chamberlain, 16 Dec. 1885, Chamberlain MSS JC 5/52/8.

163 Lefevre to Chamberlain, 6 Jan. 1886, Chamberlain MSS JC 5/52/59.

164 Lefevre to Rosebery, 24 Dec. 1885, Rosebery MSS box 62. Labouchere's earlier summary of the terms of Parnellites would accept, published in *The Times*, had also appeared generally acceptable to Lefevre.

165 Citations above are from the Stansfeld MSS.

166 W.H.G. Armytage, 'The Railway Rates Question and the Fall of the Third Gladstone Ministry', *English Historical Review*, vol. lxv, January 1950, 18–51: P.M. Williams, 'Public Opinion and the Railway Rates Question in 1886', ibid., lxvii ,37–73. As to the true degree of its Tory origins, cf. Cranbrook to E. Stanhope, 31 Mar. 1886, 'I see Mundella speaks of the Railway Bill as ours in its main principles but I do not remember that it was ever brought completely under discussion' (Stanhope MSS).

167 To Leader, 13 May 1886, Leader MSS.

168 Mundella MSS folio viii.

169 Spencer to Mundella, 31 Dec. 1885, loc. cit.: Mundella to Spencer, 4 Jan. 1886, Spencer MSS.

170 No correspondence from Campbell–Bannerman to Spencer relating to the period of the home rule ministry has survived in the Spencer MSS.

171 Spencer MSS.

172 Campbell–Bannerman to Spencer, 8 Jan. 1886, Spencer MSS.

173 Campbell–Bannerman to John Ross, 28 Apr. 1886, 41232 f. 231.

174 Speech at Edinburgh, *Scotsman*, 6 May 1886.

175 Bryce to Dr R.J. Bryce, 17 May 1886, National Library of Ireland MSS 11010.

176 Ibid.

177 Granville to Playfair, 27 Mar. 1886, Playfair MSS.

178 Sir Edward Russell, op. cit., 290.

179 Ramm, ii, 439.

180 Mrs Gladstone to Mary Drew, n.d. [4 Feb. 1886], 46223 f. 244.

181 Granville to Playfair, loc. cit.

182 Gladstone to Rosebery, 24 Mar. 1886, Rosebery MSS: cf. Dalhousie to Derby, 7 Nov. 1885, Derby MSS, 'I have not been very well of late and have got out of the trick of sleeping properly. The doctors recommend a long sea voyage.'

183 Mrs Gladstone to Mary Drew, n.d. [22 Mar. 1886], 46223 f. 277.

184 Dalhousie to Derby, 30 Aug. 1885, Derby MSS.

185 Dalhousie to Gladstone, 7 Sept. 1885, 44492 f. 69.

186 Ramm, ii, 438.

187 *Edward Marjoribanks, Lord Tweedmouth 1849–1909: Notes and Recollections* the Marchioness of Aberdeen (his sister) ed. (1909), 17.

188 The Marquis and Marchioness of Aberdeeen, *More Cracks with 'We Twa'* (1929), 204.

189 Arnold Morley in *Edward Marjoribanks*, 42. The editor of the *Scotsman*, Charles Cooper, wrote of him 'Few men have ever shown more astuteness and more diligence than he had shown in promoting the home rule cause in Scotland' (Cooper, *An Editor's Retrospect* (1896) 417).

190 For testimony to his success see A.L. Brown, Radical M.P. for the Border Burghs, in *Edward Marjoribanks*, 45 ff.

191 *More Cracks with 'We Twa'*, 203.

192   F.W.Hirst, *Early Life and Letters of John Morley*, ii, (1927), though highly informative, stops short at 26 Jan. 1886. It can be supplemented from Morley's *Recollections*, D.A. Hamer's intellectual biography, *John Morley, Liberal Intellectual in Politics* (1968), and Garvin's *Chamberlain*. All these works throw more light on Morley's differences with Chamberlain, than on his activities in office in 1886.

193   Morley to Spencer, 14 Aug. 1886, Spencer MSS.

194   Morley to Aberdeen, Haddo MSS box 4: Morley to Houghton, Crewe MSS.

195   We owe this information to Professor K.Robbins, Grey's latest biographer

196   Monroe's family have no papers relating to his political career.

197   Hamilton to Spencer, 28 Mar. 1886, Spencer MSS. Naish was not fifty when he died in 1890. For other evidence of Naish's distress over the contemplated legislation, see *I. H. S.*, loc. cit. (Mar. 1969), 325.

198   Private information.

199   Bryce to Gladstone, 12 Mar. 1886, 56447.

200   Memo and separate letter from Russell to Gladstone, 17 Mar., loc. cit.

201   R.Barry O'Brien, *Lord Russell of Killowen* (1901) ch. xi.

202   R.B.Haldane, *An Autobiography* (1929), 35–9, 112: Sir A.E.Pease, *Elections and Recollections* (1932) 220, commenting on Davey's poor showing as candidate for Stockton. Haldane had worked under and with Davey.

203   Memo. by S.Walker to Spencer, 10 Mar. 1886, following a talk between them the previous day: 56447. Enquiries were unsuccessfully made in Ulster about the survival of Walker's papers. There is no published memoir of Walker, Naish, MacDermot, or Davey.

204   Churchill to Salisbury, 16 Nov. 1885, Salisbury MSS.

205   Salisbury to Churchill, 16 Nov. 1885, Churchill MSS ix 1066a.

206   Johnston's diary, 11 June 1886, PRO NI D880/2/38.

Book Two

Part One

Where not otherwise stated, all dates in this section refer to 1885.

1   *E. H.J.*, 1 Jan.

2   *C.J.*, 1 Jan.

3   Ibid., 2 Jan.

4   Chamberlain to Dilke, 3 Jan., 43887 f. 2.

5   *E. H.J.*

6   PRO CAB 41/19/1.

7   Chamberlain to Dilke, 3 Jan., loc. cit.: Dilke's memoirs, 43939 f. 17. Regarding both stretches of south-east African coast, note Derby to Granville (copy), 25 Dec. 1884, Derby MSS 920 DER/21: 'There is no foreign claim possible in either of these localities' yet fearing an overnight German settlement.

8   For details, see below, 7 Jan.

9   Hartington to the Queen (copy), 3 Jan., Devonshire MSS 340/1611.

10   *C.J.*

11   Rosebery's journal, 3 Jan., hereafter cited as *R.J.*

12   Gladstone to his wife, 2 Jan., Glynne–Gladstone MSS.

13   *R.J.*, 3 Jan.

14   Rosebery to Mrs Gladstone, 5 Jan., Glynne–Gladstone MSS.

15   *R.J.*

16   *E. H. J.*, 5 Jan.
17   Chamberlain to Dilke, 3 Jan., 43887 f. 2.
18   *C. J.*
19   *E. H. J.*
20   The report of this cabinet prepared by Gladstone for the Queen was not written till 5 Jan., owing to his illness and absence from London (see PRO CAB 41/19/2).
21   *C. J.*: see below, 7 Jan.
22   Carlingford to Spencer, 7 Jan., Spencer MSS.
23   PRO 30/29/134.
24   44547 f. 159.
25   Carlingford to Spencer, 7 Jan., Spencer MSS. Carlingford was in favour of an expedition.
26   Received by Wolseley, 8 Jan.: copy, dated 7 Jan., Devonshire MSS 340/1615.
27   *In Relief of Gordon*, A. Preston ed. (1967), 108.
28   Hartington to the Queen, 7 Jan., Devonshire MSS 340/1616.
29   Hartington to Gladstone, 9 Jan., 44147 f. 207.
30   Same to same, 15 Jan., ibid., f. 214.
31   *C. J.*, 7 Jan.
32   Dilke's memoirs, 43939 f. 21.
33   *C. J.*, 7 Jan.
34   43939 f. 22.
35   *R. J.*, 22 Jan.
36   PRO CAB 41/19/3.
37   *C. J.*, 20 Jan.
38   Hartington to Duchess of Manchester, 20 Jan., Devonshire MSS.
39   44147 f. 221.
40   *C. J.*, 20 Jan.
41   Hartington to Duchess of Manchester, loc. cit.
42   Spencer to Granville, 25 Jan., Granville MSS, PRO 30/29/29A.
43   19 Jan., Harcourt MSS.
44   Carlingford to Spencer, 21 Jan., Spencer MSS.
45   *C. J.*, 21 Jan.
46   For this distinction, see Derby's draft tel., later cancelled, circulated to cabinet c. 11–16 Feb., Derby MSS 920 DER/23, stating H. M. G. were 'quite unprepared' to contribute to local costs.
47   Ramm, ii, 318–20.
48   PRO CAB 41/19/4: Dilke MSS, op. cit., f. 41.
49   Hartington to Duchess of Manchester, 22 Jan., Devonshire MSS.
50   44646 f. 14.
51   *E. H. J.*, 22 Jan.: *R. J.*, 28 Jan.
52   Wolff to Churchill, 25 Jan., Churchill MSS iv 547.
53   The letters, or some of them, from Hamilton to Seymour, have found their way into the Glynne–Gladstone MSS.
54   For a totally predictable series of cabinet minutes in which all ministers flatly denied responsibility for the leakages, see W. E. Gladstone MSS, new deposit, 56451.
55   Dilke MSS, 43939 f. 55.
56   Mrs Gladstone to Mary Gladstone, n.d. but 5 Feb., 46223 f. 184.
57   Ibid. (second letter of same date) f. 185.
58   B. Holland, *Life of the Duke of Devonshire 1833–1908* (1911) ii, 11: Dilke MSS, 43939 f. 55.
59   Hartington to Gladstone, 5 Feb., 44147 f. 237.

60   PRO CAB 41/19/5. Not described in Carlingford's, Dilke's or Hamilton's diaries.

61   Baring had put forward a proposal for dealing with the Egyptian bond-holders, which was discussed at this cabinet. There was no wish to pursue Baring's plans (44646 f. 29). This was probably but not certainly the same issue as that recorded above concerning Egyptian railways.

62   44646 f. 29. Cf. Derby to Childers, 31 Jan., copy, Derby MSS 920 DER/21, reminding Childers that at a meeting of the colonial committee of the cabinet in May 1884, 'it was decided, very much against my opinion, but on grounds of diplomatic necessity which it seemed impossible to resist, that an inquiry should be made into the German [land] claims. Granville pressed upon us the Egyptian difficulty, and the danger of offending Bismarck by a refusal.' Derby added that the inquiry was almost certain not to support the German claims. Derby's wish that Britain rather than the colony should bear the cost of the inquiry was a cause of strained relations between Derby and Childers at this time. The inquiry, conducted by a mixed commission of one Englishman and one German, pro-duced an agreed report on 15 Apr., which was quickly accepted by Britain. On 21 May a payment of £10,620 in respect of German claims closed the matter, which had dragged on since 1883 (when Bismarck revived it) principally because of Derby's firm rejection of German demands (see *Further Correspondence relative to Land Claims in Fiji*, 1884–5, C. 4433, May 1885).

For Selborne's view of the Fiji land question, see Selborne to Derby, 15 Apr. 1885, Derby MSS, stressing the paramount importance of native rights, and praising the Governor, Sir A. Gordon (a High Churchman who was in intimate correspondence with Selborne, especially on church matters), for allowing no one 'to oppress the native race...' Selborne had taken a similar strong line about New Guinea (see text, 16 Feb.) and his moralistic approach to imperial expansion in Fiji and New Guinea may be relevant in construing his unexpectedly strong interest in African affairs.

63   Despite the bellicose discussion, another telegram of very tepid character was despatched during the day 'Send following instructions to Lord Wolseley: If the Mahdi should make any proposals to you, it is the desire of the cabinet that you should transmit them immediately to HMG for their consideration' (H. M. G. to Baring, copy 7 Feb. 44646 f. 46).

64   Hartington to Duchess of Manchester, 8 Mar.

65   The description of this meeting is based on Dilke MSS, op. cit., f. 61 (topics 1–8): C.J., 7 Feb. (for the course of discussion on topic 2): PRO CAB 41/19/6 for a statement of decisions on topics 1, 2, 3, and 6): and E. H.J. (topics 1–3).

66   C.J., 9 Feb.

67   Ibid.

68   £2.75m. according to E. Hamilton: £2m., 'excluding the cost of operations in Egypt or the Sudan' according to Gladstone.

69   Mrs G. Cornwallis-West, op. cit., 117, referring to evening of 9 Feb.: Borthwick edited the *Morning Post*.

70   In Dec. 1884 the cabinet had agreed on a circulated proposal that St Lucia Bay should be annexed to Natal, although Gladstone had minuted 'I can hardly conceive it to be necessary or reasonable to place a *permanent* establish-ment, doubtless attended with expense, at a point like this solely on account of these rather undefined apprehensions. Might not Germany be informed in a friendly way of our manifest title?' (Derby MSS, 920 DER/22).

71   Dilke, op. cit., f. 64: PRO CAB 41/19/7.

72   Carlingford to Spencer, 10 Feb., Spencer MSS.

73   Pencilled note from Dilke to Chamberlain, probably written during this cabinet: 43887 f. 58.

74 10 Feb. 1885, Rosebery MSS box 61.
75 *The Times*, 12 Feb.: 44646 f. 35.
76 A. Preston ed., op. cit., 141.
77 Dilke, op. cit., f. 67: C.J., 9 Feb., for views at Monday's cabinet. Cf. Ramm, ii 335–6, for Gladstone's and Granville's strong sense they had been in the right at this cabinet.
78 44646 f. 35.
79 Col. R. H. Vetch, C.B., *Life, Letters, and Diaries of Lieut-General Sir Gerald Graham, V.C., G.C.B, R.E.* (1901) 284–306.
80 Ramm, ii, 316.
81 Gladstone to Granville, 10 Jan., ibid. 317.
82 Gladstone to Hartington, 9 Jan., 44547 f. 161.
83 Gladstone to Granville, 8 Jan., Ramm, ii, 316.
84 Ibid.
85 Ibid.
86 Tel. to Baring, copy, Granville MSS, PRO 30/29/134.
87 PRO CAB 41/19/8: E. H.J.: Lady Knightley's diary, 11 Feb. (Hartington): Robert Brown, *Mr Gladstone As I Knew Him and Other Essays* (1902). Brown was an obscure antiquary whose essay on Gladstone (pp. 7–36) was devoted to the proposition that the G.O.M. was never too busy for scholarly pursuits.
88 Crewe, op. cit., i, 221, gives 2½ hours, in contrast to press reports as above.
89 R.J., 16 Feb.
90 C.J., 16 Feb.
91 Rosebery did not record Gladstone as present, and his only comment was 'We came to a resolution of one sort or another' (R.J., 13 Feb.).
92 R.J., 16 Feb.
93 PRO CAB 41/19/9: Dilke, op. cit., f. 73.
94 C.J., 16 Feb.
95 44646 f. 38.
96 R.J., 17 Feb.
97 C.J., 17 Feb.
98 PRO CAB 41/19/10: Dilke, op. cit., f. 75: 44446 f. 44.
99 Minute in Hartington's hand, 12 Feb., Derby MSS 920 DER/20.
100 Dilke, loc. cit.
101 Ibid., f. 77.
102 Ibid., f. 78: also reported in almost identical language by Dilke to Grant Duff, 20 Feb., Dilke MSS, 43894 f. 171.
103 C.J., 20 Feb.
104 Ibid.
105 Minutes dated 12 Feb., Derby MSS loc. cit.
106 PRO CAB 41/19/11: Dilke, loc. cit.
107 C.J., 20 Feb.
108 *Hansard, 3*, vol. 294, col. 902.
109 R.J., 20 Feb.
110 Dilke, loc. cit.
111 According to Dilke, 43939 f. 8: the memorandum is not in the collected cabinet papers.
112 Points 1–6 based on PRO CAB 41/19/12.
113 Dilke MSS, 43913 f. 118.
114 On Gladstone's division list, Spencer's name has been crossed out of the ministers who supported resignation. But there is no evidence that Spencer changed his mind.
115 43939 f. 84: C.J., 28 Feb.

116 Hartington to Duchess of Manchester, 1 Mar.: cf. Granville to Hartington, 28 Feb., Devonshire MSS 340/1674, putting strong case for resigning.

117 R.R.James, *Rosebery* (1963), 166.

118 Hartington, loc. cit.

119 Dilke's notes in pencil written at the cabinet table itself give Grosvenor's name in brackets beside that of Gladstone, in a list of those wishing to remain in office. Dilke's cabinet 'division list' differs only from that given above, in showing Selborne as voting for both sides at once. Whether this means a change of front by Selborne, or simply confusion by Dilke, is open to doubt (Dilke MSS, 43913 f. 118).

120 56452.

121 Hartington, loc. cit.

122 Hartington to Duchess of Manchester, 19 Feb.

123 Ibid.

124 Dilke, op. cit., f. 92. For Gladstone's illness 'with cold and hoarseness' since the last cabinet, see R.A.J.Walling ed., *The Diaries of John Bright* (1930) 524, referring to 2 Mar.

125 C.J., 7 Mar.

126 Hartington to Gladstone, 5 Mar., 44147 f. 256.

127 On 5 Mar. Derby had announced that St Lucia bay was claimed by England, both by precedent and by current occupation, but that owing to German objections, negotiations were still in progress (*Hansard*, 3, vol. 295, col. 61). On 8 June, Derby said the whole question was settled, no further claims being likely to be made by Germany (ibid., vol. 298, col. 1395).

128 C.J., 7 Mar.

129 PRO CAB 41/19/13.

130 C.J., 7 Mar.

131 Hartington to Duchess of Manchester, 8 Mar.

132 Dilke, op. cit., f. 95.

133 C.J., 12 Mar.

134 Ibid.

135 Copy, 56452.

136 Gladstone's letter to the Queen reporting on the cabinet of 12 Mar. (PRO CAB 41/19/15) has been fragmented, at least as it appears in the PRO files, a note at the top stating 'First part missing'. However, an accurate copy of the middle section of Gladstone's letter, in an unidentified hand, immediately precedes it (PRO CAB 41/19/14), while the remaining missing section of the letter has been filed at PRO CAB 41/19/20.

137 The opinions on arrests were minuted on 8 Mar. and those on the title on 11 Mar. (Granville MSS PRO 30/29/145).

138 R.J., 13 Mar.

139 Ibid.

140 According to C.J., 13 Mar., Bismarck's difficulty was about the stoppage of the Egyptian sinking fund by Northbrook: according to Hartington, Bismarck now wanted to omit the clause terminating the lawsuit of the Caisse against the Egyptian government. Hartington doubted 'very much whether anything will ever make the old man friendly' (Hartington to Duchess of Manchester, 15 Mar.).

141 PRO CAB 41/19/16: 44646 f. 56 (where it is misdated 14 Mar.).

142 C.J., 20 Mar.

143 Dilke noted 20,000 as the figure. Chamberlain was in agreement with the move, saying he was all for showing a bold front irrespective of what course was finally taken. The telegram informing Dufferin of the decision was sent at 4.30 p.m. (Dufferin MSS, D 1071 H/M1/7 p. 4.).

144   *E. H. J.*
145   *R. J.*, 20 Mar.
146   Undated and unaddressed note by Selborne, Dilke MSS, 43913 f. 119.
147   Dilke, op. cit., f. 100.
148   PRO CAB 41/19/17: 44646 f. 62: *R. J.*, 20 Mar.
149   Referred to in *E. H. J.*, but incorrectly dated Tuesday, 23 Mar.: also incorrectly dated Monday, 23 Mar., in *R. J.*
150   Kimberley to Dufferin, 2 Apr., PRONI Dufferin MSS D 1071 H/M1/3 p. 47: *C. J.*
151   *R. J.*, 23 Mar. (misdated).
152   *E. H. J.*, 24 Mar.
153   *C. J.*, 24 Mar.
154   *R. J.*, 29 Mar.
155   PRO CAB 41/19/18.
156   *C. J.*, 27 Mar. Two days later Hartington said privately that he would resign 'if Suakin were given up except under pressure of force majeure as regards Central Asia' (*R. J.*, 29 Mar.).
157   *H. J.*, 27 Mar.
158   Based on PRO CAB 41/19/19: Dilke, op. cit., f. 103: *E. H. J.* and *C. J.*
159   *D. D.*, 18 May.
160   44646 f. 71.
161   Dilke MSS, 43939 f. 110.
162   *C. J.*, 4 Apr.
163   Based on *C. J.*, 4 Apr.: cypher telegrams from Gladstone and Granville to the Queen, 4 Apr., PRO CAB 41/19/21: Gladstone to the Queen, 4 Apr., PRO CAB 41/19/22: Gladstone to Childers, 5 Apr., Childers MSS 5/165.
164   *E. H. J.*, 4 Apr.: Chamberlain to Dilke, 43887 f. 91.
165   For Gladstone's views on Wolseley's alarmist letter, see Gladstone to Hartington, 2 Apr., 44148 f. 5, arguing that most of the grounds given for the advance on Khartoum were now untenable, and referring to his suggestion, by an earlier telegram to Hartington, that the cabinet meet to consider Wolseley's letter.
166   Based on PRO CAB 41/19/23: *E. H. J.*
167   56452.
168   Hamilton to Rosebery, 11 and 12 Apr., Rosebery MSS box 25: Rosebery to Primrose, 11 Apr., and to Hamilton, 12 Apr., 48610.
169   44646 f. 77.
170   Dilke, op. cit., f. 108.
171   PRO CAB 41/19/24.
172   PRO CAB 41/19/27. This is the misplaced part of a letter, undated by Gladstone but misdated 14 Apr. in another hand and filed accordingly. The contents of the letter establish that it was in fact the first part of PRO CAB 41/19/24 referring to 11 Apr.
173   Selborne to Gladstone, 10 Apr., 44298 f. 167.
174   Granville to Rosebery, 12 Apr., Rosebery MSS box 61.
175   'As to getting out of Sudan, Mr G "I am not prepared to go on upon any terms, Russia or no Russia". Not finally decided'. (Dilke MSS, 43913 f. 123).
176   Hartington to Rosebery, 11 Apr., Rosebery MSS box 61.
177   *R. J.*, 13 Apr.
178   See printed cabinet memorandum, 22 Apr., 'Opinion of the Law Officers with regard to the Suppression of the Bosphore Egyptien', Derby MSS 920 DER 58/1. The law officers found 'much to be said' for the view that the closure of the printing establishment 'was wholly illegal'.
179   Gladstone wrote of the French 'demand, shall I say a command' as a

symptom of a situation in which 'there is none so poor who may not scoff at us,so long as we shall not have shaken ourselves free of our present unnatural entanglements' (Gladstone to Selborne, 13 Apr., Selborne MSS 1869 f. 27).

180   44490 f. 117.
181   R.J., 13 Apr.
182   Not in *List of Cabinet Papers, 1880–1914.*
183   The above account generally is based on PRO CAB 41/19/25.
184   R.J., 13 Apr.
185   E.H.J.
186   R.J., 13 Apr.
187   56452.
188   PRO CAB 41/19/26.
189   E.H.J.
190   C.J., 14 Apr.
191   E.H.J. Just before the cabinet, Northbrook told Carlingford, who had missed the previous three cabinets, that Hartington and perhaps Childers were likely to resign, not over shelving the Khartoum campaign, but over announcing that it was to be shelved (C.J., 14 Apr.). Rosebery had called on Hartington that morning and found him with Childers 'who is resigning too' (R.J., 16 Apr.).
192   Hartington to Rosebery, 18 Apr., Rosebery MSS box 61. The more Hartington told Rosebery of his intention to resign, the more he elicited in return sustained and highly flattering arguments for his carrying on (Crewe, op. cit., i, 236).
193   R.J., 15 Apr.
194   Gladstone to Selborne, 13 Apr., Selborne MSS 1869 f. 27. Gladstone's cabinet notes, however, referred to Freycinet's 'improved tone'.
195   PRO CAB 41/19/28.
196   R.J., 15 Apr. Baring had, according to Rosebery, written a letter of 14 pages on 3 Apr., and again subsequently, urging that the Khartoum expedition be given up.
197   Gladstone's cabinet notes, 56452.
198   Dilke op. cit., f. 115: R.J., 15 Apr.
199   PRO CAB 41/19/29.
200   E.H.J.
201   Ibid.
202   E.H.J.
203   PRO CAB 41/19/30.
204   R.J., 20 Apr.
205   Dilke's memoirs, op. cit. ff. 87, 111.
206   44149 ff. 336–41.
207   44646 f. 97.
208   PRO CAB 41/19/31.
209   C.J., 21 Apr.
210   E.H.J.
211   Chamberlain to Rosebery, 20 Apr., Rosebery MSS box 61. Dilke later wrote that on 21 Apr. 'I decided that I could not yield and said so' (undated memorandum in Dilke's hand, Dilke MSS, 43913 f. 131). Edward Hamilton wrote to Dilke on 21 Apr. after the cabinet asking him to reconsider his stand (ibid., f. 128).
212   R.J., 21 Apr.
213   E.H.J.
214   R.J., 24 Apr., printed Crewe, op. cit., i, 235–6. Because the disagreements about the despatch appeared impossible to resolve until after a further cabinet,

Rosebery slipped away at 7.30, only to find the following day that they had subsequently agreed and sent the despatch.

215 E. H. J.

216 PRO CAB 41/19/32.

217 Ibid.

218 Hartington to Duchess of Manchester, 25 Apr.

219 E. H. J.

220 Hartington, loc. cit.

221 C. J., 25 Apr. But cf. R. J., 25 Apr., referring to the same toning down of wording, but placing it as settled in committee the previous night.

222 For membership, see 1 May below.

223 C. J., 28 Apr.

224 PRO CAB 41/19/33: Dilke, op. cit., f. 139, listing exactly the same items, in rather different order of business.

225 E. H. J., 29 Apr.

226 C. J., 29 Apr.

227 Based chiefly on C. J.: also Dilke, op. cit., f. 130, and J. A. Spender, *Campbell-Bannerman* (1923) i, 83 (with Campbell-Bannerman's memorandum on Irish government of 30 April printed in full). Gladstone's cabinet minutes record the appointment of this Irish committee, with membership as above, but without the names of Hartington, Lefevre, and Childers. Carlingford's name was written over that of Kimberley, with Rosebery crossed out. The terms of reference of the committee, appointed during the cabinet of 28 April, were 'to prepare for consideration a modified crimes bill: to consider question whether any provisions should apply to U.K.: also on local govt bill and land purchase' (44646 f. 108).

228 PRO CAB 41/19/34. According to Gladstone's cabinet notes, a telegram from Dufferin was also before this cabinet.

229 Dilke, op. cit., f. 140.

230 R. J., 2 May.

231 E. H. J., 2 May.

232 R. J., 2 May.

233 Gladstone to his wife, 2 May, Glynne–Gladstone MSS.

234 E. H. J.

235 Misdated 'Thursday 6 May' in Gladstone's cabinet minutes.

236 The two cabinets of 2 and 7 May are not recorded by Carlingford, though he was well and in London at that time and appears (according to *The Times*) to have attended the very important meeting on 7 May. There are indications that about this time Carlingford fell some weeks behind in entering up his diary.

237 44646 f. 117.

238 Dilke, op. cit.: R. J., 7 May.

239 His view had weight, in that the Gladstones and Chamberlain had dined with him the previous evening, and had a long political talk after the ladies left (R. J., 8 May).

240 E. H. J. The cabinet of 9 May is not mentioned by Hamilton.

241 Ibid.

242 Dilke, op. cit., f. 144.

243 PRO CAB 41/19/36. According to C. J., 9 May, Selborne and Northbrook were treating the issue of the evacuation of Dongola as a possible cause of resignation.

244 Dilke, loc. cit.

245 Cf. Granville MSS PRO 30/29/145.

246 R. J., 9 May.

247 PRO CAB 41/19/36.

248   R.J., 9 May.

249   C.J., 9 May.

250   R.J., 9 May.

251   Based on *E.H.J.*: Crewe, op. cit., i, 225: Harcourt to Gladstone, 44199 f. 208: Dilke, op. cit., f. 146: *R.J.*, 11 May.

252   Rosebery puts this down to his having 'consulted his friends' and mentioned in particular that Chamberlain was in constant communication with O'Shea (*R.J.*, 12 May).

253   Dilke, op. cit., f. 147.

254   C.J., 12 May.

255   Spencer to Hartington, 13 May, Devonshire MSS 340/1771.

256   C.J.

257   R.J., 15 May.

258   Based on 44646 f. 127: C.J.: Dilke, op. cit., f. 148: PRO CAB 41/19/37.

259   Gladstone's report to the Queen on this cabinet is incorrectly bound in the volume of cabinet papers for 1886 in the Public Record Office, where it is to be found under the reference CAB 41/20/19, dated 16 May (which in 1886 would have fallen on a Sunday, a most implausible day for a cabinet). Context also makes it clear that the letter belongs to 1885 and is incorrectly filed under 1886.

260   R.J., 16 May.

261   Granville MSS, PRO 30/29/145, 15 and 16 May.

262   Minutes by Rosebery and Carlingford, 19 May, and by Granville, n.d. but May, in Devonshire MSS 340/1779: earlier minutes by Carlingford and Rosebery c. 20 Apr. 1885, ibid. 340/1735.

263   44646 f. 133, n.d. but probably 16 May.

264   J.A.Spender, *Campbell-Bannerman*, i, 82.

265   Dilke to Mrs Pattison, n.d. but 21 May, Dilke MSS, 43906 f. 75.

266   Dilke memoirs 43939 f. 150.

267   R.J., 12 July.

268   Labouchere to Gladstone, 16 and 23 Jan. 1887, 56449.

269   'Mr G. will resign at the end of the session. I rather doubt Hartington being able to form a govt' (Dilke to Grant Duff, 21 May, Dilke MSS, 43894 f. 179).

270   'I was amazed, and at once wrote to resign. I afterwards got hold of Chamberlain... If a cabinet is held, we shall not attend' (Dilke to Lefevre, copy, 20 May, Dilke MSS, 43913 f. 135).

271   Lefevre saw himself only as taking up a bargaining position, and actually thought that Spencer's concessions should be accepted, at least until a settlement of the Afghan crisis was reached (Lefevre to Dilke, 28 May, in two letters, Dilke MSS, 43913 f. 140).

272   Based on Dilke's memoirs, f. 151, and 44149 ff. 347–54, (Gladstone–Dilke letters of 20–21 May). Rosebery only learned of the resignations, which took place in the afternoon of 20 Jan., through a letter from Reginald Brett, an entirely 'unofficial' personage, reaching him that evening (*R.J.*, 20 May) – a curious instance of the real routes through which cabinet politics operated.

273   Dilke to Chamberlain, c. 9 Feb. 43887 f. 58.

274   Henry Sidgwick's diary.

275   R.J., 21 May. Rosebery left London for Germany on the evening of 21 May, and returned to town early in the morning on 29 May.

276   C.J.: *The Times* did not record this meeting as being a proper cabinet council.

277   PRO CAB 41/19/38.

278   G.E.Buckle ed., *The Letters of Queen Victoria*, second series, (1926) iii,

652–5. The Queen sent the letter to Carlingford on 28 May, and to Conservative leaders later in the year (see C.J., 107n).

279   E.H.J., 25 May.

280   30 May, Devonshire MSS 340/1785.

281   R.J., 2 June.

282   Dilke, op. cit., f. 181.

283   R.J., 5 June.

284   44312 f. 128. Gladstone's plans for his future were increasingly centred on Ireland: cf. Granville to Derby, 3 June, Derby MSS 920 DER/20, saying 'Gladstone adheres to his engagements with Spencer but is stronger than ever in favour of the Dublin Govt'; and Mrs Gladstone to Lady F.Cavendish, n.d. but prob. early summer 1885, 'Two things [Uncle William] is very strong about: that he should not go without a cry (he never yet has) or without old colleagues, but there is no doubt that the Irish legislation is there. Lord Hartington received a serious letter not long ago in which he opened his whole heart to him about his Irish plans.' On 6 June the premier was described as 'extremely well and lively' (Herbert to Henry Gladstone) Glynne–Gladstone MSS.

285   C.J., R.J., 5 June.

286   For Hartington's insistence that the leak be brought before the cabinet, see Hartington to Gladstone, 29 May, 44148 f. 75. For Chamberlain's denial, and his defence that other papers had printed the story, see Garvin, *Chamberlain*, i, 613.

287   44646 f. 138. For Hartington's continuing objections to an announcement on Irish local government, as envisaged in the Spencer–Dilke compromise, see Hartington to Gladstone, 29 May, 44148 f. 75, arguing this would be an unprecedented attempt to commit a future parliament and a future ministry.

288   Gladstone to Spencer, 5 June, 44312 f. 128.

289   Ibid.

290   R.J., 5 June. According to the unsubstantiated testimony of E.H.J., Gladstone was talking privately on 7 June of asking Spencer and Rosebery to change places.

291   44312 f. 128.

292   PRO CAB 41/19/39.

293   44646 f. 140.

294   Dilke, op. cit., f. 183.

295   Selborne to Gladstone, 44298 f. 183. Selborne had protested at the 15 May cabinet against dropping the public meetings clause of the crimes bill.

296   R.J., 8 June.

297   44646 f. 147: C.J.

298   PRO CAB 41/19/40.

299   Herbert Gladstone's diary, Glynne–Gladstone MSS.

300   Fragment in Mrs Gladstone's hand, n.d., Glynne–Gladstone MSS; see also Mrs Gladstone to Lady Frederick Cavendish, 11 June, loc. cit., stressing the shock and disappointment of defeat.

301   Ibid.

302   A.Elliot's diary, 9 June.

303   Sir E.Clarke, *The Story of My Life* (1918), 240.

304   Akers-Douglas to Salisbury, 9 June, Salisbury MSS.

305   Stansfeld to a friend, 12 June, Stansfeld MSS.

306   Clarke, loc. cit.

307   Herbert to Henry Gladstone, 9 June, Glynne–Gladstone MSS. See also G.W.E.Russell ed., *MacColl* (1914) 114–5, asserting that the whip sent out – not till Saturday night – was a four-line one on ordinary paper, not a five-line one indicating serious danger: that Liberal M.Ps were allowed to leave without

hindrance, Barran for instance going home to Leeds and another Liberal leaving the House at 10 p.m. because he felt off colour: and that Hubbard, the Tory taxation pundit, had told a Liberal minister that he and perhaps other Tories would support ministers on the merits.

308 Clarke, loc. cit.
309 C.J., 9 June: Dilke, op. cit., f. 187.
310 Dilke, ibid.
311 Kimberley's memoirs, Rosebery MSS box 111.
312 Crewe, op. cit., i, 241.
313 Kimberley, loc. cit.
314 44646 f. 149 (Gladstone's notes).
315 C.J.
316 Crewe, loc. cit.
317 West, op. cit., ii, 239.
318 Entry of 9 June in Queen Victoria's Journal, Royal Archives.
319 R.J., 10 June.
320 Ibid., 11 June.

Part Two

Unless otherwise stated, all dates can be taken to refer to the period June 1885–February 1886.

1 H.W.Lucy, *Peeps at Parliament* (1904), 297.
2 50044.
3 50063a.
4 H.W.Lucy, *Gladstone* (1895), 172.
5 Northcote's diary, 50063a, f. 422; hereafter cited as N.D.
6 D.D.
7 J.S.Flynn, *Sir Robert N.Fowler, Bart., M.P.* (1893) (Carlton): Lady Knightley's diary, 9 June.
8 N.D.: Lady Knightley's diary, 9 June.
9 Manners to Rutland, 10 June, Rutland MSS: Lady Knightley's diary, 12 June.
10 E.H.J.
11 Cranborne to Churchill n.d. but 11 June, Churchill MSS v 624, countermanding an earlier note from Salisbury to Churchill (ibid. 620a) written at 4.45 p.m. just after receiving the royal summons and asking Churchill to call 'tonight after dinner or tomorrow morning'.
12 R.J., 12 July.
13 Q.V.J., 12 June.
14 D.D., 11 June.
15 Q.V.J., 16 June.
16 N.D., f. 424.
17 Q.V.J., 12 June.
18 50020 f. 117.
19 Ibid., f. 119.
20 Ibid., f. 127.
21 Ibid., 15 June (Churchill's terms): Lady Knightley's diary, 13, 15, and 20 June 1885 (on taking office) and 20 May 1884, (Churchill's character).
22 Q.V.J., 15 June.
23 Salisbury to Harrowby, 15 June, Harrowby MSS new series vol. 4, giving appointment for 6.30, with undated explanatory note in Harrowby's hand.

24 Manners to Rutland, 15 June, Rutland MSS.
25 50020 f. 127.
26 *Q.V.J.*, 17 June.
27 50020 f. 127.
28 Richmond MSS, 871/D 38.
29 Manners to Rutland, 17 June, Rutland MSS: cf. cabinet of July 4 below.
30 Smith was invited to the meeting, which was at 1.30 p.m. (Hambleden MSS, PS 9/27, Salisbury to Smith, 18 June).
31 D.D. 18 June.
32 Salisbury to Richmond, 21 June, Richmond MSS, 871 D/39.
33 N.D., f. 430.
34 D.D. 20 June.
35 N.D., f. 431: Harold E. Gorst, *Much of Life is Laughter* (1936), 142.
36 D.D. 21 June.
37 Cranbrook's diary, 22 June, Cranbrook MSS: hereafter cited as C.D.
38 N.D., passim.
39 C.D., 23 June: N.D., f. 431.
40 C.D., 25 June.
41 N.D., loc. cit.
42 A. Elliot's diary.
43 C.D., 26 June: Lady Knightley's diary, 25 June.
44 Confusingly dated 25 June in G.E.Buckle ed., *The Letters of Queen Victoria, 1862–85*, iii, 681, and in Salisbury's original letter. Cranbrook's diary, on the other hand, misdates this cabinet as taking place on Saturday June 27. It is quite clear from *The Times* and from contextual indications in the above sources that both Salisbury and Cranbrook were wrong.
45 C.D., 27–8 June.
46 N.D., f. 435.
47 C.D., 2 July. Cranbrook apparently misdates this (as other) cabinets, as taking place on Thursday, because of his confusing habit of writing his entries a day in arrears.
48 Stanhope to Carnarvon, 1 July, PRO 30/6/55/3, is the main source for this cabinet.
49 Carnarvon to Salisbury, 1 July, Carnarvon MSS.
50 Winn to Salisbury, 20 June, Salisbury MSS.
51 C.D., 5 July.
52 The date is slightly uncertain. Justin McCarthy, *Reminiscences* (1899), ii, 111, merely dates the interview 'Saturday'. Hardinge, *Carnarvon*, iii, 164, gives the morning of 6 July, citing a memorandum of the conversation by Carnarvon.
53 Justin McCarthy and Mrs Campbell Praed, op. cit., 10. For Vincent's role, see S.H.Jeyes and F.D.How, *The Life of Sir Howard Vincent* (1912), ch. x, 'The Carnarvon Interview'.
54 McCarthy, op. cit., ii, 112.
55 McCarthy and Praed, op. cit., 12, for McCarthy's undated letter which could conceivably refer to the second Carnarvon–McCarthy encounter (Dec. 1885). For Mrs Jeune's luncheon, Lady Knightley's diary, 12 July 1885.
56 McCarthy, loc. cit.
57 Lady Gwendolen Cecil, *Life of Robert, Marquis of Salisbury*, (1931), iii, 155–164.
58 Ashbourne to Carnarvon, 8 July: PRO 30/6/56/59.
59 Ibid., 9 July: PRO 30/6/56/62.
60 Carnarvon to Ashbourne, 9 July, Carnarvon MSS.
61 *Standard*, 13 July.

62   Cranbrook to Carnarvon, 12 July, PRO 30/6/55/5, is the only source for the business of this cabinet.

63   Harcourt to Cross, 27 and 28 July, 51274.

64   Based on Salisbury's report to the Queen.

65   Harrowby to Carnarvon, 14 July, Carnarvon MSS.

66   Carnarvon to Beach, 15 July, St Aldwyn MSS.

67   Salisbury to Beach, 16 July, ibid.

68   Walsh to Carnarvon, 21 July, Carnarvon MSS.

69   Harrowby to Carnarvon, 22 July, Carnarvon MSS.

70   Based on a letter from Salisbury to the Queen, dated 20 July, and referring to a cabinet 'yesterday'. There is no evidence for a cabinet on Sunday 19 July, an unlikely event in any case. It is presumed that Salisbury confused his dates, and was in fact writing on Sunday 19th July.

71   C.D., 18 July.

72   Salisbury to the Queen, 20 July, (copy), Salisbury MSS D/86/148. The incoming Conservatives had shown little despatch in dealing with a question which some of their predecessors had regarded as urgent as long ago as May.

73   Dyke to Carnarvon, 18 July, PRO 30/6/57/82.

74   Salisbury to Carnarvon, 22 July, PRO 30/6/55/9.

75   R.J., 28 July 1886.

76   Harrowby to Carnarvon, 22 July, PRO 30/6/55/8. Carnarvon's memorandum on the need for enquiry into Irish education (PRO 30/6/58/129) was dated 16 July.

77   PRO 30/6/55/9.

78   Ashbourne to Carnarvon, 22 July, PRO 30/6/58/132.

79   Salisbury to Carnarvon, PRO 30/6/55/9.

80   C.D., 25 July.

81   The parliamentary elections (medical relief) bill, originally brought in by Collings, 15 June.

82   Salisbury to the Queen, 24 July, Salisbury MSS D/86/150.

83   Dyke to Carnarvon, 23 July, PRO 30/6/58/136.

84   Ashbourne to Carnarvon, 25 July, PRO 30/6/56/70.

85   C.D., 29 July.

86   Carnarvon to Ashbourne, 1 Aug. 1885, Ashbourne MSS B26/12: 'You will be much interested to hear that I have had a remarkable conversation which lasted 1¼ hours, and that I shall hope to give you all details on my return...'

87   Lady G. Cecil, op. cit., 157.

88   Printed *in extenso*, Hardinge, *Carnarvon*, iii, 178–80, but not traced in Salisbury or Carnarvon MSS: see also letters by Carnarvon's daughter, Lady Burghclere, in *The Times*, 29 Nov. and 1 Dec. 1930. The custodian of the Salisbury MSS could not trace the document.

89   McCarthy, op. cit., ii, 113. R. Barry O'Brien's substantial biography of Parnell contains no description of the above meeting.

90   *Hansard*, 7 June 1886, vol. 306, col. 1181 (Parnell): ibid., 1199 (Beach's denial): ibid., 1200 (Parnell's disclosure): ibid., cols. 1256–60 (Carnarvon's admission of 10 June).

91   *Parl. P.* 1886, C. 4614.

92   C.D., 3 Aug.

93   Cranbrook to Carnarvon, 4 Aug., PRO 30/6/55/11; Carnarvon to Harrowby, 5 Aug., Harrowby MSS lii 138.

94   Based on Salisbury's report to the Queen.

95   C.D., 7 Aug.

96   This letter, written on 7 Aug., is in the Salisbury MSS. According to Salisbury, its contents 'were not more than they expected, and I am sure they

will be careful not to use language of extravagant hopefulness' (Salisbury to Carnarvon, 12 Aug., PRO 30/6/55/12).

97 Ibid.

98 Ashbourne to Carnarvon, 11 Aug., PRO 30/6/56/74.

99 Based on Salisbury's letter to the Queen.

100 H.J.Hanham, 'The Creation of the Scottish Office, 1881–87', *The Juridical Review* 1965, 228–32.

101 *R.J.*, 14 Aug.

102 *Q.V.J.*, 27 June.

103 Ashbourne to Carnarvon, 20 Sept., Carnarvon MSS, referring to a letter on these lines sent by the latter to Salisbury on 18 Sept.

104 Harrowby to Carnarvon, 5 Sept., ibid.

105 Churchill to Carnarvon, 27 Aug., ibid.

106 Manners to Carnarvon, 28 Aug., ibid.

107 Iddesleigh to Carnarvon, 12 Aug., ibid.

108 Ibid, 7 Sept.

109 Carnarvon to Harrowby, Harrowby MSS lii 144–5.

110 Beach to Carnarvon, 25 Sept., Carnarvon MSS.

111 Churchill to Salisbury, 1 Oct., Salisbury MSS.

112 *Irish Historical Studies*, vol. xvi, 163: W.S.Churchill, *Lord Randolph Churchill*, i, (1906), 459–61. Both accounts are non-contemporary, both are probably based on Holmes' selective memory in later life only, and both may reflect anxiety to wipe away any trace of earlier political frailties.

113 Churchill to Carnarvon, 21 Sept., Carnarvon MSS.

114 Hardinge, op. cit., iii, 194–5.

115 N.D., f. 437.

116 Ibid.

117 Ibid.

118 Ashbourne MSS.

119 Salisbury MSS D/86/174.

120 D.D., 9 Oct.

121 C.D., 10 Oct.

122 Smith to Duke of Cambridge, 9 Oct., copy sent by Churchill to Beach, St Aldwyn MSS.

123 Richmond to Salisbury, 20 Dec., Salisbury MSS class E.

124 Based on Cross to Richmond, 28 Dec., Richmond MSS 871/D 82: Salisbury to Cross, 26 Dec., 51263: Argyll to Cross, 16 Dec., 51274: Richmond to Cross, 22 and 25 Dec., 51267.

125 Salisbury MSS class E. A further and apparently unproductive ministerial meeting about the crofters' question took place at Dover House on 12 Jan., attended by the lord advocate (Macdonald), the solicitor-general for Scotland (Robertson), Arthur Balfour, and C.Dalrymple, Scottish whip from June 1885 but without a seat since the elections (D.D., 12 Jan.). There is no evidence that this last meeting was called to consider possible legislation.

126 Salisbury to Queen, 9 Oct. (copy): Salisbury MSS D/86/178.

127 Smith to Carnarvon, 13 Oct., PRO 30/6/54/13.

128 Salisbury to the Queen, 23 Oct., copy, Salisbury MSS D/86/188.

129 Ashbourne to Carnarvon, 23 Oct., PRO 30/6/55/29.

130 Hanham, loc. cit., 233: Richmond to Cross, 28 Oct., 51267. L.P.Curtis, *Coercion and Conciliation in Ireland 1880–1892* refers to cabinet meetings on 31 Oct. (p. 61) and 20 Dec. (p. 65). In our view these did not occur. The death of Lord G.Hamilton's father on 31 Oct. had no discernible effect on his political activities, barely visible at the best of times.

131 Harrowby to Carnarvon, 21 Nov.: PRO 30/6/55/34.

132   McCarthy's diary for 1885, National Library of Ireland MS 3701. The diary is so devoid of entries that its chief interest lies in its being a present from Lady Ely.

133   Justin McCarthy, op. cit., ii, 113, which says very little of their talk: McCarthy and Praed, op. cit., 17, says even less.

134   Memo of conversation with McCarthy, 13 Dec., Carnarvon MSS PRO 30/6/67/32.

135   In W.S.Churchill, op. cit., ii, 25, accounts of the proceedings on 14 and 15 Dec. are conflated to produce a single non-existent meeting on 16 Dec.

136   PRO 30/6/127/21 and PRO CAB 37/16/64: written by Carnarvon on 7 Dec. but printed on 11 Dec. and often referred to by latter date.

137   Based up to this point on Salisbury's report to the Queen.

138   PRO 30/6/127/6.

139   See PRO 30/6/127/18.

140   Churchill to Carnarvon, 18 Dec., Carnarvon MSS, PRO 30/6/55/49, replying to a letter from Carnarvon of 16 Dec. asking for suggestions about Irish university policy.

141   Churchill to Salisbury, copy, 16 Dec., Churchill MSS x 1177a.

142   References occur in Ashbourne's autobiographical notes in the Ashbourne MSS, and in PRO 30/6/55/47.

143   C.D., 16 Dec.

144   Ibid., 17 Dec.

145   Churchill MSS x 1174.

146   Churchill to Akers-Douglas, Chilston MSS U 564, C128/5.

147   Churchill MSS x 1177a and b.

148   Carnarvon to Cranbrook, 19 Dec., Cranbrook MSS T 501/262.

149   Salisbury MSS class E.

150   Beach to Churchill, 25 Dec., Churchill MSS x 1210.

151   Churchill to Carnarvon, 2 Jan., PRO 30/6/55/57: also Salisbury to Richmond, 3 Jan., Richmond MSS 8/9 f. 95, 'We practically gave up all the abnormal methods of seeking a vote of confidence; and hope that Gladstone will give us our opportunity on the Address.'

152   PRO 30/6/55/60.

153   Iddesleigh to W.H.Smith, 27 Dec., Hambleden MSS PS 9/96.

154   Beach to W.H.Smith, n.d. late Dec., Hambleden MSS PS 9/98.

155   Cranbrook to Carnarvon, 17 Dec., and Carnarvon to Cranbrook, 19 Dec., Carnarvon MSS.

156   Churchill to Carnarvon, 18 Dec., Carnarvon MSS, PRO 30/6/55/49. Cf. Churchill to Carnarvon, 19 Oct., thanking him for notes of an interview with the Archbishop, and agreeing that an 'understanding between the Tory Govt and the Irish Bishops on the education question may possibly have a most powerful effect on Irish politics.'

157   Churchill to Smith, 3 Jan., Hambleden MSS.

158   For definite evidence of Carnarvon's absence, see Carnarvon to Salisbury, 1 Jan., Salisbury MSS class E.

159   Salisbury to Richmond, 3 Jan., Richmond MSS 8/9 f. 95. Harrowby however thought that this cabinet had decided that the Speech, on 21 Jan., would be followed by bringing forward county government, and then going on to Churchill's procedural schemes (to Carnarvon, 3 Jan., PRO 30/6/55/60).

160   The letters, written on 20 and 23 Dec., are printed in *extenso* by Viscount Gladstone, *After Thirty Years* (1928), 396–8.

161   Churchill to Carnarvon, 2 Jan., Carnarvon MSS PRO 30/6/55/57.

162   As an instance of the vagueness of even the sharper ministers' recollections of such not unimportant points, note Northcote to Salisbury, 17 June 1886,

Salisbury MSS: 'Gladstone appears to be putting about a report of communications with us, and his offer to assist us in dealing with the Irish question... Halsbury, who is here, says he has no recollection of any such communication: but I think you mentioned one in cabinet, and that our general impression was against opening negotiations.'

163 C.D., 3 Jan. By 3 Jan. Carnarvon had reversed his earlier opinion, shared by Manners and Churchill but opposed by Salisbury, in favour of Wolseley as his successor. Salisbury opposed Wolseley, not because military rule would look bad, but because he rightly held Wolseley to be 'a bad hand at keeping his own counsel.' (Carnarvon to Churchill, 3 Jan., Carnarvon MSS, reversing opinion: Salisbury to Carnarvon, 3 Jan., loc. cit., opposing Wolseley). Churchill was on 2 Jan. still pressing Wolseley on Salisbury in conversation and associating his appointment with 'a policy of resistance to Home Rule' (Churchill to Carnarvon, 2 Jan.). Carnarvon's letters at this time painted a gloomy picture ('I anticipate a good deal of trouble' he wrote to Smith on 7 Jan.) and urged ad hoc relief of distress. Carnarvon had however a new bright idea, that of placing the facts before the Pope in the hope of breaking up that 'Union of the Nationalist and Clerical Parties' which was responsible for the grave situation (Carnarvon to Salisbury, 30 Dec.: described as too dangerous, Salisbury to Carnarvon, 3 Jan.: reiterated as having a value 'almost beyond calculation', Carnarvon to Salisbury, 6 Jan., but never brought before the cabinet).

164 Carnarvon to Salisbury, 1 Jan., Carnarvon MSS, PRO 30/6/55/52: Carnarvon to Ashbourne, 1 Jan., loc. cit. 30/6/55/53: draft, not exactly numbered, but loc cit. 30/6/55: see also above, cabinet of 15 Dec.

165 PRO CAB 37/17/5.

166 St Aldwyn MSS, PCC/77 n.d. but Dec.–Jan.

167 49695.

168 *Standard*, 9 Jan.

169 Churchill to Carnarvon, 9 Jan., Carnarvon MSS, PRO 30/6/55/72.

170 Ibid.

171 C.D., 10 Jan.

172 Churchill to Carnarvon, 9 Jan., loc. cit.

173 See above, 9 Oct.

174 Ashbourne to Carnarvon, 9 Jan., PRO 30/6/56/115: confirmed by Churchill to Carnarvon, 9 Jan., loc. cit.

175 Carnarvon to Cranbrook, 11 Jan., Cranbrook MSS, T 501/262.

176 C.D., 16 Jan.

177 *Standard*, 13 Jan.

178 C.D. 16 Jan.

179 N.D., 6 Feb.

180 Misdated '17th Jan. 1886' in G.E.Buckle ed., *The Letters of Queen Victoria, 1886–1901*, i, 10, and in the original letter from Salisbury to the Queen, PRO CAB 41/20/1.

181 For confirmation of the voting, see N.D., 6 Feb.

182 Salisbury to Churchill, 16 Jan., Churchill MSS xi 1302 b.

183 C.D., 16 Jan.

184 16 Jan., Salisbury MSS.

185 N.D., 6 Feb. The atmosphere in the House when it met was at first sight more friendly to a hard line than Churchill had expected.

186 Churchill to Salisbury, 16 Jan., Salisbury MSS.

187 Ibid.

188 Churchill MSS xi 1305.

189 Salisbury to Smith, 17 Jan., Hambleden MSS.

190 Salisbury to Carnarvon, tel., 22 Jan., claiming the new arrangement was

'only settled late on Wednesday night': Carnarvon to Salisbury approving Smith, n.d., Carnarvon MSS.
191 N.D., 6 Feb.
192 Churchill MSS xi 1307a.
193 Salisbury MSS class E.
194 Iddesleigh MSS, 50020 f. 140.
195 56447.
196 G.E.Buckle, ed., op. cit., i, 17.
197 C.D., 26 Jan.
198 Askwith, op. cit., 167. However, a letter written by Smith to Salisbury on 17 Jan. (Salisbury MSS class E) indirectly confirms James' report that Salisbury contemplated resignation owing to cabinet divisions on coercion. Smith wrote 'We should make ourselves ridiculous, if we went out simply because we could not agree in the Speech.' All agreed on breaking the League: 'the difference between the large majority of the cabinet and the minority, is one of time. All, Beach perhaps excepting, admit that a bill will be necessary, if not now, in a fortnight's time.'
199 To Lady John Manners, 24 Jan., Salisbury MSS D47/270.
200 Smith to Churchill, 25 Jan., Churchill MSS xi 1332.
201 Churchill MSS x 1331.
202 Loc. cit., xi, 1334.
203 Askwith, op. cit., 153.
204 Smith's arrival is misdated 26 Jan. in Sir H.Maxwell, op. cit., ii, 164.
205 C.D., 27 Jan.
206 Ibid.
207 Manners to Salisbury, 27 Jan., Salisbury MSS D/48/390.
208 Devonshire MSS.
209 Manners to Rutland, 27 Jan., Rutland MSS.
210 D.D., 27 Jan.
211 Lady Knightley's diary, 27 Jan.
212 Devonshire MSS.
213 Ibid.
214 G.E.Buckle, ed., op. cit., i, 27.
215 Salisbury MSS D/86/247.

Part Three

Unless otherwise stated, all dates below refer to the period December 1885–June 1886.
1 W.E.Gladstone, *Speeches in Scotland* (Edinburgh 1885) iii, 168.
2 Ramm, ii, 146.
3 For Acland's letters to his wife 11–13 Dec. 1885, see A.H.D.Acland ed., *Memoirs and Letters of the Rt. Hon. Sir Thomas Dyke Acland* (priv. pr., 1902): for MacColl, see G.W.E.Russell ed., *MacColl*, 118–26, for correspondence of 9–28 Dec. 1885 between MacColl, and Salisbury and Gladstone. For guests at Hawarden, the prime source is the Visitors' Book at Hawarden Castle, kindly made available to us by Sir William Gladstone as regards Dec. 1885/Jan. 1886 (there were no entries 11 Jan. 1886–Aug. 1886). The Visitors' Book records the visits of Grosvenor, Spencer, Granville, Wolverton and Rosebery, not necessarily on their day of arrival, but omits Acland and MacColl. MacColl's visit to Salisbury the day after he preached at Hawarden was already arranged by 9 Dec., when MacColl sent his own home rule scheme to Salisbury. The willingness of

the latter to receive MacColl *c.* 9 Dec. and to talk quite freely to him on 14 Dec. contrasted sharply with his very firm rebuffs to further approaches made after the cabinet of the 15th.

4   MacColl to Salisbury, 19 Dec., printed Russell, *MacColl*, loc. cit.
5   Ibid., 28 Dec.
6   MacColl to Gladstone, 28 Dec., ibid.
7   Gladstone to MacColl, 23 Dec., printed loc. cit., 256.
8   Ibid.
9   Non-political guests entered in the Visitors' Book were Mary Lyttelton (28 Dec.), Lord Lyttelton, Spencer G. Lyttelton (2 Jan.), Margaret Cowell Stepney (6 Jan.), William Dampier (9 Jan.) who was probably an obscure genealogist of lowly origins, and Lucy Cavendish (11 Jan.).
10   Gladstone to Hartington, 2 Jan., 56447.
11   56447.
12   Gladstone to Hartington, 2 Jan., loc. cit.
13   Gladstone to Grosvenor, 7 Jan., loc. cit.: copy sent by Gladstone to Spencer, 9 Jan.
14   Ibid.
15   Mrs O'Shea to Gladstone, 6 Jan., 44269 f. 277, enclosing a memorandum probably in Parnell's hand, in which the Irish demands were put as a parliament with unrestricted control over Irish affairs, and the compulsory expropriation of landowners.
16   Gladstone to Mrs O'Shea, 9 Jan., 56447.
17   *H.J.*, 30 Dec.
18   Until the last moment there were strong hopes that Granville would attend, whereas Dilke was only asked as an afterthought, of doubtful relevance in view of his probable absence from the next Liberal ministry on moral grounds (Hartington to his father, 29 Dec., Devonshire MSS 340/1875).
19   Crewe, op. cit., i, 254: Hartington to Dilke, 29 Dec., 43896 f. 189.
20   43927 f. 21.
21   44148 f. 192.
22   Hartington to Granville, 2 Jan., Granville MSS PRO 30/29/22a: cf. Hartington to Spencer, 3 Jan., Spencer MSS.
23   Ramm, ii, 421–2. Hartington perhaps received and refused a compensating invitation to Hawarden (*E.H.J.*, 6 Jan.). Gladstone saw no justification for complaints from one with 'whom he maintains he has communicated freely' (ibid., 2 Jan.). Hartington's refusal to visit may mean little if linked with the funeral of his aunt at Chatsworth, which he attended.
24   Gladstone to Hartington, 2 Jan., loc. cit.
25   Spencer to Rosebery, 30 Dec., cited Crewe, op. cit., i, 254–6. The original is not with the Rosebery MSS in the National Library of Scotland, but Spencer's draft survives at Althorp.
26   *E.H.J.*, 2 Jan.
27   Harcourt to Chamberlain, 4 Jan., proposing a posse comitatus to stop Gladstone, and 7 Jan., Chamberlain MSS JC 5/38/40 and 41. These are the only two letters from Harcourt to Chamberlain in the Chamberlain MSS between New Year 1886 and after Chamberlain's resignation.
28   Harcourt MSS box 6.
29   Morley to his sister, 8 Jan., printed F.W. Hirst, *Early Life and Letters of John Morley* (1927) ii, 276.
30   Royal Archives RA C/37/171.
31   Northbrook to Spencer, 7 Jan., Spencer MSS: Campbell-Bannerman to Spencer, 8 Jan., ibid: J.A. Spender, *Campbell-Bannerman*, i, 95–7. Trevelyan's biographer omits all mention of the meeting, while the mention in Sir B. Mallet,

Northbrook (1908), 226, adds nothing. A. Elliot, the future Liberal Unionist, declined an invitation, as he would not have done 'had I heard sooner that Trevelyan and Campbell-Bannerman were to be there' (Elliot to Craig Sellar, n.d. but early Jan. 1886, Elliot MSS). Campbell-Bannerman's engagement book (41249a) gives the dates of the meeting as 5–7 Jan., which may be on the early side in view of the epistolary evidence. Other ministers, and in particular Gladstone, showed no interest in the meeting and their letters did not refer to it.

32 Morley, *Gladstone* (1903) iii, 280, citing diary.

33 *E. H. J.*, 2 Jan.

34 Ibid.

35 Granville to Selborne, 13 Jan., Selborne MSS 1869 f. 115.

36 *R. J.*, 11 Jan., giving E. Hamilton's view: Dilke said he had come at Hartington's instance (*E. H. J.*, 12 Jan.). This raises the possibility that Hartington's lax and Gladstone's pained view of Dilke's moral blemishes were determined by short term considerations of purely political tactics, Dilke having a greater interest than anyone else in preventing the early formation of a Gladstone government, his certain exclusion from which would set the seal on his exclusion from high politics. Gladstone at this stage (but not later) certainly had every reason to wish to establish that Dilke was beyond the pale. The quietening effect on Chamberlain, for one thing, was quite remarkable.

37 Dilke to Chamberlain, 11 Jan., Chamberlain MSS JC 5 /24 /159.

38 Dilke's memoirs, 43940 f. 104: visits of 12 Jan. described in Crewe, op. cit., i, 257, as a formal shadow cabinet, but this reflects confusion with the meeting on 21 Jan. Shaw-Lefevre, who had lost his seat, was not among those invited to see Gladstone (Lefevre to Rosebery, 24 Dec. 1885, Rosebery MSS box 62).

39 'Lord H. came and had a good talk yesterday. Uncle W. seemed not dissatisfied with it' (Mrs Gladstone to Lady F. Cavendish, n.d. but Wed. in Jan. 1886, Glynne-Gladstone MSS).

40 *E. H. J.*

41 Churchill to Salisbury, 13 Jan., Churchill MSS xi 1290b: also Thorold, *Labouchere*, 284, and Grey to Earl Grey, 15 Jan., Grey MSS, showing knowledge of the dinner but misdating it Sunday.

42 Mrs Gladstone to Lady F. Cavendish, n.d. but Wed., Jan. 1886, Glynne–Gladstone MSS.

43 Harcourt to Hartington, 9 Jan., Harcourt MSS box 6.

44 Ripon to Gladstone, 20 Jan., 56447.

45 E. Hamilton to Herbert Gladstone, 14 Jan., W. E. Gladstone MSS, 56447: the quotation is from a letter received by E. Hamilton from Sir Robert on 13 Jan.

46 *R. J.*, 14 Jan.

47 *E. H. J.*, 14 Jan.

48 Gladstone to Grosvenor, 7 Jan., copy, 56447: copy sent by Gladstone to Spencer, 9 Jan.

49 A. Elliot's diary, 15 Jan.

50 *E. H. J.*, 15 Jan.

51 Diary of Lady Dorothy Stanley, 18 Jan., Chamberlain MSS JC 8 /2 /2. Callan was defeated in 1885 by his fellow Nationalists, and in 1885–86 was working closely with the Tories: see C. J., 141n.

52 56447 (Gladstone's letter): Lady Knightley's diary, 16 Jan. (Spencer).

53 Dilke to Chamberlain, 18 Jan., Chamberlain MSS JC 5 /24 /160.

54 *E. H. J.*, 19 Jan.

55 Gladstone to Granville, 18 Jan., copy, 56447.

56 Goschen to his wife, 19 Jan., cited Elliot, *Goschen*, ii, 7.

57 Mrs Gladstone to Lady F. Cavendish, 20 Jan., Glynne–Gladstone MSS.

58 Goschen to his wife, 20 Jan., cited Elliot, *Goschen*, ii, 8.

59 R.R.James, op. cit, 177.
60 At the previous weekend Lefevre was at Mentone (*Standard*, 18 Jan.).
61 Selborne to Granville, 10 Jan., Granville MSS PRO 30/29/22a.
62 Dilke's memoirs, loc. cit., f. 106. But for a different view, see Gardiner, *Harcourt*, i, 560.
63 Mrs Gladstone to Mrs Drew, n.d. but Friday, 46223 f. 236.
64 Chamberlain MSS JC 8/5/1/15: printed, C.H.D.Howard ed., Chamberlain, *A Political Memoir 1880–92* (1953), 177–8.
65 Labouchere to Herbert Gladstone, 22 Jan., Viscount Gladstone MSS, 46019 f. 159.
66 For Parnell's supposed views, see Labouchere to Chamberlain, 22 Jan., cited Thorold, *Labouchere*, 286–8.
67 R.J.
68 Courtney's journal.
69 Grey to Earl Grey, 25 Jan., Grey MSS.
70 R.J., 25 Jan.
71 Gladstone to Harcourt, 31 Jan., 56447.
72 Mrs O'Shea to Gladstone, 23 Jan., offering conditional support, 44269 f. 280: W.E.Gladstone to Mrs O'Shea, 26 Jan., copy, W.E. Gladstone MSS additional deposit, 56447.
73 56447.
74 West, op. cit., ii, 258.
75 Gladstone to Argyll, 27 Jan., 56447, 'There need be no fears connected with the division of last night. It was the safest we could have, and at the proper time when the question comes up for consideration in connection with new local authority I feel very confident it can be properly adjusted. Ireland is now the overwhelming question... The Peers of the late Govt are generally, I think, in a very reasonable state of mind?'
76 Hartington to Duchess of Manchester, 27 Jan., Devonshire MSS.
77 Mrs Gladstone to Lady F.Cavendish, Glynne–Gladstone MSS.
78 Gladstone to Spencer, 27 Jan., Spencer MSS.
79 Sir John Mowbray, *Seventy Years at Westminster* (1900), 303.
80 West, op. cit., ii, 259.
81 Though the Ponsonby MSS exist in private hands, we have failed to inspect this extensive and possibly important collection, which we understand Mr. Adrian Preston hopes to edit.
82 Arthur Ponsonby, *Henry Ponsonby* (1942), 208.
83 Ibid.
84 Ibid. As early as 24 Jan., Ponsonby had approached Rosebery and asked him whether it would be possible for the Queen to send for Hartington. Rosebery had rejected the idea very sharply (R.R.James, op. cit., 178), at least partly on Hartington's behalf. Ponsonby kept Rosebery informed of his endeavours to persuade the Queen to send for Gladstone, though the two men were not otherwise on close terms (Ponsonby to Rosebery, 27 and 28 Jan., Rosebery MSS box 43.)
85 The timing of the discussion was certainly appropriate, for that afternoon's *Pall Mall Gazette* carried the results of a questionnaire it had sent to all Liberal candidates at the previous elections. The most salient point to emerge, apart from a wide belief that the Irish vote had turned the day against the Liberals in the boroughs, was a virtually unanimous demand for 'a firm and consistent foreign policy' as the area where improvement in Liberal leadership was required. There was no doubt this was aimed at Granville. Incidentally, opinion as to whether home rule would gain or lose votes for the Liberals was completely divided.
86 Crewe, op. cit., i, 257.

87 Ponsonby to Rosebery, 27 Jan., Rosebery MSS box 43.
88 R.R.James, op. cit., 178.
89 *E. H. J.*, 28 Jan.
90 Crewe, op. cit., i, 258.
91 *R. J.*, 30 Dec.
92 See above, 14 and 15 Jan.
93 Diary of Lady Dorothy Stanley, 3 Feb., Chamberlain MSS JC 8/2/2.
94 Devonshire MSS.
95 Gladstone to Mrs O'Shea, secret, copy, 29 Jan., 56447.
96 T.R.Buchanan, M.P., to A.Elliot, 29 Jan., Elliot MSS.
97 *E. H. J.*, 29 Jan. Harcourt the previous day had thought there was still a chance of getting Hartington, but his surmise was probably already out of date.
98 Morley, *Recollections*, i, 210, citing his own diary.
99 *R. J.*, 29 Jan.
100 G.W.E.Russell, *Fifteen Chapters of Autobiography* (1914) 277: Lucy Masterman, *Mary Gladstone* (1930), 378. West erroneously implies (op. cit., ii, 260) that Ponsonby's call was on the night of 27–28 Jan.
101 Ponsonby, op. cit., 207.
102 Ibid.
103 *Queen Victoria's Journal* in the Royal Archives, cited below as *Q.V.J.*
104 Ibid.
105 Askwith, op. cit., 160.
106 44771 ff. 29–38.
107 *R. J.*
108 *E. H. J.*, 9 Jan.
109 Ibid., 27 Jan.
110 Ramm, ii, 424.
111 44771 f. 29.
112 Ramm, ii, 424.
113 R.F.V.Heuston, *Lives of the Lord Chancellors 1885–1940* (Oxford, 1964), 102.
114 44771 f. 46.
115 *E. H. J.*, 27 Jan.
116 Askwith, op. cit., 164.
117 By a coincidence Mrs O'Shea wrote to Gladstone on 30 Jan. offering to arrange negotiations between Parnell and the government 'of the nature of those which took place with Lord Salisbury on the Redistribution bill' (44269 ff 284–291). Her initiative was entirely disregarded.
118 Hartington to Gladstone, 30 Jan., 44148 f. 212.
119 44148 f. 220. When H.Brand wrote to Hartington the same day (5 Feb.), however, reporting his decision to refuse office and expecting his leader's approval, Hartington once more said that he would not stand in the government's way, and that it was 'necessary that those who thought some concession to Irish demand practicable should place their proposals before the country' (Devonshire MSS 340/1930, for Brand's letter: ibid., 340/1931, for Hartington's reply of the same date). On 4 Mar. Brand told Blunt that he regretted refusing office (W.S. Blunt, op. cit., 34).
120 Hartington to Duchess of Manchester, 30 Jan.: cf. Hartington to his father, 30 Jan., Devonshire MSS 340/1924.
121 James to Hartington, 31 Jan., Devonshire MSS.
122 James to H.Gladstone, 31 Jan., Viscount Gladstone MSS, 46038 f. 19, received by H.Gladstone at 10.30 p.m. on Sunday at 21, Carlton House Terrace.
123 Askwith, op. cit., 165.
124 James to Mundella, 4 Feb., Mundella MSS folio iv.

125 Lady Trevelyan's diary of the parliament of 1892–95. Trevelyan MSS.
126 James to Hartington, 31 Jan., Devonshire MSS.
127 Morley, *Recollections*, i, 211–2.
128 Chamberlain to Gladstone, 30 Jan., 44126 f. 132: printed by C.H.D. Howard ed., op. cit., 187–8: the letter is confined to his agreement to serve with 'unlimited liberty of judgement and rejection'. Chamberlain's formal letter of agreement to join the ministry reached Gladstone at 3 p.m. on Sunday, 31 Jan. (44771 f. 46), asking however for some office other than the Admiralty.
129 Ibid. f. 136.
130 44771 f. 43, dated 30 Jan.: see Askwith, op. cit., 162–3.
131 *E.H.J.*
132 Chamberlain's statement in his *A Political Memoir*, 188, that an interview between him and Gladstone took place at an unspecified time on Sunday, 31 Jan., is entirely uncorroborated by any evidence. What Chamberlain claims was said on Sunday, had in fact already been discussed at Chamberlain's second interview with Gladstone on Saturday. It is clear that Chamberlain wrote a letter to Gladstone on Sunday, though this is not printed in *A Political Memoir*, and this is probably the source of his confusion.
133 Morley, *Recollections*, ii, 213–4, citing his own diary: much of the narrative follows Morley's account.
134 44771 f. 46.
135 Morley to Gladstone, 2 Feb., 44255 f. 54.
136 Brett's journal, 29 Jan., 1 Feb. Brett's contempt for his confidant at this time was profound.
137 Ramm, ii, 427.
138 Cf. E. Hamilton to Herbert Gladstone, 56447.
139 44771 f. 47.
140 Harcourt to Gladstone. 31 Jan., 44200 f. 15.
141 Herbert to Henry Gladstone, 12 Feb., Glynne–Gladstone MSS.
142 Events had moved in rapid succession here. Before leaving London on Monday, Gladstone had written to Granville, strongly hinting at the Colonial Office as the best solution. Also on Monday fairly early, Spencer had been round to see Granville and 'at last today extracted a relinquishment of the F.O., but he is determined to be Colonial Minister' (*R.J.*, 1 Feb.). Granville then sent, through Herbert Gladstone, a telegram of general agreement to Gladstone, which reached him while at Osborne.
143 *Q.V.J.*, 1 Feb.
144 Royal Archives R A C/37/210.
145 L. Masterman, op. cit., 379.
146 *E.H.J.*, 1 Feb., 15 Jan.
147 *H.J.*
148 Ibid.
149 R.R. James, op. cit., 179.
150 *H.J.*, 30 Dec.
151 Ponsonby to the Queen, 1 Feb., Royal Archives RA C/37/209.
152 *E.H.J.*
153 West, op. cit., ii, 261.
154 *H.J.*
155 Ibid; and *R.J.*, 2 Feb., commenting 'It is an awful scrape'.
156 Gladstone had sent Hamilton round before dinner to let the Prince have the latest list of appointments: the Prince was keenly interested and well satisfied, and heaved a sigh of relief that Childers was not to have the War Office (*E.H.J.*).
157 *R.J.*, 2 Feb.

158   Rosebery's copy of Kimberley's revised version of his original diary, 1 Feb. 1886, Rosebery MSS box 111.

159   *Standard*, 3 Feb. W.H.Smith suspected that this interview might be the harbinger of an open or tacit coalition to deal with Ireland (Smith to Ashbourne, 2 Feb., Ashbourne MSS). Gladstone's notes of the meeting (44771 f. 66) refer only to naval and foreign affairs, Italy, Russia, Austria and Bulgaria being particularly discussed.

160   *H.J.*, 2 Feb.

161   Ibid.

162   Northbrook to Selborne, 7 Feb., Selborne MSS 1869 f. 157. By July, Northbrook was calling Gladstone 'the most conscienciously [sic] unscrupulous leader there has ever been in the history of English Parties', (Northbrook to Dufferin, 30 July, Northbrook Collection, MSS Eur. C 144/5, India Office Library). *The Times* had stated with confidence that Northbrook would join Gladstone's ministry, and Selborne wrote with alarm (3 Feb.) of Northbrook having accepted office (Selborne to Sir A. Gordon, Selborne MSS 1874, f. 67.) For other correspondence showing the general assumptions about Northbrook's position, see Ponsonby to the Queen, 31 Jan., reporting Gladstone's belief that Northbrook 'probably will join' (Royal Archives RA C/37/207): Ponsonby to the Queen, 3 Feb., reporting that Gladstone on 2 Feb. thought that in view of difficulties about Ripon, 'he might recommend Lord Northbrook instead' as lord president (loc. cit., C/37/228): and the Queen to Gladstone, 3 Feb., wishing Northbrook 'who understands India' had gone to the India Office (loc. cit., C/37/230).

163   Morley to Gladstone, 2 Feb., and Gladstone to Morley, 2 Feb., 44255 f. 54.

164   Cf. Duke of Cambridge to the Queen, 9 Feb., Royal Archives RA C/37/285, describing him as 'a very nice calm and pleasant man, well known to all here and who knows the War Office work and with whom I have no doubt I shall be able to get on very smoothly and well, whereas Mr Childers was not a *persona grata* here, as you well know and I think was more imbued with his own interests and vanity than the good of the Army.'

165   Ponsonby to the Queen, 2 Feb., Royal Archives C/37/215: ibid., 3 Feb., C/37/228.

166   For Gladstone to Chamberlain, 2 Feb., offering the L.G.B., see 44126 f. 139: for Chamberlain's acceptance, 2 Feb., see ibid. f. 140.

167   C.H.D.Howard ed., op. cit., 188.

168   Fitzmaurice, *Granville*, ii, 483.

169   Gladstone to Chamberlain, 8 Feb., 44126 f. 146.

170   But without Rosebery, who wrote 'Sat in all day in case I was wanted, but I was not' (*R.J.*, 3 Feb.). Rosebery appears not to have been consulted about any appointments except those of his Foreign Office subordinates – the first of many signs that he was still not seen as part of the real power structure of the party.

171   *E.H.J.*, 6 Feb.: one of only two recorded applications for office at this time, the other being that of Goldsmid.

172   By '47 people, Tories, Liberals, doctors, artists, diplomatists' (*R.J.*, 3 Feb.).

173   Trevelyan to Gladstone, 2 Feb., 44335 f. 195.

174   Brett's journal, reporting conversation of 24 Feb. with Rosebery.

175   Kay–Shuttleworth to Trevelyan, 15 May, Shuttleworth MSS.

176   Morley, *Gladstone*, iii, 294.

177   44771 f. 51. According to Mrs Gladstone, Goschen's visit was 'mainly because Hartington wished him to see Father' (Mrs Gladstone to Mrs Drew, n.d. but Wed., 46223 f. 242).

178   Campbell-Bannerman's diary, 41249a, as regards his appointment only: other information from H.J. and Gladstone's notes.
179   Shuttleworth MSS.
180   Earl of Morley's journal, 48292 f. 7.
181   44771 f. 51.
182   H.J., 3 Feb. Gladstone had from the start considered that the expense of re-election would deter Lorne from taking office (Ponsonby to the Queen, 1 Feb., Royal Archives RA C/37/209), and, re-election or not, he was being talked of as too poor for so expensive a post (Mrs Gladstone to Mrs Drew, n.d., 46223 f. 243). Moreover, Lorne's Irish programme, as known to Gladstone, consisted only of buying out all Irish landlords and creating elected provincial assemblies with limited powers. 'A national parliament should not be granted', Lorne asserted, except as a last resort (Lorne to Gladstone, 20 Sept. 1885, 44492 f. 104). Lorne subsequently unsuccessfully contested Bradford Central as a Liberal Unionist in 1892, and was eventually returned for S. Manchester in 1895 as a unionist. His views on home rule were published as a pamphlet by the Irish Unionist Alliance. Yet in 1886 the real objection to his taking his place as the obvious head of a Gladstonian administration in Dublin came neither from him nor from Gladstone, but from the Queen, on account of his royal connections.
183   R.J., 3 Feb.
184   Mrs Gladstone to Mrs Drew, n.d., 46223 f. 243.
185   44771 f. 47. For Gladstone to Wolverton, 31 Jan., see copy, 56447, 'For the sake of the object in view I by no means exclude the consideration of a scheme such as you have sketched – I should be glad if you were to see Spencer upon the principle of it.' Gladstone thought however that it would be unwise for him to take on finance as well as Ireland!
186   44771 f. 57. The five pages of the relevant volume of Mrs Flower's (Lady Battersea's) diary covering the home rule crisis have been excised, the gap extending from 4 Feb. to Dec. 1886 (47938).
187   Gladstone to Playfair, 2 letters, and Playfair to Gladstone, all 3 Feb., Playfair MSS.
188   Sir T. Wemyss Reid, *Memoir of Lyon Playfair* (1899), 352–3.
189   Heneage to Spencer, 17 Mar., Spencer MSS.
190   Sir Alfred E. Pease, op. cit., 105. It is not clear what Pease had in mind, but Heneage had certainly committed himself up to the eyes against home rule in a lurid and abusive letter published in *The Times* of 2 Jan.
191   44771 f. 58, 61.
192   H.J., 4 Feb.
193   Sellar to Elliot, 21 Dec., Elliot MSS.
194   44771 f. 57.
195   Sellar to Elliot, 8 Feb., Elliot MSS.
196   Gladstone to Ponsonby, 18 Feb., Ponsonby MSS, 45724 f. 187.
197   Salisbury to the Queen, 6 Feb., Royal Archives RA C/37/262.
198   Broadhurst to Gladstone, 22 Dec., Gladstone MSS new deposit, 56446.
199   Lady Monkswell, *A Victorian Diarist ... 1873–95*, ed. Hon. E. C. F. Collier (1944), 180.
200   Aberdeen to Rosebery, 5 Feb., Rosebery MSS box 63.
201   M. Pentland, *A Bonnie Fechter* (1952), 44.
202   Brett's journal, 5 Feb.
203   D.D.
204   Q.V.J., 6 Feb.
205   Elliot, *Goschen*, ii, 28.
206   Royal Archives RA C/37/247a.
207   Q.V.J., 8 Feb.

208   44200 f. 26.
209   Salisbury to Rosebery, 4 Feb., Rosebery MSS box 63.
210   Q.V.J., 7 Feb.
211   Lord Suffield, *My Memories 1830–1913*, ed. Alys Lowth (1913), 335–6.
212   Ponsonby to the Queen, 6 Feb., Royal Archives RA C/37/270.
213   Q.V.J.; typescript memo, 8 Feb., loosely inserted into journal.
214   Salisbury to Akers-Douglas, 9 Feb., Chilston MSS U 654 C 18/6.
215   Same to same, 26 Nov. 1885, ibid. C 18/3.
216   C.D., 7 Feb. The Queen was here virtually repeating Salisbury's words to her on 6 Feb. (see above).
217   The Duchess refused because of John Morley's appointment: 'every post brings her letters from Irish friends' describing themselves as 'beggars' (St Albans to Granville, 12 Feb., Granville MSS PRO 30/29/22A).
218   Ramm, ii, 429–30. The conversation with St Albans discussed above is of greater interest because it occurred on a day when, probably for the first time since leaving Hawarden, Gladstone was able to set to work in earnest on Ireland, sketching out his ideas which he then discussed with Granville (Mrs Gladstone to Mrs Drew, n.d., 46223 f. 253).
219   St Albans to Goschen, 18 Feb., printed, Elliot, *Goschen*, ii, 37, also in P. Colson, *Lord Goschen and his Friends*, 77. Cf. Lord Brabourne's political journal, Dec. 1885/Jan. 1886, discussing the Hawarden kite: 'I shall not be in the least surprised if Gladstone, on the first good opportunity, takes a highly indignant and patriotic tone, and entirely disclaims ever having entertained the project imputed to him' (Brabourne MSS, U 951 F 27/10). The opinion that nothing had really happened could be put forward as an intelligent tactical insight at any time between the kite and the leakages about resignations in mid-March.
220   This was not self-delusion: the Duke was a friend of Chamberlain and had shown radical leanings at the previous election by making a speech favouring free schools and short parliaments (Morley to Chamberlain, 24 Oct. 1885, Chamberlain MSS JC 5/54/663).
221   St Albans to Rosebery, 15 Feb., Rosebery MSS box 63.
222   The family had moved in to Downing St the previous day: 'here we are back in the old shop' Mrs Gladstone wrote happily to Mrs Drew (n.d., 46223 f. 253).
223   C.H.D. Howard ed., op. cit., 189–90: memo by Chamberlain on Irish land purchase printed, n.d., ibid. 190–3.
224   R.J.
225   R.J.: *Henry Broadhurst, M.P, The story of his Life From a Stonemason's Bench to the Treasury Bench, Told by Himself* (1901), 301.
226   Harcourt to Gladstone, 20 Feb., Harcourt MSS.
227   H.J., 15 Feb. The same source reports Gladstone as saying to E. Hamilton that morning 'Thank God, I have at last got a Chancellor of the Exchequer who knows how to put his foot down.'
228   R.J.: Chamberlain to Dilke, 3 Jan. 1885, Dilke MSS, arguing 'in favour of showing our teeth in China, Madagascar, etc.' (43887 f. 2).
229   H.J.: Harcourt's entry adds 'nothing has yet been said in the cabinet about Ireland'.
230   41219 f. 1.
231   Printed memoranda signed by Wolseley, Brackenbury, and Buller, 11 Feb. and by Col. Grove, 19 Feb., urging reoccupation, are in the Harcourt MSS together with rebuttals by Harcourt dated 16 Feb. and 17 Feb.
232   For Peters' and Kelly's earlier activities, see Paul Smith, *Disraelian Conservatism and Social Reform* (1967), 311 n.
233   Grey to Earl Grey, 19 Feb., Grey MSS.

234 Spencer to Gladstone, 19 Feb., and Archbp Walsh to Gladstone, 17 Feb., 56447.

235 Mary Drew's diary, 17 Feb., 46262 f. 11.

236 Trevelyan to Rosebery, 19 Feb., Rosebery MSS box 19.

237 56447.

238 Brett's journal, reporting a conversation of 24 Feb. with Rosebery.

239 Cf. Campbell-Bannerman to Harcourt, 10 Feb., Harcourt MSS box 9, refusing to reconsider his proposed increase in army estimates of two millions.

240 'Notes at cabinet Feb. 22 1886' (typescript copy), Harcourt MSS.

241 Childers to Harcourt, 23 Feb., Harcourt MSS box 11.

242 Childers was in no doubt that the crisis was mainly due to Harcourt's obstinacy, since the service ministers were quite prepared to make the sort of concessions that they were generally expected to make in such a situation (Childers to Gladstone, 21 Feb., 44132 f. 212).

243 *R.J.*, 24 Feb.

244 *R.J.*, 25 Feb.

245 *Q.V.J.*, 6 Feb.

246 Sidgwick's diary, *passim*: cf. 'Bryce strongly in favour of a temporising policy, the necessity of avoiding splits in the party and so forth. Thinks it difficult to find any satisfactory alternative to granting Ireland a separate legislature. The Irish would then settle down and so forth.' – A. Elliot's diary, 17 Jan. 1886.

247 Diary of Lady D. Stanley, 3 Mar., loc. cit.

248 For a full account, see Holmes' memoir in *Irish Historical Studies*, vol. xvi, no. 63 (March 1969).

249 Speech to the Eighty Club, 5 Mar.

250 Hartington to Bright, 8 Mar., 43388 f. 19.

251 *Q.V.J.*, 5 Mar.

252 Mrs Gladstone to Mrs Drew, n.d. (7 Mar. ?), 46223 f. 259.

253 44771 f. 208: Garvin, op. cit., ii, 185. Chamberlain dated his memorandum, which included a scheme of local government, 17 Feb. The other paper referred to above cannot be identified precisely among a number of drafts, but may be Gladstone's memorandum of 2 Mar., 44632 f. 145.

254 Based on diary of Lady Dorothy Stanley, 8 Mar., loc. cit., as regards conversation: and Mrs Gladstone to Mrs Drew, n.d. but Sat., 46223 f. 259. Mrs Gladstone referred to 'a quiet dinner of eight at Sir C. Forster's: Childers, Dean Vaughan, Miss Tennant, and us', but gave the dates as 5 Mar., as against 7 Mar. implied in the copy of the Tennant diary. In view of Gladstone's illness on 7 Mar., Mrs Gladstone's dating for the dinner must be preferred.

255 Mrs Gladstone to Mrs Drew, n.d., 46223 f. 261.

256 Mrs Courtney's journal, 7 Mar., cited G. P. Gooch, *Life of Lord Courtney* (1920), 254.

257 Mrs Gladstone to Mrs Drew, n.d., 46223 f. 264.

258 Sir William F. Butler, *An Autobiography* (1911), 332–9.

259 *R.J.*, 8 Mar.: Granville to the Queen, 8 Mar., Royal Archives RA B 37/33a.

260 *Q.V.J.*, 10 Mar.

261 44771 f. 72.

262 *Standard*, 11 Mar.

263 Grey to Earl Grey, 11 Mar., Grey MSS.

264 44667 f. 33.

265 Walling ed., op. cit., 535.

266 Ministers were defeated 132–114 on the Vote for the Parks (11 Mar.). Childers therefore wrote on Friday asking Gladstone to put the matter to Saturday's cabinet. It is uncertain whether it ever came before the cabinet, records of petty business done being peculiarly incomplete in 1886.

267 13 Mar., PRO CAB 41/20/10.

268 *R.J.*, 13 Mar.

269 44200 f. 82. Harcourt called exclusion of the Irish a sine qua non.

270 44313 f. 60.

271 44667 f. 35.

272 44335 f. 199.

273 15 Mar., 44126 f. 154.

274 15 Mar., ibid. f. 160. For Chamberlain's agreement to postpone his resig
nation, 16 Mar., see ibid. f. 162.

275 Mrs Gladstone to Mrs Drew, n.d., 46223 f. 268.

276 Walling ed., op. cit., 535.

277 W.S.Blunt, op. cit., 36–8.

278 Spencer to Granville, 17 Mar., PRO 30/29/22A.

279 Pease, op. cit., 113: Lubbock's diary, 17 Mar., for the harpers.

280 Based on *R.J.*, 17 Mar.: Milner to Goschen, 18 Mar., Milner MSS box
182: *Hansard*, ccciii, 1057–1131.

281 44667 f. 44.

282 Milner to Goschen, 18 Mar., Milner MSS box 182. Milner was passing on
to Goschen what Lord Ebrington, a Goschen Whig, had heard from Hartington.
Cf. the circulation in the lobby at this time of a supposed remark by Chamberlain
that he would 'sweep Gladstone out of public life' (Stephen E.Koss, *Sir John
Brunner: Radical Plutocrat 1842–1919*, (1970) 77).

283 Robert Brown, F.S.A., *Mr Gladstone As I Knew Him and Other Essays*
(1902), for the Chaldaeans: for the dinner, F.Lockwood to his father, 20 Mar.,
in A.Birrell, *Sir Frank Lockwood*, (Nelson, ed. (1910)), 164–6: for further praise
of tea by Gladstone, see Julia Cartwright ed., op. cit., 229.

284 West, op. cit.. 269.

285 Bright, *Diaries*, 536.

286 *R.J.*, 22 Mar. Cf. above for Gladstone's flattery of Harcourt, n. 227.

287 44667 f. 50.

288 Balfour to Salisbury, 22 Mar., Salisbury MSS.

289 44667 f. 51.

290 *Standard*, 24 Mar.

291 44667 f. 92.

292 *Q.V.J.*, 23 Mar.

293 Ibid., 24 Mar.

294 C.D., 24 Mar.

295 Mrs O'Shea (?) to W.E.Gladstone, 25 Mar., Gladstone MSS new deposit
56447, followed by tel. of denial disowning letter, 26 Mar.

296 Ibid., 26 Mar. For lack of Unionist appreciation of Goschen's activities
see Churchill to Salisbury, 28 Mar., Churchill MSS xii 1438b: 'Goschen has been
to Windsor, probably intriguing. Henry James abused Goschen to me very much
this morning. I really think the Queen might do worse than imitate Silly Billy
when he dismissed Lord Melbourne.'

297 There were no formal letters of resignation from Chamberlain and
Trevelyan subsequent to those sent on 15 Mar. and almost at once put in abey
ance. The formalities of resignation were concluded 27 Mar., by letters from
Gladstone to Trevelyan (44335 f. 205), and to Chamberlain (Chamberlain MSS
JC 5/34/55: printed, C.H.D.Howard, op. cit., 199), informing them that the
Queen had accepted their resignations, which could now be made public.

298 Granville to Playfair, 27 Mar. 1886, Playfair MSS.

299 44667 f. 53.

300 At dinner on 24 Mar. Trevelyan had advocated 'greater powers to the
Executive, local government, cutting down Irish representation by one half

(Sir Alfred E.Pease, op. cit., 117). Cf. *R.J.*, 26 Mar., partly confirming above account; 'Trevelyan resigned as to care of law and order'. Trevelyan tried to make his disbelief in an impartial Irish police central to his resignation, (thus stressing his official experience), but fell at times into contradictory veins of apologetic, e.g. his remark 'the real question is one of money ... Gladstone believes these Irishmen are to be trusted ... when, added Mr Trevelyan, they are quite resolved not to pay a single penny' (diary of Lady Dorothy Stanley, 30 Mar.).

301 *R.J.*, 26 Mar.
302 For the 26 Mar. cabinet from Chamberlain's angle, see his *A Political Memoir*, 198–9.
303 Morley, *Recollections*, i, 296.
304 Gladstone to Arnold Morley, 20 Apr., 44548 f. 146.
305 Mrs Gladstone to Mrs Drew, n.d. but Sat., 46223 f. 281.
306 *The Times* and *Daily News*, 29 Mar.
307 Mrs Gladstone to Mrs Drew, loc. cit.: for Dalhousie's letter of 24 Mar. cited earlier, see 44496 f. 34.
308 Bright, *Diaries*, 538.
309 Churchill to Salisbury, 29 Mar., Churchill MSS xii 1438 c.
310 McCarthy and Praed, op. cit., 34, giving McCarthy's interpretation at the time.
311 Ibid.
312 Churchill to Salisbury, 30 Mar., Churchill MSS xii 1440 a.
313 Harcourt's name did not appear in the list of those attending printed in *The Times*. However, Harcourt's name appears in Gladstone's note of those summoned, 44667 f. 62. E.Hamilton recorded the attendance of all those given above in his diary.
314 *E.H.J.*
315 A note by Rosebery in the Gladstone MSS must refer to this meeting: 'Will you let me off the adjourned cabinet? I do not think I can possibly attend.' Rosebery's absence, reported by *The Times* without explanation, is confirmed but not explained by his journal.
316 The first printed draft was dated 31 Mar. (44667 f. 73).
317 *H.J.*, 1 Apr.
318 A.Ponsonby, op. cit., 259.
319 *Standard*, 3 Apr.
320 Childers to Playfair, 3 Nov. 1885, Playfair MSS.
321 Childers to J.M.Carmichael, Gladstone's secretary, 2 Apr., Childers MSS 5/181.
322 Cooper to Childers, 28–30 Mar., loc. cit., 5/178. Extensive inquiries have failed to unearth any trace of Cooper's papers.
323 Childers to Carmichael, 3 Apr., loc. cit., 5/183.
324 *Times*, 19 May.
325 C.Cooper, *An Editor's Retrospect*, 405.
326 Holmes Ivory, Edinburgh lawyer and Secretary of Scottish Liberal Club, to Rosebery, 14 Dec. 1892, Rosebery MSS box 29.
327 Chamberlain however did know Cooper and had discussed home rule with him. In May 1885 Chamberlain 'had a talk with Cooper the other night and found him in favour of a scheme for Scotland which is exactly my own for Ireland' (Crewe, op. cit., i, 225).
328 Mrs Gladstone to Mrs Drew, n.d., 46223 f. 285.
329 Bright, *Diaries*, 539.
330 Gladstone to Morley, 3 Apr., 44255 f. 68.
331 *H.J.*, 4 Apr.

332 During a division on this day Gladstone went up to one of the gravest City men among the Tory backbenchers and talked to him for a long time about W. E. Forster, lately dead: a curious instance of his capacity for desultory conversation (see J. S. Flynn, op. cit.).

333 Morley to Gladstone, 5 Apr., 44255 f. 70.

334 West, op. cit., ii, 270.

335 44496 f. 171: R. F. V. Heuston, op. cit., 105.

336 Salisbury to Hartington, Devonshire MSS 340/1961: Lady G. Cecil, op. cit., iii, 299.

337 PRO CAB 41/20/14.

338 44667 f. 78.

339 6 Apr., Childers MSS 5/185.

340 R. J., 6 Apr.

341 Cooper, op. cit., 411.

342 R. J., 7 Apr.

343 Hartington to Goschen, 7 Apr., printed Elliot, *Goschen*, ii, 38.

344 Morley to Primrose, Gladstone's private secretary, 8 Apr., 56447: the letter, beginning 'If you think fit, you may tell Mr Gladstone that I have just had an interview westwards; . . . ', suggests either conspiratorial deviousness, or more obviously a simple lack of a close working relationship between Gladstone and Morley at this time even when it was most indicated.

345 R. J., 9 Apr.

346 Salisbury to Harrowby, n.d., Harrowby MSS.

347 Chilston MSS, C 18/7.

348 Manners to Rutland, 9 Apr., Rutland MSS.

349 Lord Arthur Russell to George Melly, 11 Apr., Melly MSS 920 MEL 31/5968.

350 'I have very strong hopes that the outcome of the present crisis will be self-government for Ireland, combined now or hereafter with federation, and that a door may thus be opened for federation with our several colonies' (Hampden to Bryce, 21 June, Bryce MSS, National Library of Ireland MS 11010).

351 44667 f. 84.

352 A. West, op. cit., ii, 271. But Bright thought Gladstone 'very cheerful and well' (Bright, *Diaries*, 540), while Mrs Gladstone said of Bright, 'he seems to me not well at all and made lots of complaints' (Mrs Gladstone to Mrs Drew, n.d., 46223 f. 288). The latter observed 'nobody in greater force than the P.M.' (46262 f. 17).

353 H. J., 12 Apr.

354 Mrs Gladstone to Mrs Drew, loc. cit.

355 Ibid., f. 289.

356 Spencer MSS. Herschell's line (since he had no other) was to press for more discussion: cf. Herschell to Harcourt, 21 Apr., Harcourt MSS box 12, expressing disquiet about several points in the home rule bill, which 'required much more consideration than it has received'. By 24 Apr. he was writing that the best description of the land purchase bill he had ever read was in an open letter from Selborne, a leading Unionist (Spencer MSS).

357 44313 f. 63.

358 'Whatever his wrongs may have been, he was most ill-conditioned – what a pity' (R. J., 14 Apr.).

359 Spencer to Harcourt, 15 Apr., Harcourt MSS box 8.

360 H. J., 13–15 Apr.

361 Harcourt to Gladstone, 15 Apr., Harcourt MSS box 9.

362 For the precise form in which Rosebery wished the decision reached at

this cabinet to be passed to the Mediterranean Fleet, see Rosebery to Ripon, 16 Apr., 43516 f. 31, giving detailed instructions for gradual escalation of pressure on Greece, increasing if necessary to a total blockade of the east coast of Greece for ships of all kinds.

363   The arms (Ireland) bill, introduced on 6 May, received its second and third readings in the Commons on 20 and 28 May, and received the royal assent on 4 June. Though Morley presented it as a bill to put down Orangeism, the Irish party made a formal show of opposition.

364   Elliot, *Goschen*, ii, 50.

365   W. S. Churchill, op. cit., ii, 90.

366   Minto to Melgund, 16 Apr., Minto MSS box 175: 48292 f. 15 (diary of the third earl of Morley, who held minor office till he resigned rather belatedly over Ireland in Apr. 1886): W. S. Churchill, loc. cit.: Caine to Chamberlain, 17 Apr., Chamberlain MSS JC 5 /10 /4.

367   R. J., 15 Apr.

368   56447, dated 16 Apr. but year not stated.

369   Copy by Rosebery, Rosebery MSS box 111.

370   44228 f. 243.

371   Chamberlain MSS JC 8 /5 /3 /15.

372   Milner to Goschen, 28 Apr., Milner MSS box 182.

373   Ibid., 25 Apr.

374   Ibid., 26 Apr.

375   Ibid., 25 Apr.

376   Diary of Lady Dorothy Stanley, loc. cit.: entry dated (in copy) 28 Mar., which is patently impossible, whereas 28 Apr. fits the text exactly.

377   *Scotsman*, 3 May: *The Times*, 4 May. *The Address of the Rt. Hon. W. E. Gladstone M.P. to the Electors of Midlothian May 1st 1886*, published in London as a National Press Agency pamphlet, is in the National Library of Scotland but not in the British Museum. It differs significantly from an MS draft (44772 f. 79). It was timed to influence the key meeting of the National Liberal Federation on 5 May, and to a lesser extent the opening of the second reading debate on 10 May.

378   No correspondence between Stansfeld and Childers on this subject has survived. Childers did tell Gladstone that he agreed in principle with Stansfeld, and that without retention of the Irish 'the bill is doomed' (memo by Childers n.d. but *c.* 7 May, 44132 f. 233).

379   44497 ff. 113–4, 134–5.

380   Mrs Gladstone to Mrs Drew, n.d., 46223 f. 316.

381   R. J., 4 May.

382   E. R. Russell to G. Melly, 7 May, Melly MSS 920 MEL 31 /5907.

383   Gladstone to Morley, 5 May, 44548 f. 82.

384   Morley to Gladstone, 8 May, ibid., f. 84.

385   Ibid., 5 May, f. 83.

386   Ibid., 8 May, f. 84. Chamberlain had written on 6 May to a certain T. H. Bolton saying that inclusion of Irish members was 'of supreme importance'.

387   Ibid., 8 May, f. 86.

388   Gladstone to Morley, 8 May, ibid., f. 85.

389   R. J., 5 May.

390   Q. V. J., 6 May.

391   E. H. J.

392   Gladstone to Stansfeld, 6 May, 44548 f. 83 (for delayed cabinet). 44667 f. 94 (for Parnell meeting).

393   Gladstone to the Queen, 8 May: PRO CAB 41 /20 /18.

394   Cf. Arnold Morley to Labouchere, 8 May, Chamberlain MSS JC 5/50/72, putting a friendly face on the decision: 'Herschell had to leave town before the end of the cabinet ... Perhaps later on it might be arranged.'

395   44289 f. 38.

396   Gladstone to Rosebery, 7 May, Rosebery MSS box 19.

397   Hambleden MSS PS 9/144.

398   Akers–Douglas' diary, 9 May, Chilston MSS, U564 F 14.

399   Viscount Chilston, 'The Unionist Alliance, 1886–1895', *Parliamentary Affairs*, vol. xiv, 194.

400   Arnold Morley to Gladstone, 9 May, 56447.

401   A résumé of most of the evidence bearing on the negotiations, apart from that in the Chamberlain MSS, may be found in J. K. Lindsay, *The Liberal Unionist Party until December 1887* (unpublished Edinburgh Ph.D. 1955), 128–44.

402   Labouchere to Chamberlain, 8 May, tel. sent 6.52 p.m., Chamberlain MSS JC 5/50/71.

403   Both memoranda have disappeared (Lindsay, loc. cit.).

404   Gladstone to A. Morley, 9 May, 44548 f. 86.

405   However, Labouchere later maintained that Gladstone only agreed in principle to the final part of the bargain, adding that the cabinet at a (mythical) meeting on 10 May had failed to agreee on a clause for insertion into the bill (Labouchere to Chamberlain, 17 May 1886, Chamberlain MSS JC 5/50/78).

406   H. W. Lucy, *Sixty Years in the Wilderness* (1911), 120–1, citing a letter of 1898 from Labouchere. For Labouchere's detailed account of the negotiations see 'The Secret History of the First Home Rule Bill', *Truth*, 14 Oct. 1908.

407   Gladstone to John Morley, 8 May, 44548 f. 86.

408   Cf. Chamberlain to Dilke, 7 May, 43877 f. 46: 'To satisfy others I have talked about conciliation and have consented to make advances but on the whole I would rather vote against the Bill than not.'

409   Mrs Gladstone to Mrs Drew, n.d. but 26 May, 46223 f. 310.

410   Balfour to Salisbury, 10 May, Salisbury MSS.

411   E. R. Russell to Melly, 11 May, Melly MSS 920 MEL 31/5906.

412   Gladstone to the Queen, 10 May, Royal Archives RA D38/74.

413   Herbert Gladstone to Labouchere, (thence to Chamberlain), Chamberlain MSS JC 5/50/76.

414   Russell to Melly, loc. cit.

415   44772 f. 107.

416   Gladstone wrote to Campbell-Bannerman on 12 May (41215 f. 13) 'It may be right to summon the cabinet tomorrow to give you your mandate and make sure of it. If it is done would 12 or 2 suit you best...' No evidence has come to light of this suggested cabinet having taken place. Some kind of ministerial meeting involving Ripon, Gladstone, and others, had earlier been expected to occur on 12 May (Ripon to Monson, Monson MSS 25/13/2/30 f. 61).

417   Figures are necessarily approximate. The well-informed London reporter of the *Scotsman* gave the attendance as Chamberlain and 49 others, with about 60 invitations issued. *The Times* reported the attendance as from 50 to 60. Chamberlain himself noted down, under the heading 'meeting May 12 1886', the names of forty-four of the M.Ps who attended, entering these in a little black book labelled 'Irish Government Bill: opinions of members' (Chamberlain MSS JC 8/6/1).

418   J. K. Lindsay, op. cit., 152: *The Times*, 13 May. The intention of this was partly to discount in advance a further definition of possible concessions which Campbell-Bannerman was expected to offer in his coming statement.

419   *Scotsman*, 13 May: *The Times*, 13 May.

420   Illingworth to Gladstone, 12 May, 44497 f. 201.

421   Guests included Lord and Lady Tavistock, Lady Hayter, Sir Henry James, Canon MacColl, the miners' leader T.Burt, and others.
422   West, op. cit., ii, 274.
423   17 May, Mundella MSS, folio iv: 'My heart is all with Mr G. You know how strangely he gave me his confidence during the last three years of his late government ... [But] I cannot bear his home rule scheme.'
424   See 29 May below.
425   James to Mundella, 17 May, loc. cit.
426   *E.H.J.*, 16 May.
427   E.Hamilton to Gladstone, 16 May, 44191 f. 69.
428   *E.H.J.*
429   Gladstone to E.Hamilton, 16 May, 44191 f. 73.
430   Gladstone to Harcourt, 12 May, 44548 f. 87: Gladstone to Morley, 19 May, ibid. f. 89.
431   Mrs Goschen to Milner, 14 May, Milner MSS box 182.
432   J.K.Lindsay, op. cit., 146: *Scotsman* and *The Times*, 15 May. Several of the Liberal Unionist committee who attended the meeting, 'reported that everyone was *very* pleased with Harty Tarty' (Mrs Goschen to Milner, loc. cit.).
433   Morley to Spencer, 16 May, Spencer MSS.
434   44255 f. 90.
435   Bright, *Diaries*, 541.
436   Akers–Douglas' diary. Brand and Craig Sellar were working under Hartington: the followers of Chamberlain had their own whip, Caine, M.P. for Barrow. Extensive inquiries have failed to locate any trace of Craig Sellar's papers and it is unlikely, given his lack of close relatives, that they will ever be found.
437   West, op. cit., ii, 277.
438   Mrs Gladstone to Mrs Drew, n.d. but Mon., 46223 f. 275.
439   Memo in Gladstone's hand, 44772 f. 111.
440   Memo on 10 Downing St notepaper, 2 a.m. 18 May, 46110 f. 102.
441   Joseph to Arthur Chamberlain, 17 May, Chamberlain MSS JC 5/11/7.
442   D.D., 18 May.
443   Memo by the Queen, 19 May, Royal Archives RA D38/84a.
444   Grey to Earl Grey, 21 May, Grey MSS.
445   *Scotsman*, 21 May: J.K.Lindsay, op. cit., 154.
446   *The Times*, 21 May.
447   *E.H.J.* The assertion by a reputable contemporary journalist, S.H.Jeyes, in his *The Right Hon. Joseph Chamberlain* (1896), 271, that Schnadhorst was called in to a special cabinet meeting on election prospects, remains not proven.
448   Lindsay, loc. cit.
449   *Scotsman*, 24 May.
450   Pease, op. cit., 133.
451   Brett's journal, 24 May.
452   Grey to Earl Grey, 21 May, Grey MSS.
453   44200 f. 122.
454   *Scotsman*, 26 May.
455   Ibid., 13 May.
456   Gladstone to Mundella, 26 May, Mundella MSS folio iii: J.Morley to Mundella, 30 May, ibid., folio vi.
457   PRO CAB 41/20/20.
458   R.J., 25 May.
459   Gladstone left Paddington at 1.45, arriving at Windsor at 2.40, and having audience during the period from about 3 to 4.30, after which he at once returned to London, walking with Ponsonby down to Windsor station (*The Times*, 26

May). The Queen departed for Balmoral the following night, Ponsonby remaining behind in London.

460 *Standard*, 26 May.

461 Morley to Ripon, 26 May, 43541 f. 6.

462 Mrs Gladstone to Mrs Drew, n.d., but night after Trevelyan's speech (therefore 25 May), 46223 f. 311.

463 44772 f. 118.

464 Mrs Gladstone to Mrs Drew, n.d. but Thursday, 46223 f. 314.

465 According to the *Scotsman*, 225 attended.

466 Chamberlain MSS JC 5/34/63.

467 Pease, op. cit., 134.

468 *The Times*, 28 May.

469 J.K.Lindsay, op. cit., 162: *Scotsman*, 28 May. Chamberlain omitted all reference to his nearly disastrous meeting on 27 May in his *A Political Memoir*.

470 Memo dated 27 May, 44647.

471 C.H.D.Howard, ed., 222, based on Caine to Chamberlain n.d., but 27 May, Chamberlain MSS JC 5/10/2.

472 'The stench last night in the House was terrible, and really alarmed members' (Manners to Rutland, 28 May, Rutland MSS).

473 Elliot, *Goschen*, ii, 72.

474 Milner to Goschen, 29 May, Milner MSS box 182.

475 Harrowby MSS, new series, vol. 4: confirmed by Salisbury to Hartington, 30 May, Devonshire MSS 340/1996, where it was argued that the Ulstermen would have voted against in any case.

476 C.D., 29 May.

477 Chilston MSS, c 18/10.

478 *Scotsman*, 1 June, has 53: Pease, op. cit., 135, made it 55.

479 *The Times*, 1 June.

480 Herbert to Henry Gladstone, 10 June, Glynne–Gladstone MSS.

481 Labouchere to Stead, n.d. ('3 a.m.'), but dated by reference to Bright's letter: W.T.Stead MSS. Cf. Labouchere to Stead, 2 June: 'The fact is that Chamberlain and Caine have only about 6 men who may be termed Chamberlainites...'; and Labouchere to Stead, 4 June, 'Hartington has a considerable following, about 40 to 55, Chamberlain only four or five'.

482 Chamberlain had written to Bright on Sunday pressing him to attend Monday's meeting (43387 f. 27).

483 Goldsmid, who voted against the second reading, had made every effort to show his sense of affinity with the ministry. 'At Ferdy Rothschild's, Sir Julian Goldsmid, a pushing Jew, conceited Hebrew, buttonholed Rosebery and begged him to get the U. Sec of State at the F.O. "I should be delighted to have you there" said Rosebery "but don't you think if you came here the F.O. would be considered rather too semitic?" ' (Brett's journal, 4 Feb. 1886).

484 J.K.Lindsay, op. cit., 165–6: Pease, loc. cit.

485 Pease, loc. cit.

486 Q.V.J., 31 May.

487 Mrs Gladstone to Mrs Drew, n.d. but 'Tuesday, sent alas Wednesday', 46223 f. 319.

488 Lindsay, loc. cit.

489 D.D., 1 June.

490 R.J., 1 June.

491 Ibid., 2 June.

492 Ponsonby, op. cit., 260.

493 Ibid.

494 Mrs Gladstone to Mrs Drew, n.d. but 'sent on Friday', 46223 f. 321. Lord

Acton dined in Downing St on two unspecified occasions in the days prior to the division, but found Gladstone too busy to talk seriously to him (Mrs Gladstone, loc. cit., f. 326).

495 Thorold, op. cit., 323.

496 *R.J.*, 6 June.

497 West, op. cit., ii, 278–81. But cf. Mrs Gladstone's report 'there he sits with a book in his hand leaving off every now and then or pacing the room' (Mrs Gladstone to Mrs Drew, n.d., 46223 f. 326).

498 Mrs Gladstone, loc. cit.

499 Pease, op. cit., 138.

500 For an account from the press gallery, see George W. Smalley, 'A Great Night in the House of Commons', in his *London Letters and Some Others* (2 vols., 1890), 226–56. Smalley wrote chiefly for the *New York Tribune*.

501 *Q.V.J.*, 10 June.

502 Herbert to Henry Gladstone, 10 June, Glynne–Gladstone MSS.

503 Grey to Earl Grey, 6 June, Grey MSS: Lady Knightley's diary, 7 June, for Chamberlain: Lubbock's diary, 7 June.

504 Pease, loc. cit.

505 A. E. Pease, son of Sir Joseph, had been uncertain of his father till the last, and was never 'more relieved than when I saw that my father's name had already been ticked off' (Pease, op. cit., 139).

506 Grey to Earl Grey, 10 June, Grey MSS.

507 Herbert Gladstone, loc. cit.

508 44647 f. 121.

509 *E. H. J.*

510 Rosebery to the Queen, 12 July, Royal Archives RA B 37/82.

511 *Q.V.J.*, 8 and 6 June.

512 Another source of royal advice was the third Earl Grey, then aged 83, who was greatly surprised on 23 May by a letter from Ponsonby asking him to pronounce on the propriety of a dissolution. Since, after the Hawarden kite, Grey had written of Gladstone's conversion to free trade as the event of the moment, his powers must have been tested to the full by the Queen's request.

513 *Q.V.J.*, 10, 11, 12 June. In addition to social motives, there was the simple fact that even had Dilke voted with the Unionists, they would still have opposed his re-election, so that he would have lost his seat in any event. Salisbury had decreed, referring to Dilke, 'We cannot make a present of a seat to a man who on every other subject is the enemy of all we care about' (Salisbury to Brabourne, 2 May, Brabourne MSS C 174/7).

514 Mrs Gladstone to Mrs Drew, n.d., loc. cit. f. 329.

Part Four

1 Reginald Macleod, Tory agent for Scotland, to Lord Lothian, 21 July, printed *The Times*, 23 July 1886.

2 See A. B. Cooke, 'Gladstone's Election for the Leith District of Burghs, July 1886', *Scottish Historical Review*, 1970.

3 Based on Kenneth O. Morgan, 'The Liberal Unionists in Wales', *The National Library of Wales Journal*, 1969: and his 'Cardiganshire Politics: the Liberal Ascendancy, 1885–1923', *Ceredigion*, 1967.

4 Lindsay, op. cit.

5 Balfour to Salisbury, 25 June, Salisbury MSS.

6 Gladstone to the Queen, Royal Archives RA C 38/1.

7   *Daily Telegraph*, 7 July.
8   Rowton to the Queen, 17 July, citing a letter from Lady Salisbury to him, Royal Archives RA C 38/4.
9   Q.V.J., 13 July.
10   Grey to Earl Grey, 14 July, Grey MSS.
11   Cranborne to Salisbury, 15 July, Salisbury MSS.
12   Derby to Hartington, copy, 12 July, Derby MSS.
13   H.A.L.Fisher, *James Bryce* (1927), i, 216.
14   R.J., 17 July.
15   *Scotsman*, 19 July.
16   Ibid., 14 and 16 July.
17   Rowton to the Queen, 17 and 19 July, Royal Archives RA C 38/4 and 5.
18   Harcourt to Rosebery, n.d. but *c*. 8 July, Rosebery MSS box 26: Mundella to Gladstone, 12 July, 44258.
19   R.J., 20 July. Cf. Gladstone's remark (to Rosebery, R.J., 22 Oct.), that he 'would not speak at all during that recess, nor have anything to do with any political question but Ireland'.
20   Tel. from Gladstone received by Queen between 4 and 5, followed by letter during the evening: tel. then sent by Queen to Salisbury at Royat (Q.V.J., 20 July).
21   Elliot's diary, 20 July.
22   See Smith to Salisbury, 19 July, in favour of coalition, Salisbury MSS.
23   'Trevelyan I hear is in favour of a coalition government': Cranbrook to Salisbury, 15 July, Salisbury MSS: Goschen to the Queen, 23 July, Royal Archives RA C 38/15.
24   Akers-Douglas to Smith, 21 July (written as if 27), Hambleden MSS PS 9/156: Cranborne to Salisbury, 15 and 16 July, Salisbury MSS: Henry Manners, Salisbury's private secretary, to Salisbury, 15 July, Salisbury MSS, reporting on meeting of leaders that morning.
25   Hartington to Goschen, 22 July, cited Elliot, *Goschen*, ii, 95–6: P.Colson, op. cit., 83–4.
26   Cf. Henry James' statement the same day 'Salisbury will ask H. to join him. H. will refuse' (James to Chamberlain, 22 July, Chamberlain MSS JC 5/46/4).
27   P.Colson, loc. cit.
28   Maria, Marchioness of Ailesbury, deserved her dinner if her remarks to Rosebery were anything to go by: 'I think Hartington and all his followers (I hope not many) behave very ill to Gladstone in seceding from him at such a moment. ... In my opinion he is the only man who can grapple with the Irish question' (2 Feb. 1886, Rosebery MSS, box 63).
29   James Morse Carmichael, Gladstone's private secretary in 1886.
30   West, op. cit., ii, 288: Mary Drew's diary, 46262 f. 27.
31   Rowton to the Queen, 23 July 7.30 p.m., Royal Archives RA C 38/14.
32   Viscount Chilston, *W. H. Smith* (1965), 211.
33   Churchill to Salisbury, 22 Aug., St Aldwyn MSS.
34   Beach to Salisbury, 25 July, copy, St Aldwyn MSS.
35   Q.V.J., 24 July.
36   Salisbury to Beach, 24 July, St Aldwyn MSS.
37   Beach to Salisbury, 25 July, copy, St Aldwyn MSS.
38   Known as Salisbury's Manners: later Duke of Rutland. A small amount of his papers while private secretary survive at Belvoir, chiefly in the form of occasionally tantalising fragments whose possible significance did not emerge during a hasty inspection.
39   Probably Devonshire MSS 340/2025, a 1,300-word memorandum.
40   Salisbury to Beach, 24 July, Lady G.Cecil, op. cit., iii, 130.
41   Q.V.J., 24 July.

42 Cranborne to Salisbury, passing on report of Tory chief whip, 24 July, Salisbury MSS.
43 Camperdown to Derby, 26 July, Derby MSS: Camperdown to Selborne, 26 July and 1 Aug., Selborne MSS 1869 ff. 197, 205.
44 For Northbrook's opposition to coalition, see Northbrook to Derby, 29 July, Derby MSS.
45 *Q.V.J.*, 24 July.
46 Elliot, *Goschen*, ii, 96–7: Colson, op. cit., 84.
47 Chamberlain to Hartington, 16 July, Devonshire MSS 340/2021: written on holiday in Italy.
48 Churchill MSS xiii 1573.
49 On Tuesday, the Queen heard from Salisbury that Lyons had declined on health grounds (*Q.V.J.*, 27 July). For the offer to Lyons, 26 July, and his refusal, 27 July, see the letters printed by Lord Newton, *Lord Lyons*, 522–3.
50 *Q.V.J.*, 28 July.
51 Ibid., 24–25 July.
52 Beach to Salisbury, 25 July, copy, St Aldwyn MSS.
53 Richmond to Salisbury, 24 July, and Harrowby to Salisbury, 25 July, Salisbury MSS.
54 Cf. Chilston, op. cit., 212 for Smith's account of ministerial movements.
55 Ibid. According to Smith, Churchill 'is anxious to tell me everything Joe has to say'.
56 Ibid., 213.
57 *The Times* reports, confirmed by Mowbray, op. cit., 303.
58 Fitzgibbon to Churchill, 27 July, copy, St Aldwyn MSS.
59 Beach to Salisbury, 28 July, copy, St Aldwyn MSS.
60 Smith to Salisbury, n.d. but docketed 27 July in Salisbury's hand, Salisbury MSS. For the offer to Cranbrook, see Salisbury to the Queen, 28 July, Royal Archives RA C 38/27.
61 Smith to Salisbury, loc. cit.
62 Churchill to Salisbury, 27 July, Salisbury MSS.
63 Churchill to Smith, 8 Nov., Hambleden MSS.
64 Halsbury to Salisbury, 28 July, Salisbury MSS.
65 M.P. Antrim 1880–85, Antrim N. 1885–87, then cr. law lord.
66 Salisbury to Halsbury, 28 July, Halsbury MSS.
67 *Q.V.J.*, 28 July.
68 Chilston, loc. cit.
69 Smith to Salisbury, 30 July, Salisbury MSS: cf. Chilston, loc. cit.
70 Ibid., 28 July, Salisbury MSS.
71 Derby MSS.
72 Gorst to Churchill, 29 July, Salisbury MSS.
73 *R.J.*, 29 July.
74 *Q.V.J.*, 30 July.
75 Churchill to Salisbury, 30 July, Salisbury MSS.
76 For party response to Churchill's promotion, note the comment of a leading backbencher not normally favourable to him: 'Randolph Churchill's leadership I am sure is right' (D.D., 30 July).
77 *R.J.*, 31 July, 1 Aug.
78 D.D., 31 July.
79 Chilston, loc. cit.
80 Salisbury to Clarke, 2 Aug., printed, Clarke, op. cit., 255.
81 *R.J.*, 2 Aug.
82 *Q.V.J.*, 25 June, 3 Aug.
83 Ibid., 3 Aug.

List of Unpublished Sources

The following materials were consulted, quotations from which appear in the text and in footnotes by kind permission of the individuals and institutions who now own them.

Ashbourne MSS, House of Lords Record Office: calendar to be published by H.M.S.O.

Austin MSS, National Liberal Club Library.

Avebury MSS: diary of Sir John Lubbock, in family hands.

Balfour MSS, divided between the British Museum and Scotland.

Bath MSS, Longleat.

Brabourne MSS, Kent County Record Office.

Broadhurst MSS, British Library of Political and Economic Science, London.

Bryce MSS, Bodleian Library, Oxford with additional material in the National Library of Ireland, Dublin.

Cabinet papers, Public Record Office.

Cadogan MSS, National Register of Archives, London.

Cairns MSS, Public Record Office.

Campbell-Bannerman MSS, British Museum.

Carlingford MSS, Somerset County Record Office.

Carnarvon MSS, Public Record Office.

Chamberlain MSS, Birmingham University Library.

Childers MSS, Royal Commonwealth Institute, London, with additional material in the Public Record Office.

Chilston MSS, Kent County Record Office.

Churchill MSS, Churchill College Library, Cambridge, with additional material in a small black metal box at Blenheim Palace, Oxfordshire.

Courtney MSS, British Library of Political and Economic Science, London.

Cranbrook MSS, Ipswich and East Suffolk Record Office.

Crewe MSS, Cambridge University Library.

Cross MSS, British Museum.

Dalrymple MSS, at Newhailes, Musselburgh, Edinburgh.

Derby MSS (15th and 16th Earls), Liverpool Record Office.

502

List of Unpublished Sources

Devonshire MSS, Chatsworth House, Derbyshire.
Dilke MSS, British Museum.
Dufferin MSS, Northern Ireland Public Record Office.
Duffin MSS, Northern Ireland Public Record Office.
Elliot MSS, National Library of Scotland.
Elliot Diaries, in family hands.
Esher MSS, Churchill College Library, Cambridge.
Gladstone MSS, British Museum.
Herbert, Viscount Gladstone MSS, British Museum.
Mary Gladstone MSS, British Museum.
Glynne–Gladstone MSS, St. Deiniol's Library, Hawarden, Flintshire.
Granville MSS, Public Record Office.
Grey MSS, Durham University Library.
Haddo MSS, Haddo House, Aberdeenshire.
Halsbury MSS, British Museum.
Hambleden MSS (papers of W.H.Smith), Strand House, Portugal Street, London.
Edward Hamilton MSS, British Museum.
Harcourt MSS, Bodleian Library, Oxford.
Harrowby MSS, Sandon Hall, Staffordshire.
Heneage MSS, Lincolnshire County Record Office.
Iddesleigh MSS, British Museum.
James MSS, Hereford County Record Office.
Johnston Diaries, Northern Ireland Public Record Office.
Knightley Diaries, Northamptonshire Record Office.
Leader MSS, Sheffield University Library.
Londonderry MSS, Durham County Record Office.
George Melly MSS, Liverpool Record Office.
Milner MSS in the Bodleian Library, Oxford by courtesy of the Warden and Fellows of New College.
Minto MSS, National Library of Scotland, Edinburgh.
Monson MSS, Lincolnshire County Record Office.
Earl of Morley MSS, British Museum.
Mundella MSS, Sheffield University Library.
National Library of Ireland MSS, Dublin containing a number of small collections relating to the period.
Playfair MSS, Imperial College Library, London.
Ponsonby MSS, British Museum.
Richmond MSS, West Sussex County Record Office.
Ripon MSS, British Museum.
Rosebery MSS, National Library of Scotland.
Royal Archives, at Windsor Castle.
Rutland MSS, Belvoir Castle, Leicestershire.
St. Aldwyn MSS, Gloucestershire County Record Office.
St. Oswald MSS, Nostell Priory, Wragby, Yorkshire.
Salisbury MSS, Christ Church Library, Oxford.
Saunderson MSS, in family hands: photocopies in Public Record Office of Northern Ireland.
Selborne MSS, Lambeth Palace Library, London.
Shuttleworth MSS, in family hands.
Henry Sidgwick's Diary, Trinity College Library, Cambridge.
Spencer MSS, Althorp Park, Northamptonshire.
Stanhope MSS, Kent County Record Office.
Lady Dorothy Stanley's Diary (extracts only), Chamberlain MSS.

Stansfeld MSS, in family hands.
W.T.Stead MSS, in family hands.
Trevelyan MSS, Newcastle University Library.
Robert Spence Watson MSS, in private hands.
Williamson memoirs (typescript), in family hands

Index

Index

Index

225–6, 231; wish to quit office, 233; and land purchase bill crisis, 239–243; on defeat of ministry, 251; and Inverness speech, 290; and resignation of, 311n., 384–6, 389, 390–4; and allotments, 323–4; and formation of 1886 ministry, 324; believes Gladstone will drop home rule, 324; dinner with Churchill, 324, 392–4, 446–7; and home rule, 327–8, 347, 383; attends Whig cabal, 331; approaches Parnell, 332; 'cordially agrees' with Gladstone, 333, 335; accepts office, 342, 346–8, 361; and local government, 361; and colonial office, 361–2; and Irish land, 371; advises Dilke, 372; on China, 374; on public opinion, 381; wishes to return to fold, 399; declines to join Liberal Unionists, 409; negotiations over reunion, xi, 416–18; and home rule division, 432; urges support for Tories, 445

Channel tunnel, 383

Chaplin, H., rebels against Northcote, 37; not desirous of office, 261; also 414, 438, 447, 455

Childers, H. C. E., predicts election result, 3n.; a liability, 15, 121; constituency, 111n., 351, 397; death of son, 134, 427; and home rule, 135, 397–8; papers, 139; and Suakin, 178; and Egypt, 181; and Africa, 188; and education, 206–7; possible resignation over Sudan, 218; and financial measures of, 193, 209, 220, 230, 235–6, 245–6; baited by colleagues, 220; withdraws resignation, 238, 245; loses seat, 317; and formation of 1886 ministry, 331, 347, 362–3; Queen objects to, 360–1; as financial mediator, 377; leaks home rule plans, 394n., 397–9; and Gladstone, 220, and Chamberlain, 222, and Rosebery, 236, and Bright, 399, and Stansfeld, 412, and Harcourt, 348; also 380, 408–9

China, 219, 289, 374

Churchill, Lord R., and H. James, 44, 323, 420; and Carnarvon, 71–2; and Parnell, 74; and Holmes, 155; James on, 420, Salisbury on, 446, 456; Queen on, 446, Gladstone on, 380, Knightley on, 264, Richmond on, 264, Cranbrook on, 283; on Cross, 287; heterodoxy, 10; absence in India, 11, 36, 38, 63, 193; and Ireland, 18, 39, 68, 237; and press, 20; returns to England, 39; attempts to reconstruct politics,

39–47; Belfast visit, 47, 114, 160, 377; *mot* on Irish bishops, 72; contempt for Ulster Tories, 75; early career in Ireland, 75–6; Norwegian holiday, 77, 438; attempts to join Gladstone, 77–8; petitions to Queen, 108; position in spring 1886, 114–15; talks to Dilke, 237; wild plans of, 238–9; dances like Cherokee, 250; papers of, 257, 259; and India Office, 262; demands retirement of Old Guard, 264; talks of Northcote premiership, 269; against upholding Spencer, 271; attacked by *Standard*, 279; on Parnell's vagueness, 285; visits Dublin, 286, 296–7; on boycotting, 287; and Burma, 288–9; and procedural reform, 293; rebuked by Manners, 293; against coercion, 302–3; twice wishes to be Irish secretary, 303, 448; dinners with Chamberlain, 324, 392–4, 446–7; summarises his career, 364; and Holmes' motion, 379; and anti-home rule demonstrations, 406; in Paris, 409; on foreign policy, 414; and tactics on home rule vote, 428; at Twickenham, 431; and Parnell's revelations, 431; health, 446n.; as foreign secretary, 446n.; speech at Dartford, 457

Civil List, select committee on, 227, 230

Clark, Sir A., doctor, 380, 391

Clarke, Sir Edward, law officer, 455

Coalition, possibility of in summer 1886, 439–44

Collings, Jesse, M.P., 27, 325, 347

Collings' amendment, 307–8, 321, 324, 331, 334, 456

Congo, 188–9

Connaught, Duke of, 288, 292

Conservatives, weakness and recovery of (1885), 35–9; and 1885 election, 40; ministerial post-election speeches, 46n.; and 1886 elections, 59–60; political style, 61–6; and Tory–Irish alliance, 66–77; legacy from Disraeli, 79; and Irish coercion, 266–7, 271, 300–1; and party meeting, 269; and budget, 271, 274; and Afghan crisis, 272, 282; defeat of, 334; shadow cabinet of, 403, 422, 428; party conference, 422; feeling against coalition, 442

Cooper, C., editor of *Scotsman*, 20, 397–8, 401

Cork, Lord, 365

Corrupt Practices Act (1883), 5

Index

Gordon, Gen., family of, 202; diary of, 210, 225
Gordon, Sir Henry, 225
Gorst, Sir J. E., 74, 269, 278, 454
Goschen, district in Africa, 278
Goschen, G. J., heterodoxy of, 10; and Sudan, 31, 36, 85n.; aims, 84–88, 100–2, 164; and Hartington, 87–8, 330–1, 337, 399, 408, 424, 442; on modern life, 92n.; attempts to form party, 97–8, 405; and Ireland, 101; Tory views of, 102; and formation of 1886 ministry, 130, 309, 347, 362; and A. Elliot, 153; and Argyll, 98n., 154, 442; consulted on Egypt, 180; and Gladstone, 204n., 330; and Churchill, 238; Chamberlain's hatred for, 325; and Morley, 330; not seen as possible premier, 335; as foreign secretary, 336; in favour of Gladstone ministry, 339; perhaps offered office by Gladstone, 363; and seats deal with Tories, 370; as committee chairman, 373; and Holmes' motion, 379; praises Smith, 389; instructs Queen, 388–390, 414, 424, 439; on Chamberlain, 389; and Edinburgh speech, 408; and Liberal Unionists, 421, 439; speech on 2nd reading, 431; and coalition, 441; as foreign secretary, 451: also 14n., 56
Graham, Gen. Sir Gerald, 219
Granville, Lord, a liability, 15, 25; papers of, 140; death of sister, 180; incompetence, 224; at Hawarden, 312; and construction of 1886 ministry, 323–30, 334–5, 337, 340, 357–8, 362, 369; and home rule, 329; and relinquishment of foreign office, 336, 340–2, 347–8, 354–6; and colonial office, 361; as possible premier, 364; and colonial premiers, 375; as mediator with Chamberlain, 385, 388; illness, 432–3, 438, 440, 452n.; also 64, 126, 128–30, 132, 135, 150, 154, 318, 333, 408–9, 415, 455, 457
Gray, E. D., owner of Freeman's Journal, 273, 338
Greece, 304–5, 341, 360, 368–9, 373–374, 381, 395, 398, 405, 412, 414, 430
Grenfell, H. R., 424
Grey, Albert, M.P., 14n., 82, 95–6, 98–100, 102–5, 108, 110, 112–13, 115, 130n., 306, 333, 382, 388, 405, 425, 432, 439
Grey, Sir Edward, 154, 430
Grosvenor, Lord Richard (Lord Stalbridge), 228, 250, 254, 313, 315, 317, 323, 326, 329, 330–1, 334, 337, 341–2, 348, 352, 358, 362, 364, 366, 406, 447
Guards, return of, desired by Tories, 270
Guthrie, Charles, 404

Halsbury, Lord, 47, 67, 252, 263, 267, 409, 452
Hamilton, (Sir) Edward, diarist, 25, 137–8, 173, 180, 186–9, 192, 194n., 201, 213–15, 225, 227–8, 233–4, 237, 244–5, 250, 254, 322–4, 328, 332, 336, 338, 340, 342, 344, 347–348, 357, 394, 420, 424, 427, 430, 443
Hamilton, Lord George, x, 46, 66, 258–9, 276, 423, 443
Hamilton, Sir Robert, Irish official, 145, 155, 326, 328, 431
Hammond, J. L., x, 136
Hampden, Lord, 403
Harcourt, Lewis, son of politician, 137, 359, 403
Harcourt, Sir W. V., Rosebery on, 401; Morley on, 153; Northbrook on, 222; Hartington on, 222; on Childers, 348; and Chamberlain, 56, 418, 421; and Goschen, 101n., 334; on democracy, 3; on election results, 3n.; intrigues against Gladstone, 25–9; and leaving Tories 'to stew', 43; character, 120; and formation of 1886 ministry, 125, 330, 334, 336–7, 347; and Ireland, 129, 226, 232, 336, 353, 358, 362; papers of, 139–140; and Egypt, 179, 211, 375; as peacemaker, 184, 231; and Sudan, 191, 205, 375; and Turks, 205; and Niger, 206; 'insulted' by Kimberley, 223–4; and Afghan crisis, 224; against Central Board, 226; against Irish land purchase, 234; favours resignation, 236; and detectives, 269; hungry for office, 317; bitterly anti-Gladstone, 321; woos Chamberlain, 321; visits Rosebery, 322–3; and Woolsack, 336, 353; and home rule, 353, 384; threatens to resign from 1886 ministry, 365, 371, 377, 395–6, 401–2, 404–5; and financial measures, 373, 377; home rule bill 'dead as mutton' 404; yachting trip, 438; against resignation, 441
Harrowby, Lord, on Northcote, 265; on lack of salary, 270; on criminal law amendment bill, 275; on party strategy, 278; and Carnarvon, 278n.; and Ireland, 285; and Canada, 291; death of relative, 307; asks to retire, 446; also 409

510

Index

Shaw-Lefevre, J. G., as potential minister under Hartington, 28; and radical junta, 42; general position, 141–3; joins cabinet, 192, 194, 197; and Sudan, 200; against resignation over Khartoum, 204; and land purchase bill crisis, 241–2; and crimes bill, 247–8; absent from shadow cabinet, 331; dropped from leadership, 341; offers to rule Ireland, 362

Sidgwick, Henry, Cambridge don, 378

Smith, W. H., and Ireland, 18, 67, 304, 306–8; offers to make room for Goschen, 102, 452; and Sudan, 270; and army, 271, 275, 290; favours coalition, 442; also 87, 254, 409

Social reforms, 16–17

Spencer, 5th Earl, and Irish policy, 153, 188, 225, 228, 248–9, 375, 386–7, 401; and Mundella, 145; and Egypt, 183; and resignation on Sudan division, 204; on Sudan, 218; plans an Irish Balmoral, 225; and Central Board, 227–8, 231; abolition of Irish viceroyalty, 234; compromise with Dilke, 246; at Hawarden, 312–13; thinks home rule ministry unlikely, 319; on Lord Aberdeen, 367; as possible foreign secretary, 358; St Albans on, 371; and formation of 1886 ministry, 324–5, 327, 329, 332, 334–6, 341, 348, 357, 359, 362, 365; also 34, 129, 131–2, 134–5, 149, 158, 276, 317, 333, 380, 443; as mediator with Chamberlain, 385, 388; on Harcourt, 396; possible resignation of, 405; and home rule campaign, 408, 438

Spurgeon, Rev. C. H., 9, 109n.

Staal, Baron de, Russian diplomat, 212, 218, 222, 224

Standard, leading Conservative organ, 279–80, 295, 299

Stanhope, Edward, as party organiser, 21; papers of, 258; anxious for Tory ministry, 261; and Scottish education, 271; and Board of Trade, 285; as foreign secretary, 451

Stanley, Col. F., 16th Earl of Derby, character and papers of, 257–8; devoted to Northcote, 262; takes colonial office, 266; and Bechuanaland, 275–6, 278; Cranbrook's doubts about, 285; accepts peerage and office, 453–4

Stansfeld, James, 134–5, 140, 143–4, 252, 311n., 388, 392–3, 412, 417, 440–1

Stead, W. T., editor, 103, 274–5

Stellaland, 278

Stephenson, Gen., 297

Stratton, conclave at, 322, 363

Stuart, Prof. James, 392, 443

Suakin, 174, 177–9, 185, 191, 193–7, 200, 207, 219, 230, 275

Sudan, decision to maintain slavery in, 207

Suez canal, 200, 219, 224

Suffield, Lord, 369

Sullivan, T. D., Parnellite M.P., on Churchill, 77

Sydney, 1st Earl, 341

Talbot, C. R. M., M.P., 437

Tennant, Sir Charles, 328

Tennant, Dorothy, diarist, 380, 410

Tennant, Margot, 454

Terry, Ellen, 431

Thornton, Sir Edward, British ambassador in Russia, 211, 213

Thring, Henry, 150, 238, 379

Times, The, on Ireland, 315

Tonga, 180

Tory–Irish alliance, as Liberal excuse, 10

Tottenham, Col. C. G., 449

Trafalgar Square riots, 4, 6–7, 369, 375–6

Trevelyan, Sir G. O., and Ireland, 17, 226, 322; and Hartington, 27, 80, 107, 440; and radical junta, 42, 141; reason for joining Gladstone, 93n., 243; and Irish deputation, 95; and Shuttleworth, 96; resignation, 135, 311n.; archives of, 138–139, 150; and Stratton conclave, 148, 322, 363; unimportance of, 148; against annexing Zululand, 174; and Egypt, 185, 187; and New Guinea, 199; and Sudan, 200, 211; against resignation, 203; and crimes bill, 226; rats on Spencer, 226, 380; for Central Board, 227; illness, 233, 235; and land purchase bill crisis, 241–3; takes office, 362–363; Gladstone on, 362; and crofters bill, 372, 376; Rosebery on, 377; on opinion in cabinet, 382; resignation of, 384–5, 388, 390–2; Mrs Gladstone on, 385; and Scottish church, 386; Goschen on, 389; and Hartington, 392; on Gladstone, 392; Brett on, 419; and Liberal Unionists, 421; on voting tactics, 429; loses seat, 439; disappears from scene, 442

T.U.C., 9

Turkey, 185, 190, 193, 205–6, 209, 231, 270n., 275, 287

Tweedmouth, Lord, 392

515